AFRICAN GENDER STUDIES

African Gender Studies
A Reader

Edited by
Oyèrónkẹ́ Oyěwùmí

palgrave
macmillan

AFRICAN GENDER STUDIES

First published in 2005 by
PALGRAVE MACMILLAN™
175 Fifth Avenue, New York, N.Y. 10010 and
Houndmills, Basingstoke, Hampshire, England RG21 6XS
Companies and representatives throughout the world.

PALGRAVE MACMILLAN is the global academic imprint of the Palgrave Macmillan division of St. Martin's Press, LLC and of Palgrave Macmillan Ltd. Macmillan® is a registered trademark in the United States, United Kingdom and other countries. Palgrave is a registered trademark in the European Union and other countries.

ISBN 1–4039–6282–0 hardback
ISBN 1–4039–6283–9 paperback

Library of Congress Cataloging-in-Publication Data

African gender studies : a reader / Oyèrónkẹ́ Oyěwùmí (editor).
p. cm.
Includes bibliographical references and index.
ISBN 1–4039–6282–0 (cloth) – ISBN 1–4039–6283–9 (pbk.)
1. Sex role—Africa. 2. Women—Africa—Social conditions. I. Oyěwùmí, Oyèrónkẹ́.

HQ1075.5.A35A376 2004
305.3'096—dc22 2004054696

A catalogue record for this book is available from the British Library.

Design by Newgen Imaging Systems (P) Ltd., Chennai, India.

First edition: July 2005

10 9 8 7 6 5 4 3 2 1

Transferred to digital printing in 2006

For
Wangari Maathai
Nobel Peace Laureate 2005
Who taught us that in order to make change,
we must take charge

Contents

ACKNOWLEDGMENTS

Grateful acknowledgment is made to the following authors and sources for permission to reprint material in this anthology:

Akyeampong, Emmanuel and Pashington Obeng. "Spirituality, Gender, and Power in Asante History" in *The International Journal of African Historical Studies,* vol. 28, no. 3, 1995. Pp. 481–508.

Amadiume, Ifi. "Theorizing Matriarchy in Africa: Kinship Ideologies and Systems in Africa and Europe," from *Reinventing Africa: Matriarchy, Religion, and Culture.* New York: Zed Books Ltd, 1997. Pp. 71–88.

Appiah, Kwame Anthony. "In My Father's House: Epilogue," from *In My Father's House: Africa in the Philosophy of Culture.* New York: Oxford University Press, 1992. Pp. 181–192.

Busia, Abena P.A. "Miscegenation as Metonymy: Sexuality and Power in the Colonial Novel" in *Ethnic and Racial Studies,* vol. 9, no. 3 (July), 1986. London: Routledge and Kegan Paul.

Fall, Babacar. "Senegalese Women in Politics: A Portrait of Two Female Leaders, Arame Diéne and Thioumbé Samb, 1945–1996," in *African Words, African Voices: Critical Practices in Oral History* edited by Luise White, Stephan F. Miescher, and David William Cohen. Indiana University Press. Pp. 214–223.

Kopytoff, Igor. "Women's Roles and Existential Identities," in *Beyond the Second Sex: New Directions in the Anthropology of Gender,* edited by Peggy Reeves Sanday and Ruth Gallagher Goodenough. Philadelphia: University of Pennsylvania Press, 1980. Pp. 75–98.

Lazreg, Marnia. "Decolonizing Feminism," from *The Eloquence of Silence: Algerian Women in Question.* New York: Routledge, 1994. Pp. 6–19.

Murunga, Godwin Rapando. "African Women in the Academy and Beyond," in *Jenda: Journal of Culture and African Women's Studies* (www.jendajournal.com) 2002, vol. 12, no. 1.

Nfah-Abbenyi, Juliana Makuchi. "Gender, Feminist Theory, and Post-Colonial (Women's) Writing," from *Gender in African Women's Writing: Identity, Sexuality and Difference.* Indianapolis: Indiana University Press, 1997. Pp. 16–34, notes pp. 156–160.

Njambi, Wairimu Ngaruiya and William E. O'Brien. "Revisiting "Woman–Woman Marriage: Notes on Gikuyu Women", in *NWSA Journal* (2000), vol. 12, no. 1.

Nnaemeka, Obioma. "Bringing African Women into the Classroom: Rethinking Pedagogy and Epistemology," in *Borderwork: Feminist Engagements with Comparative Literature*. Pp. 301–317.

Nzegwu, Nkiru. "Questions of Identity and Inheritance: A Critical Review of Kwame Anthony Appiah's *In My Father's House*," in *Hypatia*, vol. 11, no. 1 (Winter), 1996. Pp. 175–200.

Oyewumi, Oyeronke. "Making History, Creating Gender: Some Methodological and Interpretive Questions in the Writing of Oyo Oral Traditions," in *History in Africa* 25 (1998), 263–305.

———. "Visualizing the Body: Western Theories and African Subjects," from *The Invention of Women: Making an African Sense of Western Gender Discourses* Minneapolis: University of Minnesota Press, 1997. Pp. 1–17.

———. "Reconstituting the Cosmology and Sociocultural Institutions of Oyo Yoruba," from *The Invention of Women: Making an African Sense of Western Gender Discourses*. Minneapolis: University of Minnesota Press, 1997. Pp. 31–79.

Pala, Achola O. "Definitions of Women and Development: An African Perspective," in *The Black Woman Cross Culturally,* edited by Filomina Chioma Steady. Cambridge, Massachusetts: Schenkman Publishing Company, Inc., 1981. Pp. 209–214.

PREFACE

Oyèrónkẹ́ Oyěwùmí

In *The Invention of Women: Making an African Sense of Western Gender Discourses* (Oyěwùmí 1997) I demonstrate that the problem of gender in African Studies is also an epistemological one. This is because the conceptual category of gender is in origin, constitution, and expression bound to Western culture. In that study, I show that the delineation of gender categories are an outgrowth of the biological foundationalism of Western thinking about society: 'The cultural logic of western social categories is based on an ideology of biological determinism: the conception that biology provides the rationale for the organization of the social world. Thus this cultural logic is actually a "bio-logic"' (Oyěwùmí 1997: ix). Such a conception of the social world is by no means universal.

Paradoxically, though gender is proclaimed to be socially constructed, the way it is used in dominant discourses implies that it is a biologically determined category. Furthermore, most of the scholars who do research on gender have derived their conceptual and theoretical tools from studies based on Western Europe, the United States, and Canada. Although some researchers have conducted studies in Africa, it is apparent that the questions and concerns that drive most studies are based upon Western European and North American experiences. Africa is used merely as a vehicle for articulating Western preoccupations and modes of understanding.

Nevertheless, the use of gender as an analytical category in African Studies is expanding. However, accounts of various African societies, such as Igbo (Amadiume 1987) and Kikuyu to give just two examples, reveal that conceptions of gender cannot be taken at their face value if we are to make sense of African cultures. From the small but expanding original research interrogating gender in African social formations, some lines of divergence from mainstream women's studies are already apparent. I wish to draw attention to two of them. First, the category women cannot be used as a synonym for gender (as is often the case in conventional women's studies research) given the fact that in many African societies social roles are not necessarily biological roles: the best examples being the categories of "wife" and "husband". As a number of studies have shown that neither these conjugal categories nor kinship classifications are sex-specific.

Secondly, because some social roles are truly socially constructed in various African societies, discussions of gender in studies of Africa do not immediately generate or link to discussions of sex and sexuality. In the dominant women's studies literature, gender and sexuality are almost identical twins; discourses of gender are necessarily discussions about sexuality. In fact, increasingly in the United States, the word gender has come to signal sexu ality. This is not necessarily the case in African discourses or institutions: social roles and sexual roles are understood to be separable. Consequently, the starting point of research on gender in Africa must be to interrogate foundational assumptions undergirding hegemonic intellectual tools while at the same time recover local epistemologies.

The anthology *African Gender Studies: A Reader* aims to do just that. Taking Africa seriously, it represents part of the effort to correct the long-standing problem of Western dominance in the interpretation of African realities. The focus of the collection is to bring African experiences to bear on the ongoing global discussion of gender, race, power, hierarchy, and other linked concepts. The topics covered include feminism, women's agency, human rights, social identities, globalization, development, the politics of knowledge and representation, and social transformation. Our concern is twofold: that Africa must be studied on its own terms, and that African knowledge must be a factor in the formulation of social theory.

The most important criterion for the selection of papers for this anthology is the extent to which they interrogate foundational assumptions and substantive issues relating to gender and women's studies, and the extent to which they incorporate African experiences into our understanding of the social world. Bringing together classic and new writings, this book includes articles that speak to a range of debates in the interdisciplinary field of women's studies and African studies, as well as those that address issues in specific disciplines such as history, literary studies, philosophy, sociology, political science, and anthropology.

The anthology contains twenty one chapters and is divided into seven sections. Preceding each segment is an overview of the articles contained within the section.

I would like to acknowledge a grant from the Center for Black Studies at the University of California Santa Barbara that enabled the publication of this volume. I especially appreciate the role of Claudine Michel, who as director of the center set aside the funds for the project, and the active support she continued to give throughout the editorial process. In addition I thank Anna Everett, the current director of the center, for her contributions. Dora Morse and Mashid Ayoub, staff members of the center, also played central roles in getting the project off the ground.

Furthermore, I wish to acknowledge the contributors for allowing me to include their work in this anthology. Taken together, their papers represent essential readings in the interdisciplinary field of African gender studies.

SECTION I

TRANSCENDING THE BODY OF KNOWLEDGE

In the opening essay "Visualizing the Body: Western Theories and African subjects," Oyèrónkẹ́ Oyěwùmí makes a case that the narrative of gendered corporeality that dominates Western interpretations of the social world is a cultural discourse and cannot be assumed uncritically for other cultures. Thus the recent discovery of gender as a universal and timeless social category cannot be divorced from the ideology of biological determinism that underpins Western systems of knowledge. Oyěwùmí concludes that gender is not only socially constructed but also historical. She then looks at the implication in African studies of uncritically imposing Western ideologies and systems of thought, arguing that Africa must be studied on its own terms.

Beyond visible bodies, the paper "Spirituality, Gender, and Power in Asante History" by Emmanuel Akyeampong and Pashington Obeng examines Asante conceptions of power which assigns a central role to spirituality in structuring authority and hierarchy. The significance of this paper is that in our quest to understand African systems of knowledge, we must be cognizant of the relevance of the metaphysical in the constitution of power, and pay attention to the ways in which spirituality undergird interpretations of the material world.

CHAPTER 1

VISUALIZING THE BODY: WESTERN THEORIES AND AFRICAN SUBJECTS

Oyèrónkẹ́ Oyěwùmí

The idea that biology is destiny—or, better still, destiny is biology—has been a staple of Western thought for centuries.[1] Whether the issue is who is who in Aristotle's polis[2] or who is poor in the late twentieth-century United States, the notion that difference and hierarchy in society are biologically determined continues to enjoy credence even among social scientists who purport to explain human society in other than genetic terms. In the West, biological explanations appear to be especially privileged over other ways of explaining differences of gender, race, or class. Difference is expressed as degeneration. In tracing the genealogy of the idea of degeneration in European thought, J. Edward Chamberlain and Sander Gilman noted the way it was used to define certain kinds of difference, in the nineteenth century in particular. "Initially, degeneration brought together two notions of difference, one scientific—a deviation from an original type—and the other moral, a deviation from a norm of behavior. But they were essentially the same notion, of a fall from grace, *a deviation from the original type*."[3] Consequently, those in positions of power find it imperative to establish their superior biology as a way of affirming their privilege and dominance over "Others." Those who are different are seen as genetically inferior, and this, in turn, is used to account for their disadvantaged social positions.

The notion of society that emerges from this conception is that society is constituted by bodies and as bodies—male bodies, female bodies, Jewish bodies, Aryan bodies, black bodies, white bodies, rich bodies, poor bodies. I am using the word "body" in two ways: first, as a metonymy for biology and, second, to draw attention to the sheer physicality that seems to attend being in Western culture. I refer to the corporeal body as well as to metaphors of the body.

The body is given a logic of its own. It is believed that just by looking at it one can tell a person's beliefs and social position or lack thereof. As Naomi Scheman puts it in her discussion of the body politic in premodern

Europe:

> The ways people knew their places in the world had to do with their bodies and the histories of those bodies, and when they violated the prescriptions for those places, their bodies were punished, often spectacularly. One's place in the body politic was as natural as the places of the organs in one's body, and political disorder [was] as unnatural as the shifting and displacement of those organs.[4]

Similarly, Elizabeth Grosz remarks on what she calls the "depth" of the body in modern Western societies:

> Our [Western] body forms are considered expressions of an interior, not inscriptions on a flat surface. By constructing a soul or psyche for itself, the "civilized body" forms libidinal flows, sensations, experiences, and intensities into needs, wants.... *The body becomes a text, a system of signs to be deciphered, read, and read into. Social law is incarnated, "corporealized"[;] correlatively, bodies are textualized, read by others as expressive of a subject's psychic interior.* A storehouse of inscriptions and messages between [the body's] external and internal boundaries...generates or constructs the body's movements into "behavior," which then [has] interpersonally and socially identifiable meanings and functions within a social system.[5]

Consequently, since the body is the bedrock on which the social order is founded, the body is always *in* view and *on* view. As such, it invites a *gaze*, a gaze of difference, a gaze of differentiation—the most historically constant being the gendered gaze. There is a sense in which phrases such as "the social body" or "the body politic" are not just metaphors but can be read literally. It is not surprising, then, that when the body politic needed to be purified in Nazi Germany, certain kinds of bodies had to be eliminated.[6]

The reason that the body has so much presence in the West is that the world is primarily perceived by sight.[7] The differentiation of human bodies in terms of sex, skin color, and cranium size is a testament to the powers attributed to "seeing." The gaze is an invitation to differentiate. Different approaches to comprehending reality, then, suggest epistemological differences between societies. Relative to Yorùbá society, the body has an exaggerated presence in the Western conceptualization of society. The term "worldview," which is used in the West to sum up the cultural logic of a society, captures the West's privileging of the visual. It is Eurocentric to use it to describe cultures that may privilege other senses. The term "world-sense" is a more inclusive way of describing the conception of the world by different cultural groups. In this study, therefore, "worldview" will only be applied to describe the Western cultural sense, and "world-sense" will be used when describing the Yorùbá or other cultures that may privilege senses other than the visual or even a combination of senses.

The foregoing hardly represents the received view of Western history and social thought. Quite the contrary: until recently, the history of Western societies has been presented as a documentation of rational thought in which ideas are framed as the agents of history. If bodies appear at all, they are articulated as the debased side of human nature. The preferred focus has been on the mind, lofty and high above the foibles of the flesh. Early in Western discourse, a binary opposition between body and mind emerged. The much-vaunted Cartesian dualism was only an affirmation of a tradition[8] in which the body was seen as a trap from which any rational person had to escape. Ironically, even as the body remained at the center of both sociopolitical categories and discourse, many thinkers denied its existence for certain categories of people, most notably themselves. "Bodylessness" has been a precondition of rational thought. Women, primitives, Jews, Africans, the poor, and all those who qualified for the label "different" in varying historical epochs have been considered to be the embodied, dominated therefore by instinct and affect, reason being beyond them. They are the Other, and the other is a body.[9]

In pointing out the centrality of the body in the construction of difference in Western culture, one does not necessarily deny that there have been certain traditions in the West that have attempted to explain differences according to criteria other than the presence or absence of certain organs: the possession of a penis, the size of the brain, the shape of the cranium, or the color of the skin. The Marxist tradition is especially noteworthy in this regard in that it emphasized social relations as an explanation for class inequality. However, the critique of Marxism as androcentric by numerous feminist writers suggests that this paradigm is also implicated in Western somatocentricity.[10] Similarly, the establishment of disciplines such as sociology and anthropology, which purport to explain society on the bases of human interactions, seems to suggest the relegation of biological determinism in social thought. On closer examination, however, one finds that the body has hardly been banished from social thought, not to mention its role in the constitution of social status. This can be illustrated in the discipline of sociology. In a monograph on the body and society, Bryan Turner laments what he perceives as the absence of the body in sociological inquiries. He attributes this phenomenon of "absent bodies"[11] to the fact that "sociology emerged as a discipline which took the social meaning of human interaction as its principal object of inquiry, claiming that the meaning of social actions can never be reduced to biology or physiology."[12]

One could agree with Turner about the need to separate sociology from eugenics and phrenology. However, to say that bodies have been absent from sociological theories is to discount the fact that the social groups that are the subject matter of the discipline are essentially understood as rooted in biology. They are categories based on perceptions of the different physical presence of various body-types. In the contemporary U.S., so long as sociologists deal with so-called social categories like the underclass, suburbanites, workers, farmers, voters, citizens, and criminals (to mention a few categories that are historically and in the cultural ethos understood as representing specific body-types), there is no escape from biology. If the social realm is determined by the kinds of bodies occupying it, then to what extent is there a social realm, given that it is conceived to be biologically determined? For example, no one hearing the term "corporate executives" would assume them to be women; and in the 1980s and 1990s, neither would anyone spontaneously associate whites with the terms "underclass" or "gangs"; indeed, if someone were to construct an association between the terms, their meanings would have to be shifted. Consequently, any sociologist who studies these categories cannot escape an underlying biological insidiousness.

This omnipresence of biologically deterministic explanations in the social sciences can be demonstrated with the category of the criminal or criminal type in contemporary American society. Troy Duster, in an excellent study of the resurgence of biological determinism in intellectual circles, berates the eagerness of many researchers to associate criminality with genetic inheritance; he goes on to argue that other interpretations of criminality are possible:

> The prevailing economic interpretation explains crime rates in terms of access to jobs and unemployment. A cultural interpretation tries to show differing cultural adjustments between the police and those apprehended for crimes. A political interpretation sees criminal activity as political interpretation, or pre-revolutionary. A conflict interpretation sees this as an interest conflict over scarce resources.[13]

Clearly, on the face of it, all these explanations of criminality are non-biological; however, as long as the "population" or the social group they are attempting to explain—in this case criminals who are black and/or poor—is seen to represent a genetic grouping, the underlying assumptions about the genetic predisposition of that population or group will structure the explanations proffered whether they are body-based or not. This is tied to the fact that because of the history of racism, the underlying research question (even if it is unstated) is not why certain individuals commit crimes: it is actually why black people have such a propensity to do so. The definition of what is criminal activity is very much tied up with who (black, white, rich, poor) is involved in the activity.[14] Likewise, the police, as a group, are assumed to be white. Similarly, when studies are done of leadership in American society, the researchers "discover" that most people in leadership positions are white males; no matter what account these researchers give for this result, their statements will be read as explaining the predisposition of this group to leadership.

The integrity of researchers is not being questioned here; my purpose is not to label any group of scholars as racist in their intentions. On the contrary, since the Civil Rights movement, social-scientific research has been used to formulate policies that would abate if not end discrimination against subordinated groups. What must be underscored, however, is how knowledge-production and dissemination in the United States are inevitably embedded in what Michael Omi and Howard Winant call the "everyday common sense of race—a way of comprehending, explaining and acting in the world."[15] Race, then, is a fundamental organizing principle in American society. It is institutionalized, and it functions irrespective of the action of individual actors.

In the West, social identities are all interpreted through the "prism of heritability,"[16] to borrow Duster's phrase. Biological determinism is a filter through which all knowledge about society is run. As mentioned in the preface, I refer to this kind of thinking as body-reasoning;[17] it is a biologic interpretation of the social world. The point, again, is that as long as social actors like managers, criminals, nurses, and the poor are presented as groups and not as individuals, and as long as such groupings are conceived to be genetically constituted, then there is no escape from biological determinism.

Against this background, the issue of gender difference is particularly interesting in regard to the history and the constitution of difference in European social practice and thought. The lengthy history of the embodiment of social categories is suggested by the myth fabricated by Socrates to convince citizens of different ranks to accept whatever status was imposed upon them. Socrates explained the myth to Glaucon in these terms:

> Citizens, we shall say to them in our tale, you are brothers, yet God has framed you differently. Some of you have the power of command, and in the composition of these he has mingled gold, wherefore also they have the greatest honor; others he has made silver, to be auxiliaries; others again who are to be husbandmen and craftsmen he has composed of brass and iron; and the species will generally be preserved in the children. . . . An Oracle says that when a man of brass or iron guards the state, it will be destroyed. Such is the tale; is there any possibility of making our citizens believe in it?

Glaucon replies, "Not in the present generation; there is no way of accomplishing this; but their sons may be made to believe in the tale, and their sons' sons, and posterity after them."[18] Glaucon was mistaken that the acceptance of the myth could be accomplished only in the next generation: the myth of those born to rule was already in operation; mothers, sisters, and daughters—women—were already excluded from consideration in any of those ranks. In a context in which people were ranked according to association with certain metals, women were, so to speak, made of wood, and so were not even considered. Stephen Gould, a historian of science, calls Glaucon's observation a prophecy, since history shows that Socrates' tale has been promulgated and believed by subsequent generations.[19] The point, however, is that even in Glaucon's time, it was more than a prophecy: it was already a social practice to exclude women from the ranks of rulers.

Paradoxically, in European thought, despite the fact that society was seen to be inhabited by bodies, only women were perceived to be embodied; men had no bodies—they were walking minds. Two social categories that emanated from this construction were the "man of reason" (the thinker) and the "woman of the body," and they were oppositionally constructed. The idea that the man of reason often had the woman of the body on his mind was clearly not entertained. As Michel Foucault's *History of Sexuality* suggests, however, the man of ideas often had the woman and indeed other bodies on his mind.[20]

In recent times, thanks in part to feminist scholarship, the body is beginning to receive the attention it deserves as a site and as material for the explication of European history and thought.[21] The distinctive contribution of feminist discourse to our understanding of Western societies is that it makes explicit the gendered (therefore embodied) and male-dominant nature of all Western institutions and discourses. The feminist lens disrobes the man of ideas for all to see. Even discourses like science that were assumed to be objective have been shown to be male-biased.[22] The extent to which the body is implicated in the construction of sociopolitical categories and epistemologies cannot be overemphasized. As noted earlier, Dorothy Smith has written that in Western societies "a man's body gives credibility to his utterance, whereas a woman's body takes it away from hers."[23] Writing on the construction of masculinity, R. W. Connell notes that the body is inescapable in its construction and that a stark physicalness underlies gender categories in the Western worldview: "In our [Western] culture, at least, the physical sense of maleness and femaleness is central to the cultural interpretation of gender. Masculine gender is (among other things) a certain feel to the skin, certain muscular shapes and tensions, certain postures and ways of moving, certain possibilities in sex."[24]

From the ancients to the moderns, gender has been a foundational category upon which social categories have been erected. Hence, gender has been ontologically conceptualized. The category of the citizen, which has been the cornerstone of much of Western political theory, was male, despite the much-acclaimed Western democratic traditions.[25] Elucidating Aristotle's categorization of the sexes, Elizabeth Spelman writes: "A woman is a female who is free; a man is a male who is a citizen."[26] Women were excluded from the category of citizens because "penis possession"[27] was one of the qualifications for citizenship. Lorna Schiebinger notes in a study of the origins of modern science and women's exclusion from European scientific institutions that "differences between the two sexes were reflections of a set of dualistic principles that penetrated the cosmos as well as the bodies of men and women."[28] Differences and hierarchy, then, are enshrined on bodies; and bodies enshrine differences and hierarchy. Hence, dualisms like nature/culture, public/private, and visible/invisible are variations on the theme of male/female bodies hierarchically ordered, differentially placed in relation to power, and spatially distanced one from the other.[29]

In the span of Western history, the justifications for the making of the categories "man" and "woman" have not remained the same. On the contrary, they have been dynamic. Although the boundaries are shifting and the content of each category may change, the two categories have remained hierarchical and in binary opposition. For Stephen Gould, "the justification for ranking groups by inborn worth has varied with the tide of Western history.

Plato relied on dialectic, the church upon dogma. For the past two centuries, scientific claims have become the primary agent of validating Plato's myth."[30] The constant in this Western narrative is the centrality of the body: two bodies on display, two sexes, two categories persistently viewed—one in relation to the other. That narrative is about the unwavering elaboration of the body as the site and cause of differences and hierarchies in society. In the West, so long as the issue is difference and social hierarchy, then the body is constantly positioned, posed, exposed, and reexposed as their cause. Society, then, is seen as an accurate reflection of genetic endowment—those with a superior biology inevitably are those in superior social positions. No difference is elaborated without bodies that are positioned hierarchically. In his book *Making Sex*,[31] Thomas Laqueur gives a richly textured history of the construction of sex from classical Greece to the contemporary period, noting the changes in symbols and the shifts in meanings. The point, however, is the centrality and persistence of the body in the construction of social categories. In view of this history, Freud's dictum that anatomy is destiny was not original or exceptional; he was just more explicit than many of his predecessors.

SOCIAL ORDERS AND BIOLOGY: NATURAL OR CONSTRUCTED?

The idea that gender is socially constructed—that differences between males and female are to be located in social practices, not in biological facts—was one important insight that emerged early in second-wave feminist scholarship. This finding was understandably taken to be radical in a culture in which difference, particularly gender difference, had always been articulated as natural and, therefore, biologically determined. Gender as a social construction became the cornerstone of much feminist discourse. The notion was particularly attractive because it was interpreted to mean that gender differences were not ordained by nature; they were mutable and therefore changeable. This in turn led to the opposition between social constructionism and biological determinism, as if they are mutually exclusive.

Such a dichotomous presentation is unwarranted, however, because the ubiquity of biologically rooted explanations for difference in Western social thought and practices is a reflection of the extent to which biological explanations are found compelling.[32] In other words, so long as the issue is difference (whether the issue is why women breast-feed babies or why they could not vote), old biologies will be found or new biologies will be constructed to explain women's disadvantage. The Western preoccupation with biology continues to generate constructions of "new biologies" even as some of the old biological assumptions are being dislodged. In fact, in the Western experience, social construction and biological determinism have been two sides of the same coin, since both ideas continue to reinforce each other. When social categories like gender are constructed, new biologies of difference can be invented. When biological interpretations are found to be compelling, social categories do derive their legitimacy and power from biology. In short, the social and the biological feed on each other.

The biologization inherent in the Western articulation of social difference is, however, by no means universal. The debate in feminism about what roles and which identities are natural and what aspects are constructed only has meaning in a culture where social categories are conceived as having no independent logic of their own. This debate, of course, developed out of certain problems; therefore, it is logical that in societies where such problems do not exist, there should be no such debate. But then, due to imperialism, this debate has been universalized to other cultures, and its immediate effect is to inject Western problems where such issues originally did not exist. Even then, this debate does not take us very far in societies where social roles and identities are not conceived to be rooted in biology. By the same token, in cultures where the visual sense is not privileged, and the body is not read as a blueprint of society, invocations of biology are less likely to occur because such explanations do not carry much weight in the social realm. That many categories of difference are socially constructed in the West may well suggest the mutability of categories, but it is also an invitation to endless constructions of biology—in that there is no limit to what can be explained by the body-appeal. Thus biology is hardly mutable; it is much more a combination of the Hydra and the Phoenix of Greek mythology. Biology is forever mutating, not mutable. Ultimately, the most important point is not that gender is socially constructed but the extent to which biology itself is socially constructed and therefore inseparable from the social.

The way in which the conceptual categories sex and gender functioned in feminist discourse was based on the assumption that biological and social conceptions could be separated and applied universally. Thus sex was presented as the natural category and gender as the social construction of the natural. But, subsequently, it became apparent that even sex has elements of construction. In many feminist writings thereafter, sex has served as the base and gender as the superstructure.[33] In spite of all efforts to separate the two, the distinction between sex and gender is a red herring. In Western conceptualization, gender cannot exist without sex since the body sits squarely at the base of both categories. Despite the preeminence of feminist social constructionism, which claims a social deterministic approach to society, biological foundationalism,[34] if not reductionism, is still at the center of gender discourses, just as it is at the center of all other discussions of society in the West.

Nevertheless, the idea that gender is socially constructed is significant from a cross-cultural perspective. In one of the earliest feminist texts to assert the constructionist thesis and its need for cross-cultural grounding, Suzanne J. Kessler and Wendy McKenna wrote that "by viewing gender as a social construction, it is possible to see descriptions of other cultures as evidence for alternative but equally real conceptions of what it means to be woman or man."[35] Yet, paradoxically, a fundamental assumption of feminist theory is that women's subordination is universal. These two ideas are contradictory. The universality attributed to gender asymmetry suggests a biological basis rather than a cultural one, given that the human anatomy is universal whereas cultures speak in myriad voices. That gender is socially constructed is said to mean that the criteria that make up male and female categories vary in different cultures. If this is so, then it challenges the notion that there is a biological imperative at work. From this standpoint, then, gender categories are mutable, and as such, gender then is denaturalized.

In fact, the categorization of women in feminist discourses as a homogeneous, bio-anatomically determined group which is always constituted as powerless and victimized does not reflect the fact that gender relations are social relations and, therefore, historically grounded and culturally bound. If gender is socially constructed, then gender cannot behave in the same way across time and space. If gender is a social construction, then we must examine the various cultural/architectural sites where it was constructed, and we must acknowledge that variously located actors (aggregates, groups, interested parties) were part of the construction. We must further acknowledge that if gender is a social construction, then there was a specific time (in different cultural/architectural sites) when it was "constructed" and therefore a time before which it was not. Thus, gender, being a social construction, is also a historical and cultural phenomenon. Consequently, it is logical to assume that in some societies, gender construction need not have existed at all.

From a cross-cultural perspective, the significance of this observation is that one cannot assume the social organization of one culture (the dominant West included) as universal or the interpretations of the experiences of one culture as explaining another one. On the one hand, at a general, global level, the constructedness of gender does suggest its mutability. On the other hand, at the local level—that is, within the bounds of any particular culture—gender is mutable only if it is socially constructed as such. Because, in Western societies, gender categories, like all other social categories, are constructed with biological building blocks, their mutability is questionable. The cultural logic of Western social categories is founded on an ideology of biological determinism: the conception that biology provides the rationale for the organization of the social world. Thus, as pointed out earlier, this cultural logic is actually a "bio-logic."

THE "SISTERARCHY": FEMINISM AND ITS "OTHER"

From a cross-cultural perspective, the implications of Western bio-logic are far-reaching when one considers the fact that gender constructs in feminist theory originated in the West, where men and women are conceived oppositionally and projected as embodied, genetically derived social categories.[36] The question, then, is this: On what basis are Western conceptual categories exportable or transferable to other cultures that have a different cultural logic? This question is raised because despite the wonderful insight about the social construction of gender, the way cross-cultural data have been used by many feminist writers undermines the notion that differing cultures may construct social categories differently. For one thing, if different cultures necessarily always construct gender as feminism proposes that they *do and must*, then the idea that gender is socially constructed is not sustainable.

The potential value of Western feminist social constructionism remains, therefore, largely unfulfilled, because feminism, like most other Western theoretical frameworks for interpreting the social world, cannot get away from the prism of biology that necessarily perceives social hierarchies as natural. Consequently, in cross-cultural gender studies, theorists impose Western categories on non-Western cultures and then project such categories as natural. The way in which dissimilar constructions of the social world in other cultures are used as "evidence" for the constructedness of gender and the insistence that these cross-cultural constructions are gender categories as they operate in the West nullify the alternatives offered by the non-Western cultures and undermine the claim that gender is a social construction.

Western ideas are imposed when non-Western social categories are assimilated into the gender framework that emerged from a specific sociohistorical and philosophical tradition. An example is the "discovery" of what has been labeled "third gender"[37] or "alternative genders"[38] in a number of non-Western cultures. The fact that the African "woman marriage,"[39] the Native American "berdache,"[40] and the South Asian "hijra"[41] are presented as gender categories incorporates them into the Western bio-logic and gendered framework without explication of their own sociocultural histories and constructions. A number of questions are pertinent here. Are these social categories seen as gendered in the cultures in question? From whose perspective are they gendered? In fact, even the appropriateness of naming them "third gender" is questionable since the Western cultural system, which uses biology to map the social world, precludes the possibility of more than two genders because gender is the elaboration of the perceived sexual dimorphism of the human body into the social realm. The trajectory of feminist discourse in the last twenty-five years has been determined by the Western cultural environment of its founding and development.

Thus, in the beginning of second-wave feminism in Euro-America, sex was defined as the biological facts of male and female bodies, and gender was defined as the social consequences that flowed from these facts. In effect, each society was assumed to have a sex/gender system.[42] The most important point was that sex and gender are inextricably bound. Over time, sex tended to be understood as the base and gender as the superstructure. Subsequently, however, after much debate, even sex was interpreted as socially constructed. Kessler and McKenna, one of the earliest research teams in this area, wrote that they "use gender, rather than sex, even when referring to those aspects of being a woman (girl) or man (boy) that have been viewed as biological. This will serve to emphasize our position that the element of social construction is primary in all aspects of being male or female."[43] Judith Butler, writing almost fifteen years later, reiterates the interconnectedness of sex and gender even more strongly:

> It would make no sense, then, to define gender as the cultural interpretation of sex, if sex itself is a gendered category. Gender ought not to be conceived

> merely as a cultural inscription of meaning on a pregiven surface (a juridical conception); gender must also designate the very apparatus of production whereby the sexes themselves are established. As a result, gender is not to culture as sex is to nature; gender is also the discursive/cultural means by which "sexed nature" or "a natural sex" is produced.[44]

Given the inseparability of sex and gender in the West, which results from the use of biology as an ideology for mapping the social world, the terms "sex" and "gender," as noted earlier, are essentially synonyms. To put this another way: since in Western constructions, physical bodies are always social bodies, there is really no distinction between sex and gender.[45] In Yorùbá society, in contrast, social relations derive their legitimacy from social facts, not from biology. The bare biological facts of pregnancy and parturition count only in regard to procreation, where they must. Biological facts do not determine who can become the monarch or who can trade in the market. In indigenous Yorùbá conception, these questions were properly social questions, not biological ones; hence, the nature of one's anatomy did not define one's social position. Consequently, the Yorùbá social order requires a different kind of map, not a gender map that assumes biology as the foundation for the social.

The splitting of hairs over the relationship between gender and sex, the debate on essentialism, the debates about differences among women,[46] and the preoccupation with gender bending/blending[47] that have characterized feminism are actually feminist versions of the enduring debate on nature versus nurture that is inherent in Western thought and in the logic of its social hierarchies. These concerns are not necessarily inherent in the discourse of society as such but are a culture-specific concern and issue. From a cross-cultural perspective, the more interesting point is the degree to which feminism, despite its radical local stance, exhibits the same ethnocentric and imperialistic characteristics of the Western discourses it sought to subvert. This has placed serious limitations on its applicability outside of the culture that produced it. As Kathy Ferguson reminds us: "The questions we can ask about the world are enabled, and other questions disabled, by the frame that orders the questioning. *When we are busy arguing about the questions that appear within a certain frame, the frame itself becomes invisible; we become enframed within it.*"[48] Though feminism in origin, by definition, and by practice is a universalizing discourse, the concerns and questions that have informed it are Western (and its audience too is apparently assumed to be composed of just Westerners, given that many of the theorists tend to use the first-person plural "we" and "our culture" in their writings). As such, feminism remains enframed by the tunnel vision and the bio-logic of other Western discourses.

Yorùbá society of southwestern Nigeria suggests a different scenario, one in which the body is not always enlisted as the basis for social classification. From a Yorùbá stance, the body appears to have an exaggerated presence in Western thought and social practice, including feminist theories. In the Yorùbá world, particularly in pre-nineteenth-century.[49] Ọ̀yọ́ culture, society was conceived to be inhabited by people in relation to one another. That is, the "physicality" of maleness or femaleness did not have social antecedents and therefore did not constitute social categories. Social hierarchy was determined by social relations As noted earlier, how persons were situated in relationships shifted depending on those involved and the particular situation. The principle that determined social organization was seniority, which was based on chronological age. Yorùbá kinship terms did not denote gender, and other nonfamilial social categories were not gender-specific either. What these Yorùbá categories tell us is that the body is not always in view and on view for categorization. The classic example is the female who played the roles of *ọba* (ruler), *omo* (offspring), *ọkọ*, *aya*, *ìyá* (mother), and *aláwo* (diviner-priest) all in one body. None of these kinship and nonkinship social categories are gender-specific. One cannot place persons in the Yorùbá categories just by looking at them. What they are heard to say may be the most important cue. Seniority as the foundation of Yorùbá social intercourse is relational and dynamic; unlike gender, it is not focused on the body.[50]

If the human body is universal, why does the body appear to have an exaggerated presence in the West relative to Yorùbáland? A comparative research framework reveals that one major difference stems from which of the senses is privileged in the apprehension of reality— sight in the West and a multiplicity of senses anchored by hearing in Yorùbá land. The tonality of Yorùbá language predisposes one toward an apprehension of reality that cannot marginalize the auditory. Consequently, relative to Western societies, there is a stronger need for a broader contextualization in order to make sense of the world.[51] For example, Ifá divination, which is also a knowledge system in Yorùbá land, has both visual and oral components.[52] More fundamentally, the distinction between Yorùbá and the West symbolized by the focus on different senses in the apprehension of reality involves more than perception— for the Yorùbá, and indeed many other African societies, it is about "a particular presence in the world—a world conceived of as a whole in which all things are linked together."[53] It concerns the many worlds human beings inhabit; it does not privilege the physical world over the metaphysical. A concentration on vision as the primary mode of comprehending reality promotes what can be seen over that which is not apparent to the eye; it misses the other levels and the nuances of existence. David Lowe's comparison of sight and the sense of hearing encapsulates some of the issues to which I wish to draw attention. He writes:

> Of the five senses, hearing is the most pervasive and penetrating. I say this, although many, from Aristotle in *Metaphysics* to Hans Jonas in *Phenomenon of Life*, have said that sight is most noble. But sight is always directed at what is straight ahead. . . . And sight cannot turn a corner, at least without the aid of a mirror. On the other hand, sound comes to one, surrounds one for the time being with an acoustic space, full of timbre and nuances. It is more proximate and suggestive than sight. Sight is always the perception of the surface from a particular angle. But sound is that perception able to penetrate beneath the

> surface. . . . Speech is the communication connecting one person with another. Therefore, the quality of sound is fundamentally more vital and moving than that of sight.[54]

Just as the West's privileging of the visual over other senses has been clearly demonstrated, so too the dominance of the auditory in Yorùbáland can be shown.

In an interesting paper appropriately entitled "The Mind's Eye," feminist theorists Evelyn Fox Keller and Christine Grontkowski make the following observation: "We [Euro-Americans] speak of knowledge as illumination, knowing as seeing, truth as light. How is it, we might ask, that vision came to seem so apt a model for knowledge? And having accepted it as such, how has the metaphor colored our conceptions of knowledge?"[55] These theorists go on to analyze the implications of the privileging of sight over other senses for the conception of reality and knowledge in the West. They examine the linkages between the privileging of vision and patriarchy, noting that the roots of Western thought in the visual have yielded a dominant male logic.[56] Explicating Jonas's observation that "to get the proper view, we take the proper distance,"[57] they note the passive nature of sight, in that the subject of the gaze is passive. They link the distance that seeing entails to the concept of objectivity and the lack of engagement between the "I" and the subject—the Self and the Other.[58] Indeed, the Other in the West is best described as another body—separate and distant.

Feminism has not escaped the visual logic of Western thought. The feminist focus on sexual difference, for instance, stems from this legacy. Feminist theorist Nancy Chodorow has noted the primacy and limitations of this feminist concentration on difference:

> For our part as feminists, even as we want to eliminate gender inequality, hierarchy, and difference, we expect to find such features in most social settings. . . . We have begun from the assumption that *gender is always a salient* feature of social life, and we do not have theoretical approaches that emphasize sex similarities over differences.[59]

Consequently, the assumption and deployment of patriarchy and "women" as universals in many feminist writings are ethnocentric and demonstrate the hegemony of the West over other cultural groupings.[60] The emergence of patriarchy as a form of social organization in Western history is a function of the differentiation between male and female bodies, a difference rooted in the visual, a difference that cannot be reduced to biology and that has to be understood as being constituted within particular historical and social realities. I am not suggesting that gender categories are necessarily limited to the West, particularly in the contemporary period. Rather, I am suggesting that discussions of social categories should be defined and grounded in the local milieu, rather than based on "universal" findings made in the West. A number of feminist scholars have questioned the assumption of universal patriarchy. For example, the editors of a volume on Hausa women of northern Nigeria write: "A preconceived assumption of gender asymmetry actually distorts many analyses, since it precludes the exploration of gender as a fundamental component of social relations, inequality, processes of production and reproduction, and ideology."[61] Beyond the question of asymmetry, however, a preconceived notion of gender as a universal social category is equally problematic. If the investigator assumes gender, then gender categories will be found whether they exist or not.

Feminism is one of the latest Western theoretical fashions to be applied to African societies. Following the one-size-fits-all (or better still, the Western-size-fits-all) approach to intellectual theorizing, it has taken its place in a long series of Western paradigms—including Marxism, functionalism, structuralism, and poststructuralism—imposed on African subjects. Academics have become one of the most effective international hegemonizing forces, producing not homogenous social experiences but a homogeny of hegemonic forces. Western theories become tools of hegemony as they are applied universally, on the assumption that Western experiences define the human. For example, a study of Ga residents of a neighborhood in Accra, Ghana, starts thus: "Improving our analysis of women and class formation is necessary to refine our perceptions."[62] Women? What women? Who qualifies to be women in this cultural setting, and on what bases are they to be identified? These questions are legitimate ones to raise if researchers take the constructedness of social categories seriously and take into account local conceptions of reality. The pitfalls of preconceived notions and ethnocentricity become obvious when the author of the study admits:

> Another bias I began with I was forced to change. Before starting fieldwork I was not particularly interested in economics, causal or otherwise. But by the time I had tried an initial presurvey, . . . the overweening importance of trading activities in pervading every aspect of women's lives made a consideration of economics imperative. And when the time came to analyze the data in depth, the most cogent explanations often were economic ones. I started out to work with women; I ended by working with traders.[63]

Why, in the first place, did Claire Robertson, the author of this study, start with women, and what distortions were introduced as a result? What if she had started with traders? Would she have ended up with women? Beginnings are important; adding other variables in midstream does not prevent or solve distortions and misapprehensions. Like many studies on Africans, half of Robertson's study seems to have been completed—and categories were already in place—before she met the Gã people. Robertson's monograph is not atypical in African studies; in fact, it is one of the better ones, particularly because unlike many scholars, she is aware of some of her biases. The fundamental bias that many Westerners, including Robertson, bring to the study of other societies is "body-reasoning," the assumption that biology determines social position. Because "women" is a body-based category, it tends to be privileged by Western researchers over "traders," which is non-body-based. Even when traders are taken seriously, they are embodied such that the trader category, which in many West African societies is non-gender-specific, is turned into "market women," as if the explanation for their involvement in this occupation is to be found in their breasts, or to put it more scientifically, in the X chromosome.[64] The more the Western bio-logic is adopted, the more this body-based framework is inscribed conceptually and into the social reality.

It is not clear that the body is a site of such elaboration of the social in the Ga world-sense or in other African cultures. This warrants investigation before one can draw conclusions that many studies are drawing on gender in African cultures. Why have African studies remained so dependent on Western theories, and what are the implications for the constitution of knowledge about African realities? Contrary to the most basic tenets of body-reasoning, all kinds of people, irrespective of body-type, are implicated in constructing this biologically deterministic discourse. Body-reasoning is a cultural approach. Its origins are easily locatable in European thought, but its tentacles have become all pervasive. Western hegemony appears in many different ways in African studies, but the focus here will be on the hand-me-down theories that are used to interpret African societies without any regard to fit or how ragged they have become.

NOTES

1. Compare Thomas Laqueur's usage: "Destiny Is Anatomy," which is the title of chapter 2 of his *Making Sex: Body and Gender from the Greeks to Freud* (Cambridge, Mass.: Harvard University Press, 1990).
2. Elizabeth Spelman, *Inessential Woman: Problems of Exclusion in Feminist Thought* (Boston: Beacon Press, 1988), 37.
3. J. Edward Chamberlain and Sander Gilman, *Degeneration: The Darker Side of Progress* (New York: Columbia University Press, 1985), 292.
4. Naomi Scheman, *Engenderings: Constructions of Knowledge, Authority, and Privilege* (New York: Routledge, 1993), 186.
5. Elizabeth Grosz, "Bodies and Knowledges: Feminism and the Crisis of Reason," in *Feminist Epistemologies*, ed. Linda Alcoff and Elizabeth Potter (New York: Routledge, 1994), 198; emphasis added.
6. Scheman, *Engenderings.*
7. See, for example, the following for accounts of the importance of sight in Western thought: Hans Jonas, *The Phenomenon of Life* (New York: Harper and Row, 1966); Donald Lowe, *History of Bourgeois Perception* (Chicago: University of Chicago Press, 1982).
8. Compare the discussion in Nancy Scheper-Hughes and Margaret Lock, "The Mindful Body: A Prolegomenon to Future Work in Medical Anthropology," *Medical Anthropology Quarterly*, n.s., 1 (March 1987): 7–41.
9. The work of Sander Gilman is particularly illuminating on European conceptions of difference and otherness. See *Difference and Pathology: Stereotypes of Sexuality, Race, and Madness* (Ithaca, N.Y.: Cornell University Press, 1985); *On Blackness without Blacks: Essays on the Image of the Black in Germany* (Boston: G. K. Hall, 1982); *The Case of Sigmund Freud: Medicine and Identity*

(Baltimore: John Hopkins University Press, 1993); *Jewish Self-Hatred: Anti-Semitism and the Hidden Language of the Jews* (Baltimore: John Hopkins University Press, 1986).

10. See, for example, the following: Linda Nicholson, "Feminism and Marx," in *Feminism as Critique: On the Politics of Gender*, ed. Seyla Benhabib and Drucilla Cornell (Minneapolis: University of Minnesota Press, 1986); Michele Barrett, *Women's Oppression Today* (London: New Left Books, 1980); Heidi Hartmann, "The Unhappy Marriage of Marxism and Feminism: Towards a More Progressive Union," in *Women and Revolution: A Discussion of the Unhappy Marriage of Marxism and Feminism*, ed. Lydia Sargent (Boston: South End Press, 1981).
11. Bryan Turner, "Sociology and the Body," in *The Body and Society: Explorations in Social Theory* (Oxford: Blackwell, 1984), 31.
12. Ibid.
13. Troy Duster, *Backdoor to Eugenics* (New York: Routledge, 1990).
14. Ibid.
15. Michael Omi and Howard Winant, *Racial Formation in the United States from the 1960s to the 1980s* (New York: Routledge, 1986). Compare also the discussion of the pervasiveness of race over other variables, such as class, in the analysis of the Los Angeles riot of 1992. According to Cedric Robinson, "Mass media and official declarations subsumed the genealogy of the Rodney King Uprisings into the antidemocratic narratives of race which dominate American culture. Urban unrest, crime, and poverty are discursive economies which signify race while erasing class" ("Race, Capitalism and the Anti-Democracy," paper presented at the Inter-disciplinary Humanities Center, University of California–Santa Barbara, winter 1994).
16. Duster (*Backdoor*) points to the widely held notion that diseases as well as money "run in families."
17. Compare Cornel West's concept of racial reasoning in *Race Matters* (New York: Vantage, 1993).
18. Cited in Stephen Gould, *The Mismeasure of Man* (New York: Norton, 1981), 19.
19. Ibid.
20. A recent anthology questions the dominant self-representation of Jews as "the People of the Book" and in the process attempts to document a relatively less common image of Jews as "the People of the Body." The editor of the volume makes an interesting point about "the [Jewish] thinker" and his book. He comments that the thinker's book "is evocative of... wisdom and the pursuit of knowledge. In this way, the image of the Jew (who is always male) poring over a book is always misleading. He appears to be elevated in spiritual pursuit. But if we could peer over his shoulders and see what his text says, he may in fact be reading about matters as erotic as what position to take during sexual intercourse. What is going on in 'the thinker's' head or more interestingly in his loins?" (Howard Elberg-Schwartz, "People of the Body," introduction to *People of the Body: Jews and Judaism from an Embodied Perspective* [Albany: State University of New York Press, 1992]). The somatocentric nature of European discourses suggests that the phrase the "People of the Body" may have a wider reach.
21. Attention to the body has not been smooth-sailing in feminism either. See Elizabeth Grosz, *Volatile Bodies: Toward a Corporeal Feminism* (Bloomington: Indiana University Press, 1994).

22. Virginia Woolf had summed up the feminist position succinctly: "Science it would seem is not sexless; she is a man, a father infected too" (quoted in Hillary Rose, "Hand, Brain, and Heart: A Feminist Epistemology for the Natural Sciences," *Signs* 9, no. 1 [1983]: 73–90). See also the following: Sandra Harding, *The Science Question in Feminism* (Ithaca, N.Y.: Cornell University Press, 1986); idem, ed., *The Racial Economy of Science* (Bloomington: Indiana University Press, 1993); Donna J. Haraway, *Primate Visions: Gender, Race, and Nature in the World of Modern Science* (New York: Routledge, 1989); and Margaret Wertheim *Pythagoras' Trousers: God Physics and the Gender Wars* (New York: Random House, 1995).
23. Dorothy E. Smith, *The Everyday World as Problematic: A Feminist Sociology* (Boston: Northeastern University Press, 1987), 30.
24. R. W. Connell, *Masculinities* (London: Polity Press, 1995), 53.
25. Susan Okin, *Women in Western Political Thought* (Princeton, N.J.: Princeton University Press, 1979); Elizabeth Spelman, *Inessential Woman: Problems of Exclusion in Feminist Thought* (Boston: Beacon Press, 1988).
26. Quoted in Laqueur, *Making Sex*, 54.
27. Ibid.
28. Lorna Schiebinger, *The Mind Has No Sex? Women in the Origins of Modern Science* (Cambridge, Mass.: Harvard University Press, 1989), 162.
29. For an account of some of these dualisms, see "Hélène Cixous," in *New French Feminism: An Anthology*, ed. Elaine Marks and Isabelle de Courtivron (Amherst, Mass.: University of Massachusetts Press, 1980).
30. Gould, *Mismeasure of Man*, 20.
31. Laqueur, *Making Sex*.
32. See Suzanne J. Kessler and Wendy McKenna, *Gender: An Ethnomethodological Approach* (New York: John Wiley and Sons, 1978).
33. For elucidation, see Jane F. Collier and Sylvia J. Yanagisako, eds., *Gender and Kinship: Essays toward a Unified Analysis* (Stanford, Calif.: Stanford University Press, 1987).
34. Linda Nicholson has also explicated the pervasiveness of biological foundationalism in feminist thought. See "Interpreting Gender," in *Signs* 20 (1994): 79–104.
35. Kessler and McKenna, *Gender*.
36. In the title of this section, I use the term "sisterarchy." In using the term, I am referring to the well-founded allegations against Western feminists by a number of African, Asian, and Latin American feminists that despite the notion that the "sisterhood is global," Western women are at the top of the hierarchy of the sisterhood; hence it is actually a "sisterarchy." Nkiru Nzegwu uses the concept in her essay "O Africa: Gender Imperialism in Academia," in *African Women and Feminism: Reflecting on the Politics of Sisterhood*, ed. Oyèrónkẹ́. Oyěwùmí (Trenton, N.J.: African World Press, forthcoming).
37. Lorber, *Paradoxes of Gender*, 17–18.
38. Ibid.
39. See Ifi Amadiume, *Male Daughters, Female Husbands: Gender and Sex in an African Society* (London: Zed Books, 1987), for an account of this institution in Igboland of southeastern Nigeria. See also Melville J. Herskovitz, "A Note on 'Woman Marriage' in Dahomey," *Africa* 10 (1937): 335–41, for an earlier allusion to its wide occurrence in Africa.
40. Kessler and McKenna, *Gender*, 24–36.

41. Serena Nanda, "Neither Man Nor Woman: The Hijras of India," in *Gender in Cross-cultural Perspective,* ed. Caroline Brettell and Carolyn Sargent (Englewood Cliffs, N.J.: Prentice Hall, 1993).
42. Gayle Rubin, "The Traffic in Women," in *Toward an Anthropology of Women*, ed. Rayna R. Reiter (New York: Monthly Review Press, 1975).
43. Kessler and McKenna, *Gender*, 7; Laqueur, *Making Sex.*
44. Judith Butler, *Gender Trouble: Feminism and the Subversion of Identity* (New York: Routledge, 1990), 7.
45. In her study (*Male Daughters*) of the Igbo society of Nigeria, anthropologist Ifi Amadiume introduced the idea of "gender flexibility" to capture the real separability of gender and sex in the African society. I, however, think that the "woman to woman" marriages of Igboland invite a more radical interrogation of the concept of gender, an interrogation that "gender flexibility" fails to represent. For one thing, the concept of gender as elaborated in the literature is a dichotomy, a duality grounded on the sexual dimorphism of the human body. Here, there is no room for flexibility.
46. The "race and gender literature" is grounded on notions of differences among women.
47. See, for example, Holly Devor, *Gender Blending: Confronting the Limits of Duality* (Bloomington: Indiana University Press, 1989); Rebecca Gordon, "Delusions of Gender," *Women's Review of Books* 12, no. 2 (November 1994): 18–19.
48. Kathy Ferguson, *The Man Question: Visions of Subjectivity in Feminist Theory* (Berkeley: University of California Press), 7.
49. My use of the nineteenth century as a benchmark is merely to acknowledge the emerging gender configurations in the society; the process must have started earlier, given the role of the Atlantic slave trade in the dislocation of Yorùbáland.
50. See chapter 2 for a full account of Yorùbá world-sense as it is mapped onto social hierarchies.
51. This is not an attempt on my part to partake of some of the reductionist discussion about the "orality" of African societies in relation to "writing" in the West; nor is it the intention of this book to set up a binary opposition between the West and Yorùbáland, on the one hand, and writing and orality, on the other, as some scholars have done. There is a huge literature on writing and orality. A good entry point into the discourse, though it is an overly generalized account, is Walter Ong, *Orality and Literacy: The Technologizing of the Word* (New York: Methuen, 1982). For a recent account of some the issues from an African perspective, see Samba Diop, "The Oral History and Literature of Waalo, Northern Senegal: The Master of the Word in Wolof Tradition" (Ph.D.diss., Department of Comparative Literature, University of California–Berkeley, 1993).
52. See Wande Abimbola, *Ifa: An Exposition of the Ifa Literary Corpus* (Ìbàdàn: Oxford University Press, 1976).
53. Amadou Hampate Ba, "Approaching Africa," in *African Films: The Context of Production*, ed. Angela Martin (London: British Film Institute, 1982), 9.
54. Lowe, *History of Bourgeois Perception*, 7.
55. Evelyn Fox Keller and Christine Grontkowski, "The Mind's Eye," in *Discovering Reality: Feminist Perspectives on Epistemology, Metaphysics, Methodology, and Philosophy of Science*, ed. Sandra Harding and Merrill B. Hintikka (Boston: Reidel, 1983), 208.

56. Ibid.
57. Jonas, *Phenomenon of Life*, 507.
58. Keller and Grontkowski, "The Mind's Eye."
59. Nancy Chodorow, *Feminism and Psychoanalytic Theory* (New Haven: Yale University Press, 1989), 216.
60. See Amadiume, *Male Daughters;* and Valerie Amos and Pratibha Parma, "Challenging Imperial Feminism," *Feminist Review* (July 1984): 3–20.
61. Catherine Coles and Beverly Mack, eds., *Hausa Women in the Twentieth Century* (Madison: University of Wisconsin Press, 1991), 6.
62. Claire Robertson, *Sharing the Same Bowl: A Socioeconomic History of Women and Class in Accra, Ghana* (Bloomington: Indiana University Press, 1984), 23.
63. TK.
64. TK.
65. Eldholm, Harris, and Young, "Conceptualising Women," 127.
66. This term is from Fuss, *Essentially Speaking.*

CHAPTER 2

SPIRITUALITY, GENDER, AND POWER IN ASANTE HISTORY*

Emmanuel Akyeampong and Pashington Obeng

Obaa na owoo ohene.
It is the woman who gave birth to the King (Asante proverb)

Available studies of Asante history have provided illuminating insights about Asante society at different points in time. These snapshots were often taken of a centralized Asante state in the eighteenth and nineteenth centuries. Ivor Wilks has provided valuable analyses of an early assimilative Asante society, marked by egalitarian social structures, and a stratified imperial Asante in the nineteenth century.[1] Wilks, George Hagan, and Larry Yarak have examined the evolution of an Asante bureaucracy or administration.[2] Kwame Arhin has offered various portraits of a centralized Asante state: the military expansion of Asante, the structure of the Asante empire, and internal social stratification in the nineteenth century.[3] The Asante empire's twilight years are captured in the works of William Tordoff and Thomas Lewin.[4] Historians, such as Jean Allman, have sought recently to redress the paucity of studies on twentieth-century Asante.[5]

While attention has been focused on Asante's political expansion and elaboration from its eighteenth-century military successes, we still lack a processual analysis of the development of power and authority in early Asante society.[6] Asante oral traditions about these earlier years are extremely murky.[7] Asante came to the notice of Europeans on the coast after its defeat of Denkyira between 1699 and 1701, thus we lack written references to Asante before 1700. Prior to 1701, Europeans writers commented on an interior state known

* The authors are indebted to Larry Yarak, David Owusu-Ansah, and the anonymous reviewers of the *International Journal of African Historical Studies* for their invaluable comments on an earlier draft of this article. This article was first presented in the Walter Rodney Seminar Series at Boston University, February 1995. The Asante state was formed by a number of Twi-speaking Akan matriclans at the turn of the eighteenth century with its capital at Kumasi, at the center of present-day Ghana. It fell to British colonial rule in 1896.

as Akanny or Akani. It appears that Europeans on the coast applied Akanny as a linguistic term to traders from the interior and that there was no state known as Akanny.[8] But a militarily prepared Asante did not spring up overnight.

This chapter examines the cultural notions that underpinned power in Asante. It explores how "cultural resources are used in guiding actions, defining goals, interpreting the experience of such 'power' relationships as domination and subordination, or even expressing legitimacy."[9] The chapter offers an interpretive analysis of the history and anthropology of power in Asante based on oral traditions, myths, proverbs, religion, ritual, philosophy, oral interviews, and other written sources. It analyzes the development of authority structures—gerontocracy, patriarchy, chieftaincy—in Asante society, pointing to the relevance of the metaphysical in Asante conceptions of power and authority. A growing recognition of the relevance of belief in the interpretation of Asante thought and action is borne out in some of the works of Thomas McCaskie.[10] In his recent book, *State and Society in Pre-Colonial Asante*, McCaskie presents an in-depth examination of the "ideological structurations" of the Asante state, and the forging of hegemonic consent rooted in the deep structures of Asante belief and knowledge.[11] But *McCaskie's examination of power in this book is very state-oriented, muting the complex negotiations that surrounded power relations in Asante society.* Civil society lacks an agency of its own outside its interaction with the state.[12] The resulting impression is the *state*'s unquestionable monopoly of power before the last quarter of the nineteenth century. In reality, the basis of the state's power was more fragile, with several real contenders in the arena of power relations. What was transpiring was not only the state's structuration of the ideological and material bases, but also an ongoing restructuration of belief and knowledge through the dynamic mediation of the interests of the rulers and the ruled.

Spirituality—as distinct from a specific religion—pervaded Asante thought and action. Religion represented a distinct activity among the Asante that revolved around beliefs and practices. Spirituality acknowledged the reality of a nonmaterial world, as the material world was seen as incapable of explaining the totality of human experience. The Asante universe contained numerous participants—spirits, humans, animals, and plants. It was a universe of experience in which some of the participants were invisible. This happens in cultures where the empirical and the meta-empirical worlds have an ongoing discourse. Although some animals and plants had a potent life-force (Twi: *sasa*), it did not necessarily make them objects of worship (the realm of religion).

The Asante universe was suffused with power. Onyame (the Supreme Being) had created a universe impregnated with his power.[13] Power was thus rooted in the Asante cosmology, and individuals and groups that successfully tapped into this power source translated this access into authority if they controlled social institutions. Authority (political power) could be monopolized, but access to power (Twi: *tumi*:, "the ability to bring about change") was available to anyone who knew how to make use of *Onyame*'s powerful universe for good or evil. As Malcolm D. McLeod points out, knowledge was the key to power: "*Many religious activities were, by definition, mysterious and secret. Most Asante did not expect to know much about their gods; to those who did knowledge was power.*"[14] And *knowledge was an acquired or an innate quality for some individuals.*

Thus, power had no gender or age delineations. So how did gerontocracy and patriarchy structures emerge in Asante society? How did Asante male elders coopt women and juniors who were spiritually powerful? Did contending powers become submerged, ready to erupt in times of crisis? Or did such powers find a place within the state structure, their potential being utilized for the corporate good? How do we understand the distribution of power between state and civil society in Asante society? To construct a model of power incorporating spirituality, gender, and age necessarily produces a relational understanding of power that sheds light on the fragile foundations of Asante chiefship and kingship, and illuminates periods in Asante history during which contending, sometimes non-royal, groups made a bid for political power. The nineteenth century, when Asante power seemed at its peak, was also the century in which monarchical power was most tested.

The rest of this paper is divided into four chronological and thematic sections that analyze the ecological foundations of pre-eighteenth century Asante society, the emergence of a militaristic, centralized state from the eighteenth century, and the crises of authority in nineteenth-century Asante. The first section examines how ecology influenced Asante social organization and early structures of authority like gerontocracy and patriarchy. The second section explores Asante militarism, chiefship, and kingship that came in the train of military success, and new nuances in Asante conceptions of power. The third section analyzes three historical periods/incidents in which state and monarchy were threatened in Asante: the 1818–1819 Gyaman war and a coup by royal wives; military defeat in the 1870s, political instability, and the rise of a spiritual, back-to-our-roots movement (*domankama*); and the British attempt to confiscate the Golden Stool and the Yaa Asantewaa war (1900) with a woman commanding Asante military forces. The fourth section concludes this essay by offering reflections on the relational nature of power in Asante history and the continuing relevance of spirituality to twentieth-century Asante notions of power. Power does not exist in a vacuum; it is interactive. Its nature and exercise are best understood by taking cognizance of the rights, obligations, and expectations of the rulers and the ruled.

COOPERATING WITH NATURE AND THE FORGING OF SOCIAL CONSENSUS

> Akwakora te ho ansa na wowoo ohene (Asante proverb)
> An old man was in the world before a chief was born

Two factors exercised profound influence on early Asante social organization: the forest environment, and the matrilineal clan system (*mmusua*, sing.

abusua). Akan groups from the basin of the Pra-Ofin rivers had began migrating north into the sparsely populated areas of the forest zone that later became Asante from the fifteenth century, partially as a response to the demand for gold and kola from the Mande region.[15] The original clan-communities that later merged to form the Asante state—Kwaman (later renamed Kumase), Nsuta, Bekwai, Kokofu, Dwaben, and Mampon—were among Akan groups that migrated north from the basin of the Pra and Ofin rivers probably in the sixteenth century. Migration north accelerated when the emergence of Denkyira and Akwamu as powerful states in the mid-seventeenth century generated political instability. The region between the Pra and the Ofin—the Adansie and Amansie districts of present-day Asante—had also become overpopulated by the seventeenth century, and migration north (away from political turmoil and towards vacant land) was a powerful attraction.[16] But north lay the unconquered forest, and the name of the early state of Kwaman (*Kwaeman*—"forest state") reflects the effort to domesticate aspects of nature.[17]

Although oral traditions on the origins of the Asante state focus on Asante's military successes and the elaboration of the state, evidence of the earlier struggles against nature, and the social organization this struggle spawned, is discernible in Asante religion, ritual, philosophy, and the *history of abusua*.This is not to assume that Asante religion and philosophy consist of static bodies of knowledge, unchanging over time. What is instructive in Asante religion, philosophy, rituals, and proverbs, is their ability to contain and reflect divergent and/or opposing views of the Asante world. We have attempted to historicize these divergent and opposing views in order to understand the changing social order in Asante. The danger of essentializing and retrojecting knowledge about the Asante is constantly present in such an endeavor. Whether we fully overcome this barrier is debatable, for the oral and written evidence on pre-eighteenth-century Asante are beset with problems of chronology and insufficient detail. But the approach does shed invaluable light on the dynamic and shifting cultural foundations of power in Asante.

The most urgent need of Asante migrants in the forest was to subsist, an imperative that demanded cooperation and the submersion of certain individual interests that could undermine the collective wellbeing. The precariousness of existence and the ever-encroaching power of the forest informed Asante thought and action. Asante *grundnorms—nkabom* (cooperation), *nkosoo* (progress), *asomdwee* (peace), *ayamyie* (generosity), *nokwaredi* (truthfulness), and *ahohoye* (hospitality)—reflect the Asante emphasis on surviving in the forest environment. McCaskie perceptively points out that:

> The Asante were and are acutely aware that their culture, in the most literal sense, was hacked out of nature. And this understanding (which is historically and materially accurate) engendered the abiding fear that, without unremitting application and effort, the fragile defensible space called culture would simply be overwhelmed or reclaimed by an irruptive and anarchic nature.[18]

The Asante were obsessed with order and feared disorder.[19] The forest or bush constituted "an area of disorder, potential power and danger."[20] The bush quickly reclaimed abandoned settlements and cultivated areas, where human exertion had become remiss. Yet its luxuriance underscored the fertility of the soil, while the forest housed powerful spirits and forces that humans could tap to their benefit.[21]

The forest loomed large in Asante religion. Onyame's shrine often contained a stone axe (*nyame akuma*), a neolithic implement which may have testified to the agrarian triumph of Asante's forest predecessors. The earth deity (Asase Yaa), was venerated and regularly propitiated, lest she withheld her abundance. The lesser deities (*abosom*), often made their initial contacts with humans through hunters in the forest. The forest monster (*sasabonsam*) and forest dwarfs (*mmoatia*) were superhuman beings that could be dangerous or helpful. Witches (*abayifo*) consorted with these forest beings. Charms (*nsuman*),[22] were taught by forest dwarfs to individuals they spirited away or were found by hunters in the stomachs of the animals they killed.[23] Spiritually powerful animals and plants with *sasa* ("force of nature") were treated with great circumspection. *The Asante universe was one in which humans coexisted intimately with spirits: no human pursuit could be accomplished without it being secured successfully first in the spiritual realm.*

It is against this background that one gains a deeper understanding of the emergence of gerontocracy and patriarchy in early Asante society. The economic underpinnings of the Asante *abusua* has been highlighted by Wilks, McLeod, and Naomi Chazan.[24] Empirical evidence has demonstrated that patriarchy originated in economic conditions, primarily to ensure the means of subsistence by organizing the recurrent activities that cultivation involved.[25] Patriarchy's growing coherence was associated with the accumulation of wealth.[26] In the precarious forest environment of Asante, age (lived experience) and knowledge (spiritual connectedness) were highly valued. Eugenia Herbert astutely comments that African beliefs about the social and natural worlds

> privilege age and gender because they are the most salient characteristics of lived experience: the most successful individuals are those who live to old age and who abundantly reproduce themselves. By extension, they are even more successful, more "powerful," if they are able to apply their ability to other domains that are seen as inherently similar.[27]

Indeed, death even enhanced the status of such successful male elders in Asante society. They became intermediaries through whom the living could communicate with the beings of the spirit world. Male elders became the earthly representatives of the ancestors (*nsamamfo*).[28] In the interest of the corporate good, juniors were encouraged to accept the wise leadership of the elders. An Asante proverb underscored the relevance of the corporate group and the importance of "belonging in" or "belonging to" such a group: *wu nni wura, aboa kye wo* ("If you have no master, a beast will catch you").[29]

It is probable that patriarchy was a later historical development in Asante society. Wilks describes the sixteenth century in Asante history as the "era of great ancestresses."[30] Oral traditions about the founding of Kumase privilege the role of women.

> One very popular tradition claims that the area or site of Kumase was discovered by Adu Nyame Bofuo, who was sent by a woman by name, Febi-a-Odeneho, to look for her husband Adu Gyamfi. The latter had earlier on moved from the cradle of the Asante nation, Adanse and Amansie areas, to the environs of Tafo. Adu Nyame Bofuo reported to the woman and her brother Oti Akenten about the availability of an ample fertile land around the environs of Tafo. This news attracted the attention of Oti Akenten who decided to move to the area to found a settlement.... Consequently, Oti met the owner of the land, Adowaa Nkarawire, and bought the parcel of land from her.[31]

Adu Nyame Bofuo stumbled upon the site of Kumase on his mission from a woman; the site was purchased from a woman.

The importance of women in the social organization of Asante is borne out by their matrilineal system and in the works of scholars such as R. S. Rattray and K. A. Busia. The axis of Asante social organization was the matrilineage (*abusua*), headed by a male elder (*abusua panin*) and a female elder (*obaa panin*). The roles of the chief (*ohene*) and the queen mother (*ohemaa*) at the state level were modelled after that of the *abusua panin* and the *obaa panin*.[32] Both occupied stools, seen as the spiritual loci of their previous ancestors. Indeed, Rattray's elderly informants held that the *ohemaa*'s stool was senior to that of the *ohene*'s. Rattray argued that this was not mere courtesy.

> In fact, but for two causes, the stool occupied by the male would possibly not be in existence at all: 1. The natural inferiority of women from a physical standpoint. 2. Menstruation (with its resultant avoidances). In other words, a woman, besides suffering from disability, cannot go to war; but for these two facts the Ashanti woman, under a matrilineal system, would, I believe, eclipse any male in importance.[33]

It will be highlighted later that war and the menstrual taboos that surround ancestral stools and shrines were crucial factors in the development of chieftaincy and kingship in Asante. It should be pointed out that some royal women overcame these feminine taboos, and three such women—Ama Sewa, Afrakuma Panyin, and Ama Saponmma—ruled in succession in the nineteenth century as chiefs of Dwaben.[34]

Students of Asante history have long been fascinated by the phenomenon of matriliny. Upon inquiring about the origins of matriliny in Asante, Thomas Bowdich was informed in the early nineteenth century that "if the wives of the sons are faithless, the blood of the family is entirely lost in the offspring, but should the daughters deceive their husbands, it is preserved."[35] Asante thought on matriliny, blood (*mogya*), and the belief that only women can transmit blood to their offspring is more complex than the stock explanation of female infidelity. The visibility of menstrual blood, and its implications for fertility and failed fertilization, the valuable role of women as biological reproducers of Asante society, and Asante (especially male) esteem and awe of childbirth promoted the notion that only women could transmit blood.[36] As one queen mother told Rattray: "If my sex die in the clan then that very clan becomes extinct...."[37]

Indeed, the viability of an Asante village was established by "a core of women...who have children there, and whose daughters there give birth to other daughters who will continue the matrilineage...."[38] This fact explains the openness of early Asante society. Wilks argues that the Akan matriclans developed as a mechanism for absorbing outsiders at a period (the fifteenth to the seventeenth centuries) when labor was critically needed for clearing the thick forest. Asante proverbs like *obi nkyere obi ase* (no one should point to other people's [non-Asante/unfree] origins) emphasize the concept of wealth in people and Asante assimilativeness. But the proverb also seeks to prevent divisiveness within the body politic, and it is possible that the organizing principle in early Asante society was cooperation (*nkabom*) among the early settlers and not only the assimilation of slave outsiders. At this early phase, according to Wilks, the matriclan was conceived of in terms of alliance rather than descent. As the agrarian order became more firmly established by the seventeenth century, the demand for non-Akan labor dropped, and blood relations to the founder of a lineage became the signifier of legitimacy within the lineage corporate group.[39] The shift in priority was reflected in the reducing number of matriclans from twelve, as cited by Bowdich in 1817, to eight when enumerated by Asantehene (king of Asante) Agyeman Prempe I in 1907, and finally down to seven by Rattray's count.[40] Parallel to the de-emphasis on assimilating outsiders was a growth in the social prominence of men over women in the social organization of the *abusua*.

The only political office open to women in the Asante state structure was that of the *ohemaa* (queen mother), who was considered a co-ruler with the king in all state affairs.[41] Although Agnes Aidoo pointed out that the queen mother's position should not be regarded "as a general index to female political activity,"[42] the very existence of the queen mother at the highest level of state organization signifies the perceived complementarity of power as both male and female. Good leadership combined "hot" and "cold" qualities: reason balanced bravery, compassion balanced inflexibility. A Twi proverb emphasizes that *obarima, woye no dom ano, na wonye no fie* ("the hero shows his courage on the battlefield, not in the house"). The unique qualities of the queen mother balanced those of the king; most important, she was the king's counsel. As Michelle Gilbert cogently summarizes, the queen mother's "main attribute is the moral quality of wisdom, knowledge, emotion, compassion, all that pertains to her as a woman and is not bestowed by male officials."[43] The disastrous careers and destoolments of Asantehene Kofi Kakari (1867–1874) and Mensa Bonsu (1874–1883), sons of the queen mother Afua Kobi, were blamed, according to Asante oral traditions, on their mother for her lack of good counsel.[44] At three levels of Asante social organization—family, lineage, and state—women were crucial in their roles as biological reproducers and as economic and social producers.[45] Though the emergence of the Asante state diminished the political visibility of women, their role as social critics[46] and as ritual specialists was germane to the functioning of the body politic. The deities themselves were gendered, and female deities sometimes required female spokespersons "who knew the ways of the deity."[47] The river deity, Asuo Abena, in Dwaben, required an *obosomfobaa* ("priestess"), and so did Buronyaa in Effiduase. Moreover, certain rituals were best performed by women: for examples, the cleansing and social reintegration of social deviants, such as kleptomaniacs and witches, through *tutuwbo*.[48] The Asante believed such anti-social acts were caused by evil spirits, and public ridicule "severs the link between the human being and the anti-social spirits."[49] Increasingly, as the Asante state established itself from the eighteenth century, female spiritual roles came to be held by women past the stage of menopause, these women being seen as "ritual men." Such old women acquired elderly privileges such as the right to cut their hair short (*dansikra*), wear their cloths in a male fashion, drink liquor, and pour libations. Childbearing women were sidelined in public affairs because of male notions about the spiritual danger presented by menstrual blood. For such women, Wilks points out that:

> Participation in affairs of state was not encouraged, for the onset of menstruation might have untoward and unpredictable consequences for those in contact, even indirectly, with the woman. The Asante attitude was most vigorously in practice in the case of the king's wives still able to bear children. They were secluded in a harem for most of the time.[50]

Such royal wives were strictly chaperoned according to an early nineteenth-century account.[51] Old age blurred the lines of gender politics, which revolved around sexuality and procreation. The early nineteenth-century career of Akyaawa Yikwan is a case in point.[52]

War and aggrandizement would usher in the Asante state and kingship. Victory would not only subjugate the enemies of Asante, but it would elevate Asante men over Asante women. War was a uniquely male preoccupation, and "Ashanti was fundamentally a military union."[53] But even in the business of war, premenopausal women could not be excluded. If Onyame (the Supreme Being) had granted women the capacity to bear life, that same gift made them the best defenders of life. And this was probably the origins of mmomomme, that distinctly female form of spiritual warfare.[54] When Asante troops were at war, Asante women in the villages would perform daily ritual chants until the troops returned, processing in partial nudity from one end of the village to the other. This ritual protected the soldiers at war, and sometimes involved women pounding empty mortars with pestles as a form of spiritual torture of Asante's enemies.[55] Gender thus did not acquire the force of a coherent mobilizing mechanism in Asante history and the wealth political ascendancy brought certain lineages was shared by both male and female members.

CONQUEST AND KINGSHIP

Nea oman adu no so, wototo no mu a, obu wo nan mu.

If it is a man's turn to rule the state and you put obstacles in his way, he breaks your leg.

According to oral traditions, centralized, sovereign government was absent in the Akan cradle of the Pra-Ofin basin in the 1500s. The small communities that existed there were bound "not by allegiance to a common sovereign but by kinship, agnatic and clan ties and linked by trade routes."[56] Internal disputes were resolved through the arbitration of the deities and their priests and priestesses, and military leadership in times of crisis was always temporary.

> The only bond of unity was worship of the principal god, Bona. In times of danger, however, the people normally looked upon the most powerful and courageous of the clan heads as their leader. The most famous was Ewurade Basa of the Asenee clan, who tried unsuccessfully to unite the various clans under his rule sometime in the sixteenth century.[57]

The advent of state formation in the Akan cradle in the seventeenth century encouraged the northward migration of Asante's ancestors ill-disposed to sovereign or monarchical rule.

But the political climate had changed permanently from the seventeenth century as European firearms entered the coastal trade, and the intensification of commerce to the south and north of the Akan cradle precipitated a struggle to control gold and kola resources and trade routes. The Oyoko clan members, who were to found Kumase, migrated north from Asantemanso (in the Pra-Ofin basin) to Kokofu and from there to Kwaman. In Kokofu, the Oyoko leader Kwabia Amanfi died, and his successor, Oti Akenten, initiated the move to Kwaman. Established clan communities already existed in Kwaman, and the most powerful of these were Dormaa, Tafo, Kaase, and Wonoo. Oral traditions stress that the new immigrants were pitched into a struggle for survival in Kwaman. The migratory phase and the conflicts in Kwaman, spawned the successive leadership of Kwabia Amanfi, Oti Akenten, and Obiri Yeboa. The role of the chief became a historical reality in the long struggle to survive in Kwaman. It is possible that parallel developments among immigrant Oyoko groups in Kokofu, Nsuta, Bekwai, Dwaben, and the Bretuo group in Mampon promoted chieftaincy there.

Wilks highlights the role of *aberempon* ("big men") as estate developers in forging the basis of the Akan state. Their control over slaves, and their exploitation of arable land and mines, led to the emergence of "berempondoms."[58] We rather emphasize conflict, conquest, and diplomacy in the emergence of the Akan states that formed the Asante union. Akan elders often refer to the age of *atutu atutuo* (migration) as a period of intense insecurity and the survival of the fittest. Founders of villages were eager to attract settlers for defensive purposes, not necessarily because they were far-sighted estate developers motivated by entrepreneurial instincts. As villages expanded, the principle of "first comers versus late comers" introduced internal stratification. This process of social differentiation may have been aug mented by the attachment of slaves or unfree labor. Diverse groups within the community resulted in competing interests, and the resolution of internal conflicts did not necessarily privilege the interests of the earliest settlers. Ongoing negotiations around the ideals, identities, and expectations of the community facilitated continuos realignment in social relations.

Although traditions are not clear about leadership before Kwabia Amanfi and whether the Oyoko clan always provided the leaders, the military successes of Obiri Yeboa assured Oyoko ascendancy and forged the nucleus of the Oyoko state of Kwaman.[59] Under the reign of his nephew, Osei Tutu (c.1685–1717?), the Oyoko state in Kwaman was renamed Kumase and the clan-states of Kumase, Kokofu, Nsuta, Bekwai, Dwaben, and Mampon merged to form the Asante union.[60] Osei Tutu became the first king of Asante with his lineage as the royal line.

It is revealing of Asante notions of power that the new nation was rooted not only in military victories, but also in complex spiritual engineering that created a sense of shared destiny. Kingship was given a divine flavor and surrounded with mystery. Max Weber perceptively pointed out the unsuitability of patriarchal leadership, born out of routine economic activities, in terms of crisis. What is needed in crisis is charismatic leadership,

> a certain quality of an individual personality by virtue of which he is set apart from ordinary men and treated as endowed with supernatural, superhuman, or at least specifically exceptional powers or qualities.[61]

Osei Tutu's greatest achievement was his ability to "routinize charismatic authority," to utilize another Weberian term, in making kingship permanent in Asante and his lineage royal. In this process he was aided by his close friend and confidante, Okomfo ("priest") Anokye.[62]

Denkyira's power followed the Akan migrants north, and the states within a radius of twenty miles of Kwaman were forced into tributary relations with Denkyira. Four of these states were also of Oyoko origin—Kokofu, Nsuta, Bekwai, and Dwaben—and Osei Tutu sought to overthrow Denkyira's oppressive overlordship by forging a military union with these states and the powerful Bretuo state of Mampon. The union effectively crushed Denkyira rule between 1699 and 1701. To ensure the permanence of this union, tradition has it that on a Friday, Anokye assembled the clan leaders of the ministates that formed the Asante union.

> It is said that on one Friday, at a great gathering of the various independent chiefs, Okomfo Anokye caused a stool to descend from the clouds and rest on the lap of Osei Tutu. Thereafter, all the assembled chiefs were asked to provide cuttings from their nails, made into "medicine" for the consecration of the stool. The Stool became known as *Sika Dwa Kofi,* the Golden Stool, whose

day of birth is Friday. Okomfo Anokye presented it to the chiefs as the soul of the Asante nation, and granted its custody to Osei Tutu and his successors.[63]

As Wilks points out, the sky was seen as the place of origin because "the Golden Stool could not have come from elsewhere and... have stronger status,..."[64] Its gold casing was also significant, for gold was the most precious metal of the Akan. And its occupant, the king of Kumase, became the head of the Asante union.

Asantehene-elect gained their legitimacy by being lowered to touch the Golden Stool three times. It was sacrilegious to "sit" on the Golden Stool, the central unifying symbol containing the soul of the nation. Its possession was what empowered the asantehene. Importantly, kingship eclipsed gerontocracy, for even a minor could become asantehene. On being "placed" on the Golden Stool, the minor acquired the combined wisdom, age, charisma, and spiritual power of his predecessors. He became "Nana" ("elder"). But the precariousness of life in the forest environment and the political fluidity of the period, as states rose and fell, put its unique twist on Asante kingship: what may be termed the "reroutinization of charisma." An Asantehene was not only expected to inherit the "charismatic heritage" of his predecessors, he was enjoined to embellish the historical script through his military exploits and moral character. Those who failed in this challenge were destooled from office.

Successive asantehene rose to the challenge from the times of Osei Tutu, and by the end of the eighteenth century, Asante exceeded present-day Ghana in size. The "highest distinction in Asante... [became] distinction in war...."[65] As war was a manly occupation, women gradually slipped into the background on the stage of Asante politics. But at a deeper level, war involved death, and women as providers of life were prevented from going to war. Asante's victory over nature and other cultures were easily expressed in the titles of the asantehene: ***kurotwiamansa*** ("the leopard"—seen as "king of the forest"), ***kwaebibirim hene*** ("king of the deep forest"), ***osahene*** ("king of war"), and ***otumfuo*** ("holder of power").[66] The subordination of Asante women was more difficult to achieve and express.

Women controlled childbirth, and people still constituted wealth in Asante.[67] Indeed, the closure of Asante society from the eighteenth century had placed a premium on blood relations. Menstrual taboos probably originated because of this male ambivalence towards the reproductive powers of women. The advent of male political power had not reduced their dependency on women. Childbearing women were circumscribed with menstrual taboos involving Asante gods, which ensured military victories, and ancestral stools that represented the new social order. The presence of menstrual women contaminated these shrines. But menstrual blood was also spiritually powerful because it was fertility fluid. In fact, the greatest Asante shrine, the Golden Stool, was periodically contaminated with menstrual blood to sharpen its power.

It is done once a year. When it comes to ***mmusumuru adee,*** when we come to cleanse something, first, we dirty it. Then they do certain things for it to come

> back with renewed power. You can make an analogy with corn. To grow corn, you put the seeds in the soil, where it rots. Then green corn stalks sprouts out of the rotten seed.[68]

The greatest indicator of masculine power was the asantehene's exclusive right to sentence people to death—to let blood flow.[69] Male power was the antithesis of female power.

> Changes in Asante religion reflected the new political order.
> Religious beliefs envisaged different states of the afterlife for the power elite and others. It was held that members of the ruling group enjoyed the same status in the after-life as in their lifetime, which justifies the ritual execution of commoners of both sexes. Commoners, correspondingly, carried on their servile activities in the after-life.[70]

From earlier religious beliefs about the omnipresence of the Supreme Being and equal access to him,[71] the asantehene became the ultimate public mediator of Asante religion. Indeed, to utter "me Nyame" ("my God") in public, instead of "God of Osei" ("Osei" being one of the titles of the asantehene), could spell death.[72] Among the central functions of the asantehene was the performance of "magico-religious" rites, especially through the *adae* and *odwira* festivals, which sought the continued blessings of Onyame, the *abosom,* the *nsamanfo,* and powerful *nsuman.* Contrary to appearances, political power in Asante remained fragile. Kumase grew in power at the expense of the union states, pitting the Kumase chiefs (*nsafohene*)—appointees of the Asantehene—against the *amanhene* (paramount chiefs of the union states), who inherited their positions. Asante politics remained fluid, "and the great officers of the kingdom, even the king himself, were subject to rapid changes of fortune."[73] Observing the Asante monarchy in 1820, Dupuis commented that "powerful as the monarchy of Asante certainly is . . . it may be considered a fabric whose foundation is subject to periodical decay, and therefore requires unremitting attention . . ."[74]

THREATS TO THE ESTABLISHED ORDER

> Nnipa nyinaa ye Onyame mma; obi nye asase ba
> All [wo]men are the children of God; none is a child of the earth.

The 1818–1819 Palace Coup

In 1820 when Joseph Dupuis visited Kumase at the height of Asante power, the asantehene had experienced a recent coup engineered by royal women. The coup plotters, led by the asantehemaa (the queen mother), timed their bid for power to coincide with Asante's war with the northern vassal kingdom of Gyaman (1818–1819). Kwadwo Adinkra of Gyaman had aroused Asante anger by making himself a golden stool to rival that of the

Asantehene. The complexity of this rebellion, with its play on spiritual power, is best captured by citing Dupuis at length.

> When the king was about to open the campaign against Gaman, he collected his priests, to invoke the royal fetische, and perform the necessary orgies to insure success. These ministers of superstition sacrificed thirty-two male and eighteen female victims, as an expiatory offering to the gods, but the answers from the priests being deemed by the council as still devoid of inspiration, the king was induced to *make a custom* at the sepulchres of his ancestors, where many hundreds bled. This, it is affirmed, propitiated the wrath of the adverse gods. The priests then prepared a certain fetische compound, which they delivered to the king, with an injunction to burn the composition daily in a consecrated fire pot within the palace; and upon no account to neglect the fire, so as to suffer it to go out; for as long as the sacred flame devoured the powder, he would triumph over his enemies.
>
> When the king joined his army he commissioned his eldest sister (then governess of the kingdom), to attend strictly to the sacred mystery, telling her that his crown and life both depended upon her vigilance, and the fulfilment of his order. He selected also three wives to whom he was more attached than the rest, to watch by turns over the mysterious rites, in conjunction with his last-mentioned sister.
>
> During the king's absence, this arbitress of fate formed a connexion with a chief of Bouromy [Bono], whose ambition suggested a plan to seat himself upon the throne.
>
> In this conspiracy, seventeen of the king's wives and their families are said to have joined; the fire-pot was broken to pieces, and the chief commenced arming his party. But the king, added my informer, who had sustained heavy losses in the early part of the war, *and was unable to account for the audacity of the enemy,* performed an incantation over a certain talisman, which gave an insight into what was transacting in the capital. He therefore dispatched a body of men under Ouso Cudjoe, who, after an impotent struggle on the part of the enemy, effectually crushed the rebellion. When the king returned home, he called a council to deliberate upon the punishment due to the offenders, and it was finally decreed that his wives should suffer death by decapitation. His sister, to prevent the profanation of spilling royal blood, was ordered to be strangled. The chief, the paramour, and all those of his party, were doomed to the most cruel deaths at the grave of the king's mother. These sentences were carried into prompt execution, and it is affirmed that above seven hundred people were sacrificed, or fell in resisting the royal forces. After this the younger sister, my present visitor, was made governess.
>
> While these butcheries were transacting, the king prepared to enter the palace, and in the act of crossing the threshold of the outer gate, was met by several of his wives, whose anxiety to embrace their sovereign lord impelled them thus to overstep the boundary of female decorum in Ashantee; for it happened that the king was accompanied by a number of his captains, who accordingly were compelled to cover their faces with both hands, and fly from the spot. This is said to have angered the monarch, although his resentment proceeded no farther than words, and he returned the embraces of his wives. But being afterwards told by some of the superintendents that these women were more or less indisposed from a natural female cause [menstruation], he was

> inflamed to the highest pitch of indignation, and in a paroxysm of anger caused these unhappy beings to be cut in pieces before his face; giving orders at the time to cast the fragments into the forest, to be devoured by birds and beasts of prey.[75]

The asantehemaa, Adoma Akosua, was not ordered to be strangled. She was replaced in office by Yaa Dufi. The former queen mother was required to live in the Nkwantanan ward of Kumase, and her descendants were barred forever from the offices of Asantehene and Asantehemaa.[76]

Thomas McCaskie has examined the relevance of this incident in his exploration of one aspect of the Asante cognitive realm—that of witchcraft.[77] McCaskie rightly points out that the plotters had no significant military or political support, yet the asantehemaa "had in her mind some expectation of success."[78] McCaskie argues that in the realm of practical politics, the rebellion was unrealistic although the answer may not be that clear-cut "in terms of the Asante understanding of the power of witchcraft . . ."[79] To begin with, McCaskie may have wrongly located this rebellion in the province of witchcraft; it manipulated spirituality, but was it witchcraft that was being tapped in this specific incident? It is possible that he sees the use of all meta-empirical powers as witchcraft. Furthermore, witchcraft is not practiced as directly as the incident suggests.[80]

The war against Gyaman was preceded by much spiritual preparation by the king, including consulting Muslim *ulama* in Kumase, and it is not necessary to distinguish between the spiritual activities of men and women by consigning that of women to the realm of witchcraft. The king and his antagonists belonged to the same cognitive world and both believed in the efficacy of spiritual power. The women deployed mystical powers to challenge the king's political power.

The omnipresence of blood in Dupuis's account—human blood sacrificed to the gods and ancestors, and menstrual blood used by royal wives against the king—is significant in understanding this attempted coup. The two types of blood featured in the account encapsulated different gender versions of power. Red signifies danger and hotness in the Asante color spectrum.[81] Blood was sacrificed to some gods because these were avaricious beings that had been brought home from the bush by hunters. These were known as *abosom brafo*—the *brafo* being the king's executioners—implying that these gods craved blood.[82] Combining two identical but different powerful fluids could misalign the balance between the physical and spiritual worlds: like the contact of menstrual blood with other powerful gods or *nsuman* that received sacrifices of human or animal blood. The asantehene's war gown (*batakari kese*) was studded with amulets and talismans, and his finger-rings also had some spiritual power. Hence his anger at discovering that the wives who came to embrace him were menstruating. The seriousness of the king's reprisals underscore how gravely he took this rebellion.

What caused the rebellion is a more difficult question. The politics of Asante queen mothers definitely had more to do with lineage and state politics than with a feminist movement, and queen mothers in the nineteenth century notably took strong positions for or against war.[83] Asante elders today remember traditions about the war against Kwadwo Adinkra of Gyaman. Obaapanin Afua Pokuaa of Amoaman recalled that this was a difficult war; had it not been for Asante's gods, the troops would not have returned victorious.[84] Even the powerful Dente shrine of Asante's vassal, Krachi, was "beseeched for the safe return of Asantehene Osei Bonsu from the Gyaman war in 1819 . . ."[85] Asante fears concerning this historic war survive in *kete* songs.[86] A section of one of the Asantehene's *kete* songs runs:

Otumfuo wo nam na ko	Otumfuo [Asantehene] who fights while walking
oko bo Gyaman	went to conquer Gyaman
. . . .	
Otumfuo, oko kum Adinkra	Otumfuo, he went to kill Adinkra
ama Oman	for the nation
yei eko bo yen	[sigh] we had our fill of fighting![87]

Did Asantehemaa Adoma Akosua believe the asantehene had unnecessarily endangered the nation? Although the war had received the enthusiastic endorsement of the Asantemanhyiamu (the National Council), we still lack an informed perspective on how nineteenth-century Asante women evaluated the success of reigns. The thoughts of nineteenth-century Asante women about this rebellion may illuminate how they perceived the exercise of political power. But what is obvious in this coup, planned and executed by royal women and wives of the king, is the convergence of the acknowledged roles of women as counsellors, social critics, givers and defenders of life, and guardians of the body politic.

THE DOMANKAMA MOVEMENT

In the late 1870s, a priest, one Okomfo Kwaku of Adwumakaase Wadie, founded an anti-witchcraft[?] cult known as ***domankama*** or ***abonsamkom***.[88] He claimed to be a reincarnation of the legendary Okomfo Anokye, and his principal followers were named after the traditional companions of Okomfo Anokye. Some of his adherents also claimed to be reincarnations of old Asante kings such as Asantehene Osei Tutu. It appears that the Asantehene Mensa Bonsu (1874–1883) initially endorsed the movement.

> Probably early in 1880 members of the movement entered Kumase and gave a display of musketry at Dwaberem, the Great Market, apparently to demonstrate their strength and militancy. Shortly afterwards, a group re-entered the capital, and firing guns, forced their way into the palace. Taking "all sorts of liberties," one of their number tried to shoot Mensa Bonsu. Following the abortive assassination attempt, the Asantehene ordered a purge of the movement.[89]

And thus ended the political threat of the *abonsamkomfo*.

McCaskie provides a solid analysis of this movement, highlighting how apprehension and uncertainty in the 1870s—British military defeat of Asante and the burning of Kumasi (1873–1874), the destoolment of Asantehene Kofi Kakari (1867–1874), Dwaben's secession from the union, and the inept rule of Asantehene Mensa Bonsu (1874–1883)—made many Asante royals and subjects long for the old days of stability and order. This explains the "conservative appeal to historic greatness"—Okomfo Anokye and Osei Tutu.[90] The *domankama* movement strove to set itself up as a political alternative to the Kumase court, establishing a court at Adwumakaase Wadie and even drawing support from the Asante royal family.[91] But the movement sits uneasily under the umbrella of anti-witchcraft cults. It indulged in witch-hunting, yet it transcended the parameters of witch-hunting in its attempt to seize state power.

A closer look at the distribution of power in Asante society may promote a deeper understanding of *domankama*. If the Asante universe was suffused with power, the potential wielders of power at any given time could be limitless. A unique feature of the Asante state was its willingness to incorporate all forms of power, a conscious realization of the fact that power could not be confined nor monopolized.[92] The office of *nsumankwahene* ("chief of medicines") coordinated the workings of these varied forms of power. The asantehene was, among other things, *okomfo panyin* (chief priest) of Asante: in periods of interregnum, even spirit possession ceased until a new asantehene was installed and all *akomfo* in the nation swore allegiance to the new king. The asantehene's praise poems state how he gained ascendancy in the socio-political order by subjugating priests and rival chiefs:

> The priest Akomaa said, "Do not kill me for I know how to mix medicines,"
> Obiri Mmireku said "Do not kill me and I shall wash the stools of your wives,"
> Abaase of Menye said "Do not kill me and I shall prepare millet for your wives,"
> You slew the hunter and took his satchel.[93]

State power subordinated and facilitated the operation of other *recognized* forms of civil power in the interest of the Asante nation.[94] Some forms of civil power, which did not conform to the state's definition of acceptable powers, may have escaped this network and gone underground. But all active forms of civil power needed the endorsement of the asantehene. This intersection of powers encompassed but transcended anti-witchcraft cults and may provide a deeper understanding of *domankama*.

Asante have the tendency to slot antisocial behavior under the rubric of *abayisem* (witchcraft), even if the activity does not conform to the operational mode of witchcraft. *Abayisem* destroyed the fabric of Asante society so the state welcomed cults that combated witchcraft, hence Mensa Bonsu's initial endorsement of the *abonsamkomfo*. Ironically, the *domankama* movement needed the civil order provided by the state to establish itself. But when it attempted to seize state power, it was perceived as having exceeded the charter of anti-witchcraft cults. It had become a political organization. As such, it could be crushed with impunity. An Asante proverb states: ***anomaa kokokyirika tu abirempon tu a, wo to no abirempon tuo*** ("If the tiny bird imitates a giant bird in its flight, it is shot down with canon"). This is a not-too-subtle statement about the consequences of over-stepping bounds. It cannot be ascertained whether ***domankama*** harbored political designs from its inception. But its career—beginning as an anti-witchcraft cult and seeking state approval—sheds light on state/civil society relations in nineteenth-century Asante.[95] Significantly, when the British threatened the Golden Stool in the recently subjugated Asante, it was a charismatic queen mother—not a religious movement—who provided political leadership. Monarchy or strong political leadership was perceived as crucial to the functioning of the Asante nation.

THE YAA ASANTEWAA WAR

British colonial rule effectively began in Asante in 1896, when the British exiled Asantehene Prempe I and several of his principal chiefs. Aware that the Golden Stool embodied the soul of the nation, the British equated the political conquest of Asante with ownership of the Golden Stool. It was the British determination to procure the Golden Stool that resulted in the war of 1900. On March 28, 1900, during a visit to Kumasi, Governor Arnold Hodgson demanded to "sit" on the Golden Stool by right of conquest.[96] The leaderless Asante nation was over-whelmed with dismay and confusion. Then Yaa Asantewaa, queen mother of the subordinate state of Edweso, galvanized the Asante into action through ridiculing male impotency in a time of national crisis.

> How can a proud and brave people like the Asante sit back and look while the whitemen took away their king and chiefs, and humiliated them with a demand for the Golden Stool. The Golden Stool only means money to the whitemen; they have searched and dug everywhere for it. I shall not pay one *predwan* [£8. 2s] to the governor. If you, the chiefs of Asante, are going to behave like cowards and not fight, you should exchange your loincloths for my undergarments (*Montu mo danta mma me na monnye me tam*).[97]

The men accepted her challenge. Asante forces besieged the governor and his entourage in the Kumase fort; war had began.

Yaa Asantewaa commanded Asante's troops and was not just a symbolic head. As a fleeing teacher informed the Basel missionaries at Abetifi:

> An old woman called Yaa Asantewaa lives in Adweso, the mother or the aunt of the chief there, a man who was sent into exile with Prempeh. Since then she has ruled the town. "She has much influence in the whole of Asante, and is the

> soul and the head of the rebellion." When the Governor invited the chiefs to negotiate with him, she sent to tell them "I have loaded my gun, and not for nothing." She is in fact sitting quietly at Adweso, but sends her orders out from there to the different camps around Kumasi.[98]

The revolt, which lasted from April to November 1900, was however weakened by the fact that only Edweso and a few areas around Kumase participated. The death of Mawere Poku, one of Yaa Asantewaa's ablest generals and the son of Gyasehene Opoku Mensah, weakened Yaa Asantewaa's resolve and encouraged her capitulation.[99]

The dynamics that propelled Yaa Asantewaa to leadership appears to be rooted in lineage politics instead of gender. Yaa Asantewaa's lineage was famous for bravery. Her ancestor, Afranie I, fought and won Lake Bosumtwi for the Asantehene.[100] And in the turmoil of nationalist politics in the 1950s, her descendant, Edwesohene Nana Kwasi Afranie, would be charged with killing the elusive Kofi Banda—a member of the Convention Peoples' Party famous for his spiritual power (and physical strength) and feared by Asantes.[101] Perhaps (with hindsight?) it was not surprising to Asante in 1900 that a leader would emerge from the lineage of Afranie, even if she were a woman.

But gender considerations certainly colored the proceedings and the consequences of the Yaa Asantewaa war. Asante men, shamed by the Edweso queen mother's taunts about male impotency, picked up their arms. And as Albert Mawere Poku recalls from his mother's account of the exile of Yaa Asantewaa, defeat was blamed on male cowardice.

> That the men did not rise up to the occasion in such an emergency infuriated Yaa Asantewaa. When she was being taken into exile, my mother told me she turned round as she was being escorted and said: "Asantefoo mmaa, me su mo" ["Asante women, I pity you"]. Someone asked: "What about us, the men?" Yaa Asantewaa replied: "Which men? The men died at the battle front." She turned and walked off.[102]

Not surprisingly, some male elders of the Afranie lineage in Edweso have tried retroactively to revise this gender script of the 1900 war: they claim Yaa Asantewaa was a man in female disguise.[103]

The suppression of the Yaa Asantewaa revolt ended the expansionist and militaristic phase of Asante's history. As Asante was subordinated to colonial rule, the seemingly infinite power of the ruling aristocracy was put in check by British rule. The exile of the asantehene and his principal chiefs, the resulting political and religious vacuum in Asante, colonial encouragement of individual capitalism, and Christian missionary activity introduced a new era fraught with insecurity. At the state and individual levels, spirituality would aid the reconfiguration of identity and concepts of power and autonomy in twentieth-century Asante.

Conclusion: Reflections on Power in Asante Society

Akokonini, gyae akuntunakuntun, na yen nyinaa ye kesua mma

O, cock, stop this ostentation, for we all came out of the egg-shell.

Far from being the definitive statement on the origins, nature, and exercise of power in Asante history, this exploratory essay has sought to extend the frontiers of discussion on power in Asante society. Significantly, it has pointed to the inadequacy of a model of physical or coercive power in understanding power in Asante.[104] Power originated in the Asante cosmos and was accessible to all. It was the control of authority structures that became the preserve of particular lineages or groups, and this historical development can only be understood from the relational perspectives of gender, age, and social stratification.

The epigrams heading the subsections in this essay have probed the nuanced relational understanding of power in Asante society. The proverbs: "A woman gave birth to the king" and "An old man was in the world before a chief was born" stress the antiquity of matriliny and gerontocracy in Asante (Akan) society. Chieftaincy and kingship were later developments that introduced the coerciveness associated with Western definitions of power.[105] This reality is captured by the proverb: "If it is a man's turn to rule the state and you put obstacles in his way, he breaks your leg." But political authority in no way monopolized access to power, for power originated in the spiritual realm. The last two epigrams underscore the belief that all were created by the Supreme Being, none was inherently superior. McCaskie attributed to "weak thought" the Asante state's inability to restructure the "foundations and origins" of Asante belief[106]—the nature of God, life after death, immortality, predestination.[107] But in actuality, the state was limited by the shared, fundamental tenets of Asante belief, some of which have been explored in this essay. Asante belief and knowledge militated against the ideological structurations of the Asante state because power was diffuse by nature and immanent in the Asante cosmos. Access to spiritual power was restricted by knowledge, but Asante awareness of the existence and nature of spiritual forces was general. The historical script, in spite of the state's rewriting of the macro-text, still revealed that wielders of *tumi* (those able to bring about change) were numerous and not limited to state personnel. This "shared history" was subject to the state's ideological structuration, but also confined the state's structurations. The distinction between "authority" (political power) and *tumi* is pertinent to this discussion.

There are two possible ways of approaching the distribution of power in Asante society. One can advocate a model of state and civil society in which the state facilitated and coordinated the harmonious working of all forms of power. The relationship between the asantehene and the various priests in Asante fits this model. The second approach is to view state power as driving underground some forms of mystical power, such as witchcraft. These submerged powers reasserted themselves when state power was compromised, weakened or nonexistent. Both are relevant views of the distribution of power, and their coexistence sheds light on the complex nature and exercise of power in Asante, as well as the distinction between authority and power. The first view highlights the state's authority and its overwhelming agency in the realm of power relations. That was the state's ideal. The second, in our view, incorporates the actual dramatization of power relations on the ground. In this sphere, the wielders of power were numerous. The reality, as Arens and Karp point out, is that "power does not emanate from a single source and social formations are composed of centers and epicenters of power in dynamic relationship with one another."[108] As the state became more centralized in Asante, Asante kings sought to promote the perception that power emanated from a central source by placing themselves at the nexus of relations between the natural, social, and supernatural worlds. The idea was to make kingship appear indispensable to the functioning of the social order.

It is important to remember that in the acquisition and distribution of power, which are always uneven, the users of power operate from different perspectives. This paper has attempted to highlight the varied and complex nature of power within the Asante cosmos. It has also examined some of the competing interests shared and expressed by real people in their relations of power. Some of the insights explored here informed Asante conceptions of power well into the twentieth century. The inaugural scene of the National Liberation Movement in September 1954 evoked Asante notions of spiritual power: the site was beside the sacred Subin River, and the proceedings were accompanied by libations and sacrifices of sheep.[109] And the power of *mmo-momme* (female spiritual warfare) was now utilized by Asante women against the rival Convention People's Party.

NOTES

1. Ivor Wilks, "Land, Labour, Capital and the Forest Kingdom of Asante: A Model of Early Change," in J. Friedman and M. J. Rowlands, eds., *The Evolution of Social Systems* (Pittsburgh, 1978), 487–534; Ivor Wilks, *Asante in the Nineteenth Century* (Cambridge, 1975).
2. Ivor Wilks, "Aspects of Bureaucratization in Ashanti in the Nineteenth Century," *Journal of African History* 7, 2 (1966), 215–33; George P. Hagan, "Ashanti Bureaucracy: A Study of the Growth of Centralized Administration in Ashanti from the Time of Osei Tutu to the Time of Osei Tutu Kwamina Esibe Bonsu," *Transactions of the Historical Society of Ghana* 12 (1971), 43–62; and Larry Yarak, *Asante and the Dutch, 1744–1873* (Oxford, 1990). Yarak argues that the nature of Asante administration was patrimonial and not bureaucratic. Yarak also examines Asante's relations with the Dutch and the people of Elmina.
3. K. Arhin, "The Financing of the Ashanti Expansion (1700–1820)," *Africa* 37 (1967), 283–91; Arhin, "The Structure of Greater Ashanti (1700–1824)," *Journal of African History* 8, 1 (1967), 65–85; Arhin, "Rank and Class among the Asante and Fante in the Nineteenth Century," *Africa* 53, 1 (1983), 2–22. See also, Arhin, "Peasants in 19th-Century Asante," *Current Anthropology* 24, 4 (1983), 471–79.

4. William Tordoff, *Ashanti under the Prempehs 1888–1935* (London, 1965); T. Lewin, *Asante before the British: The Prempean Years, 1875–1900* (Lawrence, 1978).
5. Jean M. Allman, *The Quills of the Porcupine: Asante Nationalism in an Emergent Ghana* (Madison, 1993).
6. Ivor Wilks, *Forests of Gold: Essays on the Akan and the Kingdom of Asante* (Athens, Ohio, 1993), Chs. 1–3, partially redresses this deficiency.
7. See the special issue on the Akan of Ghana in *Ghana Notes and Queries*, 9 (1966); and the papers on the symposium on the city of Kumasi in *Research Review Supplement* 5 (1993).
8. K. Y. Daaku, "Pre-Ashanti States," *Ghana Notes and Queries* 9 (1966), 11.
9. W. Arens and Ivan Karp, "Inroduction," in W. Arens and Ivan Karp, eds., *Creativity of Power: Cosmology and Action in African Societies* (Washington, DC, 1989), xiv.
10. See, for examples, T. C. McCaskie, "Accumulation, Wealth and Belief in Asante History I: To the Close of the Nineteenth Century," *Africa*, 53, 1 (1983), 23–43; T. C. McCaskie, "Accumulation, Wealth and Belief in Asante History II: The Twentieth Century." *Africa*, 56, 1 (1986), 3–23; and T. C. McCaskie, "People and Animals: Constru(ct)ing the Asante Experience," *Africa*, 6, 2 (1992), 221–44.
11. T. C. McCaskie, *State and Society in Pre-Colonial Asante* (Cambridge, 1995).
12. See Ibid., Ch. 3 on civil society.
13. Kwame Gyekye, *An Essay on African Philosophical Thought: The Akan Conceptual Scheme* (New York, 1987), 75. Michelle Gilbert, "Sources of Power in Akuropon-Akuapem: Ambiguity in Classification," in Arens and Karp, eds., *Creativity of Power*, 59–90, makes a similar observation about diverse spiritual sources of power among another Akan group. However, the belief structure of the Akuropon-Akuapem as portrayed by Gilbert differs from the Asante case examined here in the collapsible boundaries Gilbert identifies between different categories of spiritual power.
14. Malcolm D. McLeod, *The Asante* (London, 1981), 57.
15. Archaeological evidence points to earlier habitation in the forests of the central Asante region, probably before the early iron age. Wilks, *Forests of Gold*, 64.
16. J. K. Fynn, *Asante and its Neighbours 1700–1807* (London, 1971), 27. "Overpopulation" must be understood as a relative concept, and the awareness of more vacant land elsewhere may encourage notions of overpopulation within a community.
17. Akwasi Abayie Boaten I, "Kumasi: Early Settlement up to the End of the 18th Century," *Research Review Supplement* 5 (1993), 4; Even in the nineteenth and early twentieth centuries, Asante's dense forests made a vivid impression on visiting Europeans. See Joseph Dupuis, *Journal of a Residence in Ashantee* (London, 1824), 15–16; and R. S. Rattray, *Ashanti Law and Constitution* (Oxford, 1929), 348–49.
18. McCaskie, "Accumulation, Wealth and Belief: I," 28.
19. T. C. McCaskie, "Okomfo Anokye of Asante: Meaning, History and Philosophy in an African Society," *Journal of African History* 27 (1986), 315–39.
20. McLeod, *Asante* 39.
21. Ibid., Ch. 2.
22. Succinctly described by McLeod, *Asante*, 57, as "conglomerations or conjunctions of materials believed to be powerful, and initially activated by having offerings made over them."

23. Akyeampong fieldnotes: Interview with Nana Kofi Akyerem, healer and diviner, Sekondi, August 15, 1994.
24. Wilks, "Land, Labour, Capital," 522; and Wilks, *Forests of Gold* 81; McLeod, *Asante* 19; Naomi Chazan, "The Early State in Africa: The Asante Case," in S. N. Eisenstadt *et al.*, *The Early State in African Perspective* (Leiden, 1988), 92–93.
25. See, for examples, Max Weber, *On Charisma and Institution Building,* edited and introduced by S. N. Eisenstadt (Chicago, 1968), 18; and Claude Meillassoux, "The Social Organization of the Peasantry: The Economic Basis of Kinship," *Journal of Peasant Studies* 1, 1 (1973), 81–90.
26. Friedrich Engels, "The Origin of the Family, Private Property, and the State," in Robert C. Tucker, ed., *The Marx-Engels Reader* (New York, 1978), 734–759.
27. Eugenia W. Herbert, *Iron, Gender, and Power: Rituals of Transformations in African Societies* (Bloomington, 1993), 2.
28. K. A. Busia, *The Position of the Chief in the Modern Political System of Ashanti* (London, 1968), 26–27; and Rattray, *Ashanti Law and Constitution*, 4–5.
29. Rattray, *Ashanti Law and Constitution*, 33–34.
30. Wilks, *Forests of Gold,* 66–68.
31. Boaten, "Kumase," 1.
32. Ernest E. Obeng, *Ancient Ashanti Chieftaincy* (Tema, 1986), Chs. 1 & 2. The imprint of the family on Asante social organization encouraged Rattray to posit an evolutionary origin for the Asante state. Rattray, *Ashanti Law and Constitution,* especially Chs. 9 & 10. It is obvious from the structure and analysis of this paper that we do not subscribe to this evolutionary argument for the emergence of the Asante state. Indeed, the sudden rise of the Asante state at the turn of the eighteenth century could have been a reason the family structure presented a model for political organization. The other dominant feature in Asante political organization—the wing formation—was a product of warfare.
33. R. S. Rattray, *Ashanti* (London, 1923), 81–82.
34. Rattray, *Ashanti Law and Constitution*, 173–74.
35. Thomas E. Bowdich, *Mission from Cape Coast Castle to Ashantee* (London, 1824), 234.
36. On the anthropology of menstruation, see Mary Douglas, *Purity and Danger: An Analysis of the Concepts of Pollution and Taboo* (London, 1966); and Thomas Buckley and Alma Gottlieb, eds., *Blood Magic: The Anthropology of Menstruation* (Berkeley: University of California Press, 1988).
37. Rattray, *Ashanti,* 79. Men were seen as transmitting *ntoro* ("spirit") to their children through their semen in the act of copulation. On the connections between water, white objects (fluids), and the spirit realm, see Emmanuel Akyeampong, "Powerful Fluids: Alcohol and Water in the Struggle for Social Power in Urban Gold Coast, 1860–1919" (Paper presented at Northwestern University, Evanston, January 1994).
38. McLeod, *Asante,* 25–26.
39. Wilks, "Land, Labour, Capital." A. Norman Klein has challenged the historicity of Wilks's model of the Akan matriclan as a social mechanism for incorporating strangers and unfree labor in the fifteenth through seventeenth centuries. Indeed, Klein questions Wilks's assumption that a huge market for slaves existed among the forest Akan in the fifteenth and sixteenth centuries,

as well as Wilks's assumptions about the place and scale of slavery. A. Norman Klein, "Slavery and Akan Origins," *Ethnohistory* 41, 4 (1994), 627–56. For Wilks's rejoinder, see Ivor Wilks, "'Slavery and Akan Origins?' A Reply," *Ethnohistory* 41, 4 (1994), 657–65. The distinction (if any) between "slaves" and "unfree labor" is crucial to this debate.

40. Wilks, "Land, Labour, Capital," 524–25; and Wilks, *Forests of Gold* 78–82.
41. Agnes Akosua Aidoo, "Asante Queen Mothers in Government and Politics in the Nineteenth Century," *Journal of the Historical Society of Nigeria* 9, 1 (1977), 2.
42. Ibid., 13.
43. Michelle Gilbert, "The Cimmerian Darkness of Intrigue, Queen Mothers, Christianity and Truth in Akuapem History," *Journal of Religion in Africa* 23, 1 (1993), 9.
44. Aidoo, "Asante Queen Mothers," 9.
45. Compare with Ivor Wilks, "She Who Blazed a Trail: Akyaawa Yikwan of Asante," in *Forests of Gold,* 329–61; and McCaskie, *State and Society,* 180–99.
46. Through *nnwonkoro* (satirical songs), women had the singular privilege of re-evaluating social behavior.
47. Akyeampong fieldnotes: Interview with Albert Mawere Poku, Accra, August 30, 1994. However, Kofi Asare Opoku, *West African Traditional Religion* (Accra, 1978), 55, points out that "the sex of the minister is not an indication of the sex of the deity."
48. For a detailed description of *tutuw-bo,* see Pashington Obeng, "Asante Catholicism: Ritual Communication of the Catholic Faith among the Akan of Ghana" (Ph.D. Dissertation, Boston University, 1991), 68–69.
49. Obeng fieldnotes: Interview with Opanin Kwadwo Kwaa, Antoa, July 19, 1988.
50. Wilks, "She Who Blazed a Trail," 335.
51. Bowdich, *Mission,* 290.
52. Wilks, "She Who Blazed a Trail."
53. J. K. Fynn, "The Rise of Ashanti," *Ghana Notes and Queries* 9 (1966), 27.
54. See Obeng, *Ancient Ashanti Chieftaincy,* 20; and McLeod, *Asante,* 28.
55. Akyeampong fieldnotes: Interview with Mawere Poku, Accra, August 6, 1994.
56. A. A. Boahen, "The State and Cultures of the Lower Guinean Coast," in B. A. Ogot, ed., *General History of Africa,* V (Berkeley, 1992), 412.
57. K. Y. Daaku, *Osei Tutu of Asante* (London, 1976), 10. Wilks, *Forests of Gold,* 91–92, points to the possible existence of "kingship" in the Pra-Ofin basin by the mid-sixteenth century, according to Portuguese sources, but these sources say nothing about the nature of Akan kingship. It is debatable whether these were "leaders" or "kings," but the process of state formation had commenced by this time.
58. Wilks, *Forests of Gold,* 95–99. Wilks, *Forests of Gold,* Chs. 1–3, essentially argues that certain concurrent factors in Akanland between the fifteenth and seventeenth centuries—Atlantic and Saharan commercial networks with the Akan exchanging slaves for gold; and convergent modes of production with hunters, free agriculturalists, slave labor, and individualistic slave-owning entrepreneurs—produced a socio-economic revolution and an agrarian population expansion that pivoted Akan states into being. Klein, "Slavery and Akan Origins," highlights some of the problems of Wilks's model. For more developed analyses of Akan/Gold Coast polities in the precolonial era, based on the modes of production model, see Emmanuel Terray, "Long-Distance

Exchange and the Formation of the State: The Case of the Abron-Kingdom of Gyaman," *Economy and Society* 3 (1974), 315–45; and Ray Kea, *Settlement, Trade and Polities in the Seventeenth-Century Gold Coast* (Baltimore, 1982). Kea argues that the period from the late seventeenth century witnessed the emergence of militarized, territorially expansionist states—Asante being a prime example—based on imperial-agrarian formation.

59. Daaku, *Osei Tutu of Asante*, 14–17.
60. Kwame Arhin, "The Political Economy of a Princely City: The Economy of Kumasi in the Nineteenth Century," *Research Review Supplement* 5 (1993), 16.
61. Max Weber, *Theory of Social and Economic Organization* (New York, 1947), 329.
62. On Okomfo Anokye, see Rattray, *Ashanti Law and Constitution*, Ch. 24.
63. Daaku, *Osei Tutu of Asante*, 29.
64. Wilks, *Asante in the Nineteenth Century*, 112.
65. Arhin, "Rank and Class," 13.
66. The Asantehene's praise poems (*apaee*) depict this double triumph over nature and cultures. See Kwame Arhin, "The Asante Praise Poems: The Ideology of Patrimonialism," *Paideuma* 32 (1986), 163–97.
67. On gender politics in precolonial Asante, see T. C. McCaskie, "State and Society, Marriage and Adultery: Some Considerations Towards a Social History of Pre-Colonial Asante," *Journal of African History* 22, 3 (1981), 477–94.
68. Personal communication. Things ordinarily tabooed in Asante society may be harnessed for their inherent spiritual power in specific rituals. During the *odwira* festival, for example, the Asantehene ordered the slaying of an ox—an act tabooed to him as a member of the *Bosommuru ntoro*—at Abogyawe, a sacred spot in front of his palace. The king's public violation of his taboo paradoxically sharpened his spiritual power. R. S. Rattray, *Religion and Art in Ashanti* (Oxford, 1927), 136.
69. For some thoughts on human sacrifice in Asante, see Clifford Williams, "Asante: Human Sacrifice or Capital Punishment? An Assessment of the Period 1807–1874," *International Journal of African Historical Studies* 21, 2 (1988), 433–41; and Ivor Wilks, "Asante: Human Sacrifice or Capital Punishment? A Rejoinder," *International Journal of African Historical Studies* 21, 3 (1988), 443–52.
70. Arhin, "Rank and Class," 9. See also, Bowdich, *Mission,* 262.
71. Enshrined in proverbs like *obi nkyere akoda Nyame* ("No one points God out to a child"); and *wo pese wo kasa kyere Nyame, kasa kyere mframma* ("if you want to speak to God, speak to the wind").
72. Akyeampong fieldnotes: Interview with Okyeame Banahene, spokesman to the asantehene, Kumasi, August 18, 1994.
73. McLeod, *Asante* 41.
74. Dupuis, *Journal* 236–37.
75. Ibid., 114–16.
76. A biography of Asantehemaa Adoma Akosua (ACBP/54) is provided in *Asantesem: The Asante Collective Bibliography Project Bulletin* 11 (1979), 14–17.
77. T. C. McCaskie, "Anti-Witchcraft Cults in Asante: An Essay in the Social History of an African People," *History in Africa* 8 (1981), 125–54.

78. Ibid., 128.
79. Ibid.
80. For a good discussion of witchcraft, atrikin, and the politics of kingship, see Alma Gottlieb, "Witches, Kings, and the Sacrifice of Identity or the Power of Paradox and the Paradox of Power among the Beng of Ivory Coast," in Arens and Karp, eds., *Creativity of Power*, 245–72.
81. On the significance of color—especially red, black, and white—in Akan thought, and Akan conceptions of "coolness" and "hotness," see McLeod, *Asante* 173; S. Breidenbach, "Colour Symbolism and Ideology in a Ghanaian Healing Movement," *Africa* 46, 2 (1976), 137–45; and J. G. Platvoet, "Cool Shade, Peace and Power," *Journal of Religion in Africa* 15, 3 (1985), 174–99.
82. Akyeampong fieldnotes: Interview with Kofi Akyerem, Sekondi, August 16, 1994.
83. Aidoo, "Asante Queen Mothers."
84. Akyeampong fieldnotes: Interview with Obaapanin Afua Pokuaa, Kumasi, August 18, 1994.
85. D. J. E. Maier, *Priests and Power: The Case of the Dente Shrine in Nineteenth-Century Ghana* (Bloomington, 1983), 38.
86. *Kete* is the exclusive preserve of chiefs, forming part of the genre of praise songs.
87. Akyeampong fieldnotes: Interview with Obaapanin Afua Pokuaa, Kumasi, August 18, 1994.
88. McCaskie, "Anti-Witchcraft Cults," provides the most detailed discussion of the *domankama* movement.
89. Wilks, *Asante in the Nineteenth Century*, 520.
90. McCaskie, "Anti-Witchcraft Cults," 131.
91. Ibid.
92. See, for examples, David Owusu-Ansah, *Islamic Talismanic Tradition in Nineteenth Century Asante* (New York, 1991); Ivor Wilks, "The Position of Muslims in Metropolitan Ashanti in the Early Nineteenth Century," in I. Lewis, ed., *Islam in Tropical Africa* (Bloomington, 1980); and T. C. McCaskie, "Innovational Eclectism: The Asante Empire and Europe in the Nineteenth Century," *Comparative Studies in Society and History* 14, 1 (1972), 30–45.
93. Arhin, "Asante Praise Poems," 194. The potential for conflict between chiefs and unsubdued wielders of mystical power or priests is highlighted by Victoria Ebin, "Transfers of Power: The King and the Secret Society in a Time of Crisis," in Arens and Karp, eds., *Creativity of Power* 273–88; and Maier, *Priests and Power.*
94. Personal communication from David Owusu-Ansah, November 4, 1994.
95. Asante youngmen, seeking political power in an emergent Ghana in which chieftaincy could become defunct, found themselves in the same paradoxical position: they needed the endorsement of the Asantehene—custodian of the Golden Stool, symbol of the Asante nation—to even become established in Asante. Allman, *Quills of the Porcupine*.
96. Rattray, *Ashanti*, 292. Gyasehene Opoku Mensah secretly sent the Golden Stool to Wawase for safekeeping. It was subsequently removed to the village of Abuabugya. In 1920 certain individuals at Abuabugya found the Golden Stool and sold the gold ornaments that adorned it, precipitating another national crisis in Asante. Colonial Reports, *Ashanti, 1921*, 21–29.

97. Aidoo, "Asante Queen Mothers in Government and Politics," 12.
98. Obrecht to Basel, July 30, 1900 (No. 1900.II.169). Paul Jenkins, "Abstracts Concerning Gold Coast History from the Basel Mission Archives" (n.p., n.d.).
99. Akyeampong fieldnotes: Interview with Mawere Poku, Accra, August 30, 1994.
100. Akyeampong fieldnotes: Interview with Mawere Poku, Accra, August 30, 1994. The oral history of Lake Bosumtwi, recorded by Agyeman Duah in 1962, does not mention Afranie I. *Asante Stool Histories Series,* As No. 10, Recorded by J. Agyemang Duah, Institute of African Studies (I.A.S.), Legon, 1962.
101. Allman, *Quills of the Porcupine,* 104. Kwasi Afranie was acquitted, partially due to insufficient evidence.
102. Akyeampong fieldnotes: Interview with Mawere Poku, Accra, August 30, 1994.
103. Personal communication from Kwasi Sarkodie-Mensah, native of Edweso, December 25, 1994.
104. The very thesis of McCaskie's *State and Society.*
105. Weber, *On Charisma,* 15, defines power as the ability to realize one's will in spite of opposition from others.
106. McCaskie, *State and Society,* 127.
107. Ibid., 104–108, and 123–26.
108. Arens and Karp, "Introduction," *Creativity of Power,* xvi.
109. See, for example, Jean Marie Allman, "The Youngmen and the Porcupine: Class, Nationalism and Asante's Struggle for Self-Determination, 1954–1957," *Journal of African History* 31, 2 (1990), 263.

SECTION II

DECOLONIZING FEMINISMS

Women's studies came out of the feminist movement in Western Europe and North America. Thus feminism is a significant ideology structuring gender discourses. Feminist scholars are the most important gender-focused constituency and the source of much knowledge about women and gender hierarchies. Though feminism has been presented as a liberatory ideology for women in Western Europe, the United States, and Canada, with regard to Africa, Asia and Latin America, it has been implicated in the colonizing practices that resemble and have benefited from centuries of European domination of other parts of the world. It is not surprising, then, that a book on African gender studies must first address the representations of African women in Western feminist discourses.

In her paper "Bringing African Women into the Classroom: Rethinking Pedagogy and Epistemology," Obioma Nnaemeka examines the structures of power in the feminist movement which belie the call for a global sisterhood. The engagement of privileged white women with other women she explains is characterized by overly simplistic binary oppositions between self and other, subject and object, margin and periphery. As a result, the construction of the African woman is appallingly one-dimensional. Nnaemeka goes on to examine the implications of this distorted image in teaching about Africa especially in North American classrooms. She asks two pithy questions: Why do we want to learn and teach about other cultures? What is the best way to educate about other cultures?

Marnia Lazreg in her essay "Decolonizing Feminism" (which gives this section its name) reminds us that difference in all its guises has been the sticking point of Western social sciences. Focusing on studies of women in Algeria and the Middle East, Lazreg shows that the problem of difference as the objectification of the Other is replayed in contemporary feminist scholarship without any consciousness that the Other shares a human bond with the feminist self. The double standard that American academic feminism brings to the study of other cultures is apparent when we contrast this with how they see their own culture. For them, Lazreg points out, their culture is not rejected wholesale but presented as perfectible. In contrast, by focusing on the sensational and uncouth in other cultures, they render them irredeemable. According to Lazreg feminist labels such as "women of color" only serve to reinscribe the privilege of the dominant group to name others.

Chapter 3

Bringing African Women into the Classroom: Rethinking Pedagogy and Epistemology

Obioma Nnaemeka

> Nothing so sentimental (or arrogant) as ignoring differences, nor so cowardly (or lazy) as overemphasizing them.
>
> —Robin Morgan

> Knowledge leads no more to openings than to closures. . . . Between knowledge and power, there is room for knowledge at rest . . . " the end of myths, the erosion of utopia, the rigor of taut patience."
>
> —Trinh T. Minh-ha

> Borders are imaginary lines.
>
> —Anonymous

Explorations into the character, possibilities, and survival of feminism and sisterhood on a global scale have led me to revisit the evolution of feminism in the West, especially in the United States, since the 1960s and to examine the question of identity in structuring and destructuring alliances. The crisis in the feminist movement in the United States is a microcosm of the problems that militate against women forming alliances across continents. The troubled history of second-wave feminism in the United States chronicles the movement from the radicalism and sexual politics of the 1960s to the theorizing and feminist politics of the late 1970s and early 1980s to the narcissism and identity politics of the 1980s. A study of this evolution raises some epistemological and pedagogical questions: How do the ways in which we construct, teach, and disseminate knowledge of the Other undermine or promote alliances between women?

As feminists take stock of years of concerted struggle, some suddenly realize that their shared experiences are expressed and articulated in a language they no longer understand. The theorizing of feminism created structures of power in the feminist movement analogous to those for which patriarchy is attacked. As positions of margin and center became delineated, the resistance of the marginalized to the imperious hegemony of that center became more apparent. Not opposed to recognizing differences, the resistance instead has challenged the creation of a hierarchical paradigm in which these differences are placed and interpreted. The theorizing and the subsequent ideologizing of feminism have culminated in the legitimation of the subject/object, self/other, center/margin dyads within the feminist movement itself. Such strategies of exclusion intensify group identification and loyalties which could ultimately fragment the movement. Identity politics or "home politics" should be not an end in itself but the means to an end, providing the initial building blocks for constructing social change. Nonetheless, the security that identity politics can offer may insulate us from forming the alliances necessary for political action. Bonnie Zimmerman cautions that a fine line separates autonomy from fragmentation: "There is a price to pay for a politics rooted so strongly in consciousness and identity. The power of diversity has as its mirror image and companion, the powerlessness of fragmentation. Small autonomous groups can also be ineffectual groups."[1]

In a television interview on December 31, 1979, Tom Wolfe characterized the decade that was closing as the "Me Decade." Feminists were part of the "Me Decade." too, and the identity question that simmered in the late 1970s intensified as the 1980s wore on. Symbols of commonality, oppression, and sisterhood, for example, through which the feminist movement sought to forge solidarity, became increasingly questioned as women began to assess these symbols in all their complexity. As oppression took on a human face, thus raising questions about difference, the issue of sisterhood, especially global sisterhood, assumed wider implications, transcending biology and genealogy. The belief that "sisterhood is global"[2] became a political matter.

Some feminist scholars continue to have faith in feminist scholarship because of, not in spite of, the fissures within it—fissures that enhance its vibrancy and relevance. Our faith, however, should not deter us from examining the sources of these fissures, and from working to prevent them from deepening and destroying women's ability to form and maintain alliances. We must therefore thoroughly scrutinize the theoretical and epistemological issues, the methodological procedures, and pedagogical questions in feminist scholarship as it addresses marginalized women, particularly African women.

In this day and age of "multiculturalism" and "pluralism," we find a corresponding shift in feminist scholarship from the theorizing of difference to theorizing diversity. Skeptics and cynics (often with good reason) might scream, "Hell, no! Let diversity be!" Theorizing diversity is a risky business; when diversity comes eyeball to eyeball with theory, it is diversity that blinks! Difficult questions remain: How can we theorize diversity without falling into the trap of erecting hierarchies, up-holding difference, and legitimating exclusions? How can we save the dynamism of diversity from the hegemonic grip of theory? Trinh T. Minh-ha brilliantly articulates the danger in the use of what Amilcar Cabral calls "the weapon of theory".[3]

> Indeed, theory no longer is theoretical when it loses sight of its own conditional nature, takes no risk in speculation, and circulates as a form of administrative inquisition. Theory oppresses, when it wills or perpetuates existing power relations, when it presents itself as a means to exert authority—the Voice of Knowledge... Difference needs not be suppressed in the name of Theory. And theory as a tool of survival needs to be rethought in relation to gender in discursive practice.[4]

The tension between theory and diversity motivates Susan Griffin's claim that any theory in which "the knowledge of oppression remains mute" will begin to destroy as it is transformed into ideology. I do not believe in theory as a purely innocuous formulation "born of genuine feeling of a sense of reality." Because many theories evolve from the distortion and manipulation of reality, we cannot totally absolve theory from the hegemony that taints ideology. I agree with Griffin when she asserts that ideology "is a martinet."[5] But isn't theory also a "martinet" in its own way? Theoretical frames also border and exclude. Our concern should be less with what is framed in and more with what is framed out, with what is silenced. In feminist scholarship, as we charge ourselves to listen to silences, particularly in women's writing, we must, with equal enthusiasm, listen to the silences imposed by theory. We must interrogate the history/histories of theory/theoretical frameworks and in so doing bring to the fore the human agency implicated in their formulation, suspecting the smoke screen of objectivity which obscures the ever-manipulative human agency. The smoke screen's illusion undermines us all.

The fundamental dissimilarity between the theorizing of difference and theorizing diversity is that the latter emphasizes the centrality of contiguity. The focus on contiguity which simultaneously recognizes difference and the possibility and/or reality of connection reminds me of a quilt. The quilt, separate patches revealing different and connected geographies and histories, suggests a lesson in possibilities, particularly the possibility of creating harmony out of contradictions. The quilt's beauty transcends aesthetics; the quilt is beautiful because it is also a powerfully political act and art. A theology of nearness—genuine connections, mutually empowering intersections, and fruitful interpenetration—must nurture the theorizing of diversity. Here lie the difficulties and the risk. Feminist theorizing and praxis must be rooted in *genuine* feminist ethics. The troubling contradictions between what we preach and write and what we do fuel the frustrations felt by many who continue to value and practice feminist scholarship.

In the last decade or so feminist scholars have bandied around the word *intersection*. For considerations of intersection to be meaningful, however, we must not embrace the term arbitrarily. Intersection must be allowed to assume its full meaning and range. We cannot talk about the intersections of class, race, gender, ethnicity, and sexual preference without carefully considering the intersection of theory and practice, without recognizing the intersections of world systems, particularly as the world gets smaller owing to technological advances that shrink distances.

We must interrogate feminist scholarship not only on theoretical but also on epistemological grounds. Instead of making the usual philosophical wanderings into epistemology, we must reframe questions about epistemology. Instead of perpetually constructing and renegotiating the so-called standpoint epistemologies, we must take a stand against epistemological inventions and manipulations. In short, we must ask fundamental questions about the manipulation of knowledge, about information management; the politics of publishing must be investigated and interrogated. Information management feeds partial or possibly distorted knowledge, which in turn undermines the intersections we theorize.

In 1980 Zed Press (London) published Nawal El Saadawi's *Hidden Face of Eve.* This edition's preface remains one of the best analyses of the Iranian revolution and of the relation between imperialism and Islam, outlining its effect on women in the Arab world. Saadawi categorically states in the preface that to understand and explain fully the condition of women in the Arab world, one must take into account foreign, particularly American, intervention in the region. This important preface, which establishes a connection between imperialism and the rise of Islamic fundamentalism, with the attendant repression of women, did not appear in the American edition published by Beacon Press, an omission that prompted a strong reaction from Saadawi:

> Yes, and here is a very subtle form of exploitation practiced, unfortunately, by feminists—so-called progressive feminists. Gloria Steinem of Ms magazine writes me a letter in Cairo and asks me for an article about clitoridectomy. So I write her an article setting forth the political, social and historical analysis, along with comments about my personal experience. She cuts the political, social and historical analysis and publishes only the personal statements, which put me in a very awkward position. People asked, how could Nawal write such a thing? She has such a global perspective on clitoridectomy, how could she write such a thing? They didn't know Steinem had cut the article. The second example is Beacon Press in Boston. I gave my book, *The Hidden Face of Eve,* to the publisher in London; he published all of the book—the preface, introduction, everything. The preface, which is a long preface, is crucial and important to the book. Beacon Press cut it without my permission, making me feel that I have been exploited and my ideas distorted. Without the preface, it appears that I am separating the sexual from the political, which I never do. To me, women who think they are liberated but who are obsessed with sexuality are not liberated. They are living a new slavery. They are obsessed by not having men around just as they were obsessed with having them around. It is the other side of the same coin.[6]

Although *The Hidden Face of Eve* has been widely read in the United States, the American audience, reading an incomplete version, is denied this powerful book's full impact. As readers of Saadawi in North America lead their war against physical excisions made on Arab girls, they should with equal enthusiasm challenge the type of excision Saadawi claims was performed on her book. Such manipulations of information have grave implications for our theorizing and praxis.

How can we theorize difference or diversity, and what are the pitfalls in such theorizing? How do we gather information about the Other? How do we organize, order, and disseminate that information? In short, how does information management contribute to our construction of a notion of self and at the same time alienate us from the Other? These are crucial questions that we, as students and teachers, confront in varying degrees. These and other related issues have led me to explore the subject in my essay titled "Bringing African Women into the Classroom." While working on this essay, I got a call from a colleague. During our conversation I told him about my topic. "Eh! Bringing African Women into the Classroom!" he sneered. "What do you mean by 'bringing'? Can't they walk? How do you bring them?" he asked. I replied, "You bring them on a leash." Although my response was meant to be a joke, in retrospect I believe I accurately described the profound objectification of African women in classrooms in the West. And as we consider the commodification of African women in Western classrooms, we must also address the issue of tokenism. Quite often the work of an African woman writer is thrown into a course syllabus in order to take care of race, gender, ethnicity, and class issues in one fell swoop, thereby creating a "multicultural course" which will in turn produce "multicultural students."

To study a culture presupposes in some ways that one is outside it. Can we teach as outsiders? Oh, yes, we can. The pertinent question, however, remains: How do we learn and teach as outsiders? In studying and teaching another culture, the teacher finds himself or herself situated at the congruence of different and often contradictory cultural currents. This point of convergence where the teacher stands has its privileges and rewards, but it is also fraught with danger. To survive at this precarious position requires a large dose of humility. Issues involved in researching, writing, and teaching about other cultures are inextricably linked to survival. Can we cross cultural boundaries and still survive? And the notion of crossing cultural boundaries is in itself problematic. What do we mean by "crossing"? Do we mean moving from one point to another, in the process abandoning one set of realities for another? It seems to me that a cross-cultural pedagogy entails not a "crossover" but a transgression whose partial enactment denies the finality implicit in a "crossover."

As students and teachers we discover that our explorations into understanding other peoples and cultures place us in an ambiguous site where we will never accomplish a "crossover" but rather stand astride cultures: our culture and other cultures. It seems to me that crossing cultural boundaries means standing at the crossroads of cultures. In other words, we must see that we enter other cultures with our own cultural baggage. The extent to which we allow narcissism and notions of self to mediate our analysis will determine the degree of distortion in our conclusions. As we learn and teach about other cultures, two fundamental questions should be asked: (1) Why do we want to learn and teach other cultures? (2) How can we learn and teach other cultures?

The first question raises the issue of intention. Charges of concern with economic advancement and professional upward mobility have been levied against some scholars, ranging from historians and social anthropologists to feminists and cultural critics, who proclaim themselves experts on Africa in general and African women in particular.[7] The same could be said about studies of other minorities in which insiders and outsiders to the minority cultures collaborate to advance themselves economically and professionally by means of distortions they invent about the minority cultures, distortions that run against the sacred nature of these cultures. As Ward Churchill writes:

> The past 20 years have seen the birth of a new growth industry in the United States. Known as "American Indian Spiritualism," this profitable enterprise apparently began with a number of literary hoaxes undertaken by non-Indians such as Carlos Castaneda, Jay Marks (AKA "Jamake Highwater," author of *The Primal Mind,* etc.) and Ruth Beebe Hill (of *Hanta Yo* notoriety). A few Indians such as Alonzo Blacksmith . . . and Hyemeyohsts Storm . . . also cashed in, writing bad distortions and outright lies about indigenous spirituality for consumption in the mass market. The authors grew rich peddling their trash, while real Indians starved to death, out of the sight and mind of America.[8]

An issue related to the methodological concerns that the second question raises is that of perspective, equally crucial to evaluating how we learn and teach other cultures. Perspective, distance, objectivity. Perspective implies possibilities, alternatives, choice. How can we choose an appropriate location to situate ourselves? How far or close should we stand vis-a-vis the subject of our analysis? In a 1961 lecture in Japan, Simone de Beauvoir affirmed that in a war situation the privileged and probably the most objective position is that of the person on the sideline, the war correspondent, who witnesses the battle but is not embroiled in the fighting.[9] Richard Wright brilliantly articulated the problematic of perspective: "Perspective is that part of a poem, novel, or play which a writer never puts directly upon paper. It is that fixed point in intellectual space where a writer stands to view the struggles, hopes and sufferings of his people. There are times when he may stand too close and the result is blurred vision. Or he may stand too far away and the result is a neglect of important things."[10] In our study and teaching of other cultures, balance and humility must mediate our choice of perspective.

Different problems arise depending on whether one teaches a culture as an insider or an outsider. As I mentioned earlier, one can teach as an outsider, but to do so requires the humility that is grounded in knowledge. Unfortunately, when teaching about Africa and African women, many outsiders prove too impatient to claim expertise. A three-week whirlwind tour of Africa does not an expert on Africa make; speed-reading two or three African novels cannot produce an expert on African literature. Sadly enough, schools in the West sustain tremendous institutional tolerance and encouragement of such expertise. As the academy provides a breeding ground for such experts on Africa and African women, it puts in place stiff requirements for the teaching of Western cultures and literatures. In such areas expertise must be proven through transcripts, graduate degrees, and teaching experience. Trivializing other cultures encourages the type of miseducation that leads to further trivializing of such cultures.

Teaching as an insider poses its own set of problems. Overidentification with one's culture leads to the type of romanticization that produces other levels of distortions. Good examples surface in some Negritude writings. The romanticization of Africa and the subsequent oversimplification of issues have led to much of the negative reaction against the Negritude movement. Furthermore, insiders can also be alienated from their own culture. A Western-educated African who teaches African culture also speaks from a position of alienation which may not necessarily be as profound as that of the outsider. Whether one teaches as an insider or an outsider, the issue of distance is crucial. It is Chinua Achebe's recognition of the interplay of identification and distance that sets him apart as one of Africa's foremost writers. With Achebe we experience a rare moment in literature where the writer balances himself or herself strategically. In spite of his Western education, Achebe remains a true son of Igboland, what the Igbos would call "a son of the soil." Immersed in his cultural and social milieu but possessing a critical eye, he simultaneously identifies with and maintains a distance from his environment. In his works Achebe narrates with charm his profound identification with and love for his environment while at the same time be recognizes its flaws, particularly those generated by foreign interventions.[11] Achebe demonstrates that a postcolonial subject can maintain a balanced view of the postcolonial condition.

The issue of balance is neglected in the one-dimensional Western constructions of the African woman—usually poor and powerless. We African women have witnessed repeatedly the activities of our overzealous foreign sisters, mostly feminists who appropriate our wars in the name of fighting the oppression of women in the so-called third world. We watch with chagrin and in painful sisterhood these avatars of the proverbial mourner who wails more than the owners of the corpse.[12] In their enthusiasm, our sisters usurp our wars and fight them badly—very badly. The arrogance that declares African women "problems" objectifies us and undercuts the agency necessary for forging true global sisterhood. African women are not problems to be solved. Like women everywhere, African women *have* problems. More important, they have provided solutions to these problems. We are the only ones who can set our priorities and agenda. Anyone who wishes to participate in our strugles must do so in the context of our agenda. In the same way, African women who wish to contribute to global struggles (and many do) should do so with a deep respect for the paradigms and strategies that people of those areas have established. In our enthusiasm to liberate others, we must not be blind to our own enslavement. Activities of women globally should be mutually liberating.

During the Gulf War the biggest issues in the U.S. media were Saddam Hussein and Saudi women. I will leave Saddam Hussein to George Bush. I was, however, intrigued by the numerous stories about Saudi women. American pronouncements regarding Saudi women suggest prevalent attitudes about other peoples and cultures. One remarkable example comes to mind. On December 27, 1990, the television show *Inside Edition* carried a segment on Saudi women, focusing less on Saudi women and more on the veil—supposedly the ultimate symbol of oppression. The first part of the segment showed us faceless Saudi women shrouded in ample yardage of black cloth. They did not speak. They were not made to speak. They moved against a powerful male presence: the male reporter who commented on their lives of abject subjugation.

Halfway through the tedious, patronizing commentary another Saudi woman appeared, a college student in Jordan. She wore Western clothes (symbols of freedom!) and perched on a red convertible (another symbol of freedom!), ready to speed away into the limitless unknown. This "liberated" Saudi woman spoke; she deserved to speak because she was "free."

At the end of the segment another male presence was installed. Bill O'Reilly appeared on the screen. With an evasive look in his eyes and a dubious smile on his lips, he asked the viewers, specifically the female viewers: "Aren't you lucky to be here?" A program designed to teach us about Saudi women turned out to be a lesson on how lucky and free American women are. After watching that program, I found that my concern was not for Saudi women, since the program gave me no meaningful information about them. My concern was for the millions of American women who went to bed that night believing Bill O'Reilly and his assurances. My concern is about the naivete and arrogance that such assurances nature. Many who teach African women writers in classrooms in the West are no different from Bill O'Reilly. As we look at other cultures, relativist arguments and arrogant feelings of superiority numb us to the realities of our own predicament. We need to be conscious of our own oppression in order to collaborate with those who are similarly oppressed.

In the classrooms where we teach and learn about other cultures, three important elements continuously interact: the text, the teacher, and the student. Each takes enormous risks in being there. The text is at risk primarily because it cannot defend itself against use, misuse, and abuse. But the essential question we should ask is this: Why do certain texts and not others on the same subject (in this case, African women) find their way into classrooms? What factors determine our choice of texts, films, and other teaching materials? Does one attribute such choices to a teacher's ignorance (the teacher does not know any better) or to the fact that particular texts and films confirm and legitimize the teacher's prejudices about other cultures and peoples? As we study and teach other cultures, do we enter into meaningful dialogue with the materials we have chosen? In order to unearth the prejudices and assumptions inherent in the materials we use, we should ceaselessly ask questions such as: Where is the writer in the text? Where is the filmmaker in the film? In short, we cannot meaningfully communicate information without first of all asking serious questions about the construction of knowledge. We should examine not only what the texts say but, more important, how the information and data in the texts came into being and are articulated. Concern with epistemological and methodological issues is therefore crucial if we are to save the text. A course syllabus not only demonstrates how much the teacher knows but also betrays the teacher's limitations and prejudices. The same could be said for compilers of anthologies, particularly those designed for use in world literature classes.

Often, token gestures of inclusion are extended to women and socalled third world writers. In such quasi-invisible inclusions, the relevance of a token contribution to the entire anthology or syllabus receives little attention. On a couple of occasions colleagues have asked me to name an African woman writer for inclusion in their course. The appropriate thing would have been for them to tell me the focus of the course and the required texts already on the syllabus. This information would determine whether I recommend the work(s) of Bessie Head, Aminata Sow Fall, Tsitsi Dangarembga, Flora Nwapa, or any other woman writer from Africa. My point here is that, contrary to current thinking and practice, African women writers are not easily interchangeable. It is not so important that Bessie Head's work appears on a syllabus as that it relates and speaks to other chosen materials. Such intertextual considerations help us derive optimal benefit from even the token inclusion we make. I once saw a literature syllabus that lumped Chinua Achebe together with *Robinson Crusoe* and Saint-Exupéry. Evidently the several missions that Saint-Exupéry flew over North Africa and the Sahara earned him the spot beside Achebe! It seems to me that Chinua Achebe and Joseph Conrad would have made a better combination.[13]

Students who flock to courses on African women do so probably for as many reasons as they take other courses, ranging from the desire to learn about African women because it is in vogue—the right thing to do in this day and age of cultural literacy and pluralism—to the possibility that other courses are filled and the students have nowhere else to go for credits. Nonetheless, many non-African (particularly Western) students who walk into courses on African women fall into a different category; almost all of them come in with expectations pretty much defined and entrenched in their minds. The teacher who teaches otherwise risks, among other things, receiving uncomplimentary evaluations for his or her unpardonable deviancy. And when African students take courses on African women, they are often called on to validate the pervasive distortions of African women's lives in texts and films. If the African students dare to think or argue otherwise, they are accused of overreacting. Tension builds up, creating a potentially explosive situation that impedes learning and understanding. Not merely an individual who disseminates information, the teacher who survives must also be a diplomat and psychologist.

Not too long ago I taught a course, "Women in Developing Areas: Power, Politics, and Culture," in a small Midwestern liberal arts college. We started by reading materials written by Judith van Allen and some African women scholars, Ifi Amadiume, Bolanle Awe, and Kamene Okonjo.[14] At the end of two weeks of intense reading, one of my students informed me that she was not getting anything out of the course. Her complaint surprised me since a few other students had mentioned to me that there was too much information to absorb. After a long discussion with the student, it dawned on me that her problem lay more with the nature of the materials we were reading, which discussed primarily the powerful positions that women occupy in indigenous African social and political formations. My student was basically asking, "Where are those excised/circumcised African women in marriages arranged by families who eventually shipped them off to be victimized by heavy-handed polygynists?" I told the student to exercise patience. Circumcision, arranged marriage, and polygyny would be discussed during the seventh and eighth weeks of class; she had only five short weeks to go! Our preconceived notions can be so strong that they get in the way of our learning about cultures and other peoples whose lives and realities transcend our cultural boundaries. As teachers we can overcome this difficulty by painstakingly and judiciously selecting materials that build a balanced syllabus.

The teaching of cultural studies often focuses on exposing differences between cultures. It seems to me, however, that we could accomplish much by teaching similarities and connections as well as differences. It makes sense politically that women, as teachers, teach connections, thereby reducing the distance between the student and the foreign culture and increasing points of interaction and identification. It is the teacher's responsibility to delineate the differences and commonalities between the student's culture and the foreign culture, without unduly establishing facile universalism and untenable connections. This methodology which I call teaching connections has been helpful to me in my teaching of African women to a Western audience, especially in teaching the three most discussed issues about African women—clitoridectomy, polygyny, and arranged marriage.

The pervasive sensationalization of clitoridectomy in Western media and scholarship leads to the equally pervasive belief in the in-completeness of most African women, a belief that basically questions our humanity. From the West an intense war led by Fran Hoskens, the guru of clitoridectomy, has raged against this "barbaric act" perpetrated against helpless African and Arab women. Women within Africa and the Arab world have equally condemned the practice. There is disagreement, however, about how to wage the war.[15] Our Western sisters have seen clitoridectomy primarily as an issue of sexuality, and the fixation with sexuality in the West helps explain the intensity of their intrusion. They denounce clitoridectomy because, according to them, it prevents African women from enjoying sex. But then, wasn't clitoridectomy initiated in part precisely to prevent women from going around and enjoying sex? This unmitigated advocacy of the enjoyment of sex most often leads to a stricter imposition of certain customs on African and Arab women. Foreigners, however well-meaning they may be, must not fail to see how they contribute to the intensification of oppressive patriarchal practices in Africa and the Arab world. The upsurge of religious fundamentalism in the Middle East and other parts of the Arab world occurs as a sign of resistance to imperialism and other forms of foreign intervention. The return to the veil arises not by accident. In the name of resisting foreign interventionism, patriarchal societies resort to rigid and heavy-handed enforcement of old ways—tradition, religious fundamentalism—which often oppress women. So by fighting our wars badly, our Western sisters inadvertently collaborate in tightening the noose around our necks.

Clitoridectomy goes beyond sexuality. It raises questions with profound social, political, and economic implications.[16] Any meaningful fight against this practice must coordinate with other battles against the political, social, and economic conditions that generated and continue to perpetuate such a practice. We must consider an issue such as this in all its complexities. We must establish linkages, teach connections. Furthermore, we must acknowledge the history and global nature of circumcision and clitoridectomy in order to situate the debate where it duly belongs. As Nawal El Saadawi rightly points out, the issue is not barbaric Africa and oppressive Islam. The issue is patriarchy:

> In Copenhagen, we had a lot of disagreement, we women from Africa and the Third World, with her [Fran Hoskens]. In our workshop, we argued that clitoridectomy has nothing to do with Africa or with any religion, Islam or Christianity. It is known in history that it was performed in Europe and America, Asia, and Africa. It has to do with patriarchy and monogamy. When patriarchy was established, monogamy was forced on women so that fatherhood could be known. Women's sexuality was attenuated so as to fit within the monogamous system. But she doesn't want to hear any of this.[17]

There are other aspects of teaching connections which I apply to my teaching of clitoridectomy. I teach clitoridectomy in tandem with teaching abuses of the female body in other cultures: forms of plastic surgery in the West and foot-binding in China, for example. For a Western audience I bring the issue home by comparing breast reduction surgery and clitoridectomy. We must not be distracted by the arrogance that names one procedure breast reduction and the other sexual *mutilation,* with all the attached connotations of barbarism. In both instances some part of the female body is excised.

Some women undergo breast reduction for some of the reasons that some young girls undergo clitoridectomy—to be more attractive, desirable, and acceptable. For the women in areas where clitoridectomy is performed, beauty is inextricably linked with chastity and motherhood. The crucial questions we must ask are: For whom are these operations undertaken? For whom must these women be desirable and acceptable? Women's inability to control their bodies is not country-specific. Abuse of the female body is global and should be studied and interpreted within the context of oppressive conditions under patriarchy. Teaching connections radically shifts the grounds for debate from racial and national particularism and idiosyncrasies to comparisons of women's oppression under patriarchy. In the American classroom I have observed that this shift interrogates and modifies the notion of self among the students, particularly the female students. They go from thinking nationality (American) to thinking simultaneously nationality, sex, and gender (American women).

Polygyny has been condemned in the West as one of the worst symbols of African women's oppression without any assessment of the advantages the practice accords women: sharing child care, emotional and economic support, sisterhood, companionship, and so on. Our Western sisters who pity us for having to share our husbands with other women forget that husband-sharing was perfected and elevated to an art form in the West. Polygyny comes from two Greek words: *poly* (many) and *gyne* (woman or wife). *Polygyny* has, therefore, two possible meanings—"many women," or "many wives." The English dictionary sanctifies only one of the two possibilities, "many wives," a limitation to which no one seems to object. I remember that the first English dictionary I used in the colonial school was written by one Michael West, a man. I gather that men still write dictionaries—English dictionaries!

Polygyny as "many women" places the Western man with one wife and one or more mistresses in the same category as the African man who legitimates his relationship with more than one woman. We must not also forget the brand of polygyny euphemistically called serial monogamy in the West. The need to qualify monogamy in this instance is suspect. As a matter of fact, an African woman in a polygamous relationship seems to be a step or two ahead of her Western counterpart living under the illusion that she is not sharing her husband: the African woman knows who else her husband is with. In teaching and understanding polygyny, the issue is not uncivilized Africa but men.

Arranged marriage is another issue used to illustrate the enslavement of African women. As I teach connections, I point out practices in the West similar to the arranged marriage for which African and Asian societies have been ridiculed. One wonders if the dating services mushrooming all over the United States do not engage in some similar arranging! I have watched with amazement the facility of arrangements conducted on the television show "Love Connection." On a couple of occasions I have witnessed the triumphant return of a "connected" couple to the show: the woman walks out jubilantly with a baby in her arms, and the man, now her husband, follows a few steps behind with a conspiratorial grin on his face. A family is established before our eyes, and we applaud. Again, in the issue of arranged marriage, it seems to me that African women are better off: they do not pay for the services for which their American counterparts pay exorbitantly. My American feminist friend has argued vehemently in favor of dating services because, according to her, the issue of choice is crucial. With a dating service a woman can decide to choose or not choose a particular "allocation." Incidentally, the day my friend argued her strong case, I saw sticking out of her bookshelf a book titled *Smart Women/Foolish Choices*. She must have bought the book in a moment of doubt.

At state in our divergent views is the issue of cultural difference. In order to teach difference, we must thoroughly examine how difference comes into being. Can we distinguish between constructed and actual difference?

Ideology thrives on differences; ideology actually constructs differences, thus hiding similarities and actual differences. Concerning African women in the classroom, what we see in most classrooms in the West is not the study of *African women* but rather the study of the *African woman,* in whatever way we choose to invent the myth. Usually the invented African woman carries a heavy load on her head and a baby strapped to her back, and holds two kids, with about four more in tow. Of course she lives in a village. She is the myth. The problem with myths is not what they reveal but what they conceal. In order to understand African peoples and appreciate the rich diversity of Africa, we must put a human face on the African continent. In teaching African peoples, and observer notes, "we need to breathe life into our classroom."[18] Distortions in the study and teaching of African concerns stem from imperialism's refusal to historicize and differentiate African space and peoples. We Africans must realize that our survival depends to a large extent on our ability to reclaim our history. As bell hooks correctly notes, "Our struggle is also the struggle of memory against forgetting."[19]

The understanding and mutual respect which can emanate from teaching connections are necessary tools for revisiting global sisterhood and reconceptualizing marginality. Sisterhood is not an abstraction which all women can claim simply on the basis of commonality of sex; it flourishes only through hard work. True sisterhood is a political act, a commonality rooted in knowledge, understanding, and mutual respect. For true sisterhood to emerge, women must realize the intersections of their personal and collective histories and recognize how and where their liminal histories touch. These points of intersection and convergence constitute sites of energy, power, and agency, sites where we can name ourselves or refuse to be named as we center our marginality. Only in full recognition of the possibilities of the marginal site may we begin to see it not as a position of loss and disenfranchisement but rather as a location of contestation, gain, and empowerment.

The epistemological issues raised here clearly indicate that knowledge must ground the teaching of connections. The battle flaring in the academy over issues of diversity and multiculturalism is more than a struggle over power and turf. The bitter fight to protect the sanctity of the canon and to exclude "marginal discourses" betrays an anti-intellectualism that I call the new illiteracy: the refusal of literate people to read, to learn, and consequently to know and grow.

The current debate over transforming the academy reveals that the issue of knowledge entails risks, both institutional and personal. Institutions may engage in the diversity business to give a polite nod to change and pluralism. They set out to burn a tree but find that they have set the forest ablaze. What ensues is the panic control we find in a crisis. Crisis management during a panic leads to the dangerous vacillation of one step forward, two steps back.

In response to this situation, I renew the call for a thorough examination of the relationship between sisterhood and knowledge. Susan Lanser's essay in this volume offers a fertile terrain for understanding and analyzing this relationship. True sisterhood grounded in knowledge (of self and others) will shield us from the alienation and disconnectedness of the voyeur-tourist in Lanser's study of *A Small Place.*

In order to teach our sisters, we must know them, not assume knowledge of them. Teaching connections makes great demands on our energy, time, and dedication. It compels us to retool ourselves through knowledge. Instead of using pluralism and multiculturalism as excuses for creating superficial and irrelevant visibility of peoples and issues that have for so long been relegated to the margins of scholarship, we should use them as modes of production for bringing about personal and societal transformation through knowledge. When I teach Mariama Ba, I do not make territorial claims to the entire field of knowledge and experience contained in her work simply because, like the author, I am an African woman. Mariama Ba's work grew out of an African tradition with which I am familiar, but it also evolved from an Islamic tradition with which I was totally unfamiliar. Her work required me to retool myself. I read the Koran and familiarized myself with Islamic culture, particularly the status of women in that culture.

The personal risks involved in teaching connections are great. The courses that are designed to teach inclusiveness and diversity stand as mirrors in which we as teachers see ourselves as well as the other alien cultural fields and cartographies of pain that come under our purview.

As we all know, self-knowledge can be frightening and humbling, but it is also necessary, healthy, and empowering. Equipped with proper and adequate knowledge, we can no longer walk though our sisters' "small place" as voyeur-tourists, but rather we becomes true sisters who are aware of how we and the institutions of which we are a part are implicated in creating our sisters' "small place."

What Lanser calls "unreal loyalties" may blind us to the full extent of our complicity and shield us from engaging in positive action informed by the transforming powers of knowledge. "Home politics" can be meaningful not only in terms of understanding and legitimating our "home" but also, and more important, in terms of understanding how our "homes" connect to and affect other "homes." Teaching connections requires that we grasp and teach sameness and difference simultaneously.

NOTES

1. Bonnie Zimmerman, "The Politics of Transliteration: *Lesbian Personal Narratives*," in *The Lesbian Issue: Essays from Signs*, ed. Estelle B. Freedman *et al.* (Chicago: University of Chicago Press, 1985), 268.
2. This is also the title of the book edited by Robin Morgan, *Sisterhood Is Global: The International Women's Movement Anthology* (New York: Anchor Press, 1984).
3. "The Weapon of Theory" is the title of chapter 14 in *Unity and Struggle: Speeches and Writings of Amilcar Cabral* (New York: Monthly Review Press, 1979), 119–37.
4. Trinh T. Minh-ha, *Woman, Native, Other: Writing Postcoloniality and Feminism* (Bloomington: Indiana University Press, 1989), 42–43.

5. See Susan Griffin, "The Way of All Ideology," *Signs* 7 (1982): 647.
6. Quoted in Tiffany Patterson and Angela Gillam, "Out of Egypt: A Talk With Nawal El Saadawi," *Freedomways* 23 (1983): 190–91.
7. Ifi Amadiume, preface to Male Daughters, Female Husbands: Gender and Sex in an African Society (London: Zed Press, 1987).
8. Ward Churchill, "Spiritual Hucksterism," *Z Magazine* (December 1990): 94.
9. Simone de Beauvoir, "Women and Creativity," in *French Feminist Thought: A Reader,* ed. Toril Moi (Oxford: Basil Blackwell, 1987), 27.
10. Richard Wright, "Blueprint for Negro Writing," in *The Black Aesthetics,* ed. Addison Gayle, Jr. (New York: Doubleday, 1971), 341.
11. See in particular Chinua Achebe, *Things Fall Apart* (London: Heinemann, 1958), and *Arrow of God* (London: Heinemann, 1960). Equally pertinent is Achebe's critique of the West in his books of essays, *Morning yet on Creation Day* (London: Heinemann, 1977), and *Hopes and Impediments* (New York: Doubleday, 1988), as well as his critique of post-independence Africa, in particular Nigeria, in *A Man of the People* and *The Trouble with Nigeria* (Enugu: Fourth Dimension Publishers, 1985).
12. An Igbo proverb.
13. Joseph Conrad's Heart of Darkness could be taught in conjunction with Chinua Achebe's *Things Fall Apart* and "An Image of Africa: Racism in Conrad's *Heart of Darkness,*" in Achebe, *Hopes and Impediments,* 1–20.
14. The recommended readings were: Ifi Amadiume, preface and introduction to *Male Daughters, Female Husbands;* Bolanle Awe, "The Iyalode in the Traditional Yoruba Political System," in *Sexual Stratification,* ed. Alice Schlegal (New York: Columbia University Press, 1977), 144–59; Kamene Okonjo, "The Dual-Sex Political System in Operation: Igbo Women and Community Politics in Midwestern Nigeria," in *Women in Africa,* ed. Nancy Hafkin and Edna Bay (Palo Alto: Stanford University Press, 1976), 45–58; Judith Van Allen, " 'Sitting on a Man': Colonialism and the Lost Political Institutions of Igbo Women," *Canadian Journal of African Studies* 6 (1972): 165–81.
15. See AAWORD, "A Statement on Genital Mutilation," in *Third World: Second Sex,* ed. Miranda Davies (London: Zed Press, 1983), 217–20.
16. See Nawal El Saadawi, preface to the English edition of *The Hidden Face of Eve: Women in the Arab World* (London: Zed Press, 1980).
17. Quoted in Patterson and Gillam, "Out of Egypt," 90–91.
18. Donna Blacker, "On Student-Centered Education," unpublished manuscript, 11.
19. bell hooks, *Yearning: Race, Gender, and Cultural Politics* (Boston: South End Press, 1990), 148. This quote is taken from the ANC Freedom Charter.

Chapter 4

Decolonizing Feminism

Marnia Lazreg

> It has already formed its concepts; it is already certain of their truth; it will assign to them the role of constitutive schemata. It's sole purpose is to force the events, the persons, or the acts considered into prefabricated molds.
>
> Jean-Paul Sartre on institutional Marxism.[1]

Writing about women in Algeria has been the most challenging task I have undertaken so far. Not only did it concretize for me the difficulty of doing interdisciplinary research, and raise theoretical/methodological issues, it has also led me to question the feasibility of writing and communicating across cultures about the subject of women. My project is not to entertain readers with one more exotic tale or shock them with another astounding revelation about womanhood in a faraway place. All I wish to do is communicate in intelligible terms another mode of being female. But this is more easily said than done.

Dealing with a subject with which people in this country are unfamiliar threatens to turn me into a social translator of sorts, a bona fide native anthropologist, writing for others about others. I have always resisted the quasiheroic stance assumed by experts on other cultures, and I have far too many questions about the validity of their knowledge claims to find comfort in mimicking them. My predicament takes on a more complex turn when it is realized that I am not writing "just" about another culture but about women from a culture with a history of distortion. Indeed, Algerian women and their culture have been mystified by more or less well-intentioned social scientists and feminists moved by something akin to missionary zeal.

Difference, whether cultural, ethnic or racial, has been a stumbling block for Western social science from its very inception. Nineteenth-century European ethnology and anthropology were established precisely to study different peoples and their institutions. However, regardless of the conceptual, theoretical, and methodological inadequacies and uncertainties in the works of many classical anthropologists and ethnologists, their interest in "difference" was a function of their desire to understand their own institutions better. This was the case with Durkheim's work on religion, Mauss on exchange and Malinowski on the Oedipus complex, to cite only a few. Although I do not wish to absolve Western anthropology of its Eurocentrism, it showed, at least in its heyday, some awareness of a common denominator between people of different cultures, a *human* bond. The notion of "cultural universals" or that of the "human mind," no matter how problematical, are expressions of such a common link between various peoples.

Contemporary American academic feminism has rejected, if not forgotten, this part of its intellectual heritage. Yet it has failed to do away with the evolutionary bias that characterizes social science in one form or another. In feminist scholarship (with a few exceptions) this bias is embedded in the objectification of "different" women as the unmediated "other," the embodiments of cultures presumed inferior and classified as "traditional" or "patriarchal." This would ordinarily be seen as a theoretical mishap were it not for the fact that academic feminists have generally denounced conventional social science as being biased against women both in its theory and its practice. They have specifically shown that it has reduced women to one dimension of their lives (for example, reproduction and house work) and failed to conceptualize their status in society as a historically evolving phenomenon. Hence, academic feminism has brought a breath of fresh air into the social science discourse on women, and has held the promise of a more even-handed, more holistic practice. Surprise is in order when one sees that women in Algeria (or in any other part of the Middle East) are still dealt with largely in ways that academic feminists do not wish to be dealt with.[2]

Women in Algeria are subsumed under the less-than-neutral labels of "Muslim women," "Arab women" or "Middle Eastern women," giving them an identity that may not be theirs. Whether the so-called Muslim women are devout, or their societies are theocracies, are questions that the label glosses over.

The one-sidedness of the prevailing discourse on difference between women would appear intolerably grotesque if it were suggested, for example, that women in Europe and North America be studied as Christian women! Similarly the label "Middle Eastern women," when counterposed with the label "European women," reveals its unwarranted generality. The Middle East is a geographical area covering some twenty-one countries (if one counted members of the Arab League) that display a few similarities and as many differences. Yet a book on Moroccan women and another on Egyptian women were both subtitled "Women in the Arab World."[3]

This reductive tendency to present women as an instance of a religion, nation, ethnicity or race is carried over from American feminists' uneasy relations with minority women. African-, Chinese- and Mexican-American women as well as Puerto Rican women have denounced their exclusion from feminist scholarship and/or the distortions of their lived reality by "white," middle-class feminists. They have also noted that academic feminism reproduces the social categorizations and prejudices that are prevalent in the larger society.

Objecting to definitions that reduce women to their skin color, Rosario Morales emphasizes that she wants "to be whole," and reminds her readers that "we are all in the same boat."[4] Going one step further, Mitzuye Yamada inveighs against the burden placed upon individual Asian-American women to "represent" their racial group and speak "in ways that are not threatening to our audiences." In this sense they are made to reinforce the stereotype of the Asian woman.[5]

These relatively new voices express the underside of difference between women, and are a welcome reminder that feminism as an intellectual practice cannot merely rest on the consciousness of wrongs done to *some* women by men. It points to the necessity of developing a form of consciousness among feminists in North America (and in Europe) that transcends their sense of specialness and embraces what is human at the heart of womanhood across cultures and races. Decentering as well as deracializing one's self is a precondition for such a venture. However, it is a complex and difficult one, as it requires giving up a sense of entitlement for some and overcoming disability for others that is undoubtedly grounded in the racialization of one's self. It is remarkable that academic feminists do not tire of referring to themselves as "white" or "of color." Damning the Algerian revolution with a stroke of a pen (over exactly fourteen pages), Sheila Rowbotham, who refers to herself as a "white middle-class woman," sums a complex history as the battle between whites and nonwhites. Although she writes about them, she surprisingly asserts that "I do not know what it is like to be Vietnamese, or Cuban, or Algerian"—all women she classifies as "Black, yellow, and brown."[6] If her color is a barrier to understanding the special circumstances of these women, whence comes the authority that made her define their lives and characterize their roles in history? What gives legitimacy to her work on women whom she admits she does not understand? Is it the very color she uses as a shield to both empower herself to write and protect herself from criticism?

Third World women in the United States who have expressed their anger and disappointment at being objectified as the irrevocably unmediated other have also assumed that very otherness. They refer to themselves as "women of color," another linguistic sleight of hand ostensibly meant to supplant but that in fact merely recycles the old expression "colored women," the racist connotations of which need no elaboration. This expression has acquired common currency and is used by academic feminists apparently as a way of recognizing the existence of difference between women. The inability to examine the language in which difference is expressed renders ineffective objections to academic feminists' failures to address difference in adequate terms. The language of race belongs to the history of social segregation. To argue that minority and Third World women have adopted the term "women of color" as a liberating means to assert their difference and escape a homogenizing Anglo-American feminist discourse begs the question. By using this label they accept its referent and bow to the social group that gives it currency. As Pierre Bourdieu put it "the constitutive power which is granted to ordinary language lies not in the language itself but in the group which authorizes it and invests it with authority."[7] It is not "women of color" who have the authority to impose the language of race but the women who implicitly claim to have no color and need to be the standard for measuring difference. "Color" does not determine sex, but, like sex, it does become an opportunity for discrimination. Like sex, color ought to be questioned as a significant category in understanding human beings. Why select color and not hair texture, shape of eyes or length of nails to define women? Who is subsumed under the awkwardly expressed and marginally grammatical expression "women of color?" Does it include women who are pink, pasty or sallow-skinned?

This cumbersome term grounds difference among women in biology, thereby presenting academic feminism with one of its most telling contradictions. Feminists have been waging a battle against sociobiology, yet they find themselves reasoning along similar lines when faced with "different" women! The term has become widespread even among feminists who claim to pursue a Marxist or socialist tradition that should have sensitized them to the pitfalls of using race or color as a defining criterion of human beings. The captivating power of the label "women of color" *reinscribes,* with the complicity of its victims, the racialization of social relations that it purports to combat.

Michel Foucault's assertion that "knowledge is not made for understanding; it is made for cutting" illustrates the knowledge effect of this biological language.[8] If there is little knowledge to be gained by identifying difference with color, the process of "cutting," or establishing divisions among individual women, of measuring the distance that separates them from one another, is made easier. Knowledge as cutting is politically grounded and pervades feminist scholarship. The expression, "the personal is political," ought to be amended by substituting race, ethnicity or nationality for the personal.

There is, to a great extent, continuity in American feminists' treatment of difference between women, whether it originates within American society or outside of it. There is, however, an added feature to feminists' modes of representation of women from the Third World: they reflect the dynamics of global politics. The political attitudes of the powerful states are mirrored in feminists' attitudes towards women from economically marginal states in a world rent asunder by the collapse of Communism.

The political bias in representations of difference is best illustrated by feminists' search for the sensational and the uncouth. Mary Daly selected infibulation as the most important feature of African women as reported to her by Audre Lorde.[9] Local customs such as polygamy and/or veiling, wherever they take place, appear decontextualized and are posited as normative absolutes.

The search for the disreputable which reinforces the notion of difference as objectified otherness is often carried out with the help of Third World women themselves. Academic feminism has provided a forum for Third World women to express themselves and vent their anger at their societies. But the Western mode of feminist practice is no free gift, any more than anger is conducive to lucid inquiry. Individual Third World women are made to appear on the feminist stage as representatives of the millions of women in their own societies.

The dissenting voice that objects to the gynocentric language of difference unwittingly reinforces the prevailing representation of herself, if only because she acquiesces in the notion of difference as opposition, as polarity. The totalitarian character of the existing representation of difference appropriates differential items haphazardly, and incorporates them into a structure that becomes autonomous and stands for the lived reality of Third World women. An abstract anthropological subject deemed "oppressed" is thus created. Studying this constructed subject is not for the purpose of understanding her as such as it is to gather documentary evidence of her "oppression." Ironically, the language of liberation *reinscribes* relations of domination.

In assessing the issue of writing about Third World women, Gayatri C. Spivak points out that "First World women" and "Western-trained women" are complicitous in contributing to the continued "degradation" of Third World women whose "micrology" they interpret without having access to it.[10] Although essentially correct, this view obscures the fact that complicity is often a conscious act involving the interplay of social class position, psychological identification and material interests. To include all the "Western-trained" women in the plural "we," which also incorporates "First World" women, is to simplify the reality of the feminist encounter between Western and non-Western women. Some Third World women find comfort in acquiring a Western-style feminist identity that presumably dissolves their cultural selves and enables them to take their distance from those who resist looking at themselves through Western feminists' eyes. The problem for Third World women is that their writing is constrained by the existence of an imperious feminist script. Thus, instead of being emancipatory, writing for them is often alienating. Their satisfaction, if any, derives from the approval they receive from their Western counterparts, or the ire they draw from them if they attempt to rewrite the script.

IDENTITY POLITICS AND FEMINIST PRACTICE

Asian-American feminists have pointed out that Third World feminists feel under pressure to choose between their feminism and their ethnicity or culture. This identification of feminist practice with Western culture has resulted in a contest between those who affirm their ethnicity or culture against "feminism" seen as a monolithic system of thought and behavior, and those who flaunt their feminism against their culture, implying that feminism stands above culture. Thus Third World female intellectuals find themselves either defending their culture against feminist misrepresentations or reveling in the description of practices deemed disreputable, but always sensational, in an attempt to reaffirm the primacy, validity and superiority of Western feminism.

A focus on the phenomenal manifestations of difference between women has also resulted in a crude politicization of race, ethnicity, color and/or nationality. Women speak as embodiments of these categories. It is only when a feminist's practice is racialized, ethnicized or nationalized that it somehow becomes worthy of interest. This form of identity feminism is sustained by the extension of standpoint theories to larger constituencies of women. Standpoint knowledge is in effect a *representation* of activity instead of the situated truth it purports to be.[11] By claiming standpoint as a foundation of knowledge, academic feminists have *produced* an activity that stands above and beyond a simple intervention of women's experience in constituted knowledge. When used by racialized women, standpoint knowledge yields an inverted double representation. They represent themselves in terms that already subsume and contain their representation.

The politicization of race, color, ethnicity and nationality is also the expression of a form of adaptation to the salience of racial thinking in the post-Civil Rights, post-Cold War era. The prevailing racialization of power relations in American society (which the corrective of affirmative action had already made palpable) is countered by the use of race/color, ethnicity and nationality as grounds and strategies of contention and resistance.

Among Third World academics this trend transcends the bounds of a simple awareness of ethnocentrism and cultural imperialism. It seeks to recenter existing knowledge, whether feminist or not. For example, Indian scholars have in the last few years focused on colonialism and postcolonialism to account for their own realities. Based on their understanding of the British colonial venture in India, they make generalizations that embrace other colonial situations which thus become ancillary props to buttress the Indian model.[12] The Indian experience, presented as normative, mediates our understanding of colonialism, a phenomenon as multiple and diverse in its expression as it was in its consequences. Such sanskritization of knowledge (feminist or otherwise) is perhaps a welcome change in centuries of Eurocentric knowledge, but it does not transform it. By focusing on India's colonial past, seen as constitutive of Indians' identity, it strikes a nostalgic note for a system of relations that needs to be overcome. In the same vein, the accommodation of African-American feminists to "white," middle-class feminism takes the form of an assertion of Black feminist epistemology grounded in the experience of slavery.[13]

Given this framework, is it possible to do scholarly work on women in the Third World that goes beyond documenting existing stereotypes? How does one put an end to the fundamental dismissal of what Third World women say when they speak a nonstereotypical language? How does one overcome the incipient ghettoization of knowledge about Third World women, who now figure in last chapters of anthologies in a space reserved for "women of color"?

Academic feminist scholarship on American women is generally critical without being denigrating, and therefore leaves hope for a better future for its subjects. American culture is not rejected wholesale, but presented as perfectible. In this respect, feminist critical practice takes on an air of normalcy that is missing in the scholarship on Third World women, especially those from North Africa and the Middle East. It appears as part of a reasonable project for greater equality. Conversely, the Third World feminist critique of gender difference acquires a maverick dimension. It is not carried out from within, with a full knowledge and understanding of the history and the dynamics of the institutions it rejects. It unfolds within an external conceptual frame of reference and according to equally external standards. It may provide explanations but little understanding of gender difference. In this sense, it reinforces the existing "*méconnaissance*" of these societies and constitutes another instance of knowledge as "cutting." Only this time, the cutters are also those who are generally "cut out" of the fellowship of sisterhood.

BEYOND THE RELIGION PARADIGM

I have explained in the past that there is continuity between the body of literature produced by colonial scholars and contemporary feminist studies of Algerian women.[14] Colonial critiques of native women and men centered on Islam (as a religion and culture), which also happens to play a predominant role in contemporary feminists' scholarship. Visions of Islam constitute links in a long chain that ties colonial and feminist practices over the past hundred years. They are articulated in a paradigm I have referred to as the "religion paradigm," which continues to monopolize and constrain writers' and their critics' thoughts (including my own) by compelling them to address its parameters or submit to them. This paradigm has recently been reinforced by the emergence of religiose movements throughout North Africa and the Middle East, thereby giving credence to a self-fulfilling prophecy.

The religion paradigm is steeped in a dual intellectual tradition, orientalist and evolutionary, resulting in an ahistorical conception of social relations and institutions. The orientalist tradition supports the notion that Islam is an archaic and backward system of beliefs that determines the behavior of the peoples who adhere to it. In the popular culture Islam also conjures up a medley of images ranging from the exotic splendor of the Arabian Nights, sequestered odalisques, to circumcised virgins. Fancy and fact mix to create a notion of massive difference. The language used to define women in North Africa and the Middle East creates and sustains their irremediable difference from other women. For example, a translation of French feminist Juliette Minces's book *Women in the Arab World* (the original title) bore the title *The House of Obedience* in an attempt to frame the reader's judgment.

The veil has had an obsessive impact on many a writer. Frantz Fanon, the revolutionary, wrote about "Algeria unveiled." Reaction to the abusive imagery of the veil fails to escape its attraction. Fatima Mernissi titled her first book, *Beyond the Veil*. In the spring of 1990 Condé Nast published an advertisement in the Sunday *New York Times* portraying a blonde woman modeling a bathing suit. She stood up waving a diaphanous white scarf above the heads of a group of veiled Moroccan women crouched at her feet. During the Gulf War the media were replete with contrasting images of veiled Saudi women and American women in combat gear. The persistence of the veil as a symbol that essentially stands for women illustrates researchers' as well as laypeople's inability to transcend the phenomenal expression of difference. Besides, veiling is close to masquerading, so that writing about women where veiling exists is a form of theater. Ironically, while the veil plays an inordinate role in representations of women in North Africa and the Middle East, it is seldom studied in terms of the reality that lies behind it. Women's strategic uses of the veil and what goes on under the veil remain a mystery.

Religion is perceived as the bedrock of the societies in which Islam is practiced. In an uncanny way, the feminist discourse on women mirrors that of the theologians. Writers invoke religion as the main cause (if not *the* cause) of gender inequality, just as it is made the source of underdevelopment in much of modernization theory. Two extreme interpretations of women have ensued. Women are seen either as embodiments of Islam, or as helpless victims forced to live by its tenets. Illustrating this second interpretation, a French-Algerian woman named an association she founded the "association of women living ***under*** Islamic law."

To break out of the totalitarianism of the religion paradigm requires a conception of religion as a process. It is misleading and simplistic to look upon Islam as a text that is learned and faithfully applied by all members of the society in which it is practiced. Emile Durkheim pointed out long ago that even a society of saints would produce its deviants. From a sociological perspective, religion may provide motivation for social action. It may then become secularized. Max Weber explained how this process took place in his controversial study, *The Protestant Ethic and the Spirit of Capitalism.* Religion may also be used as a mechanism of legitimation of inequality, or as a protest against it. Islam should not be analyzed differently from the ways in which other religions have been, without making it meaningless. If it were possible to isolate an independent variable that holds the key to all social ills (as is usually done in the case of Islam) we would undoubtedly have reached the utopia of a positive society that Auguste Comte, the founder of sociology, had in mind.

The point is neither to dismiss the role that Islam plays in women's and men's lives, nor to inflate it. More importantly, it is to study the historical conditions under which religion *becomes significant* in the production and reproduction of gender difference and inequality. The historicization of the relationship between gender and religion permits an appreciation of the *complexity* of the lives of women hitherto subsumed under the homogenizing and unitary concept of "Muslim." This approach further introduces a phenomenological dimension by relying on the lived experiences of women rather than textual injunctions and prescriptions made for them. It also helps to identify and explain lags that often develop between lived experience (in its social, political and economic forms) and religious dogma.

In the Algerian case, to place religion within a historical framework means introducing other equally powerful factors, such as colonialism, development policy, socialism, democratization and so on, that interact with religion in complex ways. Historicizing religion and gender is different from determining how each phenomenon appeared at various points in time. It sheds light on conclusions based on such a limited view of history. For example, one trend of thought maintains that where local customs survived the advent of Islam, women are freer.[15] Another trend points to the deleterious effects that the survival of pre-Islamic customs has had on women whose rights as spelled out in the *Quran* have been violated.[16] What matters is not so much that customs inimical to the Islamic spirit have survived, but through what process religion accommodates practices that appear to contradict its principles.

THINKING DIFFERENTLY ABOUT WOMEN

I began this book ten years ago, when I became interested in feminist theory and the role it assigns "other" women. Unhappy with the culturalist conception that attributed to Islam a powerful causative significance, I initially inquired into the conditions under which religious norms did not affect women's behavior by looking at women's involvement in the war of decolonization which took place from 1954 to 1962. As I proceeded to study the social changes that had taken place among women since 1962, it became clear to me that to understand the present I had to understand the past, especially the colonial past which still haunts the present. Colonialism and its interface with the economy and religion overdetermine any study of Algerian women in complex ways that have yet to be understood. I am thus compelled to revisit two formidable realities, colonialism and Islam, that have defeated more than one scholar.

To write intelligibly about colonialism, for a formerly colonized person such as myself, is as difficult as it is to search one's childhood for possible clues to things that happen in adulthood. Besides, the cacophony of voices clamoring about colonial and "postcolonial" discourses has recently filled academic halls so pervasively that it has trivialized references to this most important event of the nineteenth century, and placed an additional burden on those seeking to come to terms with it. Finally, the intractability of the effects of colonial domination on natives' minds and behavior well after its institutional structures were dismantled makes its analysis always frustratingly tentative.

Apart from confronting all the issues pertaining to Third World women discussed above, writing about Algerian women must deal with the crucial problem of the audience it necessarily assumes. I am writing in English about a reality that is generally unfamiliar to an English-speaking audience. The problem is not only linguistic; it is also one of sharing with an audience a history and culture, a frame of mind, significant silences, and a multitude of things that are said but dispense with explanations—all that makes writing a fulfilling and emancipatory act. A solution to the assumption of an audience, without which I could not write this book, came to mind as I remembered a discussion I had in Algiers in 1988 with a young female sociology instructor who had given me her doctoral dissertation to read. In answering a question I had asked her about her lack of reference to the role played by family law during the colonial period, she asserted that "they had no such law then." I suddenly realized how misunderstood and remote was a past that was in fact quite recent for the generation of women who came of age after the colonial era. It is that generation that I have chosen to keep in mind as a fictitious audience that might become real should this book be translated some day. It is a different generation that does not share with its parents a memory of the colonial past, and is increasingly detached from the old agrarian and community-based value system. Through a combination of ill-devised school curricula and exposure to culturally hybrid media messages, it is very naive about its history and cultural roots.

The critical approach adopted in this book and its virtual audience make it an act of transgression. I assume no race, color, ethnicity or nationality as a legitimating ground for writing it. It has no identity politics and does not aim at being politically correct. Algerian women including myself have no privileged "standpoint" or perspective that makes them closer to a feminist truth than any other women. Like many women and men, they are caught up in an intricate historical web from which they are trying to disentangle themselves with the means available to them.

THE QUESTION OF METHOD AND THEORY

Ideally, writing about women in Algeria should be so transparent as to simply reflect their reality unmediated, a sort of "degree zero" writing. Instead it is strenuous. I struggled to avoid being a social translator, just as I struggled to avoid speaking for others who, although very much like myself, might certainly feel differently from me. The most painful struggle was against the temptation to speak in the name of illiterate women who do not have access to the written word. Even if speech is respectful it still has the capacity to silence. I have chosen to let them "speak" by describing the games they played, the songs they sang, the customs they practised.

Throughout their precolonial and much of their colonial history Algerian women wrote very little, if at all. Having no direct written testimony from women, I decided to have recourse to chronicles, monographs, travelers' accounts and essays written by Algerian men as well as by French men and women. The French colonial sources present a serious problem, as they vary in quality and commitment to colonial ideology. Nineteenth-century, self-serving, colonial accounts of native Algerians are a bizarre mix of curiosity, awe, prejudice, contempt and, at times, romanticism. They yield insight into the colonial psyche and thus help to appreciate the role Algerian women and men played in French colonists' self-understanding. My role in shifting through colonial writings was a delicate one. Having been born during World War II, I am familiar with some of the customs and practices referred to in the literature as well as the changes that have affected them. My personal knowledge, which I supplemented with interviews of women in their seventies, enabled me to have a referent point in determining whether an account was accurate. However, there are problematic practices with which I am not familiar. In this case, I recounted them only if they had been written about by more than two authors.

Given the ideological nature of colonial writings and the sparseness of information about how women lived immediately before the French invasion, I undertook archival research at Aix-en-Provence to examine records kept by the Arab Bureaus during the military phase of Algeria's occupation. I reckoned that these records, confined to reporting daily events that came to the attention of military officers, would be least tainted by personal prejudice. They were. However, my purpose was not to write the history of Algerian women in the nineteenth century, but to get a sense of the dislocations wrought upon them by a radical change in their society.

Studies of Algeria and its people began to take a more dispassionate, even if questionable, and at times objective outlook at the turn of this century, as colonial social science became institutionalized. However, studies of women remained, with a few exceptions, patronizing, onesided and generally unable to comprehend their subjects' lives. The dearth of information by women in the nineteenth century and the first half of the twentieth century brings up the issue of silence in a multiple form. Silence as the absence of public voice is not synonymous with absence of talk or action. In fact, Algerian women acted throughout their history in ways that made their silence quite eloquent. Their silence was at times *circumstantial*, or the result of social, cultural or personal circumstances, such as trusting that the state would defend their rights and keeping quiet until these rights were grossly violated. At other times it was *structural*, or dictated by historically determined structures such as the colonial requirement that speech be expressed in French, thus disabling those who could not speak the language. *Strategic* silence was and still is a voluntary act of self-preservation when a woman feels it is better to keep quiet than to incur someone's wrath or disapproval.

To capture the richness and fullness of women's lives during the colonial era, and remove them from the crushing weight of colonial misapprehension, I introduced the *time* dimension in my analysis. Algerian women's lives were embedded in a different temporal order from French women, even though they lived during the same time. The time dimension enabled me to grasp the different meanings Algerian women attached to their activities, as well as the hostile or patronizing attitudes that French women exhibited towards those who did not share their time. Cultural temporalities set them apart, but often intersected with economic and political temporalities which brought them together as antagonists.[17]

Finally, accounting for women's lives under conditions of silence poses the question of intersubjectivity in all its starkness. Women's daily activities, the rituals they performed, the games they played, their joys and sorrows constitute the foundation on which families and their reproduction were and still are based. While the contents of these acts may be different, families in other human societies have similar foundations. Negative images of women are so widespread and powerful that they deprive their victims of subjectivity and agency and stand for their identity. The genetic structuralist view expressed by Lucien Goldmann provides a tentative answer to this massive problem that plagues the study of Algerian women. It is based on the principle that all human behavior is significant in the sense that "it can be translated into a conceptual language as an attempt to solve a practical problem."[18] If applied to women, this perspective makes it possible to study them as active agents in their lives instead of passive victims. It sensitizes the researcher to the signifying import of mundane activities, and restores individuality to women where it was annihilated by the unbridled empiricist bias at the heart of the prevailing academic feminist practice. Finally, it helps to problematize the written word when it substitutes itself for women's voices. This is no mean achievement within the Algerian context.

It might be argued that structuralism is structuralism. Calling it "genetic" only underscores its fundamental inability to accommodate the role played by the individual in shaping structures, if not changing them. Perhaps. But the problem is not to choose between structure and individual. Both must be taken into consideration if we are to understand women's (and men's) relation to society and to themselves. The foundation of genetic structuralism is unquestionably a necessary anthropological starting point. In addition, Goldmann's conception of the "transindividual subject" (just like Jean-Paul Sartre's "transcendental ego") constitutes another starting point for exploring the notion of intersubjectivity in the social sciences.[19] The transindividual subject is a construct that construct that incorporates *and* sublates the determinations of social class and class consciousness, ideology and the social frameworks of knowledge. The transindividual subject is also a real subject keenly conscious of these determinations and the influence that the group has on her/his thoughts. More importantly, the transindividual subject is a *critical* subject engaged in a ruthless criticism of all partial worldviews including her/his own.

For Goldmann, this subject aims at reaching what he terms a "maximum class consciousness" that incorporates elements of the consciousness of other classes. This restrictive goal may be enlarged to embrace a multicultural, multisocial consciousness that is aware of social class as well as race and sex divisions. In a word, it must reach for a truly *world* vision, as distinguished from the Weberian "worldview." Such a world vision is predicated upon a decentering of the self that must shed its narrowly defined identity trappings. Presumably, it is more difficult for women and men whose identities are formed in powerful countries to shed these trappings, as they provide a reassuring sense of entitlement.[20] But the transindividual subject is a project-in-the-making and not a preformed mold which women (at least those doing research across cultures) ought to engage.

Writing about women in Algeria is akin to entering the Pascalian wager.[21] It involves taking the risk of sounding naive and utopian, and failing in the attempt to aim at a new form of humanism based on a reassertion of the primacy of the human over the cultural. However, it also brings with it the possibility of winning the wager. Entertaining the thought of research as a wager is accepting the fact that it is uncertain, and that all of us, identity feminists, humanists, hardnosed scientists and others are part and parcel of the processes that made research on Algerian women fraught with uncertainty, and "expropriated [their] moral outrage."[22]

NOTES

1. Jean-Paul Sartre, *Search for a Method* (New York: Vintage, 1963), p. 37.
2. The use of the concept "Western" in this book does not connote any ontological meaning. It refers to individuals who inhabit the space identified as the "West" which happens to coincide with industrialization and/or past colonial empires. The concept of "Third World" is as inadequate as "West" especially now that the so-called "Soviet Bloc," which occupied the space of a Second World, no longer fits the Cold-War terminology.
3. Fatima Mernissi, *Beyond the Veil* (New York: Shenkman, 1975); Nawal El-Saadawi, *The Hidden Face of Eve* (Boston: Beacon Press, 1980).
4. Rosario Morales, "We Are All In The Same Boat," p. 91. in Cherrie Moraga and Gloria Anzaldua, eds., *This Bridge Across My Back* (N.Y.: Kitchen Table, Women of Color Press, 1983), p. 91.
5. Mitsuye Yamada, "Asian Pacific American Women and Feminism," *Ibid.*, p. 71.
6. Sheila Rowbotham, *Women, Resistance, and Revolution* (New York: Vintage, 1974), pp. 244–47.
7. Pierre Bourdieu, *Outline of a Theory of Practice* (Cambridge: Cambridge University Press, 1977), p. 21.
8. Michel Foucault, *Language, Counter-Memory, Practice,* D. F. Bouchard, ed. (Ithaca: Cornell University Press, 1977), p. 154.
9. Audre Lorde, "On Open Letter to Mary Daly" in Elly Bulkin, M. B. Pratt and B. Smith, *Yours in Struggle* (New York: Long Haul Press, 1984), pp. 94–97.
10. Gayatri Chakravorty Spivak, " 'Draupadi' by Mahasveta Devi," in Elizabeth Abel, ed., *Writing and Sexual Difference* (Chicago: University of Chicago Press, 1982), pp. 261–82, especially translator's foreword.
11. Pierre Bourdieu, *Outline of a Theory of Practice*, p. 2.
12. See Ranajit Guha, ed., *Subaltern Studies VI: Writings on South Asian History and Society* (Delhi, Oxford and New York: Oxford University Press, 1989).
13. Patricia Hill Collins, *Black Feminist Thought: Knowledge, Consciousness and the Politics of Empowerment* (New York: Routledge, Chapman and Hall, 1991).
14. See Marnia Lazreg, "Feminism and Difference: The Perils of Writing as a Woman on Women in Algeria," in *Feminist Studies,* vol. 14, no. 1, Spring 1988.
15. Margaret Smith, *Rabi'a the Mystic and Her Fellow Saints in Islam* (Amsterdam: Philo Press, 1974), pp. 148–54.
16. Reuben Levy, *The Social Structure of Islam* (Cambridge: Cambridge University Press, 1959).
17. I am indebted to Stephen Kern's *The Culture of Time and Space 1880–1918* (Cambridge: Harvard University Press, 1983) for helping me to appreciate the significance of perceptions of time and cultural change.
18. Lucien Goldmann, "Genetic Structuralism" in *Sciences humaines et philosophie* (Paris: Editions Gonthier, 1966), p. 151.
19. *Ibid.*, p. 60.
20. In anthropology Clifford Geertz argues for the maintenance of such identities by emphasizing that researchers' relation to natives is purely cognitive. See his *Local Knowledge: Further Essays in Interpretive Anthropology* (New York: Basic Books, 1983), ch. 8.

21. Lucien Goldmann, *The Hidden God: A Study of the Tragic Vision in the Pensées of Pascal and the Tragedies of Racine* (New York: Routledge and Kegan Paul, 1964), ch. 1.
22. Barrington Moore Jr., *Injustice: The Social Bases of Obedience and Revolt* (New York: M. E. Sharpe), pp. 500–05.

Section III

Reconceptualizing Gender

By focusing on the social institutions of marriage, kinship, and family in a number of African societies, the papers in this section expose alternative conceptions of the social world and the place of gender in it. Ifi Amadiume's contribution "Theorizing Matriarchy in Africa: Kinship Ideologies and Systems in Africa and Europe," considers the charged concept of matriarchy and posits that it was the traditional form in African social structures. Her critical review of three anthropological classic texts on African social systems draws our attention to the pitfalls of imposing Eurocentric paradigms.

In "(Re)Constituting the cosmology and socio-cultural Institutions of Oyo-Yoruba" Oyèrónké Oyěwùmí, reveals that seniority rather than gender is the basis of Yoruba kinship categories and social institutions. In the process she systematically dismantles the gender edifice that had been imposed by earlier scholarship in the interpretation of Yoruba realities. Consequently, Oyěwùmí posits that gender is not only a social construct but also historical.

In his paper "Kò Sóhun tí Mbe tí ò Nítàn (Nothing Is that Lacks a [Hi]story): On Oyěwùmí's *The Invention of Women*" presents a conceptually grounded reading of gender in Yoruba society. He offers a rich autobiographical reflection provoked by Oyěwumi's discussion of gender as a category in Yoruba centered intellectual discourses. Adeeko draws our attention to the role of "publics" and the idea of the subject in the construction gender in colonial and post-colonial African societies. He concludes that scholarship must do thorough critiques of mistranslations and imposed concepts like gender if we are to construct a "historical history" of African societies.

Similarly, in "Women's Roles and Existential Identities," Igor Kopytoff brings to bear a comparative eye as he contrasts Suku (Zaire) notions of social identities with Western constructions. Kopytoff concludes that Suku identities are role-based (what people do) as opposed to existential (what people are). Consequently, he argues, gender categories in suku society are more fluid than those in the West, which makes for a certain openness and occupational flexibility.

Wairimu Ngaruiya Njambi and William E. O'Brien bring knowledge up-to-date with regard to the institution of woman-to-woman marriage, which tends to be cast as anachronistic in much of the existing literature. Their paper "Woman-Woman Marriage: Notes on Gikuyu Women," is based on interviews they conducted in Gikuyu households in Central

Kenya. The article examines a range of issues, including the nature of the institution, the complex variety of reasons for its existence, and the way it functions today. Based on their case study they postulate some connections and disconnections between this kind of marriage and the dominant type between men and women, which has implications for our understanding of gender.

Chapter 5

Theorizing Matriarchy in Africa: Kinship Ideologies and Systems in Africa and Europe*

Ifi Amadiume

My major problematic in this chapter is the theorization of the vexing concept of matriarchy, not as a totalitarian system—that is, the total rule governing a society—but as a structural system in juxtaposition with another system in a social structure. Using contemporary data, I intend to throw into doubt certain established Eurocentric certainties about the origins and social character of kinship.

It has become increasingly clear that there is a major point of difference between Eurocentric scholarship and an Afrocentric perspective, particularly as represented by the work of the African scholar Cheikh Anta Diop, on the so-called scientific reconstruction of both human origins and the origins of social forms, especially the institutions of kinship, kinship ideologies and the state (Chcikh Anta Diop, 1991).[1] It is these key differences in the understanding of matriarchy that I am attempting to highlight in this chapter and I shall, hopefully, establish the possibilities for a creative theoretical formulation of gender and empowerment in African social histories.

Henry Maine's Patriarchal Theory: The Persistent European Model

Adam Kuper (1988) has provided a useful assessment of nineteenth-century European male theorists of kinship and descent. What seems clear to me from his review is that, in spite of the general claims to a comparative historical perspective, these theories were derived from specifically Indo-European histories but applied well beyond the European experience. Other peoples and their cultures were seen through European eyes, with the result that the so-called scientific reconstructions were full of subjective bias, prejudice and falsifications, as demonstrated by Cheikh Anta Diop (1991).

The nineteenth-century debate on kinship became simplistic when seen as a dichotomized choice between matriarchy and patriarchy as the determinant of the total social structure, and as a general progressive evolution from one system to the other. Yet it was not the structural relationship of institutions in a society that was studied, but the jural codes—that is, the instrument devised for ruling and not the character of that which is to be ruled or controlled. Thus, from his legal background, Henry Maine (1861) theorized a totalitarian patriarchy: a primordial patriarchal despotism for the human race. His one general gender history is known as the Patriarchal Theory, which forms the basic patriarchal paradigm in European philosophical and political thought. His so-called comparative jurisprudence was strictly limited to the Roman patriarchal agnatic corporate group system. Here, the central focus of power was the father, and the factual importance of motherhood kinship structure and history was denied.

On the origins of wider society itself, Maine's theory stated a movement from status to contract with the idea of citizenship and individualism. From this strictly European experience, Maine concluded that individualism and social contract were the highest form of civilization and superior to kinship-based status systems. Since African systems were seen as status systems and lacking the concept of state, they were placed on the lowest rung of the ladder of development and civilization. The implication of this position is that the oppressive rule of absolute patriarchy is the highest form of civilization. Diop (1991) has argued that this basic patriarchal ideology was reproduced at the state level in the European model, but that the actual concept of state came to the Europeans from Egyptian Africa as a result of direct colonialism.

Having thus developed a theory of a primordial patriarchy, and a progressive development from family societies, to gens (house), to houses, to "tribes," and then to societies of territory and state, Maine (1871) found supportive evidence from the German village community and that of an Indian Hindu village. Both had had direct Aryan influences. Maine's data were therefore based on Indo-European social history, and his theory became known as the German model.

Cheikh Anta Diop and the Matriarchy Theorists

Diop would have no quarrel with the Patriarchal Theory of Henry Maine as long as it is limited to Indo-European social history. His disagreement was with generalized evolutionist theorists of kinship, marriage and mother-right/matriarchy, such as J. M. McLennan (1865; 1876), L. H. Morgan (1871) and J. Bachofen (1861). They postulated a progression from barbarism and savagery in primitive sexual promiscuity, to matrilineal descent, to matriarchy and mother-right, and, finally, to masculine imperialism in patriarchy, monogamy and the nuclear family. All these so-called scientific reconstructions were based on ethnographies of nineteenth-century Australian Aborigines, eighteenth-century Iroquois Indians, ancient Greeks, Imperial Romans, ancient Germans, and ancient Hebrews.

Diop does not follow the theory of a general evolution, but is specific about where and when patriarchy came into being as the ideological superstructure of a specific socio-economic formation (Diop, 1991). He traced the origin of patriarchy to the nomadic proto Indo-Europeans (the Kurgans), who came from the Eurasiatic Russian Steppes between the Caspian and the Black Seas. Diop attributed to them all the inequities of a violent sociocultural formation, namely nomadism, patriarchy, the veneration of warrior deities, and the domestication of the horse—the instrument of conquest and mass destruction. It was these nomads who, in 3400 BC, invaded and wiped out the ancient European civilization which Diop claims originated from the Cro-Magnoids in the south and the last Negroids from Africa. Acording to Diop:

> patriarchy became solidly established in the Indo-European societies at the end of the Iron Age, with the arrival of the Dorians in Greece. This occurred in Rome, Persia, Aryan India, Greece, etc.; and it is inconceivable to project a matriarchal past onto the very people who were the vehicles of patriarchy, particularly the Dorians. All evidence suggests that these were people who went from hunting to nomadic life without ever experiencing the sedentary phase. It was only afterwards with the conquest of the agricultural regions, that they became sedentary. (1991: 20)

Diop (1989) postulated four cradles or histories of kinship and gender: Africa as the agricultural matriarchal south, Europe as the nomadic patriarchal north, the Mediterranean basin as the middle belt where matriarchy preceded patriarchy, and Western Asia as the zone of confluence.

In all the so-called scientific comparative reconstructions by nineteenth-century theorists, African data were left out. It is significant that it was African data that effectively overturned theories of a general evolution of kinship. The concept of matriarchy as female rule has been the main reason why the idea was ruled out as non-existent in history. Diop mashalled an array of empresses and queens from as far back as the fifteenth century BC and through into recent history, from Ethiopia, Egypt and the rest of Africa—to challenge this Eurocentric conclusion. He argued that in precolonial Africa there was no transition from matriarchy to patriarchy, since the social structure was essentially matriarchal in the sense of female rule, female transmission of property and descent, and man being the mobile element in marriage or sexual union. Fundamental changes in the African social structure began with Arabo-Islamic invasions (Diop, 1987), and became more far-reaching under European imperialism (Diop, 1989).

Contemporary African Data and the Matriarchy Debate

It would be easy to dismiss all these 'reconstructions' as based on long dead and static ethnographies and therefore irrelevant to contemporary issues. Yet the problem of history and continuity cannot be so easily ignored, as Emmanuel Terray (1972) argued in his essay on Morgan's *Ancient Society* (1877) and its importance for contemporary anthropology. The relevance of historical materialism is the fact that one can look at continuity, reversibility, transitory systems, aggregates, borrowing from systems, actual processes of negotiation and new formations; but, more importantly, one can locate instances of cultural imperialism following foreign invasions. In a colonial conquest, radical change derives essentially from forces external to a social structure. Colonial rules are violent impositions, and are maintained by violence (see Chapter 4 in this book and Amadiume, 1992).

On the question of kinship structures in contemporary social formations, Diop points out dynamic social processes which overturn any strict theories of a single progression or pattern of change. He maintains that it is the material condition and not race which determines the structure of kinship and its patterns of change or evolution. Far from seeing a complete transformation from matriarchy to patriarchy as an event completed in ancient times, Diop maintains that these processes are still taking place today:

> This transitional phase, the passage from matriarchy to patriarchy, is rich in information for sociology. We see at work the very historical and material conditions that have given rise to both the matrilineal and patrilineal systems and the avuncular relationship.
>
> Kinship, filiation, inheritance, all derive essentially from the privileged social situation of the spouse who remains in his or her clan and therefore hosts the other. (1991: 116)

Citing Evans-Pritchard and Robert Lowie, Diop refers to their data on the Nuer, the Ouehi of Ivory Coast, Hupa Indians, Pueblo Indians, the Hidatsa, Owambo of South Africa and the Khassi of Assam. In all these cases, filiation was matrilineal and the child bore the name of the mother's clan. Husbands went to wives. However, the child's name changed according to where the child went. If the wife moved to the husband's clan, the child took its father's clan name. Diop did not therefore take woman exchange as given, as is stipulated by the alliance theory—that is, woman as an object to be exchanged by Lévi-Strauss's men (Lévi-Strauss, 1969).

I believe that this objectification of woman is the main failing of McLennan (1865); although, according to Kuper (1988), he effectively overturned Maine's theory of primordial patriarchy by focusing on the actual means of reproduction—the mother. However, I believe that he unfortunately postulated the thesis of exogamy and wife-capture. He therefore saw women as objects to be moved, owned or shared, a central thesis of the alliance theory which saw woman as an exchangeable and stealable object, while men generated hostility and managed warfare. This line of thinking consequently led to the theory of a universal incest prohibition to mark the triumph of "culture" over "nature" and, by association, the exchanged woman.

From his study of wide-ranging "primitive people" and Indian polyandry and infanticide, Mclennan had made the important point that the first kinship system had to be traced through the one constant and certain person—the mother, since at first, biological fatherhood was unrecognized. After this, there was wife-sharing by a set of brothers. With the practice of polyandry, society was getting close to the recognition of fatherhood. Then finally with levirate, fatherhood became recognized, since this implied ownership. There then followed the development of economic property and rules of inheritance and, therefore, agnation. Following this formulation, family came at the end and not at the beginning as postulated in the Patriarchal Theory from the German model.

It seems to me that the main problem in these theories of kinship is the construction of woman as an object to be moved or owned. If kinship is determined through the one constant and certain person—the mother—and if we remove the concept of movement and ownership and focus on the African concept of collectivism and usufruct access to land, we are back to the basic matriarchal tripartite structure or what I might call the matriarchal triangle consisting of mother, daughter and son. These kinship terms should be seen as classifications in a grouped collective sense and not in the European individualistic sense.

By focusing on this structure and the wide-ranging possibilities of shift of power, we can at least theorize about structural change, and compare the social dynamics of coexistence of different but interracting cohesive systems. This cuts out the limitations of theories based on assumptions and the racism of unilinear evolutionism or simultaneous universal transformations.

Writing on the transformation in African dynastic matriarchy in ancient Egypt between the Third and Fourth Dynasties, Diop (1991: 105) argued that there was plenty of evidence of ancient or indigenous feminine forms showing designation of uterine descent through daughters. Egyptian *sat* equals daughter, and *sent* equals sister. Whether a woman is called daughter or sister, it seems to me, would depend on the gender focus. If the mother is the focus, she is daughter. If the son is the focus, the same mother's daughter becomes sister. With transition to patriarchy/matriliny, as in the Wolof example, *sat* equals grandson, descent, which is a derivation from *sant,* the proper name of a clan which perpetuates the family line and is derived from the family line of the mother. With a patriarchal shift of focus, the reference is to the sister of the uncle in a matrilineal system. In this way, there was transmission of rights and perpetuation of the clan through sisters, who in actual fact are a mother's daughters.

The matriarchal structure of kinship, or the matriarchal triangle of power, was reproduced in African queendoms as the tripartite power-sharing system. The names of the queens were uttered jointly with those of the kings on the throne to be occupied. Diop refers to Ibn Battuta's testimony on fourteenth-century Mali that men were not named after their fathers; that genealogy was traced through the maternal uncle; and that sons of the sister inherited to the exclusion of his own children (ibid.: 107).

The origin of culture based on Lévi-Strauss's (1969) theory of incest taboo depends entirely on belief in the exchange of women. In the old matriarchy proper and its tripartite mother-focused system, if incest was allowed, as in ancient Egypt (Reed, 1974), Burundi, etc., the children would come from daughters/sisters who remained at home. If incest was not allowed, children would still come from daughters/sisters remaining at home in the so-called matrilineal system, or as a result of the widely practiced woman-to-woman marriage, or male daughter institutions. With the old system of marriage where men provided agricultural labour for sexual access to a woman's daughters, children would still come from daughters/sisters who remained with their mothers. These practices, particularly the institution of woman-to-woman marriage, mean that neither exchange nor ownership need take place. The matricentric structure does not need to be dismantled for the purpose of reproduction.

The whole thesis of incest taboo as marking the beginning of civilization, following the assumption that clanic organization is founded on incest taboo and that clanic organization marks the progression from animality/nature to order/civilization, in actual fact only explains the beginning of patriarchal exchange and ownership. It does not explain the beginning of social regulation on sexual relations, for there is an assumption that the matricentric unit is not itself already a cultural construct—that is, that the mother or the woman cannot make culture and rules. She does not have a distinct social unit or material base for that mode of production. Yet in the African data, the matricentric unit is an autonomous production unit; it is also an ideological unit.

Diop says that the pure state of matriarchy was only at the truly elementary stage of the first emergence of the matriarchal clan, and was characterized by avuncular inheritance. Is he calling matriliny matriarchy? Or is he saying that matriliny is a characteristic of matriarchy? He makes the important point, however, that mistakes made in analysis of matriarchy result from studying clans in Africa which have already undergone very complex evolution.

The notion of the pure primitive stage in Africa used by anthropologists is a fallacy and has led to a racist "othering," maintaining a constant savage and primitive Africa to a civilized, high-cultured Europe (Mudimbe, 1988). As Diop (1987) argued and demonstrated in his reconstruction of precolonial Black Africa, with his 2000 years' historical depth study of ancient African socio-political systems, African societies had been densely populated and extensively centralized under empires and monarchies in well-developed urban cities and with thriving international commerce. Diop called it the period of detribalization which lasted up to the sixteenth century.

Under the territorial state of the African dynastic state model, seemingly autonomous villages were in actual fact subjects of the citybased monarch (Diop, 1991). African societies had again retribalized to different degrees during the period of the Atlantic Slave Trade from the sixteenth century, following the Trans-Saharan Slave Trade and the weakening of authentic ancient African empires by Arabo-Islamic conquests and imperialism (Diop, 1987). Regression and decline then intensified under European colonization and the imposition of the European state system. As Diop writes, as a result of all these forces of change, "[t]here was then a co-existence of tribal and monarchical elements as well as varied systems of filiation that misleads the observer who is not perspicacious" (Diop, 1991: 119).

It is these varied coexisting systems that interest me, particularly how under our very eyes gender valued colonial influences are leading to specific types of radical change in the structures of kinship. These types of transformation did not take place either in the centralization in the ancient monarchies or under Islamic colonialism, as Diop acknowledged that even in the African monarchies "the matriarchal system was subjacent" (ibid.). Instead of "subjacent," I have called it juxtaposition of systems (Amadiume, 1987).

In contrast to African socio-political systems, even under colonial pressures of change, in Indo-European societies there was an absence of a *matrius* opposite a *patrius* in the juridical role (Diop, 1991: 121). This to me explains the source of the Patriarchal Theory. Diop is very concerned to show that these historical structural differences in social structures between Europe and Africa had nothing to do with race, but with changes in the material condition.

Similar arguments concerning the varied character of African systems of filiation were made by Wendy James (1978) in her critique of Engels's theory of a historical loss of woman power as a result of property and ownership. Whereas Diop's thesis stressed the difference in ideological construct, that of Frederick Engels (1891) was based on a materialistic construct. However, in a moral sense, both arrived at the same conclusions. Diop characterized the Aryan Greek and Roman cultures of Europe as idealizing the patriarchal family, war, violence, crime and conquests. Guilt, original sin, pessimism and individualism pervaded their moral ethics. Their women were home bound and denied a public role and power, being totally under the control and ownership of fathers and husbands to whom they were chattels (Diop, 1989).

Based on ethnographic and historical reconstruction, Engels made the following contrast: non-class and pre-class societies were based on an egalitarian tribal order in which sexual (gender) egalitarianism reigned. Everything was communally owned and people fulfilled their subsistence needs. Families in the European sense did not exist, rather there were large communistic households which were centred on women and where decisions were reached consensually. Women's kinship bonds formed the basis of women's solidarity.

This egalitarian, woman-centred and caring society was overturned by men (we do not know precisely when, how and why) with the introduction of the notion of ownership, which saw woman as property and a thing to be owned. This, to Engels, was the beginning of class societies and associated characteristics of ownership, inequality, the male-centred family as an economic unit, the dependent wife and decline in the social status of woman, and the appropriation and exploitation of surplus production for exchange. Engels's indictment of European patriarchy and capitalism was articulated in strong moral language, in expressions such as "the slave of his lust and a mere instrument for the reproduction of children" (about the servitude of the European woman to man); "icy water of egotistical calculation"; and "callousness" (about the logic of capitalism).

These transformations led to changed gender relations with state intervention in the family, as industrial production was presented as the valued public and power domain. On the other hand, labour in the family was considered domestic and a valueless private domain. Hence, as argued by a tendency in European feminist scholarship, the universal subordination of woman is directly related to her domestic role (Rosaldo and Lamphere, eds, 1974). This was yet again a generalization from a specifically European experience.

Like Diop, James countered that the historical experience of African women was different, since they had relative structural power in all institutions of social organization, but failed to theorize this reality of empowerment. She looked at descent from anthropological data, pointing out that Africa is the major home of matriliny, which she defines as "the systematic tracing of descent through women". This matriliny remains dominant in some regions, while in some cases it belongs to recent history, hence James' expression "the persistence and resilience of matriliny among many of the populations of the continent" (1978: 141).

One of the disagreements which James had with Engels's formulation was the representation of matriliny and female rule as the samething. This suggests that James is saying that matriliny (the tracing of descent through women) is not matriarchy, that is, "female rule". To her, the supposed historical passage from matriarchy to patriarchy "belongs to the realm of myth and fantasy rather than history" (ibid.: 143), and the evidence used for matriarchy echoes the Amazon myth of the ancient Greeks. So, we are quite clear that James understands matriarchy as "female rule". Having dismissed matriarchy, James concerned herself with patrilineal and matrilineal descent systems, assessing which of them is more stable politically and which gives way to the other.

James dismissed Engels's assumption of the mutual exclusiveness of modes of lineal descent and a universal unilinear evolution, stating four reasons:

1. There is no clear link between gender and a specific line of descent, that is to say, power and authority of a specific gender are not linked to a type of descent system. As James put it, "In fact it would not even be agreed by modern anthropologists that such a correlation can be found" (1978: 143).
2. There are dual descent systems and non-unilineal modes of reckoning inheritance and succession.
3. The persistence of matriliny in sophisticated political organizations.
4. Continuing relevance of matriliny as a metaphor (biological connection between generations), and matriliny as a moral system.

By dismissing the link between gender and a particular type of descent, specifically the possibilities of authority and power for women in matriliny (Schneider and Gough, 1961; Fox, 1967; Schlegel, 1972), I believe that European anthropologists were misled by their own ethnocentrism into insisting on a general theory of male dominance in all types of descent systems. However, it is on the structural analysis of the metaphorical symbolism of matriliny (biological connection between generations or motherhood) and the matriarchal ideological construct generated from this symbolism that Eurocentric scholarship has failed African Studies.

The importance of Diop's comparative historical perspective is in his understanding of matriarchy/matriliny as a shift of focus from man at the centre and in control to the primacy of the role of the mother/sister in economic, social, political and religious institutions (Diop, 1989). In the anthropological framework, these are the institutions which make up a society or a social system. The European writers did not seem to have had a parallel historical experience of motherfocused systems to draw from. Their patriarchal paradigm was taken from the fixed point of the father. This affected their understanding and interpretation of African data. They kept looking for man as father or man as the axis around which all rotated, or man as the owner and the controller of everyone and everything. James called it the "patrifocal syndrome".

The invisible, transitory or distant role of man as father in African kinship was extremely difficult for the European mind to accept, as can be seen from James's quotes from famous anthropologists such as Lévi-Strauss (1969), Evans-Pritchard (1965), and I. M. Lewis (1976). These European men were perplexed by the imagined "conflict between male domination and citizenship traced through women," as Lewis put it. Since they assumed male dominance, citizenship traced through women was a strange phenomenon. The general position was that the seizure of political control by women would transform matriliny to matriarchy, and artificial insemination would make things very different. Consequently, there was a failure to see the culturally constructed invisibility of the father role as approximate to artificial insemination.

Unlike the Europeans, Diop as an African had no difficulty in talking about a "matriarchal regime". James in contrast rejected the application of matriarchy, suggesting an alternative view of matriliny which focuses on ideas of citizenship and identity, authority, status and ties of loyalty, instead of focusing on structures of power, and therefore contradictions and conflicts. Following Evans-Pritchard, she concluded that on the status of women, one is dealing with "a moral question".

In genealogical representation of a so-called patrilineal society, women are left out, but in a matrilineal diagram, individuals are defined through female links. Consequently, James writes:

> Society is more than a diagram, and where the matrilineal principle is enshrined, for whatever practical or symbolic purpose, the nodal position by women must be more than a diagrammatic matter. There must surely be evaluative connotations, even a theory of the central focus provided by women in the definition of social relations stemming from the matrilineal principle. The granting of a key position to women in the logical, formal ordering of wider relations surely invites us to look further, not necessarily for "female rule" in a crude power sense, but for equally strong affirmations of the central qualities, even the primacy, of women's position. (1978: 149)

James goes on to provide examples of the centrally creative role of women in production and reproduction in African societies: founding a family, building a household, and the respected and honoured role of motherhood. This motherhood is "represented as a central social category, from which other relationships take their bearing—particularly connections with the next generation" (ibid.: 150). Yet James does not describe the organizational unit for the sociocultural construc-tion of these roles, because she is avoiding an analysis of power and conflict—that is, politics. The result is an inhibited analysis of matriarchy; a refusal to see what is staring one in the face!

This is evident in the interpretation which she gives to the case studies cited. On Rattray's 1920s Ashanti data, James points out the prevalence of matriliny, the primacy of the mother as a central fact on which Ashanti ideas focus, the physiology of reproduction as the metaphorical symbol. Consequently, James settled for the term "matrifocality" as "an indigenous view of the moral primacy of biological motherhood in the definition of social relations" (ibid.: 150). In Ashanti society, matrifocality was expressed in socio-economic terms and a jural framework of matrilineal descent groups.

This so-called matriliny is therefore both concrete and ideological. It is through their mother and not through their mother's brother that men trace status, rank and rights. The matrilineal group holds and transmits property. Had James included a study of the political organization, she would have seen the reproduction of the matricentric unit, the tripartite matriarchal triangle at the superstructural level in the centralized political systems, as pointed out by Annie Lebeuf (1963). This would again bring back the much dreaded term "matriarchy".

In her second case study, the Uduk of the Sudan-Ethiopian border, James again points out the relevance of matrifocality in the reckoning of status and the social structure: "in personal and moral terms the mother is the key figure in the kinship world of the Uduk" (1978: 153). Behind the seemingly patrilineal organization there is a matrifocal logic. Having listed several so-called patrilineal societies in Africa in which it is possible to perceive underlying matrifocal ideas, James concludes, 'patrilineages are artificial constructs built up from the fragments of many natural matrilines' (ibid.: 156).

I believe that this is a very important statement which needed to be developed for an analysis of the socio-economic basis of the ideological construct of matrifocality. Matrifocality is a cultural construct even if the metaphor used derives from the female reproductive role. It throws into question the derogatory dismissal of these ideas by European feminists as essentialist and limiting to women's choices. It seems to me that the important thing here is the ideological message generating the notions of a collectivism of love, nurturance and protection derived from womb symbolism. As James says of most African societies, whether patrilineal or matrilineal, "there is a deeper and historically more enduring level at which the nature and capacity of women are given primacy in the definition of the human condition itself" (ibid.: 160).

James acknowledged that the European experience and fundamental theory of the family are patrifocal. This has led to biased comparisons and caused difficulties in the present analysis of matriliny, just as it affected the nineteenth-century debate on matriarchy. Significantly, James saw bridewealth and the exchange of woman as the key factor responsible for patriarchal formation. If there is not bridewealth, the system shifts back to matriliny. Contrary to James, I am arguing that with matriliny, there is already a shift of focus or power in the matriarchal triangle from mother to son, who in matriliny is seen as the all-important uncle. Yet he is a son, a brother, a husband, an absentee/invisible father, as well as an uncle.

THE MATRICENTRIC UNIT AND THE IDEOLOGY OF MATRIARCHY IN FOUR AFRICAN ETHNOGRAPHIES

In the critique of Claude Meillassoux (1964) and Emmanuel Terray's (1972) analysis of the lineage mode of production of the Guro of Ivory Coast, I argued that both men imposed a Eurocentric concept of 'natural family' on the Guro data (see Introduction, this volume). In detailing the productive units and the processes of production in order to analyse the socio-economic formations in Guro domestic mode of production, the very basic kinship unit—the matricentric production unit—was left out. Its structural importance was therefore not taken into account.

It is a common error which stems from a definition of reproduction derived from a European patriarchal paradigm which sees woman as an object of exchange. Marriage is consequently presented as a mechanism of physical and social reproduction of the group. Woman in this formulation starts off as an object in a patriarchal exchange and transaction. She is not seen in her autonomous status as mother. Yet the motherhood paradigm is culturally recognized as an autonomous unit, as we have already seen in African constructs of kinship in a few ethnographies.

I have argued that the recognition of the motherhood paradigm prevents the error of taking patriarchy as given, or as a paradigm. Both matriarchy and patriarchy are cultural constructs, but patriarchy is one step above the motherhood paradigm. This is the basis of my distinction of the household as the matricentric unit, and family as a wider construct involving the head of one or more household matricentric units. As I have already argued, the matricentric unit does not need to be dismantled for the purpose of reproduction. Also with the practice of woman-to-woman marriage the family need not be headed by a male.

In order further to press my point about the structural presence of a basic matriarchal system in the social structures of traditional African societies, I examine the following evidence from four ethnographic texts on contrasting African societies.

Nnobi case study (Amadiume, 1987) In the Igbo rural village of Nnobi in contemporary Nigeria, the paradigmatical gender structures of kinship in the indigenous society[2] are in binary opposition. They are expressed or represented concretely, metaphorically or symbolically in the *Obi* (ancestral or family house) which is male, and the *Mkpuke* (the matricentric unit or mother and child compound) which is female. The following is a sketch of the dynamic systems:

Obi—male	*Mkpuke*—female
Headship = *diokpala* (first son) *di (dibuno)* = husband • the person has a male status in cultural classification of gender • in biological sex-gender the person can be man or woman.	**Headship** = Mother–wife–mother • the person is culturally classified as female, even when playing the role of *di* = husband.
The unit composition Headship over: • one or more *Mkpuke* units (matricentric units or households) • therefore family	**The unit composition** • matricentric = mother and siblings • therefore household.
Economy • dependent on *Mkpuke* productive units for labour, raw food and cooked food.	**Economy** • the smallest production unit • autonomous • has its own farm or garden.
Ideology • patriarchal in ideology of *umunna* (common fatherhood) • jural force • competitiveness • masculinism, valour • force, violence.	**Ideology** • matriarchal in ideology of *umunne* (common motherhood) • moral force • collectivism • ideals of compassion, love, and peace.

In Nnobi matriarchy as an ideological superstructure, there is a dialectic between the matricentric production unit and the relations of production. Therefore, those who ate out of one pot were bound in the spirit of common motherhood. This basic ideological superstructure was reproduced at wider levels of social organization in the political order. In the all-encompassing matriarchy, all Nnobi were bound as children of a common mother, the goddess Idemili, the deity worshipped by all Nnobi.

The matriarchal ideology thus provided the logic of overall administration. There were four named days in a week, each of these was also a market day and was named after the goddess in honour of whom the market was held. In these names—Oye, Afo, Nkwo, Eke—the Igbo achieved a logical configuration of a space/place, a time/day and a goddess. Most of the festivals which provided the yearly calendar in the seasonal rhythm of village life were in celebration of life-cycle events and productivity associated with the goddesses.

In the Igbo dual-sex political system (Okonjo, 1976; Amadiume, 1987), the titled women were central to consensual decision making and controlled the marketplaces. In Nnobi, it was *Ekwe* titled women, the earthly representatives of the goddess Idemili, who controlled the village Women's Council, holding overall veto rights in village assemblies. The *Ekwe* system can therefore be seen as a political matriarchal system, which was, however, in dialectical or structural relationship with the *umunna* based patriarchal system, both in dialogue with each other. The middle ground for manoeuvre is a third classificatory system: the nongendered collective humanity, *Nmadu*, person, which is again based on non-discriminatory matriarchal collectivism, as a unifying moral code and culture generating affective relationships as opposed to the political culture of patriarchy, imperialism and violence.

In Meyer Fortes's data on the Tallensi (1959, 1987), contradictions in the kinship system can be glimpsed, despite suppressed and fragmented information, which suggest that there is a missing system in dialogue with the male-centred patriarchal system. But as a result of the enthnocentric bias of the European ethnographer, the partial and monologic experience of the son became a model for the whole society. Yet a dual-gendered system was in operation. One can consequently accuse Fortes of masculinization of data—a very European syndrome.

The structural significance of female ancestresses and spirits was not analysed from the *soog* kin ideological system, which appears to provide an alternative matriarchal kinship based moral ideological system. The *soog* kin concept, we are told, extended beyond the framework of the lineage and clan. It was in complementary opposition to clan relations and was based on trust and amity. There was, therefore, another ideological system in opposition to patriarchy, but its socio-economic base and the processes of its reproduction were not described.

Similarly Paul Riesman's Jelgobe data (1977) provide a whole set of gendered symbolism in binary opposition in *wuro* (house) equals female equals woman, and *ladde* (bush) equals male equals man. *wuro* and *ladde* appear to constitute the basic paradigmatical structures of matriarchy and patriarchy, with the father remaining as an outsider to the *wuro* structure. The woman builds and owns the hut, and as such was addressed as head of the house, *Jam suudu*. From this structural unit is derived a whole set of matriarchal meaning and ethics symbolized in the concept of *suudu*—a place of shelter, hut for people, nest for birds and bees, envelope for a letter, a box or case where anything rests or sleeps. Customs, rules and morality binding the wider patrilineage of *Suudu baaba,* the father's house, were derived from this womb symbolism.

In Maurice Bloch's Merina data (1986), we again see two gendered systems of kinship. The matricentric kinship was considered the biological kinship linking children to their mothers and their siblings. At birth, therefore, humans were only matrilineally related. There was a close bond between children of two sisters. The other kinship system is that of descent which was determined by elders. In accordance with these two distinct systems, two systems of belief were reproduced or elaborated in ritual, forming a symbolically gender-valued opposition. Under the heading of female we have woman, the house, household, dispersal, south, division, kinship, and heat; under that of male we have, man, the tomb, the clan, unity, north-east, sanctity and order.

A third category was the Vazimba autochthonous category considered to be the original owners of the land and natural fertility. Vazimba cults were usually dominated by women. There were, therefore, three ideological sys tems: the matricentric system dominated by a motherhood ideology; the descent system dominated by elders and a patriarchal ideology; and an invisible/inverted/externalized matriarchy in the Vazimba category. In these four ethnographic texts there is a juxtaposition of systems. The matricentric structures generated alternative moral systems available to social subjects, male or female, in the course of social relations. The presence of these fundamental matriarchal systems generating love and compassion means that we cannot take the Oedipal principle of violence as a basic paradigm or given in the African context, as Meyer Fortes unfortunately introduced it into African Studies. The balancing matriarchal system acted as a constraint on the patriarchal structure, checking the development of totalitarian patriarchy and monolithism which are typical of the Indo-European legacy. Out of the European legacy emerged the concept of cultural or moral society as a solid monolith glued together by ritual. That ritual meant patriarchal ideology equals society, equals power, equals state.

Much has been written in denounciation of studies focusing on origins. Yet for colonized people, historical depth and continuity on which a non-colonial status and identity depends is an imperative as strongly demonstrated by Diop (1987, 1991). The advantage in looking at kinship from the perspective of historical origins is in the sense of meaning, in order to locate the origin of a social concept or phenomenon. Others have argued that kinship is best analysed as a phenomenon being created in history, in which case, kinship would therefore be subject to change. Again the problem in this approach, from the point of view of colonized people, is the question of which history is seen and in which history an event is to be contextualized? In any case, there is the fundamental question of what was the original character of that which is undergoing change.

NOTES

* This chapter was first presented as a paper at the interdisciplinary conference on Matrilineality and Patrilineality in Comparative and Historical Perspective, University of Minnesota, 30 April–3 May 1992; and at the workshop. Women and Work: Historical Trends, 7–10 September 1992. Centre for Basic Research, Kampala, Uganda.

1. See Ifi Amadiume, 1992. In this paper, I looked at the comparative scientific methodology used by Diop in his study of the ideology of gender in state formations in his 5000 years' historical perspective on socio-political formations and transformations in Egypt/Africa and Europe. I showed specifically how Diop saw the moral philosophy of different types of states as gendered. Hence, he made a contrast between the pacifist ideological superstructure of the so-called Asian Mode of Production (AMP) societies, particularly the matriarchal Egyptian/African model, and the warlike morality and militaristic values of the patriarchal Greco-Roman city state.

2. Data here are presented as static only for the purpose of analysis. The processes and effects of systemic masculinization by British colonization and the imperialism of the neo-colonial Europeanized state on this society has been dealt with elsewhere. See Amadiume, 1987 and Chapter 5 in this book.

BIBLIOGRAPHY

Amadiume, Ifi, 1987, *Male Daughters, Female Husbands: Gender and Sex in an African Society*, Zed Books, London/New Jersey.

——, 1992, "Gender and social movements: the relevance of Cheikh Anta Diop's *Civilization or Barbarism*." (Paper presented at CODESRIA 7th General Assembly on the theme Democratization Processes in Africa: Problems and Prospects.)

Bachofen, J., 1861, *Das Mutterrecht*, Benno Schwabe Co. Verlag, Basel.

Bloch, Maurice, 1986, *From Blessing to Violence: History and Ideology in the Circumcision Ritual of the Merina of Madagascar*, Cambridge University Press, Cambridge.

Diop, Cheikh, Anta, 1987, *Precolonial Black Africa: a Comparative Study of the Political and Social Systems of Europe and Black Africa, from Antiquity to the Formation of Modern States*, Lawrence Hill & Co., Westport, USA.

Diop, Cheikh, Anta, 1989, *The Cultural Unity of Black Africa: The Domains of Matriarchy and Patriarchy in Classical Antiquity*, Karnak House, London.

——, 1991, *Civilization or Barbarism: An Authentic Anthropology*, Lawrence Hill Books, Brooklyn, New York.

Engels, Fredrick, 1891, *Origin of the Family, Private Property and the State* (4th edn), Lawrence and Wishart, London.

Evans-Pritchard, E. E., 1965, "The position of women in primitive society," in *The Position of Women in Primilive Society and Other Essays in Social Anthropology*, Faber, London.

Fortes, Meyer, 1959, *Oedipus and Eob in West African Religion*, Cambridge University Press, Cambridge.

——, 1987, *Religion, Morality and the Person*, Cambridge University Press, Cambridge.

Fox, Robin, 1967, *Kinship and Marriage*, Penguin, London.

James, Wendy, 1978, "Matrifocus on African women," in Shirley Ardener (ed.), *Defining Females: The Nature of Women in Society*, Croom Helm, London.

Kuper, Adam, 1988, *The Invention of Primitive Society: Transformation of an Illusion*, Routledge, London.

Lebeuf, Annie, 1963, "The role of women in the political organization of African societies," in Denise Paulme (ed.), *Women of Tropical Africa*, University of California Press, Berkeley.

Lewis, I. M., 1976, *Social Anthropology in Perspective*, Penguin, London.

Lévi-Strauss, C., 1969, *The Elementary Structures of Kinship*, Eyre and Spottiswoode, London.

Maine, Henry, 1861, *Ancient Law*, John Murray, London.

——, 1871, *Village Communities in the East and West*, John Murray, London.

McLennan, J. M., 1865, *Primitive Marriage*, Black, Edinburgh.

——, 1876, *Studies in Ancient History*, Quaritch, London.

Meillassoux, Claude, 1964, *L'Anthropologie économique des Guro de Côte D'Ivoire*, Mouton, Paris.

Morgan, L. H., 1871, *Systems of Consanguinity and Affinity of The Human Family*, Smithsonian Institute, Washington.

——, 1877, *Ancient Society*, Macmillan, London.

Mudimbe, V. Y., 1988, *The Invention of Africa: Gnosis, Philosophy, and the Order of Knowledge*, Indiana University Press and James Currey, Bloomington and Indianapolis.

Okonjo, K., 1976, "The dual-sex political system in operation: Igbo women and community politics in midwestern Nigeria," in N. J. Hafkin and E. G. Bay, (eds), *Women in Africa: Studies in Social and Economic Change*, Stanford University Press, Stanford, CA.

Rattray, R. S., 1923, *Ashanti*, Clarendon Press, Oxford.

——, 1927, *Religion and Art in Ashanti*, Clarendon Press, Oxford.

——, 1929, *Ashanti Law and Constitution*, Clarendon Press, Oxford.

Reed, Evelyn, 1974, *Woman's Evolution from Matriarchal Clan to Patriarchal Family*, Pathfinder Press, New York.

Riesman, Paul, 1977, *Freedom in Fulani Social Life*, The University of Chicago Press, Chicago.

Rosaldo, M. Z. and Lamphere, L. (eds), 1974, *Woman, Culture, and Society*, Stanford University Press, Stanford, CA.

Schlegel, Alice, 1972, *Male Dominance and Female Autonomy: Domestic Authority in Matrilineal Societies*. HRAF Press, New Haven.

Schneider, D. and Gough, K., 1961, *Matrilineal Kinship*, University of California Press, Berkeley.

Terray, E., 1972, "Historical materialism and segmentary lineage-based societies," in *Marxism and "Primitive" Societies*, Monthly Review Press, New York.

Chapter 6

(Re)constituting the Cosmology and Sociocultural Institutions of Ọ̀yọ́–Yorùbá

Articulating the Yorùbá World-Sense

Oyèrónkẹ́ Oyěwùmí

Indisputably, gender has been a fundamental organizing principle in Western societies.[1] Intrinsic to the conceptualization of gender is a dichotomy in which male and female, man and woman, are constantly and binarily ranked, both in relationship to and against each other. It has been well documented that the categories of male and female in Western social practice are not free of hierarchical associations and binary oppositions in which the male implies privilege and the female subordination. It is a duality based on a perception of human sexual dimorphism inherent in the definition of gender. Yorùbá society, like many other societies worldwide, has been analyzed with Western concepts of gender on the assumption that gender is a timeless and universal category. But as Serge Tcherkézoff admonishes, "An analysis that starts from a male/female pairing simply produces further dichotomies."[2] It is not surprising, then, that researchers always find gender when they look for it.

Against this background, I will show that despite voluminous scholarship to the contrary, gender was not an organizing principle in Yorùbá society prior to colonization by the West. The social categories "men" and "women" were nonexistent, and hence no gender system[3] was in place. Rather, the primary principle of social organization was seniority, defined by relative age. The social categories "women" and "men" are social constructs deriving from the Western assumption that "physical bodies are social bodies,"[4] an assumption that in the previous chapter I named "body-reasoning" and a "bio-logic" interpretation of the social world. The original impulse to apply this assumption transculturally is rooted in the simplistic notion that gender is a natural and universal way of organizing society and that male privilege is its ultimate manifestation. But gender is socially constructed: it is historical and culture-bound. Consequently, the assumption that a gender system existed in Ọ̀yọ́ society prior to Western colonization is yet another case of Western dominance in the documentation and interpretation of the world, one that is facilitated by the West's global material dominance.

The goal of this chapter is to articulate the Yorùbá world sense or cultural logic and to (re)map the Yorùbá social order. It challenges the received assumption that gender was a fundamental organizing principle in Old Ọ̀yọ́ society. To this effect, there will be an examination of social roles as they were articulated in a number of institutions, including language, lineage, marriage, and the market. The social categories of *ìyá* (mother), *bàbá* (father), *ọmọ, aya, ọkọ, àbúrò* (see below on the translation of these terms), *ẹ̀gbọ́n* (elder sibling or relation), *aláwo* (diviner), *àgbẹ̀* (farmer), and *oníṣòwò* (trader) are presented and analyzed. Acknowledging the dangers of mistranslation of key concepts, I will use Yorùbá terminology as much as possible. Using Yorùbá vocabularies of culture—my knowledge of Yorùbá society acquired through experience and research—I will interrogate a range of feminist, anthropological, sociological, and historical literatures, and in the process I will critically evaluate the notion that gender is a timeless and universal category.

Yorùbá language and oral traditions represent major sources of information in constituting world-sense, mapping historical changes, and interpreting the social structure. Documented accounts that I will refer to include the writings of the Reverend Samuel Johnson, a pioneering Yorùbá historian and ethnographer, and the memoirs and diaries of European travelers and missionaries of the nineteenth century. Finally, in conceptualizing the past, the present is not irrelevant. All of the institutions that I describe are not archaic—they are living traditions.

PUTTING WOMAN IN HER PLACE

Gender as a dichotomous discourse is about two binarily opposed and hierarchical social categories—men and women. Given that, I should immediately point out that the usual gloss of the Yorùbá categories *obìnrin* and *ọkùnrin* as "female/woman" and "male/man," respectively, is a mistranslation. This error occurs because many Western and Western-influenced Yorùbá thinkers fail to recognize that in Yorùbá practice and thought, these categories are neither binarily opposed nor hierarchical. The word *obìnrin* does not derive etymologically from *ọkùnrin*, as "wo-man" does from "man." *Rin*, the common suffix of *ọkùnrin* and *obìnrin*, suggests a common humanity; the prefixes *obìn* and *ọkùn* specify which variety of anatomy. There is no conception here of an original human type against which the other variety had to be measured. *Ènìyàn* is the non-gender-specific word for humans. In contrast, "man," the word labeling humans in general in English that supposedly encompasses both males and females, actually privileges males. It has been well documented that in the West, women/females are the Other, being defined in antithesis to men/males, who represent the norm.[3] Feminist philosopher Marilyn Frye captures the essence of this privileging in Western thought when she writes, "The word 'woman' was supposed to mean *female of the species*, but the name of the species was 'Man.'"[6] In the

Yorùbá conception, *ọkùnrin* is not posited as the norm, the essence of humanity, against which *obìnrin* is the Other. Nor is *ọkùnrin* a category of privilege, *Obìnrin* is not ranked in relation to *ọkùnrin*; it does not have negative connotations of subordination and powerlessness, and, above all, it does not in and of itself constitute any social ranking. Another reason *ọkùnrin* and *obìnrin* cannot be translated into the English "male" and "female" is that the Yorùbá categories only apply to adult human beings and are not normally used for *ọmọdé* (children) or *ẹranko* (animals). The terms *akọ* and *abo* are used for male and female animals, respectively. They are also applied to some fruit trees like the papaya and to the abstract idea of a period in time, that is, the year. Thus *akọ ìbẹ́pẹ* is a papaya tree that does not bear fruit; and *odún t'ó ya 'bo* is a fruitful (good) year. "May your year be fruitful [*yabo*]"[7] is a standard prayer and greeting at the beginning of the Yorùbá new year, which is signaled by the arrival of the "new yam." Because *akọ* and *abo* are not oppositionally constructed, the opposite of a good (*abo*) year is not an *akọ* year. An unproductive year is a year that is not *abo*. There is no conception of an *akọ* year. A fruitless pawpaw tree is an *akọ* tree. A fruitful pawpaw tree is not described as *abo*; rather, a fruitful tree is considered the norm; therefore, it is, just referred to as a pawpaw tree. I cite these examples to show that these Yorùbá concepts, just like *ọkùnrin* and *obìnrin*, which are used for humans, are not equivalent to the English "male" and "female," respectively. Thus, in this study, the basic terms *ọkùnrin* and *obìnrin* are best translated as referring to the anatomic male and anatomic female, respectively; they refer only to physiologically marked differences and do not have hierarchical connotations like the English terms "male/men" and "female/women." The distinctions these Yorùbá terms signify are superficial. For ease of deployment, "anatomic" has been shortened to "ana" and added on to the words "male," "female," and "sex" to underscore the fact that in the Yorùbá world-sense it is possible to acknowledge these physiological distinctions without inherently projecting a hierarchy of the two social categories. Thus I propose the new concepts *anamale, anafemale*, and *anasex.* The need for a new set of constructs arose from the recognition that in Western thought, even the so-called biological concepts like male, female, and sex are not free of hierarchical connotations.[8]

Indeed, the Yorùbá term *obìnrin* is not equivalent to "woman" because the concept of woman or female conjures up a number of images, including the following:

1. those who do not have a penis (the Freudian concept of penis envy stems from this notion and has been elucidated at length in Western social thought and gender studies);[9]
2. those who do not have power; and
3. those who cannot participate in the public arena.

Hence, what females *are not* defines them as women, while the male is assumed to be the norm. The aforementioned images are derived from the

Western experience and are not associated with the Yorùbá word *obìnrin*. Since the conceptual language of gender theories is derived from the West, it is necessary to view these theories as *vectors* of the issue they are designed to explain. Unlike "male" and "female" in the West, the categories of *obìnrin* and *ọkùnrin* are primarily categories of anatomy, suggesting no underlying assumptions about the personalities or psychologies deriving from such. Because they are not elaborated in relation and opposition to each other, they are not sexually dimorphic and therefore are not gendered. In Old Ọ̀yọ́, they did not connote social ranking; nor did they express masculinity or femininity, because those categories did not exist in Yorùbá life or thought.

NECESSARY DISTINCTIONS WITHOUT DIFFERENCE

The Yorùbá terms *obìnrin* and *ọkùnrin* do express a distinction. Reproduction is, obviously, the basis of human existence, and given its import, and the primacy of anafemale body-type, it is not surprising that the Yorùbá language describes the two types of anatomy. The terms *ọkùnrin* and *obìnrin*, however, merely indicate the physiological differences between the two anatomies as they have to do with procreation and intercourse. They refer, then, to the physically marked and physiologically apparent differences between the two anatomies. They do not refer to gender categories that connote social privileges and disadvantages. Also, they do not express sexual dimorphism[10] because the distinction they indicate is specific to issues of reproduction. To appreciate this point, it would be necessary to go back to the fundamental difference between the conception of the Yorùbá social world and that of Western societies.

In the previous chapter, I argued that the biological determinism in much of Western thought stems from the application of biological explanations in accounting for social hierarchies. This in turn has led to the construction of the social world with biological building blocks. Thus the social and the biological are thoroughly intertwined. This worldview is manifested in male-dominant gender discourses, discourses in which female biological differences are used to explain female sociopolitical disadvantages. The conception of biology as being "everywhere" makes it possible to use it as an explanation in any realm, whether it is directly implicated or not.[11] Whether the question is why women should not vote or why they breast-feed babies, the explanation is one and the same: they are biologically predisposed.

The upshot of this cultural logic is that men and women are perceived as essentially different creatures. Each category is defined by its own essence. Diane Fuss describes the notion that things have a "true essence . . . as a belief in the real, the invariable and fixed properties which define the whatness of an eniity."[12] Consequently, whether women are in the labor room or in the boardroom, their essence is said to determine their behavior. In both arenas, then, women's behavior is by definition different from that of men. Essentialism makes it impossible to confine biology to one realm. The social world, therefore, cannot truly be socially constructed.

The reaction of feminists to conservative, male-dominant discourse was to reject it totally as a vehicle of oppression. Feminists then went on to show that the existence of two sexes, which has been regarded as an "irreducible fact,"[13] is actually a social construction. In the process of challenging the essentialism of male-dominant discourses, many feminist writings treated all distinctions between men and women as fabrications.[14] Thus the fact that women bear children is not given the attention it deserves; instead it is located on a continuum of what are called "gender differences." It is given the same degree of importance as the fact that women have less body hair than men. Thus despite the relentless feminist assault on mainstream essentialism, feminist constructionism contains, within it the very problem it seeks to address. Like the traditional male-dominant discources, feminism does not entertain the possibility that certain differences are more fundamental than others. That women bear children calls for a distinctive assessment. If Western conservative discourses collapse the social world into biology by seeing all observed differences between men and women as natural, feminism maintains this lack of a boundary between the social and the biological by homogenizing men and women and insisting that all observed differences are social fabrications. This is the problem.

Undoubtedly, in a postchromosomal and posthormonal world in which genes are said to determine behavior, and science is the unassailable source of wisdom on all things, it is difficult to imagine that acceptance of distinctive reproductive roles for men and women would not lead to a creation of social hierarchies. The challenge that the Yorùbá conception presents is a social world based on social relations, not the body. It shows that it is possible to acknowledge the distinct reproductive roles for *obìrin* and *ọkùnrin* without using them to create social ranking. In the Yorùbá cultural logic, biology is limited to issues like pregnancy that directly concern reproduction. The essential biological fact in Yorùbá society is that the *obìnrin* bears the baby. It does not lead to an essentializing of *obìinrin* because they remain *ènìyàn* (human beings), just as *ọkùnrin* are human too, in an ungendered sense.

Thus the distinction between *obìnrin* and *ọkùnrin* is actually one of reproduction, not one of sexuality or gender, the emphasis being on the fact that the two categories play distinct roles in the reproductive process. This distinction does not extend beyond issues directly related ro reproduction and does not overflow to other realms such as the farm or the *ọba's* (ruler's) palace. I have called this a distinction without social difference. The distinction in Yorùbáland between the way in which anatomic females pay obeisance to their superiors and the way in which anatomic males do is useful in elaborating the distinct but ungendered consideration of pregnancy. Any casual observer would notice that in the contemporary period, *obìnrin* usually *kúnlẹ̀* (kneel down, with both knees touching the floor) when greeting a superior. *Ọkùnrin* are seen to *dòbálẹ̀* (prostrate themselves, lying flat on the ground and then raising their torsos with arms holding them up in a push-up pose). Some might assume that these two distinct forms of greeting are constructions of gender, yielding social valuations and difference. However, a simple association of anatomic females with kneeling and anatomic males with prostrating will not elucidate the cultural meanings of these acts. What is required is a comprehensive examination of all other modes of greeting and address, how they are represented in a multiplicity of realms, and how they relate to one another.

When anatomic females pay obeisance to the *ọba* (ruler), they have to *yııkà*—in which case they lie on their sides, propping themselves up with one elbow at a time. In practice, *íyııkà* looks like an abbreviation of *ìdòbálẹ̀*. It appears that in the past, *ìyııkà* was the primary mode of female obeisance to superiors. But over time, kneeling has become dominant. Thus, it would seem that the preferred position for paying obeisance for all persons, whether *obìnrin* or *ọkùnrin*, is for the "greeter" to prostrate to the "greetee." I would assert that the contingencies of pregnancy led to the *ìyııkà* modification for anatomic *obìnrin*. It is obvious that even pregnant *obìnrin* can *yııkà*, but they cannot prostrate easily. Johnson lends historical background to this interpretation. In the late nineteenth century, he observed that the mode of saluting a superior involved "the men prostrating on the ground, and the women sitting on the ground and reclining on their left elbow."[15] The predominance of *obìnrin* kneeling is a more recent development. In fact, female prostration can be seen even today. I have observed *obìnrin* prostrating themselves in the *ọba*'s palace in Ògbọ́mọ̀sọ́. Moreover, a common stance of worship of the deities is the *ìdòbálẹ̀*, irrespective of anatomic type.[16] Therefore, the disassociation of *obìnrin* from prostration is uncalled-for. Similarly, the disassociation of *ọkùnrin* from kneeling is unwarranted.[17] In Yorùbá cosmology, there is the conception of *àkúnlẹ̀yàn*, literally "kneeling to choose"—which is the position that all persons assume in front of Ẹlẹ̀dá (the Maker) when choosing their fate before being born into the world. On closer examination, it is clear that kneeling is a position used not so much for paying homage as for addressing one's superior. All persons who choose to address the *ọba*, for example, whether *ọkùnrin* or *obìnrin*, will of necessity end up on their knees. This is not difficult to understand, given that it is impractical to engage in long conversations in the *ìyûkà* or *ìdọ̀bálẹ̀* positions. In fact, the saying *ẹni b'ọ́ba jiyàn ô yíò pẹ́ lórí ìkúnlẹ̀* (someone who would argue with the *ọba* must be prepared to spend a long time in the kneeling position) alludes to this fact. Further, we know from Johnson's writings that the *aláàfin* (ruler) of Ọ̀yọ́ traditionally had to kneel down for only one person—an *obìnrin* official of the palace. In explicating the nature of the office and duties of this official—the *ìyámọdẹ* (a high official who resides in the palace compound)—Johnson writes:

> Her office is to worship the spirits of the departed kings, calling out their Egúngúns in a room in her apartments set aside for that purpose. . . . The king looks upon her as his father, and addresses her as such, being the worshipper of the spirit of his ancestors. *He kneels in saluting her, and she also returns the salutation, kneeling, never reclining, on her elbow as is the custom of the women*

> *in saluting their superiors.* The king kneels for no one else but her, and prostrates before the god Ṣàngó, and before those possessed with the deity, calling them "father."[18]

The propitiations and thank-offerings to the lineage ancestors during the first two days of the Egúngún (annual festival of ancestor veneration) are named *ìkúnlẹ̀*.[19] Finally, *ìkúnlẹ̀* was the preferred position of giving birth in traditional society and is central to the construction of motherhood. This position, *ìkúnlẹ̀ abiyanmọ* (the kneeling of a mother in labor), is elaborated as the ultimate moment of human submission to the will of the divine. Perhaps the fact that the mode and manner of acknowledging a superior does not depend on whether s/he is an anamale or anafemale indicates the nongendered cultural framework. A superior is a superior regardless of body-type.

It is significant that in Yorùbá cosmology, when a body part is singled out it is the *orí* (head), which is elaborated as the seat of individual fate (*orí*). The word *orí* thus has two closely intertwined meanings—fate and head. *Orí* has no gender. The preoccupation with choosing one's *orí* (fate, destiny) before one is born into the world is to choose a good one. In Ifá discourse,[20] there is a myth about three friends who went to Àjàlá, the potter, the maker of heads, to choose their *orí* (fate, heads) before making their journey to earth. The anasex of these three friends is not the issue in this myth, and it has nothing to do with who made a good choice and who did not. What is of importance is that due to impatience and carelessness, two of the friends chose a defective *orí* while only one of them chose a good *orí:*

> They then took them to Àjàlá's [the Potter's] store-house of heads.
> When Oriseeku entered,
> He picked a newly made head
> Which Àjàlá had not baked at all.
> When Orileemere also entered,
> He picked a very big head,
> Not knowing it was broken.
> The two of them put on their clay heads,
> And they hurried off to earth.
>
> They worked and worked, but they had no gain.
> If they traded with one half-penny,
> It led them
> To a loss of one and one-half pennies.
>
> The wise men told them that the fault was in the bad heads they had chosen.
> When Afùrwàpẹ́ arrived on earth,
> He started to trade.
> And he made plenty of profit.

When Oriseeku and Orileemere saw Afùwàpẹ́, they started to weep and said the following:

> "I don't know where the lucky ones chose their heads;
> I would have gone there to choose mine.

> I don't know where Afûwàpé chose his head.
> I would have gone there to choose mine."[21]

Afûwàpé answered them, saying in essence that even though we choose our heads from the same place, our destinies are not equal. Rowland Abiodun elaborates this distinction between *orí-inú* (inner head or destiny) and the physical *orí* (head), and in discussing the importance of *orí-inú* for each individual he makes a number of telling points:

> A person's Ori-Inu is so crucial to a successful life that it is propitiated frequently, and its support and guidance are sought before undertaking a new task. For this reason, personal Ori shrines are indispensable and are present in homes, *irrespective of sex*, religious belief, or cult affiliation, and in the performance of virtually all sacrifices, ancestral worship, and major and minor festivals, Ori features prominently, since it determines their favorable outcoinc.[22]

The purpose of the foregoing explorations of some apparent distinctions in Yorùbá social life is to problematize the idea that the distinction between *obìnrin* and *ọkùnrin* necessarily concerns gender. Gender is not a property of an individual or a body in and of itself by itself. Even the notion of a gender identity as part of the self rests on a cultural understanding. Gender is a construction of two categories in hierarchical relation to each other; and it is embedded in institutions. Gender is best understood as "an institution that establishes patterns of expectations for individuals [based on their body-type], orders the social processes of everyday life, and is built into major social organizations of society, such as the economy, ideology, the family, and politics."[23]

The frame of reference of any society is a function of the logic of its culture as a whole. It cannot be arrived at piecemeal, by looking at one institutional site or social practice at a time. The limitations of basing interpretations on observation without probing meanings contextually immediately become apparent. Next, attention will be turned to specific institutions in Ọ̀yọ́ society, explicating them to map cultural meanings and ultimately to understand the world-sense that emerges from the whole. In the final analysis, comprehension comes from totalizing and situating the particular into its self-referent context.

SENIORITY: THE VOCABULARY OF CULTURE AND THE LANGUAGE OF STATUS

Language is preeminently a social institution, and as such it constitutes and is constituted by culture. Because of the pervasiveness of language, it is legitimate to ask what a particular language tells us about the culture from which it derives. Language carries cultural values within it.[24] In this study, I am not so much interested in taking an inventory of words as in teasing out the world-sense that any particular language projects.

Seniority is the primary social categorization that is immediately apparent in Yorùbá language. Seniority is the social ranking of persons based on their chronological ages. The prevalence of age categorization in Yorùbá language is the first indication that age relativity is the pivotal principle of social organization. Most names and all pronouns are ungendered. The third-person pronouns *ó* and *wọ́n* make a distinction between older and younger in social interactions. Thus the pronoun *wọ́n* is used to refer to an older person, irrespective of anatomic sex. Like the old English "thou" or the French pronoun *vous, wọ́n* is the pronoun of respect and formality. *Ó* is used in situations of familiarity and intimacy.[25]

In social interactions and conversations, it is necessary to establish who is older because that determines which pronoun to use and whether one can refer to a person by that person's given name. Only older persons can use another's name. It is possible to hold a long and detailed conversation about a person without indicating the gender of that person, unless the anatomy is central to the issue under discussion, as with conversations about sexual intercourse or pregnancy. There is, however, considerable anxiety about establishing seniority in any social interaction. It is almost sacrilegious to call someone who is older by name; it is regarded as uncultured. The etiquette is that in the initial meeting of two people, it is the older person who has the responsibility and privilege first of asking, *Ṣ'álàfíà ni?* (How are you?). Because who is older or younger is not always obvious, the pronoun of choice for all parties meeting for the first time is *ẹ*, the formal second-person pronoun, at least until the seniority order has been determined.

Kinship terms are also encoded by age relativity. The word *àbúrò* refers to all relatives born after a given person, encompassing sisters, brothers, and cousins. The distinction indicated is one of relative age. The word *ẹ̀gbọ́n* performs a similar function. *Ọmọ*, the word for "child," is best understood as "offspring." There are no single words for boy or girl. The terms *ọmọkùnrin* (boy) and *ọmọbìnrin* (girl) that have gained currency today indicate anasex for children (deriving from *ọmọ ọkùnrin* and *ọmọ obìnrin*, literally "child, anatomic male" and "child, anatomic female"); they show that what is privileged socially is the youth of the child, not its anatomy. These words are a recent attempt at gendering the language and reflect Johnson's observation of Yorùbáland in the nineteenth century. Commenting on the new vocabulary of the time, he noted that "our translators, in their desire to find a word expressing the English idea of sex rather than of age, coined the . . . words 'arakonrin,' i.e., the male relative; and 'arabinrin,' the female relative; these words have always to be explained to the pure but illiterate Yoruba man."[26]

Ìyá and *bàbá* can be glossed as the English categories "mother" and "father," respectively, and to English speakers they may appear to be gender categories. But the issue is more complicated. The concept of parenthood is closely intertwined with adulthood. It is expected that people of a certain age have had children because procreation is considered the raison d'être of human existence. It is the way things are and have to be for the group to survive. Although the uniqueness of the *ọkùnrin* and *obìnrin* roles in reproduction is coded in language, the most important attribute these categories indicate is not gender; rather, it is the expectation that persons of a certain age should have had children. Unlike the English concepts of mother and father, *bàbá* and *ìyá* are not just categories of parenthood. They are also categories of adulthood, since they are also used to refer to older people in general. More importantly, they are not binarily opposed and are not constructed in relation to each other.

The importance of the seniority principle in Yorùbá social organization has been acknowledged and analyzed variously by interpreters of the society. It is the cornerstone of social intercourse. The sociologist N. A. Fadipe captures the range and scope of this principle when he writes, "The principle of seniority applies in all walks of life and in practically all activities in which men and women are brought together. The custom cuts through the distinctions of wealth, of rank, and of sex,"[27] He goes on to show that seniority is not just about civility; it confers some measure of social control and guarantees obedience to authority, which reinforces the idea of leadership.

It should also be stressed, however, that seniority is not just a matter of privilege in everyday life. It is also about responsibility. In the socialization of children, for example, the oldest in a group is the first to be served during meal times and is held responsible in cases of group infraction because this older child should have known better. The supreme insult is to call a person *àgbàyà* (senior for nothing). It is used to put people in their place if they are violating a code of seniority by not behaving as they should or are not taking responsibility. If a child starts eating from the common bowl first and fails to leave some of the food for the junior ones, s/he is chided with *àgbà'yà*. There is no notion of "sissy" or "tomboy."

Unlike European languages, Yorùbá does not "do gender";[28] it "does seniority" instead. Thus social categories—familial and nonfamilial—do not call attention to the body as English personal names, first-person pronouns, and kinship terms do (the English terms being both gender-specific/body-specific). Seniority is highly relational and situational in that no one is permanently in a senior or junior position; it all depends on who is present in any given situation. Seniority, unlike gender, is only comprehensible as part of relationships. Thus, it is neither rigidly fixated on the body nor dichotomized.

The importance of gender in English kinship terminology is reflected in the words "brother" (male sibling) and "sister" (female sibling), categories that require conscious qualifiers in Yorùbá conceptualization. There are no single words in Yorùbá denoting the English gendered kinship categories of son, daughter, brother, sister. Qualifiers have to be added to the primary categories in order to make the anasex of the relation apparent. The absence of gender-differentiated categories in Yorùbá language underscores the absence of gender conceptions.

The importance of seniority-ranking has attracted the attention of scholars of Yorùbá culture. American anthropologist William Bascorn, who did ethnographic work in the 1930s, made the following observation: "Yorùbá kinship terminology stresses the factor of seniority including relative age as one of its manifestations, which is so important in relationships between members of the clan. . . . Sex is of relatively little importance, being used only to distinguish 'father' and 'mother.' "[29] Likewise, British ethnographer J. S. Eades, writing about fifty years later, underlined the importance of age in social interactions: "Many older Yorùbá do not know when they were born, but they do know precisely who is senior or junior to themselves because being older confers respect and deference. The junior members of the compound are expected to take on the 'dirtier' and more onerous tasks."[30] The absence of gender categories does not mean that the Yorùbá language cannot describe notions or convey information about male and female anatomic differences. The critical point is that those differences are not codified because they did not have much social significance and so do not project into the social realm.

The differences between the Yorùbá and English conceptualizations can be understood through the following examples. In English, to the question, "Who was with you when you went to the market?" one might answer, "My son." To the same question in Yorùbá, one would answer, *Ọmọ mìi* (My child or offspring). Only if the anatomy of the child was directly relevant to the topic at hand would the Yorùbá mother add a qualifier thus, "*Ọmọ mìi ọkùnrin*" (My child, the male). Otherwise, birth-order would be the more socially significant point of reference. In that case, the Yorùbá mother would say, *Ọmọ mìi àkóbí* (My child, the first born). Even when the name of the child is used, gender is still not indicated because most Yorùbá names are gender-free.

In contrast, in English-speaking, Euro-American cultures, one can hardly place any person in social context without first indicating gender. In fact, by merely mentioning gender, Euro-Americans immediately deduce many other things about people. In the English language, for example, it is difficult to keep referring to one's offspring with the non-gender-specific "child." It is not the norm to do this; it may be considered strange or suggest a deliberate withholding of information. Kathy Ferguson, a feminist mother and scholar, recognized this:

> When my son was born I began a determined campaign to speak to him in a non-stereotypical fashion. I told him often that he is a sweet boy, a gentle boy, a beautiful boy, as well as a smart and strong boy. The range of adjectives may have been impressive, but there was a predictability in the nouns: whatever variation existed, it rotated around that anchor word boy. The substitution of gender-neutral nouns ("you're such a terrific infant, such an adorable child, such a wonderful kid"), was unsustainable.[31]

A Yorùbá mother does not need to trouble herself about such things. The problem of constant gendering and gender-stereotyping does not arise in the Yorùbá language. The anchor word in Yorùbá is *ọmọ*, a non-gender-specific word denoting one's offspring, irrespective of age or sex. *Ọmọdé* is the more specific term for young child(ren). Though *ọmọ* is often translated as "child," it does not show any age restriction. A seventy-year-old mother would refer to her forty-year-old as *ọmọ 'mì* (my child).

LINEAGE HIERARCHIES: THE *Ilé*, JUNIOR CONSORTS, AND SENIOR SIBLINGS

The previous sections have focused on the sociocultural meaning of certain linguistic concepts in order to understand Yorùbá cosmology. In this and the following sections, my focus shifts somewhat to a number of specific social institutions and practices, with the purpose of further documenting the Yorùbá social world and world-sense. Yorùbá have been urbanized for centuries; we live in towns—settlements that are characterized by large populations engaged in farming, trade, and a number of specialized craft occupations. Individual identity is reckoned in terms of ancestral town of origin. In the 1820s, Hugh Clapperton, a European traveler who passed through Ọ̀yọ́, identified by name thirty-five towns.[32] The Reverend T. J. Bowen,[33] an American Baptist missionary, estimated the population of some towns in 1855: Ọ̀yọ́ at eighty thousand; Ibadan at seventy thousand; Ilorin at one hundred thousand; and Ede at fifty thousand. Until its fall in 1829, Ọ̀yọ́ was dominant, being the center of a thriving empire.[34] It is against this background that the following discussion becomes clearer.

The primary social and political unit in Ọ̀yọ́-Yortùbá towns was the *agbo ilé*—a compound housing the group of people who claimed a common descent from a founding ancestor. It was a landholding and titleholding sociopolitical unit that in some cases practiced specialized occupations such as weaving, dyeing, or smithing. These units have been described as corporate patrilineages in the anthropological literature.[35] Most of the members of a lineage, including their conjugal partners and their children, resided in these large compounds. Because marriage residence was in general patrilocal, the presence in the compound of anafemale members and some of their children has often been discounted in the literature. The labeling of these compounds as corporate patrilineages is the most obvious example of this lack of acknowledgment. The implications of this reductionist labeling will be discussed later.

All the members of the *ìdílé* (lineage) as a group were called *ọmọ-ilé* and were ranked by birth-order. The in-marrying anafemales were as a group called *aya ilé*[36] and were ranked by order of marriage. Individually, *ọmọ-ilé* occupied the position of *ọkọ* in relation to the in-coming *aya*. As I noted earlier, the translation of *aya* as "wife" and *ọkọ* as "husband" imposes gender and sexual constructions that are not part of the Yorùbá conception and therefore distort these roles. The rationale for the translation of the terms lies in the distinction between *ọkọ* and *aya* as owner/insider and nonowner/outsider in relation to the *ilé* as a physical space and the symbol of lineage.[37] This insider–outsider relationship was ranked, with the insider being the privileged senior. A married anafemale is an *abilékọ*—one who lives in the house of the conjugal partner. This term shows the centrality of the family compound in defining the status of residents. The mode of recruitment into the lineage, not gender, was the crucial difference—birth for the *ọkọ* and marriage for the *aya*. Since there were no equivalents in the Western cultural logic, I have chosen to use the Yorùbá terms in most places. Henceforth, the specific sexual *ọkọ* of an *aya* will be called her sexual conjugal partner.

In theory, it was only the sexual conjugal partner of the *aya* who had sexual access. The rest of the *ọkọ*, his siblings and cousins, regardless of anatomic sex, were also her *ọkọ* but did not sexually engage her. Some might claim that there was a possible gender distinction among *ọkọ* since in this heterosexual world only the anamales could copulate with an *aya*. Such a reading would be incorrect because in the universe of *ọkọ*, it would have been sacrilegious for anatomic males older than an *aya's* particular conjugal partner to be sexually involved with her—again, the predominant principle at work was seniority, not gender. According to the system of levirate, younger members of the family upon the death of an *aya's* conjugal partner could inherit rights in and access to the widow if she so consented. An older person could not inherit from the younger. Anafemale *ọkọ* were not left out even in this form of inheritance; they too could inherit rights to the widow, while the sexual privileges were then transferred to their own anamale offspring if need be. Therefore, it is clear that there was no real social distinction between the anafemale *ọkọ* and the anamale *ọkọ*. Furthermore, because of the collective nature of the marriage contract, it was possible to imagine a marital relationship that precluded sex—other rights and responsibilities being paramount.

The hierarchy within the lineage was structured on the concept of seniority. In this context, seniority is best understood as an organization operating on a first-come-first-served basis. A "priority of claim"[38] was established for each newcomer, whether s/he entered the lineage through birth or through marriage. Seniority was based on birth-order for *ọmọ-ilé* and on marriage-order for *aya-ilé*. Children born before a particular *aya* joined the lineage were ranked higher than she was. Children born after an *aya* joined the lineage were ranked lower; to this group, she was not an *aya* but an *ìyá* (mother). It is significant to note that the rank of an *aya* within the lineage was independent of the rank of her conjugal partner. For example, if an old member married an *aya* after his own offspring had married, she (the father's *aya*) ranked lower than all the offspring's *aya*, because they preceded her in the lineage. This occurred regardless of the fact that he, as an elderly member of the lineage, might rank higher than everyone else. This fact again shows that each person's rank was independently established and underscores my point that the timing of entry into the clan, not gender, determines ranking.

The hierarchy within the lineage did not break down along anasex lines. Although anafemales who joined the lineage as *aya* were at a disadvantage, other anafemales who were members of the lineage by birth suffered no such disadvantage. It would be incorrect to say, then, that anatomic females within the lineage were subordinate because they were anatomic females. Only the in-marrying *aya* were seen as outsiders, and they were subordinate to *ọkọ* as insiders. *Ọkọ* comprised all *ọmọ-ilé*, both anamales and anafemales, including children who were born before the entrance of a particular *aya* into the lineage. In a sense, *aya* lost their chronological age and entered the lineage as "newborns," but their ranking improved with time vis-à-vis other members of the lineage who were born after the *aya* entered the lineage. This fact dovetails very nicely with the idea in Yorùbá cosmology that even actual newborns were already in existence before they decided to be born into a specified lineage. So the determinant for all individuals in the lineage was when their presence was recorded. The organization was dynamic, not frozen in place as gendered organizations are wont to be.

Against this background, the following statement by anthropologist Michelle Rosaldo is misleading and a distortion of Yorùbá reality: "In certain African societies like the Yorùbá, women may control a good part of food supply, accumulate cash, and trade in distant and important markets; yet when approaching their husbands, wives must feign ignorance and obedience, kneeling to serve the men as they sit."[39] It is clear in this statement that the word "wives" is automatically universalized to refer to all anafemales, while the term "men" is used as a synonym for husbands, as in Western societies. As explained earlier, these are not the meanings of these categories in Yorùbá language and social structure. What this statement fails to point out is that in the Yorùbá context, the term *ọkọ* (translated here as "husband") encompasses both anamale and anafemale. Therefore, the situation described in the quote cannot be understood in terms of gender hierarchy, as Rosaldo has done. Indeed, the same courtesies, such as kneeling, referred to in the above passage were accorded by *aya* to the anafemale *ọkọ*, members of their marital lineages, as a matter of course. Another interesting caveat is that mothers used *ọkọ 'mì* (literally, "my *ọkọ*") as a term of endearment for their own children, signifying that these children, unlike themselves, were insiders and belonged in their marital lineage.

In a study based in Lagos, anthropologist Sandra T. Barnes, using a feminist framework, assumes that Yorùbá anafemales are subordinate to anamales. Thus she interprets the observed deferral of *obìnrin* as a deferral to male authority figures. She then postulates a contradiction between her observation and the cultural ethos that "women are as capable as men."[40] Barnes misinterprets whatever it was that she observed. The paradox that she articulates here is of her own making since hierarchy and authority, as I have consistently shown, to this day do not depend on body-type (more commonly known as gender). Furthermore, Barnes's interpretation of the proverb *Bọ́kùnrin réjò tóbìnrin paà kéjò ṣáá ti kú* (If a man sees a snake and a woman kills the snake, what is important is that the snake should be dead), which she cites as proof of the cultural ethos of gender equality,[41] is simplistic because she assumes the proverb is timeless. A more attentive reading of the proverb suggests the presence of gender categorization and hints at a contestation, if you will, of ongoing claims regarding the capabilities of *ọkùnrin* and *obìnrin*. A more contextualized reading would place the proverb in the historical context of the recent colonial transformations in which in certain circles group interests are being put forward in the idiom of gender.

Inside the lineage, the category of members called *ọkọ* were anamales and anafemales, but the category *aya* appeared to be limited to just anafemales. Beyond the lineage, however, this was not the case. Devotees of the *òrìsà* (gods/goddesses) were referred to as the *aya* of the particular *òrìsà* to whom they were devoted. The devotees were *aya* to particular *òrìsà* because the latter enjoyed the right of ownership / membership, just like members of a lineage enjoyed the right of membership vis-à-vis in-marrying *aya*. The devotees were outsiders to the shrine, which was home to the *òrìṣà*. Indeed, S. O. Babayemi, a Yorùbá social historian, observing devotees of the deity Ṣàngó, notes that male worshipers, "like the female members . . ., are referred to as wives of Ṣàngó."[42]

The foregoing elucidation of the occurrence of the social category of anamale *aya* in the religious realm should not be discounted by relegating it solely to this realm. Yorùbá society was not and is not secular; religion was and is part of the cultural fabric and therefore cannot be confined to one social realm. As Jacob K. Olupona, the historian of religion, notes: "African religion, like other primal religions, expresses itself through all available cultural idioms, such as music, arts, ecology. As such, it cannot be studied in isolation from its sociocultural context."[43]

Within the lineage, authority devolved from senior to junior, the oldest member of the lineage being at the helm. Because, in general, most of the adult anafemale *ọmọ-ilé* were assumed to be married and resident in their marital compounds, there is a tendency in the literature to assume that the oldest and most authoritative member was invariably an *ọkùnrin*. This is not correct for a number of reasons. The cultural institution of *ilémosú* referred to the presence of adult anafemale *ọmọ-ilé* in their natal lineages. *Ilémosú* was associated with the return to natal lineages of anafemale *ọmọ-ilé* after many years of marriage and sojourn in their marital compounds. The adult *obìnrin* members of the lineage were known collectively as the *ọmọ-ọsú*.

If the anafemale member was the oldest person present in the lineage, then she was at the apex of authority. The presence of anafemale *ọmọ-ilé* and their children in their natal lineages was not uncommon given the fact that patrilocality was neither universal nor a permanent state in many marriages. In many status-privileged lineages, female *ọmọ-ilé* did not necessarily move to their marital lineages even after marriage. Samuel Johnson noted that "some girls of noble birth will marry below their rank, but would have their children brought up in their own home, and among their father's children, and adopt his totem."[44] Similarly, N. A. Fadipe recognized that

> if the mother's family is influential, a child may lean towards the maternal uncle more than he leans towards his own father. Whether the mother's family is influential or not, if at any time a man felt himself being crowded out either physically or psychologically from his own extended-family, he would find a welcome in the compound occupied by his mother's family.[45]

Although Fadipe went on to argue that a person's rights in his/her mother's family are somewhat more limited than in his/her father's family, the fact that certain lineages trace their ancestry through a founding mother suggest that there is reason to challenge this claim. Additionally, there are historical figures like Efúnṣetán Aníwúrà, the Ìyálóde of Ìbàdàn, who in the nineteenth century was one of the most powerful chiefs in the polity. She had risen to this position of preeminence by having claimed the leadership of the Olúyòlé lineage, which was actually the lineage of her mother's birth.[46] In the contemporary period, my own personal experience and research corroborate the findings of Niara Sudarkasa, who conducted her study in Aáwẹ́, an Ọ̀yọ́ town, in the early 1960s. Sudarkasa writes:

> When a man has been brought up in his mother's compound, and resides there with his wives and children, he would usually be regarded as part of the male core of the house even though he belongs in his father's lineage. . . . There is the case of a man in his sixties whose father's compound is Ile Alaran in the Odofin quarters but has lived in his mother's compound (Ile Alagbẹdẹ) since he was a very young boy. This man is a member of his father's lineage, he has property rights which accrue from membership in the *idile*, and his adult sons may build houses on the land in Ile Alaran. Nevertheless, this man built a two-story house at Ile Alagbẹdẹ and is the most influential man in that compound. He is referred to by the members as the Bale. . . . Whenever a member of Ile Alagbede is involved in a dispute with a person of another compound, it is to this man that the Bale of the other compound would look for settlement of the matter.[47]

Notwithstanding the fact that in the literature the head of the family is usually described as the *baálẹ̀* (the eldest anamale), there are lineages even today that are led by anafemales. In Ògbómọ̀ṣọ́ in 1996 there were two female village heads—Baálẹ̀ Máyà and Baálẹ̀ Àrójẹ—representing their lineages and holding the hereditary titles. These females were first citizens of both their lineages and the village. It is, then, a gross misrepresentation to assume that anatomy necessarily defined the line of authority inside the lineage. The oldest residents of the lineage were usually the *ìyá*—the mothers of the lineage. These were the old mothers who were usually in a position of authority over their children, including any *baálẹ̀* who was one of their offspring. They were collectively known as *àwọn ìyá* (the mothers), and no major collective decisions could be made without their participation individually and as a group. Because they were usually the longest-living residents of the lineage, they controlled information and carried the lineage memory. Considering that this was an oral-based society, one can begin to appreciate the importance of their positions.

The privileged position occupied by *àwọn ìyá* can be shown by considering the dominant role of the *ayaba* (palace mothers) in the politics of Old Ọ̀yọ́. The power associated with longevity was institutionalized in the role of the *ayaba* in the political hierarchy of Ọ̀yọ́. I will discuss this in the next chapter, but it is important to note here that their power derived from experience and memory, "as many of them [had] lived through the reign of two or more Alaafin."[48] The *ayaba* were next in line of authority to the *aláàfin*, and they wielded the power of the rulership in both the capital and the provinces. The household head in the Ọ̀yọ́ setting should not be interpreted as some de facto or de jure leader who was in control of all decisions. Since the lineage was segmented and was a multilayered and multigenerational group in which a variety of collective, sometimes conflicting and individual, interests were represented, the notion of an individual head of household is more misleading than elucidating. In the *agbo ilé* (compound), power was located in a multiplicity of sites, and it was tied to social role-identities that were multiple and shifting for each individual depending on the situation.

Gender as a Theoretical and Ideological Construct

As I have demonstrated repeatedly above, in Western discourses, gender is conceived as first and foremost a dichotomous biological category that is then used as the base for the construction of social hierarchies. The body is used as a key to situating persons in the Western social system in that the possession or absence of certain body parts inscribes different social privileges and disadvantages. The male gender is the privileged gender. But these observations are not true of the Yorùbá frame of reference. Thus gender constructs are not in themselves biological—they are culturally derived, and their maintenance is a function of cultural systems. Consequently, using Western gender theories to interpret other societies without recourse to their own world-sense imposes a Western model.

Edholm, Harris, and Young conclude that "the concepts we employ to think about *women* are part of a whole ideological apparatus that in the past has discouraged us from analyzing *women's* work and *women's* spheres as an integrated part of social production." [65] I could not agree more with the idea that concepts are part of the ideological apparatus. However, these scholars fall into the very ideological trap they elucidate—they deploy the concept "women" as a given rather than as a part of the "whole ideological apparatus." Woman/women is a social construct, although it is invoked asocially and ahistorically. There were no women in Yorùbá society until recently. There were, of course, *obìnrin*. *Obìnrin* are anafemales. Their anatomy, just like that of *ọkùnrin* (anamales), did not privilege them to any social positions and similarly did not jeopardize their access.

The worldwide exportation of feminist theory, for example, is part of the process of promoting Western norms and values. Taken at its face value, the feminist charge to make women visible is carried out by submerging many local and regional categories, which in effect imposes Western cultural values. Global gender-formation is then an imperialistic process enabled by Western material and intellectual dominance. In effect, one of the most important recommendations that emerges from my analysis of Yorùbá society is that in any consideration of gender construction, researchers should be concerned about not only the "whatness"[66] of gender but also the "whoness"—because one determines the other. That is, when scholars say that gender is socially constructed, we have to not only locate what it is that is being constructed but also identify who (singular and plural) is doing the constructing. To return to the building metaphor used earlier, how many of the bricks for erecting the edifice come from the society in question? How many from scholars? And, finally, how many from the audience?

The problem of gender in African studies has generally been posed as the woman question, that is, in terms of the issue of how much women are oppressed by patriarchy in any given society. Women and patriarchy are taken for granted and are therefore left unanalyzed and unaccounted for. However, in mapping the Yorùbá frame of reference, it became clear that the social category "woman"—anatomically identified and assumed to be a victim and socially disadvantaged—did not exist. Assuming the woman question a priori constitutes an unfounded application of the Western model, privileging the Western way of seeing and thereby erasing the Yorùbá model of being.

In conclusion, what the Yorùbá case tells us about gender as a category is that it is not a given. Thus, as an analytic tool, it cannot be invoked in the same manner and to the same degree in different situations across time and space. Gender is both a social and historical construct. No doubt gender has its place and time in scholarly analyses, but its place and its time were not precolonial Yorùbá society. The time of "gender" was to come during the colonial period, which will be discussed in subsequent chapters. Even in reference to those periods, gender cannot be theorized in and of itself; it has to be located within cultural systems—local and global—and its history and articulations must be critically charted along with other aspects of social systems.

NOTES

1. Old Ọ̀yọ́ refers to Ọ̀yọ́-ile (Ọ̀yọ́ "home"), the original space that was settled. There are many other Ọ̀yọ́ that were occupied at different historical time periods before the establishment of New Ọ̀yọ́ in 1837. The distinction I wish to draw, however, is between New Ọ̀yọ́, which was established in the nineteenth century, and all the previous Ọ̀yọ́. Ọ̀yọ́ was many places, spatially speaking, but my allusion is to one culture and its continuities, despite a lot of movement. This chapter, then, is concerned with the period before die monumental changes of the nineteenth century. According to Robert Smith, "The Oyo of the alafin are three: Oyo-ile, Ọyo-oro, . . . and lastly New Oyo. Although only these three bear the name 'Oyo,' tradition recounts that, since their dispersion from Ile-Ife . . ., the Oyo people have settled in sixteen different places" ("Alafin in Exile: A Study of the Ìgbòho Period in Oyo History," *Journal of African History* 1 (1965): 57–77). For the history and social organization of Ọ̀yọ́, see the following: Samuel Johnson, *The History of the Yorubas* (New York: Routledge and Kegan Paul, 1921); S. O. Babayemi, "The Rise and Fall of Oyo *c.* 1760–1905: A Study in the Traditional Culture of an African Polity" (Ph.D. diss.,

Department of History, University of Birmingham, 1979); J. A. Atanda, *The New Oyo Empire: Indirect Rule and Change in Western Nigeria, 1894–1934* (Bristol, England: Longman, 1973); Robert S. Smith, *Kingdoms of the Yoruba* (Madison: University of Wisconsin Press, 1969); Robin Law, *The Oyo Empire c. 1600–c. 1836* (Oxford: Clarendon Press, 1977); Toyin Falola, ed., *Yoruba Historiography* (Madison: University of Wisconsin Press, 1991); Peter Morton-Williams, "An Outline of the Cosmology and Cult Organization of the Oyo Yoruba," *Africa* 34, no. 3 (1964): 243–61.

As to the term "world-sense": it is a more holistic term than "worldview" because it emphasizes the totality and conception of modes of being.

2. Serge Tcherkézoff, "The Illusion of Dualism in Samoa," in *Gender Anthropology*, ed. Teresa del Valle (New York: Routledge, 1989), 55.
3. Gayle Rubin, "The Traffic in Women," in *Toward an Anthropology of Women*, ed. Rayna R. Reiter (New York: Monthly Review Press, 1975).
4. Judith Lorber, *Paradoxes of Gender* (New Haven: Yale University Press, 1994).
5. Simone de Beauvoir, *The Second Sex* (New York: Vintage Books, 1952).
6. Marilyn Frye, *The Politics of Reality* (Trumansburg, N.Y.: Crossing Press, 1983), 165.
7. In his book *Visions and Revisions: Essays on African Literatures and Criticism* (New York: Peter Long, 1991), Oyekan Owomoyela attempts a gendered reading of this saying. But, in my view, he is just imposing Western gender thinking on Yorùbá (81).
8. See, for example, Thomas Laqueur, *Making Sex: Body and Gender from the Greeks to Freud* (Cambridge, Mass.: Harvard University Press, 1990); and Judith Butler, *Gender Trouble: Feminism and the Subversion of Identity* (New York: Routledge, 1990).
9. Nancy Chodorow, *Femininities, Masculinities, Sexualities: Freud and Beyond* (Lexington: University of Kentucky Press, 1994).
10. For a discussion of sexual dimorphism and the need to integrate biological and social constructs, see Alice Rossi, "Gender and Parenthood," *American Sociological Review* 49, no. 1 (1984): 73–90.
11. The title of a recent book is especially appropriate in this regard; see Elizabeth Grosz, *Volatile Bodies: Toward a Corporeal Feminism* (Bloomington: Indiana University Press, 1994).
12. Diana Fuss, *Essentially Speaking: Feminism and the Nature of Difference* (New York: Routledge, 1989), xi.
13. Suzanne J. Kessler and Wendy McKenna, *Gender: An Ethnomethodological Approach* (New York: John Wiley and Sons, 1978).
14. See, for example, Judith Butler's discussion of sex as fiction in *Gender Trouble*.
15. Johnson, *History of the Yorubas*, 65.
16. Personal communication with Dr. Jacob K. Olupona, historian of Yorùbá religion.
17. Ibid. Johnson claims that during the Egúngún festival, there is an overnight vigil at the graves of the ancestors; it is called ìkúnlẹ̀ because the whole night is spent kneeling and praying (31).
18. Ibid., 65; emphasis added.
19. Ibid., 31.
20. Ifá is one of the most important knowledge systems in Yorùbáland, producing a vast storehouse of information on the society in the divination verses. Ifá is the *òrìṣà* (god) of divination.

21. Wande Abimbola, *Ifa: An Exposition of Ifa Literary Corpus* (Ìbàdàn: Oxford University Press, 1976), 131–32. It is only in the English translation that the anasex of the three friends becomes apparent or constructed.
22. Rowland Abiodun, "Verbal and Visual Metaphors: Mythical Allusions in Yoruba Ritualistic Art of Ori" *Word and Image* 3, no. 3 (1987): 257; emphasis added.
23. Lorber, *Paradoxes of Gender*, 1.
24. Ngugi Wa Thiong'o, *Decolonising the Mind: The Politics of Language in African Literature* (London: James Currey, 1981).
25. Ifi Amadiume, *Male Daughters, Female Husbands: Gender and Sex in an African Society* (London: Zed Books, 1987), makes a similar point about the non-gender-specificity in the Igbó subject pronoun (89).
26. Johnson, *History of the Yorubas*, xxxvii.
27. N. A. Fadipe, *The Sociology of the Yoruba* (Ìbàdàn: Ìbàdàn University Press, 1970), 129.
28. Candance West and Don Zimmerman, "Doing Gender," in *The Construction of Gender*, ed. Judith Lorber and Susan A. Farrell (Newbury Park, Calif.: Sage, 1991).
29. William Bascom, *The Yoruba of Southwestern Nigeria* (Prospect Heights, Ill.: Waveland Press, 1969), 54.
30. J. S. Eades, *The Yoruba Today* (London: Cambridge University Press, 1980), 53.
31. Kathy Ferguson, *The Man Question*, 128.
32. Hugh Clapperton, *Journal of 2nd Expedition into the Interior of Africa* (Philadelphia: Carey, Lea, and Carey, 1829), 1–59.
33. T. J. Bowen, *Central Africa* (Charleston: Southern Baptist Publication Society, 1857), 218.
34. For a discussion of Yorùbá urbanism, see the following: E. Krapf-Askari, *Yoruba Towns and Cities: An Inquiry into the Nature of Urban Social Phenomena* (Oxford: Clarendon, 1969); and Akin Mabogunje *Urbanization in Nigeria* (London: University of London Press, 1968).
35. For example, Peter C. Lloyd, "The Yoruba Lineage," *Africa* 25, no. 3 (1995): 235–51.
36. Today, they are called *ìyàwó ile*. The term *ìyàwó* seems to have supplanted *aya*. In past usage, *ìyàwó* meant specifically "bride," but now it has been, extended to mean "wife."
37. Compare Karen Sacks, *Sisters and Wives: The Past and Future of Sexual Equality* (Urbana, Ill.: University of Illinois Press, 1982).
38. I borrowed the phrase "priority of claim" from Niara Sudarkasa's study of the Awẹ́, a Yorùbá community. My usage differs, however, in that I do not accept that gender is part of its composition. See Niara Sudarkasa, "In a World of Women: Fieldwork in a Yoruba Community," in *The Strength of Our Mothers* (n.p., 1996).
39. See Michelle Rosaldo and Louise Lamphere, eds., *Women, Culture, and Society* (Stanford, Calif.: Stanford University Press, 1974), 19–20.
40. Sandra T Barnes, "Women, Property and Power," in *Beyond the Second Sex: New Directions in the Anthropology of Gender*, ed. Peggy Reeves San-day and Ruth Gallagher Goodenough (Philadelphia: University of Pennsylvania Press, 1990).
41. Jacob K. Olupona, *African Traditional Religions in Contemporary Society* (New York: Paragon House, 1991).

42. S. O. Babayemi, "The Role of Women in Politics and Religion in Oyo" (paper presented at the Institute of African Studies, University of Ìbàdàn, seminar entitled "Women's Studies: The State of the Arts Now in Nigeria," November 1937).
43. Olupona, *African Traditional Religions*, 30.
44. Johnson, *History of Yorubas*, 86.
45. Fadipe, *Sociology of the Yoruba*, 126.
46. Bolanle Awe, *Nigerian Women in Historical Perspective* (Lagos, Nigeria: Sankore, 1992), 58, 65.
47. Niara Sudarkasa, *Where Women Work: A Study of Yoruba Women in the Market Place and at Home*, Museum of Anthropology, Anthropological Papers 53 (Arm Arbor: University of Michigan Press, 1973), 100.
48. Babayemi, "Role of Women," 7.

Chapter 7

Kò Sóhun tí *Mbe* tí ò Nítàn (Nothing Is that Lacks a [Hi]story): On Oyèrónké Oyěwùmí's *The Invention of Women*

Adéléké Adéèkó

> The fundamental category "woman"—which is foundational in Western gender discourses—simply did not exist in Yorùbáland prior to its sustained contact with the West.
>
> —Oyèrónké Oyěwùmí

> Obìnrin na woman for Yorùbáland.
>
> —Fela Anikulapo Kuti

For questioning many governing axioms of African gender studies, Oyèrónké Oyěwùmí's *The Invention of Women: Making an African sense of Western Gender Discourses* often elicits strong reactions from its readers. The book asserts forcefully that scholars of gender in Africa, especially Yorùbá societies, fit their observed facts to learned western notions about women with little regard for the social history of their subjects of study. The book also argues insistently that African kinship terms constitute a significant source of knowledge yet to be uncovered and analyzed for what they can teach us about the "world-sense" of African societies. Oyěwùmí contends that scholars who are not willing to pay close attention to the African "world-sense," particularly as it is compressed in the "word-sense" of African communities, cannot say a lot that is profound about the situation of gender in Africa. I outline in this short reflection ways in which Oyěwùmí's analysis has enabled me to begin to "make sense" of my Yorùbá "gender" experiences. The remarks offered here are deliberately written in an autobiographical style because Oyěwùmí's book answers many questions I have accumulated over many years.

In my youth, I was taught both in school and at church to accept the following: (i) the English word "man" means "*o*kùnrin" in Yorùbá; (ii) "woman" means "obìnrin"; (iii) husband means "*o*k*o*"; (iv) wife means "aya" or "ìyàwó"; (v) father means "bàbá"; (vi) mother means "ìyá" or "màmá"; (vii) female means "abo"; (viii) male means "ak*o*"; and (ix) child means "*o*m*o*." At home, my mother either called me by my given name or addressed me as "*o*k*o* mi" ("my husband"). When describing me to others, then I was "*o*m*o*" ("child"). At 72, my mother still calls me her "*o*k*o*" (husband). I cannot remember her referring to my father directly as "*o*k*o* mi" ("my husband"). He was always "Iba Lékè" (Lékè's father) to her, and she was always "Iye Lékè" (Lékè's mother) to him. My mother had special names she alone used for children born in my father's household before she married into the family. These people are now much older, some of them grandparents. She still refers to them either by those peculiar names or by their children's name. For example, my oldest (half)sister (my father's first child) was either "Aríyàálò" (one who has a mother to depend on") or "Ìyá Ìbejì" (the mother of twins she later became and which all of us called her until she died). Prior to her having children, other older people in the family called my sister Adé*so*lá. I and all her younger siblings, regardless of anatomical distinctions, called her "àntì mi" (my older female sibling). This term, we should note, carries a meaning that is completely different from its English language source, "auntie." One of my older brothers was *E*niaf*é* (the lovable one) until he had his first child and became Bàbá Tolú (Tolú's father). His given name (àbís*o*) is "Bí*ó*dún."

When I was about to get married to Táíwò, a woman I met through a friend (far away from our hometown) and whose parents I never knew at all, our fathers said they are related in some distant past. Màmá Òkè-Ìf*è* (a much older person whose authority on family history superseded our fathers') intervened, saying that the relationship our fathers spoke of was too far back to prevent the marriage. Màmá Òkè-Ìf*è* (literally, the mother from Òkè-Ìf*è*) moved in with her natal relatives, specifically Táíwò's father, after her husband, a native of Òkè-Ìf*è*, died. When my mother learned of this tangled relationship, she started referring to Táíwò as "*o*k*o* mi" (my husband), the same term she uses for virtually everyone in my father's household. After marriage, Táíwò became "*o*k*o* mi-aya mi" (my husband-my wife) to my mother. She never calls her "*o*m*o* mi" (my child). My mother calls my wife her "husband" because Táíwò is my father's relation (although Màmá Òkè-Ìf*è* has said she is not). My mother also calls her son's wife her own wife because she is married to Táíwò through me. In essence, my mother calls me and my wife her husband. If what I learned at school is right, I am sharing a "wife" with my mother! Given this logic, I also share a "wife" with my father-in-law because I am also an "*o*k*o*" (husband) to my mother-in-law, although she has never called me this to my hearing. I would explain why in a moment. In the same vein, Táíwò's siblings are also my mother's "*o*k*o*," that is, my wife's siblings are my mother's "husbands." Oyěwùmí's argument in *Invention* gives us the intellectual framework for discovering the logic that underlies these terms. I learned from this book that these are not Yorùbá metaphoric terms for gender universals but meaningful articulations of social relationships as they are organized by that society.

I should add that I left my hometown, Ìjẹ̀bú-Imuṣin, at 12, and Táíwò has never lived there for more than two weeks continuously, because her parents, both teachers, lived most of their working lives in other towns. When we met, she was a nurse at a state hospital in Abẹ́òkúta, and I was a high school teacher at Modákẹ́kẹ́, two cities located in two different states and about 300 kilometers apart. That is to say we were both living far away from "home," and we never knew each other as people from the same "hometown." We have both been living in the United States for over 18 years now. Surprisingly, Táíwò, like many other Yorùbá women I know in Colorado, calls our children, including girls, "*ọ*k*ọ* mi" (my husband). When I asked our American born children if they were ever puzzled about this term, they just smiled. I am not sure my explanations made any sense to them.

I still remember my concern for a woman I flew with from Lagos to New York about a decade ago. This person who was going to join her husband in Minneapolis asked me in English (after learning that I live in the U.S.) to confirm if it is true, as one of her "wives" (ìyàwó) at home had told her, that Minneapolis is far from New York. I was concerned for her because if she were to ask an American this question, someone may take her words to mean what she did not intend.

Although my mother calls my wife "*ọ*k*ọ* mi" (my husband) my mother-in-law does not address me in the same way. This is not because I am not her "*ọ*k*ọ*" (husband), but because kinship terms (especially gender related ones) used in contemporary Yorùbá societies reflect the "public" to which each speaker belongs. My mother-in-law is a retired school "headmistress" and the only wife of my father-in-law. He was a school headmaster. My father was a carpenter, and my mother, the second of his three wives, sells fish at our hometown market. My wife's parents participate in the operations of what Oyěwùmí, after Peter Ekeh, calls the Nigerian "civic public." This public developed under the supervision of the British, and its main means of sustenance are "the military, the police, and the civil service." My parents operate most of the time in the "primordial public" where old habits and obligations still bear a lot of moral freight. In Peter Ekeh's original formulation, the African public split into two during colonialism:

> there are two public realms in post-colonial Africa, with different types of moral linkages to the private realm. At one level is the public realm in which primordial groupings, ties, and sentiments influence and determine the individual's public behavior. . . . *The primordial public is moral and operates on the same moral imperatives as the private realm.* On the other hand, there is a public realm which is historically associated with the colonial administration and which has become identified with popular politics in post-colonial Africa. It is based on civil structures: the military, the civil service, the police, etc. Its chief characteristic is that it has no *moral* linkages with the private real. . . . *The civic public in Africa is amoral and lacks the generalized moral imperatives operative in the private real and in the primordial public.*" (92)

I have quoted Ekeh at length because its terms are very important to Oyěwùmí's interpretation of the history of gender formations in Yorùbá societies. The only major difference is that Oyěwùmí extends colonialism to mean Europeanization generally. She also adds that "the civic-public is male-dominant and the primordial-public is gender-inclusive" (154). Ekeh and Oyěwùmí are supported by Wole Soyinka's report in *Aké* that Abeokuta women of the civic public used to be called "oníkaba" (frock wearers [like European women]) and those of the primordial public "aró*so*" (wrapper wearers). In the hometown of my youth, western educated women were called "olórùka" or "alárédè" (ring wearers).

In the "civic" public sphere, old relationships are maintained very selectively. Hence my wife, like my far less schooled mother, calls our children "*o*k*o*" (husband) but does not refer to my siblings with this term as she normally would, had all of us been living within the primordial sphere. My mother-in-law does not call me "*o*k*o*" (husband) and is more likely to refer to me as "*o*m*o*" (son) mainly because I am her *son*-in-law. In the "primordial" sphere, this would be a strange thing for her to call me because of my father's "relationship" to her husband. Had my mother-in-law been operating exclusively in the primordial sphere and had followed Màmá Òké-Ífẹ̀'s recollections, she would have called me her "àna," the term for relatives of people married into a family.

It is also my observation that first generation male members of the "civic" public tend to be more sexist in their relationship to women. This is because the "civic" public constructed under the aegis of Christian, European mercantile, and colonial institutions was the main agent of introducing new ideologies of gender to the Yorùbá society. The earliest "civic" Yorùbá men gave advancement opportunities to their sons first and their daughters thereafter. My grandfather, an Anglican Church catechist and school teacher, stopped my mother from studying further after elementary school. According to my mother, her father believed that girls' schooling only ends up in the kitchen. To follow Oyěwùmí, my grandfather borrowed his gender model from what he observed in the mission house and not in Ìl*ó*t*ò*, his home village. As things were, my grandfather's action permanently stalled my mother's further advancement into the "civic" sphere. I believe my mother's account because I witnessed this practice as a very young kid when some of my elementary school classmates could not go on to high school because their parents (most of them operating within the "primordial" public) wanted to reserve their truly meager resources for the advancement of their sons. In the history of gender formations proposed by Oyěwùmí, this practice differs radically from tradition in that there were no futureless "daughters" in primordial structures. It also shows the profound impact of the emergence of the "civic" public on Yorùbá societies. In many instances where the polygamous father is the "breadwinner," the traditional system of inheritance is acknowledged by sending one son, from each matricentered unit (ìdíigi) to school; where there is no son, a daughter is sent to school to represent her own matri-segment. Mothers who have the means pick up the difference of what the "breadwinner" cannot cover. When they do not have the means, their daughters' education and advancement into the civic public can be stalled.

The general prayer, which is to say desire, in the primordial public is a rapid and hitch free movement into the "civic" public. The parochial ethos of the civic public is keenly sought because it is constructed as the only pathway to *ọ̀*làjú (being civilized and modern). The civic public's structures of feeling and acting are also backed by persuasive and repressive social practices. When I started schooling in 1964, one condition of our enrolment is that we were to give our "father's" name. Those of us who had older siblings in school had no problem with what to say. That was not the case for others. There was this boy, called Bí*ọ̀*lá (not his real name). His father's nickname was "àtùpà" (the lamp), short form of "àtùpà t*ọ̀*l*ọ́*run tàn kò s*ẹ́*ni tó lè páá" (the lamp lighted by God cannot be put out by a human being). When Bí*ọ̀*lá was asked his father's name, he simply said: "Àtùpà" (the lamp). Our teachers burst out laughing loud at Bí*ọ̀*lá's ignorance of his father's "name." Since the teachers lived among us, they knew the "real" name; they corrected Bí*ọ̀*lá and taught him his patronym. In 1964, Bí*ọ̀*lá learned his patronym in school and began his journey into the esteemed civic public sphere.

Oyěwùmí said repeatedly in her book that Yorùbá society has always been patrilocal. Hence women cannot be "*ọ*k*ọ*" (husband) in their marital household, neither can they be "aya" (wife) in their natal household. After marriage, girls can grow up to be "aya" (wife) in another household. But they never give up their "*ọ*k*ọ*" (husband) status in their natal household. Boys, like their sisters, would be "*ọ*k*ọ*" to all the wives who marry into the household of their birth. I agree with Oyěwùmí that this is not a privilege conferring arrangement for males, who never get to be "aya" (wife). This point needs repeating that "*ọ*k*ọ*" (husband) and aya (wife) are situational and relational terms. "*Ọ*k*ọ*" (husband) and "*ọ*m*ọ*" (offspring/child) are terms that all Yoruba individuals, regardless of sexual anatomy, acquire and retain from birth till death through social relationships anchored in lineage and family life.

Being an Ìj*ẹ̀*bú-Yorùbá man moving out of the "primordial" into the "civic" public, as his parents wished, Oyěwùmí's book answers many questions I have developed in my moving back and forth within these two publics. Having been a "husband" since I was born, one statement has a particular resonance for me: "The Yorùbá category *ọ*k*ọ* [husband] includes what in English a married woman would call husband and sister-in-law; therefore it is not gender-specific but denotes lineage membership" (160). The term does not indicate the possession (or lack of possession) of an anatomic part but a location in a nexus of relations.

When Fela sings "obinrin na woman for Yorùbáland," what does he mean? I would submit that he is articulating the school sense of "woman": "the receptacle that passively receives [man's] *product*" (Irigaray 18). Any one who enjoys Fela's music cannot but agree that his thoughts belong to the "civic" public despite his relentless claim of "primordial" allegiances. Fela's music and countless other means of formal and informal education glamorized the language of sexism for many Nigerian men of my generation.

When Oyěwùmí claims that "woman" did not exist in Yorùbá social discourse, she means that in the Yorùbá *primordial public* the idea of the human "subject" does not automatically approximate the "masculine." That is to say "obìnrin" became "woman," "*o*kùnrin" became "man," "ìyá" became "mother", "bàbá" became "father," "*o*ba" became "king," "*o*m*o*" became "son," and, for that matter, "Ès*ù*" became "Satan" in the process of Europeanization, or modernization (*ò*làj*ú*) to many people. In order for us to construct a *historical history* of Yorùbá societies, I learned from the book, the cultural mistranslations that produced the current assumptions about gender demand trenchant critiques. She is not asking us to stop doing gender studies in Yorùbá societies: she insists, instead, that African gender scholars should first constitute the genealogy of their objects of study.

Oyěwùmí does not claim some ahistorical exceptionalism for Yorùbá societies. Her examples show, for instance, that because a female cannot be both "*o*k*o*" (husband) and "aya" (wife) in her natal household, the incest taboo operates in Yorùbá societies. But the patrilocality that operated this rule in "primordial" Yorùbá publics does not invalidate the specific subjectivity (or *orí* [inner head]) of the individual that moves from one household to another. The woman who becomes "aya" (wife) in another household does not cease to be "*o*k*o*" (husband) in her natal household. Nowadays men and women of the civic public are instructed to abandon their extended natal households and cling exclusively to their spouses. They are even instructed to change their school-taught patronymy for their husband's. Oyěwùmí's analysis makes it very clear that contemporary gender practices in the civic sphere should not be unquestioningly treated as if they are universal and timeless.

REFERENCES

Ekeh, Peter P. "Colonialism and the Two Publics in Africa: A Theoretical Statement." *Comparative Studies in Society and History* 17:1 (January 1975): 91–112.

Irigaray, Luce. *Speculum of the Other Woman.* Trans. Gillian Gill. Ithaca: Cornell University Press, 1985.

Kuti, Fela Anikulapo. "Expensive Shit."

Oyěwùmí, Oyèrónk*é*. *The Invention of Women: Making and African Sense of Western Gender Discourses.* Minneapolis: University of Minnesota Press, 1997.

Soyinka, Wole. Aké: *the Years of Childhood.* New York: Random House, 1981.

Chapter 8

Women's Roles and Existential Identities

Igor Kopytoff

A commonplace yet puzzling phenomenon has given rise to this exploration. Why is it that in many changing "traditional" societies, where the burdens of inequality so obviously rest on women, we see women claiming and assuming positions of political power with relative ease? One thinks of Indira Gandhi in India, Sirimavo Bandaranaike in Sri Lanka, Corazon Aquino in the Philippines, Benazir Bhutto in Pakistan, Khalida Zia Rahman and Skeikh Hasina Wazed in Bangladesh, Shirley Kuo in Taiwan . . . the list is a long one. By contrast, in the United States, with its long-standing egalitarian ideology and progressivist tradition, the election of a women president remains elusive and the reality of women cabinet members rare. Moreover, what occurs at the top of the political pyramid in these "traditional" societies also happens at lower political levels and in bureaucracies and the professions. One encounters innumerable cases of women smoothly pursuing independent careers that put at their beck and call unresentful male subordinates.

Nor does the conventional liberal wisdom that conflates "traditionalism" and "conservatism" with "sexism" always hold in the West. After all, the first British woman prime minister turned out to be a Tony rather than a Liberal or a Laborite, and in the American Congress, more women members have been Republican than Democrat.

This does not mean that the assumption of new careers by women in all these instances has necessarily been easy. But it does mean that the conventional view of these matters is somehow out of tune with the facts. The problem clearly calls for a new perspective on the dynamics of gender roles. I shall begin the task here by examining these roles among the Suku of Zaire—a society in which I have done ethnographic fieldwork and whose cultural subtleties are consequently more accessible to me than those of the larger Third World societies I have mentioned.

The Suku, numbering about 100,000, live in hamlets and small villages scattered across the rolling savannas of southwestern Zaire (for a brief general sketch of Suku society, see Kopytoff, 1965). Traditionally—that is, before the colonial period and into the 1950s—they were organized into small matrilineages averaging some thirty five members. The division of labor followed gender very closely. Subsistence agriculture was entirely in the hands of women, who also kept chickens, did a little fishing in the swamps, and trapped small rodents. The women kept house, cooked, gathered firewood, and carried water. Their one craft was pottery, and a few engaged in herbalism.

Men did no subsistence agriculture. But they did keep miniscule gardens of herbs, tobacco, bananas; occasionally and more recently, some imported "European" vegetables and tended small groves of raffia palm from which they extracted fiber and "wine." They hunted and trapped wild animals and kept the larger domestic animals—goats, pigs, and hunting dogs. Most of Suku craftwork was done by men: they built houses; they made baskets and wove raffia cloth, mats, fishing weirs, and nets; they manufactured all the household utensils; and they did the woodcarving. The outstanding male craft specialist was the blacksmith, who produced hoes, knives, arrow-points, and axes. In addition, the men controlled the professions, involving medical practice, divination, dispute settlement, and the organization of rituals such as circumcision. The men also held the formal political positions, such as the headmanship of lineages, various chieftainships, and the kingship.

A Terminological Excursion

Now, to move directly toward the central issue of this discussion, let me point at once to an omission from my lists of occupations of men and women. I did not include among men's occupations the impregnation of women and their provision of semen in the production of children. Nor did I point out that it is the women and not the men who bore children. Had I mentioned these occupations in the same breath as woodcarving and household chores, the average reader would have been startled. But why? The question raises some serious cognitive and cultural issues.

I am, of course, writing as an anthropologist, within the anthropological tradition of listing certain things when describing the division of labor by gender. In this tradition, one explains who weaves baskets and who makes pots but not who gives birth to children. The latter piece of data is "obvious" and it is redundant and pedantic to mention it. Childbearing by women is "natural" and shows no cross-cultural variation—unlike basket weaving and pottery, which are variable, "cultural," and worth mentioning.

This way of approaching the division of labor by gender is indeed more anthropological than Western. After all, in many Western groups, people would draw the line differently between what is obviously natural and what is arbitrarily cultural. They might, for example, insist that women are no less "naturally" meant to do household chores, rear children, and support their husbands' egos than they are meant to bear children. That is, which roles in a society are seen to belong naturally to certain persons and which are seen as being in some sense artificial is itself a cultural artifact. Granted that bearing children is part of what we assume to be a core (physiological, psychological, sociological) of objectively natural functions that go with femaleness, no society restricts itself to that core in its definition of what is "natural." And even the core's boundaries are by no means objectively obvious, as the various shifts in anthropological ideas on the subject over the past century have shown.

In the folk anthropology of a society, the distinction between what is natural and what is artificial (or to the anthropologist, "cultural") is reflected in its treatment of social identities and the roles associated with them. This statement requires a brief terminological excursion.

I owe my use here of the term "social identity" to Goodenough (1965), who incisively clarified Linton's (1936) original conceptualization of role and status. Beginning with role (an easily observable piece of behavior), Linton carried his theoretical discussion toward the more abstract status—that is, in the direction of social structure. By contrast, Goodenough began the discussion with the individual in a given concrete ethnographic setting, and moved in the direction of cognition, identity, social psychology, and culture. Briefly defined, social identity (recognized by a native term) is an aspect of the social (as opposed to personal and idiosyncratic) self. In this perspective, a social structure may be said to consist of actors who are expected to behave in terms of their various social identities (such as in the English terms father, policeman, teacher, doctor, prime minister, and so forth, in our society).

I would like to suggest here that in examining social roles in a society, it is useful to make a further distinction within Goodenough's notion of social identity. The distinction is between what people in a society regard as *existential* social identities and those they regard as *role-based*. Some social identities are culturally defined as having to do with what people "are" in a fundamental sense, indicating a state of being (for example, in the West, father, woman, or priest). This is in contrast to social identities that are culturally perceived as being derived from what people "do" that is, identities based on their roles (for example, physician, teacher, or policeman).

Some features of an existential identity and the roles attached to it (what they visibly do) are culturally defined as immanent in the state of being: people do *X* because of what they are. Thus, in the West, certain nurturing roles are immanent in the existential identity of father. By contrast, in role-based identities, the causal relationship is reversed: people are *X* because of what they do. The identity here is circumstantial, derived from the role that has been taken on, and the identity lapses when the role is shed. To say that *X* has a policeman's identity is a shorthand way of saying that *X* performs a certain kind of role. The identity is a label for a role and it does not exist in and of itself, the way an existential identity—qua state of being—does.

Roles and features that are culturally defined as immanent in an existential identity are, of course, relatively immutable and subject only with great difficulty to social renegotiation. People do not welcome the subtraction from existential identities of their established immanent features, and they resist the addition to them of new immanent features, especially when these threaten to contradict established ones. On the other hand, there are other features of existential identities that, even if prevalent, are not regarded as immanent. Such features are far more open to debate and negotiation. To take a rather trivial example, even fifty years ago the wearing of skirts by women in America, though a prevalent feature of the female identity, was not an immanent one, as the wearing of pants by men was and still is. As a result, the expansion in the wearing of pants among women in the 1960s did not entail any serious debate.

Let me now apply these distinctions to male and female roles among the Suku.

GENDER IDENTITIES AND ROLES AMONG THE SUKU

Traditionally, a Suku was a human being (*mutu,* pl. *batu*) not immediately upon birth but rather after a "coming-out" and naming ritual—the first rite of passage in the life cycle—that took place several weeks after birth. At this time, formal recognition was given to the child's sex as well as to the socially crucial existential identities of membership of one's matrilineage and that of one's patrikindred (for a sketch of the organization of these groups, see Kopytoff, 1964). Circumcision, traditionally at the age of sixteen or older, took the male into social adulthood—he became a *yakala* (pl. *bakala*), a "man" as in the narrower English term for a postboyhood male. Although no ritual marked the onset of menarche (or of menopause) in the female, she became a "woman" in the narrower sense of adult woman (*muketu,* pl. *baketu*) with the onset of menstruation. I shall focus my discussion here on such mature men and women.

Looking back, I realize that in my conversations with the Suku there emerged a kind of operational definition for existential identities and the immanence of their features. The definition rested on the form taken by explanations of a role's raison d'être. To begin with the simplest case, the reason given for the fact that women bore children was simply that "they are women." The role of childbearer was seen as flowing directly out of the woman's identity—out of her state of being a woman. The appeal to this existential identity constituted a terminal explanation for her role of childbearer; the statement was sufficient and nothing more needed to be added to it. That, in the case of childbearing, this explanation should be terminal seems obvious to us—because we happen to share it. (And we are tempted to think that we share it because the relationship between woman and childbearer is biologically given. True, but the terms of the relationship may be reversed. It is conceivable that, in some societies, the term we might gloss as woman may in reality be seen as an immanent feature of the existential identity of childbearer.)

The Suku proffered similar terminal explanations for roles that were not so obvious to the foreigner. Thus, a woman could not be initiated as a lineage head and she could play one but not another ritual role because, again and without further explanatory ado, "she is a woman." This mode of explanation obviously leaves very little room for logical probing or social negotiation.

What is significant for the argument of this essay is that, among the Suku, few immanent roles were specifically linked to the man or the woman qua existential identities. This is not to say that these roles were not important, but importance focused on the symbolic rather than the pragmatic aspects of life. Among these immanent roles, the ones that loomed largest for a woman were, precisely, childbearing (with its great weight as a realization of the female identity) and the profoundly immanent role, in this matrilineal society, of reproducer of offspring on whom she conferred their crucial existential identity of members of their corporate kin group. Certain rituals involving "medicines" required participation by a woman, others by a man, and still others by both. The "contamination" by dangerous "medicines" through the sexual act followed different rules with women and men. The ritual initiation into chiefly positions was restricted to men, and so were hunting, warfare, and ironworking (all three ritually encrusted occupations), as well as house building and toolmaking. Men were said to do these things simply "because they are men."

A complex system of reciprocal existential identities, with associated immanent features, was found in the sphere of kinship relations (father–son, mother's brother–sister's son, older brother–younger brother, and so forth), of what we like to call ritual kinship (as in blood brotherhood and the adoption of acquired persons—"slaves"—into the kin group), and of certain entirely ritual spheres (such as the identity of Kita, see Kopytoff, 1980). All of these identities and relations, it should be noted, were heavily ritualized.

One set of identities deserves special comment—that of husband and wife. The immanent roles associated with them were clearly defined but they were few in number. They focused primarily on the various dangers of ritually unsanctioned sexual unions. But most features of the husband–wife relationship (though they could have mystical significance) involved the contractual side of marriage. Here, bridewealth transactions established (and renegotiations could change) the precise rights of the mates in one another and in the children. These rights were not immanent in the husband–wife relationship as such. They included such matters as the wife's role as grower and maker of food and as provider of sex to the husband; and the husband's role of provider of meat, cloth, and utensils to the wife. In brief, the numerous roles that Westerners consider to be immanent in the identities of husband and wife derived, among the Suku, from specific and discrete contractual, circumstantial, and negotiable arrangements. The boundary between the immanent and the circumstantial was reflected in two sets of terms. When the immanent features of the marriage were involved, this was better conveyed by using the terms *mununi* (husband) and *mukasi* (wife). On the other hand, the contractual and circumstantial features were better conveyed by the terms *yakala* (literally man, male) and *muketu* (literally woman, female). The distinction is reminiscent of the two terms used for wife in French: *épouse,* with its implications of legalism and formality, and *femme,* conveying sociability and informality. The more formal Suku set of terms was, in fact, rarely used, simply because the contexts in which they were relevant were rare. The statement by Vellenga (1983: 145) about Akan marriage—that "generally it could be said that marriage was considered more of a *process* that a state of being"—conveys very well the flavor of the nonexistential side of Suku marriage arrangements.

When pressed further for explanations, my Suku informants attributed the immanence of certain roles in certain existential identities to the nature of human existential identity itself, as in the case of injunction against sex between siblings. The immanence of other roles they attributed to the "injunctions of Suku elders/ancestors" (*misiku mya bambuta*). Here, the Suku posited a Suku existential identity separate from their neighbors'. More recently, however, with the growing awareness of startling variations in customs, such explanations have become less satisfying. When I once mentioned to a group of Suku that in some parts of Africa women are "circumcised," the information was greeted with disbelief and hilarity. One person, who had literally fallen on the ground with laughter, asked in jest whether women in those places also impregnated women. In Suku folk anthropology, to be circumcised was as immanent a feature of being a man as the begetting of children. Circumcision was not a variant practice but an invariant, "natural" attribute of masculinity—of human masculinity before the appearance of uncircumcised Europeans and, since then, of African masculinity (though my story about female circumcision among some distant Africans suddenly threw uncertainty over that). Circumcision was also, above all, a "natural" nonattribute of femininity—the sort of thing that a Suku anthropologist might think it pedantic to mention in a report on gender attributes in a foreign society, in the same way that Western anthropologists think it pedantic to mention childbearing as an attribute of femininity.

But when it came to the fact that Suku women did agriculture, the reason given was not that "it is because they are women," or that there was an ancestral injunction that women should do agriculture. The Suku recognized that there is a kind of custom that is different from one naturally or ancestrally imposed. This is the *mutindu* or *mpila,* or, in the Kikongo-based lingua franca of the area, *faso* (from the French *façon*). The distinction between the two kinds of customs is, of course, reminiscent of Sumner's (1906) classic distinction in sociological theory between the coercive "mores" and the merely habitual "folkways," that is, "social practices." What I refer to as immanent features of existential identities carry the kind of coercive force that Sumner's mores do; in contrast, like practices, the circumstantial features of existential identities do not.

The Suku recognized that they shared some of their practices with their neighbors, and they could point to specific instances of the diffusion of practices in the region. Practices were seen as changeable and some were known to have changed within Suku society. There was nothing startling, then, in the idea that some Suku practices may be reversed among other peoples—that, in another society, for example, men might do subsistence agriculture and women might weave baskets.

Agricultural work by women was not a matter of ancestral injunction but rather a practice. As I have mentioned, Suku men did traditionally do some planting inside the village and in the form of little gardens of herbs, tobacco, and imported vegetables. In the late 1940s, men had begun to plant coffee trees in the very few places in Sukuland where the soil allowed it. My suggestion that men might plant manioc, the staple food, if there were a market for it, was acceptable. However, the idea of planting it for one's own consumption was rejected on pragmatic grounds. They could do it, but it would make no sense since the women already planted all the food they needed. I do not wish to convey the impression that these pragmatic discussions lacked all emotional overtones. Suku men did not like to engage in agriculture and they did feel somewhat demeaned when they did, even if, as in the case of coffee, the profits seduced them into it. But the point is that they were seducible for pragmatic reasons. Not doing agriculture was a circumstantial feature of male identity and a socially negotiable one.

The overwhelming majority of the tasks that I have mentioned as being on the women's side in the division of labor were of this circumstantial rather than immanent kind—matters of negotiable practice. Unlike mores and "injunctions from the elders/ancestors," which are self-justifying and beyond rational discussion and rational defense, circumstantial features of women's identities could be discussed and defended, even if the defense was circular. For example, when I raised the issue of men planting subsistence crops, one of the reasons advanced for their not doing so was that since women cooked, they might as well know what they are cooking. Later, when I broached the idea of cooking by men, I was told that since women grew the food, they knew it and might as well cook it. And when I reminded them of the earlier argument, the response was not embarrassment at having been caught at a fallacy but rather a triumphant reassertion of it all along the lines of "that's exactly right, you see, these things go together." The point is that the strands in this circular functionalist web are pragmatic, and the very possibility of engaging in such a defense implies the negotiability of these particular gender roles.

To the extent that the new occupations introduced in the colonial period had no established place in the Suku folk anthropology of gender, all of them lacked immanence and represented circumstantial roles. Their relationship to gender should thus have been negotiable—in principle. In fact, a certain amount of cultural pre-sortment occurred. Some of this was achieved by obvious equations—a policeman's or soldier's role easily joined that of warrior and hunter as an attribute of male social identity. But whether these new roles were unquestionably immanent in the male existential identity remained unclear (it is significant, I think, that in many parts of Africa where women had never been warriors, they nevertheless have become soldiers without any sense of profound anomaly). Many other new roles, such as schoolteachers, clerks, or nurses, had no obvious traditional counterparts. Pragmatically, however, their allocation was conditioned by the fact that the women had little time to spare beyond their routine work while the men were definitely, in the economist's language, underemployed.

It was largely in these terms that the embryonic modernization of the Suku area began to take shape after the Second World War. For example, in the matter of cooking—traditionally, a circumstantial but almost universally female role among the Suku—the issue was sorted out very early on. Suku males took work as cooks for resident European and African officials; the job, with its regular pay, gave them some status. Similarly, young men took on jobs caring for expatriate children—an occupation that traditionally fell on the women. The women's heavy responsibilities would not allow them to become engaged as nannies or indeed as anything else. One might be tempted to say that men took on these jobs *because* it gave them money and status. This explanation would be too easy. The far greater status and rewards of being a Christian schoolteacher, for example, would not have been sufficient to make men even remotely consider the possibility of abandoning circumcision. The Christian missionaries from the beginning did not press the attack on what they recognized as a pagan but non-negotiable feature of men's existential identity.

Although growing vegetables for sale to the small local stranger community was rather more frequently done by men, some women did it too in the midst of their busy schedules. The little trading that was available in this economically depressed region was again done mostly by men, though a little by women. Clerking was all done by men at the beginning, but then literacy was until the 1950s almost monopolized by them. As more women became literate, a few of them began to move into clerkish positions.

In brief, the definition of many old roles and most of the new roles meant that these roles remained open to both genders—in principle. Their statistical distribution was, however, skewed, and that for pragmatic reasons. But even pragmatically Suku women did not invariably give preference to old established roles. This is shown by the emergence among the Suku of that contemporary pan-African figure: the free woman. Unlike other groups closer to the centers of modernity, the Suku had very few such free women—in the late 1950s, a few score at most. But this makes their emergence no less significant as a systemic cultural phenomenon.

The colonial authorities of what was then the Belgian Congo recognized a formal status of *femme libre*. In the official view, a free women was one who had detached herself from the obligations and constraints of African custom. She could claim to be subject not to the customary tribunal but to that held directly by colonial administrators enforcing the written legal code of the colony. This creation of a legal status was a case of law following African sociological reality. Legalities aside, de facto free women had been a feature of most colonial African societies.

Among the Suku and neighboring peoples, free women engaged in such varied occupations as traders, small businesswomen (such as keepers of the rudimentary shops, hotels, bars, and restaurants in African townships), prostitutes, temporary concubines of expatriate European and African functionaries, and common-law wives of the relatively de-tribalized and mobile males involved in the modern sector (mechanics, drivers, male nurses, businessmen, clerks, and the like). Free women often moved between these various roles. When they had children, these either joined the burgeoning urban population or were brought up by their mother's relatives back in the village. The children had no problem of social placement among these matrilineal populations, being automatically members of their mothers' kin groups.

What was the social position of these free women from the Suku point of view? They were simply women who had not married, for whom nobody had paid bridewealth, and who exercised scarcely any of the main traditional female occupations, that is, cultivation and minor crafts. But their existential identity as women remained intact. They bore children and, like other women, thereby asserted their womanhood. They conferred on these children what was in women's power to confer—that essential quality of "blood" that made these children members of their matrilineage. In principle, they could fulfill any of the women's ritual roles.

If they were not, in fact, called upon by their kin groups to take up female ritual roles, the reason was practical, for these roles imposed considerable constraints on sexual activities. If many of them did not bring up their own children, this conformed with certain traditional understandings. As in most of Africa (where fosterage of children is very widespread), rearing children (as opposed to bearing them) was not a role immanent in a Suku woman's existential identity. The task was easily delegated to other relatives, sometimes for the convenience of parents, sometimes at the request of relatives. A childless woman might ask her sister to let her have a "spare" daughter to bring up and help out around the house (as elsewhere in Africa, children represented an important part of domestic labor resources).

The negotiability, in Africa, of various aspects of the marital and parental role is striking from the Western perspective, where so many immanent features are embedded in the identities of husband/father and wife/mother. For example we are now aware of the very wide distribution throughout Africa of what Herskovits (1938:i: 319–22) first called "woman-marriage" in Dahomey (for example, see Strobel 1982: 120–21). In this kind of marriage, it is possible for a woman, by paying bridewealth for another woman, to acquire the legal role of "husband" to that woman and the legal role of "father" to her children (the children being sired by a designated male who does not thereby acquire legal paternal rights in them). The very possibility of a woman being a "husband" and "father" puts very vividly to the test the Western cultural assumptions about which features are naturally immanent in the woman's social identity. But "woman-marriage" is only one expression of a more general tendency in African cultures to have a great variety of different kinds of heterosexual unions, all surrounding the woman's existential identity with negotiated arrangements whose formal recognition makes them all akin to what Westerners feel compelled to see as some kind of "marriage." Thus, Herskovits lists thirteen kinds of such unions for Dahomey, and Vellenga (1983: 145) refers to twenty-three for the Akan (for an example of the bewildering number of strategies such systems permit, see Bledsoe, 1980). In this perspective, the Suku free woman represented a radically stripped down version of essential Suku womanhood—stripped, that is, of most of its traditional panoply of circumstantial features, with the remaining existential core being endowed with a set of new circumstantial features and roles.

It is not surprising, then, that at no time had I heard anyone disparage Suku free women as "loose" or suggest that they were doing anything they should not or not doing something they should. The flavor of the attitude is conveyed by the fact that some informants compared free women to nuns, African and European, whom the Suku saw as having taken on special circumstantial roles rather than, as in the Christian view, having adopted a profoundly new existential identity. The difference, amid the similarities, between the free woman and the nun was that the nun had also chosen to agree not to bear children. When people expressed moral judgments about free women, they talked not about the category as such but about the conduct of some individuals within the category. A promiscuous trader woman, whose promiscuity led to unseemly public behavior, would be condemned in the same way that a married woman would. The same held for a full-time prostitute whose behavior (but not her role) might or might not be shameful.

The absence of evaluative comments on such role transformations is related to another aspect of the Suku definition of woman's existential identity. The Suku did not focus on *what* in some essentialist sense that existential identity—what we would call womanhood—was. The identity of woman existed as a concept, but it was not described in terms of some general internal content. In effect, there was no general pattern of "femininity," no generic "feminine role" as such, describable in terms of some characterological qualities.

Linton (1945: 130) coined the term status-personality to indicate the linkage, in a given society, between a particular status and the personality configuration required by that status. For example, we generally recognize that to be a successful psychologist or university administrator calls for a personality different from what it takes to be a successful army sergeant. We may transfer Linton's idea to Goodenough's concept of social identity and talk of an identity-personality.

In discussing chieftaincy—an existential identity established by a ritual—the Suku very willingly described the identity-personality desirable in rulers. The chief should be dignified in bearing, reserved, slow to anger, judicious, generous, nurturing, stern with transgressions but understanding and forgiving. Similarly, one could easily elicit broadly sketched identity-personalities (in such reciprocal existential relationships as that of father–son or mother's brother–sister's child) and narrowly sketched ones for diviners, judges, or guardians of ritual medicines. I could never, however, elicit an identity-personality for either woman or man as such. Characterologically, that is, males and females were not differentiated, the character of a particular person being regarded as a matter of individual variation that cross-cut gender. One sometimes heard it said that women in their childbearing years had a greater tendency to be talkative and impulsive and to lack discretion. But this was not said of women in general. And the traits were also said to be present in some individual men. It is significant that I have not heard anyone say about an indiscreet man that he was "like a woman"—a very common formulation in Western, Middle Eastern, and, I am sure, other societies.

The Suku do not say that "women should not be forward." What they will say is that a woman should be quiet on such and such an occasion, as should also a man on certain occasions. The Suku do not say that "women should be obedient." They will say that a wife should obey her husband in certain contexts, as a son should obey his father in certain contexts. Even when disapproving of breaches of roles immanent in the identity of the post-pubertal woman, the Suku would not phrase the issue characterologically, as is done in so many societies, by saying: "Do not walk naked in the street because women should be modest." What they will say is: "Do not walk naked in the street because it is shameful for big women to walk naked in the street." The avoidance of characterological judgments is related to the general pattern of what might be called "externality" in African cultures—the unwillingness to probe into the inaccessible interior of persons (precisely what modern Westerners so excel at). The African preference is for dealing with behavior in terms of external and visible features, without conflating them into a global statement about the interior person.

In any analysis of women's roles in a given society, it is important to discover whether the society conceptualizes a singular identity of "woman" (as the West does), and whether that identity is kept quite distinct in certain contexts from such identities as wife, or adolescent, mature, or post-menopausal females. Thus, among the Suku, while there was no answer to the question of what women are or of how they should behave in general, such a description was available for the identity of a wife. But the description—in any case clearly contextual—was bare: above all, a Suku wife should be respectful of her husband and her in-laws, as he should be of her and his in-laws. Beyond that, being a wife entailed circumstantial features and roles, defining not what one was but what one did, such as providing food and sex, cooking, and keeping house. These task-oriented roles were derived from the contractual side of Suku marriage, which involved negotiated payments by the husband. Legally, a wife was to fulfill these roles without also paying a personality-role. If she failed in her obligations, the failure was legal, and narrowly so. For example, if one's mate misused one's property, one could take him or her to court, but this act did not threaten the marriage itself.

An analogy will perhaps clarify the point: in some contemporary American marriages, the wealth of the respective mates is kept legally separate. How each chooses to use it is a matter lying outside the obligations immanent in the marriage relationship. A spendthrift with his or her money is immune from accusations of being a spendthrift in the context of the marriage partnership. Since marriage in America is an overwhelmingly existential relationship, such variations in marriage are regarded in main-stream American culture as having been deliberately put outside of the marriage relationship. In Africa, on the other hand, such negotiated variations *constitute* the marriage in one of its several possible guises.

In this perspective, the African free woman is at the extreme of a continuum of acceptable women's roles, including her relationship with men. To a Westerner, one end of the continuum is clearly recognizable as "marriage" while the other end appears as a most ephemeral relationship with one or more men. The significance of the free woman lies in showing the ease with which an apparently radical transformation of women's roles can occur by what is in fact a slight variation in role shedding and role acquisition. Many other African women, Suku and others, have gone some but not all the way on this road. And more recently, they have taken these transformations in new directions—into the professions, the bureaucracy, and politics. They perform these new roles with little evidence of being victims of the kind of wrenching role conflicts that so often accompany the careers of their Western, and especially American, sisters. These transformations have taken place without any notable public debate in most African societies (some Islamic African societies being apparent exceptions that demand, however, close analysis).

The free African women were usually seen as a new phenomenon, attributable to the destabilization of old customs by modern forces. But the phenomenon clearly has deeper cultural roots. Together with the principles that underlie it, it is widely distributed in Africa, and the dynamics of identity I have described have worked as smoothly and thoroughly in the big cities as in backwaters such as Sukuland. All this militates against the idea that the free African woman has arisen only since colonial times or solely in response to modern conditions. A considerable literature has developed (for one review, see Strobel, 1982) that indicates this. We are now also aware of the large number of African women who rose as large-scale entrepreneurs and political and even military leaders in the past (see, for example, Sweetman, 1984). The literature also points to the wide specific variation in the social condition of African women in different places and historical periods. What I would stress here is that these concrete variations become understandable precisely because they deal with the circumstantial elements (that are highly responsive to external changes) that cluster around a very narrow existential core.

WOMEN'S IDENTITIES IN THE WEST

The crucial question I have been posing is this: granted that most and perhaps all societies posit that being a woman is an existential identity with a set of features immanent in it, how many such immanent features are there and what are they? Or, to put it most simply, the problem of women's roles is not whether a society recognizes women as being different from men (they invariably do) but how it organizes other things around the difference.

I am not competent to extend this perspective from the Suku and Africa to other areas of the Third World. Let me try, however, to bring the perspective to the very different situation found in the West and more particularly in the United States. What is there, then, in the modern Western conceptualization of women's identities and roles that makes the Western configuration so different?

Two things come immediately to attention: (1) the astonishingly greater number of immanent features associated with the Western woman's existential identity, and (2) the elaborate interior characterization of the Western female existential identity itself—what Betty Friedan (1963) so aptly called the feminine mystique.

The modern American conception of womanhood—by which I mean the most recent and still culturally dominant synthesis in mid-twentieth-century "mainstream" American culture—had been in the making over the preceding century and a half of Anglo-American history. Its emergence was part of a larger transformation that included the spreading cultural hegemony of an expanding middle class that became the carrier of a progressivist ethos of antitraditionalism, individualism, egalitarianism, and democracy. Before that, both in northwestern Europe (see, for example, Howell, 1987) and in America (Jensen, 1987), role definitions were rather differently and more loosely organized.

In the modern synthesis, the range of the immanent features of womanhood is very wide indeed and it is familiar enough to need hardly any extensive discussion. In addition to the role of childbearer, the woman's identity has come to include numerous immanent features embodying a vast array of responsibilities. There is the rearing, socialization, and education of one's own children, in a society where "correct" socialization is believed to determine the child's future success in life. There is the role of providing a physically and psychologically encouraging ambience at home for the husband. There is the management of the social life and social calender of the family unit. There is housekeeping, which merges into the more elusive homemaking. There is the responsibility to present to the world attractive and physically cared-for house, children, husband, and, not least, one's own self as a significant indicator of the state and status of the family. And, perhaps hardest of all, there is the requirement of presenting to the world a characterologically, rather than merely behaviorally, defined femininity: charm, docility, good sense, seductiveness, controlled sexuality, a certain impracticality in business matters combined with a no-nonsense managerial efficiency in home matters, and so on.

These features began to be built up gradually, beginning early in the nineteenth century, with the development of what Matthews (1987) refers to as the cult of domesticity. Increasingly, the identity of wife-mother came to be seen as immanent in the very identity of being a woman. This was not always so. In the nineteenth century, the spinster—like the bachelor, widow, and widower—was culturally well-recognized as an alternative identity (see, for example, Chambers-Schiller 1984). The identity had its own cluster of integral roles (including such roles as schoolteacher, nurse, nanny, or companion) and was not unlike the alternative gender identities of nun and priest. But by the mid-twentieth century, spinsterhood and bachelorhood ceased to be seen as equal and mature identities in and of themselves. They became increasingly defined as incomplete identities, representing an unachieved journey toward the mature identity of married person. The redefinition was further exacerbated by the invasion of American popular culture by psychology and especially a vulgarized Freudianism; spinsterhood changed from an alternative identity into a flawed one, into a public statement of sexual, and therefore existential, incompleteness. The very terms spinster, bachelor, widow, and widower became somewhat embarrassing and began to drop out of common usage, to be replaced by the vague "single." Not surprisingly, this trend coincided with the questioning of the existential legitimacy of the identities of nun and priest.

By the mid-twentieth century, American society seemed to have arrived at the point where most small-scale societies like the Suku have been all along—where all "normal" men and women are somehow incomplete unless they are married and have progeny. But there is a difference with African societies that lies in the circumstance that each of the American gender identities is encrusted with numerous immanent features. Many unmarried African women could repair their incompleteness and have mates and children by resorting to one of a dozen or more available recognized unions. The modern American woman can achieve this "normal" identity only by way of marriage, with its burdensome and cumbersome package of immanent roles. Once existentially complete, she can then turn to other occupations. But everyone is realistic enough to know that few can manage that with any ease, and if a woman does, the achievement is publicly recognized by the obligatory and congratulatory aside about how it had all been done without her ceasing to be a woman-wife-mother. To give such high praise is to reiterate the rarity of success in reconciling the role contradictions. And if success is rare, then it is too risky to entrust to women such crucial positions as, say, the presidency of a company, let alone of a country.

The sheer weight of the American woman's immanent role-load continues to make the taking on of other identities and roles a daunting prospect. It is true that the workload of Suku women's roles was heavier and more time-consuming, but the roles themselves were overwhelmingly circumstantial and negotiable. In America the existential identity is enveloped in a huge mantle of non-negotiable roles. If an American woman wishes to take on a new circumstantial role (say, that of professional), she cannot easily trade it for an old one (say, that of her family's hostess).

Moreover, if an American woman wishes to chip away at the immanent roles, the dominant liberal social ethos often makes this course of action ideologically and pragmatically difficult. An ethos of personal achievement discourage the delegation to others of tasks considered to be properly one's own. An egalitarian ethos frowns upon the hiring of the less advantaged as servants to do onerous tasks, and it also makes the social handling of the inherently unequal relationship with servants difficult (in a way that a class society does not). An individualistic ethos prizes individual privacy; this makes the presence of servants and their involvement in the intimate details of everyday life uncomfortable (in a way that aristocratic societies do not, with their exclusion of the lower orders from the community of manners and their notorious lack of personal shame before servants). And just when the use of servants becomes increasingly unacceptable, the use of relatives as surrogates for the fulfillment of one's roles becomes increasingly difficult, for the ethos of antitraditionalism questions the sincerity and the obligatory nature of culturally mandated relationships, including those of kinship, and extols instead voluntary relationships.

While there is some room for rearranging housekeeping roles, many of the other roles immanent in womanhood are by their nature utterly non-negotiable. A woman can scarcely delegate to someone else the psychological caretaking of her husband. Nor can she, while pursuing her education or profession, delegate entirely to others the rearing of her children, steeped as the task is in innumerable psychological subtleties; to do so would make her an "unnatural mother" in her own eyes no less than in others'. Moreover, the greater the sheer number of immanent roles, the greater the chances of substantive conflict with new circumstantial roles that one might be contemplating—for example, conflicts between schedules demanded by a job and by the socialization of one's children.

But the greatest source of difficulties may be traced to the development of a characterological model of existential womanhood itself. The existence of this model in the West is itself part of the rise of individualism and the idea that a knowledge of their "internal" core yields a superior understanding of people. This internal perspective leads, in turn, to especially subtle characterological formulations of existential social identities, be they of gender, race, or ethnicity. Once an internal personality-like characterization of womanhood exists, the problem arises of its congruence with the identity-personality (Linton's status-personality) of various occupations. For example, can one who is "naturally" docile, impractical, and seductive take on occupations demanding aggressiveness, hardheadedness, and professionalism? For the American woman, the conflict between different pursuits is very often existential—a personality conflict that also involves values, responsibilities, and ethics. This is in contrast to the Suku, for whom, in the absence of a characterological model of womanhood, the conflict is pragmatic.

The issue is further complicated by the different views of the relationship between the natural and the cultural. In the Hobbesian and Durkheimian views, society is an artificial—hence, cultural—construction that transcends and often contradicts nature. On the other hand, American folk anthropology (and, frequently, American social science) is Lockean, seeing society as a natural phenomenon beholden to natural laws. Hence, to Americans, social change must conform to the demands of Nature. And it is Nature (as revealed by Science) that, in the absence of an active deity, becomes the validator or invalidator of proposed social changes.

This poses special problems in dealing with gender roles. If what is natural is right, then whatever one believes or wishes to be right must be proven natural; and whatever one wishes to be wrong must be shown to be unnatural. This injects American debates over social policy with an extraordinary amount of theory, measurement, and scientific pretensions. In so eminently cultural an issue as civil or educational rights, the opposing sides both argue over the latest word on I.Q. tests and the latest ruminations of social scientists. For the same reason, in the first flush of feminist agitation, one saw the drive to demonstrate scientifically the biological equivalence between the sexes, while antifeminist rhetoric seized on the latest experiment to claim biological nonequivalence. The legitimacy of civic arrangements is made to depend on the latest reports from the laboratories.

In the popular expression of this system, when a role hitherto played by men (as, for example, the role of secretary and typist at the turn of the century) is taken up by women, the new reality is eventually justified on natural grounds. This can be accomplished relatively quickly, given the shallowness of modern historical awareness (itself a part of its antitraditionalism). Once an occupation threatens to become the preserve of one gender, there occurs a flight from it by the other—not unlike the flights that make for ethnic successions in American neighborhoods.

What I wish to stress here is that the development in the modern West of what we generally think of as the basic progressivist package of values has been a double-edged weapon when it came to the transformation of women's roles. Egalitarianism, individualism, personal independence, refusal to exploit others for one's personal comfort, and the need for an objective and scientific rather than a traditional (and therefore "arbitrary") basis for social action—even as these values called for redefining gender roles in an egalitarian direction, they also rigidified these roles and made venturing into new roles and occupations for either sex more difficult. It is an obvious paradox that the liberation of the servant girl necessarily imposed, in practice, more domestic chores on her mistress. Other such paradoxes are more than practical. The humanitarianism that specifically banished women from work in the mines, for example, necessarily gave moral sanction to the idea that women are existentially unfit to do certain kinds of men's work.

CONCLUSION

We find ourselves back where we began—with the puzzle of "traditional" rather than "progressive" societies producing women prime ministers and assertive professionals that take on with startling ease positions hitherto reserved to men. My analysis depended primarily on a paradigmatic contrast between Africa and the United States. It left untouched the question of what specifically this says about gender conceptualizations in the West outside of the United States and in the rest of the Third World (a label without much content in any case). I can only hope that at least the mode of my analysis and the terms I have coined for it can be usefully applied elsewhere in the elucidation of similar problems.

A final point—in my discussions with colleagues, I have sometimes encountered a reaction worth noting. They point out that, after all, the Indira Gandhis and the Corazon Aquinos get where they are "not on their own" but "because" of their relationship to their fathers and husbands. And if Third World professional women often find it easy to pursue their careers and to administer men, it is "because" they live in a class society in which servants make their independence of action possible and in which lower-class men are used to accepting orders from superiors, whatever their gender. These objections do not always apply to Africa, with its mostly classless traditional societies, but they deserve an answer with respect to places such as India.

The objections are really expressions of disapproval of the social conditions that allow Third World women of the higher classes to be free of certain burdens. At the very least, the critics refuse to be impressed with women's progress when the costs of success are so culturally unacceptable. This argument, then, is essentially about price. It also reflects the contradictions within the modern progressivist ethos that I have discussed, an ethos whose many different values are not all reconcilable. Western progressivist ideology is notoriously cultureless, while the structure of identities and roles cannot exist, even in the abstract, in a sociocultural vacuum. To say that it is Indira Gandhi's kinship position that has given her power is precisely to say that in many societies certain factors (unpalatable though they are to the Western progressivist ethos) do override gender distinctions in a way that they cannot be overridden in America. In India, the kinship-dynastic factor overrode them twice: first it transmitted the political charisma of a man, Pandit Nehru, to a woman, his daughter Indira Gandhi, and then from her to a man, her son Rajiv. The factor of gender, that is, worked in both directions. What the critics would have liked was for Indira Gandhi to have achieved it entirely on her own. But how, speaking concretely? Like Margaret Thatcher, perhaps? But ideology intrudes....

That a hierarchical or class structure may give some women authority over some men merely reminds us that societies will always rely on many different kinds of criteria when they confer or transfer authority: family connections, class, caste, religion, education, race, majority or minority status—the list is endless. Each of them has at one time or another, in one place or another, been considered objectionable. It has been left to our age to consider all of them objectionable. In societies where existential social distinctions—based on what we usually call "ascribed statuses"—have been drastically reduced (as they have been in most Western societies), those that do remain, gender included, will be all the more visible and irritating to progressivist sensibilities. All of these different systems of gender identities and roles carry their particular social costs—costs in terms of their own values and costs in terms of the values of observers from other societies. How such costs are to be compared and weighed is a question that belongs in a forum other than this one.

BIBLIOGRAPHY

Bledsoe, Caroline. 1980. *Women and Marriage in Kpelle Society.* Stanford: Stanford University Press.

Chambers-Schiller, Lee Virginia. 1984. *Liberty, A Better Husband—Single Women in America: The Generations of 1780–1840.* New Haven: Yale University Press.

Friedan, Betty. 1963. *The Feminine Mystique.* New York: Norton.

Goodenough, Ward H. 1965. "Rethinking 'Status' and 'Role': Toward a General Model of Cultural Organization of Social Relationships." In *The Relevance of Models for Social Anthropology,* M. Banton, ed. London: Tavistock.

Herskovits, Melville J. 1937. "A Note on 'Woman Marriage' in Dahomey." *Africa* 10: 335–41.

——. 1938. *Dahomey: An Ancient West African Kingdom.* 2 vols. New York: J. J. Augustin.

Howell, Martha C. 1987. *Women, Production, and Patriarchy in Late Medieval Cities.* Chicago: University of Chicago Press.

Jensen, Joan M. 1987. *Loosening the Bonds: Mid-Atlantic Farm Women, 1750–1850.* New Haven: Yale University Press.

Kopytoff, Igor. 1964. "Family and Lineage among the Suku of the Congo." In *The Family Estate in Africa,* Robert F. Gray and P. H. Gulliver, eds., pp. 83–116. Boston: Boston University Press.

——. 1965. "The Suku of Southwestern Congo." In *Peoples of Africa,* James L. Gibbs, Jr., ed., pp. 441–78. New York: Holt, Rinehart, and Winston.

——. 1980. "Revitalization and the Genesis of Cults in Pragmatic Religion: The Kita Rite of Passage among the Suku." In *Explorations in African Systems of Thought,* Ivan Karp and Charles S. Bird, eds., pp. 183–212. Bloomington: Indiana University Press.

Linton, Ralph. 1936. *The Study of Man.* New York: Appleton-Century.

Linton, Ralph. 1945. *The Cultural Background of Personality.* New York: Appleton-Century.

Matthews, Glenna. 1987. *"Just a Housewife": The Rise and Fall of Domesticity.* New York: Oxford University Press.

Strobel, Margaret. 1982. "African Women." *Signs: A Journal of Women in Culture and Society* 8: 108–31.

Sumner, William Graham. 1906. *Folkways: A Study of the Sociological Importance of Usage, Manners, Customs, Mores and Morals* (1959 ed.). Boston: Ginn.

Sweetman, David. 1984. *Women Leaders in African History.* London: Heinemann.

Vellenga, Dorothy Dee. 1983. "Who Is a Wife? Legal Expressions of Heterosexual Conflicts in Ghana." In *Female and Male in West Africa,* Christine Oppong, ed., pp. 144–55. London: Allen and Unwin.

Chapter 9

Revisiting "Woman–Woman Marriage": Notes on Gikuyu Women

Wairimu Ngaruiya Njambi and William E. O'Brien

Studies of women who marry women in Africa are relatively few in number and generally dated, with few recent contributors. Based on interviews in central Kenya with Gikuyu[1] women involved in "woman–woman marriages," this study critiques the extant literature, focusing on two key issues. Most authors have perceived narrow conditions and functionalist purposes for explaining woman–woman marriages. Our interviewees typically express complex reasons for marrying women, suggesting that woman–woman marriage is a flexible option within which women may pursue a range of social, economic, political, and personal interests. We also critique the concept of "female husband," suggesting that while the "husband" role can be male or female, the term is not so easily separated from the male connotations it implies in western contexts.

> I ask myself, "What is it that women who are married to men have that I don't have? Is it land? I have land. Is it children? I have children. I don't have a man, but I have a woman who cares for me. I belong to her and she belongs to me. And I tell you, I don't have to worry about a man telling me what to do!."—Ciru, married to Nduta

Introduction

The practice of women marrying women is somewhat common in certain societies in West Africa, Southern Africa, East Africa, and the Sudan (O'Brien 1977). Yet, besides a total lack of discussion in the popular media, what is typically called woman–woman marriage is the subject of a very small body of academic literature.[2] Early scholarship is limited to the margins of several colonial-era ethnographies such as those of Evans-Pritchard, Herskovits, and Leakey. Leakey ([1938] 1977), for example, writing on Kenya's Gikuyu over six decades ago, devoted only two pages to woman–woman marriages out of a 1,400-page, three-volume, ethnography.[3] More recent work remains equally marginal. Precious few writings address woman–woman marriage practices exclusively (e.g., Amadiume, 1987; Burton, 1979; Krige, 1974; Oboler, 1980); within others the subject remains little more than a footnote (e.g., Davis and Whitten, 1987; Mackenzie, 1990; Okonjo, 1992). Since O'Brien's (1977) call for field research into woman–woman marriages more than two decades ago, there has been no study of Gikuyu woman–woman marriages, and few studies anywhere else. Our study attempts to revive this dormant discourse in relation to the Gikuyu.

Based on interviews with members of households containing woman–woman marriages, we attempt to provide images of this institution as practiced in central Kenya. Relying upon these women's voices, we present these Gikuyu woman–woman marriages in relation to major themes in the literature.[4] On the one hand, we critique what appear to us as narrow and deterministic accounts of the circumstances under which woman–woman marriages take place, as presented by some authors. Particularly challenging to such accounts are these Gikuyu women's expressed reasons for marrying, all of which go beyond the limited scenarios previously suggested by others. Leakey, for example, in his work on the Gikuyu, provides only a single circumstance in which such marriages can occur. Conversely, our attention is on the ambiguities and flexibility inherent in women's decision to marry women. In addition, we point to the strong emotional bonds to one another expressed by these women, shedding critical light on the omissions of purely functionalist perceptions of woman–woman marriage relationships. We also challenge the generalized conceptualizations of women who initiate such marriages as "female husbands." That term, used by Leakey and virtually all other authors on the topic, regardless of cultural context, imposes a "male" characterization upon a situation where none necessarily exists. Emphasizing a term such as "female husband" prompts sex-role presumptions that do not fit these Gikuyu women, who bristle at the implied male-identification regarding their roles.

This study is based on interviews with women in eight households in a small village in Murang'a District in central Kenya. This case study approach does not attempt to portray a generalized picture of woman–woman marriages, but relies upon the women's situated words to explain why they have married women, allowing them to present their own illuminating perspectives (see Smith, 1987). A more comprehensive survey of woman–woman marriages would be welcome as a means of answering questions regarding the prevalence of the practice as well as general demographic characteristics of such households, but was beyond the small scope and limited resources of this project.[5]

The Gikuyu are the largest ethnic group in Kenya, generally occupying the administrative unit of Central Province. "Kikuyuland," as it is commonly called, is bounded by Nairobi to the south and Mt. Kirinyaga (Mt. Kenya) to the north, the Rift Valley and Nyandarua Range (Aberdares) to the west, and the Mbeere Plain to the east. The Province is subdivided into three administrative districts: Kiambu District on the northern outskirts of Kenya's capital Nairobi; Nyeri District in the environs of Mt. Kenya; and Murang'a District, considered the spiritual heartland of the Gikuyu, in the center. Typically referred to as the Central Highlands region, the topography of much of the province is characterized by a series of ridges and valleys. This landscape has influenced the relatively decentralized customary political organization and land tenure rules among the Gikuyu, though such customary arrangements now co-exist with national political and state land tenure regimes (Mackenzie, 1990; Muriuki, 1974).

Most of the woman–woman marriage households in the study engaged in peasant farming for a living, dividing their agricultural production between cash crops and subsistence crops, a pattern typical of this rural setting. However, some of the women were engaged in other occupations including shop ownership, market trading of small commodities, and, in one case, *matatu* (mini bus) driving. The initiators of these relationships, who are called *ahikania*, were all landowners, and the households all had modest living standards similar to most others in the locality. Though the interviews took place in a rural setting, two of the subjects were residents of Nairobi, while another lived and worked in a nearby small urban center.

The majority of the *ahikania* were middle-aged at the time of marriage, and two were in their early 30s. All of the *ahiki*, the women who accepted the marriage offer, were between the ages of 20 and 30 when they were married. Education patterns of the subjects shows that most of the initiators of the marriages were educated through the traditional Gikuyu educational system of *githomo gia ugikuyu*: one had a high school education, one primary school. Almost all of the women who accepted the marriage offer had at least a primary school education. The wide range of age and education suggests to us that woman–woman marriage continues to be a relevant potential life-option for Gikuyu women.

Kuhikania, the process of getting married, and *uhiki*, the marriage ceremony, takes place in the same manner for woman–woman marriages as with woman–man marriages. In fact, there is no separate term to differentiate a woman–woman marriage from a woman–man marriage. Even the term which describes the marriage initiator, *muhikania*, is used to describe a woman or a man.[6] As woman–woman marriages are not sanctioned by the various Christian churches in the region, *kuhikania* and *uhiki* continue to be performed through customary guidelines. The woman seeking a marriage partner, the *muhikania*, announces, either through a *kiama* (a customary civic organization) or through her own effort, her desire to find a marriage partner, or *muhiki*. Once the word is out, interested women go to visit, and once a suitable partner is found the muhikania's friends and family bring *ruracio* (gifts associated with *uhiki*) to those of the future wife and vice-versa. *Uhiki* takes place after this gift exchange and is performed with ceremonial blessings, termed *irathimo*, by elders of both families as the new wife moves into the *muhikania*'s house.

WOMAN–WOMAN MARRIAGES AND FAMILY DEFINITIONS

While woman–woman marriage may be familiar to most anthropologists, at least in passing, the topic remains relatively obscure to most people outside Africa. In family studies discourse, the topic is pushed to the extreme margins by an historical fixation on western nuclear families as a universal ideal. This normative presumption of nuclearity makes it very difficult for particular non-western family forms, such as the woman–woman marriages in this study, to be evaluated as anything but bizarre novelties. As Skolnick and Skolnick argue:

> The assumption of universality has usually defined what is normal and natural both for research and therapy and has subtly influenced our thinking to regard deviations from the nuclear family as sick or perverse or immoral. (1989: 7)

Several features of western nuclear family ideology go to the root of its alleged functionality: the notions of monogamy and permanence, compulsory heterosexuality or opposite-sex relationships, and the perceived need for a father figure (Scanzoni *et al.*, 1989). The Gikuyu woman–woman marriages we studied challenge this thinking on all counts. Not only are the adults involved in these marriages of the same sex, but also there may be more than two, and the form of the family is not necessarily permanent (as an ideal) once a union is made, but may change periodically. Furthermore, men are often absent from such relationships, though they may be involved in married relationships as spouses of woman who initiate woman–woman marriages.

One example of such a relationship in our study is Kuhi's household. In this complex case, Kuhi (a woman) and Huta (a man) were originally married to each other. Later, they decided together that Huta would marry a second woman, Kara, creating a polygynous marriage.[7] Later still, Kuhi entered into a woman–woman marriage with a woman named Wamba. Wamba came to that family as Kuhi's marriage partner, and to assist in raising the children of that household. In this particular case, Wamba could have a sexual relationship with Huta (whom she also informally regarded as a husband), and was not restricted from having sexual relationships with other men outside their household. Later in her life, while still married to Kuhi, Wamba married a woman named Wambui. The result is that this single household contains four marriages: two woman–man marriages and two woman–woman marriages. Such complex relationships do not break any "rules," expectations, or ideals of woman–woman marriages, but are an accepted aspect of such relationships in Gikuyu contexts.

Krige (1974), a central figure in the woman–woman marriage literature, focuses her critique on the common presumption of opposite-sex partners as the basis for all marriage. She suggests that definitions of marriage, even when accounting for cross-cultural difference, tend to emphasize the male–female relationship as paramount. Some authors have attempted to incorporate woman–woman marriages into this universal presumption by suggesting, as does Riviere (1971), that the woman who initiates a marriage to a woman is playing the role of a man and can therefore be counted as male. Hence, Riviere (1971) rejects the notion that woman–woman marriages prove exceptions to the idea of opposite sex partners as the basis for marriage. Krige argues, however, that the woman she refers to as the "female husband" has no necessary male characterization: to count "female husbands" as "men" imposes a western assumption that "husband" is automatically associated with maleness (1974). As we suggest later, in these Gikuyu woman–woman marriages, the so-called "female husbands" do not identify their roles with maleness, providing support for Krige's position. Unlike Krige, however, we question even the use of the term "female husband."

The idea of same sex relationships has spurred discussion of the sexuality of women in such marriages. A few texts imply that there may be sexual involvement in these marriages. Herskovits, for example, suggested that Dahomey woman–woman marriages sometimes involved sexual relations between the women (1937). Davis and Whitten go so far as to state that the main issue in explaining these relationships generally is over whether reasons for such partnerships are in fact "homoerotic" or strictly socio-economic (1987: 87). While sexuality was not directly discussed in our interviews, we can glean from the experience that this dichotomy makes little sense.[8]

In our Gikuyu locale, women in these relationships did not talk about sexual involvement with one another, although some did indicate sharing the same bed at night. However, in South Africa, Lovedu woman–woman marriages imply no sexual involvement according to Krige's (1974) suggestion, while in Kenya the Nandi eliminate even the possibility of a sexual relationship in such marriages according to Oboler (1976). At best, given the ambiguity in this Gikuyu context, one might borrow Obbo's assertion regarding the Kamba of Kenya that while there may be no clear indication of sexual relations among women in these marriages, we simply cannot dismiss the possibility (1976). We agree with Carrier that this possibility has been too quickly dismissed by some authors, and suggest that the subject deserves more careful investigation (1980). At the same time, we question the assumption that sexual contact is the only factor that determines whether one should be considered as "homosexual" (see Martin, 1991).

On the other side of the dichotomy, to suggest that such relationships are based solely on socio-economic factors like access to land and other resources or lineage ignores the close emotional ties experienced by these women. Such functionalist views have strongly influenced historical, and still-held stereotypes of African marriages generally. African family relations, compared to the privileged, western nuclear family form, are often portrayed as relatively primitive since they are presumed to be based on practical considerations alone, such as access to resources, as opposed to having a significant emotional aspect (e.g., Albert, 1971; Ainsworth, 1967; Beeson, 1990; Kilbride and Kilbride, 1990; Le Vine, 1970). The women interviewed help undermine such rigid notions, demonstrating clear emotional commitment to the women they marry. For example, one participant, Nduta, proclaims her feelings for her ***muka wakwa***, or co-wife, Ciru:[9]

> No one dare to disturb my co-wife in any way, and especially knowing what I would do to them. No one dares point a finger at her. I tell her to proudly proclaim her belongingness to me, and I to her. . . . What I hate most is when people come to gossip to me about my co-wife's whereabouts or whom they have seen her with. I don't care as long as she is here for me now and even after I am gone. . . . Regardless of what she does, she is here because of me. Then why should I tell her what to do and what not to do. She is a free woman. And that is what I want her to be. So, when they come here to gossip, I tell them to leave her alone. She is mine and she is here on my property, not yours. . . . She who sincerely loved me and I loved back, let her stay mine. It is she who shall enshrine and take over this household when my time comes. (in interview)

In addition to expressing love (***wendo***) for Ciru, Nduta also alludes to the fact that Ciru is not restricted from having sexual encounters with men outside the woman–woman marriage relationship. Such liaisons, however, in no way undermine Ciru's reciprocated love and appreciation for Nduta. In a separate interview, Ciru, who has been married to Nduta for over 25 years, presents her deep feelings for her marriage partner:

> I know that some people do talk negatively about our marriage. Although honestly I have never caught anybody personally. But I ask myself, "What is it that women who are married to men have that I don't have? Is it land?" I have land. "Is it children?" I have children. I don't have a man, but I have a woman who cares for me. I belong to her and she belongs to me. And I tell you, I don't have to worry about a man telling me what to do. Here, I make all the decisions for myself. Nduta likes women who are able to stand on their own, like herself. I do what I want and the same goes for Nduta. Now I'm so used to being independent, and I like that a lot. I married Nduta because I knew we could live together well. She is a very wonderful woman with a kind heart. (in interview)[10]

While functionalist interpretations perceive African family relationships in terms of the purposes they serve in the functioning of a society, our interviewees highlight the complex and intertwined aspects of relationships that one would expect to find in a discussion of any committed, caring marriage partnership, undermining prevailing notions of the non-emotional African "Other."

One other point in the ideology of the nuclear family that remains strong, even among scholars, but is challenged by the woman–woman marriage data, is the alleged need for a father figure to maintain "functionality" (Cheal, 1991). Regardless of how diversified family lifestyles become, the presence of a father, whether played by the biological father or a father figure, is very much preferred and privileged over his absence. Long ago, Malinowski (1930) wrote that "in every society a child must have a socially recognized father to give the child a status in the community" (in Skolnick and Skolnick,

1989: 8), and "illegitimacy" was considered to be a sign of social breakdown. Illegitimacy still is regarded as such by many, and there is a resurgence of this ideology in the family studies literature, as well as in popular family discourse (Scanzoni *et al.*, 1989). The presence of a father is apparently not so important in many woman–woman marriages. During interviews, some women downplayed the importance of men in their households. Of the eight households in our study, six did not include permanent relationships with male partners. Among these six households, it seemed clear based on our interviews that male involvement with children, beyond procreation, was restricted, even identities of designated male genitors could not be revealed. Ciru's comments support the view that males are viewed principally as friends and/or sex partners with no claim on children or property. What does she desire from men? Not much, apparently, except perhaps sex, and she can get that when she wants on her own terms:

> I have freedom to have sex with any man that I desire, for pleasure and for conceiving babies. And none of these men can ever settle here at our home or claim the children. They can't. They are not supposed to, and they know that very well. They come and go. (in interview)

Nduta's comments present the same lack of interest in having a man around as the ideal situation, expressing the independence provided by keeping men out of the household:

> We have no interest with a man who wants to stay in our home. We only want the *arume a mahutini* [men met in "the bush," a term for "male genitors"]—meaning those who are met only for temporary needs. *The meaning for this is for a woman to be independent enough so that she can make her own homestead shrine.* Ciru sees also that I myself do not keep a man here. What for? To make me miserable? If I kept a man here who will then start asking me for money to buy alcohol, where would I find such money? No, I won't agree to live like that. It is better for one to look after oneself. It is better for one to look after oneself. (in interview, emphasis added)

Another case that downplays the importance of a male presence is that of Mbura, who had been married to a man, though he had died over 40 years ago. She was more recently married to a woman, Nimu, who subsequently left after a couple of years. Mbura was later married to a woman named Kabura on the last day of this fieldwork. Mbura responds as well to the question of the place of men in the woman–woman marriage household, adding that, to her, men are not trustworthy, though she still appreciates their temporary presence:

> Men, even the good friends, know that they are not welcome here. They are here just for a visit and to leave. Whatever they come here to do, they must leave. They cannot be trusted. That is not good. One is given respect and that's all. (in interview)

Despite the fact that the other two households in the study *did* have men present as partners of one of the ahikania, or marriage initiators, the need for a "father figure," an ideal of most heterosexual nuclear families is clearly not a universal reality for all family situations.

BEYOND COMMON EXPLANATIONS

An overview of the literature on woman–woman marriages in African societies might tempt a reader to make three intertwined cross-cultural generalizations. The first generalization regards access to children. Sudarkasa suggests that the basis for woman–woman marriage, as with African marriages generally, is the desire "to acquire rights over a woman's childbearing capacity" ([1986] 1989: 155). That is, the woman who initiates a marriage seeks access to children that she herself does not have. Rights over childbearing capacity are often linked to a second general theme: that children are desired by such women as a means of transferring property through inheritance. Krige suggests that woman–woman marriages contracted "as a last resort in raising a male heir to perpetuate the name and inherit the property of a man . . . seems to be its most common form" (1974: 29). Connected to both general circumstances is the third common assertion that women's "barrenness" is a fundamental factor prompting woman–woman marriages. In fact, one of the most widely held general assumptions, as Burton points out, is that woman–woman marriages must involve women who cannot themselves have children (1979). Evans-Pritchard's account of the Nuer suggests that almost exclusively it is "barren" women who make such marriages (1951). Langley, speaking of the Nandi, said that three types of women practiced woman–woman marriage: those childless married women who are too old for childbearing, childless widows, or a childless wife unable to conceive (1979; see also Talbot [1926], 1969 and Oboler, 1980). Finally, Leakey asserts that among the Gikuyu it is childless widows beyond childbearing age who marry women in order to continue their husbands' lineages ([1938] 1977).

Leakey's description of Gikuyu woman–woman marriage practices encompasses all three generalizations ([1938] 1977). He claims that woman–woman marriages occur when a man leaves property to a widow beyond childbearing age, when no other male inheritor is present (such as a brother, half-brother, son). This widow is then expected to marry a woman who would bear her a son with the help of a designated genitor, who has no rights over the children or property.

By offering such a narrow scenario, Leakey denies flexibility and variation regarding the circumstances under which Gikuyu woman–woman marriages take place. Positing such limited "rules" for woman–woman marriages can be hazardous not only when applied across cultures, but also when applied *within* a single culture or locale, as our Gikuyu examples demonstrate. Gikuyu women in our relatively small study sample, living within a very proscribed spatial setting, expressed multiple and heterogeneous reasons for marrying women, defying the circumscribed explanations provided by Leakey, as well as others across the African continent. The women initiating these marriages pursued various objectives: companionship to appease loneliness, to be remembered after death, to have children to increase the vibrancy of the household, to fulfill social obligations in accordance with indigenous spiritual beliefs, and not least to avoid direct domination by male partners in a strongly patriarchal society, including men's control of both the women's behavior and household finances.

Our study does not deny the inability to bear children, inheritance, or lineage as partial explanations for some, or even many, Gikuyu woman–woman marriages. Expressed reasons for marrying women in our study *did* often include the desire for the *muhikania* to have a child to inherit property and/or to perpetuate her family lineage. However, such explanations are never offered as the exclusive reasons, nor are they offered by all women. Such women appear to have much greater latitude in choosing how and why they participate in woman–woman marriages. For example, situations that defy Leakey's account include those in which women who are already married to men (who are still alive) and have their own children then initiate *uhiki*, or marriage, with a woman, as in the above described case of Kuhi (married to Wamba).

Mbura's explanation for *kuhikia*, or marrying a woman superficially resembles Leakey's account, since she expresses a desire for children that she herself cannot bear, as indicated in the following statement:

> I married Nimu because I could never have children myself. I did not even give birth to children who later died, nor did I experience any miscarriage. I remained the way I came out of my mother's womb. And now I'm getting old and there is no way I can sit, think and decide to have a baby because my time is over, unless *Ngai's* [God's] miracle happens to me [she laughs].[11] I think a lot about how my husband left me and how I can't have a baby. That is why a cry of a baby makes me happy and sad at the same time. One has to realize how special a child is. . . . So, when I think about all these things: how I can't have a child, how my husband died and left me nothing, and how I have this illness, I ask *Ngai wenda mdathima na mutumia ungi* [God, please bless me with another woman]. . . . "Won't you please send that woman here to my home." Who knows, that woman might . . . give me a child. . . . Don't you see when I die I will be satisfied that I have left somebody in that home, who shall continue and revive that home? (in interview)

While she seems to portray a conventional account—marrying a woman to have a child to continue a lineage—Mbura's explanation is more complicated, indicating a desire for children beyond their role as inheritors of land and name. This is not to suggest, however, that lineage is not important in Mbura's decision to marry a woman. But the lineage she seeks to perpetuate is not necessarily her husband's, as Leakey and others would argue. Rather, Mbura is most interested in being remembered herself, as she indicates in the following statement:

> If I were to die even as we speak, that would be the end of it. I would be completely forgotten. No one would ever mention my name. That is simply because

> there would be no one to carry on my name. Since my husband died he is still remembered by many. But the key reason why he is still remembered is because of me. Someone may pass through here and demand to know "Whose home is that?" Then turn around and ask, "What about the next one?" One would reply, "Did you know so and so? This is his wife's home." Now do you see that the reason he is being remembered is because of me? Because I can be seen. But if I were to die, who will make me be remembered?...That is why the idea of marrying another woman came to me. Even now as we speak, if *Ngai* would bless me with another woman I would appreciate her.

Mbura continues, suggesting that companionship to appease loneliness is another strong motivation for marrying a woman:

> Let me tell you, I'm not the only one or the first one to marry a woman. And certainly, there are many others out there like me. I'm all alone just like that. No husband, no child. Just poor me. No one is here to keep me company or even to ask me "Did you sleep well?," except for occasional visits by some people like those you met here the other day. (in interview)

While Leakey's explanation may partly account for Mbura's case, Nduta's case clearly has emerged under a set of circumstances not fully considered by Leakey. First of all, Nduta's decision is the result of women's collaboration, namely between Nduta and her mother-in-law. Nduta married a man named Ndungu with whom she had three sons and a daughter. However, early in their marriage, her husband and their three sons were poisoned to death by some people in her husband's clan who wanted their land. After their deaths, Nduta's mother-in-law advised her to marry a woman as a way of protecting their family and land from male relatives who were trying to take her land, a sign of the tenuous hold that women have over land in Gikuyu society (Mackenzie, 1990). Rather than being victimized by men within their family, Nduta's case shows how women collaborate to look out for one another to protect women's interests:

> When a woman is left alone, she should not be frightened, but must be brave. You must make yourself a queen, otherwise, be a coward and everything you stand for will be taken away from you by those who are hungry for what you have.... If you were a woman, and you had properties, you will be the first one to be stolen from by the men who thought they were more important than women. So, she must act....I had a lot of properties and if it were not for *karamu* [the "pen"] that cheated me out of many of them, I would still have a lot.[12] I lost many of them because I was a woman and I had no sons. So, my mother-in- law advised me to marry my own woman because all my people had been finished [i.e., killed] except for my daughter. And that is the piece of advice that I myself chose to follow. So I married her. When I married her [Ciru], she said "It is better to live with a woman. I'm tired of men." I responded, "Is that so?! I love that." We became good friends and partners and thereafter I gave *ruracio* to her family. (in interview)

Mackenzie, in discussing gender and land rights in Murang'a District, also describes woman–woman marriage as a strategy for Gikuyu women to prevent male relatives from stealing land from them (1990). She suggests that such women who marry other women appropriate custom as a source of legitimation, attempting to manipulate customary tenure rules to their advantage. Gikuyu land tenure is complex, given the coexistence of customary and state rules. Customary tenure in Murang'a District is based on the *mbari*, or sub-clan system in which local *mbari* elders control and allocate use rights to land. While during the 1950s and 1960s, colonial and independent governments implemented a system of individual land ownership, individual title did not fully supplant the *mbari* system. Both tenure systems are utilized based upon circumstance and interests, and are often manipulated to the advantage of men and detriment of women (Mackenzie, 1990).

Compared to both Nduta's case and Mbura's, Mackenzie discusses a woman (referred to as "WG") who, "being without sons, chose to 'marry' a woman on her husband's death to prevent her brother-in-law from snatching their holding of 5.6 ha" (1990: 624). Mackenzie's account acknowledges these women as agents who are able to resist the strong patriarchal tendencies of their society. However, despite this important contribution, Mackenzie's brief account describes the circumstances of woman–woman marriages largely in terms provided by Leakey, limiting the option to widows who marry women to provide male inheritors. Thus, Mackenzie does not present other factors expressed by our interviewees, such as Mbura's emphasis on loneliness, desire for children, and a wish to live in a vibrant household.

While Nduta does not claim loneliness as a factor in her decision, her explanation also diverges somewhat from Mackenzie's, as well as Leakey's, scenario. Nduta's case is similar to Mackenzie's and Leakey's images of woman–woman marriage presented by those authors in that she had been married to a man who died and she had no sons (they died as well). However, upon marrying a woman after her husband's death, she asserts that she could have passed her land to her daughter, Ceke. Indeed, Ceke was given half of Nduta's land. While Nduta explained that she could have left all of her land to Ceke, she decided against doing so because she did not want to constrain her daughter with the social expectations that "staying at home" entails:

> ... I didn't want my daughter, Ceke, to stay here. I gave her freedom to fly and land wherever she wanted. That is the same freedom that brought me here. So why would I want to hold her here? Women like to go far. They don't like to be held down at their birth home. (in interview)

While the issue of inheritance is important in Nduta's case, related to her difficult struggle as a woman to maintain control over land resources, Nduta adds an important dimension drawn from Gikuyu mythology. This reason becomes clear when we hear Nduta, who is about 90 years old, speak of her dead sons who, she says, visit her in her sleep to thank her for marrying a woman:

> *Roho wa anake akwa makwrire* [the spirits of my dead sons] come to visit me to show appreciation for what I have done for them. One time they came and told me, "Thank you, mother for marrying Ciru for us. We are very grateful for bringing us dead people back home again. We are grateful indeed. For that we will always be watching over you. Nothing will ever harm you. We will take care of you." And then I would say, "If I didn't marry Ciru for them, who else would I have married her for?" Then the other day they came to tell me that I have got only five years to live; that I'm going to die soon [she laughs hard]. I said, "Is that so? Thanks a lot and may *Ngai* be praised!" That is fine for me. I need rest. (in interview)

Nduta's sons died long ago, very young, and had not been able to accomplish much in their lives. Some Gikuyu still believe that if someone dies suddenly, his or her life activities can be carried out as if they are still alive so that their opportunities would not be denied. Thus, when their mother married Ciru, she married her in the same way her sons would have married had they lived. In this sense, even though these sons were already dead, they feel quite at home because of Ciru's presence.

While Nduta's and Mbura's cases push the limits of Leakey's narrow inheritance-focused account of woman–woman marriage, the case of Nduta's daughter, Ceke, falls largely outside the scope of his scenario. Ceke's decision to marry a woman appears to be heavily influenced by the example set by her mother, who acted as a role model. However, unlike her mother she was at the same time still married and living with her husband, Ngigi, together with her daughter, Wahu, along with Wahu's six children. Having grown attached to Wahu's children, Ceke was insecure about whether Wahu would move away with them, leaving Ceke in a household without children. Ceke's marriage to a woman (Ngware) was thus viewed as a way Ceke could have more children. Ceke's intention was that her wife, Ngware, would have children with her husband, Ngigi. After having a child, however, Ngware left the household. Ceke and Wahu (her daughter) then reached an agreement that the children would be welcome to remain with Ceke even if Wahu decides to leave:

> Although my daughter was living with me at the time, and had all these children that you see here, I did not know what to expect from her. I did not know whether one day I will wake up and find her gone with all her children that I personally have raised and who actually call me *maitu* [mother], or whether she had already made up her mind that she will never leave. I made that move of wanting to find out when my wife [Ngware] left us. After that, my husband and I made an agreement with Wahu that she will live with us permanently and that if she will ever feel like leaving, her children that we have raised as our own will be welcome to remain with us where they are already guaranteed good care as well as land settlement when they grow up. In any case, this is her land too, you know. Since we have got no other children, everything we have belongs to her and her children and to my other son borne by my wife before she left. (in interview)

While this example supports the general claim that women marry women to acquire rights over childbearing capacity (Sudarkasa [1986], 1989), Ceke's decision is not linked to property inheritance, "barrenness," or widowhood: the three essential criteria for a Gikuyu woman–woman marriage, according to Leakey. Like Mbura, Ceke's strong desire for children was an important factor in her decision. The option of woman–woman marriage as a means to fulfill this desire was immediately apparent, given the influence and example of her mother, Nduta.

Finally, we have already alluded to the more overtly political motivations for marrying women expressed by some of our interviewees. The relative freedom from male control, which appears to be built into Gikuyu woman–woman marriages, is expressed most forcefully by Ciru and Nduta in previous quotations. Recall, for example, Nduta's conversation with her then wife-to-be, Ciru, who commented, "I'm tired of men," to which Nduta responded, "I love that." And Nduta's comment about why she doesn't live with a man, stating "What for? To make me miserable?" Recall also these women's comments regarding the sexual freedom they find in these relationships. And finally, recall the opening quote in which Ciru states that her woman–woman marriage allows her to avoid having "a man telling me what to do."

These examples demonstrate that flexibility, heterogeneity, and ambiguity appear as guiding principles in explaining such marriages, rather than being governed by somewhat rigid social rules, as the literature so often implies. However, contributions to the woman–woman marriage literature have continually, since the early-twentieth century, presented these relationships in functionalist terms. Cheal suggests that functionalist explanations continue to be perceived as having a "subterranean" influence on the study of families, describing such relationships in terms of "the ways in which they meet society's needs for the continuous replacement of its members" (1991: 4). Our alternative has been to present the institution of woman–woman marriage, at least in the Gikuyu context, as a flexible option available to women within which they may pursue any number of interests: political, social, economic, and personal.

WHAT'S IN A NAME? RETHINKING THE "FEMALE HUSBAND"

Another area of concern for us in the literature is the unquestioned use of the term "female husband," the general term used to describe women who initiate woman–woman marriages. Mackenzie (1990), in the above section, uses the term to describe such women in the Gikuyu context, as did Leakey ([1938] 1977) many decades earlier. Regarding the Nandi in Kenya, Oboler defines the term "female husband" as the woman who initiates the woman–woman marriage, as a woman "who pays bridewealth for, and thus marries (but does not have sexual intercourse with) another woman, and by doing so, becomes the social and legal father of her wife's children" (1980: 69). Evans-Pritchard

(1951), Herskovits (1937), and Seligman and Seligman ([1932] 1965) all connect the female husband to these gendered characteristics. More recently, Oboler opens her paper with a quote from one of her female informants:

> No, I don't [carry things on my head]. That is a woman's duty and nothing to do with me. I became a man and I am a man and that is that. Why should I assume women's work anymore? (1980: 69)

Oboler argues that among the Nandi, male and female sex-roles are so strictly divided, especially regarding property management issues, that female husbands are literally defined by others and themselves as men in order to resolve the sex-role contradiction.

Not surprisingly, the major debate regarding the term "female husband" is over the male social traits often attributed to such women. Some have criticized the emphasis placed on gendered assumptions regarding sex-roles. For example, Krige suggests that one cannot assume that female husbands generally are taking on male roles (1974). Rather, one must carefully study sex roles in particular societies. For the Lovedu, Krige points out that numerous roles involve both males and females. Oyěwùmí, writing about the Yoruba, argues that local terms for both "husband" and "wife" are not gender-specific since both males and females can be husbands or wives (1994). As a result, as Burton (1979: 69) contends, the assumption that "husband" and "male" are automatically connected "confounds roles with people" since "husband" is a role that can be carried out by women as well as by men. Amadiume (1987), Burton (1979), Krige (1974), Oyěwùmí (1994), and Sudarkasa (1986) all suggest that in many societies, "masculinity" and "femininity" are not as clearly defined categories as they are in the West; presuming that "husband" automatically connotes "male" and that "wife" connotes "female" imposes western sex-role presumptions on other societies, ignoring local ambiguity regarding these roles (Sudarkasa [1986], 1989).

While our study supports views that women initiating marriages are not characterized as "male," we question the continued use of the term "female husband" to describe such women. Burton (1979), Krige (1974), and Sudarkasa (1986), while criticizing those who confuse social roles with genders, implicity suggest that the term "female husband" is adequate and that the only task is to transform its connotative meaning.

We argue that the term "female husband" should be reconsidered on the grounds that the male connotation of "husband" cannot be so easily disposed of; just as the term "wife" conjures an association with "female," so does "husband" with "male." Especially in contexts where gender roles are ambiguous, this implicit association will easily mislead readers to impose western presumptions upon woman–woman marriages. Thus, in our view, efforts to theoretically disassociate gender from such role-centered terms—like "husband" and "wife" in this instance—imposed originally by western researchers in colonial contexts, will in a practical way continue to impose a male/female dichotomy.

Some early colonial-era ethnographers might be interpreted as ambivalent and uncomfortable in the application of the term "female husband." Talbot ([1926] 1969) and Herskovits, for example, both write the concept as *female "husband"* (1937). That approach to the term "husband" (in quotes) seems to acknowledge that the term applies only imprecisely, even problematically, to women who initiate marriages to women, and is used only for lack of a more appropriate term. Others' use of the term, such as that of Evans-Pritchard (1945; 1951) and Leakey ([1938] 1977), shed the ambivalence of previous ethnographers, thereby legitimizing the term *female husband* as a concept for use by future researchers.

For most, however, the male connotation of the term was with little doubt intended in most early writings, given the apparently widespread presumption of male identification with the roles of such women. The functionalist perspectives of the times presumed a clear, gendered division of roles in family settings, making it difficult to apply any concept but "husband" to what appeared to them as the dominant role in these relationships. We acknowledge that there is nothing essential about the term "husband" that necessitates domination and control. But we also acknowledge, as does Oyěwùmí, that historically the term "husband" in most western contexts is normally associated with the role of "breadwinner," "decision-maker," and "head of household" (1994). We feel that the use of the term "female husband" serves to mask the relatively egalitarian woman–woman marriage relationships we encountered. Sudarkasa even acknowledges that, generally, there is no necessary subordination in woman–woman marriages, and that in many societies many aspects of decision-making and control over resources are parallel and complementary (1986).

The relative absence of domination, for example, is evident in the terms the women used to describe one another. The women interviewed never used the Gikuyu term for "husband" *(muthuri)* to describe their partners. Instead, they consistently referred to each other using the terms *mutumia wakwa* and *muka wakwa*, which when used by these women translates as "co-wife," or *muiru wakwa*, which translates as "partner in marriage," indicating the mutual respect and relative equality between them. While most women in our study who initiate the marriages tended to be women with social influence and/or relatively greater material wealth, within the marriages both women interpreted their relationship as semiotically and materially equal.

Furthermore, women in our study rejected any male-association with their position of initiator of the marriage. None of the women interviewed indicated that they aspired to be like "males." What follows is Nduta's perception of herself in relation to the seeming "maleness" of her marital position:

> I stayed at Nairobi for three weeks at my daughter's house, and when I came back they were joyfully shouting "She is back!" And because I brought them bread just like other men who work in the city do around here, the children started shouting, "Here comes our *baba* [father]! Our *baba* has arrived! Our

> *baba* has arrived!" (she laughs). I called them *ndungana ici*.[13] "Who told you that I am your *baba*?" (she laughs again). So I asked them, "Is that what you see me as? I'm not your *baba*. But thank you for appreciating that I can also bring bread home." Therefore, even when you see me quarrel with them sometimes, I don't store those quarrels in my heart. I brought this family together not to destroy it but to care for it. (in interview)

Nduta is being teased by her children, who called her *baba*, because of the bread she brought from the city, just as men with urban jobs do when they visit their rural homes, not because her position as initiator of the marriage automatically connotes male characteristics.

As a tentative alternative to "female husband" we have been using the phrase "marriage initiator" to describe women in that position. However, we acknowledge that such description can be problematic, especially if it is used to focus more attention on the "initiator" at the expense of the agency of the one "initiated" into the marriage. We also acknowledge that descriptions of such concepts will differ from one culture to another.

Avenues for Future Research and Conclusions

This article addresses the neglected topic of woman–woman marriages in Africa, relying upon Gikuyu women to speak about issues that have lain dormant for a number of years. Our effort has been to challenge researchers on the topic to rethink the ways in which such relationships have been represented up to this point.

Future research must rely more heavily on the voices of Gikuyu women to investigate this subject, not necessarily as a "better" and "authentic" way to tell these women's stories, but also as a constant reminder that these women have typically not had opportunities to speak and tell their own stories. Research must become sensitized to the idea that local voices relate the complexities, ambiguities, and heterogeneity involved in practices of woman–woman marriage, and in the analysis of how these practices take place and how the women involved perceive them. We do not suggest that because these Gikuyu examples suggest flexibility, ambiguity, and heterogeneity that all African woman–woman marriages are the same. Rather, we raise the possibility that earlier explanations import assumptions that obscure different interpretations.

A number of issues regarding Gikuyu woman–woman marriage remain. Our study did not investigate, for example, the prevalence of such marriages among the Gikuyu. Early in the twentieth century, Leakey simply stated that such relationships were "not uncommon," while our own sampling in the early-1990s (perhaps surprisingly) uncovered eight households within a small locale ([1938] 1977). A census of these households might show woman–woman marriages to be more common and persistent than the silence in the literature would imply. Oboler's survey among a Nandi community in Kenya's Rift Valley suggested that three percent of households contained woman–woman marriages (1980). However, her small sample does not necessarily mean that this rate of woman–woman marriages is the same for Nandi society generally nor does it say much of anything about other societies containing woman–woman marriages.

Another issue that needs further exploration is the emergence and transformation of Gikuyu woman–woman marriages during the 500 year history of the Gikuyu. Muriuki offers evidence that the matriarchal origins of Gikuyu society had been superseded by patrilineal and patrilocal social and political organization by the mid-seventeenth century (1974). It is certainly not clear, but perhaps Gikuyu woman–woman marriage is a remnant of a matriarchal past. While nothing has been written of origins, more recent twentieth-century social transformations have without doubt profoundly impacted practices of woman–woman marriage. As with other indigenous practices, Christian churches have severely and unfairly questioned the morality of woman–woman marriages, and have, in turn, shaped public opinion. For example, recent baptism guidelines from the Catholic Church in Kenya include their policy on, in their words, "woman who 'marry' other women."

> In regard to this traditional practice, the first step is to insist that this arrangement be given up completely and that meantime [sic] all those involved, plus any other persons directly responsible for the arrangement, be denied the sacraments. After the women have separated completely, each one will be helped separately and any infants will be baptised. (Kenya Catholic Bishops, 1991: 21)

Such official condemnation impacts public perception by suggesting that such marriages represent an affront to Christian values.[14] To our knowledge, no opinion poll has been conducted among the Gikuyu, a predominantly Christian ethnic group, which might give a clear indication of public attitudes. Such a poll has been conducted in Nigeria, where Okonjo suggests that 93.5 percent of 246 Igbo women surveyed disapproved of woman–woman marriage, a perception undoubtedly influenced by decades of Church Pressures (1992). Similar disapproval in our study locale might be evident in that at least some households appear to face a certain amount of open hostility coming mostly in the form of teasing. For example, Nduta complains about the teasing she sometimes endures from neighbors, some of whom refer to her as a "man" (*muthuri*) simply because she is married to a woman:

> ... for these people laugh at me saying that I am a man. I'm not a man. I'm neither a man nor a woman. That is who I am, like a decent being. So I tell them. I have to be strong. Well, I'm not a man. (in interview)

Perhaps twentieth-century social changes, which have seriously dislocated, though not completely eliminated many indigenous institutions, fosters an ambivalence toward woman–woman marriage as a practice that is simultaneously acceptable, yet also incurs hostility. The acceptability of woman–woman marriages is evident in the fact that despite some hostility, these Gikuyu woman–woman marriages are in no way secretive or hidden. All of the women in the study underwent a marriage ceremony to affirm their relationships, a ceremony no different than that for an opposite sex, indigenous (i.e., non-Christian) Gikuyu marriage. Like other marriages, woman–woman marriages are facilitated by clan elders from both women's families (rather than priests or ministers), and involve an exchange of gifts between both families as well as dances and food. Such marriages are clearly not "underground" in any way.

Silence among feminists regarding the issue of woman–woman marriages is another issue. By now, it has been well documented that well-meaning feminists from western contexts have often represented "Third World women" in problematic ways. A common view is that of a linear women's emancipation, suggesting that societies have moved through evolutionary stages from women's oppression toward liberation, with western feminists having made the greatest progress and "Third World women" still mired in more overt forms of oppression. As a result, Third World women, a problematic category in itself, are often described by feminists "in terms of the underdevelopment, oppressive traditions, high illiteracy, rural and urban poverty, religious fanaticism, and 'overpopulation'" that appear to rule their lives in relation to those in the relatively liberated West (Mohanty, 1991: 5). Such a linear view ignores what in many cases are long histories of women's empowerment and resistance, demonstrated here by woman–woman marriages.

By marrying women, these Gikuyu women are clearly radically disrupting the male domination that operates in their everyday lives. Their stories may begin with land and struggles over material resources, but they are also stories of love, commitment, children, sexual freedom, vulnerability, and empowerment. The "implosion" of all these things makes these women's stories unique and all the more compelling to feminists who are constantly searching for unique practices of feminism that resemble, but are not engineered by, western feminism (Haraway, 1997).

NOTES

1. "Gikuyu" is the indigenous spelling of what is commonly referred to as "Kikuyu."
2. Other terms include "woman-marriage" and "woman-to-woman marriage."
3. Moreover, he apparently did not even get his information on the topic from women involved in such relationships. Discussing his data-collection strategy, Leakey indicates that he relied solely upon male informants to learn about the topics discussed, presumably including woman–woman marriages.
4. The names of interviewees have been changed to protect their identities.
5. This research was originally part of a graduate thesis project in Family Studies. The interviews took place between May and August of 1992.
6. Note that multiple Gikuyu terms seem to describe the same concept. Choice of term depends upon the context in which the concept is employed. For example, while "marriage initiator" in one context is expressed as *muhikania*, the plural form of the concept is *ahikania*.

7. It is important to acknowledge that in most cases polygynous marriages among the Gikuyu come as a result of negotiation between the first wives and husbands.
8. While the sexuality of the women involved in woman–woman marriages is clearly one of the most interesting unresolved issues on the topic, the Human Subjects Review Board reviewing the research proposal decided that the topic was too sensitive, and therefore declared such questions off limits.
9. Interviews were conducted in the Gikuyu language and were translated by the primary author.
10. *Miario miuru*, or "negative talk," that is mentioned by Ciru in this quotation points to fundamental changes that have occurred in Gikuyu society over the course of the twentieth century with colonialist religious and educational training. These changes are reflected in complex local attitudes toward indigenous practices and are discussed briefly in the last section of this paper.
11. *Ngai* commonly translates as "God," although the Gikuyu term carries no gendered connotation.
12. *Karamu*, or "the pen," refers to the use of title deeds (by those who could read and write—mainly men) that conferred private ownership of property since the 1960s. This private ownership was started under colonial rule and undermined (though it did not eliminate completely) more customary land tenure rules (Mackenzie, 1990).
13. *Ndungana ici* is a derogatory term that translates most benignly as "You Stink!" However, the term also has sexual connotations, and is only used by elders to criticize misbehavior of younger people.
14. Related to condemnations of woman–woman marriage practices are official condemnations of homosexuality as expressed in recent homophobic statements by Presidents Moi of Kenya, Museveni of Uganda, and Mugabe of Zimbabwe, who referred to homosexuals and homosexual practices in terms such as "scourge," "abominable acts," and "lower than pigs and dogs" respectively. Some in Africa argue that the lack of local African terms for "homosexual" is evidence that homosexuality is foreign to Africa. However, in the Gikuyu language there is no term for "heterosexual" either. Should this be taken as evidence that sexual relationships between women and men do not exist? Among the Gikuyu, male-to-male sexual contact is traditionally prohibited; but prohibition suggests to us that such practices are already in place.

REFERENCES

Ainsworth, Mary D. Salter. 1967. *Infancy in Uganda: Infant Care and the Growth of Love*. Baltimore, MD: Johns Hopkins University.

Albert, Ethel M. 1971. "Women of Burundi: A Study of Social Values." In *Women of Tropical Africa*, ed. D. Paulme. Los Angeles: University of California Press.

Amadiume, lfe. 1987. *Male Daughters and Female Husbands: Gender and Sex in an African Society*. London: Zed Press.

Beeson, R. W. 1990. "The Clinical Distribution of Family Systems." *International Journal of Contemporary Sociology* 27: 89–127.

Burton, Clare. 1979. "Woman-Marriage in Africa: A Critical Study for Sex-Role Theory?" *Australian and New Zealand Journal of Sociology* 15(2): 65–71.

Carrier, Joe. 1980. "Some Comments on Woman/Woman Marriage in Africa." *Anthropological Research Group on Homosexuality Newsletter* 2(3): 2–4.

Cheal, David. 1991. *Family and the State of Theory*. Toronto, Canada: University of Toronto Press.

Davis, D. L., and R. G. Whitten. 1987. "The Cross-Cultural Study of Human Sexuality." *Annual Review of Anthropology* 16: 69–98.

Evans-Pritchard, E. E. 1945. *Some Aspects of Marriage and the Family Among the Nuer*. Livingstone, Northern Rhodesia: The Rhodes-Livingstone Institute.

——. 1951. *Kinship and Marriage Among the Nuer*. Oxford, UK: Clarendon Press.

Haraway, Donna. 1997. *Modest Witness@Second Millennium. FemaleMan Meets OncoMouse: Feminism and Technoscience*. New York: Routledge.

Herskovits, Melville J. 1937. "A Note on Woman Marriage in Dahomey." *Africa* 2–3: 335–41.

Kenya Catholic Bishops. 1991. *Guidelines for the Celebration of the Sacrament of Baptism for Infants and Special Cases*. Nairobi, Kenya: St. Paul Publications.

Kilbride, Philip Levey and Janet Capriotti Kilbride. 1990. *Changing Family Life in East Africa: Women and Children at Risk*. University Park: The Pennsylvania State University Press.

Krige, Eileen Jensen. 1974. "Woman-Marriage, With Special Reference to the Lovedu—Its Significance for the Definition of Marriage." *Africa* 44: 11–37.

Langley, Myrtle S. 1979. *The Nandi of Kenya: Life Crisis Rituals in a Period of Change*. London: C. Hurst and Company.

Leakey, Louis S. B. (1938) 1977. *The Southern Kikuyu Before 1903*. New York: Academic Press.

Le Vine, R. 1970. "Personality and Change." In *The African Experience*, Vol 1, eds. J. N. Paden and E. W. Soja. Evanston, IL: Northwestern University Press.

Mackenzie, Fiona. 1990. "Gender and Land Rights in Murang'a District, Kenya." *The Journal of Peasant Studies* 17: 609–43.

Malinowski, Bronislaw. 1930. "Parenthood, the Basis of Social Order." In *The New Generation*, ed. Calverton and Schmalhousen, 113–68. New York: Macauley Co.

Martin, Biddy. 1992. "Sexual Practice and Changing Lesbian Identities." In *Destabilizing Theory: Contemporary Feminist Debates*, eds. M. Barrett and A. Phillips, 93–119. Palo Alto, CA: Stanford University Press.

Mohanty, Chandra T. 1991. "Under Western Eyes: Feminist Scholarship and Colonial Discourses." In *Third World Women and the Politics of Feminism*, eds. C. T. Mohanty, A. Russo, and L. Torres, 51–80. Bloomington: Indiana University Press.

Muriuki, Godfrey. 1974. *A History of the Kikuyu 1500–1900*. New York: Oxford University Press.

Obbo, Christine. 1976. "Dominant Male Ideology and Female Options: Three East African Case Studies." *Africa* 46(4): 371–89.

Oboler, Regina Smith. 1980. "Is the Female Husband a Man? Woman/Woman Marriage Among the Nandi of Kenya." *Ethnology* 19: 69–88.

O'Brien, Denise. 1977. "Female Husbands in Southern Bantu Societies." In *Sexual Stratification: A Cross-Cultural View*, ed. A. Schlegel, 109–26. New York: Columbia University Press.

Okonjo, Kamene. 1992. "Aspects of Continuity and Change in Mate Selection Among the Igbo West of the Niger River." *Journal of Comparative Family Studies* 23: 339–60.

Oyěwùmí, Oyèrónké. 1994. "Inventing Gender: Questioning Gender in Precolonial Yorubaland." In *Problems in African History: The Precolonial Centuries*, eds. R. Collins *et al.*, 244–50. New York: Marcus Wiener Publishing, Inc.

Riviere, Peter G. 1971. "Marriage: A Reassessment." In *Rethinking Kinship and Marriage*. A.S.A. Monographs, No. 11, ed. R. Needham. London: Tavistock Publications.

Scanzoni, John, Karen Polonko, Jay Teachman, and Linda Thompson. 1989. *The Sexual Bond: Rethinking Families and Close Relationships*. Newbury Park, CA: Sage.

Seligman, C. G. and B. Z. Seligman. (1932) 1965. *Pagan Tribes of the Nilotic Sudan*. London: Routledge and Kegan Paul.

Skolnick, Arlene S., and Jerome H. Skolnick. 1989. "Introduction: Family in Transition." In *Families in Transition*, 6th ed., eds. A. S. Skolnick and J. H. Skolnick, 1–18. Boston: Scott, Foresman and Company.

Smith, Dorothy E. 1987. *The Everyday World As Problematic: A Feminist Sociology*. Boston: Northeastern University Press.

Sudarkasa, Niara. (1986) 1989. "The Status of Women' in Indigenous African Societies." In *Feminist Frontiers II: Rethinking Sex, Gender, and Society*, eds. L. Richardson and V. Taylor, 152–58. New York: McGraw-Hill, Inc.

Talbot, Percy A. (1926) 1969. *The Peoples of Southern Nigeria*. London: Cass.

Section IV

Gender Biases in the Making of History

Feminist researchers have identified the male-bias in the constitution of knowledge, especially historical knowledge. They have not only exposed the dominance of political history in organizing the field but have also called attention to the invisibility of women in historical writings. Consequently, feminist historians have developed a new subfield called women's history even as they advocate the use of gender as an analytical category in the study of any historical subject.

Oyèrónké Oyěwùmí, in her contribution "Making History, Creating Gender: Some Methodological and Interpretive Questions in the Writing of Oyo Oral Traditions," goes beyond the issue of gender bias in the constitution of history by questioning whether in the long duration of African history we can assume gender categories and treat men and women as timeless social identity groups. She demonstrates the connections between Eurocentric bias and male bias documented in African historical writing.

In his paper "Gender Biases in African Historiography," Paul Tiyambe Zeleza takes up the feminist call for the gendering of history and does a systematic accounting of the role of gender in the writing of African history. He then goes on to look at the different ways in which historians attempt to redress this gender bias and to reconstruct African history, particularly women's history.

The essay "Senegalese Women in Politics: A Portrait of Two Female Leaders," by Babacar Fall documents the career of two women politicians. It is a work of contemporary political history, which uses oral sources to reconstruct the pioneering political contribution of Arame Diene and Thioumbe Samb in the face of class and gender discrimination and marginalization. The paper demonstrates that a full understanding of Senegalese politics during this period is impossible if historical writing remains androcentric, and limits itself to only male subjects who are literate in colonial languages.

CHAPTER 10

MAKING HISTORY, CREATING GENDER: SOME METHODOLOGICAL AND INTERPRETIVE QUESTIONS IN THE WRITING OF OYO ORAL TRADITIONS[1]

Oyèrónké Oyěwùmí

I

Of all the things that were produced in Africa during the colonial period—cash crops, states, and tribes, to name a few—history and tradition are the least acknowledged as products of the colonial situation. This does not mean that Africans did not have history before the white man came. Rather, I am making distinctions among the following: firstly, history as lived experience; secondly, history as a record of lived experience which is coded in the oral traditions; and finally, the recently constituted written history. This last category is very much tied up with European engagements with Africa and the introduction of "history writing" as a discipline and as profession. But even then, it is important to acknowledge the fact that African history, including oral traditions, were recorded as a result of the European assault.

This underscores the fact that ideological interests were at work in the making of African history, as is true of all history. As such, tradition is constantly being reinvented to reflect these interests. A. I. Asiwaju, for example, in a paper examining the political motivations and manipulations of oral tradition in the constitution of Obaship in different parts of Yorubaland during the colonial period writes: "in the era of European rule, particularly British rule, when government often based most of its decisions over local claims upon the evidence of traditional history, a good proportion of the data tended to be manipulated deliberately."[2] This process of manipulation produced examples of what he wittily refers to as "*nouveaux rois* of Yorubaland."[3]

Since the colonial period, the way in which Yoruba history is being reconstituted has been a process of inventing gendered traditions. Men and women have been invented as social categories, and history is presented as being dominated by male actors. Female actors are virtually absent and where they are recognized, they are reduced to exceptions. Bolanle Awe makes a similar observation when she writes that piecing together "women's history" has been difficult because of "the dearth of information [about women's achievements], particularly documentary evidence, that some outstanding women in history have been mistaken for men and their achievements, attributed to male rulers!"[4] In an earlier paper Awe alluded to a distinction between African historiography, with its male bias and African oral traditions, which are inclusive of all segments of the population.

My own concern is not with "women's history," *per se*. Rather, the focus, more fundamentally, is to question the historicity of the gendered interpretation of Oyo oral traditions in the work of many contemporary historians. The goal is to draw attention to the fact that writing Yoruba history has been a process of gender attribution in which kings and men have been created from oral traditions which were originally free of gender categories. Elsewhere I have shown that gender-based social categories, be they kinship or occupational designations, are absent in the indigenous conception.[5] Instead, the differences coded in the Yoruba frame of reference were age-based; thus seniority, not gender, was the language of status.

In order to trace and account for the process of genderizing Yoruba history and political institutions, I interrogate the work of Samuel Johnson, the pioneering historian of the Yoruba, and other writers who have touched on the question of gender in Oyo historiography.[6] Issues about language, the collection and cultural translation of oral traditions, the transmission of knowledge, and the social identity of historians will be addressed. In the first part of the paper, I interrogate specifically the dynastic lists of *alaafin* (rulers) that have been presented by various local and foreign recorders of the past. These lists purport to show that male rulers were the norm, and that any females among them were exceptions. The question posed is this: given the non-gender-specificity of Oyo names, pronouns, and social categories, how have historians deciphered the gender of all the *alaafin* on the lists?

Put another way, considering the difficulty of identifying anatomical sex at a spatial and temporal distance in Yoruba language, how were the "recorders" of these lists able to identify particular rulers as male, especially those who ruled before the nineteenth century, a period in which there were no written eyewitness accounts? N. A. Fadipe, the Yoruba sociologist, noted one important aspect of the problem of deciphering sex in Yoruba language at a spatial and temporal distance from the subject: the "introduction of the third person singular personal pronoun *o* into a passage of written Yoruba, in which persons and things of various genders have previously been mentioned, is apt to prove irritating... because *o* may mean he, she, or it."[7]

Despite this "problem," a survey of the documentation of Oyo history shows that all the categories that were gender-free have now become gendered and male-specific.[8] *Omo* (offspring) have been turned into sons, aburo/egbon (siblings) into brothers, *alaafin* and *oba* into male rulers popularly known as kings (gendered male). Having been reduced to exceptions, females occupying thrones have been routinely demoted to regents. How do we account for this process of genderization which is ultimately a patriachalization of Oyo history?

II

The story of the publication of the Reverend Samuel Johnson's *The History of the Yorubas* is fascinating in itself, though there is no space to tell it here. Suffice it to say that even though the original manuscript had been completed in 1897, it was not published until 1921. Johnson was a Yoruba, a Saro, whose legacy to his people was a documentation of their history.[9] There is no question that his motive for writing was nationalistic and his role in the documentation of Yoruba history cannot be overstated. Robin Law, a historian of the Oyo empire, asserts that:

> The historical traditions of Oyo did not constitute a history of Oyo, until put together for this purpose by a literate historian such as Johnson. In an oral society, there is not so much a traditional history as a range of historical traditions, each tradition (or at least each group of traditions) with its own function and institutional context.[10]

Although one could not disagree with Law's pronouncement on Johnson's seminal role in constituting the historiography, from the perspective of the Yoruba the various *itan* (narratives) and information encoded in *oriki* (praise poetry) constitutes their account of the past with or without Johnson's intervention. It must be emphasized that the late realization in postmodern Western historical traditions that points of view are implicated in historical documentation, and that historical facts at any given point in time are a result of contestation, is not new but have always been factors that are taken into account in the presentation of Yoruba historical traditions. *Itan* and *oriki* are critically deployed in Yorubaland with their perspectival role in mind.

The Reverend's influence on Yoruba historiography cannot be overestimated, either at the level of written history or oral traditions. In fact his work is being reabsorbed into Yoruba oral traditions in a process of feedback.[11] Like any pioneer, Johnson's work has been critiqued by a number of scholars and commentators. His bias in favor of the state of Oyo has been noted, and his Christian partisanship has been acknowledge.[12] From the perspective of this study, however, what is of interest is Johnson's gendered interpretation of the dynastic list—purportedly showing that all the *alaafin* who have ruled Oyo since its inception have all been male except one. B. A. Agiri has done a comprehensive critique of many aspects of Johnson's account.[13] Robin Law and Robert Smith have raised questions about the factuality of this list *vis-à-vis* the number of *alaafin*, the chronology of the events, regnal lengths, and even the order in which these rulers were said to have reigned.[14] What has attracted little attention is the unquestioned assumption that male *alaafin* were the universal norm, and any females among them were exceptions, and only regents for that matter.

Based on his interviews with the *arokin*, official historians of Oyo, Johnson compiled a dynastic list reproduced here from the appendix of his book.

1. Oduduwa
2. Oranyan
3. Ajaka
4. Sango
5. Ajaka
6. Aganju
7. Kori
8. Oluaso
9. Onogbogi
10. Ofiran
11. Eguoju
12. Orompoto
13. Ajiboyede
14. Abipa
15. Obalokun
16. Ajagbo
17. Odarawu
18. Kanran
19. Jayin
20. Ayibi
21. Osiyago
22. Gberu
23. Amuniwaiye
24. Onisile
25. Labisi Regent Iyayun
26. Awonbioju
27. Agboluaje
28. Majeogbe
29. Abiodun
30. Aole
31. Adebo
32. Maku
33. Majotu
34. Amodo
35. Oluewu
36. Atiba
37. Adelu
38. Adeyemi

Of the thirty-nine names represented, Johnson differentiates Oduduwa and Oranyan as historical kings who did not reign in Oyo. The fourth *alaafin* Ajaka was said to have been called to the throne twice. Iyayun, a female, is mentioned as having ruled only as a regent. The rest of the thirty-six names listed are presented as male *alaafin*.

However, Johnson's own elaboration of the history of succession and the evidence presented by other historians, show that there is reason to believe that some of the *alaafin* who ruled Oyo before the nineteenth century were female. For example, A. L. Hethersett, another Yoruba local historian, who served as the chief clerk and interpreter for the British in Lagos in the 1880s and 1890s, put together from oral tradition on Oyo dynastic list in which *Gbagida*, was identified as a female alaafin.[15] The name Gbagida also appeared in Johnson's work, but only as a term of admiration and the nickname for *alaafin* Onisile, the twenty-fifth ruler on his list.[16] If anything, this confusion demonstrates that looking at "proper" names is not sufficient for determining the maleness or femaleness of any *alaafin*. Indeed, Johnson himself had asserted that in Yoruba culture, "proper names rarely show any distinction of sex, the great majority of them apply equally well to males and females."[17]

More recent scholarship has also identified Orompoto, the twelfth ruler on Johnson's, list as female. In addition, two other previously unmentioned *oba*—Adasobo (*alaafin* Ofinran's mother), and Bayani (*alaafin* Sango's sister) have come to notice. Robert Smith, who collected oral traditions from various categories of officials in Igboho and New Oyo in the 1960's made the following observation: "...account of the military success of Orompoto's reign...confirmed that the warlike *Orompoto* was a woman... One informant at New Oyo added that *Orompoto* reigned for twenty years... as a woman king (*oba obinrin*)."[18]

The presence of female rulers certainly raises questions about the assumption of an all-male succession system. For one thing, the female *alaafin*, irrespective of their numbers, cannot be dismissed as exceptions, unless there is a clearly stated rule from which they were being excepted. Thus far, no such rule has been shown to exist. The more fundamental question raised by the presence of female *alaafin* is not why their numbers are few, because that is not yet known for a fact, but how gender, female or male, was assigned in the first place. In other words, the issue is not why only four *alaafin* are identified as females, but how the rest of them were identified as males. The larger question concerns the nature of historical documentation and the orientation and identity of the "documenters."

Johnson was aware of the gender-free nature of Yoruba categories in relation to English, and expressed reservations about the influence on Yoruba of English gender categories. Nevertheless, his Western and Christian training had already shaped his perceptions about the linkages among gender, leadership, and cultural custodial knowledge. The presence of a male-biased gender ideology is indicated in the introduction to his book, when he urged his other "brethren" to follow in his footsteps and inquire about the histories of other parts of Yorubaland "because it may be that oral records are preserved in them which are handed down from *father to son*."[19] In line with Western ideology, Johnson's phrasing locks out females from the historical transmission and knowledge production process. Nonetheless, it could be argued that the apparent gender bias in Johnson in the preceding quote is superficial, being merely a matter of translation. However, I would disagree with this line of reasoning because language is important in and of itself; and secondly, Johnson's gender bias goes beyond language and his world view is becomes clearer as we examine the totality of his writings on historical events and Oyo cultural institutions.

In any interview process, the formulation of inquiry can be a clue to the nature of information sought, and shapes how such knowledge is to be organized. Law notes that:

> Oral information is normally offered only in response to a question, and both its content and its form are greatly influenced by the questions asked...The problem about literate historians' use of oral traditions is not so much that they falsified what they heard (though this undoubtedly sometimes occurred) as that by the very process of seeking out oral information, they changed its character.[20]

Johnson relied exclusively on what he collected from the *arokin* (royal bards) for information about the earlier period of Yoruba history.[21] However, his account could not have been identical to what he heard from the *arokin* for the following reasons: first, the difference in nature between oral history and written history;[22] then the relationship between language and translation; and finally, the mediating and interpretive role of Johnson the recorder, which he himself commented on. For instance, he observed that the *arokin* often presented him with different versions of some events, one can only surmise that he, as the literate historian, selected one from these and then reconciled it with the grand narrative of Oyo history he was in the process of producing.

Johnson's biases were likely to have affected his role as a recorder of oral tradition, particularly at the points of collection, translation, and transmission. From the perspective of this study, the most problematic aspect of his interpretation is the notion that succession to the throne have always been male-exclusive. Though there is no record of the questions he asked the *arokin* to elicit the information he collected from them, it is possible to speculate on what form of interrogation he used. Law has suggested that Johnson might have asked: "How many Kings of Oyo have there been, and in what order did they reign?"[23] What is interesting is the implication of these questions in Yoruba translation, since it is likely that Johnson rendered them in Yoruba rather than in English.

My interest is in the first part of the question which I have translated as: Oba/*alaafin meelo lo ti gun ori ite ni isedale ilu Oyo*? Clearly, the importance of language cannot be overemphasized as a code for transmitting or interpreting perceptions and values framing otherwise factual information. In the two languages, the preceding question differ in one crucial sense namely that in English, king is a male category, while in Yoruba, both *oba* and *alaafin* are gender-free, making the translation of one into the other at best obfuscatory. In effect, though Johnson listened to what the information-keepers had to say, but because of the frame of reference gap as shown in the divergence in the language structure—English is gender-coded, Yoruba is not—the *arokin* may have given a response to a question that he did *not ask*: how many rulers (male and female) have there been? Thus when the royal bards gave him the names of rulers, they had no reason to specify gender (since gender specificity was not in their frame of reference), while Johnson, having asked for *oba* which he interpreted as kings (a male-specific Western category), would have assumed that all the names presented to him identified male rulers. Neither *alaafin* nor *oba* are gender-specific; therefore they do not translate as *king*.

Still, beyond Law's wording of the question, it is possible to initiate narratives of the past by posing the question differently. For example, "*tal'o te ilu yi do? tani o tele e?*" (Who founded this polity? who followed?) is a common way of starting history lessons in Yorubaland.[24] Because the question is gender-free in Yoruba, the names presented in the *arokin's* response cannot be identified as specifying male or female gender. Oranyan or Sango was the founder of Oyo, but neither the names nor the deed of founding a polity itself suggest any gender-specificity; in the oral traditions, both males and females have been known to found lineages and towns and polities. For example, there are numerous oral traditions about the person of Oduduwa the Yoruba progenitor and the first "mythical" ruler on Johnson's list.[25] According to some *Itan*, Oduduwa was male, and in some others female. The burning question remains what method a recorder of the past like Johnson used to decide the appropriate gender for any particular ruler, especially that of those who reigned before the nineteenth century, for which there were no eyewitness accounts?[26]

The most important point in the discussion of gender in Oyo historiography is that gender categories did not exist; as such, sex was not a point of reference, it had no significance in the elaboration of the powers of the *oba* and therefore apparent references to male or female, when they do occur, are incidental in the constitution of the historical personages. By the same token, since gender was not the basis of social categorization in the Yoruba cultural ethos, the *arokin* would have had no reason to indicate the sex of any of the rulers they named in response to Johnson's questions. But, since Johnson took for granted a male-exclusive right to succession, there would have been no reason for Johnson to inquire explicitly about the sex of any particular *alaafin*.

This then brings the discussion back to the focal question asked at the beginning of this paper: given that Oyo-Yoruba names were not gender-specific, and considering the fact that succession and inheritance were not gender-based, how did Johnson know the gender of each *alaafin*? How did he know, for instance, that *alaafin* Onisile, the twenty-fifth *alaafin* on his list, was male? The simple answer is that he did not know. Johnson simply took for granted that *alaafin* were "kings," and therefore male, since this was perceived to be the natural order of things given what obtains in a Western milieu, where his educational training and sensibility had been formed.

Robin Law has asked the question how truly traditional is traditional history. Using Yoruba oral tradition as a case study, he concluded that "Johnson's kinglist was not a traditional one, but a creation of his own. Or, rather, perhaps, a creation of the *Arokin* under Johnson's influence . . . There is no need to believe that any of Johnson's *Alafin* are inventions."[27] Law is perhaps correct to assume that Johnson did not invent any particular *alaafin*; however, the attribution of a male gender to almost all of them is nothing but an invention. The invention lies in the reinterpretation of the institution of *alaafin* as akin to European kingship (gendered male) and the logical constitution of the occupiers of such a position as males serving unspecified but distinct male interests. The list itself may not have been invented intentionally, but the gender of particular rulers was invented unconciously. The wording of Johnson's hypothetical question to the *Arokin* in the penultimate Law quote reflects the dilemmas of "translating cultures"—the problem is clear in many writers reference to these gender-free ruler's lists as "kinglists" (gendered male). In the next section I undertake a more detailed examination of the process of creating androcentric institutions in Oyo history and culture.

III

The issue of defining what the exact rule of succession in Old Oyo is essential. Historians such as J. A. Atanda, relied on Johnson for an understanding of succession in Old Oyo.[28] Others, like Law, observed that "the mechanics of succession at Oyo are imperfectly known," but in spite of that observation he went on to cite what is termed in this study, Johnson's hypothesis of "*aremo* succession."[29] Agiri concluded that "nothing specific could be remembered about early succession patterns and that Johnson remedied this deficiency in the way he thought most appropriate."[30] What is at issue is precisely what Johnson thought was most appropriate and why he thought that this was the most likely mode of succession, and its implications for the understanding of Oyo past and present.

According to Johnson Old Oyo succession was male-exclusive—access being based on primogeniture. In the earlier days, he claims that "the eldest son naturally succeeded the father."[31] But as Agiri reminds us, "there was at least one occasion, even during the earliest period, when a son Egunoju, was succeeded by his *sister* Orompoto."[32] And Smith reports that "informants at New Oyo have said that Ofinran began his reign under the regency of his mother Adasobo."[33] Johnson elaborated the early system of succession:

> The very first official act of the new King after his coronation is to create an Aremo.... The title is conferred on the eldest son of the sovereign in a formal manner, the ceremony being termed the "christening" as of a newly born child, hence he is often termed "omo" (child) by way of distinction.... When the King is too young to have a son, or his son is a minor, the title is temporarily conferred upon a younger brother, or next of kin that stands in place of a son, but as soon as the son is of age, he must assume his title.[34]

An interesting part of Johnson's elucidation of the position of the *aremo* is the notion that it changed over time, in that there was a period during which because of the suspicion of patricide of some previous *aremo*, it became part of the law and constitution that the *aremo* reigned with his father and had also to die with him.[35] Even with the alleged changes, Johnson maintains that, succession remained male-exclusive. A male successor he postulates, is chosen among the "members of the royal family, of the one considered most worthy, age and nearness to the throne being taken into consideration."[36]

However, a reappraisal of Johnson's narrative brings to light certain information that is not accounted for by the framework of a male-exclusive succession. The social category *aremo* needs to be deconstructed by providing the cultural institution context. The term *aremo* actually means first-born. We see this common usage of the term in the *oriki* of *alaafin* Ladugbolu (1920–1944) as recorded by J. A. Atanda:

> *Aremo Awero, b'e ba nlo 'le mole*
> *Teru t'omo ni o yo*
> *B'e ba ri baba.*

> The first born of Awero, when one goes to Mole House,
> Both slave and freeborn would rejoice
> At seeing the father.[37]

Awero is the personal *oriki* (cognomen) of a female, presumably, therefore, this is *alaafin* Ladugbolu's mother's name, and Ladugbolu is addressed here, as his mother's first born. This does not mean, however, that he was also his father's first born, considering that the royal family is usually polygamous. In everyday usage, there would be many first borns in the palace: the question is whose?

It cannot be overemphasized that the problem of translation looms large. When Johnson wrote that the crown fell to Ajaka's son, Aganju, or that Onigbogi was one of the sons of Oluaso, he was probably translating the Yoruba word *omo* into the English son.[38] It could well have been translated as daughter of, or even brother of or sister of (when siblings are of different generations, then the younger is referred to as the *omo* of the older one). In fact, the best translation of *omo* in this context is "descendant of or relation of." It should also be noted that there is no indication as to the gender of the person being descended from, there is often no reference to mother or father and since a subject can equally inherit is from both father and mother, one cannot assume one gender. Recall that Ofinran, the tenth *alaafin* on Johnson's list, was said to have inherited the throne from his mother Oba Adasobo. A number of *alaafin* were more explicitly identified with their mother's heritage—most notably Sango, whose mother was said to be a Nupe royal blood. Hence Sango's appellation, "*omo Elempe,*" the descendant of Elempe, ruler of the Nupe.[39]

Having translated the gender-free *aremo* into the gender-specific Crown Prince, Johnson was faced with the task of accounting for what happens if the first-born is female, since there is really only one first-born that is socially recognized. He did this by ascribing to the female *aremo* the title of "Princess Royal," which was supposed to be conferred formally in the same way as that of Crown Prince.[40] However, after her investiture, the female *aremo*'s formal role seem to end. This perspective could derive from the general practice whereby, in the larger society, on marriage female offspring take up residence in the household of their conjugal family—marriage residence being patrilocal. However, patrilocality was not universal. It was also commonplace for female offspring of royalty to stay in their natal compounds even after marriage. This practice is encapsulated in the saying, *omo oba o ki n'gbe le oko*,[41] (royal female offspring do not dwell in their marital house). Rather, they usually stayed and raised their children in their natal lineages. Johnson himself did observe that "some girls of noble birth will marry below their rank, but would have their children brought up in their own home, and among their father's children and adopt his totem."[42] That the children of such royal female offspring were raised in the royal household introduced the possibility of succession passing through females, as acknowledged by Johnson: "the right to the throne is hereditary, but exclusively in the male line or the male issue of the King's daughters."[43]

Johnson's historical accounts of succession for some of the *alaafin*, however, contradict the hypothesis of male-exclusive succession. Two are discussed below. One concerns Osinyago, the twenty-first *alaafin* on his list. According to Johnson, "*Osinyago* who succeeded to the throne was equally worthless.... His first born son, like his father, was of a grasping propensity, which led to his early death. The second child though a female, was masculine in character, and *she considered the rank and privileges of the Aremo (Crown Prince) her own.*"[44]

When the theory of male-only succession is used, it would seem commentworthy and virtually revolutionary, that *Omosun*, the female offspring, made a bid for the throne. More ridiculous than shocking is the fact that her behavior as depicted suggests that she did not seem to have been aware of her exclusion from the throne on account of her sex. On the other hand, if the fact of ungendered succession is accepted, it becomes obvious why she would regard the throne as her entitlement: she could not be aware of any restriction of her claim to the throne simply because there was no such restriction. The origin of the dispute between Omosun and her male cousin shows that she had been involved in governance since the dispute between the two arose over "the right of appointing a new Aseyin at the death of the then king of Iseyin [a tributary state of Oyo]."[45] Her concomitant masculinization by Johnson is another pointer to his Western gendered consciousness in which female leadership can only be accounted for by the infusion of a certain dose of masculinity.

Another questionable account of succession is in regards to Johnson's presentation of Iyayun, as an *ayaba* (royal consort) who allegedly became a regent. He writes about this *alaafin:* "During *Kori's* minority, *Iyayun* was declared regent; she wore the crown, and put on the royal robes, and was invested with the *ejigba*, the *opa ileke* and other royal insignia and ruled the kingdom as a man until her son was of age."[46] In the traditional Oyo-Yoruba inheritance system, inheritance devolves through consanguinal and not conjugal lines. The question then arises as to the whereabouts of all the other members of the royal family, the large pool of siblings, parents, and cousins, from which it would have been more likely to select a successor.

The practice of regency in Europe, in which the throne passes to a wife through her minor son, is in principle alien to Yoruba culture. Thus it is not likely that an *iyawo* (spouse) who is not regarded as a member of the lineage, would have been allowed to take over the throne under any circumstance. In fact, it would have been most unacceptable to the royals and the Oyo Mesi (council of chiefs) who would have regarded it as the ultimate usurpation. Johnson may have introduced this alien concept of succession through conjugal ties instead of the normative mode of succession based on blood ties to explain what he considered to be an exception—a female occupying the throne—having been glaringly convinced that this ruler's female sex could not be glossed over.

An alternative explanation—given the evidence—is that Iyayun was on the throne simply because she was a descendant of the previous *alaafin*, who might have been her father, mother, brother, sister, uncle, or aunt. In other words, she was more likely to have been an *omo oba* (descendant of a previous ruler) rather than an *ayaba*. There may indeed have been some confusion over the identity of Iyayun, in that Johnson also presents her as an *omo oba* (royal offspring) from one of the provincial towns, which raises the question of what her natal identity really is?[47]

It is also probable that there is confusion about the order of succession, in that Iyayun may have reigned before her son, and that he actually inherited the throne from his mother. In any case, it is difficult to accept that she was an *ayaba* who came to occupy the throne. The role of the *ayaba* was separate, different, and it was formalized. In authority they were only secondary to to the *alaafin* in the political hierarchy, occupying many different positions; offices that Johnson himself went to great lengths to explain.[48] From the point of view of this paper, the issue of female regency is considered to be largely fabricated, being the easiest way to reconcile the historical fact of a female occupying the throne with Johnson's working assumption of a male-only succession system.

In the light of the foregoing, Robert Smith's account of *alaafin* Orompoto, quoted again below in greater detail, can be evaluated. Smith collected oral traditions from the *arokin* in the 1960s, gaining information that had not been recorded by Johnson.

> This account of the military success of Orompoto's reign makes surprisingly the assertion at lgboho, confirmed reluctantly by the authorities at New Oyo, that the warlike Orompoto was a woman, sister and not brother of Egunoju. The most specific account is that she took over the government because of the youth of Ajiboyede, Egunojo's son. One informant at New Oyo added that Orompoto reigned for twenty years, not merely as a regent (*adele*) but as a woman king (*oba obinrin*).... *The persistent reference to Orompoto as a woman becomes more feasible when it is recalled that there has already been at least one, possibly three female regencies in earlier Oyo history.*[49]

In this case, *Orompoto* was an *omo oba* (royal offspring) in her own right. The fact that she reigned instead of her brother's son does not mean she was a regent (a temporary representative of a true ruler). This is not the first instance of collateral succession even in Johnson's account. Plausibly, she reigned because she was the appropriate person to be on the throne at that time, given that in Yoruba culture, children's inheritance rights were not automatically superior to those of siblings. Her attributed reign of twenty years also suggests that she was recognized to be a genuine *alaafin* in her own right. What is pertinent with regard to the interpretive role of the scholar, is that even when Smith quotes an informant as specifying that Orompoto was a "woman ruler," he still has to strive to grapple with the concept of female rulership, which he can only justify by framing it with the regency concept—just as Johnson did before him. Since *oba* is not sex-specific in Yoruba, the new phrase *oba obinrin* (woman ruler) is awkward. It would be interesting to know how the coupling of those two words came into being and who put them together.

In my own research, I have not come across a gender-specific qualification such as *baale obinrin* (woman village head) for the present-day female ruler of Maya, a village that used to be under Oyo jurisdiction.[50] The present *baale* is Oloye Mary Igbayilola Alari; she is female and I was able to conduct a series of interviews with her in Ogbomoso in March 1996.[51] She was made the *baale* on 20 December 1967 by the late Soun of Ogbomoso, Olajide Olayode, which meant that she had already spent twenty-nine years in office. Oloye Igbayilola was the unanimous choice presented by her family for the office. During our conversation I asked why she was chosen by the family and whether anyone had raised objections to her claiming the title because she is female. She replied that there had been no such objection, but that she had in fact been drafted by her family members, who had come to the conclusion that she was the best person in the family to do the job.

In Aroje, another village in the Ogbomoso environs, there was another female ruler. I made several attempts to interview her but was unsuccessful. Unfortunately, she died in May of 1996. The present Soun of Ogbomoso, Oladunni Oyěwùmí, who made her the *baale* told me that she was the rightful person for the throne. The Soun pointed out that in certain Yoruba polities and lineages male gender is not a prerequisite to occupying the throne.

Like Johnson, other historians evidence the same unresolved dilemmas about gender in Yoruba history. Law questions the claim in Heatherset's list that Gbagida, the twenty-fifth *alaafin* on Johnson's list, is female: "the claim that this ruler is female is difficult to account for."[52] Law does not explain why such a claim is difficult to accept, but given the sociocultural ethos and historical evidence, his own dismissal of female rulers needs to be scrutinized. One cannot overemphasize the point that interpreters of Oyo history have yet to explain how they deciphered the gender of each *alaafin* on the various lists. Conversely, the idea that the female royal offspring were disenfranchised is equally difficult to sustain, given the existence of present-day female rulers, given the lack of evidence that most of the listed *alaafin* were male, and given Yoruba inheritance and succession systems. Many contemporary historians seem to be creating Oyo history in a cultural vacuum; if they paid attention to other institutions, cultural values, and practices, it would have been clear that some of their basic assumptions needed to be accounted for rather than be taken for granted.

Smith has noted that the Oyo dynastic list may have been considerably shortened because many earlier *alaafin* have been forgotten "because they descended from the female line and were later replaced by descendants in the male line."[53] Peel confronted the same problem of gender and the rulers' list in the state of Ilesha, another Yoruba domain. According to him, despite the oral narratives concerning at least six female rulers, none of the contemporary ruling houses wanted to claim descent from these females, as they believed it would weaken their claim to the throne. This echoes the reported reluctance by the authorities in New Oyo to confirm to Smith that *alaafin* Orompoto was a woman, and again underscores the need to determine the precise time in Yoruba history at which the presence of women in rulership, power, and authority became perplexing to certain sections of the population. Thus for Peel, "it is impossible to know what has happened to produce the tradition of so many 'female' *Owa* rulers, though a sociologist's strong inclination is to believe that the problem lies in the [retelling of] tradition rather than the event."[54]

Although the political systems of the different Yoruba states should not be homogenized, Peel's observation is relevant to this discussion. To remove the gender-bias, however, his observation needs to be restated. Thus the concern should be not what happened to produce the tradition of so many females, but what happened to produce the tradition of so many males and male-only succession in the retelling of Oyo history. When and why has the tradition of female succession become invalid in many of these polities?

In the contemporary period, in line with this masculinization trend, the general aristocracy seems to have also been masculinized along with the *alaafin*. Thus there is without evidence an assumption that members of the *oyo Mesi* (council of chiefs), the *omo oba* chiefs (royal offspring titleholders), the *arokin* (royal bards and historians) were all male. The *ayaba* (royal consorts), mothers of the palace who held various key authority positions in the political hierarchy, appear to be the exception to the rule of male dominance in the political hierarchy of Old Oyo, as presented by historians beginning with Johnson. Smith did collect information from the Iyanaso and other wives of the late *alaafin* Ladugbolu, and S. O. Babayemi in his work gives a detailed account of their role in the political system.[55]

In the interpretation of oral traditions, many writers, local and foreign, assume that the phrase "descendant of" in genealogies denotes a succession of father to son, even when it is clear that numerous successions pass from sibling to sibling. Peel noted the widespread father-to-son preference in the elaboration of historical succession of rulers in many West African states and concluded that:

> This is no doubt a translation of its closest genealogical analog . . . It is very common in West African dynasties with a widely rotating succession that an early period is alleged to have had a father-to-son succession, which is so easily and economically explained as an artifact of the later genealogical system itself, that we would be very chary of assuming a real change of succession without clear additional evidence.[56]

Peel is certainly correct about this rendering of succession in English as father-to-son, but one cannot always assume that in the African languages and cultures, the oral traditions are equally male-exclusive in law, letter, and spirit. Taking the father-to-son analog as gospel, Peel infuses it with new life by postulating a Yoruba model of historical reconstruction based on the saying *baba ni jingi* (your father is a mirror), which he interprets as the idea that "the physical appearance, aptitudes, spiritual affinities, social position of a father as best echoed in his sons."[57] Even if one accept his interpretation that the saying is about lineal inheritance, he is simply incorrect to suggest that inheritance of any kind—including physical appearance—devolves only from father to son. Such an interpretation is not suggested by the evidence. In practice, both male and female offspring do inherit from the father. The saying *baba ni jingi* is part of a larger unit—a poem which articulates Yoruba ideas about parental bonds and inheritance in which *both* mother and father are represented.

> *Iya ni wura*
> *Baba ni jingi*
> *nijo iya ba ku ni wura baje*
> *nijo baba ba ku ni jingi wo'mi*
>
> Mother is gold
> Father is a mirror
> When mother dies the gold is ruined
> When father dies
> The mirror drowns (my translation)

Finally, it should be noted that from the Yoruba perspective, fathers can also be reincarnated in their daughters, given the fact that anatomical attributes are not privileged and do not determine social practices. For example, recall Johnson's explication of the office of the Iyamode, one of the female high officials in the palace as embodying the spirit of the alaafin's "fathers."[58] In fact, one of the rites associated with the birth of a child is a consultation with a *babalawo* or diviner priest to (*gbo ori omo na*) establish the spirit of the ancestor incarnated in the child. There is no gender specificity as to where ancestral spirit shows up, since female children often embody male ancestors. In the religious realm also, spirit possession does not discriminate based on anatomical sex: Sango, the thundergod, manifests itself in both male and female devotees. The primary problem of rendering Yoruba history and indeed other aspects of the culture, then, is the imposition of the Western, overly physicalized and gendered model of apprehending the world. Perhaps the *baba ni jingi* conceptualization is appropriate if we all agree that the *baba* (father) in question is the West. Yoruba historiography mirrors Western history, as many other African scholars have argued.[59]

IV

The problems of interpretation of Yoruba history and culture, particularly with regard to the issue of gender, can also be attributed to the linguistic and cultural translation of Yoruba into English. This can be demonstrated, using the two major sources of oral tradition, *itan* (historical narrative) and *oriki* (praise poetry). In 1988 a group of historians visited Oyo to record the views of the *arokin* on their "own professional activities and history."[60] In response, one of the *arokin*, the *Ona-Alaro*, told the following *itan* (narrative), to highlight their role as consolers of the *alaafin* in time of crisis. One of the researchers, P. F. de Moraes Farias, reports the response in both Yoruba and English.

> *Ti nnkan ba tise Oba, oba oo pe won o lo pe wa wa.*
> *Ti awon ijoye ba tiso bayii pe nnkan bayii o ti se Oba bayii, oba bayi nnkan se e ri. Oba bayi nnkan se e ri, yoo baa poun naaa gba, Oloun lo wi pe o wa bee. O le je pe omo oba kan le wa ko je pe omo re doodu eni-abi-asole doodu re, ko fo sanle ko ku, gbogbo awon ti won wa lodo re o ni le wi. Won o loo gbe e pamo. Ni won o waa pe, "E lo pArokin wa". Laa wa so pe, Bayii, bayii, bayii, a gbo pomo re bayii o si; omo ti Lamoin bayii naa si wa bee, omo ti Lakesegbe naa si wa bee, yoo baa poun gba. Awa laa loo so.*[61]
>
> If something happens to the Oba, the Oba [the alaafin] will send for us. As soon as *his* Chiefs tell us that such and such a thing has happened to the Oba, [we will tell him about] another Oba to whom something similar also happened. So *he* will say that he accepts [gba] it because it is Olorun's making. Suppose a prince, the first born of the Oba [alaafin] dies The courtiers will not dare give the news to the Oba. They will go and hide the corpse. Then they will say, "Go and call the Arokin". Then we will tell *him:* "We hear that this son of yours has died. We hear that this son of yours has died. The son of so-and-so [an Oba] once died in the same way. And so did the son of somebody else [another oba]." And then the alaafin will say he accepts [gba] it. We are the one's who will go and tell him.[62]

In a number of ways the translator of this piece has been careful. Most notable is the rendering of the ungendered Yoruba words "*Lamoin*" and "*Lakasegbe,*" into the apparently non-gender-specific English "so-and-so" and "somebody else." Because the Hausa/arabic derived loan-word "*Doodu,*" which has become part of Oyo vocabulary, is sex-specific, being a male designation, the translation of the first "*omo oba* (child of ruler)" as "Prince," is acceptable. However, the subsequent references of "*omo,*" which are gender-free in the Yoruba original also end up being translated into "son." Similarly, there is nothing to indicate the sex of the hypothetical *alaafin* but s/he is transformed into a male in the English translation by the use of the pronouns "he," "his," and "him." Thus do all the characters in the story acquire the male gender, even though with the exception of a reference to "*Doodu*" in the case of one character, there is nothing in the *arokin*'s Yoruba speech to warrant such an assumption for the rest of them, who number at least three.

The same distortion and inaccuracy is replayed in the next *itan*, which the *arokin* narrate. The protagonist is another *omo oba* named as Akuluwe, who this time is a female. This is indicated in the fact that the *alaafin* told the Onikoyi to make her his *aya* (bride).[63] Farias suggests that a female was necessary in this story because the action depended on the protagonist being taken away—embarking on a journey; and since the logic of Oyo marriage is for the female to be taken away, then it follows that a female protagonist was indispensable to the story. There is an element of overinterpretation in making such an assumption. Besides the fact that it was commonplace for female royals on marriage not to move to their marital lineages, male royals offspring lived in the provinces, so they too made journeys in and out of the

Oyo metropolis all the time. The *itan* is as follows:

> *Oba to je tele Orananyan, Oba Ajaka Dada Ajuon ti adape re n je Oba Ajaka I'Oyoo ile, omo kan soso t'o bi... Gbogbo Oyo Mesi loun o fe e, ko fe won. Won won-ribaa Baale ilu, ko fe won. Gbogbawon to loun o fe... Okoyi lo loun o fe. Oba ni ko lo fi s'aya. Ngba Onkoyi n lo, too n mu loole, ibi ti ile su won si, won pe ibe ni Gbongbon. O wa sunbe. Oorun ti won waa sun nbe, ni gba tile ee mo ile jo... Omo Oba jona, o jona si ilu yen. Ngba Onkoyi waa dele, o wi pe Oun daran o! Omo t'Oba foun, oun lo ku... Won ni o pe awon omoo re, pelu sekere ii. Onikoyi ni babanla baba ti wa.*
>
> The Oba [*alaafin* of Oyo] who ruled after Oranmiyan, Oba Ajaka Ajuon, this is is his name. Oba Ajaka at Oyo Ile. *He had one daughter.* All the Oyo Mesi [members of the royal council] said they wanted to marry her, but she refused. She also refused the Baale [chiefs] of many towns. All the ones she said she wouldn't marry... then she said she would marry the Oba of Ikoyi, and the Allafin gave her hand in marriage. When the onikoyi was taking her home, nightfall caught them at Gbongbon. During the night, the house in which they slept caught fire... the princess was burned to death... He was told to call upon his own children with this sekere. The Onikoyi is our grandfather...

In the Yoruba original, this female offspring is said to be *alaafin Ajaka*'s "*omo kansoso to bi*"[64] (ruler's one *and only child*) (my translation). In the Farias translation, it is rendered as "the only daughter." This is inaccurate because it gives the impression that Ajaka had other children—sons—thereby minimizing the gravity of her death. This in turn compromises the point of the story being told by the *Ona-Alaro*, which is to establish the origins of the institution of *Arokin* in Oyo history. The *Ona Alaro* (an *Arokin)*, recounted that the institution developed to console a particular *alaafin* in the moment of the greatest crisis of his life as a parent and a ruler—the death of her/his only child. The oral account as rendered in Yoruba is clearly different from the English version in letter and in spirit. It would be interesting to know how the *arokin* would have reached to the English version, since it clearly undermines the import of their institution in that the task of consoling a ruler who has lost an only child is more weighty than that of consoling one who has lost one of many children.

Next, this discussion explores the relationship between gender and *oriki* the other important source of information about the past. Can *oriki* shed light on the gender of historical figures? According to Bolanle Awe, there are three forms of *oriki* dealing with human achievements:

[1] *Oriki ilu* (towns), deals with the foundation of a town, its vicissitudes and its general reputation among its neighbors.
[2] *Oriki orile* (lineages), gives the characteristics of a patrilineage by focusing attention on a few illustrious members whose attributes are supposed to typify the main features of the lineage.
[3] *Oriki inagije* (individual personalities), deals mainly with individuals. The poem could outline those qualities that mark him (or her) out for

distinction or it could be a combination of these and his/her pedigree, in which case some of the *oriki orile* is included.[65]

As Awe articulated, the *oriki* of individual personalities (also called *oriki borokini*, that is, praising of important persons) are the most informative for historical reconstruction. She further asserted that:

> Oriki inagije . . . could be a very fruitful source for historical reconstruction . . . Because its scope is more limited in the sense that it concentrates on one individual and therefore covers a relatively shorter period of history, the oriki can give detailed and direct information which can be more easily fitted into available historical evidence on the period.[66]

Since the *oriki inagije* are portraits of important personalities, it would seem that information about the gender of the person in question would be readily available. But even then, as Awe immediately pointed out, "this type of oriki is not always easily available for the more remote period of Yoruba history."[67] The focus of the present paper is the pre-nineteenth century period, since this was the same period in which other sources of evidence are lacking. Consequently, there are serious limitations on relying on *oriki inagije* to decipher the gender of Oyo rulers. Karin Barber, in a paper on *oriki*, suggested that the events of the nineteenth century provided ample opportunity for self aggrandisement, to the extent that the number of notable personalities increased exponentially and that the genre of *oriki* of notable personalities itself witnessed not only amplification but stylistic changes in performance.[68]

To go back to the question of delineating the gender of historical figures, it may be possible to discern this by using personal *oriki* (cognomens) which appear to be gender-specific. Proper names do not indicate gender, but those cognomens which also function as names seem to suggest gender-specificity. Adeboye Babalola asserted that personal *oriki*, unlike given names, are an indication of what the parents hope for a particular child.[69] Unlike cognomens, names usually denote the circumstances of birth. Alake, Adunni, and Alari are cognomens associated with females, while Alamu, Akanni, and Alade are a few associated with males. It is possible therefore that if in the *oriki* or *itan* the cognomen of the personality is given, then one may be able to ascertain sex. For example, in the *oriki* of the lineage of *oko* contains the following lines:

> *Aare Alake jibola Alake Ajiboro loko . . .*
> *Aare Alake omo agede gudu Oba Igbaja.*[70]
>
> The leader Alake *Ajiboro loko . . .*
> The leader *Alake*, one that fought fiercely killing without mercy, the ruler of Igbaja.

Since Alake is the personal *oriki* of a female, these lines show that the Oko lineage has a revered founding female ancestor. One major drawback to relying on cognomens is that they are not always used instead of proper names. In Johnson's dynastic list, for example, only one or possibly two names appear to be cognomens; namely Ajagbo and Atiba, which are male cognomens. The thirty-six other names listed are given names and are therefore not gender-specific. Similarly, none of the 142 lines of *oriki* of Balogun Ibikunle, a notable nineteenth-century figure presented by Awe in her study, contains any mention of his cognomen, although we learn that he is the father of 'Kuejo and we also learn the names of myriad other notable personalities whom he engaged in war.[71] The point is that personal *oriki* are not always forthcoming in this respect.

Even then, another problem that arises when the cognomens are mentioned in a particular *oriki* genre is to determine who is specifically being addressed, since there is a proliferation of names. Karin Barber collected the *oriki* of Winyomi, a founding father of Okuku. The following lines provide a good illustration of this problem:

> Winyomi Enipeede Head of the Hunters
> Aremu, blocks the road and doesn't budge, Enipeede, one who fills the coward with apprehension . . .
> Alamu said "If you get into trouble to the tune of two thousand cowries"
> He said, "Your own father will take his cut of the settlement"
> European cloth does not wear well
> Winyomi said "what it is good for is showing off."[72]

In this there are a number of appellations, and presumably all refer to Winyomi; however the presence of the two cognomens—Aremu and Alamu—suggest that reference is to more than one person, since an individual can have many given names but usually only one cognomen. Indeed, this issue raises the question of conflation of identities in *oriki* that makes it difficult to untangle the genealogical detail and individual identities presented. Barber correctly asserted that a "social history that attempted to use *Oriki* to recover patterns of personal relations would meet with . . . difficulties. *Oriki* do not record the genealogical relationships of the subjects commemorated in the *Oriki* . . . Genealogical relationship . . . seem actually to be obscured rather than clarified or preserved, by the *Oriki*."[73] It is also true that a history that purports to assign gender to personalities on the basis of *oriki* allusions alone is also fraught with problems. Furthermore, as Barber shows, even the "I" of an *oriki* chant moves continually "between male and female, adult and child, insider and outsider, specific and generalized persona."[74]

The *oriki* genre with its multiplicity of references, carries within it an indeterminacy with regard to questions of individual social identity. Another source of complication in regard to the issue of shifting identities, lies in the fact that the different units of the *oriki* have different sources, and variable dates of composition, even though they are recited *as if* they derive from one source and one lineage. Individual identity in Old Oyo derived from communal identity, and a subject's *oriki* would include lines from both the maternal and paternal lines. In performance, however, all the events and attributes appear to pertain only to one descent line.

Finally, because particular physical and moral attributes have their own stock epithets, they introduce another lack of specificity even into the individualized *oriki inagije*. A number of attributes that have their own poems are tallness, shortness, generosity, and dancing ability. These are introduced to enhance any personality with the said attribute during an *oriki* performance.[75] If a male or female subject is being addressed, and if s/he is identified as tall or short, the appropriate epithet would be incorporated.

It is no wonder then that Barber, who sought to make a distinction between male and female *oriki*, concluded that such a distinction is not possible. Writing about the *oriki* of prominent women, she observed that "these *oriki* are very close in tone and in imagery to the personal *oriki* of big men. There are no recognizably 'women's *oriki*.'"[76] But the evidence is clear that there are no men's *oriki* either. Steeped in the male-as-norm framework of the West, Barber is using men as the measure. Consequently, she continues to project erroneously the idea that there are men's *oriki* though there are no women's *oriki*. There are neither men's *oriki* nor women's *oriki*. *Oriki* in Yorubaland are gender-free in all regards.

In a Western-dominated world in which gender is produced and invoked as an ontological, timeless, and a universal category, there is naturally a preoccupation with establishing gender. It must be understood, however, that in the Yoruba past, gender categories were not part of the frame of reference; gender, therefore cannot be used as the fault-line in the reconstruction of the past. In the contemporary period, invocations of gender has to take into account the history of genderization which would include a consideration of the role of scholars in the process of history-making.

V

Thus far this discussion of the process of grafting gender onto Yoruba history and culture has addressed the creation of "men," as exemplified by the masculinization of universal authority categories such as the aristocracy in general, and the *alaafin* in particular. Running *pari passu* was a complementary and equally important process, the creation of "women" by scholars in general. This particular process rests on acceptance by these scholars of three questionable assumptions: first, the genderization of Yoruba society, in which the universal world sense is split into male and female; secondly, the notion that male dominance and privilege is the natural manifestation of the differentiation; and thirdly, that by implication the residual societal attribute of deprivation is ascribed to females. With man assumed to be the measure of all things, when confronted with incontrovertible evidence about females who were in positions of power and authority, the tendency is to explain them away as exceptions, as temporary representatives of men or male interests, or as stooges of the oppressive patriarchy, or to reduce their significance by positing that they held sway over other females only.

Against a background in which social identify is gendered and an idea of "status of women" is introduced projecting females as forever unempowered, the work of the pioneering Yoruba social historian, Bolanle Awe—well-known for going beyond the eventcenteredness that characterizes the field of history—has been invaluable in presenting an alternative tableau. In a paper entitled, "The Iyalode in the Traditional Political System of the Yoruba," she endeavored to place the office of the Iyalode squarely among the pantheon of Yoruba political positions in which it belonged.[77] There is no mention of an Iyalode in Johnson's account of the powerful mother-officials who dominated the political hierarchy of the Oyo metropolis. The person that he identified as being in charge of the market is the Eni-oja. "she is in charge of the King's [*alaafin's*] markets, and enjoys all the perquisites accruing therefrom . . . She has under her (1) the Olosi who has joint responsibility with her for the market, and (2) the Aroja or market keeper, an officer whose duty it is to keep order, and arrange the management of the market, and who actually resides there."[78]

Johnson's omission inevitably suggests that there was no such titled office in Old Oyo, and lends credence to the idea that the title Iyalode is more associated with the provinces and was elaborated at a later historical time period, probably with the development of new states like Ibadan following the fall of Old Oyo in 1836. In my conversations with the Soun of Ogbomoso, Oba Oyěwùmí,[79] he mentioned that there are a number of chieftaincy titles in presentday Ogbomoso, such as the *Otun* and *Osi*, that are not historical, but were constituted only in recent history owing to the influence of Ibadan.[80] He went on to say that Ibadan is a republic, whereas Ogbomoso and Oyo are monarchies. As such, these newly imported chieftaincy titles were at odds with the monarchical organization. I asked whether the Iyalode title which is now present in Ogbomoso is one of the Ibadan imports. Oba Oyěwùmí pointed out that the title was not traditional to the Ogbomoso polity. In the interview with the Iyalode of Ogbomoso, Oloye Oladoja Aduke Sanni, she said that the first Iyalode was installed in Ogbomoso only during the time of the Yoruba wars.[81] In fact she noted that the first Iyalode had been conferred with the title in recognition of her bravery during those troubled times. This would make the title a relatively recent addition in Ogbomoso.

Johnson, however, does mention an Iyalode in some of the provincial towns but of great significance is that his account did not tie her to the market, suggesting a wider arena of power. Nevertheless, an interrogation of the office of Iyalode is necessary to this study, given the way in which the office has been elaborated as a prototype of female leadership, and its deployment without regard for historical time and differences in pan-Yoruba political organizations.

The particular appellation Iyalode is associated with Ibadan in particular, a state that emerged within the Oyo political system in the nineteenth century. It was also known in Abeokuta, another new state. In other polities such as

Akure and Ondo, there were two chieftaincy titles, *Arise* and *Lobun*, respectively, which were also known to be held by women. However, it should not be assumed that all these titles had the same meaning and function throughout Yorubaland, since to do so would be to level and homogenize political posts that were in operation in different politico-cultural centers at different historical time periods. Indeed, a number of scholars have documented the differences in the organization of Yoruba states which show why chieftaincy titles, basis, and functions of particular titleholders cannot be assumed to be the same. Awe acknowledges this when she observes that "[i]t is clear that it is impossible to make sweeping generalizations about the position of the Iyalode or of women generally within the Yoruba political system."[82]

Given the interrogatory mission and ongoing scrutiny of the building blocks of knowledge, and the reappraisal of Yoruba historiography, it is perhaps cogent to re-examine some of the basic assumptions in the historiography of the Iyalode. The title Iyalode means "Mother of Public Affairs" and, according to Awe, the holder of that office was the voice or spokesperson of women in government.

> Her most important qualifications were her proven ability as a leader to articulate the feelings of women . . . and . . . in contrast to the male chiefs, who would be involved in the organization of war, the reception of foreign visitors, and so on, it is not unlikely that the women chiefs would be involved in the settlement of disputes between women, the cleanliness of the markets, and other female concerns.[83]

It is apparent that these observations are based on several erroneous assumptions: that women and men constituted separate social categories with differing interests; that the office of Iyalode represented a women's chieftaincy system separate from and parallel to that of men; that the female anatomy of the Iyalode was a primary qualification for office; that the alleged predominance of females in trading occupations implies that markets were female concerns. The prefix *iya* (mother), suggest a female. But it also means older woman, and is therefore an indication of adulthood, seniority, and consequently, responsibility and status. Thus Iyalode can also be translated as older female in charge of public affairs. *Iya* and *baba* are normally used as prefixes in describing the engagements of a particular adult female or male respectively. Thus a male chief is called *baba isale* (older male, leader); a female food seller—*iya olonje* (older female seller of food); and a male cloth weaver—*baba alaso* (adult male of cloth-maker).

However, the other part of the title—*ode* (public affairs)—goes beyond the person, indicating that the responsibilities of the office encompass a much wider domain than is commonly attributed to it. Someone in charge of the markets, would have had authority over the community's economy—regulating supply and demand, product pricing, allocation of stalls, tolls, fees, and fines. Furthermore, if the background of Yoruba polities heavily engaged in warfare and the emergence of Ibadan or Abeokuta as military states is considered, the connection between war and the economy becomes clearer. Hence it was perhaps no coincidence that in the nineteenth century, Iyaola, the first Iyalode of Ibadan, was given the title because of her contributions to Ibadan's war efforts. According to Awe, "[l]ike the male chiefs, she contributed her quota of soldiers to Ibadan's ad hoc army where a corps of domestic slaves were trained to fight."[84]

Similarly, Madam Tinubu, after an illustrious career, received the title of Iyalode of Abeokuta in "appreciation of her bold deeds." These included the supply of guns and ammunition to Abeokuta soldiers, during the wars between Abeokuta and Dahomey.[85] As for Efunsetan, another Iyalode of Ibadan, her interest in public affairs extended to foreign affairs. Well-known for her extensive wealth, Efunsetan constituted formidable opposition to the ruler of Ibadan Aare Latosa. Awe records that, "she challenged [Latosa's] foreign policy that alienated Ibadan from her neighbors, and resisted his domestic policy that tended towards the establishment of sole rule, contrary to Ibadan's tradition of oligarchic government."[86] Thus from Awe's accounts, the careers of the individual Iyalode—Iyaola, Madam Tinubu, and Efunsetan—suggest that they were not circumscribed by any considerations of gender since there were no such restrictions. The general national interests such as the economy, domestic policy, defense, and foreign affairs did not fall outside their purview.

There is also the question of which women the Iyalodes were supposed to be concerned with. The general assumption is that a major constituency were an-female traders. Because of the predominance of females in the occupation of trading, in the literature the term *trader* has become virtually synonymous with "market woman," which in turn is used interchangeably with the word "woman." Thus an *egbe* (guild) of traders which is an occupational or professional guild is misrepresented as a women's group, whereas the *raison d'être* of a traders' *egbe* is for the members—females and males—to come together to enhance their business.

Traders are not categorized on the basis of anatomy; nor does the ability to sell goods inhere in the female anatomy. Rather, the type of goods, trade distance, etc., determines their interests. Hence, for instance, even if all food sellers are female and belonged to a food sellers guild, this does not make it a women's group, because the qualification for membership does not derive from the anatomy, but from the commonality of their economic activity. On the question of whether a legitimate argument can be made about the statistical prevalence of females in a particular trade or the other, see my discussion of statistical categoricalism in the previous paper as I interrogated the division of labor.[87] Suffice it to say that the question of gender and numbers does not arise from the Oyo frame of reference, although of course it fits in very well with the Western biological framework. The question itself already presupposes gender categories as a natural way of organizing society, a claim that is challenged by Oyo cosmology and social organization.

Thus if the Iyalode had jurisdiction over disputes within the marketplace, or regulatory responsibility for environmental sanitation, or if they served as a channel for communication between people in the marketing profession and governmental authorities, describing them as being concerned with women's interests would seem the result of a conceptual straitjacket. It does not afford the ambiance of perception which acknowledges more comprehensively the iyalode's functions.

This brings the discussion to the task of determining what in Old Oyo society could have constituted a distinctly women's political interest, which the iyalode or any feminized female official was supposed to represent. From what is known about Old Oyo's political and social organization, anatomical females were, alongside males, arrayed around diverse interests deriving from class, occupation, lineage, and so on. Some of these interests, such as those of the *iyawo* (females married into a lineage) and *oko* (females born into a lineage) sometimes conflicted. Within the Old Oyo political system, the most significant conflicting tendencies were between the *alaafin* on one hand, and the *Oyo Mesi* (the council of chiefs) on the other.[88]

In the elaborate palace administrative machinery which protected the interest of the *alaafin* against the *Oyo Mesi* were the *ayaba* females comprising the royal consorts. Specifically, the positions they occupied included the royal priesthood of Sango, the national religious denomination of *Orisa* worship. There were also in the administration, the *Ilaris* (female and male) some of whom served as bodyguards. As Awe observed of the powerful mothers in the palace: "they were . . . in a position of great influence because they had direct access to the king. Even the *Iwarefa*, his highest officials, had to go through them to arrange rituals, festivals, and communal labor. Tributaries of the Oyo kingdom could only approach the *alaafin* through them."[89] In fact, Awe further suggests that their positions were said to "undermine the effectiveness of the iyalode." that is, if in fact there was such a chieftaincy. The disjuncture between the powerful mother-officials and the alleged *iyalode* in itself suggests a dissonance that preempts the homogenization of females as a sociopolitical category.

The foregoing again illustrates that a gendered framework of analysis is an alien distortion seriously limiting the understanding and rendering of precolonial Yoruba history. Considering that anatomical maleness is not regarded as a qualification for other chieftaincy posts and political representation of corporate interest by ward chiefs, presenting the office of the *iyalode* as one for which the primary qualification is anatomical femaleness, results in the exceptionalization of the *iyalode*. Similarly, presenting her as being concerned solely with women's interests, which in the context of precolonial Yorubaland are conceptually difficult to decipher as being separate from societal interests, has the consequence of feminizing the post, and thereby eroding its significance.

VI

In light of the prevailing thesis here that Yoruba society was not organized along gender lines, the focus of this section is to analyze the images of Esie.

These are a collection of stone sculptures numbering over 1000 pieces located in Esie, a Yoruba town of Igbomina composition in present-day Kwara State. Most Igbomina claim Oyo origins. The images have been dated to the twelfth to fourteenth centuries, and they range in height from fourteen centimeters to over one meter, and comprise soapstone figures representing men, women, children, and animals. Scholars have always been concerned about the relationship between art and the social order, and whether art reflects society or responds to the same structural principle as the social organization. In a paper on Yoruba verbal and visual arts, Drewal and Drewal correctly assert that "the structure of the arts and the structure of society are homologous and reflect Yoruba aesthetic preference but, more importantly, that these structures are a concrete manifestations of Yoruba conception of the nature of existence and being. They articulate ontological thought."[90]

The origins of the stone images of Esie, as they came to be known, remain a great mystery, especially as they apparently did not originate in the present site but seem to have been transported there. This is interesting, because many of the pieces weigh over 50 pounds, some even more than 100 pounds. They were brought to the attention of the Western world in 1933 by H. G. Ramshaw, school superintendent for the Church Missionary Society. Subsequently, a number of European scholars visited the site and wrote about the Esie images. The most comprehensive work to date, *Stone Images of Esie, Nigeria*, by Philips Stevens, was published in 1978. The book fulfils the twofold mission of evaluating the ethnographic and archeological data and presenting an extensive photographic catalog.[91] The aim in this section is to interrogate Stevens' gender-specific interpretation of them, as well as to evaluate the assumption of historians of Yoruba art about the naturalness of gender. Ethnographic data should provide clues to comprehending the images and allow for a reverse dialectic—an interpretation of the images as clues to ethnography.

Stephens describes the variety of the sculptures in the Esie collection:

> Most are seated on stools; a few are standing. Some apparently reveling, laughing, playing musical instruments; most of them are armed as if for war. Their features suggest a great diversity of influences . . . The figures have been propitiated since the latter part of the 18th century when the present inhabitants claim to have arrived on the site and found them.[92]

The Esie sculptures are a concrete (literally!) manifestation of the Oyo Yoruba conception of the nature of being and existence as determined by lineage membership and social roles, which are not defined by gender. At the heart of one of the gendered renderings of the Esie Images is the fact that many of the figures are carrying arms, including daggers, bow, and quivers. The images appear to depict social roles. Stevens writes that "fully one-third (about 325) of the pieces are female, and of these about a quarter (85) are armed, as if for war."[93]

Using the framework of a lineage-determined division of labor rather than a gender-based one, it is clear that the images, both female and male, represent the *omo-ile* (offspring) of one the lineages associated with warfare and hunting, such as Eso, Oje, or Ile Olode. Thus the arms-bearing females are more likely to be *omo* (offspring) than *iyawo* (females married into the lineage), and, as I have demonstrated elsewhere, the position of a female offspring in a lineage does not differ from that of the male, both deriving role authority from lineage membership.[94] Stevens, however, perceives these "militaristic females" as aberrant and then proceeds to genderize their weapons:

> Of the total number of such militaristic figures, an interesting correlation does appear: men are archers and wielders of daggers; the women carry cutlasses. In fact, no figure that is positively female (T35 is questionable) wears a quiver; only a few of the males hold cutlass.[95]

In this manner, gender is fostered as a given, and realities that cannot be accounted for by the fabrication are thus exceptionalized. Interestingly, once the notion that all the figures holding cutlasses are female, is accepted, it becomes virtually impossible to look at a cutlass-carrying figure without seeing a female. In other words, once the gender of the figures is assumed and the gender-appropriateness of the weapons is assumed, then the weapons become a way of identifying gender and vice-versa.[96] The process is at best circular. It should be reiterated that there is nothing in Oyo culture that disociates females from carrying cutlasses or machetes. In his analysis of the metal staff of Orisa Oko, the Yoruba god of agriculture, C. O. Adepegba had this to say: "the Yoruba word for staff seems inappropriate as the square-ended flat-edged object resembles a sword or cutlass than a staff.... The staff is meant for female devotees: male devotees carry strung cowries."[97] Even if one were to subscribe to the notion of gender-specificity in Yoruba life, Adepegba's assessment of Orisa Oko shows that "women" are the cutlass carriers, which is diametrically opposed to Stevens' working assumption that male figures are the more likely to carry weapons.

This leads to a fundamental question concerning what otherwise appears obvious—how viewers are able to determine the gender of each of the figures themselves. Stevens seems to acknowledge that apprehending gender at a spatial and temporal distance in Yoruba discourse can be an ambiguous adventure, and proffers some guidelines.

> In West African sculpture, determining the intended sex of the figure is difficult. Where they are exposed, the genitals are certain indicators but the breasts are sometimes equally pronounced in both sexes. Hairstyles, jewelry and dress do not appear to correlate sexually in the Esie collection . . . I have relied on breast accentuation . . . where the breasts are more than mere nubs, I have designated the figure as female.[98]

But using the breast as an index of gender still has certain limitations. In real life many women do not have breast accentuation, which is probably a better indication of female youthfulness—prime motherhood—than just femaleness.

Also several figures are wearing bow straps covering their breasts or nipples, which makes it impossible to determine breast accentuation. Consequently, Stevens' statistical analysis of how many figures are female and his correlation of sex to weapon type reveals more about the workings of a gendered gaze than it does about the images themselves.

Another scholar who has written about the Esie Images is John Pemberton, as part of his rendering of the Oyo visual world and religious iconography. However, it appears that his representations are not only gendered, but illustrate what a number of feminist and other scholars have postulated about western visual arts: that is, the gaze is always a male gaze—the beholder is male. In a beautifully illustrated book entitled *Yoruba: Nine Centuries of Art and Thought*, Henry Drewal, John Pemberton, and Rowland Abiodun, display samples of Yoruba art forms with commentary situating them in their different locations. In the section on Oyo art, Pemberton comments on one of the Esie pieces, which he identifies as a male:

> Seated male figure, Esie . . . The artist conveys the authority of his subject in the composure of the face and the directness of the gaze, as well as the seated position and gesture . . . The expressive power of this carving is that the artist not only depicts a social role but makes one aware of a person who held the role . . . There is a fleshy quality in the once-powerful shoulders and arm. One feels the weight of the man in the abdomen as it protrudes above the sash and in the spread of the hips as he sits on the stool.[99]

Pemberton also comments on a comparable (in posture and composure) figure which he identified as female, thus:

> Seated female figure . . . The Esie female figure holds a cutlass, which rests on her right shoulder as a symbol of office. . . . Note the delicate scarification marks on her forehead. The height of her elaborate coiffure is equal to that of her face, emphasizing the importance of the head. . . . The head and face of the woman are exquisitely modeled. She has an elaborate hairstyle, powerful forehead above deeply recessed eyes, and a fullness of the lips. The strings of beads around her neck, her youthful breasts, and the fullness of her abdomen are evidence of her beauty and power as a woman.[100]

It should be recalled that, since among the Esie figures there is no purported gender-specificity in coiffure, scarification, or adornment, the marked difference in how these two images are presented becomes apparent. The male image is discussed in terms of social roles, the female in terms of adornment. The authority of the man is vested within him—composure, gaze, gesture; the woman's authority derives from a symbol. The spread of the male's abdomen spells weightiness, the fullness of the female, beauty. Even where the word power is used to describe her, it is in the context of her womanhood—the "power of a woman"—to do what? In popular Nigerian parlance today, this allusion would be taken to mean "bottom power." In other words her power is not about authority but derives from her ability to exercise influence based on the commodification of sexuality. Such a delivery mimics the presentation of female beauty to a male voyeur in European art.

Yet, using the ungendered model postulated by this work, it is possible to comprehend that the Esie figures are not depicting power and authority in a sex-specific manner as Pemberton's interpretation suggests. For example, the youthfulness of some of the identifiable females and their depiction as figures with authority could suggest that they are in their natal lineage (probably a hunting one), which then explains the naturalness of their carrying arms. From the perspective of using the images as evidence for certain social claims, this interpretation suggests that the figures are best analyzed as a collection—a reflection of the prevalent communal ethos—not as individual characters without a context. As I have argued above, until recently war in Yorubaland was not conceptualized as a masculine activity.

The gendered gaze is also apparent in Pemberton's renderings of religious iconography, exemplified by that of Sango, the thunder god. For example, all his selections of religious worship show female devotees and priests. Most of them are in what he interprets to be subservient positions, whereas most of the males are in authority positions. Yet it is clear from other sources that even the *alaafin* prostrates before the god Sango, and before those possessed of the deity calling them "father."[101] According to Pemberton, "[t]he unpredictable capricious self-serving *Orisa* is also the one who imparts his beauty to the woman with whom he sleeps. He is the giver of children."[102] Such language as seen in Pemberton's commentary is imbued with implicit sexual references which suggest that the female priests worship the god as a male sexual figure. He claims that Sango is praised by women in a song:

> Where shall I find *Jebooda*, my husband?
> He dances as he sings with us.
> He-who-destroys-the-wicked-with-his-truth . . .
> He-who-spends-a-long-time-in-Oya's-grove;
> For when we wake up,
> You who serve the whole world, father of *Adeoti*,
> I will pay homage to you my father.[103]

Contrary to Pemberton's assumption, it is not only "women" who worship Sango. The term "husband" is a mistranslation of the Yoruba word *oko* in the text, and in no way constitutes evidence that only females use such a chant. Sango is the *oko* of his worshippers because he is the house-owner and they are the outsiders. It is accepted terminology for devotees and priests of *orisa* (religious deities or gods) to be called *iyawo* (consort). Recall S. O. Babayemi's assertion that "...male worshippers...like the females members...are referred to as wives of *Sango*."[104] Indeed Pemberton does include a photograph of a "wife" of another god, *Orisa Oko* in the collection.

The relationship between Sango and his congregation is neither gendered nor sexualized. Sango is not the only *orisa* who gives children. Apart from the fact that children are the ultimate gift with which any god can present to a devotee, there are at least two female deities, *Oya* and *Osun* who are specifically worshipped for their ability to give children. Therefore it is erroneous to attribute Sango's children-giving powers to his male anatomy.

While the sexualization of Sango worship may have made it difficult for Pemberton to acknowledge the *orisa's* male devotees, the same cannot be said for James Matory, who reveals another facet of the sexualized view. He interprets the categorization of the male adherents as *iyawo*—which he glosses as wife—as a sign of symbolic if not actual homosexuality. In the Geertzian mode of "thick descriptions [inventions]," his interpretations are so thick they curdle. Thus in Matory's writing, Sango priests appear as drag queens and transvestites. His dissertation, "Sex and the Empire that is No More: A Ritual History of Women's Power Among the Oyo-Yoruba," explores the symbolism of the Yoruba verb "*gun*" which he glosses as "to mount." He explicates: "indigenous lay testimony illustrates Oyo's rise and fall in dramatic images of gender relations. This imagery I, like other scholars, have glossed as 'mounting', which in Oyo religion and politics structures the delegation of authority from god to king, king to subject, husband to wife, and ancestor to descendant."[105]

From the preceding quote, it is obvious that the very premise on which Matory rests his study is alien to the Yoruba conception. Categories like "king" are absent and the so-called lines of authority he presents are fabrications, in that authority does not flow in the directions he has articulated, and of course gender categories are absent. No flow of authority between *oko* and *iyawo*, for instance, can be characterized as a gender-flow since both categories encompass male and female. Likewise, his introduction of homosexuality into Yoruba discourse is nothing but an imposition of yet another foreign model. Wande Abimbola, a scholar of Yoruba history and oral traditions, has raised doubts about the sexualized interpretation of Oyo history. As Matory records, Abimbola questions "whether the verb *gun* carries the implications of the English verb to mount.... Third, but concomitantly, he believes that I [Matory] exaggerate the gender correlates of Spirit possession (gigun) in the Oyo-Yoruba context."[106]

From the perspective of the present argument, sexuality, like gender, is considered to be a social and historical construct. Therefore, in order to determine if a sexualized interpretation is applicable to the Old Oyo setting, it becomes necessary to define what is normally male and female—identified in the culture, noting the historical time period and the changes through that time.

The case of hair adornment springs to mind. Sango priests are noted for their hairstyles—a corn rowed hairdo traditionally called *kolese*. Sango worship was the official religion of the Oyo court. This hair style is often interpreted by scholars as a sign that they are trying to enact femaleness. For example, Babayemi writes that for male worshippers to be accepted, "they must dress up their hair as women." While there is a contemporary notion that hair-plaiting and adornment is associated only with females, it is recent, not timeless, and is by no means universal—witness the elaborate hairstyles of many of the Esie stone figures.

In Ogbomoso I conducted interviews with the Awise Elesin Ibile chief Oyatope—chief of the practitioners of indigenous religion—who is also the priest of Oya (a female god).[107] His hair was in braids and he told me that priests of Oya, just like Sango priests after initiation, are never to cut their hair; therefore, for ease of grooming, they braid it. The emphasis here is not on braids but on never cutting the hair. Consequently, it is possible that the focus of many scholars on braids is a misguided emphasis in terms of deciphering meaning, the real issue is not why braids but why they do not cut their hair.

Nevertheless, hairstyle does have significance in Oyo history. There was a special class of bureaucrats and *alaafin*'s messengers called *Ilari*—named by their hair style. According to Johnson, "the term *Ilari* denotes parting of the head, from the peculiar way their hair is done. They are of both sexes and number some hundreds, even as many as the King desires." It is also common in current times to see male rulers and chiefs in eastern Yorubaland with cornrowed hair at certain festivals. Consequently, any analysis of hairstyle in Yoruba society cannot assume gender. Such an enterprise is best done within the context of the symbolism and metaphysics of hair and the *ori* (head) on which it stands.[108] This interpretation must also acknowledge the cultural locality and the socio-religious context. For instance, the genesis of the ceremonial coiffure differs from the religious. There are also different styles of corn rows, considering that the *kolese* may have a different symbolism from the *suku* style, for example. In the light of a host of complexities, it is difficult to sustain the view that male corn rowing is a sign of transvestism.

Finally, it is proper to assess the existence of institutions like the *oro* which function today as male-exclusive institutions in that when *oro* rituals are in process, in some Oyo towns, women are confined inside their compounds. In the light of my thesis that indigenous cultural norms were traditionally gender-free, the most pertinent question are: what is the origin of the *oro* institution and when did it emerge in Oyo? What is the nature of women's exclusion taking into account the permutations of the various identities commonly submerged under the concept of women. For example, a restriction on child-bearing females has a different meaning than a universal one. If *oro* is an old institution, did its character change over time? What are its implications with regard to access and the exercise of power for different sections of the population.

These are all empirical questions that cannot be answered by simply declaring that *oro* is off limits to women. Indeed, from the evidence that we have at this time, both *oro* and *ogboni* another contemporary institution in Yoruba polities are all new, being nineteenth-century additions to the sociopolitical structure of Oyo. Agiri and Atanda have researched the institution of *oro* and *ogboni* respectively. They have also touched on the linkages of these institutions with the Egungun cult, which is seen as supremely Oyo, and therefore plays a central role in the government of Oyo. According to Agiri, "in the case of Oyo, . . . available evidence suggests that the *Oro* was introduced there during the nineteenth century by the Jabata immigrant group. Here, the paramountcy of the egungun has never been in doubt...The egungun are associated with the important religious matters of state."[109]

Obinrin do participate in Egungun and the most important official, the *ato*, is a female. The marginalization of the *oro* in Oyo politics is in sharp contrast to the centrality of both the Egungun and Sango cults. The marginality of *oro* suggests its newness and foreignness in the Oyo cultural milieu. The more interesting question then would be how to comprehend the existence in one and the same polity of the dominant Sango cult, which is controlled by the mothers of the palace, and the *oro*, which purports to exclude women, a gender bias that is said to embrace even the all-powerful *ayaba* (mothers of the palace).

In his consideration of the Ogboni cult which is usually coupled with *oro*, Atanda criticized the interpolation of institutions in New Oyo on Old Oyo as Morton Williams had done in his speculations about the institutions of Old Oyo.[110] Atanda concluded:

> Whatever the case, the point being emphasized is that Ogboni cult became a factor in the government of Oyo only with the foundation of the new capital in the nineteenth century. There is therefore no basis for the present tendency of talking of the role of the cult in the government of the Old Oyo Empire which came to an end at the beginning of the nineteenth century and before the cult was introduced into the Oyo polity by alaafin Atiba. In other words, the error should be avoided of interpolating what is a nineteenth century phenomenon into the earlier history of Oyo.[111]

There is no question that the nineteenth century was a period of rapid and monumental changes in Oyo, primarily because of the civil wars and its permutations with the increasingly dominant and multifarious presence of Europeans—and Westernized Yoruba like Johnson—in the society. The impact of the changes of that period are still being felt and acted out. The nature and type of institutional transformations that took place are still not completely understood. The gendering of Oyo institutions and the attendant patriarchalization are the most important for this study. In the nineteenth century gender categories and consequent androcentrism became apparent in some of the discourses, institutions, and interpretations of history.

The source of Fadipe's irritation lies not in the Yoruba language but in the more recent imposition on the society of the European predilection for gender categorizing. One cannot blame the Yoruba for not creating gender constructs. The real problem is the mistranslation and distortion that have resulted from the process of imposing Western models in the reconstruction of Yoruba past.

Ultimately, the argument being made in this paper is not about whether females have been constructed as absent among the Oyo-Yoruba rulers, but about the presentation of the alaafin as men; also, it concerns the projection of the power of the rulers as being founded on the existence of male privilege and male interest. Consequently, the idea that privilege inhered in the male body type, was introduced into the scholarship about the Yoruba, independently of Yoruba cultural ethos and parameters of information coding, and therefore, without justification. Furthermore, in the process of constituting the history of Oyo, men were invented as a category from a universe that was gender-free; there was no an-sex-specification in access to offices by law, in language or in the cultural ethos. In creating kings, men were logically created and were then handed the rulership of the Empire, while the residual part of the society (what ever that was supposed to be) was carved out to be the domain of another category labeled women. This process derived from the uncritical assumption that Western categories were universal. Thus as Yoruba oral traditions became part of global history, they necessarily acquired the coloring of the dominant cultural institutions of their time—both Western secular and Christian. In these traditions, power and authority are believed to be the prerogative of the male sex and therefore gender interests were at the base of political institutions.

Thus the challenge for historians and other scholars is that in the same way that some may adduce evidence as to why, for example, the Oyo polity was not superior to that of Ile-Ifethey should provide evidence for a gendered reading of Yoruba traditions. They should further show proof that a system of rulership existed that was based on male-interest and male-only succession. Before scholars can make the kind of male-dominant claims that they have assumed, evidence has to show that the political hierarchy was dominated by males, secondly, that maleness constituted a particular social interest that promoted males as a group over females, and finally that such a gendered system is timeless.

Much of Oyo-Yoruba history has been written in the traditional event-centered mode of historical documentation in all of its overrepresentation of wars, kings and great men. This focus has led to the idea that male actors dominated, around an undefined male interest, to the detriment of and virtual absence of "women." In the previous article, I have shown that gender categories did not exist, as such, gender was not an organizing principle in Old Oyo society. Seniority defined by relative age was the dominant principle. Thus, social categories like men and women and other categories like kings deriving from an elaboration of anatomic distinctions did not exist. Oyo social categories were gender-free in that the anatomy did not constitute the basis for their construction and elaboration. Access to power, exercise of authority, and membership in occupations all derived from the lineage, which was regulated within by age, and not sex.

Consequently, the critical point being made here about gender in Old Oyo historiography, is what this work terms the invention of "women" and of course "men" as social categories, which are constructs elaborated on the presence or absence of certain body parts. This invention was not systematic. Rather, its original impetus was rooted in the assumption that gender is a natural way of categorizing in any society and that male privilege is its ultimate manifestation. This assumption was carried forward from European history as the model of global history, and because of colonization and the educational training of historians of African origin, many have not made a departure from the Western model which they have in the main accepted as given.

It is important to understand that the issue being raised is not a polemical objection to a male-dominated society. The focus rather, is an attempt to systematically scrutinize the building blocks of historical knowledge. What is being questioned is the claim in Yoruba historiography that old Oyo society was male-dominant, when no evidence has ever been adduced for this position. In Oyo, both history and tradition were reconstituted during the colonial period, and the indigenous world sense and frame of reference have been subverted in the process of constituting the new social categories—men, women, and kings in particular.

Having questioned the social identity of scholars and its effect on their interpretations of Oyo history, there seem to be a need to examine the gender conceptual gap in the cultural translation of Yoruba sensibilities into English and vice versa. This fact raises the question of the relationship between Yoruba categories, which are truly gender-free therefore generic and English categories, which privilege the male even when they appear to be generic. Given that the study and reconstruction of Yoruba history are undertaken by both Yoruba and Euro-American historians, there is a possibility that when the historians of Yoruba origin use the word "king" for example, they may mean a gender inclusive category like the Yoruba Oba. A number of historians, even as they write about king lists and kings, do not seem to be questioning the historicity of female alaafin (Babayemi, Agiri, Asiwaju for example) which leads the issue to whether they assume the category "king" to be gender-neutral like oba or alaafin. The reverse seems to be the case for many of the Europeans. (I examine the question of language, literature, cultural translation, and audience in paper 5.) The argument here is not that contemporary African historians are less androcentric than their Euro-American counterparts. Rather, the point is that the way in which English is being used may reflect different language and cultural realities. My experience of English language-use in Nigeria suggest such a possibility. Indeed, words and the meanings attached to them are ultimately decipherable only within the larger societal frame.

Barber's own work itself shows very clearly that oriki is neither male exclusive in subject matter, nor female exclusive in performance or composition. The limitations of her research is actually a limitation imposed by her insistence on using Western gender categories even as she correctly asserted that the Yoruba world is not dichotomized into male and female. More specifically, her insufficient appreciation of the fact that the oriki of the lineage are as much the product of female as well as male members of the lineage. The character and identity of a lineage derives from the personality and remarkable deeds of any member of the lineage which is then generalized to all the other members. The following passage is a good illustration of the nature of lineage oriki. Barber presents us with the oriki of Babalola, a prominent male member of the Elemoso lineage:

> Babalola, the child opens its arms, the child delights its father,
> The way my father walks delights the Iyalode.
> Enigboori, child of the father named Banlebu ["meet me at the dye-pits"]
> If people don't find me in the place where they boil ijokun dye
> They'll meet me where we go early to pound indigo,
> Enigboori, that's how they salute the father called "Banlebu"[my emphasis].

In the interpretation of this oriki provided to Barber by the elderly sister of Babalola being saluted, it becomes clear that the emphasized lines are actually a reference to a daughter of the compound who is noted for her sexual liaisons. The lines are actually interpreted to mean that "If you don't find her in one place you'll surely find her in another"—in other words, in the house of some man or other!" Yet, these are the lines from the lineage oriki which is being used to salute a prominent male member of the family. What this shows is that the character and identity of the lineage as projected in *oriki orile* (lineage oriki) is an emblematization of characteristics derived from past observations coupled with present behavior of any person in the lineage regardless of ex. The more fundamental implication of this fact, is the question of the nature of Oyo lineages. The idile (lineage) have been called patrilineages in the scholarly literature but as I showed in paper two, the concept distorts more than it illuminates what actually goes on inside these lineages and the local conception of them. Mothers, female offspring and *iyawo* are as central in the determination of the identity and characteristics of these institutions as are fathers and male offspring. The patrlineage is not so much the father's house but the father's house as inflected by the mother's identity. Thus, even children of the same father but different mothers are not inserted into the lineage in the same way neither would their personal oriki be identical or necessarily similar as these also draw from the mother's background.

A good example of what I have interpreted as the assumption that obaship is a gender-free institution is demonstrated in A.I. Asiwaju's account of the state of Ketu, in southern Yorubaland. He recounts a most interesting event which incidentally is consigned to a footnote in his book. In his discussion of the proliferation of *alaketu*, ruler of a Western Yoruba pre-colonial state that now straddles Nigeria and the Republic of Benin, he counted three claimants to the title in the 1970's. One was a female from Brazil: "One other Alaketu, a woman, based in Bahia, South America even visited Nigeria in 1974 with such pomp that she tended to eclipse the existence of the West-Africa based ones!"[112] That Asiwaju does not subject the an-sex of the self-styled *Alaketu* from the Yoruba Diaspora to analysis nor see it as a cultural aberration may be due to his recognition that succession in many pan-Yoruba states was not gender-based, and that therefore the appearance of a female ruler needed no explanation.

NOTES

1. One of the earliest scholarly engagements with African oral tradition as history is Saburi Biobaku, "The Problem of Traditional History with Special Reference To Yoruba Traditions," *JHSN* (December 1956). The present paper is based on a chapter in my *The Invention of Women: Making an African sense of Western Gender Discourses* (Minneapolis, 1997).
2. A. I. Asiwaju, "Political Motivation and Oral Historical Traditions in Africa: The Case of Yoruba Crowns," *Africa*, 46 (1976), 113–47.
3. Ibid., 116.
4. Bolanle Awe, "Introduction" in *Nigerian Women in Historical Perspective* (Lagos, 1992), 7.
5. See Oyeronke Oyěwùmí, "Inventing Gender: Questioning Gender in Precolonial Yorubaland" in *Problems in African History*, ed. Robert Collins (New York, 1993).
6. For aspects of his biography see J. F. Ade Ajayi, "Samuel Johnson: Historian of the Yoruba," *Nigeria Magazine* (1964), 141–46, and Phillip Zachernuk, "Samuel Johnson and the Victorian Image of the Yoruba," in Toyin Falola, ed., *Pioneer, Patriot, and Patriarch: Samuel Johnson and the Yoruba People* (Madison, 1993), 33–46.
7. N. A. Fadipe, *The Sociology of the Yoruba* (Ibadan, 1970), 63.
8. I hesitate to call it a problem because it is not a Yoruba-generated one. Rather, it is an issue that has arisen with the imposition of western values and practices which are imbued with gender, which is an ontological category in their thinking and social arrangements.
9. The Saro also called Akus and recaptives were liberated slaves who had been settled in the British colony of Sierra Leone. Many originated in Yorubaland, sold during the Atlantic slave trade, but had been liberated by the British squadron on the West African coast during the abolitionist phase of British expansion. In 1843, after being Westernized and Christianized, they started returning to Yorubaland and were to play a decisive role in the penetration of Western values and goods among the Yoruba. By the middle of the nineteenth century, they had become an elite group in Lagos and Abeokuta. They represented the internal factor that facilitated the colonization of Yorubaland. They also brought literacy and Western schooling to Nigeria. Bishop Ajayi Crowther—the first African Anglican Bishop in Africa—was one of them and he was instrumental in reducing Yoruba into writing. Indeed, the varied role of individual Saro and the collective in the history of modern Nigeria cannot be overstated. See Jean Kopytoff, *Preface to Modern Nigeria:Sierra leonians in Yorubaland*, 1830–1890 (Madison, 1965), for a history.
10. Robin Law, "How Truly Traditional Is Our Traditional History? The Case of Samuel Johnson and the Recording of Yoruba Oral Tradition," *HA* 11 (1984), 197.
11. For a discussion of feedback in other African oral traditions see David Henige, "The Problem of Feedback in Oral Tradition: Four Examples From the Fante Coastlands," *JAH*, 14 (1973), 223–25.

    For a discussion of Johnson and feedback in Yoruba history see B. A. Agiri, "Early Oyo History Reconsidered," in *HA* 2 (1975).
12. Ibid., 1.

13. Ibid.
14. R. Smith, "Alafin in Exile: a Study of the Igboho Period in Oyo History," *JAH* 6, (1965), 57–77; "Law, How Truly Traditional,"
15. "Law, How Truly Traditional," 207–11.
16. Samuel Johnson, *The History of the Yorubas* (London, 1921), 176.
17. Ibid., xxxvii.
18. Smith, Alafin in Exile, 68.
19. Johnson, *History of the Yorubas*, vii, with emphasis added.
20. Law, "How Truly Traditional," 199.
21. Curiously, he does not mention the female *akunyungba* (royal bards) or the *ayaba* (royal consorts) as one of his sources.
22. See Henige, "Feedback," and Law, "How Truly Traditional," for some of these disjunctures.
23. Law, "How Truly Traditional," 213.
24. I want to thank Olufemi Taiwo for his generous contribution in our discussions on this o this issue.
25. See *Ife: The Cradle of a Race*, ed. I. A. Akinjogbin (Port Harcourt, 1992).
26. There are no known references to Oyo written records earlier than the seventeenth or early eighteenth centuries. Invariably, the earliest eyewitness accounts are European accounts.
27. Law, "How Truly Traditional," 213.
28. J.A. Atanda, *The New Oyo Empire* (London, 1973).
29. Law, "How Truly Traditional?"
30. Agiri, "Early Oyo History," 5.
31. Johnson, *History*, 41.
32. Agiri, "Early Oyo History," 5.
33. Smith, *Alafin in Exile*, 64.
34. Johnson, *History*, 47
35. Ibid., 41.
36. Ibid.
37. J. A. Atanda, *New Oyo Empire*, 210; my translation.
38. Johnson, *History*, 155.
39. B. A. Agiri, "Early Oyo History," 9. Agiri argues that Sango may not have been a real individual, but that myths about him developed to explain the period of Nupe control over Oyo.
40. Johnson, *History*, 47.
41. There is also another meaning that female royal offspring do not make stable marriage partners.
42. Johnson, *History*, 86.
43. Ibid, xx.
44. Ibid., 173, with emphasis added.
45. Ibid.
46. Ibid., 156.
47 Ibid., 155. There is indeed some general confusion in the literature as to the lineage identity (are they wives or daughters?) of the female officials in the Oyo political hierarchy. The confusion is compounded by the fact that in English, they are called "queens" or "ladies of the palace." Smith, "Alafin in Exile," alludes to the confusion.
48. Johnson, *History*, 63–67. See also S. O. Babayemi, "The Role of Women in Politics and Religion in Oyo," paper presented at the Seminar on Women's

Studies: The State of the Arts Now in Nigeria, Institute of African Studies, Unioversity of Ibadan, November, 1987.

49. Smith, *The Alafin in Exile*, 32, with emphasis added.
50. What might need further analysis though is the fact that the word *baale* seems to derive from *baba*, which means "father."
51. Transcripts of recorded interview conducted in Ogbomoso on 3 and 26 March 1996. I also have in my possession an autobiographical pamphlet given to me by the Baale herself. *Iwe Itan Kukuru Nipa Ilu Maya (Ayetoro).*
52. Law, "How Truly Traditional," 210.
53. Smith, "Alafin in Exile," 75n52.
54. J. D. Y. Peel, "Kings, Titles, and Quarters: a Conjectural History of Ilesa," *HA*, 6 (1979), 126.
55. S. O. Babayemi, "The Rise and Fall of Oyo" (Ph.D., University of Birmingham, 1990).
56. Peel, "Kings, Titles, and Quarters," 129.
57. Peel, "The Pasyt in the Ijesha Present," *Man* ns 19 (1984), 113.
58. Johnson, *History*, 65.
59. A. Temu and B. Swai, *Historians and Africanist History: A Critique* (London, 1981).
60. P. F. de Moraes Farias, "History and Consolation: Royal Yoruba Bards Comment on Their Craft," *HA*, 19 (1992), 263–97.
61. Ibid., 275.
62. Ibid., 270, with emphasis added.
63. Ibid., 275.
64. In the Yoruba Bible the same expression is used to indicate that Jesus is the only son of God. The implications of the non-gender specificity of the Yoruba term *omo* to refer to Jesus has not been studied.
65. Bolanle Awe, "Praise Poetry as Historical Data: The Example of Yoruba Oriki," in *Africa*, 44 (1974), 332.
66. Ibid., 348.
67. Ibid.
68. Karin Barber, "Documenting Social and Ideological Change Through Yoruba Personal Oriki: A Stylistic Analysis," *JHSN*, 10/4
69. Adeboye Babalola, *Awon Oriki Borokinni* (Ibadan).
70. S.O. Babayemi, *Content Analysis of Oriki Orile* [undated] 168–69.
71. Awe, "Praise Poetry," 340–46.
72. Barber, *I Could Speak Until Tomorrow: Oriki, Women, and the Past in a Yoruba Town* (Edinburgh, 1991), 198.
73. Ibid.
74. Ibid., 259.
75. Babalola, *Awon*, 7–9.
76. Ibid.
77. Bolanle Awe, "The lyalode in the Traditional Yoruba Political System"; in Alice Schlegel, ed., *Sexual Stratification: A Cross-Cultural View* (New York, 1977).
78. Johnson, *History,* 66.
79. As it happens, Oba Oyěwùmí is my father; I have had numerous conversations on all these questions with him.

80. For the rise and influence of Ibadan see Bolanle Awe, "The Rise of Ibadan as a Yoruba Power" (D. Phil., Oxford University, 1964).
81. Interview conducted at her residence in Ogbomoso on 7 July 1996. Transcript is available.
82. Awe, "Iyalode," 157
83. Ibid., 147–48.
84. Ibid., 153.
85. Oladipo Yemitan, *Madame Tinubu: Merchant and King-Maker* (Ibadan, 1987), 47–48.
86. Awe, "Iyalode," 152
87. Oweyumi, Invention of Women, 76.
88. See for example, the discussion in J. A. Atanda, *New Oyo Empire.*
89. Awe, "Iyalode," 151.
90. M. T. Drewal and H. J. Drewal, "Composing Time and Space in Yoruba Art," *Word and Image*, 3 (1987), 225.
91. Philips Stevens,*Stone Images of Esie, Nigeria* (New York, 1978).
92. Ibid., 22.
93. Ibid., 65.
94. Oyěwùmí, "Inventing Gender."
95. Ibid.
96. John Berger, *Ways of Seeing* (London, 1972), 45–64.
97. C. O. Adepegba, *Yoruba Metal Sculpture* (Ibadan, 1991), 31.
98. Stevens, *Stone Images*, 65.
99. John Pemberton, "The Oyo Empire" in Henry Drewal, John Pemberton, Rowland Abiodun, and Allen Wardwell, *Yoruba: Nine Centuries of Art and Thought*, (New York, 1989), 78, with emphasis added.
100. Ibid., 82.
101. Johnson, *History*, 65.
102. Pemberton, "Oyo Empire," 162.
103. Ibid.
104. S.O. Babayemi, "The Role of Women in Politics and Religion in Oyo."
105. James Matory, "Sex and the Empire That Is No More" (Ph.D., University of Chicago, 1992), 6.
106. Ibid., 538.
107. Interview conducted in his residence in Ogbomoso on 16 March 1996. Transcripts of recorded interview available.
108. See Rowland Abiodun, "Verbal and Visual Metaphors: Mythical Allusions in Yoruba Ritualistic Art of Ori," *Word and Image* 3 (1987), 257.
109. B. A. Agiri and T. Ogboni "Among the Oyo-Yoruba," *Lagos Notes and Records*, 3 (1972), 53.
110. Peter Morton-Williams, "An Outline of the Cosmology and Cult Organization of the Oyo Yoruba," *Africa*, 34 (1964), 243–61.
111. J. A. Atanda, "The Yoruba Ogboni Cult: Did It Exist in Old Oyo?" *JHSN* 6/4 (1973), 371.
112. Asiwaju, "Political Motivation," 113. It should be recalled that, according to Johnson, the polity of Ketu was one of the original polities founded by Oduduwa's children. In the case of Ketu, however, it is said that because this child of Oduduwa was female, the deed of founding passed to her son.

CHAPTER 11

GENDER BIASES IN AFRICAN HISTORIOGRAPHY

Paul Tiyambe Zeleza

INTRODUCTION

In the last two decades the literature on African women has grown rapidly. This can be attributed to several factors, including the political impetus of the women's movement and the crisis of conventional development theory and practice, and the consequent rise of the women-in-development project. For the discipline of history, more specifically, interest in women's history has been spawned by the widening horizons of historical epistemology and research, especially the growing interest in, and the development of, new approaches to social history. Until recent times historians preoccupied themselves with political history. They tirelessly described political developments, wars and battles, and celebrated the lives of great men (Barraclough, 1978; Conkin, 1989; Himmelfarb, 1987).

Despite the proliferation of the literature on women, including women's history, women remain largely invisible or misrepresented in mainstream, or rather "malestream," African history. They are either not present at all, or they are depicted as naturally inferior and subordinate, as eternal victims of male oppression. Alternatively, the romantic myth is advanced that the roles of women and men were equal and complimentary in good old, harmonious, pre-colonial Africa, or the lives of notable, exceptional, heroic women are celebrated (Imam, 1988). In short, in most institutions of higher learning in Africa women's history is still marginal and lacks recognition and academic respectability (Awe, 1991: 211).[1] This situation is, of course, not peculiar to African history. It applies worldwide, and to the social sciences in general.[2]

This chapter seeks to do four things. First, it will demonstrate the inadequate representation of women in African history by looking at some of the most frequently used texts. Second, an attempt will be made to identify some of the reasons for this by examining the dominant paradigms in African historiography. Thirdly, the chapter outlines the reconstructions of women's history made by feminist historians. These historians face two interrelated challenges. The first is to recover, empirically, the lives of women and restore their story to history. The second challenge is theoretical, to deconstruct the conventional historical paradigms and devise new ones which will rid history of its inherent androcentrism, in order to redefine and enlarge the scope of the discipline as whole, to make historical reconstructions more inclusive, more comprehensive, and more complex. The final part, then, suggests some ways of gendering African history.

The Invisible Women

The authors of African history textbooks differ in their approaches and research methods, in the subjects they examine, the interpretations they advance, and in their ideological outlooks. But they have two things in common: they are predominantly male and sexist in so far as their texts underestimate the important role that women have played in all aspects of African history. In more extreme cases women are not even mentioned at all, or if they are, they are discussed in their stereotypical reproductive roles as wives and mothers. The language used often inferiorises the women's activities, or experiences being described. Also, women's lives are usually cloaked in a veil of timelessness: the institutions in which their lives are discussed, such as marriage, are seen as static. In viewing them as unchanging, as guardians of some ageless tradition, women are reduced to trans-historical creatures outside the dynamics of historical development.

A survey of some of the most widely used history textbooks clearly demonstrates these biases. The chapter will examine three categories of texts: general histories that are continental in their coverage, regional histories, and histories of particular themes, such as political, economic, and social history. With each text, the chapter tabulates the space devoted to women in the text and in the illustrations, if any, and the general thrust of those references in terms of content.

The General Histories

Eight sets of general histories were examined. They are all written by prominent historians of Africa, both African and Africanist. None is a woman. Some of them do not even mention women in their indexes. This is true of Tidy and Leeming's (1981) two volume text, *A History of Africa* and Afigbo *et al.* (1986) *The Making of Modern Africa,* also in two volumes. Volume One of the latter book looks at Africa in the nineteenth century and Volume Two at Africa in the twentieth century. I looked at the revised edition published in 1986. "This very popular text," the blurb at the back proclaims, "has been thoroughly revised to include the most up-to-date developments in research and historiography." The two texts have 372 pages each, making for a total of 744 pages, none of which is specifically devoted to women. The illustrations are hardly any better. Out of the sixty illustrations in Volume One women appear perfunctorily in two. Volume Two is a little better. Out of 80 illustrations women appear in 13, mostly in the background. Only in three are they the central focus of attention.

The most comprehensive studies which seek to summarise current significant knowledge in African history are the UNESCO *General History of Africa* (1981–1993) and the Cambridge *History of Africa* (1975–1986) both published in eight thick volumes.[3] Both studies have very little to say about women. An examination of Volumes 6 and 7 of the UNESCO *General History* and volumes 5–8 of the Cambridge History dealing with the nineteenth and twentieth centuries, periods upon which reconstructions of African women's history have concentrated, amply bears this out. Volumes 6 and 7 of the UNESCO *General History* have 861 and 865 pages, respectively. Women are mentioned only on 4 and 14 pages, respectively. In Volume 6, the women are mentioned with reference to Chokwe women who followed their husband traders (p. 302), provision of education for Egyptian girls by the Coptic Church (p. 347), women as gold washers in Asante and Lobi (p. 690), and sexual relations between diaspora African men in Europe and European women (p. 759), while in Volume 7 they are mentioned with reference to their fertility patterns (five pages) and polygyny (four pages). It needs to be noted that the references to women on these pages are mostly restricted to a sentence or two. As for visual representation, out of 125 illustrations in Volume 6 women appear in 20. Only in ten of them are women represented alone. The women depicted are mostly either slaves or queens. In Volume 7 women appear in 11 out of the 96 illustrations. Only in two of these illustrations are the women the central characters.

The same pattern can be seen in the Cambridge History. Women appear on three pages out of 517 pages in Volume 5; ten out of 956 pages in Volume 6; 30 out of 1063 pages in Volume 7; and nine out of 1011 pages in Volume 8. Of the three references in Volume 5, one is to Creole women traders, the other to Chokwe acquisition of slave women, and the third is to the growing numbers of European women in the colonial enclaves towards the end of the nineteenth century. Interestingly, in this volume marriage is mentioned on 8 pages without even referring to women at all! In Volume 6 the references are to women's agricultural work (on four pages), women as "assets" or "pawns" for chiefs, local lords, and elders (on four pages). The last two are on young women migrating to towns in southern Africa and the importation of British female domestics to South Africa. The bulk of the references to women in Volume 7 are to women's resistance against colonial rule, specifically pass laws in South Africa and taxation in Nigeria. Next comes references to the increased agricultural burden on women as a result of expanded cash crop production, the imposition of forced labour and male labour migration. Interestingly, most of the references are to women in Southern Africa. Women in Central Africa are referred to only on one page, East African women on two pages, North African women on three pages, and West African women on six pages. It is quite remarkable that in Volume 8 which deals with the period 1940–1975, for which there is abundant literature on African women in development, there is only one reference to women as producers! Indeed, in this volume women are largely mentioned in passing, with reference to urban migration, employment, seclusion, and apartheid pass laws.

The single volume general histories are no different. Basil Davidson's (1991) revised and expanded edition of his celebrated *Africa in History*, has only one reference to women, in which the author states rather blandly that "generally, all women in Africa suffered, as most of them have continued to suffer, from more or less gross forms of discrimination imposed by men" (p. 191). In Curtin, *et al.* (1978) African History which, we are told, "celebrates the coming of age of *African history*, representing a quarter of a century of research by scholars from Africa, Europe and America," and in which "less emphasis is given to political history and more to social, economic and intellectual trends," women are mentioned only on nine out of the 612 pages, and appear in one out of 25 illustrations. On five of the nine pages, women are mentioned or alluded to in relation to polygyny, in which they are depicted merely as commodities that were circulated. In the remaining references, a paragraph is devoted on page 161 to discussing, in static terms, gender inequality in early East Africa. This is followed, on pages 559 and 566 by sketchy discussions of two paragraphs each, first of the impact of male migrant labour on women during the colonial period, and second, of gender imbalances in settler and non-settler colonial cities. The longest section dealing with women, tries to examine, in three paragraphs, the 1929–1930 women's "riots" in Nigeria known as the Aba "women's war." The lone illustration with a women's representation is a piece of sculpture, whose caption reads: "Kneeling woman holding a bowl, from Luba, Zaire, Buli workshop. Such statues were used by Luba kings. White porcelain clay with supernatural powers was kept in the bowl. This is a utensil of sacred kingship." This is all the authors have to say about gender relations in this society! [4]

There are more references to women in Robert July's (1992) latest edition of *A History of the African People*. They appear on 20 out of the book's 593 pages and in seven out of the 78 illustrations. But the descriptions and depictions are very sexist. Women are portrayed either as high status queen-mothers or merely as pawns and commodities that were distributed by male elders. According to the author, they were valued in pre-colonial societies primarily for their fertility (p. 548), and by the Europeans as concubines (p. 146), for they were otherwise part of the rural "unproductive population" (p. 405). Indeed, in July's account women are discussed in the same breath as children, debtors and slaves in the pre-colonial era (p. 125), and as children, the aged, and the infirm in the colonial era (p. 406). Women's lives are seen as static, as shown by the fact that the longest section on women, which revealingly comes towards the end of the book (pp. 546–47), discusses women "in traditional African society," thereby glossing over the impact of colonialism, and then jumps to contemporary discrimination against women, which the author attributes largely to "widespread ignorance among African women concerning the specific details of their own rights." In the illustrations we mainly see the women walking. When they are doing something, like pounding grain, it is before a background of a drought-stricken landscape, the effect of which is to reinforce the futility of their efforts. The ravaged landscape becomes a metaphor of their utter helplessness and victimisation by, and in a perverse way affinity to, nature.

The victimisation, indeed infantilization, of women is no less explicit in Freund's (1984) self-proclaimed radical book, *The Making of Contemporary Africa*, which is written, it is claimed, "from a materialist perspective [that] provides a refreshing reinterpretation of the complex events in sub-Saharan Africa since the eighteenth century. It also serves," the blurb continues, "as a succinct introduction to the history of modern Africa, incorporating in the text a critical appraisal of the best scholarship in recent years." However, women, who are mentioned on 22 out of the 357 pages, but hardly shown in any of the 12 illustrations, are treated no better than in the other books examined above. Almost invariably, they are mentioned as "dependents," together with youths, clients and slaves whether in the pre-colonial period (p. 63), or the colonial period (pp. 129, 131, 134). Women and youths are mentioned interchangeably when examining their entry into wage labour (p. 147) and colonial cities (p. 183). For a study claiming to be informed by historical materialism, it is rather strange that before the nineteenth century men and women are shown to have lived in an oversimplified, static, and homogeneous world, in which the men hunted and the women grew and prepared food (pp. 19–20), until, behold, the Europeans brought cassava which "may have freed women from agricultural labour," never mind that "the evidence for this is very limited" (p. 45). The marginalization of women extends to the bibliography. Publications on African women are given only one paragraph in a fifty-page select bibliography.

The Regional Histories

The regional histories display the same tendencies. There are those that totally ignore women, and others that mention them in passing. The few that discuss women in slightly more detail still betray androcentric biases. I have examined five regional histories, covering each region of the continent. Needless to say, regional history is unevenly developed, reflecting no doubt different historiographical traditions, patterns of colonization and decolonization, and the varied constructions of regional identities.[5] By comparing different editions, some of the regional histories under survey clearly demonstrate that women's history has yet to penetrate the thick walls of androcentrism that encircle African historiography.

An example of a regional history that does not mention women is Abun-Nasr's (1975, 1987) *A History of the Maghrib*. In the second edition published in 1975 women are not even indexed. In 1987 the author published a revised volume that "supersedes" the previous two editions. He was compelled to do so, he states, because "our knowledge of Maghribi history has advanced rapidly and new perspectives for interpreting it were opened by research in which Maghribi historians have participated in an outstanding way" (p. xi). The new book is certainly more detailed: it has 455 pages compared to 422 pages for the 1975 edition. But it resembles the earlier editions in one fundamental way: women are still totally ignored. So much for the "new perspectives".

Women are also largely absent from the regional histories of southern and eastern Africa that I looked at. They are not mentioned in the first edition of Denoon and Nyeko's (1972, 1984) *Southern Africa Since 1800.* Neither are they mentioned in the second edition of 1984, which was undertaken, the authors tell us, because of the "very great changes in the quality and quantity of information available. In order to accommodate the new evidence, and the new ideas which have been circulated," they conclude, "we could not simply make the small changes which are often introduced into the second edition of a book. Instead, we found we had to re-write the book, developing a new framework for this evidence and for these ideas." This new evidence and the new ideas apparently have yet to discover women or gender. As for the illustrations, out of 23 in the first edition, only three show women, one of a woman barely discernible in a group of men, another of semi-naked women, and the third of women and girls smiling to the camera before a background of a shanty location. In the second edition, the offending picture of naked women has been removed, but the other two retained. In a third picture a handful of school girls are shown as part of the Soweto uprising; they are walking behind a large group of school boys. Thus there are still three pictures depicting women, but now out of 26 illustrations.

Omer-Cooper's (1987) textbook is not much better in terms of the illustrations. Women appear in 18 out of the 115 illustrations. They are prominently featured in only six out of the 18, and only in one do they appear alone. This is a picture of women leaving jail with their fists raised in defiant gesture. In the actual text, women are mentioned on seven out the 297 pages, with reference to marriage (on three pages), Zulu military settlements, royal women, and pass laws (on one page each).

The same skewed coverage of women is evident in the standard history texts on East Africa. Women are not mentioned in Ingham's (1965) study, or Ogot's (1973) widely used text, *Zamani.* Women are also notable for their absence in Volumes I and II of the three Volume *Oxford History of East Africa* (Harlow and Chilver 1965). In Volume III women are mentioned on ten out of 691 pages, mostly in connection to their marriage patterns, fertility, and morals as perceived by missionaries and other colonial ideologues (pp. 405–08). Women's political activities are mentioned very briefly on two pages, noting the formation in Tanzania in the 1950s of a Council of Women by a certain Lady Twining and a women's section in the Tanganyika African National Union (TANU), respectively (pp. 185, 187). As for women's productive roles, the book is largely silent, except to note, in a sentence put in brackets, that "(women, except for those who had found freedom, at a price, in the towns, did what they had always done)" (p. 512).

The situation is not much better with Ajayi and Crowder's *History of West Africa* (1985), the standard textbook on West African history. According to the index of Volume 1 of the 1976 edition[6] women are mentioned on four pages out of the book's 649 pages. The textual material is confined to fleeting statements on the institution of women chiefs in the Ondo area of the

Yoruba, and the active role played in political life by women relations of the king in the Wolof and Serer kingdom. There are 26 additional references to women which can be culled from the text. They include the three references to Queen Amina, and the 11 and 12 references to matrilineal and patrilineal systems, respectively. On "the legendary exploits" of Queen Amina the author murmurs that "her conquests and achievements may have been exaggerated" (p. 561). As for the statements on the matrilineal and patrilineal systems, they are often presented in the anthropological present, and no attempt is made to analyse how they developed, or the content of gender relations they embodied. For example, we are told (p. 464), without explanation, that in Djoloff the predominant matrilineal system gradually gave way to the patrilineal system. Volume 2 of the 1976 edition, which covers the nineteenth and twentieth centuries, has, surprisingly, even fewer references to women. There is only one reference to the category "patrilineal," none to "matrilineal." No remarkable woman is mentioned. Half of the references to women, made on six pages in a book of 764 pages, are on the impact of the nineteenth-century jihads. The famous 1929 Women's Aba riot is given short shrift in two sentences.

A comparison between the 1976 and 1985 editions shows little improvement in terms of gender coverage and analysis. The example of Volume 1 will suffice. In the 1985 edition, according to the index, there are two additional pages that refer to women. The additions are on women as slaves (pp. 640–41). In the meantime, references to matrilineages and patrilineages have been reduced to two pages each, and if one adds references to marriage and family, there are 12 other references to women. In addition to those directly referring to women and Queen Amina in the index, women are mentioned on 22 pages, less than the number in the 1976 edition. And yet the 1985 edition is 93 pages longer than the former edition!

The most extensive coverage of women among the regional histories I examined was found in Birmingham and Martin's (1983) *History of Central Africa*. The fact that it was first published in 1983 may have something to do with it. Also, unlike the texts examined above, one of its editors is a woman. Volume One deals with the pre-colonial period, while Volume Two focuses on the colonial and post-colonial periods. In the first volume women are mentioned on 59 out of the book's 315 pages, and in the second volume on 53 out of the 432 pages. In both volumes, however, women are mostly referred to in relation to marriage. References to women and marriage can be found on 35 out of the 59 pages where women are mentioned in Volume One and on 30 out of the 53 pages in Volume Two. The bulk of the remaining references deal with women as timeless victims of a ferocious patriarchal order. In Volume One women are mentioned as subordinate agricultural labourers and as slaves on nine pages each. In Volume Two women's labour, whether in the agricultural or the urban economy, is mostly discussed as an appendage of male migrant labour. Predictably, the remaining contexts in which women are mentioned centre on women's infertility and prostitution.

The Thematic Histories

It would appear that women's invisibility is no less marked in the historical studies dealing with specific themes. It is most apparent in studies dealing with political history, and slightly less so in texts on economic and social history. Out of the seven studies on nationalism and decolonization that I examined, four do not mention women at all (Davidson, 1978; Mazrui and Tidy, 1984; Hargreaves, 1988; and Gifford and Louis, 1988). In Rotberg and Mazrui's (1970) massive collection on *Protest and Power in Black Africa*, women are not indexed, but one of the contributions is on a woman religious and nationalist leader, Alice Lenshina of Zambia (Roberts, 1970). That is one out of 35 contributions. In Gifford and Louis's (1982) *The Transfer of Power in Africa*, which is 654 pages long, women are mentioned only once, not in the actual text, but in the bibliographic essay, where a study on women's involvement in the Algerian revolution is noted and the point made that this involvement "did not lead to an improvement in their condition in a Muslim society. Once independence was achieved, a traditional reaction scuttled the advances they had started to make" (p. 534). De Braganca and Wallerstein's (1982) three volume reader on African liberation movements only contains two documents by women: one is by Zanele Dhlamini on women's liberation in South Africa prepared on the occasion of the South African Women's Day in 1972 (Dhlamini, 1982), and the other by Sinclair (1982), President of the South African women's organization, Black Sash, replying to a newspaper article disputing claims that conditions in South Africa in 1970 were improving. The cover of Volume 2, in which there is no document by a woman, shows a male soldier with a gun receiving a pumpkin from a woman, who is balancing another pumpkin on her head while holding a third by her other arm. The message is clear: men are the fighters, women the food providers. So much for the transformative power of liberation struggles!

Three of the six books on economic history that I looked at also do not mention women or deal with the question of gender (Munro, 1976; Wickins, 1981; Issawi, 1982). The other three make very feeble efforts to do so. In Rodney's (1982) renowned *How Europe Underdeveloped Africa* women are mentioned on six out of 312 pages. Brief references are made to the exploitation and oppression of women in the Maghreb (p. 55), the women Amazon warriors in Dahomey (p. 121), and women's limited access to education during the colonial period (pp. 251, 266). The most detailed treatment of women comes in the last chapter on the impact of colonialism on Africa. Ironically, it outlines the role of women in "independent precolonial Africa." The author discusses the "two contrasting and contradictory tendencies." On the one hand, women, especially "in Moslem African societies," were exploited and oppressed by men through polygamous arrangements. But they were also accorded respect and enjoyed a "variety of privileges based on the fact that they were keys to inheritance," on the other. Indeed, "women had real power in the political sense, exercised through religion or directly within the politico-constitutional apparatus" (p. 226). It is quite strange that in an economic treatise women's economic roles are hardly addressed.

In Hopkins' (1973) *An Economic History of West Africa* and Austen's (1987) African Economic History only the barest allusions are made to women's economic roles. Hopkins refers to women on six out of 337 pages in two contexts: in connection with household labour and local trade. He notes that in the (timeless) pre-colonial era, West African "societies distinguished between the labour of men and women, though the line was not always drawn at the same point" (p. 21). As for trade, women's involvement is portrayed as having been restricted to local trade on the grounds that "local trade was a convenient adjunct to household and, in some societies, farming activities" (p. 56). Recent studies have shown that women were also involved in long distance trade (Afonja, 1981; White, 1987; Amadiume, 1987). Despite its publication almost a decade and half after Hopkins' study, Austen's book is far less satisfactory both as an economic history text and in its coverage of women. Women are mentioned on ten out of 294 pages, either in passing (sometimes even in brackets as on p. 180), or invoked to support dubious contentions. For example, Austen denies that the Atlantic slave trade had a negative demographic impact on Angola because women "who are the key determinant of reproduction in any human population" were left behind (p. 96). He also disputes that colonial cash production undermined domestic food supplies for women continued their "traditional" food producing activities (pp. 139, 145).

The most extensive coverage of women in the studies I examined was found in books on labour and social history published in the 1980s. Earlier labour history studies tended to ignore women. For example, women are notable by their absence in the two renowned labour history studies published in the 1970s: *The Development of An African Working Class* (Sandbrook and Cohen, 1975) and *African Labour History* (Gutkind *et al.* 1978). Two relatively recent labour histories compare favourably to this. One is by Stichter (1985) and the other by Freund (1988). In Stichter's *Migrant Labourers,* women are discussed on 82 out of 225 pages. In fact, two of the seven chapters are specifically devoted to women. In Freund's *The African Worker*, women are featured on 28 out of 200 pages. Stichter's analysis on women centres on two main issues. First, the effects of male labour migration on women where it is argued that male labour migration led to changes in the traditional division of productive labour between men and women. Women's workload increased as they took on tasks previously done by men and became heads of households. They showed initiative by adopting new agricultural strategies and trading roles, or by migrating to the cities. Secondly, in Chapter 6 Stichter examines women as migrants and workers by looking at the factors behind female labour migration, the patterns of women's employment, and the forms of women's consciousness and struggle.

Stichter seeks to celebrate women's active involvement in the labour process, but in the end she idealises colonialism as a force that liberated

African women from ruthless patriarchal control. In "African pre-capitalist societies," she asserts, women's status was not dissimilar to that of slaves and serfs' (p. 148). This contention is based on an uncritical acceptance of anthropological theories on "domestic," "lineage" or "patriarchal" modes of production according to which male elders controlled the labour of junior males and women of all ages.[7] Not only is the conceptualisation of modes of production problematic, as demonstrated above, but gender relations in pre-colonial Africa cannot be generalized.[8] As Freund states, "the rights of male elders to appropriate surplus in African societies varied immensely" (p. 6), so that "it is a tricky business to generalise for sub-Saharan Africa as a whole on the question of women and labour exploitation" (p. 83). However, Freund's own examination of women and the labour process (concentrated on pp. 81–90) is far less satisfactory than that provided by Stichter. It lacks any systematic historical analysis, for unconnected and undeveloped points are thrown around on women's labour in the household, informal sector, factory work, and domestic service. That says something about the author's valuation of women as historical subjects.

A similar problem can be seen in the books on social history that I examined. While efforts are made to incorporate women, they are still depicted either as marginal or weak. For example, although several authors in *Peasants in Africa: Historical and Contemporary Perspectives* (Klein, 1980) refer to rural women, women are never depicted as central to the peasant production systems, societies, struggles, and transformations being analysed. In Feierman and Janzen's (1992) collection, *The Social Basis of Health and Healing in Africa* in which women are considered on 58 out of the 487 pages, the women are largely discussed with reference to their fertility patterns, rather than their role as healers, unlike men. We are also told of male perceptions of disease rather than female perceptions. In a rare comparison of male and female medical practitioners, we are informed that among the Zulu women practice medicine in a "clairvoyant" manner while men practice in a "nonclairvoyant" manner (Ngubane 1992). In Illife's (1987) ambitious, but disappointing, tome *The African Poor: A History,* women are discussed on about 100 out of 387 pages. But Illife's poor women, like his poor in general, are timeless victims of Africa's seemingly primordial structural poverty. They are invariably "unsupported" or "unattached" women, that is, women without men, the unmarried, widowed, and sterile women. Nothing could save them from poverty, neither wit nor informal sector activities. And they could not turn to poverty relief institutions or their own social welfare and support networks for these institutions and networks were poorly developed or non-existent. Their only salvation lay in marriage. In short, married and dependent women are invisible from the ranks of Illife's poor.

African Historiographies and Women's History

The relative underdevelopment of African women's history can partly be attributed to the fact that, as Bolanle Awe (1991: 211) has argued, "compared with the history of many other parts of the world, the writing of the history of Africa itself is a fairly recent development." Few would dispute that history as a discipline is intrinsically empirical. That does not mean, however, that historical reconstructions are not based on deeply held philosophical assumptions, or specific theoretical frameworks often borrowed from the other social sciences. In the last three decades, as demonstrated in earlier chapters, three paradigms have dominated mainstream African historiography: the nationalist school, which was dominant from the time of decolonization to the early 1970s; the underdevelopment or dependency perspective, which held sway from the late 1960s to the late 1970s; and the Marxist approach which gained ascendancy in the 1970s and early 1980s. This periodization is not meant to denote neat sequential stages, for elements of all three paradigms have coexisted at any one time in the last three decades and, indeed, continue to do so, as shown in Chapter 7 on imperialist historiography.

As noted earlier, in reconstructing African history, the nationalist historians were preoccupied with eradicating imperialist and racist myths that Africa had no history prior to the coming of the Europeans, and in devising new methods of research to recover African history (Ki-Zerbo, 1981; Vansina, 1985; Henige, 1982). This fixation with celebrating and laying the empirical framework of African civilizations not only consumed the historians" energies, but also blinded them to gender analysis. These historians sought to reclaim and glorify Africa's great states, cities, and leaders. In short, nationalist historiography was primarily political and elitist. It had little to say about the "masses," whether men or women, or social and economic history. Almost invariably, exploitation and oppression were discussed only in reference to colonialism. Thus in its epistemology, nationalist historiography had neither the conceptual tools nor the ideological inclination to deal with class or gender hierarchies, exploitation and struggles in African history.

For their part the historians using the dependence paradigm focused primarily on the economics of exploitation, but in spatial, not social or class terms. Development and underdevelopment were seen as integrated and dialectical processes, linking and reproducing the differentiated spatial configurations of Europe and Africa, "metropoles" and "peripheries," "centres" and "satellites," the "North" and the "South," "developed" and "developing" countries, the "First" and "Third" worlds. Consequently, the central problematic of dependence historiography was to unlock and explain the process by which surplus from Africa and the peripheries in general was drained, expatriated, or appropriated by Europe or the metropoles in this integrated world capitalist system. Unequal exchange, whether of products or labour costs, became the pivot around which the entire process of western development and "Third World" underdevelopment spun. The dependence paradigm produced a static, frozen history of Africa, one in which external forces played the predominant role. It is a history of inter-national, not class, relations and struggles. Whenever class is alluded to, it is often used as a derivative and functionalist category, simply as one among the many factors that mediate dependence and underdevelopment. If dependence historiography ignores class, it has proved stubbornly blind to gender analysis.

On this score, Marxist scholars were hardly any better, despite their vigorous critiques of both nationalist and dependency historiographies. Marxist historians were too preoccupied with fitting African histories into the Marxian modes of production, or inventing tropicalized varieties, and articulating them with the capitalist mode during colonialism, to delve seriously into gender analysis. Besides, class, not gender, is the central problematic of traditional Marxism. Women's oppression is seen as a secondary phenomenon, a symptom of capitalist oppression. As argued in the classic Marxist study on women, *The Origin of the Family, Private Property, and the State* by Engels (1972), women's oppression originated with the introduction of private property. Contrary to popular perceptions, this study does not offer a concrete historical analysis but an abstract model based on dubious anthropological data (Lane, 1976). The inadequacy of the traditional Marxist paradigm has given rise to other feminist frameworks, including radical feminism and socialist feminism, which seek to comprehend the role of class as well as gender, race, and nationality, among other social constructs, in the creation of women's oppression and liberation (Jaggar and Rothenberg, 1984; Hirsch and Keller, 1990; Hutchful, 1996).

It can be seen, therefore, that none of the three dominant paradigms used in reconstructing African history takes women's history and women's oppression seriously.[9] Not surprisingly, women are either absent or marginal in the historical studies examined above, which were in one way or the other inspired by these frameworks. Thus the challenge that faces feminist historians is not only one of recovering women's history, of redressing balances, but also one of developing new theoretical frameworks that better explain the real world. In this endeavour, feminist historians have been busy deconstructing the hierarchical conceptual dualisms that seek to encase women's lives in the worlds of "nature" and the "family," and the "private" and "domestic" spheres, as distinct from the supposedly male worlds of "culture" and "work," and the "public" and "political" spheres. To begin with, the binary vision contained in these dualisms, such as the private/public divide, misrepresents the interdependence and interconnectedness of social reality and processes. Moreover, these distinctions and dichotomies are not universal, whether as empirical realities, or as conceptual categories. They arose in a specific European historical context[10] and are derived from Enlightenment thought (Foster, 1992: 3–6).

Historians concerned with gender analysis have to guard against both essentializing and universalising the experiences of particular, mostly white middle-class western, women. "There are startling parallels," writes Spelman (1988: 6), "between what feminists find disappointing and insulting in Western philosophical though and what many women have found troubling in much of Western feminism". All too often race, ethnicity, and class are inserted as "additive analyses." The unfortunate result is a discourse that is patently racist, especially when spurious comparisons are drawn between racism and sexism and the latter is depicted as being a more "fundamental" form of oppression, for it distorts and ignores the reality of Black women who experience both forms of oppression.

In North America the ethnocentrism and "white solipsism," as Rich (1979) calls it, of western feminist scholarship has come under sustained attack from African-American and African-Canadian feminists and other so-called "women of colour".[11] These criticisms have caused white middle-class feminists considerable discomfort, guilt, and sometimes reappraisals of their intellectual and political practices. The problems of feminist ethnocentrism or Eurocentrism are even more blatant when it comes to studies of women in the so-called "Third World" (Sievers, 1989; Afary and Lavrin, 1989; Reinharz, 1992). In African studies the Eurocentric virus afflicts not only women's studies but all the social science disciplines and the humanities, especially when it comes to the construction of "theory" and the writing of regional or continental surveys and syntheses (Imam and Mama, 1994). Western Africanists, who are by their very existence implicated in western dominance, have often not displayed the necessary reflexivity and "epistemic humility," to borrow Pierson's (1991) term. African scholars, including feminists, have fought vigorously against this "intellectual imperialism." Despite their criticisms, ethnocentric practices are still alive and well in western feminist scholarship on Africa as can be seen in the recent special *Signs* issue on Africa which blithely justifies the absence of contributions from African women scholars.[12]

Our review of the literature has so far been derived mostly from the criticism of *content*, the poor coverage of women, the tendency to view women's lives as peripheral and unchanging, all of which reflect the absence of concepts that tap women's historical experiences. Little has been said about *methodology*, that is, the actual techniques and practices used in the research process. How do the methodologies of the three historiographical frameworks compare with the trends in feminist research?

Feminist researchers use a variety of methods. But they all arise, according to Fonow and Cook (1991a: 2), "from a critique of each field's biases and distortions in the study of women." Their work tends to display, they argue, reflexivity, action-orientation, and attention to the affective components of the research, among other things. Feminist historians, more specifically, have embraced oral history as a key method to recover women's experiences and voices from androcentric notions, assumptions, and biases which dominate "malestream" history everywhere. As one author has put it, "women's oral history is a feminist encounter because it creates new material about women, validates women's experience, enhances communication among women, discovers women's roots, and develops a previously denied sense of continuity" (Reinharz, 1992: 126).[13] Women's history is also unusually interdisciplinary in its approach.

Of the three paradigms, it would seem that nationalist historiography, has more in common with feminist history in terms of *methodology* than with either the dependence or Marxist perspectives, both of which rely on traditional social science research methods. Nationalist historians prize oral tradition, which they believe enables them to recover African experiences and "voices," that is, African perceptions of their lives, their consciousness, often silent in the arid and self-serving written records of colonial functionaries. Oral sources remove the cloak of invisibility enveloping many aspects of African history. Confronted with limited or non-existent written sources, nationalist historians were also unusually open to the use of a wide range of sources, from oral traditions and historical linguistics, to the findings of anthropology and the natural sciences. This made interdisciplinarity an important feature of nationalist historical scholarship. Thus feminist and nationalist historians tend to privilege oral methods in their efforts to dismantle deeply entrenched biases and recover the history of long suppressed, exploited, and humiliated groups of people.

The goal of nationalist historiography was to bring Africa and Africans back into history. In this sense it was an emancipatory project. But nationalist historiography did not deviate from the contours of western historiographies, from which it borrowed most of its questions and assumptions. It sought to demonstrate that Africa had built civilizations comparable to those of Europe. To what extent can women's history escape such a fate? Is restoring women to history enough? Is women's history to develop as an autonomous field of research, or is its aim to reformulate and transform history as a whole? Women's history is slowly gaining ground in many countries but there are already signs of its ghettoization.[14] Those who would wish to avoid this trajectory suggest going beyond writing women's history by writing gender history. Women's history focuses specifically on women's experiences, activities and discourses, while gender history provides analyses concerning how gender operates through specific cultural forms (Newman, 1991: 59).

RESTORING AFRICAN WOMEN TO HISTORY

In African history feminist historians are still largely at the stage of restoring women to history, of writing what Lerner (1979: Chapters 10–12) has called "compensatory" and "contribution" history, rather than of writing gender history.[15] The last two decades have seen rapid growth in the literature on African women. Most of it is the work of anthropologists, sociologists, and development specialists. The number of historians writing about the historical experiences of African women is still relatively small but growing.[16] Already the days when African women were painted with the brush of exotica and seen as a monolithic group afflicted by eternal victimization seem to be long gone. Explanatory models of women's oppression derived from European and American history and racist anthropology have come under challenge and been stripped of their univerzalistic pretensions. African women are no longer seen as being cloaked in veils of "tradition" from which they were gradually liberated by "modernity," for the concepts "tradition" and "modernity" have been exposed for their ahistoricity and ethnocentrism.[17]

The themes that preoccupied anthropologists for ages, such as kinship, marriage, fertility, sexuality, and religion are being re-examined as historical processes. Moreover, feminist historians are beginning to examine more systematically the historical development and construction of women's culture, solidarity networks, and autonomous social spaces. The importance of women's economic activities is being demonstrated, whether it is in agriculture, trade, or crafts and manufacturing. Researchers have also shown that women actively participated in pre-colonial politics, both directly as rulers and within arenas viewed as the female province, and indirectly as the mothers, wives, sisters, daughters, and consorts of powerful men. Women's involvement extended to military participation, both as individuals accompanying male troops and as groups of actual combatants. It can no longer be doubted that during the colonial era women actively participated in nationalist struggles. They either organised their own groups and fought against colonial policies which they saw as inimical to their interests, or they joined male-led nationalist movements. Colonialism is seen to have had a contradictory and differentiated impact on men and women, as well as on the women themselves. The more nuanced accounts reveal that while the position of most women declined during the colonial era, women also took initiatives that reshaped their lives and challenged the colonial order.

In terms of periodisation, most of the literature concentrates on the nineteenth and twentieth centuries. Women's history before 1800 is still largely tentative. The rest of this section presents a brief bibliographic survey of women's history in different parts of the continent.[18] For the period before 1800 the few works on women in the Western Sudan focus mainly on three themes, first, the political role played by women leaders, such as Amina; second, the impact of Islam on the gender division of labour and women's position in society; and third, the growth of women's slavery with the expansion of the trans-Saharan slave trade (Sweetman, 1984; Callaway, 1987; Robertson and Klein, 1987). For the West Coast and its hinterland the literature has dwelt on women's active participation in trade, production and state formation, and increased social stratification among women (Afonja, 1981; Awe, 1977; Brooks, 1976). The historiography on eastern and southern Africa has featured the role of queen mothers, marriage and kinship systems, and the role of women in production (Young, 1977; Leacock, 1991; Kaplan, 1982; Mbilinyi, 1982; Sacks, 1982; White, 1984; van Sertima, 1985; Kettel, 1986).

The historiography on women becomes more voluminous for the nineteenth century. The analysis tends to be richer in empirical detail and displays more theoretical sophistication. For Western Africa Aidoo (1981) emphasises the central role that Asante queen mothers played in the nineteenth century. Wilks (1988) looks into the life of one remarkable woman in Asante. Hoffer (1972) and Boone (1986) discuss how female solidarity among the Mende enabled some women to become chiefs and exercise political power. White (1987) sensitively charts out the development of women traders in Sierra Leone. Carney and Watts (1991) show that the intensification of agricultural production in the Senegambian region from the mid-nineteenth century was both a social and gendered process. Mann (1985, 1991) explores women's urbanization in Lagos by looking at the changing forms of marriage and social status for elite women and their access to landed property, capital, and labour in the second half of the nineteenth century. Roberts (1984) suggests that the growth of local slavery freed elite Maraka women from agricultural labour and allowed them to expand textile manufacturing which they controlled. In her penetrating study, Amadiume (1987) delineates the changing constructions of gender and sex roles in Igbo society. Boyd (1986) writes of the Fulani women intellectuals produced by the jihads, while Imam (1991) brilliantly charts out the development of seclusion in Hausaland before and after the establishment of the Sokoto Caliphate as well as during and after the colonial period.

The nineteenth century was also a period of rapid change in eastern and southern Africa. The expansion of commodity production, which sometimes included the slave trade, appears to have facilitated the subordination of women in some societies. Such appears to have been the case among the Mang'anja in southern Malawi (Mandala, 1984), the southern Tswana (Kinsman, 1983), the Maasai, (Talle, 1988), and in southern Mozambique (Isaacman, 1984). In other societies, women's productive roles, economic autonomy, property rights, and household relations were transformed by the adoption of new technologies, such as the plough, as has been demonstrated in the case of Basotho women (Eldridge, 1991), or as a result of political change, such as the reorganization and expansion of the military system as has been demonstrated in the case of the Nandi of Kenya (Gold, 1985), which led to the progressive removal of male labour from the homesteads, and the intensification of female labour time in household production. Women responded to these changes in various ways. Their solidarity, as well as opposition and accommodation to their growing subordination, was articulated through song and poetry (Gunner, 1979), the formation of spirit possession cults, dance, improvement, and puberty rites associations (Strobel, 1979), the manipulation of ritual and prophetic power and conversion to Christianity (Comaroff, 1985). In addition, some resorted to casual labour and prostitution, selling and buying land, or tried to put their role as food producers to good effect (Clark, 1980; Crummey, 1981, 1982; Spaulding, 1984; Alpers, 1986; Kapteijns, 1985).

Analyses of women in nineteenth century North Africa have also become more sophisticated as historians abandon the idealist biases, according to which the status and role of women in these societies is primarily attributed to the ideas and values contained in Islamic religious and juridical texts. It has become quite clear that this approach ignores the fact that the formal texts do not tell us much about the changing realities of women's lives in the extremely diverse societies and countries that make up the so-called "Muslim world" (Beck and Keddie, 1978; Keddie, 1979; Keddie and Baron, 1991; Tucker, 1983; UNESCO, 1984; Jansen, 1989; Ahmed, 1992). The literature on Egypt makes it clear that the exploitation of peasant women increased in the course of the century thanks to agricultural "modernization," state centralization, labour and military conscription, and the progressive decline of the extended family as a semi-autonomous unit and the consequent consolidation of family property around men. At the same time, however, some elite women acquired land either through purchase, inheritance, usually in the absence of male children, or grants from male relatives, especially a father (Tucker, 1985). Seclusion of middle class women appears to have increased as the old merchant classes became marginalised due to the imposition of state trading monopolies and as the wives of the "new" urban-based petite-bourgeois professionals were increasingly cut off from their husbands' professional lives and relegated to the domestic sphere (Cole, 1981). All these changes provoked debate about the position of women in society. The feminist discourse was conducted among the intellectuals, including men (Cole, 1981; Kader, 1987; Philipp, 1978; Cannon, 1985).

For women's history in the twentieth century, the impact of colonialism has, predictably, featured prominently. Many of the writers already referred to in the preceding paragraph examine how African women were affected by the imposition of colonial rule. They demonstrate that colonial patriarchal ideologies combined with indigenous patriarchal ideologies tended to reinforce women's subordination, exploitation and oppression. Many elite women were progressively marginalised as they lost their political power and control over trading and manufacturing activities. But there were other women who took advantage of the expanding petty commodity markets (Ekejiuba, 1967; Johnson, 1978), or who sought to retain their autonomy by migrating to the rapidly growing colonial towns and cities where they often engaged in trading activities, beer brewing, domestic service, and sometimes prostitution, thanks to the acute demographic imbalance between the sexes (Little, 1973; Bujra, 1975; van Onselen, 1982; Gaitskell *et al.*, 1983; Robertson, 1984; White, 1990). The expansion of cash crop production and male labour migration increased women's workloads, while at the same time their ability to appropriate the products of their labour declined (Boserup, 1970). Migrant labour was particularly prevalent and its negative effects on women especially evident in Southern Africa (Muntemba, 1982; Wright, 1983; Walker, 1990). There were, of course, some societies where women did succeed in retaining and even improving on their previous autonomy, if only temporarily (Hay, 1976; Mandala, 1984).

All these developments produced acute tensions in gender relations, to which the colonial state responded by tightening restrictive customary law, which led to important changes in family structure and created new forms of patriarchal power (Chauncey, 1981; Hay and Wright, 1982; Chanock, 1985; Roberts, 1987). By far the topic that has attracted the most attention is that of women's resistance to colonial rule (Denzer, 1976; Rogers [Geiger], 1980, 1990). The studies range from those that examine specific activists (Denzer, 1981, 1987; Okonkwo, 1986a; Rosenfeld, 1986; Brantley, 1986) and events, such as the Aba Women's War of 1929 (van Allen, 1976; Ifeka-Moller, 1975), the Anlu's Women's uprising in the Cameroons (Ritsenthaler,

1960), the spontaneous uprisings of South African women in the late 1950s (Bernstein, 1985) and their participation in the struggles against apartheid generally (Goodwin, 1984; Mandela, 1984; Kuzwayo, 1985; Barret, 1986), to general analyses of women's involvement in nationalist struggles in various countries (Steady, 1975; Denzer, 1976; Mba, 1982; Walker, 1982; Weiss, 1986; Geiger, 1987). It is now abundantly clear that women were actively involved in the wars of national liberation, such as Mau Mau (Likimani, 1985; Kanogo, 1987; Presley, 1991), and those in Algeria (Gorden, 1972), the Portuguese colonies (Urdang, 1979, 1984), Namibia (Cleaver and Wallace, 1990), and Eritrea (Wilson, 1991). Studies are also beginning to appear on women's active involvement in labour movements and struggles (Robertson and Berger, 1986; Zeleza, 1988a; Mashinini, 1991).

For the post-colonial period much of the literature has focused on whether or not women's position and status has improved or deteriorated with independence. The scope of subjects covered is wide, ranging from women in the rural and urban economies and women's participation in state politics and development projects, to changes in the structure of marriage and kinship. The literature shows that in many countries women's rural production has become more commodified since independence. In addition to farming, women in regions afflicted by the growing crises of subsistence have increasingly resorted to petty trading and wage labour to make ends meet. Commodification has increased the differentiation of rural women and made it more complex (Afonja, 1981, 1986; Guyer, 1984; Okali, 1983; Crevey, 1986; Newbury and Schoepf, 1989).

Research on African women has privileged rural over urban women, perhaps because the vast majority of African women are still rural dwellers (Simmons, 1988; Davison, 1988, 1989). But it is quite clear that the number of women migrating to and living in cities has risen considerably (Sudarkasa, 1977; Adepoju, 1983; Perold, 1985; Stichter and Parpart, 1988). Much of the literature on urban women has tended to focus on their activities as traders or informal sector operators. Those studies that deal with women in wage employment have demonstrated that while women's employment has grown rapidly in many countries since independence due to economic expansion, increased women's access to education, changes in family structure, and struggles by the women themselves for economic independence, women still tend to be crowded in low-paying service jobs and have to juggle with the burdens of the double day (Selassie, 1986; JASPA/ILO, 1986b, 1986c, 1986d, 1986e, 1986f, 1988; Zeleza, 1988b; Stichter and Parpart, 1990).

The studies done on women's participation in state politics demonstrate that women have been excluded and marginalized from the political process, despite their active involvement in the independence struggles. In some countries women, especially petty traders, have been targeted as scapegoats and attacked by states facing acute economic problems.[19] The literature has also amply demonstrated that until quite recently most government and international aid organizations primarily focused on men rather than women in their development projects. This was gradually changed thanks to the growth of the feminist movement and the food crisis in many African countries. The "women in development" movement and ideology was born. But it has done little, to date, to empower the vast majority of Africa's economically exploited and politically marginalized women (Brian, 1976; Nelson, 1981; Lewis, 1984; Mbilinyi, 1984; Overholt *et al.*, 1985; Swantz, 1985; Munachonga, 1989). This is true even in the self-styled "socialist" regimes (Haile, 1980; Urdang, 1983; Fortman, 1982; Seidman, 1984).

But African women in the post-independence era have not been passive victims. They continue to struggle both individually and collectively against their exploitation, oppression, and marginalisation, and to push open the doors to economic, political, social, and cultural empowerment (Obbo, 1980, 1986; Stamp, 1986; Dolphyne, 1991).

GENDERING AFRICAN HISTORY

It is quite evident that a lot of work has been done to recover women's history, but much more needs to be done. Also, the history that has so far been recovered has yet to be fully incorporated into the mainstream of African historical studies. Feminist historians, therefore, have to pursue a two-pronged agenda: writing women's history and gender history. Women's history, or "herstory," is often seen as a reconstruction, a retrieval, of women's experiences, expressions, ideas and actions. Gender has been defined as the changing social organization and symbolic representation of sexual difference, the primary field within which or by means of which power is articulated or signified. As a concept it offers an epistemological redefinition of historical knowledge as construction rather than reconstruction (Scott, 1988: Chapters 1 and 2). To put it simply, it is said that in women's history the primary focus is on women, while in gender history it encompasses both men and women as gendered subjects.

Apart from its explanatory power, the growing importance of gender as an analytical category reflected growing frustration among feminist historians at the relatively limited impact that women's history was having on mainstream historical studies.[20] There were also those who may have adopted the term "gender" merely as a synonym for women because it sounded more objective and neutral than "women," and thus gave their work academic legitimacy. Moreover, its popularity was probably helped by the proliferation of studies on sex and sexuality. It can further be argued that the concept of "gender" offered the reductionist paradigms of Marxism and psychoanalytic theory a much-needed face-lift. Unfortunately, women's history and gender history have increasingly come to be seen in oppositional and hierarchical terms. This reproduces the very binary thinking and dichotomous models feminist historians have been at pains to discard.[21]

The elevation of gender history over women's history may appear more "radical" and inclusive, but can in fact play into the hands of anti-feminists and legitimate exclusionary practices in academia. Courses in women's history can be opposed on the grounds that gender is integrated in the mainstream courses when that is in fact not the case. This is, for example, the situation in Canada where, Pierson (1992: 138) points out, there is no "positive evidence that the paucity of women's history courses results from mainstream adoption of gender as "a useful category of historical analysis, leading to an integration of gender history and the history of women's past experiences into non-women's history courses, undergraduate and graduate."[22]

Women's history and gender history, are mutually reinforcing, and need to be pursued simultaneously by feminist historians. In concrete pedagogical terms this means devising curricula that contains specific courses in women's history and consciously incorporating feminist perspectives in mainstream courses. Creating and maintaining specific courses in women's history is based on a recognition that women's history represents "a field of knowledge production which has its own history, formed by both the politics of women's liberation and intellectual developments within history and in associated disciplines" and that there are methodological frameworks that are specific to women's history and women's studies in general (Allport, 1993). Women's history, in short, must not be seen as a temporary necessity, something that is not "real history." Women's history is, both on an empirical and theoretical level "one of the most exciting historical specializations today" and by its very existence is instrumental in "deconstructing mainstream historiography. By emphasizing the 'other side' of history, women instead of men, the implicit male perspective of historiography that has obliterated women becomes explicit. This process is 'pivoting the centre' of dominant historiography. It exposes normative and expressive rules of both historical writing and teaching" (Grever, 1991: 77).

The actual content of the courses in women's history, and the teaching methods, will of course vary, reflecting, no doubt, different national histories, women's experiences, and intellectual traditions. Underpinning courses in women's history, epistemologically and pedagogically, should be feminist theorizing that recognizes difference and the gendered nature of all social relations and works on the immediate environment to achieve political action (Foster, 1992: 10–25). These courses must not only be offered at the university level, but at the primary and secondary school levels. Needless to say, this is likely to be met by resistance from the educational authorities in many countries. The strategies to overcome such resistance will necessarily vary. But such endeavours and struggles are unlikely to go far without organization. Feminist historians need to make women's history visible by organising all kinds of activities, penetrating the councils that design syllabuses and set examinations, and by publishing new material. Without new course books the case for women's history is unlikely to be advanced. In other words, in addition to publishing sophisticated articles, monographs and books on women's history for use at the university level, feminist historians have to undertake the far less glamorous task of publishing new material for schools.

Advancing gender history and mainstreaming entails gender-balancing courses and making gender as fundamental as, say, class as a category of historical analysis. Taking gender seriously as a conceptual tool for understanding the human past challenges the conventional periodizations based on political events and cultural and religious shifts in which men were preponderantly involved,[23] and transcends the traditional questions and problematics, constructs of significant events, and the theories and explanatory models of social change (Scott, 1988; Kelly-Godol, 1984).

Gendering history is a process that involves a series of curricular changes, whose ultimate objective is a balanced and inclusive curriculum, in which women's and men's past experience can be understood together. A number of stages have been suggested in developing a gendered history curriculum (Schuster and van Dyne, 1984; Schade, 1993). Confronted with a curriculum in which women are absent, the feminist historian could begin by searching for and incorporating the missing women within the conventional paradigms. This would essentially be a story of the heroines, of the great women leaders, warriors, traders, thinkers, and so on. This could be followed, or accompanied, by offering specific lectures within the course on women experiences during the period under discussion.

This gradualist or additive approach is problematic. Introducing women's history into the curriculum through a few "exceptional" examples does little to change the existing paradigms. In fact, a subtle, and perhaps unintended, message may be imparted to students: that since some women did succeed the failure of others to do so may be ascribed to their lack of motivation, ability, and other individual attributes. This serves to deny the reality of oppressive structures. Adding a couple or so lectures may make women seem anomalous, the material about them marginal to the core knowledge covered in the curriculum. This is merely to suggest that the larger goals of curriculum transformation must not be lost in well-meaning, but token, gestures which do not challenge the conventional paradigms.[24]

The questions of gender, class, and other social constructs that shape historical change, such as race and ethnicity, must be discussed explicitly. One way of confronting androcentric historiographical biases and promoting gender history is to use "battling readings" throughout the course. This involves using readings from "regular history" and "women's history" for every topic discussed. This forces students to confront different constructions of history and the differentiated participation of men and women in historical processes. For example, in discussing trade in nineteenth century West Africa one can pit Hopkins's (1973) *An Economic History of West Africa* and White's (1987) *Sierra Leone's Settler Women Traders.* In studying the pre-colonial iron industry Haaland and Shinnie's (1985) *African Iron Working* can battle it out with Herbert's (1993) *Iron, Gender, and Power.* For a general survey of African history the "battling textbooks" can be *African History* by Curtin *et al.* (1978), and Johnson-Odim and Strobel's (1990) *Restoring Women to History.*

This enables the students and the teacher to systematically question the existing paradigms, the validity of the conventional definitions of historical periods, causality, and normative standards of what constitutes significant knowledge, and the incorporation of gender as a category of analysis.[25] A gendered curriculum would embody an inclusive vision that explores history as "ourstory," a complex, ambiguous, and contested story of the human experience, a story based on difference, diversity and inequality, rather than sameness, uniformity, and generalization.

A gendered historiography would, for example, demonstrate that migration, one of the beloved themes in African historiography involved more than the heroic adventures of male warriors and leaders, that essentially it entailed the expansion of productive, distributive, and demographic frontiers in which both men and women played a fundamental, but differentiated role, and gender relations, divisions of labour and ideologies were often reconstructed in the process. Migrations would no longer be depicted as dramatic but simplified events, rather as complicated, if prosaic, social processes. Gender would also help decode the symbolisms, ideologies and structures of state formation and the changing nature of hegemony and social struggle. Analysis of imperialism and colonialism would certainly be deepened, for imperial conquest articulated the misogynist constructions of "manliness" and "otherness" and the reconfiguration of African gender relations and sexuality featured centrally in the justificatory baggage of the colonial project. For its part, economic history would lose its neat and dualistic analytical categories that strictly separate productive from distributive activities, "traditional" from "modern" societies, "subsistence" from "market" economies, "informal" from "formal" sectors, "unproductive" from "productive" labour, "private" from "public" spheres, for it would be shown that women either straddle both, or their involvement in one reproduces the other. The male labour power that is mobilised for the "modern," "market," "formal," "productive" and "public" spheres would hardly exist without women working in the "unremunerated" ("unproductive" in the lexicon of neo-classical and Marxian labour theories) "traditional," or "subsistence," or "informal," or "private" sectors. Thus it would be clear that the dualisms of conventional economic historiography do not represent distinct, separate spheres, but integrated activities structured by gender and class.

CONCLUSION

The examples could go on. But the case for gender history, I believe, has been made. Gendered history offers an opportunity both to bring women to the historical centre stage and to make history a truly comprehensive study of the human past in all its complexities. The pursuit of gender history should not, however, be at the expense of women's history as a separate and distinct branch of knowledge and history. Feminist historians can, and wherever possible should, work on both fronts simultaneously. Privileging one over the other is to fall into the very binary dichotomies and hierarchies of "malestream" historiography and western philosophy that feminists and African historians have been struggling against all these years. Gender history cannot go far without the continuous retrieval of women's history, while women's history cannot transform the fundamentally flawed paradigmatic bases and biases of "mainstream" history without gender history. Ultimately our goal is both to understand women for their own sake, much as we try to understand workers or peasants for their own sake, as separate windows into aspects of the human past, and also to probe and capture our shared, but varied, diverse and unequal, historical experiences and relations as human beings.

Mainstreaming African women's history and gendering African history are immense tasks. It needs the collaboration of both female and male historians who are informed by feminist perspectives and committed to a deeper and broader understanding of the human past than is possible by using the conventional androcentric paradigms. More concretely, there is need for comprehensive and up-to-date surveys of women's courses offered in the Social Sciences and Humanities and Arts departments in African universities, as well as of faculty hiring by gender. Also, the importance of developing and disseminating bibliographic guides and syllabi cannot be overemphasised. Bibliographies of works by African scholars and published in Africa would help significantly: African feminist researchers need to be more aware of each other's work and use that to build relevant paradigms instead of always borrowing theories manufactured in the West. Many of the existing bibliographic surveys mostly contain works published in the western countries by Africanists.[26] Moreover, systematic work needs to be undertaken to generate national, regional, and continental syntheses and other materials on various aspects of women's history. The compilation of source materials on women's history, both written and oral, for research and which could also be used as primary readers in history courses, would be particularly useful.

NOTES

1. It would be interesting to find out how many departments of history in African universities offer specific courses in women's history.
2. This is quite evident from the papers in the collection by Offen *et al.* (1991), which cover about 25 countries in Europe, North and South America, Africa, and Asia. See Kleinberg, (1988); Carroll (1976); Angerman *et al.* (1989). In the social sciences the usual practice is for women to be taught largely in segregated women's studies departments. See Hess and Ferree (1987); Nielsen (1990); Reinharz (1992).
3. All the editors of both series and almost all the contributors are men. At the time research for this chapter was conducted Volume 8 of the UNESCO series had not yet come out, hence its omission in the analysis that follows. This volume shows a slight improvement over the previous ones, with women being mentioned on 38 out of the 934 pages of text. Nothing to brag about.
4. In the 1995 second edition there is an expanded coverage of women, but only to 17 pages out of 530 pages of text.
5. In the Orientalist constructions of North Africa, for example, the region is often seen as part of the "Middle East," the "Arab" or "Muslim" world, rather

than an integral part of Africa. See Said (1979). Attempts to divorce North Africa, especially Egypt, from the mainstream of African history, were spawned by nineteenth–century European racist historiography. See Bernal (198, 1991). For problems of defining regions in Africa as historical units during different periods, and in relation to colonial configurations, see Zeleza (1984, 1985).

6. Volume one has no woman contributor, while volume two has one out of 16 contributors.
7. See especially the work of Terray, 1972; Meillassoux, 1981; and Seddon, 1978.
8. This point is made, and demonstrated powerfully, in Mandala (1990); also see, Zeleza (1993). This will also be demonstrated below when we examine the reconstructions of women's history attempted to date.
9. To be sure, as Foster (1992: 3) has argued, "the Liberal and Marxist discourses have been stretched to include women but the dominant assumptions still exclude a feminist perspective. They cannot accommodate feminist interests which threaten the very foundation on which these theories rest."
10. Bock (1991) observes that the old dichotomies are simply being replaced by equally problematic new ones, notably, gender/sex (social construction of male and female roles/biological differentiation between men and women), equality/difference, and integration/ autonomy. She argues that the dichotomy between "social" gender and "biological" sex 'does not resolve but only restates the old "nature" versus "culture" quarrel. Again, it relegates the dimension of women's body, sexuality, motherhood and physiological sexual difference to a supposedly pre-social sphere, and it resolves even less the question of precisely what part of women's experience and activity is "biological" and what part "social" or "cultural" (p. 8). It is often also not realized that "the dichotomous distinction between sex and gender is largely specific to the English language" (p. 9). Also see K. Offen, R. Pierson and J. Rendall, "Introduction," in K. Offen *et al.*
11. See, for example, the influential work of Bell Hooks (1981; 1984; 1988). The anguished debates between white women and women of colour can be seen in some of the books on women's history and feminist methodology already referred to, such as Offen *et al.* (1991); Jaggar and Rothenberg (1990); Hirsch and Keller (1990). Also see, *Feminist Review*, Nos. 22 and 23, 1986; Joseph and Lewis (1986); Lemer (1990); Stasiulis (1990).
12. Discussed in greater detail below. It is this attitude that leads Parpart (1992: 171–79) to argue (after noting that African women have challenged the widespread habit of western Africanists at conferences to discuss African women's experiences without engaging African women scholars themselves) that the question of who does research on African women's history "is a red herring."
13. The author notes that there are, of course, many types of oral history and various reasons why feminists use them. Also see Gluck (1979). Some feminist historians note that oral historians sometimes do not adequately question the concepts they use. For example, they may want to demonstrate women's marginality, when the women concerned may not see themselves as marginal, see Geiger (1990). Others are not convinced that oral history helps in "liberating" the voices of oppressed women, see Personal Narratives Group, eds., 1989.
14. For the ghettoization of women's history and marginalisation of gender history in Britain see Jane Rendall, in Offen *et al.*, 1991.

15. This history seeks, she argues, to write about women missing from, and describing their contribution to, traditional history. This constitutes, in her view, "transitional women's history," which she distinguishes from women's history that studies the actual experiences of women in the past on their own terms, and what she calls "universal history," a holistic history synthesising traditional history and women's history. The latter is what increasingly came to be referred to as gender history.
16. For detailed bibliographic surveys, see Robertson (1987); *Canadian Journal of African Studies* 22 (3), 1988, *Special Issue on Women;* and the well-written monographs on so-called sub-Saharan Africa and the so-called Middle East, a large part of which covers North Africa, in Johnson-Odim and Strobel (1988).
17. Historians have amply demonstrated that many practices and values which are considered "traditional" today, including those in the sphere of gender relations, were invented during the colonial period, see Ranger (1989) and Chanock (1985). Increasingly anthropologists have come to the same view, but in typically convoluted post-structuralist deliberations, see Comaroff (1980) and Moore (1986).
18. This section relies heavily on Johnson-Odim and Strobel (1988), and Zeleza (1993).
19. For example, in the 1980s the Nigerian military government increased its attacks on market women as Nigeria entered a period of economic crisis partly brought about by declining oil revenues. The women traders were blamed for high inflation and shortages, see Dennis, 1987. On relations between the Nigerian military and women see Mba, 1989.
20. Scott (1988: 3) gives this as one of the main reasons she turned to gender as an analytical framework in feminist history.
21. For a compelling critique of Scott's post-structuralist feminist historiography, see Hall, 1991; also see Schwegman and Bosch, 1991; and Newman, 1991. Bock (1991) and Sangster (1995) have argued forcefully for the deconstruction of the dichotomy between women's history and gender history. For her argument that gender history is not more encompassing, does not offer more profound insights, and is not theoretically more sophisticated than women's history, Sangster, a distinguished Canadian feminist historian, has been widely condemned by her younger colleagues (personal communication), one more indication of how vicious sectarian academic battles can be.
22. Pierson's (1992) data shows that the number of women's history courses in Canadian universities remains abysmally low, accounting for less than 3% of the total number of courses offered.
23. For example, in European history, the glory that was the Renaissance, the period during which men (elite men) saw their intellectual horizons widen, loses its glow with revelations that women became more subordinate and restricted than in earlier centuries, see Kelly (1984).
24. This point is made particularly well in the American context by Higginbotham, 1990. The *Women's Studies Quarterly,* has done several special issues on incorporating feminist perspectives in various Social Science disciplines, including Economics and Psychology with their rigid, positivist, and pseudo-scientific paradigms and models. See Vol. 18, Nos. 1&2 devoted to curricular and institutional transformation; Vol. 18 Nos. 3&4, to "Women's Studies in Economics"; Vol. 20, Nos. 1&2, to "Feminist Psychology: Curriculum and Pedagogy."

25. In my third year African history class that I taught at Trent University, I experimented with this method, and it was fascinating watching the students becoming more aware that "doing" history is as gendered as the historical processes they were trying to understand. For example, in my tutorial on the "Islamic Revolutions in West Africa in the Nineteenth" century I used Chapter 12 in Curtin *et al.* (1978) ("The Commercial and Religious Revolutions in West Africa"); Murray Last (1985) ("Reform in West Africa: the Jihad Movements of the nineteenth century," in Ajayi and Crowder, eds.); Boyd (1986) ("The Fulani Women Poets," in A. H. M. Kirk-Greene and M. Adamu, eds.); J. Boyd and M. Last (1985) ("The Role of Women as 'Agents Religieux', in Sokoto"); Kapteijns (1985) ("Islamic Rationales for the Changing Roles of Women in the Western Sudan" in Daly, ed); and J. Carney and M. Watts (1991) ("Disciplining Women? Rice, Mechanization and the Evolution of Mandinka Gender relations in Senegambia").
26. See, for example, the recently published bibliographic guide by Fong (1993). The absence or under-representation of works on women by African scholars in standard Africanist historiographic surveys is staggering as can be seen, for example, in Robertson (1987).

CHAPTER 12

SENEGALESE WOMEN IN POLITICS: A PORTRAIT OF TWO FEMALE LEADERS, ARAME DIÈNE AND THIOUMBÉ SAMB, 1945–1996

Babacar Fall

Presenting a portrait of a political leader is not common among Senegalese historians. The most well-known examples of such portraits are of renowned leaders or high-ranking officials in the hierarchy of political parties or the state. This paper goes against this tendency. It outlines and analyzes the career paths of two women who have variously marked Senegalese political evolution: Arame Diène and Thioumbé Samb.

The primary sources used for the article are interviews conducted with these two women. The women's testimony is part and parcel of the documentation collected by the oral history workshop at the Université Cheikh Anta Diop. The interviews took place in 1994, 1995, and 1996.

The interviewers chose to conduct the interviews as open discussions. Preliminary meetings were held to define the interviews' objectives and expected results. These first meetings allowed trust to build between the informants and the research team.

The principal difficulty was the transcription in French of the testimony obtained in the national language, Wolof. The narrators, illiterate, were unable to validate the transcribed testimony. Nevertheless, an accurate transcription was assured by repeatedly listening to the interview tapes.

Through their testimony, two adversaries in Senegalese political life, Arame Diène and Thioumbé Samb, have told their stories and their views of the principal events that marked their way. To understand the scope of this testimony, which was analyzed as a primary source, it is essential to understand the context of Senegalese political life. Such an understanding gives a singular sense of these women, whose paths are mapped out and compared by examining their political itineraries.

THE CONTEXT OF SENEGALESE POLITICAL LIFE

There are strong traditions in Senegalese political life, although they are limited to the four municipalities that benefited from French citizenship: Dakar, Gorée, Rufisque, and Saint-Louis. Since 1848, Senegal has elected a representative to the French parliament. Until 1914, only whites and mulattos were elected. In 1914, a black, Blaise Diagne, acceded to the position of deputy for the first time. Upon Diagne's death in 1934, Galandon Diouf succeeded him to the parliament and dominated political life until 1941. Following the Second World War, the electorate grew with the Law of Lamine Guèye of May 7, 1946, which gave French citizenship to all nationals of overseas territories. Political life was expanding.

Political leaders all came from among the educated elites. Lamine Guèye was known as an attorney. Léopold Sédar Senghor was a professor of grammar. Cheikh Anta Diop and Abdoulaye Ly combined their political activities with their professions as historians. Caroline Diop, the first woman elected as a deputy to the Senegalese National Assembly, was an elementary school teacher who had earned her degree at the Ecole Normale for girls in Rufisque. Such education confers status and gives access to leadership positions. During the first half of the twentieth century, advanced schooling for boys was encouraged (Coquery-Vidrovitch, 1994: 239), but only assimilated or "cultivated" girls were enrolled in school. Because of the limited number of women who had attended school, the political elite was mostly masculine.

Nevertheless, women were present on the political scene. Sought after by educated political leaders because of their electoral weight and their abilities in mobilizing other social groups, they were nonetheless victims of prejudice. In addition, they were often given a weak role in decision-making. They ensured the liveliness of political meetings: they were the ones who sat on the sidelines and "applauded," according to Arame Diène. With their colorful clothing, they gave such functions an air of festivity.

The dominant image of the woman participating in political life is that of the socialite woman providing some folklore. But after 1945, women acquired the right to vote and now constitute a significant electoral weight because of their effective participation in elections. But even if they in large part ensure victory, they are no less confined to the symbolic representation. Caroline Diop is one example.

A renowned teacher and great orator having a significant electoral influence, she has been engaged in political life since 1945. Nevertheless, she was only elected and invested as the first female deputy in 1963. That is to say, women's electoral and political weight is not reflected in access to high-profile positions. This largely explains the weak presence of women in Senegalese historiography. Also, it is difficult to describe the role of women in the Senegalese political arena if the historian uses classic, official sources. That is nevertheless the challenge addressed by this essay. In addition, it attempts to reconstitute the paths of two women who are atypical militants, in that they did not receive an elite education in a French assimilationist school. Arame Diène and Thioumbé Samb are products of the popular tradition. Not having attended school, they gradually thrust themselves onto the political chessboard to become leading figures of female militancy. They have taken paths that are similar but divergent, and, above all, marked by different luck.

COMMON TRAITS

With their strong personalities and great abilities for social mobilization, both women come from the same milieu: the Lebou ethnic group, constituting the native population of Dakar. In addition, they are both self-made women. While the political leaders come predominantly from the elite intelligentsia formed in the French schools, these two women are the product of a "popular" culture. They did not attend the French schools. They are among those categorized as illiterate and traditionally destined to remain at home. The social status of women, which tended to marginalize them and keep them from the public sphere, hampered the emergence of female political leaders (Fall, 1989).

Nevertheless, both played a significant role in the women's movement of their respective parties: Arame Diène is affectionately called the "mother" of the Socialist Party,[1] while Thioumbé Samb was vice president of the women's movement of the Senegalese Democratic Union (UDS)[2] and a founding member of the Union of Senegalese Women.

Arame Diène and Thioumbé Samb entered the political world in 1945 and 1946, respectively. They influenced opposition political groups until 1983.

Arame Diène declares with pride that she got into politics in 1945/46, following a family tradition. Her parents were among the notable Lebous. "We were with Goux Alfred, who is a *toubab* [white]. We fought to support Goux, the mayor of Dakar. The choice was dictated by loyalty to Galandou Diouf, allied to Goux Alfred and, above all, a friend of my father. After his death, only Goux was left. It was he whom we knew in Dakar. When Lamine Guèye ran against him, I stayed with Goux, following the family tradition. Of course, Lamine Guèye had a large following. He was very politically aware. He was a son of Senegal, a native of Saint-Louis. Yet he lived in France and there was no link between him and my Lebou family. God wanted Lamine Guèye and his party, Le Bloc Noir, to win the 1948 elections."

When Senghor became active in politics at Guèye's side, Arame Diène's family stayed with Alfred Goux. But with the rupture between Guèye and Senghor in 1948, Senghor created the Senegalese Democratic Bloc (BDS) and found support among the Lebou community in Dakar.

Arame Diène states, "Senghor joined us on our position and decided to come with us. The old Lebous, all notables, were still there: my grandfather Alieu Codou Diène; Ousmane Diop Coumba Pathé, who is the father of Mamadou Diop, the current mayor of Dakar; El Hadj Falla Paye, the father of Alioune Badara Paye, who was director of the Dakar Fair; El Hadj

Ibrahima Diop, at the time the Grand Serigne of Dakar; El Hadj Assane Ndoye; and Mbaye Diagne Dégaye." The elders met, talked with Senghor, and promised to support him against Lamine Guèye. The political agreement sealed between Senghor and the Lebou community largely determined the selection of Abbas Guèye, a leading figure of the syndicalist movement, as a candidate for Deputy of Senegal.

Abbas Guèye was a native Lebou and held the prominent position of general secretary of commercial syndicats. At the primary elections of 21 October 1945, Lamine Guèye's French Section of the Socialist International (SFIS) and Senghor's BDS shared the two seats. But in the 17 June 1951 elections the BDS took both seats. Abbas Guèye was elected. On the evidence of a pact linking the members of the Lebou community to Senghor's BDS, the Lebou were satisfied with the final electoral agreement (Ly, 1992: 11).

Thioumbé Samb also became involved in politics in support of Abbas Guèye. She explains, "Since Abbas Guèye is Lebou, the Lebou community came together to support his candidacy for the position of deputy. My husband, who was a member of the Senegalese Democratic Union (UDS/RDA), had given me permission to join the BDS youth group. After the victory of the BDS, I stopped my primary activity and in 1947 joined my husband in the Senegalese Democratic Union."

Arame Diène points out that "at that time politics was different than today. Yes! At that time if someone wanted to be represented in the elections they were the ones who financed the campaign...[but] with Senghor, it was the commitment and the money of the partisans that allowed his election....[T]he men and women both contributed."

Arame Diène was affected by the loss of political ethics among the militants who are presently fighting each other for honors in the Socialist Party. She remembers that yesterday's militants showed greater commitment and motivation than those of today. Currently, political involvement is equated with material, financial gain. Political allegiance to a party, especially the one in power, is bought. Arame Diène criticizes this search for gain as "political nomadism," and consoles herself by remembering the pure sentiments that gave the militants of her generation the determination to fight for a cause. The same bitterness grips Thioumbé Samb when she says, "Today it's a game: see how much money can be siphoned off, have a good time."

In their intellectual profiles, Arame Diène and Thioumbè Samb are the opposite of the "cultivated" elite who earned their degrees in French schools. They did not attend school, but take pride in having been among the first militants, in the heroic phase of their party's formation. Arame Diène is proud to remember that during that time it was "us, the ignorant nobodies, who cheered and applauded, who fought, were insulted, and all that comes with it until our party was on its feet!"

Thioumbé Samb explains the reasons for her lack of schooling: the Lebous, especially, did not like to enroll girls in school. School was seen as a waste. It was thought to corrupt one's soul with cunning and trickery. It was the place where one could "learn how to win without being right," according to the Grande Royale, one of the key characters in Cheikh Hamidou Kane's book *The Ambiguous Adventure* (1961: 165).

But faced with the schooling imposed by the whites, the first children sent to learn were captives, followed by the sons of the leaders, and then other children. Girls, however, considered those who held to tradition, the soul, and the culture, had to be preserved. They were not to have any contact with the French school.

Apart from these resemblances, these two women had very dissimilar paths through life.

Two Diverse Fortunes

Thioumbé Samb was shaped by the UDS/RDA, the radical nationalist party which was created in Senegal after the constitutive Congress of the African Democratic Assembly, held 18 October 1946. This party counted on the training of its militants to enable them to cope with the ostracism and repression imposed by colonial power. Thioumbé Samb observes that the strength of the UDS, which was directed by Abdoulaye Guèye Cabri and Ba Thierno, lay in its militants' education and training. According to her, "the other political groups were preparing their militants for fights, insults, and praise, while the UDS/RDA was emphasizing the education of women."

> [W]e had high school students as our teachers; they taught us after 6:00, after they had finished their classes. We who lived in the Guele Tapée neighborhood, we were assigned Racine Ndiaye, who taught us how to take care of certain formalities, notably how to sign the bottom of a document... because we formed delegations to go ask around the governor's delegation for authorization to hold political meetings... and we were only given authorization to meet in movie theaters. We talked to the owners of the theaters, who let us use their theaters from 3:00 to 6:00. We did that to educate the militant [women] so that they would realize that they could take the reins of the country, which had become independent.

In 1957 the principal parts of the BDS and the UDS/RDA merged to create the Senegalese People's Bloc (BPS), which in 1958 became the Senegalese Progressive Union (UPS). This political group, since 1986 called the Socialist Party, had managed to dominate the Senegalese political chessboard since 1947.

But at the time the BPS was created, parts of the UDS/RDA rejected the pro-colonial reform line of the new party and prepared to put on its feet a political group that was heir to the anticolonial traditions. Thioumbé Samb was strongly involved with this group, which was directed by Majhmout Diop, a pharmacist who was a native of Saint-Louis. The project ended in Thies on 15 September 1957 with the creation of the African Party for Independence (PAI), the Marxist nationalist party. Between 1957 and 1983 Thioumbé Samb distinguished herself as the foremost leader of the PAI.

But in 1983, Thioumbé Samb rejoined the Socialist Party with hopes of participating in the construction of the country under the leadership of President Abdou Diouf. This change of allegiance in one way marks the end of a political career. It was a failure, because what appeared to be a political revival turned out to be more of a retreat from the political scene. This is a historical irony for one who had fought as a militant for so long, first for the Senegalese Democratic Union (UDS) section of the African Democratic Assembly (RDA), then for the African Party for Independence (PAI). All these political organizations represented the nationalist wing in the fight against the colonial system.

Arame Diène, a militant first in pro-colonial, then in neocolonial, reform, took part in the Senegalese Democratic Bloc, which became the Senegalese Progressive Union and then in 1976 the Socialist Party. She had a more fortunate destiny than her rival Samb. In 1983, her political career reached its summit with her election as deputy to the National Assembly. She took her revenge on the intellectuals who had joined the party only in their own interest. In analyzing her rise, Diène describes her great political insight. In fact, she characterizes her nomination for deputy as marking an epochal change in national political values.

In 1981, Prime Minister Abdou Diouf had succeeded Léopold Sédar Senghor as president. He set out to gain a new mandate, and the elections of 1983 offered Arame Diène a great opportunity. She recounts her interview with Diouf regarding the Socialist Party's choices for parliamentary candidates:

> I went to see him as the regional official for Dakar because they could not ignore me and accept some other woman, since it was I who had won the region. I told him, "Mister President, I came to see you because I heard that you were going to appoint eight women to the list of deputies and I'm the official of the region. When Senghor was here, our movement had the strength to elect me, but I wanted to be deputy; he would have rejected this request, because he only believed in those who'd been educated, but I know that you are aware of the realities of the situation and I'm part of the 'Lebou reality'." He responded, "If the regional union presents you as a candidate, then I'll put you on my list."
>
> So my union nominated me with no problem. They nominated my substitute, Ramatoulaye Seek, as well. God blessed us; we were both elected. Another woman, Aida Mbaye, was the offical of the regional union of Tambacounda—she was a native of Saint-Louis and she was not schooled either. She was nominated by her regional union and then elected to the National Assembly.

For Arame Diène, a new head of the Senegalese state led to a change in the criteria for promotion. As long as Senghor was president, she had resigned herself to being deprived of the honors of a position as deputy. She expresses it this way: "If Senghor were still there, I'd never be deputy. Senghor only believes in those who were educated. Abdou Diouf also believes in diploma-holders, but he knows the realities. He combined the two."

Arame Diène interprets this change in the criteria for advancement as progress. She indicates that by the 1988 elections, "we were two women and two men, there were four of us, so it seemed that things had evolved.... Already in 1983, Aida Mbaye and I were two 'ignorant women,' not educated, within the National Assembly, but we were not insignificant." She knows she has come a long way. According to her, her election is also the reward for her patience and her sense of political opportunity. She expresses her satisfaction using philosophy as well as humor to evaluate her political development. "Politics is not a sprint, but a marathon. If you are in a hurry, you'll go nowhere; it's step by step, progressing slowly. Look at everything I went through before becoming deputy in 1983."

This determination animates her while she measures the difficulties facing her participation in the game of the parliamentary institution. She tells of the incident that allowed her to become known as a full-fledged member: "When I had been elected deputy for the first time, during a parliamentary session I was seated next to a male deputy, and when I asked for the floor, he answered in a mocking tone, 'If you want the floor we won't give it to you, because here we speak French.' I responded, 'Oh really! So today the National Assembly is going to break up [laughs], because if I have to be in an Assembly where I cannot express myself, I'm leaving.' I raised my hand and the president of the National Assembly said to me, 'Okay, Arame, I'll register your name. You'll speak Wolof because we can't elect someone whom we don't allow to speak, can we?' [laughs] I was the first to speak Wolof at the National Assembly."

During parliamentary sessions, Arame strictly limited her participation: "I don't speak when the sessions are about defense, finances,... but as soon as it's about farmers, health, women, and children I speak in Wolof; but what I say is clear and comprehensible to everybody—we all understand Wolof." With this attitude, Arame Diène refuses to play the role of benchwarmer. On the contrary, she is proud of her position as deputy and is determined to justify it.

Pride and disappointment are evident in the intersecting paths of these two female leaders of Senegalese political life.

Cross-Examination of Two Life Narratives

The reconstruction of these two women's paths opens up the field of historical discourse to oral sources. Giving their voices back to these two women who did not attend French schools enabled them to tell their own stories. They remembered events and rediscovered the logic and sense of their political commitment within the framework of the facts. Listening to their voices also gives us a sense of their ability to interpret the events in which they played determining roles.

The two people discussed here are among the "forgotten" of Senegalese historiography for two reasons. First, our collective memory is generally male. Second, they are not political stars or heroes. They are ordinary citizens who, by chance, were invited to recount their lives. Once past initial surprise that researchers were interested in their careers, they realized that their political activities had become visible, and participated in the rewriting of their stories. Consequently, they are very self-confident and describe their preoccupations, the state of their souls, even their evaluations of history. The resulting testimony is not a eulogy, but rather a reconstructed memory of another period of time: a past visited with an undisguised nostalgia.

Arame Diène is satisfied to have remained loyal to a political tradition and to see the result of her efforts. Her involvement having been rewarded after thirty-seven years of service, she repeats that politics is a long-distance race. She is conscious of remaining among the people and also shares her honors and disappointments with her extended family. Changing political circumstances have validated her journey. Her understanding of changing power structures allowed her to make her way to the National Assembly, which for a long time had been reserved for the French-schooled political elite. Consequently, she is no longer part of the anonymous mass of militants who toil in support of other political leaders. She is now an active player and intends to assume a central role in the community. She takes pride in the prestige she enjoys in the Socialist Party and among the general public.

Arame Diène, content with her success, contrasts greatly with Thioumbé Samb, who is a disappointed leader, bitter and retreating from the political scene. Samb, who was among the first activists in the fight for independence, now feels frustrated and marginalized. She was not one of what she calls "the beneficiaries of independence." Her quasi-solitary life in Fann Hock, the old PAI seat, contrasts with the opulence of Arame Diène's family home, located in the popular quarter of Medina in Dakar.

Thioumbé Samb does not try to hide her bitterness. The PAI militant, who was arrested and imprisoned in Saint-Louis in 1960 during the municipal elections, sees herself as a martyr. "We who fought for independence are forgotten today," she declares. Her disappointment is even stronger because she was a victim of humiliation and repression under Senghor's regime and, with the PAI, went underground between 1960 and 1976. Following the PAI's legalization, she was active in politics from 1976 to 1983, always on the side of Majhmout Diop.

In 1983, the final step for Thioumbé Samb was her decision to rejoin the Socialist Party, which she had fought for thirty-six years. After two months of what seemed a warm welcome, she came up against the hostility of her new allies, who still viewed her as a rival. Between the two leaders, past animosity was replaced with the fear that the newcomer would crystallize old resentments among the women in the Socialist Party in Dakar. Thioumbé Samb was uncomfortable in her new position. She realized too late that her disappointment was the price of her costly decision to renounce her past connection to the opposition. Her political naïveté turned into instability. She lost big in the game of political alliances.

Arame Diène is proud to declare herself a long-distance runner who has won. Thioumbé Samb only finds consolation by retreating to the memory of a certain past when, in 1957, the PAI awarded her the gold medal of the Women's Union of Senegal. She shows visitors her photo collection as supplementary testimony to the prestigious role she had in Senegalese political life.

One cannot be insensitive to the disappointment, even the drama, that she feels in the face of the almost total indifference of her milieu. Sharing Thioumbé Samb's disappointment, a female member of the research team leaves her with this comment: "History is unfair." But shouldn't we also acknowledge that history is ironic as well?

NOTES

This essay was translated by Laura Gardner, with the help of Eric Prieto, Ph.D.

1. The Socialist Party in Senegal is the heir of the Senegalese Democratic Bloc, created by Léopold Sédar Senghor in 1948 after breaking with Lamine Guèye's French Section of the Socialist International (SFIS), and of the Senegalese Progressive Union, founded in 1958. The Socialist Party has governed Senegal since independence.
2. The Senegalese Democratic Union (UDS) is the Senegalese section of the African Democratic Assembly (RDA), founded in 1946 by Houphouët Boigny. This nationalist party, which had sections in different territories of French West Africa and French Equatorial Africa, had weak support in Senegal, where political life was dominated by the SFIS and then the Democratic Bloc.

BIBLIOGRAPHY

Awa, Kane. 1995. "Femmes et politique: des récits de vie et/ou de pratiques de quelques militantes sénégalaises." M.A. thesis, University Cheikh Anta Diop.

Coquery-Vidrovitch, Catherine. 1994. *Les Africaines: histoire des femmes d'Afrique noire du XIXème au XXème siècle.* Paris: Editions Desjonquères.

Fall, Rokhqyq Gningue. 1989. "Femmes et pouvoirs politiques en Afrique—L'exemple du Sénégal." In *Cultures en crise: quelles alternatives pour les femmes africaines?*, 63–65. Special issue of *Fippu—Journal de Yewwu Yewwi, pour la libération des femmes.*

Jewsiewicki, Bogumil. 1987. "Le Récit de vie entre la mémoire collective et l'historiographie." In *Récits de vie et mémoires vers une anthropologie historique du souvenir*, ed. Fabrice Montal and Bogumil Jewsiewicki, 213–46. Paris: L'Harmattan.

Kane, Cheikh Hamidou. 1961. *L'aventure ambiguë.* Paris: R. Julliard.

Ly, Abdoulaye. 1992. *Les Regroupements politiques au Sénégal, 1965–1970.* Dakar: Codesria.

Section V

Writing Women: Reading Gender

The papers in this section are focused on the representation of African women by others, their own self-representation as they come into voice, the role of gender in African women's writings, and indeed how they perceive their roles given the histories of oppression and marginalization. The seminal position of Joseph Conrad's *Heart of Darkness* in African literature in colonial languages is well known. However, despite the engagement of a whole series of African writers with this novel, not much has been made of the African woman "at the heart of the Heart of Darkness," as Abena Busia puts it. Her paper "Miscegenation as Metonymy: Sexuality and Power in the Colonial Novel" certainly begins to challenge the absence of women as colonial subjects in literary representations, as she interrogates issues of gender, race and sexuality in the colonial enterprise.

How does one do a feminist analysis of post-colonial African literary texts without reproducing the dominant Eurocentric modes of reading, many of which have been found to be inadequate for this genre? This is the task that Juliana Makuchi Nfah-Abbenyi sets for herself in "Gender, Feminist Theory, and Post-Colonial (Women's) Writing." She offers us a postcolonial theory of African literary criticism in which she postulates that novels in themselves are theoretical texts: "the theory is embedded in the polysemous and polymorphous nature of the narratives themselves." As such, she submits that Africans are not simply receivers of theory but makers also. With regard to gender in African women's writings, she suggests some important themes, including identity, difference, motherhood, sexuality and female solidarity.

The literary text is by no means the only place to look for the writings of African women; in fact, it may not be the oldest form in which African women engaged. The original work of Audrey Gadzekpo on the history of gender and gender discourses in the Gold Coast suggests that there is a longer if hidden history of women's participation in the print media. In her never before published paper, "The Hidden History of Women in Ghanaian Print Culture," she deconstructs Ghanaian press history charting the contributions of women as columnists, editors, journalists, readers, and occasional contributors from its nineteenth-century inception. She concludes that the female writing subject was able to insert herself into this medium in ways that allowed her voice to be heard, and thereby gaining the opportunity to act as an author of her own social history.

Chapter 13

Miscegenation as Metonymy: Sexuality and Power in the Colonial Novel

Abena P. A. Busia
Rutgers University

I invoke the shade of Joseph Conrad: imperial and colonial novelists inscribe within their works a multitude of fictions at whose core is the notion of the "otherness" of the locations of those outposts of progress whose recollection threatens the memory. The possibility of the darkness of their own hearts keeps them repeating Marlowe's journey, so I evoke Conrad, for he it is, alien exile though he may be, whose own "tenebrous" language "inchoates" for me an equally alien, or alienating, tradition.

At the heart (or should I say the climax?) of *The Heart of Darkness,* written nearly one hundred years ago, stands a distressed black woman, the very symbol of frenzied passion, agitated, uncontrollable, powerless, inaudible, and certainly functionally inarticulate.

> And from right to left along the lighted shore moved a wild and gorgeous apparition of a woman. She walked with measured steps, draped in striped and fringed cloths, treading the earth proudly, with a slight jingle and flash of barbarous ornaments. She carried her head high . . . She must have had the value of several elephant tusks upon her. She was savage and superb, wild eyed and magnificent; there was something ominous and stately in her deliberate progress. And in the hush that had suddenly fallen upon the whole sorrowful land, the immense wilderness, the colossal body of the fecund and mysterious life seemed to look at her, pensive, as though it had been looking at the image of its own tenebrous and passionate soul . . . She stood looking at us without a stir, and like the wilderness itself, with an air of brooding over an inscrutable purpose.[1]

Conversely—and adversely—at the other end of the journey sits "The Intended," the woman for whom or on whose behalf, it seems, Kurtz's whole ridiculous venture is embarked upon.

> She came forward, all in black, with a pale head, floating towards me in the dusk. She was in mourning. It was more than a year since his death, more than a year since the news came; she seemed as though she would remember and mourn for ever... I noticed she was not very young—I mean not girlish. She had a mature capacity for fidelity, for belief, for suffering. The room seemed to have grown darker, as if all the sad light on this cloudy evening had taken refuge on her forehead. This fair hair, this pale visage, this pure brow, seemed surrounded by an ashy halo from which the dark eyes looked out at me. Their glance was guileless, profound, confident, and trustful. She carried her sorrowful head as though she were proud of that sorrow, as though she would say I—I alone know how to mourn for him as he deserves.[2]

It is for this woman the "noble lie" is told. The unspeakably transformed Kurtz, with whom the African woman has presumably been intimate, is unfit for the European woman even to hear about.

The differences in the evocation of these two women are crucial. The Intended is portrayed against a well delineated background, the source of that mercantile capitalism which Marlowe is at pains to question. Her setting is replete with detailed descriptions of buildings and corridors; a visual and tactile concreteness gives form to her existence, and she can speak and be heard. The locale of the black woman is strikingly different; she arises out of the blank spaces on the map of Marlowe's childhood, and the palpable darkness against which she is summoned is its only substantial element. Everything else about the place, including the woman, is incoherent. The black woman is conjured up out of a void, a fissure or space out of which there can be, for her, no coherent or comprehensible language—not because it cannot be uttered, but because, as Marlowe makes quite clear, her language cannot be heard, and it is this singular factor which has had bearing on the representation of black women in imperial discourse.

However, these apparent and very obvious contrasts between the women, one black and dressed in glitter, the other pale and dressed in black, like a photographic negative and its image, are at one and the same time germane, and vitally irrelevant. The whole "benighted" journey of enlightenment takes us from one to the other and back again, but only the men move. The two women are both essentially trapped where their men find them, as fixed points of conflicting desires, and the century of drama enacted between the spaces they each occupy has been one in which they have been pawn and prize; both of them.

I need to make clear what kind of novel it is I am speaking about, what legacy it is Conrad leaves in his wake. Expatriate novels of Africa, whatever broad category of literary convention they may fall into,[3] remain, on the whole, male-dominated imperial fictions. The continent of Africa herself, and the pronoun is apropos, serves as an excuse, a suggestive, well-manhandled partner for the European male to exploit, an oppositional frame of reference for the working out of symbolic dramas of which she is not so much the subject, as the object. The desire to conquer her, and to have this conquest mean something, first possessed Henty's schoolboy master of the world who unfortunately grew—bigger if not up—and not so much metamorphosed, as exposed his camouflage. He appears in today's texts as the sexist and fundamentally pernicious mercenary, fighting increasingly more dubious battles, he was, from the point of view of the reluctant and recalcitrant natives at least, always threatening to be.

Imperial and colonial novels inscribe within them several fictions, which are ultimately choreographed around the question of *power,* and however "innocent" such stories as those by Henty or Haggard may appear to be, their effect is to encode in the popular mind the superiority of the white male dominant class, against the inferiority of the colored peoples of the earth—the conquest of whom is "not a pretty thing when you look at it," and despite Marlowe's contention, few of the colonized have found in the act any *idea* which redeems it. In the literary discourse of the world of the colonial novel we have habitually isolated three species of being—European men, European women, and "natives." We are used to discussing the imperialism of the colonial novel with respect to the colonized peoples, but this concentration on the black/white divide has led to a disguising of yet another fiction inscribed by these texts; that of the "subject" nature of females in general, white or black. The parallel and equally powerful discourse of imperialism over the female is an integral part of the structuring metaphors of these texts.

The novels which make up the canon of Imperial and Colonial fiction are mostly written by men, and even when written by women they are primarily about men, and concern the professional and middle-class ethics of the Europeans who both write the works and people their pages. This is an environment in which rigid codes of social behaviour are enacted, and Europeans are segregated amongst themselves according to professional affiliation, rank, and class, with maverick social behaviour strictly censored. Within this literature, the cast of characters, as well as the dramas they enact, are demonstrably severely circumscribed,[4] revolving as they do around the problematics of moral confusion, social disruption, ostracism and death. These works reflect for public consumption that which is said to be the inevitable result of trying to live in, and manage, an unmanageable continent; like a bitch on heat Africa proves uncontrollably insatiable.

In the development of the genre, as historical circumstances changed, and the empire had not so much to be conquered as administered, Haggard's proud boast that there was "not a petticoat in sight"[5] became less frequently heard as the presence of women in the colonies slowly, but significantly, altered colonial life and its literature. Imperial conquest is the role of men, and thus colonies exist primarily to be controlled and lived in by men, in barracks and clubs, and women complicate this rather simple issue. The whole question of the presence of women—black, white, or otherwise—is problematic, for in this genre *women* are functionally subordinate to begin with; even white women. Thus with the introduction of women into the colonial novel, the men betray another fiction; the struggle for order, which naturally remains the primary function of Englishmen in foreign parts, becomes delineated in terms of sexual behaviour and misconduct. Female sexuality, troublesome at the best of times in male literature, is regarded with an attitude bordering on neurotic in the already tortured relationships on display in the colonies. The sex element runs as a strong undercurrent through out these works, and the tensions induced by the strong social and moral codes are thus expressed in terms of sexual comportment, for it seems that amongst Europeans in the far-flung parts of empire, great social and political pressure manifests itself in the form of all kinds of deviant sexual behaviour. Like the colonized countries they all inhabit, woman also becomes a subject space.

Monogamous heterosexual marriage amongst white couples is the norm, and sexual deviancy from this norm (most commonly represented by an act of potential or actual adultery) is used as an indicator of the moral standing of the characters concerned, and to dramatize the extent of social and moral breakdown. The sexual "deviation" goes the whole range of misconduct from European men trying to have sex with each other, or each others' wives, to European men and women having sexual encounters with both African men and women. All such acts become indicators of moral accountability. The question of sex becomes an obsession, as the walls between male and female remain essentially erect, and the treatment of women as rigid as the treatment of Africa. Sex becomes deeply symbolic, with miscegenation the *bête noire* of a deep, dark colonial nightmare always threatening to raise not so much her head, as her tail.

Let us deal first with the impact this has upon white women. For the most part they are manipulated by having their sexuality dealt with in a restrictive number of ways. White women as sexual beings are preferably ignored, otherwise they are looked upon as frigid, chaste or virginal, or, at the other extreme, seen as just plain whorish. This gives rise to a situation where there are two kinds of white women. In the first place, there is the hero's wife, whose role is to be supportive, whether or not she succeeds. She is generally a virtuous and sensitive woman, sharing the concern of the mission of his life which has brought him to Africa to begin with. But though the moral union between them is strong, the physical union is often inadequate. Then there is the hero's own personal "temptress," the symbol and agent of his social and moral breakdown, and the moral burden of the tale centres around a man who becomes incapable of keeping the two kinds of women distinct. The heart of the matter is that the "other woman" is always more beautiful than the wife, and the relationship between herself and the hero, being based purely on gratifying sexual attraction, potentially or actually destroys him (for whether or not the liaison is consummated depends upon how much of a "villain" he is supposed to be).

This schematic arrangement results in the placing of the white woman as the vehicle of damnation or the ultimate prize for the *hero*. In these political novels, one of the key factors in determining who the true hero is, is to see who ends up with the virtuous white woman, for whoever is beloved by her is rewarded. Furthermore, the men frequently see the necessity to conquer the woman as an integral part of their colonial adventure. However, a paradox is thus created for the moral hero who, because of the scathing attitude towards the whole idea of sexuality,[6] is not supposed to desire the fulfillment of his conquest.

One further restriction placed upon European women arises from the fact that the distinctions between what is sexually permitted to the man, and what the woman, remain extremely rigid. The more they speak (I mean really speak, not chit-chat), the more sexuality, but the less sexual respectability, they have. There is a sense in which, ***with the singular and significant exception of their continued access to language*** in these works, the position of white women since the "sexual revolution" of the last twenty years has perhaps been "reduced" almost to the level black women have always occupied. This is made almost glaringly obvious in a work such as *Rivers of Darkness*,[7] where a female French doctor, the innocent victim of the "coverup" of a professional scandal by her male colleagues, is sent in disgrace to Mozambique. At the medical kangaroo court which condemns her, she is judged justifiably guilty, the proof positive being the revelation that though a single woman, living alone, she took "the pill" as a matter of course, a habit which clearly makes her capable of any low and reprehensible deed.

This doctor is not alone in her predicament, for single women in Africa are invariably in flight from some kind of emotional turmoil involving a man, and more often than not in flight from some kind of past they wish to keep concealed. That is to say, white women are not *allowed* to be voluntarily sexual beings. Being in Africa is supposed to give them the opportunity to repent of their passions, and sublimate them by acquiring a sober sense of duty and falling in love with a man who does not acknowledge their sexuality.

For colonial Europeans, sexual behaviour is considered reprehensible, even by those who enjoy it, and is of course attributed to being in "Africa." In an almost anthropomorphic manner, the continent herself is endowed with a teeming female sexuality which affects everything within her.[8] As in the description of Conrad's gorgeous apparition, the emphasis is on sex and fertility. African vegetation is abundant and luxuriant, African women are tempting, reproductive sex objects, who both allure and repel. The promiscuous nature of the continent in her luscious and uncontrollable fertility affects the Europeans, the men in particular, and they give way to whatever temptations cross their paths, a weakness which always leads to social ostracism and often self-destruction. Even when the terrain is desert, it is the lonely barrenness of that landscape which makes them succumb!

This response to the continent has a devastating effect on the women of the place. The correct imperial response to African women becomes complicated by the sexuality of the *continent*. However, where there are two sorts of white woman, there is only one sort of black; sex objects. Black women seldom have names, for they are not so much people as presences—*fleshy* presences to be sure, but seldom accorded even the shadowy amount of dramatic substance with which Conrad endows his apparition. Black women are actually seldom present as players on the stage, and when they are, they do not speak, only white women have voices—black women have no vocabulary, and few gestures. Unlike their European counterparts in a colonial context, their words and actions are significantly absent from the vocabulary of public symbols. Whenever white women are present, they have the whole nexus of dramatic events organized around their existence, whereas black women are rarely presented as if they were viable human beings. They affect the dramatic action as symbolic spaces rather than as characters or personalities in their own right. The black woman remains an unvoiced object, most often to be found prone, legs spread, lurking in the shadows of a bedroom. It is required of black women not only that they be sexual, but above all that they be silent.

My illustrations of the consequences of this subordination and silencing of the black woman are taken from Margery Perham's *Major Dane's Garden* and David Caute's At *Fever Pitch.*[9] *Major Dane's Garden* presents a singular dramatization of the elision of the black woman's voice. In this novel Blaker, the young British D.O. (and his name is truly apropos), exposes his weakness of moral purpose by taking up the offer made to him by a black woman in need of a judicial favour, and sleeping with her to solace his loneliness. In complete contrast to Rhona, the English heroine who virtuously avoids the noble man she loves, the black woman actively seduces a man who is a moral failure, and whom she does not love. It is this act which precipitates the major political and diplomatic crisis of the novel, yet the African's motives are never fully explained; her own voice is not heard at all, and her story is only partially recorded and reported through the words of the European male:

> Now I must tell you why I am writing in this curious way. There was a dispute in court about a betrothal. I need not tell you the details. They were a striking couple: the woman, Khedichu, was the most beautiful Somali I have ever seen. She stood as straight as a spear and had regular features, a European profile. The man, Ibrahim, was a well-known warrior of an important house, a scarred, impassive person in a spotless tobe. I couldn't decide the point, and sent them to the kathi. That night, when I was sitting upon the veranda, Khedichu suddenly appeared, as if out of the ground, and came up to me, walking beautifully. She implored me to do this and not to do that. I gathered that she had very secret reasons for not wanting to marry Ibrahim, but she dared not say so because Ibrahim, having a great reputation to keep up, would kill her—and someone else. She would do anything in the world for me, if only I would help her. Rhona, I am not pretending this was the first time, but, you see, Khedichu was a very important person. We talked late. You can finish the story for yourself—Ibrahim's secret, threatening message to me, my realization of the futility of trying to arrest him. Have I mentioned that Ibrahim was a famous warrior? I have no doubt he will keep his word. Whatever happens, for the sake of you and Chard and Dane, I must not let this scandal come out. So the odds are all against me; I am a sitting bird for Ibrahim and his friends.[10]

We will not comment on what it is that makes her appear beautiful, and note only that like Conrad's woman she is strongly identified with the place itself, *appearing as if out of the ground.* In great contrast to Rhona, the married white woman who also has two men in addition to her husband in love with her, yet resists all temptation—remaining "chaste" even after it is clear her marriage is over and she has a passionate desire for Dane—Khedichu clearly has the unwanted Ibrahim, the unnamed other man, as well as Blaker, the last two at least of whom she takes to bed. Furthermore, not only is she left unvoiced, but the act of miscegenation between herself and Blaker, is rendered literally unspeakable. Blaker can not even write down what it is he has done. (Rhona, once she gets over the shock of realization, is suitably disgusted: "Pity left her. How could he? He had seemed so *clean* and young, and he said he loved her. Her cheeks flushed, burned, throbbed" [emphasis mine].) It is imperative to recognize that this unvoiced incident is the central dramatic event of the tale. The subsequent murder of Blaker by Ibrahim, followed by the immediate military response to his death, precipitate both the major political and personal dramas of the novel, and bring the colony to the brink of disaster. However, the events leading to this murder are only given in the account cited above, where everything fundamental is left unsaid and dependent upon interpretation.

The staging of the two women as oppositional is fundamental; Rhona is the battle prize, in the struggle for political power and manhood, between her husband Major Cavell and the hero Major Dane. Her husband actually articulates the fact that whoever is beloved by her gains the upper hand, and both men see the mastery of her as a part of the battle to master the land. She bestows her affection, switching allegiance, at the crucial moment, to the noble man whose politics are ascendant. The moral victor is the one the white woman loves, the man who can truly tame both the woman and the land by *seeding a garden* in the barren deserts of Abyssinia. In great contrast, the moral failure is the "boy" who sleeps with the black woman, and his literally unspeakable act of miscegenation is appreciated only through inference. Following the customary pattern, it is the person the powerful Europeans wish to condemn who singles himself out by indulging in an actual, physical liaison with an African woman.

The combination of the two factors of sex and race serves to make miscegenation the ultimate taboo, abrogating unto itself the suggestion of taintedness or evil. It is thus one of the central problems at the heart of these works. In general the *kind* of contact between the races is variable, and changes with the times, nonetheless, even at its most prevalent and liberal, the amount remains minimal, and subject to even more restrictive rules, overt or covert. But all interracial sex is regarded as a serious breach of conduct, and few novels are bold enough to broach the subject *overtly,* as a subject to be discussed by the characters within the texts themselves, with any conscious seriousness, still less with any notion of the possibility of its acceptability. When broached at all it is more often simply dismissed as unconscionably aberrant behaviour. Much of the time the problem is such anathema that not everyone even troubles to mention it. However, it remains always a threat, in the background, representing the feared final transgression, and occasionally, the characters do transgress.

White men are given more liberty in their sexual behaviour, and within certain limits their sexual mores are not questioned. They are only questioned when they begin to disrupt the British social order. Therefore the most frequent, and the most tolerated kind of inter-racial contact—precisely because not threatening to the British social order—is that of English men with African women, preferably prostitutes. Blaker's error was that he allowed his lusts to interfere with the sanctity of the administration of British justice. White men, seen with peculiar frequency lusting after the black female flesh of a people they continue to hold in contempt, are granted a curious lust which needs must be satisfied. That is, if you wish to sleep with a black woman you may do so, so long as she remains a prostitute, so long as you don't want to bring her to the club, and so long as you don't spread the disease that she is almost certainly going to give you. But if you start taking the whore seriously, that is unacceptable. Sex after all is permissible only under limited circumstances, even with white women, and marriage to other than a white woman should be unthinkable.

In contrast, there is no flexibility in attitude towards women in relationships with black men, particularly as the vary notion of white female sexuality is articulated as problematic to begin with. Sexual relations with a black man is *always a disaster* for the European woman, and she can under no circumstances be forgiven for marrying an African man; this would be beyond the pale, so to speak. Where a European woman voluntarily enters a relationship with an African man, she is shown, at the most sympathetic, to have been fundamentally and grievously in error. More often the consequences are socially catastrophic, and she is exposed as a degenerate and a social outcast who must make some terrible form of recompense. A quite vindictive example of this latter appears in John Wylie's *Riot*[11] when a young English woman married to a Ghanaian politician is symbolically punished for this union by being brutally raped by several African men the night of the riot which her husband's political colleagues had been instrumental in encouraging. Such relationships continue to be disastrous, as in the breakdown of all three marriages in Carol Christian's *Into Strange Country,* Alun Williams' *Valleys of Shadow*, and William Boyd's *A Good Man in Africa*.[12] The desire for any *intimate* union willingly entered into between the two races is regarded as strange country indeed.

Sex between the races is never a good thing. Without exception, when it takes place, it is an unhealthy relationship with dire consequences. If there were any doubt as to the acceptability of such behaviour, we need only look at its fruits, literally and symbolically. Where there are children born of such a union who live, they are frequently the most morally degenerate of beings: villainous, treacherous, manipulative degenerates who, contrary to genetic laws of breeding, manage to inherit both the most repulsive physical and spiritual traits of their parents.[13] Generally it is the black man who sheds these undesirable and undesired children upon the white female, and this is naturally considered a greater tragedy and a more abhorrent violation than the shedding of the white man's seed in the body of the black woman. The black woman herself seems more prone to spread diseases and death. If the death does not come directly, it eventually comes indirectly through her anyhow—as for example in the case of Blaker—because the relationship puts the man in an untenable position which in the end can only be resolved by his death. Time and again, the European man who has an encounter with an African woman which he permits to interfere with his judgement and mode of behaviour as an Englishman, ends up destroyed or dead.

There is one most fascinating novel in which this situation is reversed, and it is the African who dies, not the European, but in this case the victim is not a woman, but a man. It is even more true and extreme in *At Fever Pitch* than in most novels that moral confusion is represented by deviant sexual behaviour. The pressure of sexual desires and the consequences of sexual infidelities dominate all the central relationships. Furthermore, the usually strained in-group relationships among the expatriates are further exacerbated by the fact that in this case the exclusive community is the British Army, and the dominant sexual passion, homosexuality. The military situation makes all the neurosis over rank and class more acute, and this can be—and is—manipulated as a vehicle for sexual control.

As always, the central characters are Europeans, but there are a number of noteworthy Africans, of whom we here single out the "black buck" Sulley. This man is the batman to one of the British Officers, and we see him, when off duty, performing admirably with black women. He in fact keeps two wives pregnant and satisfied. However, he is subsequently seduced by Michael Glyn, his homosexual British master, an effectual rape which leaves him emasculated, and, most crucially, abjectly craving more of "that bed palaver thing" with his master. The chain of events which follows gives rise to the possibility of a radical interpretation of the colonial encounter, and transforms this text into one of the very few *potentially* liberating texts of its kind.

In this novel, as a consequence of his sexual behaviour, the hero *faces* what conquest can do to subject peoples, and does not like what he sees. Michael Glyn comprehends the reality that his mastery rests on an emasculation; Sulley must by force be made as if a woman—with all the implications this carries concerning the idea of the feminine—and then killed as a consequence of his desires. The implications of the analogy between this man as representative of the colonized, peoples are salutory; the colonial encounter produces a debilitating and ultimately fatal desire, *but it is a desire nonetheless.* Furthermore, the homosexual British officer is, after the consequent death of Sulley, initiated by a coloured female prostitute into a slaughterous "manhood" on election night. His first ejaculation into the body of the black woman is closely followed by, and becomes identified with, his frenzied triggering of a spray of bullets into a mutinous crowd, killing dozens of Africans. The one who conquers also truly loses control, and recognizes that there is nothing further to do but leave, abandoning the Africans to face the irreparable damage he has done.

Colonization in this text is *not* a good thing for any of the parties involved; nonetheless, what is interesting for our purposes is the manner in which the powerlessness of the black woman in particular is rendered more stark in this novel. As a colonial text is ultimately fails to be truly revisionist, and again, it is in the representation of the black *woman* that this failure is dramatized. We have in effect the total emasculation of the virile black male, which has a correspondingly devastating effect on the black woman. The two wives are in a subordinate position anyway, then the man who masters them is further mastered by the white man, and prefers that subjugation, leaving the women further subjugated. What is most pernicious, where they are concerned, is that their husband, after his rape, is said to crave sex with his white male master, and for his sake not only neglects them but beats them into submission. They accept his spiritual and physical violence in silence, then turn on *each other* in their desperation. In this manner they dramatize Michael Glyn's definition of womanhood as "sublime impotence," and expose the unacknowledged association between both groups of men which alienates the subordinate, silenced African women.

But what matter? We must ask why it is that this pattern repeats itself over and again; to what end is this subjugation of the female being done? We are viewing these texts in the specific context of the light they shed on representations of the colonial encounter. Much has been said concerning the representation of the colonial native as the European "other,"[14] but as those studies done are based on texts in which African males are very much present, but scant notice is taken of the practical non-existence of African *females*, I here maintain that this analysis is strictly one of the "othering" of the African *male* as the reverse of his European counterpart.[15] Thus, where it could be said that in the colonial novel the colonized male encounters not himself but his antithesis, the colonized woman encounters only erasure. She sees herself only in silent spaces. The unvoicing of the black woman is literal, and her essence projected only as a void. It is the meaning of this "void" that we must consider.

Viewed from the (disad)vantage point of the African woman, colonial literature is in the end simply about power. What these works as a body reveal is the relentless, ethnocentric will to power—not so much as a subject of their discourse, though this is very often the case, as in their "strategic formation"[16] which betrays a collective struggle for, and manipulation of, power. This power, whose legitimacy is suspect, in literature as in life, is maintained through the sheer force of repetition which becomes tantamount to the repeated use of force. It is of course as true for colonized men as for women that their texts collectively read as an articulation for mastery, but for women that articulation in its very nature betrays an ambivalence. This is a body of works whose strategic formation is one of power, but the locus of that power is the silenced body of the African female. What is crucial is the manner in which sex becomes metonymic, with miscegenation standing on the lowest rung of the metaphoric ladder of values and behavioural norms by which all characters are judged.

Given the aims of the colonial novel, to reflect the attempt at order in an alien and hostile territory, the imagery of sex can only betray a deep conflict: the juxtaposition of conquest and desire, and of empowerment and violation. As one of the leading metaphors for the idea of imperial conquest is that of the mastery of the woman, and since also the body of the continent is feminized, the mastery over colonial space becomes represented through the metaphor of rape. Given the violence of this sexual metaphor, desire cannot be satiated without conquest, nor power attained without violation. In each case the one cannot be achieved without the other, for the only way to conquer the woman is to succumb to her. Whether it be the white woman or the black the result is a paradox.

If we focus on the representation of each kind of woman in turn, the dilemma at the core of this paradox will be made more clear. In the case of the white woman, it is she who is situated as the rewards of victory. Given the formal structural relationships within which the heroes are confined, in order to be the victor, and deserve the prize woman, it is necessary to win her love, but at the same time never to claim her by consummating that love. (Not at least whilst still in the colonies!) Passion, though the most ennobling of emotions to feel and share, is the most debasing of instincts to succumb to. Thus, it is necessary (as does Major Dane) to demonstrate that you can have mastery over the woman, but never (as Kurtz apparently did) to *exercise* that power. Deflected sexuality must rather be channelled, in Dane's case naturally, by creating a garden in the desert of Abyssinia. But we rarely *witness* either the final conquest of the land, or the *fruitful* consummation of the relationship with the white woman. So the exercise of mastery can never be completed; the woman must be ever present to be won again, and the desire for conquest finds its own justification. Yet at the same time the perpetuation of that situation is only possible through the affected rejection of the supposed object of desire, whether it be the woman or the land—a rejection which is never truly *enacted,* as, for the most part, the territory is not abandoned nor yet does the woman remain unloved.

If we then substitute the body of the black woman, identical in the representation with the land itself, for that of the beloved, the paradox remains. If the hero does not take the silent African woman who is *said* to be willingly yielding, he does not rule her, or her space. If he conquers her, and consummates the relationship, he has failed, by committing that unspeakable act which cannot ultimately be sanctioned. Furthermore, if that be done, he invariably falls prey to Kurtz's dilemma—separated from the impelling body of the white "intended" and falling prey to the compelling body of the black, he might also inherit Kurtz's epitaph "he dead."[17] Kurtz, like Blaker, dies *because* he succeeds in the necessary "violation" which legitimizes his existence. Thus the unclean act becomes conquest itself; according to the rules of its own war, the conquest of the colonized body can never be sanctioned or legitimized, and the colonial text remains always at odds with itself.

Thus the obvious reading would be to interpret these works as if the relationships with white women legitimated the colonial presence, and those with black women dramatized a confession of guilt over the colonial encounter. As with Kurtz and his intended, conquest is said to be done at the behest of the inviolate white woman, but always performed at the expense of the black. But this again would deal only with that which is vocalized, rather than with that which remains structurally unrepresented; we are always left with the figure of the black woman, deliberately evoked as the essential spirit of the land, whose voice is silenced, if not usurped altogether.

In a fiction which perpetuates a myth of order in the need for conquest, and through the structuring of the relationship between *Europeans* perpetuates conquest and desire, the real fiction lies at one and the same time concealed and yet incomprehendingly exposed. The colonial is never truly encountered. The strategy succeeds in perpetuating a fiction, but the truth lies in that which cannot be said. Colonial literature does *not* become confessional, with the pattern of conquest and domination truly reconsidered in the contrasting structural relationships between white and black women. What these works give us is a justification of the colonial venture, with the real questioning of legitimacy still unattempted. The glance is deflected, with that which is *posited* as the representative spirit of the place never fully envisioned. Despite the energy of her potential to act, the wildly passionate woman on the banks remains a "gorgeous apparition" whose words appear inaudible.

Finally, therefore, the colonial subject is not represented by the "othered" male, as the discourse pretends, but remains unrecognized still in the purported silence of the black woman, and thus, in the literature, unheard. The strategic formation of power supposedly legitimated by these texts becomes a self-betraying manoeuvre in which the supreme fiction is that of the deliberate usurping of the voice of the supposedly willing African woman, rendering her falsely inarticulate. Metonymic sexuality both masks and betrays the unvoiced paradox; desire objectified as the body of "the intended" remains the continued justification for the colonial venture, but "brooding over an inscrutable purpose," it is the "mysterious life" of the black woman who in her "silence" voices judgement.

NOTES

1. Joseph Conrad, *The Heart of Darkness* (1898) (New York: Norton, 1971), p. 62.
2. *Ibid.*, p. 76.
3. There are two accepted conventions concerning these categories, which can be broadly labelled the "political-romance" and the "adventure." See D. Hammond "The Image of Africa in British Literature of the Twentieth Century" (Ph.D. Columbia University, 1963), p. 37, and Jeffrey Meyers, *Fiction and the Colonial Experience* (Ipswich: Boydell Press, 1973), p. vii.
4. This rigid structuring of the dramas enacted was the subject of my dissertation "Re-presenting Africa: Patterns of Experience in British Novels 1948–1980" (D. Phil., Oxford University, 1984).
5. Rider Haggard, *King Solomon's Mines* (1898) (New York: Dover Publications, 1951), p. 243.
6. This disavowal of sexuality is, however, one of the singular changes between the hero of the colonial and the post-colonial novel. Heroes of books by such

writers as Wilbur Smith, for example, set great store by their sexual prowess, and for them the ultimate accolade is to be seen, publicly, to "get the girl." Furthermore, as one response in colonial fiction to the sexual revolution of the 1960s has been a reaction against women which further restricts the representation of their sexuality, the opposing nature of these trends has set virginity once again at a premium. Thus, the new hero's woman is preferably a virgin if one can be found, but, given their scarcity, almost any woman will do.

7. Ronald Hardy, *Rivers of Darkness* (New York, G.P. Putnam's Sons, 1979).
8. See D. Hammond, *op. cit.* ch. IV.
9. Dame Margery Perham, *Major Dane's Garden* (New York: Africana Publishing Corporation, 1970). David Caute, *At Fever Pitch* (London: Andre Deutsch, 1959).
10. Perham, *op. cit.,* p. 190.
11. John Wylie, *Riot* (London: Secker & Warburg, 1954).
12. Carol Christian, *Into Strange Country* (London: Allen & Unwin, 1958), Alun Williams, *Valleys of Shadow* (Swansea: Christopher Davies, 1976), William Boyd, *A Good Man in Africa* (London: Hamish Hamilton, 1981).
13. See H.R. Collins, "His Image in Ebony: The African in Fiction During the Age of Imperialism" (Ph.D. Columbia University, 1951), pp. 218–23; Sarah Milbury-Steen, "Contrasting and Reciprocal Views of Africans and Europeans" (Ph.D. Comparative Literature, University of Indiana, 1975), pp. 156–59.
14. See for example J. Meyers, *op. cit.,* ch. 3. D. Hammond, *op. cit.,* Introduction. Milbury-Steen, *op. cit.,* ch. 1. H.A.C. Cairns, *Prelude to Imperialism* (London: Routledge & Kegan Paul, 1965), ch II, and chs. V & VI, for the influence of this notion on British ideas and actions.
15. Even in Homi Bhaba's provocative article "Of Mimicry and Man: The Ambivalence of Colonial Discourse," *October* 28 (Spring 1984), for example, it appears that his "man" is strictly male. As in Naipaul and all his other references, his analysis reads as if based upon observations regarding mimic *men,* and the colonized woman seems again absent from the debate.
16. The term is of course Edward Said's. See *Orientalism* (London: Routledge & Kegan Paul, 1978), p. 20.
17. Walter Ong in his fascinating psychological analysis "Truth in Conrad's Darkness" (*Mosaic,* University of Manitoba, Vol. XIII, no. 1), argues that the Intended is polarized as "western consciousness without self-knowledge," and is the real "horror" which impels Kurtz's journey of discovery. If we consider the place of the African woman in such a reading, the encounter with full self-knowledge—the bringing to light of the unconscious self which both is, and is at, "the heart of darkness"—becomes contemporaneous with the encounter with her; at the end of the journey the "other" becomes confounded with the self, yet this self-recognition still destroys. At the end of the journey it is still only the "horror" herself, and the Marlowe who permits her her narcissistic self-delusions, who remain alive in their *known* world. For us then, the question still remains: why is it that Marlowe who faces his unconscious represented as "Africa," somewhat vicariously through Kurtz, as Ong points out, rather than, like Kurtz, through the exercise of his own will, remains alive whereas Kurtz, who faces a "darkness" directly associated with the African woman, dies as a consequence.

Chapter 14

Gender, Feminist Theory, and Post-Colonial (Women's) Writing

Juliana Makuchi Nfah-Abbenyi

The concept of gender has influenced, defined, and oriented much of feminist discourse in the past three decades. Donna Haraway has stated that all the modern feminist meanings of gender have roots in Simone de Beauvoir's insight that one is not born a woman. Gender, explains Haraway, is a concept that developed to "contest the naturalization of sexual difference in multiple arenas of struggle. Feminist theory and practice around gender seek to explain and change historical systems of sexual difference, whereby 'men' and 'women' are socially constituted and positioned in relations of hierarchy and antagonism."[1] According to Elaine Showalter, gender has been used within Anglo-Saxon discourse to stand for the social, cultural, and psychological meaning imposed upon biological sexual identity. She further states that while earlier feminist literary criticism was interested primarily in women and women's writing, "[t]he introduction of gender into the field of literary studies marks a new phase in feminist criticism, an investigation of the ways that all reading and writing, by men as well as women, is marked by gender."[2] Feminist scholars were now able to theorize gender beyond the limits of sexual difference. This shift was necessary and significant because sexual difference had been central to the critique of representation in feminist writings and cultural practices of the 1960s and 1970s. Indeed, Sandra Harding has referred to feminist inquiries into the sex/gender system as "a revolution in epistemology."[3] Feminist theorists in recent decades have thus generally drawn from the diversity inherent in feminism(s).

Gender and Feminist Theory

Most feminists differentiate sex from gender.[4] Sex is understood as a person's biological maleness or femaleness, while gender refers to the nonphysiological aspects of sex, a group of attributes and/or behaviours, shaped by society and culture, that are defined as appropriate for the male sex or the female sex.[5] Gender is not a given at birth; only the actual biological sex is. Gender identity then begins to intervene through the individual's developing self-conception and experience of whether he or she is male or female.

Feminist theory has introduced gender as an important category of analysis—one with sociological, cultural, political, anthropological, historical, and other implications, depending on what aspects of gender the theorist is most interested in elucidating.[6] For some feminists, gender is a system of meanings within cultures used to categorize male and female sexuality in hierarchical terms. They argue that men and patriarchal ideologies control women's reproductive and sexual capacities, and that as a result, women are trapped by their reproductive anatomy and by a dogma of compulsory heterosexuality.[7] Other feminists have rewritten the woman's body and reconceptualized the feminine,[8] while others bring to the forefront the importance of mothering and early identification to gender relations, with the assumption that the family is the primary site of gender struggle.[9] Gender has also been seen as a play of power relations that offers men's and women's activities as public and domestic respectively. This opposition rigidly controls the organization of production and manipulates the division of labor into "male" and "female" categories.[10] Some feminists have argued that gender is a social and/or cultural process involving a complex set of relations that inevitably interlock with other relations of age, race, class, ethnicity, ideology, etcetera.[11] Still others stress the importance of the politics of spaces, locations, margins, and identities as they interlock with and alter gender relations.[12] The concept of gender therefore comes to feminist theory and criticism from many different areas.

Feminist literary criticism has for some time sought to apply some of the insights provided by gender theory. But within African literary circles, feminist literary criticism began to gain some ground only as of the late 1980s. As Jean O'Barr rightly points out, the concept of gender is still "rarely a theme for analysis" among African critics.[13] Consequently, the theories on gender that will ground my arguments will more often than not be Western theories. For this reason, I have chosen to include this theoretical chapter, which I deem necessary and important because of my primary sources; and also because, although I am writing this book in North America for a predominantly North American audience, I am also strongly aware of the African audience that must not, cannot, be excluded from its readership.

As an African literary critic working with Western feminist theories, I am confronted with the issue of what I can appropriate for the purposes of my feminist analysis of an African, postcolonial literature. I have therefore opted to take a critical look at some of the different approaches to gender that have been formulated within various areas of feminist theory and criticism, which relate specifically to issues centered on women's bodies; and also to look at how issues of identity and difference directly influence the construction of subjectivity in women's bid for agency and self-determination. I would posit that gender and feminist theory, especially *vis-a-vis* identity, sexuality, and difference, has not been formulated in ways that are wholly adequate and appropriate for African, "Third World" women's lives and literature. This does not in any way suggest that existing "Third World" or post-colonial theory is not without its own pitfalls.

POST-COLONIAL LITERARY THEORY

Some critics of "Third World" or post-colonial literature have suggested methods for the reading of these texts that I believe are more often than not grounded in Eurocentric thinking and biases. If Frederic Jameson, for one, views "all third-world texts" as "necessarily" national allegories, Homi Bhabha speaks of an ambivalence in colonial discourse that is captured within post-colonial texts in the form of "mimicry."[14] I contend that it is limiting to treat these texts simply as national allegories or reflections of colonial experience. Although I agree with Bhabha that there is, often, an "ambivalent" element of mimicry embedded in colonial discourse and reflected/transgressed in/by post-colonial texts, I will argue that some of these texts—including the ones I will be analyzing—decisively move beyond "camouflage" and beyond being "almost the same, but not quite." These texts present the cohabitation of a multiplicity of contradictions that cannot be contained only in an "ambivalent," mimetic economy. Such texts can be read as representation that is much more than just "mimetic" and/or oppositional, or continually producing a slippage. My interest lies not with the constant fracturing and undermining of colonialist discourse but, rather, with how these texts offer alternative scripts that subvert internal systems of power, texts whose gaze is not necessarily directed toward the colonialist text.

Ashcroft, Griffiths, and Tiffin take this discussion one step further when they write in their 1989 book, *The Empire Writes Back: Theory and Practice in Post-Colonial Literatures*, that

> The idea of "post-colonial literary theory" emerges from the inability of European theory to deal adequately with the complexities and varied cultural provenance of post-colonial writing.... Post-colonial theory has proceeded from the need to address this different practice. Indigenous theories have developed to accommodate the differences within the various cultural traditions as well as the desire to describe in a comparative way the features shared across those traditions. (11)

Although the need for a post-colonial literary theory is undoubted, the difficult issue becomes one of "developing" theo[ries] that in themselves do not simply reflect Eurocentric tendencies. Such theories should neither position these literatures only in opposition to the center (for example, Salman Rushdie's statement on the back cover of the book that "the Empire writes back to the centre") nor posit false notions of the universal. Arun Mukherjee has questioned "the totalizations of both the post-colonialists and the post-modernists that end up assimilating and homogenizing non-Western texts within a Eurocentric cultural economy."[15] The problem with such totalizations, as some critics have argued, is that the term "post-colonial" ends up being a monolithic term that ignores historical specificity and the vital differences between the experiences of colonization, past and present, among both white settlers and non-white (post)colonials.[16] Mishra and Hodge have argued that such homogenization "is clearly aimed at making the diverse forms of the post-colonial available as a single object on the curriculum of the centre,"[17] while Stephen Slemon maintains that center/periphery dichotomies end up "privileging the kind of post-colonial writing which takes resistance to colonialism as its primary objective."[18] As Mukherjee has rightly stated:

> When post-colonial theory constructs its centre-periphery discourse, it also obliterates the fact that the post-colonial societies also have their own internal centres and peripheries, their own dominants and marginals. . . . When it focuses only on those texts that "subvert" and "resist" the colonizer, it overlooks a large number of texts that speak about these other matters [of race, class, gender, language, religion, ethnicity].[19] (6)

An undifferentiated concept of postcolonialism and postcolonial theory therefore not only robs the so-called postcolonials of their differences but also ignores the power relations inherent in such totalizing categorizations. For, within the broad "post-colonial" category, and further, within those internal centers and peripheries of post-colonial societies, post-colonial women and post-colonial women's writing would "require a different order of theorising, since postcolonial women are like a fragment, an oppositional system, within an overall colonised framework. Women therefore function here as burdened by a twice disabling discourse."[20] I will add that women are not just "a" fragment, but multiple fragments burdened by a discourse that is disabling in multiple ways. As we will see in later chapters, this heterogeneity is captured and contested in post-colonial women's writing using a variety of methods. What is therefore important here for me is the fact that there can be no one, "unified" post-colonial literature or theory, just as there is no one, "unified" feminist theory, but rather feminist theories that offer diverse and differing voices within feminism(s).

When one speaks of the development of indigenous theories as mentioned by Ashcroft, Griffiths, and Tiffin, much therefore depends on one's point of view. I do agree that some indigenous theories have been developed to accommodate the West as well as the differences within various indigenous cultural traditions, but I will add that these theories also question the predominance of the West. It is my contention that indigenous theories have always been there, in the languages and cultures of Africa, in orally transmitted texts, and later on in published fiction. They were not looked into or read as such, however. This point already forecasts the most important theoretical argument that I will make in this chapter, which is that the novels I am analyzing are theoretical texts. The theory is embedded in the polysemous and polymorphous nature of the narratives themselves. These texts reinscribe and foreground teleological, ontological, and epistemological insights and praxes relevant to the specific histories and politics that preceded the fictional texts. I contend that "indigenous" theory is autonomous, self-determining, and exists in unconventional places like fictional texts; such theory can qualify as a kind of performance in print. Werewere Liking's writing offers a good example of what I am talking about. Her writing is heavily grounded in Bassa rituals. Bassa oral tradition therefore provides the theoretical foundation and framework on which her fictional texts are built. In order to fully understand her work, one must have some understanding of the theoretical fabric embedded in her writing and into which the writing is woven. When a *mvet* (instrument) player or griot narrates a *mvet* (epic poem) late into the night, continuing for hours on end, there is a theoretical framework that governs and directs his or her oral performance. In *African Oral Literature: Backgrounds, Character, and Continuity*, Isidore Okpe-who maintains that:

> African oral literature is studied side by side with modern African literature because many modern African writers consciously borrow techniques and ideas from their oral traditions in constructing works dealing essentially with modern life. These writers would like to feel that even though their societies have changed drastically from what they were several generations ago and even though they communicate with the world in a language that is not their own, there must be certain fundamental elements in their oral traditions that they can bring into their portraits of contemporary life.[21]

That is why, when I read the texts in this book as fictionalized theory or as theorized fiction, feminist gender theory will find itself both alongside and embedded in the texts.

I will also use personal insights and speak in the first person so as to distance myself from subject/object dichotomies. Feminist theory has reclaimed personal experience and, by so doing, has opened up a space within academe that has hitherto been deemed non-academic, non-abstract. But, although feminist theory has lifted the ban on the first person, it has not necessarily included my personal voice. I am even more comfortable with including my personal insights because African women as scholars and critics have not often had the chance to bring their own voices and experiences to bear on most scholarly research available in print (in articles or especially in book-length analyses). My critical analysis, sometimes grounded in my everyday experience as African woman, can only enrich the arguments that will be made, given that I will be "finding and naming critical theory which is African, melding it with western feminist theory and coming out with an overarching theory that enriches both western and African critical perspectives: [breaking] the cycle of dependency on western critical theory."[22] I also come from an oral traditional background that encourages and demands communal participation in day-to-day creative activities. The personal voice, especially during sessions of oral literature and performance, is encouraged and valued. That is why Achebe once described African art and literature as a "restoration of celebration."[23] The individual voice and participation, therefore, are part and parcel of the theoretical and (communal) critical process. I agree with Barbara Christian who, while condemning what she regards as "the race for theory" driving Western literary criticism, also urges minority and Third World critics to develop ways of reading their own literatures that do not necessarily reflect the often prescriptive ideas of the Western literary theoretical establishment.[24] I also value Henry Louis Gates' suggestion that the challenge of the critic of Afro-American literature is "not to shy away from literary theory, but rather to translate it into the black idiom, *renaming* principles of criticism where appropriate, but especially *naming* indigenous black principles of criticism and applying these to explicate [their] own texts."[25] That is why Anthonia Kalu has argued that it "has become necessary and, in fact imperative, that new approaches to the problem incorporate African ways of knowing. However, that avenue requires the development of strategies that enable the African scholar/researcher to address the African problem from an authentic viewpoint."[26] Or, as aptly put by Kenneth Harrow: "Change and a literary tradition are inextricably linked. To deny African literature the emergence of its own tradition [and critical theories, I might add] is to deny it the power to differ from 'world' literature, or European literature. And to accept that difference without accepting the process of emergence is to impute a stagnation to one corner of literature while generally accepting the power of writers [and critics] to create traditions elsewhere."[27]

My aim in this chapter is therefore twofold: one, to provide a critical discussion on aspects of gender that are relevant to my analysis of gender relations in the novels I am examining, given that gender theory is only beginning to make its way into African literary criticism. Two, to modify (where necessary) or express some of my arguments in ways that can be valuable to a feminist critique of gender in the context of African literature, given that most of the feminists who were writing the theories under consideration did not have African women or their literatures, cultures, or societies in mind. Frankly, Western feminists and critics are notorious for neither reading nor citing Third World critics nor giving them the place within theoretical discussions that they deserve (except for the few that have been "recognized," integrated, and named, and therefore fall within their parameters of thinking). We are often referred to as scholars who cannot and do not "theorize." Such statements are meant to keep us ("Third World" scholars) perpetually at the consumption end of Western theory, as opposed to the production end. They reinforce what Ketu Katrak has described as a "new hegemony being established in contemporary theory that can with impunity ignore postcolonial writers' essays, interviews, and other cultural productions while endlessly discussing concepts of the 'Other,' of 'difference,' and so on."[28]

I contend that African writers and critics are not merely receivers but are makers of theory as well. The nature of their theories and the "rules" (for lack of a better word) that govern their theoretical production and practice is that which needs to be outlined, given that Western readers often have a narrow or limited perspective. I agree with Adrienne Rich's suggestion that theory is nothing else but "the seeing of patterns, showing the forest as well as the trees—theory can be a dew that rises from the earth and collects in the rain cloud and returns to the earth over and over. But if it doesn't smell of the earth, it isn't good for the earth."[29]

RETHINKING FEMINIST THEORY AND POST-COLONIAL WOMEN'S WRITING

The institutions of motherhood and heterosexuality have become central to feminist analysis of gender and sexuality.[30] Although Catherine MacKinnon has stated that sexuality is *the* locus of male power,[31] radical feminists have championed the notion that women's oppression and the disparity in gender relations is to be found in sexual asymmetry (the division of society into two distinct biological sexes) and the sexual division of labor—in the patriarchal, universal male control of women's sexual and procreative capacities. They have challenged the patriarchy's control of women's bodies, especially the constitution of sexual difference through the phallic symbolization described by Freud and Lacan, and have reclaimed the irreducible reality of women's concrete experiences.[32] Sexual asymmetry and women's lack of control over their bodies as it relates to their procreative capabilities and sexual pleasure have thus received much attention within feminist criticism.

I find these contributions valuable, but I will also argue that sexual asymmetry is not as clearly distinct nor as universal as some theorists present it to be. The Nigerian feminist and sociologist, Ifi Amadiume, has shown in *Male Daughters, Female Husbands: Gender and Sex in an African Society* how Igbo women of Nnobi in Eastern Nigeria once drew power from the fact that male-female relationships were mediated by flexible gender ideologies. Obioma Nnaemeka has noted that this flexible gender system permitted women "to assume positions of wealth, power, and authority which, under strict gender definition, would have been the preserve of men."[33] Though not a common phenomenon throughout Africa, and though sometimes class-related, such flexible gender ideologies are important to the discussion of texts by African women writers, given that issues of sexuality and male domination will be grounded in specific cultural tenets associated with male–female social and sexual relationships. For example, Buchi Emecheta shows in her writing how when women are displaced out of the rural areas where the sexual division of labor grants women certain roles and autonomy, and move to urban areas where flexible gender systems are almost non-existent, women often find themselves in a disadvantaged position compared with their men.

What Amadiume describes accounts for a different and new argument within feminist theorizing on sexual asymmetry, male domination, and women's sexuality. Without necessarily glorifying pre-colonial gender relations in these societies, it must be noted that most of the flexible gender relations she describes were rigidified during colonial rule and have become part of the post-colonial heritage in African urban communities. These more rigid, masculinist gender roles failed to assimilate the earlier gender-integrated power structures in which women played major roles. Certain gender roles became fixed in that they had to be performed by either men or women. Among the Ibgo, for instance, indigenous spiritual practices empowered women in the person of the powerful goddess Idemili. Women assumed the roles of goddesses and their high priests could be men. There were also male deities with female high priestesses. When women became Christians, the powerful goddesses were dethroned. Women could no longer assume the roles of deities that had the right to stand in judgement over men or humankind. Of special relevance is the fact that men were generally powerful, but so too were/could be women.

Amadiume has been criticized by Elleke Boehmer for "not always deal[ing] satisfactorily with the continuing predominance of *de facto* patriarchal authority in the community, and the status commanded by the roles of son and husband." I would insist, though, that the separation of gender from sex roles not only creates a clearly defined women's sphere but also accounts for what Boehmer describes as "the independence and self-coherence of women's lives within that 'sphere.'"[34] A good example of the effects of this separation is seen in our (West African) local market economies, where women have long established their own places in the public sphere and are a powerful force to reckon with. In Beba, where I come from, women have spaces/rituals that are exclusive to women that men cannot invade, though they can share in, and vice versa. An example would be our *ndzang* (women's) and *ndoto'* (men's) dances. Either gender can partake in the celebration, on the sidelines, but cannot take control of the space/ritual. The separation of gender from sex roles provides unique spheres, spaces, and locations from which women can constitute and construct identities.

The feminists discussed earlier have limited their analyses of gender inequality to woman's biology and/or her sexuality and how it has been sanctioned either by patriarchy or by the Phallus. Women's sexuality is, on the one hand, controlled by an unbalanced sexual division of labor that manipulates women's procreative activities; on the other hand, woman's body is presented as a pleasure-based entity whose drives have either been sanctioned or repressed. Adrienne Rich's and Monique Wittig's condemnation of compulsory heterosexuality and the marginalization of lesbian women is crucial to delineating the ways in which these practices affect gender relations. But, the critique of motherhood (that views women as forced mothers) and heterosexuality (that views women as sexual slaves), despite its emphasis on women and their rights over their bodies, can be problematical to most African women simply because motherhood and family have historically represented different experiences and social practices to Western and African women. Motherhood is a theme that runs through the writings of many African women writers, and they question whether women are merely forced mothers and/or sexual objects. Emecheta and Bâ show how the presence or absence of children can have devastating and/or empowering impacts on women's lives.

Whereas many Western women may view multiple childbirth as both oppressive and restrictive (to their work, careers, economic well-being, et cetera), most African women find empowerment in their children and families. They use their status as mothers to challenge some of the demands their cultures place on them. They even use this status to make demands and obtain tangible concessions for themselves. Emecheta and Bâ, for example, illustrate how a woman who is a senior wife has at least three things that stand in her favor. These she can use with impunity: one, her position of senior wife; two, her status as a mother; and three, her status as the mother of sons, since her sons are the direct heirs to the family's property. The major problem for African women will not necessarily reside in control over their bodies or motherhood as such, but with a combination of other interrelated issues, such as discriminatory cultural and patriarchal practices that give better socio-economic and/or political status to mothers, especially mothers of sons as opposed to mothers of daughters (Adaku, one of Buchi Emecheta's characters, suffers discrimination on the basis of the gender of her children, who are all girls); the lack of sex education for young teenage girls; birth control that is nonexistent or subject to restrictive policies; infant mortality and insufficient health care facilities that force some women to lose children and bear more to make up for the numbers that they really desire, or have more children in their search for the sons that they might not have. We will see in the following chapters that the women writers do not separate these issues either. They are all problematized as different facets of women's struggle against patriarchal oppression in their societies.

Women's pleasure and the denial of pleasure for women has also been one of the thorny issues addressed by feminists. In an African context, the exclusive theorization of the erotic is not without its pitfalls, as that conception of the woman's body as openly pleasurable to the ***woman*** is not often openly debated by either men or women. For some men, woman's pleasure is not spoken of or meant to be spoken about. In some cases, it can be spoken about so long as it gives credit to their virility—in other words, so long as the Phallus both as sexual organ of pleasure and as transcendental signifier is affirmed. For others, women can affirm their pleasure so long as it is done in private with other women-friends; otherwise, she is seen as a slut! The expression of sexual pleasure becomes an even thornier issue in instances of polygamy. As we will see in the next chapter, the protagonist of *The Joys of Motherhood*, Nnu Ego, resents her co-wife, Adaku for her open display of pleasure. The senior wife of a male character in the same novel dies the night that her husband openly gives pleasure to his mistress in their courtyard.

For women, the picture is slightly different. Women do talk among themselves about their bodies. Women teach one another secrets and practice rituals concerning sexuality that they hand down from generation to generation. They sometimes talk about their sexual pleasure, but it is more often than not in relation to that of men. In most African societies where women's pleasure is most often inferred from what they say or do, from how they say or do it, in their day-to-day interactions with men, the theorization of their pleasure as exclusive to women would drive an intolerable wedge between men and women. Moreover, a theory of sexuality that limits itself to the presence, lack of, or denial of sexual pleasure is not only problematical but also negative to those women in Africa who have had to undergo the cruel practices of "female circumcision." I am aware of the fact that some critics might find the expression "female circumcision" to be inappropriate because of the obvious connotation of maleness/manhood in the term "circumcision"; and also because the pain and trauma, as well as the infection, hemorrhaging, sickness, and death that sometimes ensue from excision and infibulation, is not comparable to that experienced with male circumcision. I am using this expression for two reasons: one, because most Africans use it; and secondly, as an all-encompassing term, given that some women writers have used the "egg ritual" in their writing, which does not have a specific term like, say, clitoridectomy, and cannot be subsumed under female genital surgeries, either.

Western feminists tend to zero in on specific issues concerning women in the "Third World," and then sensationalize those hand-picked issues for Western consumption. Many other equally important (contextual) problems that plague the lives of these women are ignored. It is not uncommon to hear some Western feminist scholars at conferences who, when they include a few sentences or paragraph(s) on "Third World" women in their paper, immediately narrow their focus to clitoridectomies/infibulation in Africa. What happens more often than not (and this is from personal experiences as well) is that African women's sexuality seems to end up being synonymous with "clitoridectomy" in Western feminist circles.[35] The fact that this practice is limited to certain areas in Africa, and that the vast majority of African women have not been victims of this awful ritual, does not seem to matter, and neither do the various and multiple contexts of their oppression(s). The fact that these women seem to be condemned and left by the wayside by feminist discourses is more disconcerting given that feminist intellectual exercises tend to stress one thing only, the inability of these victims to experience sexual pleasure.[36]

What I find negative is the fact that a good majority of the feminists who address this issue often *do not* delve into the reasons why it happens, nor do they propose any solutions that can be helpful in the lives of these women. We are told that circumcision takes away their pleasure for life. This is sometimes followed by a plethora of examples that depict African men as inherently savage and violent. What ends up happening is unfortunate, given that in the bid to match African women's (sexual) victimization with African men's brutal nature/patriarchy, the women seem forgotten or remain in the shadow of the discussion that is (supposedly) about them and their sexuality. This issue is particularly problematical to me because my awareness of female circumcision was sparked and has been sustained only since my arrival in North America (Canada and the United States).

I have often wondered why concerned Western feminists do not crusade, for instance, for funding to set up psychotherapeutic clinics (something

Western, of which they have a better understanding, although these might not necessarily work) in the countries involved, or more practically, to crusade for funding to be made available to local women's networks in the countries involved, so that these African women, who have proven time and time again that they are masters at networking, can afford to travel (given the economic status of most women) around their communities/countries, come together, talk to one another and seek solutions as individuals within groups, to solving the problems that touch their lives in so many important ways. Local women can therefore obtain valuable counseling and support from each other that can empower them either to collectively or individually protest against this practice (something that is happening already) and/or enable them to deal with their loss, heal, and live fulfilling sexual lives.

The Malian feminist, Awa Thiam, interviewed many African women who spoke and offered viewpoints about their experiences of excision and/or infibulation. Thiam assesses some reasons that are mythical, cultural, and historical associated with these practices. She concludes that the struggle against these practices can work only if the current social structures are challenged within the countries involved. Men and women need to be informed and educated, "so that everyone may take a stand against them."[37] The Egyptian physician, feminist, and activist Nawal el Saadawi has demonstrated in her book *The Hidden Face of Eve*[38] that the circumcision of girls exists in and is re-enforced by a plethora of conditions within patriarchy that range from socioeconomic, to cultural, to political reasons. For example, those who perform these acts find them economically profitable and resist change because they will lose one or their only means of making a living. Underdevelopment and poverty are therefore closely linked with the practice. Men use this practice as a cultural and political weapon to keep women in a position of subjugation in a society where the hierarchization of sexes is important to men, so that they can always define the female sex as inferior to the male sex, thereby legitimizing the prevalent male control over the female sex and especially over her sexuality. Saadawi also describes the devastating psychological traumas that circumcised women suffer, and are, therefore, in dire need of clinics or spaces within which a healing process can begin and thrive. She is convinced that the practice of clitoridectomies, excision, and/or infibulation on women cannot be separated from all the other economic, cultural and political conventions that have fostered, influenced and still advocate its existence. She insists on "recognizing linkages between the individual, community, society, and state" (xv). To dissociate these phenomena would be dangerously limiting and would lead to obvious stereotypical assumptions and definitions, especially of the women who are scarred for life by these practices. Getting men and women, and especially women, to stand together and challenge these social structures is of the utmost importance. I contend therefore that, when (all) African women's sexuality is restricted to an issue of sexual pleasure, reductive and negative feminist politics are the result. In her insightful essay, "Arrogant Perception, World Travelling and Multicultural Feminism: The Case of Female Genital Surgeries," Isabelle

Gunning cautions us that "as feminists, we must develop a method of understanding culturally challenging practices, like female genital surgeries, that preserves the sense of respect and equality of various cultures. The focus needs to be on multicultural dialogue and a shared search for areas of overlap, shared concerns and values."[39] It is our inability to develop complex methods of understanding and describing "culturally challenging practices" that I find wanting in feminist discussions on this subject.

Let me use an example from my specific cultural experience to illustrate this point. Violence against women among the Beba is considered a taboo; indeed beating one's wife is as serious a crime as committing suicide through hanging. Both acts are punishable by Beba custom. The perpetrators of battery are made to pay heavy fines. In the case of hanging, libations have to be carried out to cleanse what is considered an abomination, the stigma from which on the one hand weighs down a family for generations, but on the other hand acts as a potent sanction and deterrent of suicide within the larger Beba community. Individuals are thus encouraged to seek other avenues within their families/society in solving their problems instead of resorting to suicide. Similarly, two things are said among the Beba: a man has no right to lift his hand to a woman; only women "physically" fight other women. A man who beats his wife is, by the same token, feminized. Although this feminization of physically abusive men can be interpreted by feminists as insulting to women, as "typical macho" behavior or as an oppressive patriarchal way of thinking, the fact remains that, within Beba culture, women are protected from male violence by the same patriarchal reasoning and punishment. Language and culture thus function in complex, challenging ways and, in this instance, offer an "ambiguous" choice. As a Beba woman I might question this option theoretically, but in practical terms, I am prepared to accept and even embrace it—the deterrence of male violence against women, against me. We need to develop a more complex outlook toward these issues. The problems that define and construct African women's sexuality, therefore, need to be explored beyond the denial or lack of sexual pleasure.

As was mentioned earlier, African women do talk among themselves about their bodies and their sexuality. They have been able to create strong woman-to-woman bonds that empower them with a valuable network of practices from which men are excluded. But the vast majority of these African women have not pushed or are not able to push these bonds to the limits of celebrating lesbian sexual pleasure. They seem to be hemmed in by repressive cultures or what Rich considers to be institutionalized heterosexuality. It is my conjecture that some homoerotic feelings could and do possibly develop between some women in Africa, but they are maintained at a primal level and do not necessarily become sexual. Homosexuality in this case becomes taboo, something whose existence is sometimes "known" but heavily repressed and rarely spoken or spoken about. We will see how Beyala uses the character Ateba to question the silences (specifically women's silences) and prohibitions that for millennia have repressed and suppressed homosexuality in the language, beliefs, customs and culture of her people.

I attended the 17th Annual African Literature Association Conference (ALA) in 1991, which was exclusively on the African woman (writer). When the issue of lesbianism in the work of Beyala was raised, the reaction of most of the African women in the audience fluctuated between indifference, anger, aggressivity, and even outright contempt. One woman said that lesbianism was not a "problem" in Africa, it simply was not "our problem." The chair of the panel, who evidently agreed, took the floor and angrily said that "we" have other pressing and more important "problems" to worry about. In not so many words, they dismissed the matter except for a vicious undercurrent of presuppositions and insinuations that permeated the room until the end of the discussion. Most African women sometimes have a presumptuous way of talking about lesbians, especially their diaspora lesbian "sisters," either as women who do not know how to handle their men, or as women who have the luxury of "buying into" a culture alien to theirs.

In other words, those women vehemently affirmed their heterosexuality. Reflecting back on this, I can conjecture that affirming their heterosexuality might appear to have been the right thing to do, strategically. Such affirmation gives us better chances of fighting gender oppression than endorsing a poorly understood and universally stereotyped lesbianism, whose chances of "public" acceptance will almost be nil in our African societies. Although, strategically, one might choose to risk this stance, I will maintain as well that this choice continues to stigmatize and perpetuate prejudice against what one can conjecture to be a "silenced" number of lesbian African women, who cannot speak openly about their sexuality and therefore cannot publicly and politically fight for their rights. Heterosexual women find themselves in an "enviable" bargaining position, but it is won at the expense of these silenced others.

I learned at the ALA conference that most African literary critics are not concerned with lesbian or gay issues because this topic is very sensitive and often controversial, or because they view other issues as more pressing. Or, they fall back on the excuse that homosexuality is shunned or repressed by their culture and thought by many not to exist. Furthermore, not many African writers address the issue of homosexuality in their writing, and even when they do, as Chris Dunton has shown in his essay, " 'Wheyting Be Dat?' The Treatment of Homosexuality in African Literature," its use is often either "crudely stereotypical" or "monothematic," one that sees homosexuality as directly linked to and grounded in the African's encounter/experience with the exploitative and alienating Other, in this instance, the West.[40] Dunton also notes that for the few writers who do "exhibit a much deeper imaginative engagement in the condition of homosexuality and in its social psychology . . . the presentation of homosexual relationships remains schematic, intentional" (444–45). I contend that the texts that will be analyzed in chapter 3 are accomplishing the opposite of what some critics are not ready to do, or are reluctant to do. Some critics, for instance, have condemned a writer like Beyala for creating a character with "homosexual tendencies," while others claim that what she writes about is not really homosexuality but strong friendships between women. These texts will thus be inscribing themselves beyond radical feminist protest and at the crossroads of African (literary) critical reticence and resistance.

Most African women would also judge a feminist rejection of heterosexuality as separatist. They would prefer to view sexuality as a contested terrain, one that, as Foucault points out, deals with "a multiplicity of discourses produced by a whole series of mechanisms operating in different institutions" and historical periods.[41] The socio-economic and political implications of male power embedded in the sexual division of labor must be combined with the multiple and varying meanings of women's bodies and sexualities inscribed in the novels that will be under discussion. There can be no clear-cut separation between sexuality, history, economics, and politics in texts that are written about women's lives in a post-colonial context, where some flexible gender ideologies have been replaced by less flexible ones, and where power relations have shifted drastically and have put women in more disadvantaged conditions. An important point that I will make is that these texts are not "duplicating," "reflecting," or "writing back" to radical feminist critiques on sexuality. They are creating a space for themselves by questioning a combination of oppressive conditions that are both traditional and specific to their colonial heritage and post-colonial context, a context that positions their protest beyond the limits of radical feminism.

Women-to-women bonding and networking has been specific to African women's existence and agency for millennia; so too, has been the complementarity of gender roles between African men and women. When a woman writer questions the repression of homoerotic bonding among women, when these writers critique marriage, motherhood, the male use of economic and political power to control women's sexuality and lived experiences, I contend that their texts are, within the context of African and postcolonial literature, doing within the canon something comparable to what radical feminist writings did for the feminist movement starting in the 1960s. The similarity lies not in content, but in the way both reinscribe identity. These texts are not just giving voice, nor are they just reinscribing the question of African women's identity; they are begging and forcing readers, critics (the majority of whom are men), to reflect on the issues that they have hitherto forgotten, neglected or simply brushed aside.

Susan Hekman has written that "[t]he subject/object dichotomy that excludes women from the realm of the subject has had a profound effect on the status of women in the modern era" (94). Hekman is here referring to the universal, unified subject, "Woman." If women have been excluded from the realm of "the subject" in Eurocentric discourses, then Third World women have been "objects" of discourses (Eurocentric, colonial and post-colonial) even more so than Western women. Being the Other of man, the Other of the West, the Other of other (Western/non-Western) women has been as problematical as the place(s) of post-colonial women "as writing and written subject."[42] African and "Third World" women seem to find themselves in an indescribable position within this metonymic chain of otherness, one that I will describe, to borrow Spivak's words, as that of "the historically muted subject of the subaltern woman,"[43] with a difference. If Spivak's subaltern woman is historically muted, I contend the reverse, which is that she has always spoken, she has spoken in alternative ways that have challenged and continue to challenge not only imperialism and colonial discourse but us, the critics as well, who have been slow to or have refused to hear and acknowledge when and how these voices have spoken.[44]

If African and "Third World" women are often left in the shadows, this brings problems of identity and difference to the forefront in post-colonial women's writing. Post-colonial women need to claim a specific identity, one that is crucial to what Patricia Collins has described as that of the "outsider within," because claiming an identity gives to all marginalized groups of women not only the chance to critique gender hierarchies within their own communities from the margins but also the dominant power structures.[45] They can fluctuate between what bell hooks has termed "the margin and the center," they can draw on what Chela Sandoval has described as "oppositional consciousness"[46] while simultaneously using what Linda Alcoff has called "positional perspectives" to construct meaning, subjectivity, and agency.[47] I will contend that African women need to claim an "identity politics" that foregrounds their ability to fluctuate between the margin and the center, wherever these margins and centers might be, but will also enable them to move beyond constructed and constituting margins and centers, creating their own margins and centers along the way.[48] As we shall see later, in Buchi Emecheta's *The Joys of Motherhood*, Nnu Ego's co-wife, Adaku, is a woman who quickly pinpoints the roots of discrimination against her and looks for methods to combat it: she sends her daughters to school instead of marrying them off; she sets up a trade, et cetera. Most of the texts that I will discuss demonstrate a conscious and constant weaving of personal identity politics and positionality.

Since different groups of marginalized women can create new spaces and social locations for themselves within the dominant culture, marginality (be it represented as racial, sexual, historical, or cultural difference) will therefore be the point of intersection for identity politics, the location where identity politics finds full expression. By creating these new spaces and locations, women take the margins to the center and vice versa. This constant shifting subsequently subverts dominant political, economic, cultural conceptions of gender, both at the center and at the margins. What this means for post-colonial women is that they can and need to problematize "their own internal centres and peripheries, their own dominants and marginals" (Muhkerjee 6). If I were to go back to Cameroon today, I would be confronted with different kinds of struggles at different levels and contexts. For example, on the one hand, I will have to explain to other scholars why I call myself a feminist, what I mean when I call myself a feminist, how I practice my feminism; and on the other hand, I will have to explain to many people why I do not want to have any more children when most of them believe that three is not enough, given my social and financial status. These are two very different battles but are very much related.

Post-colonial women therefore have to make use of multiple identity, of the "I" that Minh-ha maintains has "*infinite layers*" (*WNO* 94).[49] They bring to the politics of identity and gender-as-difference, as otherness, a struggle that must actively involve the dominant and dominated, the colonizer and colonized, the First and Third Worlds. That is why, Minh-ha contends, the story of gender-as-difference is a story that places both insiders and outsiders in an arena of contestation and negotiation, because:

> The moment the insider steps from the inside she's no longer a mere insider. She necessarily looks in from the outside while also looking out from the inside. Not quite the same, not quite the other, she stands in that undetermined threshold place where she constantly drifts in and out. Undercutting the inside/outside opposition, her intervention is necessarily that of both not-quite an insider and not-quite an outsider ("Not You" 76).[50]

What this means is that identity must be constantly constructed in the context of other identities, always shifting depending on whom one encounters. We will see in the next chapter how, in Dangarembga's *Nervous Conditions*, the protagonist's cousin Nyasha's identity constantly shifts depending on her (re)actions toward her father, her mother, or her cousin, Tambudzai. Fixed identity must therefore be de-stablized and by so doing, fixed relations of gender and power hierarchies can also be dis-organized. This disruption creates simultaneous margins where sexual difference or gender inequalities will find themselves in potentially fluid, though still problematized, shifting locations. African women can, therefore, not only fluctuate between and within identities and subject positions, they can redefine their racial, cultural, historical difference(s).

My arguments can be summarized as follows: my treatment of identity here synthesizes post-colonial and gender theory and moves beyond the strictly "academic" parameters that are assigned to critical theory and practice. This book not only confronts the lack of and neglect of women's fiction writing but, in the same vein, is reclaiming and recovering this fiction and a practice of theory not common to feminist politics and praxis. Recovering women's fiction, therefore, also belongs in the realm of indigenous theory. I emphasize the point that these texts move beyond conventional academic definitions of theory. For instance, after she bears a (male) child, Nnu Ego is told, "You are now a woman," or "You have become a woman." These statements are loaded with a number of gender-related definitions: It is as if gender were discontinuous (as if she is not a woman until the birth of a child then confers womanhood and femininity); is sometimes biologically achieved or lost; and in her cultural context ushers in a status that can either be rejected or assumed and manipulated.

The theoretical framework that I have delineated will show how the writings of African/post-colonial women writers create and redefine the new spaces in the margins of feminist and hegemonic discourses. When Spivak asks, "Can the subaltern speak?" she is also questioning the "desire to conserve the subject of the West, or the West as Subject" (271). My analysis begins in the next chapter with three writers: Buchi Emecheta, Ama Ata Aidoo, and Tsitsi Dangarembga. This chapter will demonstrate how they have reconstituted and reconstructed the multiple, shifting, and sometimes contradictory identities and subjectivities of African women in their writing. They show how these same contradictions are valuable and empowering tools necessary to subverting gender(ed) dichotomies and exigencies, contradictions that are paramount to describing African women's identity, subjectivity, and agency.

NOTES

1. "'Gender' for a Marxist Dictionary: The Sexual Politics of a Word," in *Simians, Cyborgs, and Women: The Reinvention of Nature* (New York: Routledge, 1991), 131.
2. "Introduction: The Rise of Gender," in *Speaking of Gender*, ed. Elaine Showalter (New York: Routledge, 1989), 2.
3. "Why has the Sex/Gender System Become Visible Only Now?" in *Discovering Reality*, ed. Sandra Harding and Merrill Hintikka (Dordrecht: D. Reidel, 1983), 314.
4. Simone de Beauvoir, *The Second Sex*, trans. H. M. Parshley (New York: Vintage, 1974); Hilary Lips, *Sex and Gender: An Introduction* (California: Mayfield, 1988); Linda Lindsey, *Gender Roles: A Sociological Perspective* (New Jersey: Prentice Hall, 1990); Judith Lorber and Susan Farrell, eds., *The Social Construction of Gender* (Newbury Park, CA: Sage, 1991).
5. Ann Oakley, *Sex, Gender and Society* (New York: Harper Colophon, 1972); Suzanne Kessler and Wendy McKenna, *Gender: An Ethnomethodological Approach* (New York: John Wiley and Sons, 1978); Ivan Illich, *Gender* (London: Marion Boyars, 1983); Robert Stroller, *Presentations of Gender* (New Haven: Yale UP, 1985).
6. For example, Nancy Chodorow, *The Reproduction of Mothering: Psychoanalysis and the Sociology of Gender* (Berkeley: U of California P, 1978); Linda Nicholson, *Gender and History: The Limits of Social Theory in the Age of the Family* (New York: Columbia UP, 1986); Linda Lindsey, *Gender Roles*, Kessler and McKenna, *Gender.*
7. Michelle Rosaldo and Louise Lamphere, eds., *Women, Culture, and Society* (Stanford: Stanford UP, 1974); Gayle Rubin, "The Traffic in Women: Notes on the 'Political Economy' of Sex," in *Toward an Anthropology of Women*, ed. Rayna Rapp (New York: Monthly Review Press, 1975), 157–210; Sherry Ortner and Harriet Whitehead, eds., *Sexual Meanings: The Cultural Construction of Gender and Sexuality* (Cambridge: Cambridge UP, 1981); Adrienne Rich, "Compulsory Heterosexuality and Lesbian Existence," in *The Signs Reader*, ed. Elizabeth Abel and Emily Abel (Chicago: U of Chicago P, 1983), 139–67; *Of Woman Born: Womanhood as Experience and Institution* (New York: W. W. Norton, 1986); Pat Caplan, ed., *The Cultural Construction of Sexuality* (London: Routledge, 1989).
8. For instance, the French feminists presented in *New French Feminisms: An Anthology*, ed. Elaine Marks and I. de Courtivron (New York: Schocken, 1981); Monique Wittig, *The Straight Mind and Other Essays*

(Boston: Beacon, 1992); Nancy Fraser and Sandra Bartky, eds., *Revaluing French Feminism: Critical Essays on Difference, Agency, and Culture* (Bloomington: Indiana UP, 1992).

9. Chodorow, *The Reproduction of Mothering*, and *Feminism and Psychoanalytical Theory* (New Haven: Yale UP, 1989).
10. Alison Jaggar, *Feminist Politics and Human Nature* (Sussex: Harvester, 1983); Nancy Hartsock, "The Feminist Standpoint: Developing the Ground for a Specifically Feminist Historical Materialism," in *Feminism and Methodology*, ed. Sandra Harding (Bloomington: Indiana UP, 1985), 157–80; Dorothy Smith, *The Everyday World as Problematic: A Feminist Sociology* (Toronto: U of Toronto P, 1987).
11. Jane Flax, "Postmodernism and Gender Relations in Feminist Theory," in Malson *et al.*, 51–73; Trinh Minh-ha, *Woman, Native, Other: Writing Postcoloniality and Feminism* (Bloomington: Indiana UP, 1989); bell hooks, *Yearning: Race, Gender, and Cultural politics* (Toronto: Between the Lines, 1990); Chandra Mohanty *et al.*, eds., *Third World Women*.
12. Audre Lorde, *Sister Outsider* (Freedom, CA: Crossing Press, 1984); Elly Bulkin *et al.*, *Yours in Struggle: Three Feminist Perspectives on Anti-Semitism and Racism* (Ithaca, NY: Firebrand, 1988); Trinh Minh-ha, "Not You/Like You: Post-Colonial Women and the Interlocking Questions of Identity and Difference," *Inscriptions* 3/4 (1988): 71–77.
13. Jean F. O'Barr, "Feminist Issues in the Fiction of Kenya's Women Writers," in Jones *et al.*, 55.
14. Frederic Jameson, "Third-World Literature in the Era of Multinational Capitalism," *Social Text* 15 (1986): 69; Homi Bhabha, "Of Mimicry and Man: The Ambivalence of Colonial Discourse," *October* 28 (Spring 1984): 126. (For a critique of Jameson, see Aijaz Ahmad, "Jameson's Rhetoric of Otherness and the 'National Allegory,'" *Social Text* 17 [1987]: 3–25.)
15. "Whose Post-Colonialism and Whose Postmodernism?" *World Literature Written in English* 30.2 (1990): 1–2.
16. See, for instance, Anne McClintock, "The Angel of Progress: Pitfalls of the Term 'Post-Colonialism,'" *Social Text* 31–32 (1992): 84–98; Ella Shohat, "Notes on the 'Post-Colonial,'" *Social Text* 31–32 (1992): 99–113; Kwame Anthony Appiah, "Is the Post-in Postmodernism the Post-in Postcolonial?" *Critical Inquiry* 17 (Winter 1991): 336–57.
17. Vijah Mishra and Bob Hodge, "What is Post(-)Colonialism?" *Textual Practice* 5.3 (1991): 401.
18. "Unsettling the Empire: Resistance Theory for the Second World," *World Literature Written in English* 30.2 (1990): 35.
19. See also Frank Schulze-Engler, "Beyond Post-Colonialism: Multiple Identities in East African Literature," in *US/THEM: Translation, Transcription and Identity in Post-Colonial Literary Cultures*, ed. Gordon Collier (Amsterdam: Rodopi, 1992), 319–28.
20. Mishra and Hodge, 408. See also Suleri 155n30, and Spivak, "Imperialism and Sexual Difference," *Oxford Literary Review* 8: 1–2 (1986): 225–40.
21. Bloomington: Indiana UP, 1992, 18. See also Eileen Julien's *African Novels and the Question of Orality* (Bloomington: Indiana UP, 1992), 7.
22. I am here borrowing the words of one of the reviewers of my manuscript, who characterizes this act as "a truly *liberating* force."
23. "African Literature as Restoration of Celebration," *New African* (March 1990): 40–43.

24. "The Race for Theory," *Feminist Studies* 14.1 (1988): 67–79.
25. Henry Louis Gates, Figures in Black (New York: Oxford UP, 1987), xxi, my emphasis.
26. "Those Left Out in the Rain: African Literary Theory and the Re-Invention of the African Woman," *African Studies Review* 37.2 (Sept. 1994): 77–95. See also Chinua Achebe, "Colonialist Criticism," in *Hopes and Impediments: Selected Essays* (New York: Anchor Books, 1989), 68–90.
27. *Thresholds of Change in African Literature: The Emergence of a Tradition* (Portsmouth, NH: Heinemann, 1993) 4.
28. "Decolonizing Culture: Toward a Theory for Postcolonial Women's Texts," *Modern Fiction Studies* 35.1 (1989): 158.
29. "Notes toward a Politics of Location (1984)" in *Blood, Bread, Poetry: Selected Prose* 1979–1985 (New York: W. W. Norton, 1986), 213–14.
30. Rich, "Compulsory Heterosexuality"; Kate Millett, *Sexual Politics* (New York: Ballantine Books, 1970); Rosemarie Tong, *Feminist Thought* (Boulder: Westview, 1989), 95–138; Gayatri Spivak, *In Other Worlds* (New York: Routledge, 1987), 80.
31. "Feminism, Marxism, Method, and the State: An Agenda for Theory," in *The Signs Reader*, ed. Abel and Abel (Chicago: U of Chicago P, 1983), 227.
32. Cixous and Irigaray in Marks and de Courtivron, eds., *New French Feminisms*, Wittig, *The Straight Mind*. Also, Hartsock "The Feminist Standpoint," and Smith, *The Everyday World as Problematic*.
33. Review of *Male Daughters, Female Husbands* in *Signs* 16.3 (1991): 611.
34. "Stories of Women and Mothers: Gender and Nationalism in the Early Fiction of Flora Nwapa," in Nasta, 14. It is worth noting that Amadiume's study also provides data that points to the fact that this flexible gender system exists in many parts of Africa.
35. I have been asked a number of times, at conferences, by total strangers, "how it feels to be circumcised." The obvious assumption itself that I am, or must be, is mind-boggling. See Nfah-Abbenyi, "Reflections of an African Woman," in the special issue on racism and gender of *Canadian Woman Studies* 14.2 (Spring 1994): 25–28; and "Why (What) Am I (Doing) Here: A Cameroonian Woman?" in *Our Own Agendas: Autobiographical Essays by Woman Associated with McGill University*, ed. Margaret Gillett and Ann Beer (Montreal: McGill-Queen's University Press, 1995), 250–61; and "Bridging North and South...Notes Towards Dialogue and Transformation," in the special issue on "Bridging North/South: Patterns of Transformation" of *Canadian Woman Studies* 17.2 (Spring 1997): 145–48.
36. See, for instance, Fran Hosken, *Genital and Sexual Mutilation of Females* (Lexington, MA: Women's International Network, 1979).
37. *La parole aux négresses* (Paris: Denoël/Gonthier, 1978), trans. by Dorothy S. Blair as *Speak Out, Black Sisters: Feminism and Oppression in Black Africa* (London: Pluto Press, 1986), 87.
38. Boston: Beacon Press, 1980.
39. *Columbia Human Rights Law Review* 23 (1991–92): 191.
40. *Research in African Literatures* 20.3 (Fall 1989): 422–48. See also Daniel Vignal, "L'homophilie dans le roman négro-africain d'expression anglaise et française," *Peuples Noirs, Peuples Africains* 33 (May–June 1983): 63–81.
41. In *The History of Sexuality, Vol. 1: An Introduction*, trans. Robert Hurley (New York: Vintage Books, 1978), 33. Diamond and Quinby have suggested in "The Feminist Sexuality Debates" that Foucault "does not particularly

illuminate the effects of the deployment of sexuality on the lives of women," *Signs* 10.1 (1984): 120. For a gendered view of some uses of Foucault to feminist readings on sexuality, see Susan Hekman, *Gender and Knowledge: Elements of a Postmodern Feminism* (Boston: Northeastern UP, 1990); Susan Bordo, "The Body and the Reproduction of Femininity: A Feminist Appropriation of Foucault," in Jaggar and Bordo, 13.

42. Trinh Minh-ha, "She: The Inappropriate/d Other," *Discourse* 8 (Fall–Winter 1986–87): 3.
43. Gayatri Spivak, "Can the Subaltern Speak?" in *Marxism and the Interpretation of Culture*, ed. Cary Nelson and Lawrence Grossberg (Urbana: U of Illinois P, 1988), 295.
44. For an example, see Benita Parry's reading of what she describes as Spivak's "deliberated deafness to the native voice where it is to be heard," in "Problems in Current Theories of Colonial Discourse," *Oxford Literary Review* 9: 1–2 (1987): 34–39.
45. Patricia Hill Collins, "Learning from the Outsider Within," *Social Problems* 33.6 (1986): 14–32.
46. "U.S. Third World Feminism: The Theory and Method of Oppositional Consciousness in the Postmodern World," *Genders* 10 (Spring 1991): 1–24.
47. "Cultural Feminism versus Post-Structuralism: The Identity Crisis in Feminist Theory," in Malson *et al.*, 324.
48. For the concept of identity politics, see The Combahee River Collective, "A Black Feminist Statement," in Moraga and Anzaldua, 212.
49. See also de Lauretis, "Feminist Studies/Critical Studies: Issues, Terms and Contexts," and Mohanty and Martin, "Feminist Politics: What's Home Got to Do with It," in *Feminist Studies/Critical Studies*, ed. Teresa de Lauretis (Bloomington: Indiana UP, 1986).
50. Also, Coco Fusco, "Managing the Other," *Lusitania* 3.3 (1990): 77.

CHAPTER 15

THE HIDDEN HISTORY OF WOMEN IN GHANAIAN PRINT CULTURE

Audrey Gadzekpo
University of Ghana, Legon

Conventional history and its discourses were constructed around the figures of illustrious men, and "important" male-centered events. In many colonial histories and histories of nationalism, women are either completely absent as historical actors, appear only in relation to male actors, or occasionally as deviants, or archetypes of good or evil.

Western formulated dichotomies such as private/public, nature/culture, reason/emotion have also contributed to the historical neglect of African women by suggesting that women were unlikely to have been in the public spheres of politics, employment and scholarship in early historical periods. So have parallel assumptions about women's subordination, oppression, and inferiority in African societies.

This chapter de-constructs Ghanaian press history from the perspective of gender by charting the contributions women made to newspapers in the Gold Coast during the colonial period. It argues that despite women's absence in secondary texts on the history of Ghanaian newspapers there was considerable female presence in both the operations and discourses of the very vibrant nationalistic press throughout much of the colonial period. Textual and anecdotal evidence show that from as far back as the last quarter of the nineteenth century through to the twentieth-century women were engaged with the press as readers, as occasional contributors, as paid and unpaid columnists, journalists and editors.

For years researchers of the Ghanaian press succumbed to "received wisdom" that the female writing subject did not exist in early newspaper culture. Except for K. A. B. Jones-Quartey's (1974) passing reference to Mabel Dove-Danquah (considered the first female journalist in Ghana) in his first volume on Gold Coast journalism and a profile he wrote on her for the centenary brochure of the Ghana Association of Writers (1975), the history of women's participation in colonial print culture in Ghana has had no lineage. The dearth of historical information on women has perpetuated a fairly common notion that women did not engage with newspapers during the colonial period.

The assumption that women were absent from newspapers is predicated on the fact that press culture is highly ritualistic and was, until recently, male-dominated. Researchers of women's press histories have also reasoned that because newspapers are a form of public speaking and women were discouraged from public speaking, few women engaged in journalism in the early days of the western press (Zoonen, 1991, 1994; Henry, 1993; Hermes, 1993; Tuchman, 1996; Perkins, 1996).

In Africa where traditionally women had strong informational roles the introduction of newspapers themselves, not biases against women's public speaking, was largely responsible for the silencing of women (Steeves, 1993). This new colonial mode of communication required literacy and money, requisites that disadvantaged women and advantaged men, who were likely to be the more educated and affluent of the genders in colonies such as Ghana. Not only did the educated male elite who published and edited newspapers become the natural communicators, who spoke on behalf of the majority uneducated population, but the highly politicized, opinionated, and querulous institutional culture of the early African press made newspapers an inhospitable site for female activity.

EARLY GHANAIAN NEWSPAPERS

From the middle of the nineteenth century right through to the period of independence in 1957 the press played a pivotal role in the emerging hybridized socio-political culture of the Gold Coast. The newspaper in colonial Gold Coast reflected elite Gold Coast society, prescribed and validated new cultural and social values, educated and socialized readers and protested on their behalf. This influential, if at times chaotic medium, reflected the dynamism of a very important period in a nascent nation and was instrumental in articulating, defining and re-defining the aspirations of the new Gold Coast man and woman.

Existing historiography has already provided substantial information on the political nature of the press in colonial Africa (Jones-Quartey, 1958, 1968, 1974, 1975; Kimble, 1963; Ainslie, 1966; Rowand, 1972; Omu, 1978; Barton, 1979; Jenkins, 1985). Through an invaluable corpus of monographs, books, journal, and newspaper articles Jones-Quartey, for example, has helped to contextualize Gold Coast newspapers and the vivid male personalities that were behind them, complementing such information with a useful chronology of existing newspapers in the colonial period.

The Gold Coast did not pioneer journalism in West Africa, that distinction belongs to Sierra Leone, where a short-lived newspaper, *The Royal Gazette and Sierra Leone Advertiser*, was started in 1801.[1] But it was in the Gold Coast that an almost exclusively African owned and edited press first took hold. Existing evidence indicates there were close to 90 newspapers of varying life spans produced in the Gold Coast between 1857 and 1957.[2] Some 22 of these entered into the field before the turn of the nineteenth century, 20 titles were launched in the first three decades of the twentieth century and more than 40 after 1930.[3] Most of these newspapers were published in Cape Coast and Accra, the locations that served variously as the administrative capitals of the Gold Coast[4] and the hotbeds of nationalist political activity.

EARLY FEMALE ENGAGEMENT WITH THE EARLY GHANAIAN PRESS

Textual evidence from newspapers indicates that despite their historical absence women were represented as readers, as illustrative figures, as writers, and as correspondents in the early Ghanaian press. As early as in the last quarter of the nineteenth century, for example, the *Gold Coast Times* implicates women as readers by posting female-directed advertisement on its pages (See *Gold Coast Times* 1874–1884). The newspaper carried notices advertising a Mrs. Jane A. Brown, a milliner, who could make dresses for ladies, and one advertising a ladies college in Finchley, U.K. Other papers reflected similar gendered advertisements such as lotions, makeup and gentle laxatives, many of which were illustrated by images of European women.

More persuasive evidence that women constituted a target readership, however, lies in the *Gold Coast Times'* promise to start a column for ladies. Even though it failed to produce the column with any degree of consistency, the fact that the *Gold Coast Times* felt a need to include a women's column is in itself suggestive of female readership. The only "Ladies Column" extant, which was carried in the July 21, 1880 issue, lacks authorial attribution and there is nothing specific to the text that leads to the conclusion it was written by a Ghanaian woman, however that dim possibility cannot be dismissed without further authentication.

Before 1930, especially, women primarily engaged with the press through correspondence between newspapers and their implied female readership. It is impossible to ascertain whether indeed this readership was real or representational, particularly as most letters carried no authorial attribution, or at best only partial gendered attribution. Even though authorship may be open to conjecture, gendermarked letters to the editor can, however, be read as a form of female activism and the range of dialogue encouraged in them as representational of the positioning of women's voices in this male-oriented sphere (Shevelow, 1989). Such letters provided women with opportunities to speak for themselves and to share feminine experiences invested with the authority of their gender (Shevelow, 1989). Admittedly, there are social implications implicit in the act of letter writing as only elite women could appear in print and we cannot surmise that they spoke to the condition of the majority of Ghanaian women. Still, female-authored letters in early Ghanaian newspapers are worth interrogating because they grapple with serious fundamental questions regarding women in a transforming society, and indicate that male-dominated cultural institutions such as the press had the capacity to accommodate heterogeneous views.

The columns of some of the earliest newspapers produce several letters ostensibly authored by women that illustrate the degree to which early female readers of newspapers were actively involved in press narratives as both consumers and participants. Typically, these letters were in response to male writers whose opinions had affronted Ghanaian womanhood in some form or fashion. An exemplar instance of this can be found in the following acerbic retort from an anonymous reader of the Ladies Column, the first women's column published in a Ghanaian newspaper:

> The ladies of Cape Coast are much obliged to Cancoanid[5] for his zeal in the vindication of our causes. It is true that we Ladies of Africa in general are not only sadly misrepresented but are made the foot-ball of every white seal that comes to our Coast... The gentleman or we should rather say biped (for we cannot call him by any other name and whom we believe is a Just Ass of P's) we say the biped, who said he could not perceive why we should seek to be clothed in European habiliments or desire to be mentally trained in the education of Europe, is only fit to be Just Ass of P's to the Boobies in Fernando Po ... We would like to ask that Donkey Clown what habiliments did his ancestors who worshipped the mistletoe and wood and stone wear?... We have been sadly abused by people of such description, and because we have said nothing they continue to abuse us with impunity... It is true had we the advantages of European ladies we should not be a whit behind and although we have not white or angelic faces we are capable of as high a degree of culture as any white lady... such clownish gentlemen would that we were still in our ignorance that they may take advantage of us.... (*Western Echo*, January 3, 1886)

This anonymous, gender-marked letter suggests there were women in Ghana in the late 1800s who were educated, socially aware, and prepared to challenge patriarchy and racism in print. By simply exercising their right to rejoinders female newspaper readers such as "one of them" wittingly or unwittingly are able to insert themselves into gendered discourses and provide counterpoints to male views. Throughout the colonial period such correspondence made it possible for women to provide alternative views to male-dominated discourses on controversial issues. A letter by "Afua of Abokobi" (*Times of West Africa*, May 14, 1934) for example, takes on a male reader for disparaging women who were in polygamous marriages by terming them "second hand women." Her rebuttal challenges the gender stereotypes and double standards of elite men and successfully articulates another perspective on the marriage debate.

Another example of the female alternate voice comes from a letter by "Yaa Amponsa" of Kumasi appealing to Governor Shenton Thomas, through a letter to his daughter Bridget, to withdraw the water and sedition bills because passing them would bring hardship to "hundreds of thousands of girls" in Ghana and Ashanti (*Times of West Africa*, March 8, 1934). Here, instead of addressing the Governor directly she positions herself as female supplicant in the traditional practice of appealing for intercession through an intermediary. Though carried in a "benign" gendered space, this interesting instance of female political satire, underscores the ways in which women's press activism presented themselves.

In a letter in which she describes herself as family head of the Amoah family and sister to Senior Divisional Chief Amoah II, a reader of the *Gold Coast Independent*, Elizabeth Johnston asserts her authority within traditional Cape Coast society by justifying her right to appoint a representative to her brother (*Gold Coast Independent* December 13, 1930, *Gold Coast Times*, December, 16, 1930). The full background to the letter is unclear but since the one that was carried by the *Gold Coast Times* was qualified by an editor's note disagreeing with her method of appointing her brother's replacement as chief, we can infer that Johnson's letter was an attempt to set the record straight regarding actions for which she was being criticized. A few weeks later she is provoked to write a rejoinder taking exception to the editor's note at the bottom of her previous letter. This takes the form of a lengthy lecture on the Fante native constitution, kinship system and traditional customs (*Gold Coast Independent*, January 10, 1931). The tone of the letter locates Johnston in the traditional role ascribed to women as custodians of culture, except that where her expertise in this area would have been normally displayed orally, the medium determined orality be substituted with textuality.

Early Ghanaian newspapers provided another avenue for women's thoughts to come before the reading public through the publication of the full or partial text of public lectures given by prominent women at literary clubs or other social organizations. Exemplar instances of writings of this kind are a lecture on "domestic training" delivered by Charlotte Quarshie-Idun to the Young People's Literary Club (*Gold Coast Independent*, April 29, 1933), one by Mercy Quartey-Papafio on "the place of the woman in the home or in the social life of the town" (*Gold Coast Times*, October 13, 1934), Ethel Dove's lecture on the "Education of Girls" (*Gold Coast Independent*, April 23 and 30 1927), and a talk by Charity Zormelo to the Nationalists Literary Society on "Education for a New Day" (*Gold Coast Independent*, May 4, 1935). The titles and substance of these lectures are instructive of the topics considered in elite women's purview, and underscore assumptions that their gender transformed them into experts on girls' education, domesticity and preparation for their assigned roles in society.

Yet another illustration of the female writing subject is represented by published poetry. In the first quarter of the twentieth century the *Gold Coast Leader* (see 1925–1928), for example, published several poems by Gladys May Casely-Hayford. The poems appeared in the newspaper during the editorship of J. E. Casely-Hayford who was Gladys' father; her mother was Adelaide Casely Hayford. Most of Gladys' poetry was romantic and personal, although she did write a few that were somewhat political, for example one "dedicated to the late Dr. Aggrey" (*Gold Coast Leader*, Oct. 21, 1928). The

Leader also provided Gladys with the opportunity to review works and to write feature articles. So for example, she reported on the proceedings of the 2nd Achimota conference (*Gold Coast Leader*, July 14, 1928), an important conference which the paper editorialized on in a subsequent issue of the paper and reviewed Creole poetry of West Africa (*Gold Coast Leader*, August, 20, 1927) and G. A. Gollock's "Sons of Africa" (*Gold Coast Leader*, September 19, 1928).

Gladys' poems were not the only female-authored poems carried in Gold Coast newspapers. There appeared to have been poems by a Georgina Ione Hansen-Hammond, who was cited by one of the *Gold Coast Leader's* more regular columns, "Mixed Pickles by Ebo," as having contributed poems to the *Leader*, and who was held up, along with Gladys Casely Hayford, as illustrative of the fact that Gold Coast women had crossed the literary barrier:

> In former times the pen, like the sword, was considered as consigned by nature to the hands of men, the ladies contended themselves with private virtues and domestic excellence. A female writer, like a female warrior was considered a kind of eccentric being that deviated, however illustriously from her due sphere of motion and was therefore rather to be gazed at with wonder than countenanced. The revolution of years has now produced an army of women writers who with the spirit of their predecessors have set masculine ability at defiance and asserted their claim. They are proving day by day that their intellect is not inferior to that of man. (*Gold Coast Leader*, October 8, 1927)

GENDERED SPACES

The most effective outlet for women's voices in the predominantly male space of the early periodical was the gendered space. Generally, media histories have shown that gendered spaces such as women's columns in newspapers, magazines, journals, radio, and television programs, are the likely sites for locating much of early female journalistic activity. The works of several researchers have richly informed our understanding of the functionality of the gendered space in print culture (White, 1970; Ferguson, 1983; Shevelow, 1989; Tuchman, 1989; Beetham, Ballaster *et al.*, 1991; Brake, 1994; Beetham, 1996; Aronson, 1997). While current debate criticizes them for "ghettoizing" rather than mainstreaming women's issues, gendered spaces were, and in many ways are, still motivated by the desire to address a perceived gap in the communication needs of their target audience.[6]

There is scant evidence of the existence of women's periodicals in colonial Ghana, although a 91-year-old informant, Marion Odamtten, claims she and a group of friends started a magazine somewhere in the 1940s that lasted into the 1950s titled *African Woman*. Indeed a 1951 *Daily Graphic* article partly confirms this by noting that Odamtten was the editress of "*Ghana Women*" *(Daily Graphic*, September 14, 1951).[7] Odamtten claimed to have edited the magazine for the Women's Progress Union, a society of which she was a founding member and admits that the magazine circulated only in the capital city of Accra, and had an estimated print run of no more than 100 copies.[8] No copy of the magazine appears to have survived although her assertions suggest women's periodical contributions may have extended beyond newspapers.

In the absence of women's magazines it was the women's column that gendered Ghanaian journalism. Women's columns in early newspapers were instrumental in forming a female reading audience organized around the textual representation of women as readers, writing subjects and textual figures situated within a reformist discourse designed to instruct and entertain them. They engaged directly with readers on specific topics as well as engaged in their lives by offering to show them how to improve themselves. While they provided a discursive space for women, they also delineated the process of simultaneous liberation and restriction that marked women's engagement with the press. At a time when women had few outlets for self-expression the women's column provided them with an enabling space, and to co-opt Beetham (1996), acted as a "kind of nursery," which allowed for all kinds of literary activity—poems, short stories, didactic articles, fashion sketches, essays and sounding-off forums. At the same time however, it was a disenabling space, limiting the location of women's writings and circumscribing what could or could not be discussed. An editor's note soliciting contributors for a women's column, is illustrative of attempts at regulating the contents of gendered spaces in early Ghanaian newspapers:

> The Editor will welcome articles for the Women's Corner on the world of fashion, on female society and the social world in general; on dancing, music and concert; on children and children's education, on indoor games and other sports such as tennis, on the home and the kitchen, and in general on all subjects, even literature, books, religion, marketing, dress-making, etc. in which the cultured lady of fashion is interested. Articles on the female view of politics for this Corner must be moderately toned in harmony with the polite taste of women. (*Times of West Africa*, March 12, 1934)

Still women's columns produced journalistic writings that bear witness to women's interventions in the public sphere. At one point or another in their publishing history, more than a third of the pre-independence newspaper titles provided space specifically addressing women. They include the *Western Echo*, the *Times of West Africa*, the *Gold Coast Independent* (second series), the *Gold Coast Times* (second series), the *African Morning Post*, the *Gold Coast Spectator*, the *Gold Coast Observer*, the *Ashanti Pioneer*, the *Accra Evening News*, the *Daily Graphic* and the *Sunday Mirror*. A few others, notably the *Gold Coast Times* (first series) and the *Gold Coast Leader*, promised women's columns but failed to deliver.

Were gendered spaces motivated by a real need for women's own space or were they just conventional? Perhaps as Kathleen Hewitt (1933) hints at in her foreword to a collection on the "Women's Corner" by Marjorie Mensah Ghanaian newspapers established women's columns so they will not be considered "behind the times." A more gracious reasoning, however, may have been that nationalist editors recognized very early on the need to include women in their reformist agenda and sought to do that through this dedicated didactic space whose primary mission was to educate and modernize the "new" Ghanaian woman. It is reasonable to also assume that in their bid to create new communities of readers, editors may have calculated that they could extend their subscription base by attracting a small but growing pool of loyal female readers. No matter, whether born of a fashion trend, or of recognition of her social and/or economic potential, or motivated by the desire to educate women, the women's column was a strong signifier of the presence of women in print culture. It was the most public arena opened up by elite men in which elite women could dialogue on "women's issues and concerns" and helped to sustain a continuous and intimate communication between early newspapers and their female readership, a relationship which sometimes extended beyond the text.

Beyond the Gendered Space

The gendered space may have been the breeding and nurturing ground for female journalistic activity, but journalism was not always gendered. It was possible for women to transcend the journalism of women's columns as well as to rise in the hierarchy of the press. Not surprisingly, the *Daily Graphic*, the paper that encouraged the most female activity, provided opportunities for acknowledged writers such as Mabel Dove-Danquah, Akua Asaabea Ayisi, Edith Wuver and Regina Addae to write on non-gendered subjects that appeared in the more general pages of the newspaper. After Independence Wuver made history by becoming the first female war correspondent in Ghana, having been sent by the paper to cover the 1962 Congo War. Regina Addae, who was initially employed as editorial secretary became the paper's first female parliamentary reporter and a current affairs columnist in the middle 1950s.[9]

Two women, Efua Scheck and Dove-Danquah, rose to become editors of newspapers in 1950, an achievement that was not replicated until 1980/1981 when Elizabeth Ohene was made editor of the *Daily Graphic*. Scheck was the assistant editor of a provincial newspaper called the *Takoradi Times* and assumed editorship in 1950 when her brother, Saki Scheck, who was the editor, was thrown in jail for 12 months for publishing seditious material.

Dove-Danquah was the *Accra Evening News'* very visible combative editor for a short period from early 1951 to the middle of that year.[10] Like Scheck she was politically active, both journalistically and otherwise. In June 1954 as CPP's candidate for the Ga Rural Electoral District, she won 3331 out of 3974 votes beating out two male opponents to become the first African woman elected by popular vote to a national legislative body. More importantly, Dove-Danquah was the indisputable doyenne of Gold Coast journalism having first entered the field by working as a columnist for the

Times of West Africa (1931–1935). Her four-decade-long career as a journalist had her corresponding for several other newspapers under various pseudonyms. She also engaged in other literary activities such as writing short stories, some of which were published in newspapers (*Times of West Africa* and *Daily Graphic*, for example) and can now be found in international literary collections.

ANONYMITY

A mistress of disguise, Dove-Danquah's journalistic versatility was exposed through a small announcement carried in the *African Morning Post*, accompanied by her picture, which notified readers that:

> Mrs. J.B. Danquah (nee Dove) whose photograph is reproduced above, will in future write articles in her own name, Mabel Danquah. She has been known under such pen names as Marjorie Mensah "*Times of West Africa;* Ebun Alakija—'*Nigerian Daily Times*' and Dama Dumas—in our own *African Morning Post*". (*African Morning Post*, January 3, 1938)

Anonymity in the early Ghanaian press appeared to have been fairly entrenched, partly because the social and political conditions prevailing in colonial Ghana required protective anonymity in order to diffuse responsibility, deflect liability from individual authors of text, and to present a unified front to readers. Anonymity shielded in particular contributors who were in government employ and who feared victimization for articulating contentious views in nationalist newspapers that were adversarial to colonial policy and authority.

There may have also been gendered reasons for female anonymity, although it was not always clear. The identities of most of the authors of early women's columns and pages were concealed behind such feminine pseudonyms as "Elena," "Joyce," "Marjorie Mensah," "Gloria," "Nana Egyiriba," etc.

Since the early Ghanaian press actively solicited articles from women, and eagerly represented the female writing subject, the primarily reason for female anonymity was unlikely to be that women feared they would not have been published on account of their gender.

Rather, a likely reason educated elite women, conditioned to be demure, may have preferred to write in anonymity was that they were afraid of "risking fame" by appearing in print. By using anonymity they were able to shy away from the "bubble notoriety" that authorial attribution would have conferred upon them. Another reason female writers preferred to operate anonymously was because of the confrontational nature of print culture. Newspapers required not only literary ability, but also a tough skin that could withstand the scrutiny of critics. Anonymity allowed contributors to maintain their privacy, and perhaps personal dignity in the face of newspaper attacks, and prevented their alienation from people they might offend in their writings.

But anonymity, no doubt, is a contributory factor to women's historical invisibility in print culture, obscuring identity and presenting difficulties for researchers interested in discovering women's varied voices in the press.

No column illustrates the vexed questions raised by authorship like the "Women's Corner" in the *Times of West Africa*[11] and the multivocality of its pseudonymous author Marjorie Mensah. The unraveling of the Marjorie Mensah mystery deserves close attention because it elucidates the manner in which anonymity was deployed in the Gold Coast press and underscores some of the implications raised by anonymously authored female texts in the second quarter of the twentieth century. Right from the inception of this column on March 12, 1931, it fueled intense intra and inter-newspaper debate over authorship, with readers contesting the gender of Marjorie Mensah and the paper reveling in the controversy. Bold headlines over reader's letters on the identity issue were augmented by well-considered comments from Marjorie Mensah herself or her fellow columnist, pseudonymed "Zadig," who wrote the "Diary of a Young Man About Town" column.

One of the earliest letters questioning Marjorie's gender came from Asuana Quartey whose main force of argument centered on the technical competence of women writers:

> I have been following closely the many interesting letters under the pen of Miss Marjorie Mensah since your paper made its first appearance in the journalistic arena. The nature of the letters, the diction, the firm grip of the writer, tend to arouse my suspicions, and probably those of many readers; and confirm me in the conviction as to the identity of the writer being a man. I mean no offence to "your lady" correspondent, but it is very unusual that West African Ladies (even those with a superior European education) could be induced to take an intelligent interest in the affairs of the country in the same breath as your lady correspondent is doing. This is a new feature in West Africa journalism, for which please accept my heartiest congratulations. (*West Africa Times*, April 21, 1931)

Another letter from a C. A. des Bordes, who also disputes the likelihood that women were adequately placed to be journalists, echoes Quartey's position:

> ...I beg to say in my few infantile stock of vocabulary, that Miss Marjorie Mensah is a man—To say she is a man, may sound differently or bring about a variety of understanding to some of your readers, but to me I say she is a man in that, the work which she has voluntarily undertaken to do, and must do as long as this paper endures for the reason that a special column is provided for her, could very seldom be accomplished by even a man except he is solely attached to the duties of the Press. Miss Marjorie Mensah's daily writing since the first publication of this valuable paper, except on two occasions when she was relieved by her woman friends, has always been a sensational problem to me in particular and very likely to many others—her sweet style of diction as a woman is to me above the par... Miss Marjorie Mensah's portrait must, if possible be printed at the side of her name in the Ladies Corner, which was for her sake provided. While it will gain for her more honor and admiration, it will give more fire to many of our women who are ambitious. Undoubtedly, Miss Marjorie Mensah had most of her training in Europe; but I dare say her

complete control of English may not wholly emanate from her European training.... (*West Africa Times*, April 24, 1931)

Other readers such as Esther Stonewall Payne (*West Africa Times*, May 11, 1931) counter the male skepticism about Marjorie Mensah's journalistic ability by arguing that her style of diction demonstrates her mental prowess and highlights the fact that "some of the ladies out here have wit enough to express their minds as equally as the men if not better."

Rival newspapers soon joined the fray over Marjorie Mensah's identity, carrying views from readers such as C. S. Adjei, for whom the Marjorie Mensah identity crisis produced a constant stream of letters. In one of his letters Adjei accuses another letter writer, Kofi Tawia, of trying to deceive "the white world into regarding our women as generally capable of contributing articles, such as those that emanate from the veiled personality of Marjorie Mensah" (*Gold Coast Independent*, August 8, 1931). A charge to which Kofi Tawia provides this spirited and insightful defense:

> Far from contending that Marjorie Mensah is not the Nom de Plume of a male correspondent of the *West Africa Times*, I have simply sought to bring home to you and your type of patriots two important facts—that the articles of "Marjorie Mensah" can possibly be the product of a female correspondent and that contrary to the general belief that our women are still swimming in illiteracy, we have today, a number of ladies, though small, who can suggest social reforms in the press and hold their own against many a man in a lot of things.... (*Gold Coast Independent*, September 12, 1931)

The columnist herself was quick to address what she termed the "literary scraps" about her identity, accusing her detractors of courting "bubble notoriety which they had sought with so much ostentation—the small consequence of seeing themselves in Print."

The Marjorie Mensah enigma soon transcended literary and social circles, and became a subject of legal contestation. In 1934 Kenneth MacNeil Stewart, a former editor of the paper, filed a lawsuit in the Divisional Courts against the *Times of West Africa*. The lawsuit was prominently reported on the front pages of the paper starting on May 11, 1934 and continued until judgment was given a few days later. Stewart, regarded as an accomplished journalist and writer of the 1930s, was suing the Guinea Times Publishing Company, proprietors of *Times of West Africa*, for copyright of the name of Marjorie Mensah. His action had been precipitated by the publication of a book containing compilations of articles from the Marjorie Mensah column. Titled "Us Women,"[12] this illustrated book was edited by Kathleen Hewitt of London and was well publicized in the *Times of West Africa* (see for example, November 2, 3 and 28, 1933). In his statement of claim Stewart alleged that with the exception of two articles, he had written all the selections in the book. But the newspaper disputed the claim stating, according to published newspaper reports, that he was not the only contributor under the "Corner" and that the name Marjorie Mensah was not invented by him, but by

Mr. Coussey, a Managing Director of the Company in conjunction with Dr. J. B. Danquah.[13] The two men had bandied several names around, including the name Regina, before settling on Marjorie Mensah.[14] But perhaps more importantly, the defense claimed when MacNeil Stewart was on staff and after he left the paper, "other people, especially Miss Mabel Dove, wrote articles under the Ladies Corner." The defense argued that "of 68 chapters in the book[15] 'Us Women' only about 8 were written by Mr. Stewart and the rest of the 60 or so were from the pen of Miss Mabel Dove." According to coverage on court proceedings, original manuscripts backed the newspaper's claims. Significantly, Danquah is reported to have said that as editor "the first article in the column was handed to MacNeil Stewart to edit, and that it had been written by Miss Ruby Papafio."[16] Upon cross-examination Danquah elaborated further on the first authorship of the column, explaining that that first manuscript by Miss Papafio on cookery was "built up by Mr. Stewart" (*Times of West Africa*, May 14, 1934).

Five days after the lawsuit was called, Mr. Justice Joseph Mervyn, St. John Yates found in favor of the defendants, set aside an interim injunction against the use of the name Marjorie Mensah by *Times of West Africa*, and awarded costs against Stewart. The report on Yates' judgment is worth quoting as it further illuminates the nature of authorship of the Ladies/Women's Corner:

> His Lordship said that the plaintiff was engaged as editor to produce the paper and no special agreement was made for that employment. There was a Ladies Corner as a feature and he wrote articles under that name in the course of his employment. But "Marjorie Mensah" was not adopted by the plaintiff as his pen name and His Lordship found as a fact that the name was invented by the Managing Director in conjunction with Mr. Coussey for the Company. Articles under the Ladies Corner were not exclusively written by the plaintiff, others did so and were paid. The ownership of "Marjorie Mensah" was not therefore in the plaintiff. (*Times of West Africa*, May 16, 1934)

This case, as reported by the newspaper, proves at least that the gender of the columnist so hotly contested was mostly, although not entirely female. As the reports suggest Marjorie Mensah was a construct of the newspaper's bosses; a construct that came with a set of expectations. More importantly, the MacNeil Stewart lawsuit also establishes Mabel Dove Danquah as the dominant and most consistent Marjorie, although not the only Marjorie as secondary historical sources have led us to believe. The interim injunction imposed upon the use of the name Marjorie Mensah in the paper during the period of the lawsuit forced the column to acknowledge other bylines—Koshie, Odarley, and Lizzie Sarbah.[17] An editor's note underneath Lizzie Sarbah's byline on May 11, 1934 explains that "in view of the pending interest in the writer of the Women's Corner Miss Mabel Ellen Dove requires us to say she is not the present writer under our Women's Corner."

It is probable that even before the lawsuit these women contributed to the paper but were made invisible by "Marjorie Mensah." On the other hand, it is entirely possible that in order to subvert the injunction these female names were used to camouflage the real author of the text, although this seems unlikely given the fact that the paper ran the risk of court censure.

The clues provided by the Marjorie Mensah lawsuit, specifically the information that Ruby Quartey-Papafio was an occasional contributor, opened up the prospect of investigating her as a possible hidden newspaper contributor also. While I was unable to establish whether Ruby Quartey-Papafio, a distinguished educationist, was concealed behind any other pseudonyms I discovered that her sister, Mercy Quartey-Papafio, later Mercy Ffoulkes-Crabbe, was the "voice" behind "Gloria." As is often the case with conjectural history the possibility that a Quartey-Papafio lurked behind a pseudonym served as the lead to tracing and interrogating more closely members of that family. It had been supposed that the Quartey-Papafio women, having been well educated, were likely and certainly capable of engaging with the press. Public lectures given by both Ruby and Mercy Papafio were occasionally excerpted in newspapers.[18] This information served as further motivation to pursue that line of inquiry.

Persistence was rewarded by luck when the 67-year-old only child of Mercy Quartey-Papafio stumbled upon information that lay buried in her mother's "tin trunk." Dorothy Jane Osuman Ffoulkes-Crabbe, an anesthesiologist had, when first approached, said she had no idea whether or not her mother was a newspaper contributor.[19] The suggestion that she might have been, however, eventually led her to investigate her mother's belongings, which had remained largely untouched since her death on June 14, 1974 at the age of 80. Among the legacy left behind by Mercy Ffoulkes-Crabbe was an innocuous primary school workbook, containing what appeared to have been attempts at writing an autobiography. The entries were written in the third person, but in Mercy Ffoulkes-Crabbe's handwriting[20] and they chronicled her illustrious career in education as well as her social activism. More importantly, an entry in the book unveiled she had another more discreet career as a newspaper columnist. Written as a notation in the top margin of a page were the following words: "Mrs. Ffoulkes-Crabbe was for a time a columnist under the penname of Gloria, of the Women's Corner of the *Gold Coast Times*, published at Cape Coast."[21] This unfinished, unpublished autobiographical material unlocked a major mystery about the identity behind a women's column, published with great regularity in the *Gold Coast Times* from 1936–1940, and in which many interesting gender debates occur. Other entries contained in the book are also enormously helpful not only in situating Ffoulkes-Crabbe more firmly as an elite Ghanaian woman, but in informing the discourses of "Gloria," her newspaper persona.

CONCLUSION

This chapter demonstrates that women played a significant role in shaping a vibrant and pivotal press in the early press in Ghana. By dismantling the textual and cultural hierarchies of scholarship that have impinged on previous press histories it has been possible to consider the totality of women's newspaper contributions and to chart a long trajectory of women's journalistic engagement. The textual evidence available from newspapers reveals the presence of the female writing subject from as early as the last quarter of the nineteenth century when women were generally thought to possess little or no literary ability. Evidence has also demonstrated that the female voice became stronger as the twentieth century progressed and peaked in the immediate pre-independence period when women worked variously as editors, as journalists, as columnists and as contributors to newspapers.

The data suggests that the history of women in Gold Coast print culture is not a history of exceptions, even if there were exceptional women, and that the female writing subject was able to insert herself in ways and spaces that allowed her a voice and through that, the opportunity to act as an author of her own social history.

Obviously, unearthing the hidden history of women in the early Ghanaian press is an open-ended task, made more difficulty by anonymity, which acts as a double-edged sword. Anonymity may have allowed women to stretch the boundaries of the possible, but it has also exacted a great historical price by concealing the identities of many noteworthy women writers and perpetuating their invisibility in the Gold Coast press.

NOTES

1. The oldest press in English-speaking West Africa was in Freetown, Sierra Leone in 1801, followed by the Gold Coast in 1822, Nigeria in 1859 and Gambia in 1883 (see Ainslie, 1966; Jones-Quartey, 1975: xxi; Echeruo, 1977; Omu, 1978; Barton, 1979).
2. Jones-Quartey (1975a) lists about 78 different titles in this time period in depositories and holdings in the African Studies Institute, University of Ghana, Balme Library, University of Ghana, Cape Coast University, Ghana National Archives, Padmore Research Library of African Affairs, and University of Science and Technology, Kumasi. The British Newspaper library in Colindale contains 32 titles most of which can be found in the Ghanaian depositories while other depositories such as Birmingham University and Akfrofi-Christaller library in Akropong list a smaller number.
3. See Appendix A for annotated chronology of newspapers in the colonial period.
4. The seat of the colonial government was officially moved from Cape Coast to Accra on 19th March, 1877, but Cape Coast remained the intellectual capital and centre of sophistication and enlightenment through to the first quarter of the twentieth century at least. It was the site of early Gold Coast elitism as manifested by a small educated group that had familiarity with European culture, adopted Western ways and was socially and economically advantaged.
5. Cancoanid is the conductor of the "Ladies Column" which published this letter. It has not been possible to determine the article that provoked such a response.
6. The recent phenomenon of male-targeted media such as magazines is noted and included in the definition of gendered space.
7. There is an obvious discrepancy in the title of the publication, which poses a problem. This was pointed out to Odamtten but she insists that it was African

Woman and not Ghana Women (letter from Helen Odamtten, daughter of Marion Odamtten, July 12, 2001). Unfortunately no copy of the magazine has been located as yet.

8. Interview with Marion Odamtten, Accra, January 31, 2001. Odamtten's children said she had shown them copies of the magazine but did not know what had happened to the copy that had been kept by Odamtten. She said she started the magazine because she wanted something to do beyond being a housewife and thought it would help in her charity work. She wrote some of the articles and named among her contributors Mrs. Samango and Aaron Ofori-Atta.
9. Interview with Regina Addae, Accra, February 2, 2001.
10. It is not quite clear exactly when she took over the editorship of the paper. It appears it was at least before April 1951 because her name was appearing on the paper as editor about then. The June 29, 1951 edition of the paper however, lists S.O. Sandy as editor, indicating that her editorship ended around that time. She appeared to have left Ghana shortly after for Freetown Sierra Leone where according to an article carried in the *Evening News* of November 27, 1951 she stayed for three months and led a women's demonstration march against the high cost of living. Jones-Quartey (1975b) also notes that in 1951 she paid a visit to her father's birthplace, Freetown where together with Constance Cummings-John, the second African woman central legislator, they organized 20,000 Sierra Leonean.
11. The *Times of West Africa* was published in Accra by Joseph Boakye (J. B.) Danquah, a prominent nationalist politician.
12. A copy of the book can be found in Cambridge University Library. It was published in 1933 by Elkin Mathews & Marrot Ltd., 44 Essex Street, Strand.
13. Unsuccessful attempts were made to crosscheck newspaper reports with court transcripts. No records were located on the case.
14. This fact may explain why in the very first Diary of a Man About Town Zadig (a.k.a. J.B. Danquah) had slipped in his introduction of the column and referred to "Regina Mensah," rather than "Marjorie Mensah." See *Times of West Africa*, March 19, 1931.
15. Each article was headed as a chapter, accounting for the number of chapters cited in the lawsuit. In actuality therefore what were 68 articles, which made up the collection.
16. *Times of West Africa*, May 12, 1934.
17. See especially the period between March 12 and May 16, 1934.
18. Mercy Quartey-Papafio's lecture on "The place of the woman in the home or in the social life of the town" was carried by the *Gold Coast Times* Oct 13, 1934. Also, the paper had, on Oct 21, 1939, carried a speech broadcast from the Accra Studio by Miss Ruby Papafio on Women's part in the war. On July 18, 1951, the *Daily Graphic* had also carried an article by Mercy K. Ffoulkes-Crabbe (nee Quartey-Papafio) titled "Our Young Women and Higher Studies." Also "suspicious" was an article in the Ladies Corner on May 18, 1931 from "Cape Coast correspondent" noting Miss Mercy Kwarley Papafio, headmistress of Government School had put a stop to an undesirable practice of schoolgirls, which Marjorie Mensah had drawn attention of her readers to. There was a sense that the article was actually a rejoinder by Mercy Papafio.
19. Dorothy Ffoulkes-Crabbe was first contacted in January, 2001 as part of the informants interviewed for this thesis.

20. Dorothy Ffoulkes-Crabbe confirmed that was her mother's handwriting in an interview on February 3, 2001.
21. She did not expand on this note, unfortunately. At the time she wrote the column (1936–1940) however, Mercy Quartey-Papafio was the headmistress of Government Girls School, Cape Coast, now called Phillip Quarcoe, a position she held from 1922 until 1948 when she retired.

BIBLIOGRAPHY

Beetham, Margaret (1990). "Towards theory of the periodical as a publishing genre." In BLAKE, Laurel *et al.* (eds.). *Investigating Victorian journalism.* New York: St. Martin's Press.

Beetham, Margaret (1996). *A Magazine of Her Own? Domesticity and Desire in the Woman's Magazine: 1800–1914.* London: Routledge.

Beetham, Margaret (2000). "The agony aunt, the romancing uncle and the family of empire: defining the sixpenny reading public in the 1890s." In BRAKE, Laurel *et al.* (eds). *Nineteenth-Century Media and the Construction of Identities.* Basingstoke and New York: Palgrave.

Bradford, Helen. "Women, gender and colonialism: rethinking the history of the British Cape Colony and its frontier zones c1806–70." *Journal of African History,* 37 (3), 1996, 351–370.

Brake, Laurel, BELL, Bill and FINKELSTEIN, David (2000). "Introduction." In Brake, Laurel *et al.* (eds). *Nineteenth-Century Media and the Construction of Identities.* Basingstoke and New York: Palgrave.

Brake, Laurel (1997). "Gendered space and the British press." In HANS, Michael, and O'Malley, Tom (eds.). *Studies in Newspaper and Periodical History: 1995 Annual.* Westport, CT and London Greenwood Press.

Brake, Laurel (1994). *Subjugated Knowledges: Journalism, Gender and Literature in the Nineteenth Century.* Basingstoke: Macmillan.

Cromwell, Adelaide (1986). *An African Victorian Feminist: The Life and Times of Adelaide Smith Casely Hayford, 1868–1960.* London & New Jersey: Frank Cass & Co. Ltd.

Easley, Alexis (2000). "Authorship, gender and power in Victorian culture: Harriet Martineau and the periodical press." In BRAKE, Laurel *et al.* (eds). *Nineteenth-Century Media and the Construction of Identities.* Basingstoke and New York: Palgrave.

Hewitt, Kathleen (ed.) (1933). *Us Women.* London; Elkin Mathews & Marrot Ltd.

Jenkins, Raymond. Gold Coast Historians and their pursuit of the Gold Coast pasts—1882–1917: an investigation into responses to British cultural imperialism by intellectuals of the Christianized, commercial communities of the townships of the Southern Gold Coast during the years of British imperial conquest and early occupation—1874–1919. Ph.D. thesis, University of Birmingham, 1985.

Jones Quartey, K. A. B. (1974). *A Summary History of the Ghana Press: 1822–1960.* Accra: The Ghana Information Services.

Jones Quartey, K. A. B. (1975a). *History Politics and Early Press in Ghana: the Fictions and the Facts.* Accra: Ghana Universities Press.

Jones Quartey, K. A. B. (1975b). "Profiles: first lady of pen and parliament— a portrait." In International Centenary Evenings with Aggrey of Africa, Anniversary Brochure. Ghana Association of Writers (GAW), December 5–6, 1975.

Raymond, Joad (1990). "The newspaper, public opinion and the public sphere in the seventeenth century." In Raymond, Joad (ed.). *News Newspapers and Society in Early Modern Britain.* London and Portland, OR: Frank Cass.
Sage, Lorna (2000). "Foreword." In Campbell, Kate (ed.). *Journalism, Literature and Modernity.* Edinburgh: Edinburgh University Press.
Shevelow, Kathryn (1989). *Women and Print Culture: the Construction of Femininity in the Early Periodical.* London and New York: Routledge.
Tuchman, Gaye, with Fortin, N. (1989). *Edging Women Out: Victorian Novelists, Publishers, and Social Change.* London: Routledge.
Tuchman, Gaye (1996). "Representation: image, sign, difference." In Baehr, Helen and Gray, Ann (eds.). *Turning it On: A Reader in Women and Media.* London and New York: Arnold.

SECTION VI

DEVELOPMENT AND SOCIAL TRANSFORMATION

Given the last five hundred years of devastation caused by the ravages of the Atlantic Slave Trade, the institutions of slavery and its attendant racial stratification of the global system, colonization and continuing predatory globalization, it is not surprising that achieving social transformation has been high on the African agenda for a long time. The discourse on development, however, pre-empted African aspirations by imposing social programs that have little or nothing to do with their needs. Achola O. Pala, in her classic paper "Definitions of Women and Development: An African Perspective," asks what development would look like from the perspective of Africans, especially African women. Her admonition that any analysis of African women must pay attention to the interplay between global economic forces and all manner of local structures and ideologies takes center stage in the next paper.

In "An Investigative Framework for Gender Research in Africa Within the Context of the Political Economy of the New Millennium," Filomena Steady gives us a comprehensive accounting of the global economic forces arrayed against Africans and a catalogue of supporting academic structures that validate the exploitation of Africa. More importantly, her paper proposes Africa-centered approaches by highlighting oppositional discourses that have challenged these Eurocentric paradigms. Steady identifies some of the methodological challenges in investigating gender in Africa and brings her knowledge and experience to bear by providing concrete answers to the Leninist question "what is to be done?"

Bogso women farmers are already doing a lot as Bertrade B. Ngo-Ngijol Banoum tells us in her contribution: "The Yum: An Indigenous model for Sustainable Development." The article exposes women's agency, and demonstrates the value of local structures in development by showcasing the contemporary uses to which Bogso women farmers (Cameroun) put the *Yum*: an indigenous community mobilizing and organizing tool rooted in the ancestral cultures of solidarity.

Chapter 16

Definitions of Women and Development: An African Perspective

Achola O. Pala

In this brief chapter, I do not propose to engage in a discussion of what development is or what an African perspective means. Rather, I wish to draw attention to points which I consider to be central to an understanding of the contemporary position of African women. It is reasonable to say that in Africa today the position of both women and men can be largely described as an interplay between two parameters. The first, which we may call dependency, comprises economic and political relationships through which our peoples have found themselves increasingly involved with metropolitan Europe (e.g., England, France, Germany, Belgium, Spain, and Portugal) and the United States of America, especially since the sixteenth and seventeenth centuries, starting with the slave trade and colonialism and continuing up to contemporary neocolonial links. The second embraces indigenous African socioeconomic norms (e.g., in food production, family ideology, property rights, and perceptions of respect and human dignity), insofar as these continue to regulate social behavior.

In other words, the position of women in contemporary Africa is to be considered at every level of analysis as an outcome of structural and conceptual mechanisms by which African societies have continued to respond to and resist the global processes of economic exploitation and cultural domination. I am suggesting that the problems facing African women today, irrespective of their national and social class affiliations, are inextricably bound up in the wider struggle by African people to free themselves from poverty and ideological domination in both intra- and international spheres.

Neither research on African development potential and problems nor specific emphasis on issues relating to the participation of African women in local economies is new. The British colonial government, for instance, commissioned and/or supported a number of studies specifically to investigate the role of women in African societies, in order to formulate policies which would "integrate" women more effectively into the colonial development. Even a quick perusal of local newspapers in a given colonial period will reveal a "concern" by the colonial government, backed by women's associations (usually made up of wives and sisters of colonial administrators and missionaries), for the education and training of African women. More recently, in the last two decades, African women's national organizations have taken up the cry for equal opportunities for women in such matters as employment and training. In every instance, it will be found that research or social protest launched on behalf of or by women themselves is invariably motivated by economic and political considerations rather than feminism per se. In some instances, the issue of women's rights is used as a means of social control; in others, it serves to consolidate the political position of individual men and women. In all cases, it is a reliable indicator of ideological alignments within a particular national or international situation.

It cannot be stated too often that up to this time research on African problems has been greatly influenced by intellectual trends from outside the continent. Like the educational systems inherited from the colonial days, the research industry has continued to use the African environment as a testing ground for ideas and hypotheses the locus of which is to be found in Paris, London, New York, or Amsterdam. For this reason, the primary orientation to development problems tends to be created on the basis of what happens to be politically and/or intellectually significant in the metropoles. At one time, it may be family planning; at another, environment; at yet another, human rights and women's social conditions. At one time, there is funding for a particular type of study; at another time, money for yet another research topic. Such continual redefinition of research priorities means that African scholars are forced into certain forms of intellectual endeavors that are peripheral to the development of their societies. Such a redefinition of research problems and programs concerning Africa sometimes manifests itself in the emphasis of research orientations which have little to offer African women. I have visited villages where, at a time when the village women are asking for better health facilities and lower infant-mortality rates, they are presented with questionnaires on family planning. In some instances, when women would like to have piped water in the village, they may be at the same time faced with a researcher interested in investigating power and powerlessness in the household. In yet another situation, when women are asking for access to agricultural credit, a researcher on the scene may be conducting a study on female circumcision.

There is no denying that certain statistical relationships can be established between such variables as fertility, power, initiation rites, and women's overall standing in the household/community. What I am trying to emphasize, however, is that a statistical relationship per se, which can be established as an academic exercise, does not necessarily constitute relevant information or a priority from the point of view of those who are made the research subjects. In essence, research efforts which seek to enhance the participation of women in contemporary Africa, whether or not they emanate from the continent, should be formulated in relation to the socioeconomic realities which African women confront today. Furthermore, as we stand between the corridors of international intellectual corporations and national ethnic class divisions, the struggle which is being waged by women at various levels for equity in access to land or educational opportunities, better nutritional standards, or lowered infant-mortality rates is by no means separate or different from efforts made at the level of analysis to understand the nature of real or putative problems facing African women today.

Two further points may illustrate some of the analytical mileage to be gained when the two basic parameters outlined above are brought to bear on understanding African women. First, in considering the issue of the impact on women of colonial and/or neocolonial socioeconomic processes, it is well to bear in mind that, although such processes have enclaved women in the reserves and exploited their labor while withdrawing men to work in wage-earning jobs, in reality wages alone cannot constitute an argument that men have benefited from those systems of oppression. In fact peoples who are dominated by a repressive regime, whether they are men or women, share a similar subordinate structural position *vis-à-vis* the dominant culture. What we must look for, then, is not how African women lost their development opportunity during colonial or contemporary neocolonial periods (since our men have also suffered the same loss) but, rather, the differential impact of such socioeconomic conditions on men and women.

In this respect, I am reminded of men in our villages who were once recruited as plantation workers or infantry soldiers to fight in colonial wars. They left their villages thinking that they would earn money or make some other fortune from earning wages in work or benefits from the army. Meanwhile, their wives worked on the land to keep the family on its feet at home. Now these men (some of them at least) are retired at home with no benefits, having spent their youth feeding the industrial and military machines of their days. In actuality they are no better off than their wives, who had to till the land to feed their children.

The alienation experienced by low-paid African (Senegalese) dockworkers and their womenfolk at the hands of French colonials is also well documented by Sembene Ousmane in his novel *God's Bits of Wood*. In another novel, *Mine Boy*, Peter Abrams vividly depicts the situation of Ma Leah, a strong African woman in the slums of Johannesburg who earns a living by brewing and selling illicit liquor. She tries to evade the police but is finally arrested and jailed. In the same story her "daughter" Eliza, who is well educated, is estranged from the slum community in which she grew up. Yet she is excluded from the community of others (white people) who have comparable educational experience. Meanwhile Xuma, a man from the rural hinterland, arrives in Johannesburg to look for work. He gets a job and even becomes a leader of his co-workers in the mines. However, he is haunted by the idea of his friend who is dying of tuberculosis, having spent all his youth in the service of the mining industry. The three—Ma Leah, Eliza, Xuma—are all earning wages, but their position as Africans in a discriminatory job market remains in reality the same.

The second point I want to consider here is a problem with the notion of "integration of women in development," an expression developed by the

United Nations and largely adopted by international aid agencies. One may well ask, "Integrating women into what development?" Historically, African women have been active in the provisioning of their families. This is a role which they play today, although they are being constricted in their efforts to feed their families by multinational corporations in food processing and agribusiness as well as by national land reform and crop programs. These women are well "integrated" into the dependent national economies. While it is possible to anticipate some structural changes through the implementation of some of the UN recommendations for special women's programs and women's bureaus or commissions, it is also likely that such institutional arrangements may serve in some instances to restrict rather than enhance the participation of women in their societies. Member states that pursue a program of development that negates equity can only be paying lip service to the issue when they agree to establish a women's bureau or commission. Such concepts as "integration of women in development" therefore require close scrutiny, in view of the fact that the majority of African peoples still operate within dependent economies. In such circumstances local participation tends to be characterized by what is sometimes referred to as "resistance to change," "apathy," or "indifference." Whenever a people have to use much of their creative energy for resistance, it means they are set back one step each time they approach a problem. The majority of Africans (men and women) find themselves in this situation. Thus questions of autonomy and self-determination still remain critical to an understanding of the problems surrounding female participation in contemporary Africa.

In ending this brief statement, I wish to reiterate what I consider to be central in understanding the position of African women today.

(*a*) Any analysis must embrace the relationship between the international and national economic systems and women's position, including expectations of women in society and the contradictions associated with and arising from these expectations at the international, national, and domestic level.
(*b*) African scholars, and especially women, must bring their knowledge to bear on presenting an African perspective on prospects and problems for women in local societies.
(*c*) Scholars and persons engaged in development-research planning and implementation should pay attention to development priorities as local communities see them. This means an effort to bring these priorities to the attention of national governments and research groups and to encourage participation by local communities in identifying issues which they consider primary in their daily lives. In this way, there need not be an artificial boundary between practical and academic research, or between policy and theoretical research, on the role of women in development.

I would close by recalling a peasant woman in rural Kenya, who said the following when I asked her what development means to her: "During the anticolonial campaigns we were told that development would mean better living conditions. Several years have gone by, and all we see are people coming from the capital to write about us. For me the hoe and the water pot which served my grandmother still remain my source of livelihood. When I work on the land and fetch water from the river, I know I can eat. But this development which you talk about has yet to be seen in this village."

REFERENCES

Amado, Jorge. *Gabriela Cravo e Canela.* São Paulo: Martins, 1959.

Azevedo, *O Cortiço.* São Paulo: Martins, 1969.

Freyre, Gilberto. *The Masters and the Slaves.* Translated by Samuel Putman. New York: Alfred A Knopf, A Borzoi Book, 1964.

Lima Barreto, Afonso Henriques. *Clara dos Anjos.* 3rd ed. São Paulo: Brasiliense, 1969.

Queiroz, Rachel de. *O Quinze. Tres Romances.* Rio de Janeiro: Livraria José Olympio Editôra, 1948.

SELECT BIBLIOGRAPHY

Adekogbe, E. "La Femme au Nigeria." *Perspectives de Catholicite*, v. 19 (3), 1960: 16–23.

Adibe, M. L., and A. Tessa. "Position and Problems of the Woman in French-Speaking Africa. II-Gabon." *Women Today*, v. 6 (3), 1964: 51–63.

"African Women Help in Rural Education and Training." *UNESCO Information Bulletin*, v. 22, Feb. 1966: 12–13.

"Africa's Food Producers: The Impact of Change on Rural Women." *Focus*, v. 25, January 1975: 1–7.

Aidoo, Ama Ata. *Anowa*. Harlow: Longmans, 1970.

——. *No Sweetness Here.* Garden City, N.Y.: Doubleday, 1971.

——. *The Dilemma of a Ghost.* Accra: Longmans, 1965.

Albert, Ethel M. "Women of Burundi: A Study of Social Values." *Women of Tropical Africa*, ed. Denise Paulme. Berkeley: University of California Press, 1971.

Al-Shahi, A. S. "Politics and the Role of Women in a Shaiqiya Constituency (1968)." *Sudan Society*, v. 4, 1969: 27–38.

Aluko, Timothy Mofolorunso. "Polygamy and the Surplus of Women." *West African Review*, v. 21 (270), 1950: 259–260.

Ames, D. "The Economic Base of Wolof Polygyny." *Southwestern Journal of Anthropology*, v. 11 (4), 1955: 391–403.

Ames, D. W. "The Selection of Mates, Courtship, and Marriage among the Wolof," *Bulletin d'Institute Francais d'Afrique Noire*, 18, nos. 1–2. 1956.

Andreski, Iris. *Old Wives Tales: Life Stories of African Women.* New York: Schocken Books. 1970.

Ardener, Edwin. "Belief and the Problem of Women." *The Interpretation of Ritual.* J. S. LaFontaine, ed. London: Tavistock, 1972.

Auber, J. "La femme dans les traditions et less moeurs malagaches." *Revue Madagascar*, 22, 1955: 43–48.
Awe, Bolanle. "University Education for Women in Nigeria." *Ibadan*, no. 18, February 1964: 57–62.
——. "The Iyalode in the Traditional Yoruba Political System" in Alice Schlegel, ed. *Sexual Stratification: A Cross-Cultural View*. New York: Columbia University Press, 1977.
Awori, Thelma "For African Women Equal Rights are not Enough," *UNESCO Courier*, v. 28 (3), March 1975: 21–25.
Baker, Tanya, and Mary E.C. Bird. "Urbanization and the Position of Women." *Sociological Review*, v. 7 (1), July 1959: 99–122.
Barkow, Jerome. "Hausa Women and Islam." *The Canadian Journal of African Studies*, v. 6 (2), 1972: 317–328.
Barthel, Diane. "The Rise of A Female Professional Elite." *African Studies Review*, v. 18 (3), Dec. 1975: 1–18.
Beidelman, T.O. *The Kaguru: A Matrilineal People of East Africa*. New York: Holt, Rinehart & Winston, 1971.
Beier, H.J. "The Position of Yoruba Women." *Presence Africaine*, 1–2 (April–July 1955): 39–46.
Berger, Iris. "Rebels or Status-Seekers? Women as Spirit Mediums in East Africa." *Women in Africa*, Nancy J. Hafkin and Edna G. Bay, eds, Stanford: Stanford University Press, 1976.
Bohannan, Laura. "Dahomean Marriage: A Revaluation." First published, 1949. Reprinted in *Marriage, Family and Residence*, Paul Bohannan and John Middleton, eds. pp. 85–108. New York: Natural History Press, 1968.
Bohannan, P. and Dalton, G. (eds) *Markets in Africa*. Evanston: Northwestern University Press, 1962.
Boserup, Ester. *Women's Role in Economic Development*, London: George Allen and Unwin, 1970.
Brain, James L. "Less Than Second-Class: Women in Rural Settlement Schemes in Tanzania." *Women in Africa*, Nancy J. Hafkin and Edna G. Bay, eds, Stanford: Stanford University Press, 1976.
——. "Matrilineal Descent and Marital Stability: a Tanzanian Case," *Journal of Asian and African Studies*, v. 4 (2), 1969: 122–131.
Brandel-Syrier, Mia. *Black Woman in Search of God*. London: Lutterworth, 1962.
Brooks, A.E. "Political Participation of Women in Africa South of the Sahara." *Annals American Academy of Political Social Science*, v. 375, January 1968: 82–85.
Brooks, George E. "The Signares of Saint-Louis and Goree: Women Entrepreneurs in Eighteenth-Century Senegal," *Women in Africa*, Nancy J. Hafkin and Edna G. Bay, eds, Stanford: Stanford University Press, 1976.
Bunbury, Isla. "Women's Position as Workers in Africa South of the Sahara." *Civilizations*, v. 11 (2), 1961: 159–68.
Calame-Griaule, G. "The Spiritual and Social Role of Women in Traditional Sudanese Society." *Diogenes*, 37, 1962: 81–92.
Caldwell, John C. *Population Growth and Family Change in Africa*. Canberra: Australia National University Press, 1968.
Chilver, E. M., and P. M. Kaberry. "The Kingdon of Kom in West Cameroon," in D. Forde and P. N. Kaberry, eds, *West African Kingdoms in the Nineteenth Century*. London: Oxford University Press for the International African Institute, 1969.

Christian, Angela. "The Place of Women in Ghana Society," *African Women*, III, 3, 1959: 57–59.
Clignet, Remi. *Many Wives, Many Powers: Authority and Power in Polygynous Families (Abure and Bete, Ivory Coast)*. Evanston: Northwestern University Press, 1970.
Crane, Louise. *Ms. Africa: Profiles of Modern African Women*. New York: J.B. Lippincott Co., 1973.
Curley, Richard T. *Elders, Shades and Women: Ceremonial Change in Lango, Uganda*. Berkeley: University of California Press, 1973.
Davidson, Basil. *Black Mother*, 4th ed. Boston: Atlantic-Little, Brown and Co., 1966.
De La Rue, A. "The Rise and Fall of Grace Ibingira." *New African*, v. 5 (10), December 1966: 207–08.
Diarra, Fatoumata Agnes. *Femmes africaines en devenir: Les femmes zarma du Niger*. Paris: Editions Anthropos, 1971.
Dobert, Margarita. "Liberation and the Women of Guinea." *Africa Report*, 15 (7), 1970: 26–28.
——. "Women in French-Speaking West Africa: A Selected Guide to Civic and Political Participation in Guinea, Dahomey, and Mauritania." *Current Bibliography of African Affairs*, v. 3 (9), September 1970: 5–21.
Dobkin, M. "Colonialism and the Legal Status of Women in Francophonic Africa." *Cahiers d'Etudes Africaines*, v. 8 (3), 1968: 390–405.
Donner, Etta. "Togba, a Women's Society in Liberia." *Africa*, v. 11, 1938: 109–11.
Dorjahn, Vernon R. "The Factor of Polygyny in African Demography," in Bascom and Herskivits, eds. *Continuity and Change in African Cultures*. Chicago: University of Chicago Press, 1959, chapter 5, pp. 87–112.
——. "Fertility, Polygyny and their Interrelations in Temne Society," *American Anthropologist*, 60 (5), 1958: 838–60.
Douglas, Mary. "A Form of Polyandry Among the Lele." *Africa* v. 21: 1–12, 1951.
——. "Is Matriliny Doomed in Africa?" *Man in Africa*. Phyllis Kaberry and Mary Douglas, eds. London: Tavistock, 1969: 121–35.
Dupire, Marguerite. "The Position of Women in a Pastoral Society." *Women of Tropical Africa*, Denise Paulme (ed.) pp. 47–92. Berkeley: University of California Press, 1971.
Earthy, E. Dora. *Valenge Women: The Social and Economic Life of the Valenge Women of Portugese East Africa*. London: Cass, 1968.
Eide, Wenche Barth and Steady, Filomina Chioma. "Individual and Social Energy Flows: Bridging Nutritional and Anthropological Thinking about Women's Work in Rural Africa: Some Theoretical Considerations," in Jerome, N., Kandel, R. F. and Pelto, G. H. eds, *Nutritional Anthropology*. New York: Redgrave Publishing Company, 1980, pp. 61–84.
Ekejiuba, Felicia "Omu Okwei: Merchant Queen of Ossomari." *Journal of the Historical Society of Nigeria*, v. 3 (4) 1967: 633–646.
Esike, S.O. "The Aba Riots of 1929." *African Historian*. (Ibadan), v. 1 (3), 1965: 7–13.
Evans, David R. "Image and Reality: Career Goals of Educated Ugandan Women." *Canadian Journal of African Studies*, v. 6 (2), 1972: 213–232.
Falade, Solange. "Women of Dakar and the Surrounding Urban Area." *Women of Tropical Africa*, Denise Paulme (ed.), pp. 217–30. Berkeley: University of California Press, 1971.
Fluehr-Lobban, Carolyn "Agitation for change in the Sudan," in Alice Shlegel (ed.) *Sexual Stratification: A Cross-Cultural View*. New York: Columbia University Press, 1977.

Fortes, M. *The Dynamics of Clanship among the Tallensi*. Oxford: Oxford University Press, 1945.

Galadanci, S.A. "Education of Women in Islam with Reference to Nigeria." *Nigerian Journal of Islam*, v. 1 (1) Jan.–June 1971: 5–10.

Gamble, David. "The Temne Family in a Modern Town in Sierra Leone." *Africa*, v. 33 (3) 1963: 209–26.

Gantin, Bernardine. "Christianity and the African Woman." *World Mission*, v. 13, Summer 1962: 13–22.

Gollock, Georgina A. *Daughters of Africa*. New York: Negro University Press, 1969 (reprint of the 1932 edition).

Goody, Esther N. *Contexts of Kinship: An Essay in the Family Sociology of the Gonja of North Ghana*. Cambridge: Cambridge University Press, 1973.

Goody, Jack. "Inheritance, Property, and Marriage in Africa and Eurasia." *Sociology*, v. 3, 1969: 55–76.

Goody, Jack and Esther Goody, "The Circulation of Women and Children in Northern Ghana." *Man*, v. 2 (2), June 1967: 226–48.

Goody, Jack and Joan Buckley. "Inheritance and Women's Labour in Africa." *Africa*, v. 43 (2), April 1973: 108–21.

Gutkind, Peter C. W. "African Urban Family Life and the Urban System." *Journal of Asian and African Studies*, v. 1 (1), 1966: 35–46.

Hafkin, Nancy J. and Edna G. Bay, eds. *Women in Africa: Studies in Social and Economic Change*. Stanford: Stanford University Press, 1976.

Hamilton-Hazeley, Lottie E. A. "The Education of Women and Girls in the Provinces." *Sierra Leone Journal of Education*, v. 1 (1), April 1966: 20–23.

Hansen, Karen Tranberg. "Married Women and Work Explorations from an Urban Case Study." *African Social Research*, v. 20, December 1975: 777–79.

Harris, J. S. "The Position of Women in a Nigerian Society," *Transactions of the New York Academy of Sciences*, v. 2 (5), 1940.

Hastie, P. "Women's Clubs in Uganda." *Mass Education Bulletin*, v. 2 (1), December 1950: 4–6.

Hay, Margaret Jean. "Luo Women and Economic Change During the Colonial Period." *Women in Africa*, Nancy J. Hafkin and Edna G. Bay, eds, Stanford: Stanford University Press, 1976.

Hecker, Monique. "UNESCO and Women's Rights: An Experimental Project in Upper Volta." *UNESCO Chronicle*, v. 16 (6), June 1970, 257–65.

Hill, Polly. "Women Cocoa Farmers." *Ghana Farmer*, v. 2 (2), May 1958: 70–71.

Hoffer, Carol P. "Mende and Sherbo Women in High Office." *Canadian Journal of African Studies*, v. 6 (2), 1972, 151–64.

Ifeka-Moller, Caroline. "Female Militancy and the Colonial Revolt: The Women's War of 1929, Eastern Nigeria." Shirley Ardener, ed., *Perceiving Women*. London: Malaby Press, 1975: 127–57.

Izzett, Alison. "Family Life Among the Yoruba in Lagos, Nigeria." *Social Change in Modern Africa*. A. Southall, ed. London: Oxford University Press, 1961.

Jeffreys, M. D. W. "The Nyama Society of the Ibibio Women." *African Studies*, v. 15 (1), 1956: 15–28.

Jellicoe, M. R. "Women's Groups in Sierra Leone." *African Women*, v. 1 (2), June 1955: 35–43.

Jiagge, J. A. "The Role of Non-Governmental Organizations in the Education of Women in African States." *Convergence*, v. (2), 1969: 73–78.

Kaberry, Phyllis M. *Women in Grassfields: A Study of the Economic Position of Women in Bamenda, British Cameroons*. 2nd edn. New York: Humanities Press, 1969.

Kane, Malmouna. "The Status of Married Women under Customary Law in Senegal." *American Journal of Comparative Law*, v. 20 (4), Fall 1972: 716–23.

Keirn, Susan Middleton. "Voluntary Associations Among Urban African Women." Brian M. du Toit, ed., *Culture Change in Contemporary Africa. Communications from the African Studies Center.* Vol. 1., Gainesville: University of Florida, 1970.

Krapf-Askari, Eva. "Women, Spears, and the Scarce Good: A Comparison of the Sociological Function of Warfare in Two Central African Societies (Zande and Nzakara)." A. Singer *et al.*, eds, *Zande Themes.* London: Oxford University Press, 1972: 19–40.

Krige, Eileen Jensen. "Girls' Puberty Songs and their Relations to Fertility, Health, Morality and Religion among the Zulu." *Africa,* v. 38 (2), April 1968: 173–98.

Lancaster, Chet S. "Women, Horticulture, and Society in Sub-Saharan Africa." *American Anthropologist*, v. 78 (3), Sept. 1976: 539–64.

Landes, Ruth. "Negro Slavery and Female Status." *African Affairs*, v. 52 (206), 1953: 54–57.

Landis, Elizabeth S. *Apartheid and the Disabilities of African Women in South Africa.* (UN Unit on Apartheid, December 1973). A. G. Bishop & Sons Ltd., Orpington, Kent.

Lebeuf, Annie M.D. "The Role of Women in the Political Organization of African Societies." Denise Paulme, ed., *Women of Tropical Africa.* London: Routledge and Kegan Paul, 1963: 93–120.

Leith-Ross, Sylvia. *African Women: A Study of the Ibo of Nigeria.* London: Routledge & Kegan Paul, 1965.

Levine, Robert A. "Sex Roles and Economic change in Africa." *Ethnology* 5 (2), 1966: 186–93.

Levine, Robert A., Klein, N. H. and Deven, C. R. "Father-Child Relationships and Changing Life-Styles in Ibadan, Nigeria." *The City in Modern Africa.* H. Miner *ed.* New York: Praeger, 1967.

Lewis, Barbara C. "The Limitations of Group Action Among Entrepreneurs: The Market Women of Abidjan, Ivory Coast." *Women in Africa*, Nancy J. Hafkin and Edna G. Bay, eds. Stanford: Stanford University Press, 1976.

——. "Economic Activity and Marriage among Ivorian Urban Women," in Alice Schlegel ed. *Sexual Stratification: A Cross-Cultural View.* New York: Columbia University Press, 1977.

Little, Kenneth "Voluntary Associations and Social Mobility among West African Women." *Canadian Journal of African Studies*, v. 6 (2), 1972: 275–88.

Lloyd, Peter C. Divorce among the Yoruba. *American Anthropologist*, v. 70 (1), 1968: 67–81.

——. "The Status of the Yoruba Wife." *Sudan Society*, v. 2, 1963: 35–42.

Magbogunje, Akin L. "The Market Woman." *Ibadan*, v. 2, Feb. 1961: 14–17.

Magdalen, M. C., Sister. "Education of Girls in Southern Nigeria." *International Review of Missions*, v. 17, 1928: 505–14.

Marie-Andre du Sacré Coeur. *The House Stands Firm: Family Life in West Africa.* Trans. Alba I. Zizzamia. Milwaukee: Bruce, 1962.

Marris, Peter. *Family and Social Change in an African City: A Study of Rehousing in Lagos.* London: Routledge & Kegan Paul, 1961.

Marshall, Gloria. "In a World of Women: Field Work in a Yoruba Community." Peggy Golde, ed., *Women in the Field: Anthropological Experiences.* Chicago: Aldine, 1970: 167–94.

——. "The Marketing of Farm Produce: Some Patterns of Trade among Women in Western Nigeria." *Proceedings of a Conference at the Nigerian Institute of Social and Economic Research*, Ibadan, 1962: 88–99.

Marshall, Gloria. "Women, Trade and the Yoruba Family," Ph.D. dissertation, Columbia University, 1964.

Mayer, Philip, and Mayer, Iona. "Women and Children in the Migrant Situation." Part IV, pp. 233–282. *Townsmen or Tribesmen.* Capetown: Oxford University Press, 1963.

Mbilinyi, Marjorie. "The Status of Women in Tanzania." *Canadian Journal of African Studies*, v. 6 (2), 1972: 371–77.

McCall, Daniel. "Trade and the Role of Wife in a Modern West African Town." A. W. Southall, ed., *Social Change in Modern Africa.* Oxford: Oxford University Press, 1961.

Mickelwait, Donald R. *et al. Women in Rural Development: A Survey of the Roles of Women in Ghana, Lesotho, Kenya, Nigeria, Bolivia, Paraguay and Peru.* Boulder: Westview Press, 1976.

Miller, Jean-Claude. "Ritual Marriage, Symbolic Fatherhood, and Initiation among the Rukuba, Plateau-Benue State, Nigeria." *Man*, v. 7: 283–95, 1972.

Molnos, A. *Attitudes Towards Family Planning in East Africa.* Munich: Weltforum Verlag, 1968.

Muhammad, Yahaya. "The Legal Status of Muslim Women in the Northern States of Nigeria." *Journal of the Centre for Islamic Legal Studies*, v. 1 (2), 1967: 1–38.

Mullings, Leith. "Women and Economic Change in Africa." *Women in Africa*, Nancy J. Hafkin and Edna G. Bay (eds), Stanford: Stanford University Press, 1976.

Mutiso, G.C.M. "Women in African Literature." *East African Journal*, v. 8 (3), March 1971: 4–13.

Nasemann, Vandra. "The Hidden Curriculum of a West African Girls' Boarding School." *Canadian Journal of African Studies*, v. 8 (3), 1974: 479–94.

Ngugi, Wa Thiong'o (James). *A Grain of Wheat.* London: Heinemann, 1967.

Nwapa, Flora *Efuru.* London: Heinemann, 1966.

O'Barr, Jean F. "Making the Invisible Visible: African Women in Politics and Policy." *African Studies Review*, v. 18 (3), December 1975: 19–28.

Ogunsheye, F.A. "Les femmes du Nigeria." *Presence Africaine*, v. 32–33, June-Sept., 1960: 120–38.

O'Kelly, Elizabeth "Corn Mill Societies in Southern Cameroons." *African Women*, v. 1 (1), 1955: 33–35.

Okonjo, Kamene. "The Dual-Sex Political System in Operation: Igbo Women and Community Politics in Mid-Western Nigeria." *Women in Africa*, Nancy J. Hafkin and Edna G. Bay, eds, stanford: Stanford University Press, 1976.

O'Laughlin, Bridget. "Mediating Contradiction: Why Mbum Women Do Not Eat Chicken." M. Z. Rosaldo and Louise Lamphere, eds., *Women, Culture and Society.* Stanford: Stanford University Press, 1974.

Olmstead, Judith. "Women and Work in Two Southern Ethiopian Communities." *American Studies Review*, v. 18 (3), December 1975: 85–98.

Omari, T. Peter "Role Expectation in the Courtship Situation in Ghana." *Social Forces*, 42 (2), December 1963: 147–56.

Oppong, Christine. *Marriage Among a Matrilineal Elite: A Family Study of Ghanaian Senior Civil Servants.* London: Cambridge University Press, 1974.

Oppong, Christine, and Okali, Christine; and Beverly Houghton. "Woman Power: Retrograde Steps in Ghana." *African Studies Review*, v. 18 (3), December 1975: 71–84.

Ottenberg, Phoebe. "The Changing Economic Position of Women Among the Afikpo Ibo." William R. Bascom and Melville J. Herskovits, eds., *Continuity and*

Change in African Cultures. Chicago: University of Chicago Press, 1959: 205–23.

Pala, Achola O. "A Preliminary Survey of the Avenues for and Constraints on Women in the Development Process in Kenya." Discussion Paper No. 218. Nairobi: Institute of Development Studies, University of Nairobi, March 1975.

——. "The Role of Women in Rural Development: Research Priorities." Discussion Paper no. 203. Nairobi: Institute of Development Studies, University of Nairobi, June 1974.

Pankhurst, Sylvia. "Ethiopian Women's Welfare Association." *Ethiopia Observer*, v. 4 (2), March 1960: 45–47.

Paulme, Denise. *Women of Tropical Africa.* Berkeley and Los Angeles: University of California Press, 1971.

Pellow, Deborah *Women in Accra: Options for Autonomy.* Michigan: Reference Publications, Inc., 1977.

Perlman, Melvin L. "The Changing Status and Role of Women in Toro, Western Uganda." *Cahiers d'Etudes Africaines*, v. 6, 1966: 564–91.

Pool, Janet. "A cross-comparative study of aspects of Conjugal behaviour among women of Three West African countries." *Canadian Journal of African Studies*, v. 6 (2) 1972: 233–59.

Razafyadriamihaingo, suzanne. "The Position of Women in Madagascar." *African Women*, v. 3 (2) June 1959: 29–33.

Richards, Audrey. *Chisungu: A Girl's Initiation Ceremony Among the Bemba of Northern Rhodesia.* London: Faber & Faber, 1956.

Ritzenthaler, Robert E. "Anlu: A Women's Uprising in the British Cameroons." *African Studies*, v. 19 (3) 1960: 151–56.

Robertson, Claire. "Economic Woman in Africa. Profit-Making Techniques of Accra Market Women." *Journal of Modern African Studies*, v. 12 (4), December 1974: 657–664.

——. "Ga Women and Socioeconomic Change in Accra, Ghana." *Women in Africa*, Nancy J. Hafkin and Edna G. Bay, eds, Stanford: Stanford University Press, 1976.

"Role of Women in National Development in African Countries." *International Labour Review*, v. 101, April 1970: 399–401.

Sa 'D Al-Din Fawzi. "The Role of Women in a Developing Sudan." *Women's Role in the Development of Tropical and Sub-Tropical Countries.* Brussels: Institute of Differing Civilizations, 1959.

Schapera, Isaac. *Married Life in an African Tribe.* Evanston: Northwestern University Press, 1965.

Schneider, Daivd M. and Gough, Kathleen (eds.) *Matrilineal Kinship*, Berkeley: University of California Press, 1961.

Schlegel, Alice. *Male Dominance and Female Autonomy: Domestic Authority in Matrilineal Societies.* New Haven: Human Relations Area Files Press, 1972.

Schuster, Ilsa. *The New Women of Lusaka*, Palto Alto, Mayfield Publishing Company, 1979.

Simons, H. J. *African Women: Their Legal Status in South Africa.* Evanston: Northwestern University Press, 1968.

Siquet, M. "Legal and Customary Status of Women." *La Promotion de la femme au Congo et en Ruanda-Urundi.* Brussels: Congres Nationel Colonial, 12th Session, 1956: 197–251.

Smith, Mary F. Baba of Karo, a Woman of the Muslim Hausa. London: Faber, 1964.

Smock, Audrey C. and Giele Janet Z. eds. *Women: Roles and Status in Eight Countries*. New York: Wiley, 1977.

Southall, Aidan W. "The Position of Women and the Stability of Marriage in Tropical Africa." Aidan W. Southall, ed., *Social Change in Modern Africa*. London: Oxford University Press, 1961.

Spencer, Dunstan S.C. "African Women in Agricultural Development: A Case Study in Sierra Leone." African Rural Economy Working Paper No. 11. East Lansing: Michigan State University, April 1970.

Steady, Filomina Chioma. Female Power in African Politics: The National Congress of Sierra Leone. Munger African Library Notes, no. 31, August, 1975.

——. "Protestant Women's Associations in Freetown, Sierra Leone." *Women in Africa*, Nancy J. Hafkin and Edna G. Bay, eds, Stanford: Stanford University Press, 1976.

——. "Male Roles in Fertility in Sierra Leone: The Moving Target." in Oppong, C. *et al.*, eds, *Marriage, Family and Parenthood in West Africa*. Canberra: Australian National University, 1978.

Steady, Filomina Chioma and Eide, Wenche Barth. "Individual and Social Energy Flows: Bridging Nutritional and Anthropological Thinking about Women's Work in Rural Africa: Some Theoretical Considerations," in Jerome, N., Kandel, R. F. and Pelto, G. H., eds, *Nutritional Anthropology*. Pleasantville, N.Y.: Redgrave Publishing Company, 1980, pp. 61–84.

Stichter, Sharon B. "Women and the Labor Force in Kenya: 1895–1964." *Rural Africana*, v. 29, Winter, 1976: 45–67.

Strobel, Margaret. "From Lelemama to Lobbying: Women's Associations in Mombasa, Kenya." *Women in Africa*, Nancy J. Hafkin and Edna G. Bay (eds)., Stanford: Stanford University Press, 1976.

——. *Muslim Women in Mombasa*. New Haven: Yale University Press, 1979.

Sudarkasa, Niara. Where Women Work: A Study of Yoruba Women in the Marketplace and in the Home. Ann Arbor: University of Michigan Press, 1973.

Suleiman, S. M. "Women in the Sudan Public Service." *Sudan Journal of Administration and Development*, v. 2, Jan. 1966: 37–53.

Suttner, R. S. "The Legal Status of African Women in South Africa." A Review Article. *African Social Research*, v. 8, Dec. 1969: 620–27.

Toure, Sekou. "The African Woman." *The Black Scholar*, v. 4 (6–7), March–April 1973: 32–36.

——. "The Role of Women in the Revolution." *Black Scholar*, v. 6 (6), March 1975: 32–36.

Uchendu, Victor Chikezie. "Concubinage among Ngwa Igbo of Southern Nigeria." *Africa*, v. 35 (2), April 1965: 187–97.

United Nations Economic Commission for Africa. "Country Report for Nigeria. Vocational Training Opportunities for Girls and Women." Addis Ababa: Economic Commission for Africa, 1973.

UN Economic Commission for Africa. Report of the Regional Conference on Education, Vocational Training and Work Opportunities for Girls and Women in African Countries. Rabat: UNECA 1971.

UNESCO Report of the Conference on African Women and Adult Education. Paris: UNESCO, 1962.

UNESCO. "Report of the Research Team Appointed by the Sierra Leone Commission for Education, Training, and Employment Opportunities for Women in Sierra Leone, 1974."

Urdang, Stephanie. *Fighting Two Colonialisms: Women in Guinea-Bissau.* New York: Monthly Review Press, 1979.

——. "Fighting Two Colonialisms: The Women's Struggle in Guinea-Bissau." *African Studies Review*, v. 18 (3), Dec. 1973: 29–34.

Usoro, Eno J. "The Place of Women in Nigerian Society." *African Women*, v. 4 (2), June 1961: 27–30.

Van Allen, Judith. "'Aba Riots' or Igbo "Women's War"?—Ideology, Stratification and the Invisibility of Women," in Hafkin, N. and Edna Bay, eds. *Women in Africa.* Stanford: Staford University Press, 1976, pp. 59–85.

——. "Sitting on a Man: Colonialism and the Lost Political Institutions of Igbo Women." *Canadian Journal of African Studies*, v. 6 (2), 1972: 165–182.

——. "Women in Africa: Modernization Means More Dependency." *The Center Magazine*, v. 7 (3), May–June 1974, 60–67.

Wainwright, Bridget. "Women's Clubs in the Central Nyanza District of Kenya." *Community Development Bulletin*, v. 4 (4), Sept. 1953: 77–80.

Walker, Alice. "The Diary of an African Nun." *The Black Woman: An Anthology.* Toni Cade, New York: The New American Library, 1970.

Well, P. M. "Wet Rice, Women, and Adaptation in the Gambia." *Rural Africana*, v. 19, Winter 1973: 20–29.

Whiting, Beatrice B. "The Kenyan Career Woman: Traditional and Modern." *Annals of the New York Academy of Sciences*, no. 208, March 1973: 71–75.

Wipper, Audrey. "African Women, Fashion and Scapegoating." *Canadian Journal of African Studies*, v. 6 (2), 1972: 329–349.

——. "Equal Rights for Women in Kenya?" *Journal of Modern African Studies*, v. 9 (3), Oct. 1971, pp. 429–42.

——. "The Maendaleo Ya Wanawake Movement: Some Paradoxes and Contradictions." *African Studies Review*, v. 18 (3), Dec. 1975: 99–120.

Wipper, Audrey. "The Politics of Sex: Some Strategies Employed by the Kenyan Power Elite to Handle a Normative-Existential Discrepancy." *African Studies Review*, v. 14 (3), December 1971: 463–82.

——. "The Roles of African Women: Past, Present and Future." *Canadian Journal of African Studies*, 6 (2) 1972: 143–46.

Women's Role in the Development of Tropical and Subtropical Countries. Brussels: Institut International des Civilizations Differentes, 1959.

Chapter 17

An Investigative Framework for Gender Research in Africa in the New Millennium

Filomina Chioma Steady

I. Introduction: Africa—A Continent in Crisis

The majority of African countries are in crisis. Economic domination through corporate globalization is the primary global strategy for economic growth. The resulting development paradigm is re-colonization through the reproduction of hegemonic tendencies that facilitate the movement of trans-national capital. Protracted recession, the debt burden, Structural Adjustment Programmes, externally-controlled privatization and an emphasis on exports are creating a cultural crisis of major proportions. The marginalization of Africa through corporate globalization has led to widespread poverty, the destruction of many African economies, social dislocation and civil strife. This is compounded by the erosion of the life-supporting capacities of many African ecosystems. Authoritarian regimes and gender-based discrimination complete the picture.

Global economic processes are producing new dimensions of structural racism through North/South and Black/White polarizations. The United Nations conference on racism held in Durban, South Africa last year recognized the correlation between corporate globalization and racism and emphasized the gendered dimensions of this correlation. Racialized women, become recruited into the international labor force as cheap sources of unprotected and migratory labor and as objects of sex tourism, trafficking and domestic servitude. The overwhelming evidence seems to suggest that gender-based hierarchies and gender subordination combined with structural racism are being reinforced by globalization African women are among the most severely affected (Steady, 2002).

The study of gender in Africa cannot escape the realities of post-colonial domination. Through the reproduction of colonial-like policies supported by international financial institutions and international corporate laws, the patriarchal ideologies of colonization are being reproduced through globalization. It is no surprise then that despite significant epistemological challenges of the postmodernist era. Eurocentric concepts, methodologies and paradigms in the study of gender in Africa over the last 30 years continue. They remain the compelling and pervasive force in presenting one-dimensional, frozen and simplified writings about women in Africa.

This chapter examines the impact of external concepts, methodologies and paradigms in the study of gender in Africa as supporting academic structures validating the exploitation of Africa. It also proposes African-centered approaches based on an understanding of African socio-cultural realities, feminist traditions and philosophies. The aim is to develop gender-focused frameworks of analysis that can bring out the multiple and varied social locations of African women while maintaining their specific identities and priorities and developing linkages with other women. Hopefully, this will allow for new approaches in gender research that will promote greater understanding of gender issues, gender equality, social transformation and women's empowerment. In this regard, the paper uses historical, cultural and post-modernist analyses to argue for an emphasis on culture. It also makes a case for the relevance of oppositional discourses. These approaches can best address and challenge both the continuities of patriarchal myths and "tradition" and the impact of colonial patriarchy and racism as they continue to be expressed in global economic domination.

II. The Persistence of Eurocentric Paradigms: New Wines in Old Bottles

Academic interests in Africa historically stemmed from the need to maintain systems of colonization and exploitation through value-maintaining ideologies that included scientific racism. Today, globalization, a new and more insidious form of domination has replaced the colonial project accompanied by corresponding neoliberal paradigms. Concepts of the African woman continue to be central to the development of these paradigms since gender is an organizing principle in the accumulation and operation of colonial and transnational capital and in the allocation of resources and privilege. What is interesting, is the way in which these paradigms continue to reproduce themselves.

The discipline of anthropology, the most influential in African Studies, had three main approaches that reinforced colonial domination and racism. Social darwinism, structural/functionalism and "acculturation" theories. Anthropology was often linked to colonialism and anthropologists helped to develop the image of the "savage" which according to Macquet, helped to justify colonial expansion and domination (Maquet, 1964).

Many of the earlier theoretical distortions were criticized as biased, myopic and based on faulty methodologies and unreliable data. Nonetheless they became reinforced through modernization theory which promoted the notion of "stages" of growth. Modernization theory is now rearing its ugly head through the prism of neoliberalism, the pillar of corporate globalization. Neo-evolutionalists echo modernization theorists through their proclivity for dichotomies. Conceptual frameworks applied to Africa are often presented in Eurocentric-oriented dichotomies of rural/urban, formal/informal, traditional/modern, developed/underdeveloped and so forth. Whatever the division, Africa always ended up on the lower rung of the social evolutionary ladder and in methodological schemes of classification.

The equilibrium model of the British school of structuralism-functionalism also had a colonial *raison d'etre.* It provided analyses of "tribal" law and order so that the "natives" could be effectively governed through the policy of "indirect rule." This policy was in effect quite misleading since the British established a number of "warrant chiefs" and "district commissioners" that served as puppets of the British colonial government. The equilibrium model mystified reality and regarded colonialism as a given (Owosu, 1975). It also ignored the destructive consequences of three centuries of the trans-Atlantic slave trade involving more than 20 million Africans (Galt and Smith, 1976).

Structuralism/functionalism continues to be relevant through the essentializing tendencies of globalization, a new form of colonization. The colonial economy has been replaced by a "new and improved" international colonial system whose structure and function depends on domination by a single functioning market controlled by the North. Today, neo-liberal paradigms justify globalization in much the same way as their antecedents, namely social Darwinism, modernization theory and structural/functionalism justified colonialism. Liberal-oriented international relations studies privilege Western political institutions within a global political system dominated by Western capital and patriarchal ideologies. (Pettman, 1996).

The "acculturation" model found mostly in studies of social change in Africa is not much different. It assumes the inevitability of assimilation to Western norms, values and lifestyles as a result of contact with the West. Seldom is the reverse shown to illustrate the impact of Africa on the West through music, religion, intellectual traditions and so forth. Acculturation studies have for the most part been concerned with what Magubane refers to as "symbols of Europeanization" and "Westernization." Such symbols are measured by European attire, occupations, education and income and have resulted in the inferiroization of African culture, values and esthetics.

Because colonialism was ignored, these studies also ignored the lack of free choice and decision-making and the role of coercion in the process of acculturation. In effect, colonialism not only blocked indigenous processes of decision-making, it also destroyed indigenous processes of knowledge generation. The result is a form of scientific colonialism sustained by scientific racism. Historical studies were no less Eurocentric and racist. Africa was presented as having no history, no civilization and no culture. Studies of the classical period have consistently denied the contributions of Africans to Egyptian civilization and to the civilizations of ancient Greece.[1]

Most of the themes of social science research fashioned by colonial conquest, imperialistic designs or neo-liberal motivations have also influenced gender studies and the feminist discourse. With the exception of Boserup, whose analysis was a critique of the gender bias in economic development (Boserup, 1970) modernization theory tends to see African women at a lower stage of development (read evolution) compared to women of the West; structuralism-functionalism imposes a functional explanation in the study of gender relations that is essentialist in nature. Acculturation studies have been replaced by "women in development" or "gender in development" studies which seek to "integrate African women in development" by making them more like Western women.

III. Oppositional Discourses

Post-colonial and post-modern discourses are providing a revisionist examination of epistemologies and paradigms. They are challenging and reframing many of the philosophical and theoretical underpinnings that are derived from a strongly positivistic, universalizing and evolutionary tradition of Western scholarship. They are concerned with the historical and modern imperatives of the global political economy. It is within this trajectory that gender research in Africa can yield the best results.

Eurocentric paradigms can lead to an abstract mapping of systems of stratification rather than to a more profound interrogation of the very institutions that determine such lines and parameters of social inquiry.

The widespread poverty among women in Africa requires an understanding of the construction of social inequality at the global level which privileges some countries and its men and women, (primarily among groups in the North) at the expense of others, notably in the South.

Revisionist historiography and the work of Diop, Bernal, UNESCO, Black Studies programs and Afro-centric paradigms are challenging the tenacity of scientific racism posing as scholarship. Revisionist historians, economists and other social scientists focusing on the impact of the international political economy on Africa have made significant contributions in challenging the scientific colonialism and racism inherent in Eurocentric scholarship. Rodney's **How Europe underdeveloped Africa** was a major milestone in this development and has been reinforced by dependency theorists. Their studies provide a basis for understanding how and why the underdevelopment of Africa has continued and how it has become intensified through corporate globalization (Rodney, 1981; Amin, 1974, 1997; Bernal, 1987; Asante, 1990; Amadiume, 1997; Fall, 1999; Pheko, 2002).

Corporate globalization, supported by neo-liberal paradigms, is the process that directs the market with the aim of ensuring the unfettered flow of transnational capital. In this process, nation states are rendered powerless through laws that protect multinational cooperation and that are regulated by the World Trade Organization International financial institutions such as the World Bank and the IMF impose conditionalities of Structural

Adjustment Programmes designed to promote macro-economic stability and through loans that stifle the economic growth of countries of the South. The result is a reverse resource flow though debt servicing of at least 14 billion U.S. dollars a year from Africa to the affluent nations in the North. This is greater than the amount received in *real* international aid.

Corporate globalization is increasing marginalization of African countries in the global economy, a process that transcends gender but that has gender implications. Globalization has a compounded effect on women because of certain structural disadvantages in the global and national division of labor and inequalities in the distribution of assets and power.

IV. Feminists of Africa and the South Challenge Eurocentric Paradigms

The Association of African Women for Research and Development (AAWORD) was among the earliest women's organizations of the South to adopt a critical approach to research and to challenge Eurocentric paradigms from a feminist and post-colonial perspective. As early as the mid 70s, it called for the de-colonization of research and established a critical gender research agenda. It also has a major research agenda on globalization (Fall, 1999). In the mid 80s, following the lead of AAWORD, The Development Alternatives for Women in a New Era (DAWN), a research organization of women of the South also challenged the destructive neoliberal model of development and its impact on women of the South.

Throughout the 80s and 90s feminist scholars of color in the South and North led an intellectual movement that challenged essentialist notions of womanhood and insisted on recognizing and interrogating difference. Crucial to this task was the need to understand how the social location of women is determined by race, ethnicity, class, status and access to privilege. Those at the lower end of the scale face powerlessness, exclusion, despair and vulnerabilities. Such constructions of social inequality confers power on some at the expense of others. (Steady, 1981; Sen and Grown, 1986; Essed, 1990; Mohanty, 1991; Imam, 1997).

a. Methodological Challenges in Investigating Gender

There are some fundamental assumptions in investigation of gender that do not fit the African reality, even when controlling for African diversity. One is the belief in the universal subordination of women. Another is the separation of the public and private spheres into gendered spheres that gave men an advantage by participating in the public sphere. From this analysis followed studies seeking to explain asymmetrical relations between men and women.

If one is to believe the universal subordination argument, then one has to ignore the ways in which social location based on race, ethnicity, class, color and so forth confers power and privilege. Furthermore, one has to question the sensitivity of the research tools used to investigate "subordination" and also the methodological approaches used to apply it cross-culturally. The "universal subordination of women" argument forces us to settle for the highly contested notion that "biology is destiny" and to ask the following questions: Whose biology? Whose destiny? Are all female biologies socially constructed the same way? What if they come in different colors? What if they are stunted by poverty and malnutrition? What if they are subject to trafficking like a commodity? What if they cannot carry a foetus to full term because of poor health?

Similarly, if one accepts that gender is a metaphor for relations of power, how do we define power? do all men have power? Do some women have power? How are the people with the most power socially constructed? In many African societies, power is not only vested in political organizations. Women can derive power from their position in religious systems, in female secret societies such as the Sande of Sierra Leone and Liberia as well as through their roles as mothers, especially when the society is matrilineal and has matrifocal ideologies.

The post-modernist challenges of the 80s by feminist scholars of the South included serious critiques of methodologies which questioned the right of Western feminists to assume dominance on feminist discourses. They also questioned their essentializing proclivities without regard to race, nationality and so forth. Mohanty, following others, also questioned the production of "Third World Women" as a homogeneous category in Western feminist texts and as subaltern subjects (Mohanty, 1985). A major critique along this line also centered on the essentialist proclivity of lumping all women in one basket without clarifying who is being spoken about and who is speaking for whom, or who has greater credibility in framing the issue (Nnaemeka, 1998).

Problems of framing are also problematic when filtered through the racist and sexist biases. For example, Narayan, writing on women of India challenges the tendency to use so called "cultural" explanations of practices like sati and dowry murders in India while ignoring murders due to domestic violence in the United States. This has led to the visibility of dowry murder in India and to the comparative invisibility of domestic violence murders in the United States. (Narayan, 1997; 95)

While not condoning harmful cultural practices with patriarchal origins, genital surgical interventions in Africa have been over sensationalized. African women are presented as savages or damaged victims worthy of nothing better than scorn. At the same time, harmful plastic surgery to reconstruct healthy vaginas, breasts and other body parts in the West are ignored. Also ignored, is the fact that they are also responding to cultural dictates that define the ideology of womanhood. Western plastic surgery, as Foucault would put it, is an example of "docile bodies" succumbing to the coercive pressures of Western patriarchal culture (Foucault, 1992).

b. African Women and the "Gender" Problematique

The term "gender" is a highly contested concept when applied to Africa. "Gender" has become the main focus of Western feminist discourse during the second wave of feminism. Like other systems of thought it has been exported to the South as a concept, an analytical tool and as a policy initiative. The domination of Western concepts and terminologies has thus become apparent in the term "gender." It is well established in development circles of the United Nations which in turn influences the agenda and budget of national governments and even academic research.

In 1981, I pointed out in the introduction to the book **The Black Woman Cross-Culturally,** that within a racist polical/economic hegemony, White women can become primary oppressors. It is now widely accepted that women are a nonessentialist category and represent diverse groups with different social locations. "Gender" can therefore mean different things to different people since it carries the ideologies of the socio-cultural context in in which it is constructed.

Without doubt, the term "gender" carries a Western bias. It tends to be myopic, inventive, and can obscure other differences. Because it is Western, it reveals white Western middle-class biases and obscures other differences based on race, class, ethnicity, religion, sexuality and so forth. In this regard, it fails to recognize the role of women themselves in other structures of oppression.

"Gender" is analogous to difference but contains within it notions of inequality and is often viewed as a metaphor representing relations of power. However, analysis of power is often restricted to male/female power relations only, ignoring power relations based on race, class, ethnicity, age, nationality and so forth. Thus the various ways in which gender has been used, namely, as a basis organizing principle of society; as a heuristic tool, as a crucial site for the application of dichotomous models and as an indicator of progress in the development process have to be questioned.

Furthermore, the term "gender" tends to represent a proclivity towards dichotomous models that do not often fully represent the African reality, although exceptions can be found. For example, a study of cultural boundaries and social interactions in Africa has argued that trans-social and transactional cultural flows are inherently gendered and that gender is a crucial site of intersection between "inside" and "outside" (Grosz-Ngate and Kobole, eds., 1999: 8).

c. Two Major Examples Challenging the Concept of "Gender" in Africa

African societies are complex and recognize exceptions to general normative rules. They use other concepts that convey a cyclical ordering of social life in addition to oppositional and hierarchical ones or on ones based on biological classification. For an example, changes in the lifecycle can alter women's status so that post-menopausal women can assume political functions and serve as elders and advisers on the same basis as men.

Similarly, female ancestors can share equal status with male ancestors. Moreover, "third genders" "agendered and trans-gendered entities" and "alternative genders" have been discovered in many parts of the non-Western world. In Africa, institutions such as "woman marriage" and the ambiguity of the gender of some deities have challenged the dichotomous model of the West.

Major challenges of the term "gender" have come from African women, the most celebrated of whom are Amadiume and Oyěwùmí. Amadiume's book, **Male Daughters, Female Husbands** was ground breaking in deconstructing the word "gender" in the Igbo context. In her analysis of sex-gender distinctions, she exposes what she described as the racism and ethnocentrism of earlier studies of Igbo society by Western scholars. She convincingly demonstrates how misleading biological categories can be in studying sex and gender since either sex can assume socially viable roles as male or female.

Oyěwùmí in **The Invention of Women,** further challenges the heavy reliance of Western scholarship on what is seen "world view" rather than what is perceived through other senses "world sense." She argues that although "gender" is deemed to be socially constructed, biology itself is socially constructed and therefore inseparable from the social". Hence the separation between "sex" and "gender" is superficial since "sex" itself has elements of construction. She insists that this "biologization" inherent in the Western articulation of social difference is by no means universal. Through imperialism it has been imposed on other cultures resulting in the imposition of the term "gender" which, being socially constructed, may not have existed at all in some societies.

She argues that "Gender" has become important in Yoruba studies not as an artifact of Yoruba life but because Yoruba life, past and present, has been translated into English to fit the Western pattern of body-reasoning. This pattern is one in which gender is omnipresent, the male the norm, and the female the exception; it is a pattern in which power is believed to inhere in maleness in and of itself. It is a pattern that is not grounded in evidence" (Oyěwùmí, p. 30).

Oyěwùmí agues that in the written discourse of the Yoruba gender is privileged over seniority only because of Western dominance in the conceptualization of research problems and in social theory. In Yoruba society, seniority takes precedence over gender and many Yoruba such as *oba* or *alafin* nouns are genderfree. The creation of "woman" as a category was one of the very first accomplishments of the colonial state since in precolonial societies, male and female had multiple identities that were not based on anatomy. "For females, colonization was a two-fold process of racial inferiorization and gender subordination" (Oyěwùmí, p. 124).

V. THE NEED FOR ALTERNATIVE AFRICAN-FOCUSED METHODOLOGIES

There is a need to critique and challenge the Eurocentric models in the study of women in Africa. Since most models are linked to political conquest through colonialism and corporate conquest through globalization, oppositional discourses inherent in various forms of Marxism, post-structuralism, post-colonialism and postmodernism are still relevant to African gender research.

Such approaches will of necessity have to include one or more of the following: a historical perspective, a holistic perspective, multidimensionality, multiple time frames, multiple levels of analysis, multiple identities and realities, relational and dynamic contexts, comparative methods, oral history, life history and so forth.

The need to link theory and praxis is essential. Given the empirical reality of poverty, economic exploitation and marginality, theory for the majority of Africans is a luxury. The thrust towards praxis will expose and centralize invisibility, voicelessness and autogenic social processes need to act and change retrograde developments. It will also help to reconcile universal and post-modernist tensions.

VI. African-Focused and Gender-Sensitive Approaches

One of the major constraints to gender research in Africa is the weak data base and the lack of a critical mass of gender researchers due to the low priority given to social science research and to the brain drain. The challenge is greater than the resources and available capacity. For example, African research on gender has to develop methodologies for criticisms and revisionist endeavours as well as methodologies for alternative research. The same standards for date gathering procedures that will satisfy the basic scientific requirements of validity, reliability and replicability have to be applied. Added to this will be new methods related to language and to indigenous systems of thought so that the framing of gender will be determined within the context of the relationship of language to culture.

Crucial to the redefining of an alternative approach to research from an African perspective will be the following: Policy-orientation; Viewpoint and value orientations, time orientation, geographical orientation, levels of analysis and an emphasis on culture. All of these factors will be conditioned by the type problem to be investigated, the kinds of data available, research instruments to be employed and the need to prioritize the research problems to be investigated (Steady, 1977).

Given the diversity of Africa, theoretical applications have to be developed through dynamic, multi-dimensional and heterogeneous methodological approaches and adjusted for contextual validity. However, it is quite legitimate to speak of an African perspective or an African reality even if only one or two African countries are indicated. This type of typological projection can become a valid heuristic tool. When one speaks of Eurocentric models, one does not have to indicate which particular European country or people is being referred to.

a. Policy Orientation

Western scholarship places a high value on theorizing and theory-building at the expense of pragmatism and relevance. Hence higher prestige is given to theoreticians. For Africa, there are many economic and social problems, not least of which is its dependency on the West and its marginalization through globalization, which theory cannot solve. Lack of interest in practical problems has been shown to lead to an insensitivity to the people studied and to an emphasis on professional advancement by the researcher.

Over 40 years ago, a European scholar Galtung in referring to what he called "scientific colonialism" compared the researcher who extracts data for professional profit to the colonialist who exports the resources out of Africa. In the following analogy, he demonstrates a parallel between the two systems of extraction and processing:

"...to export data about the country to one's own country for processing into manufactured goods, such as books and articles....is essentially similar to what happens when raw materials are exported at a low price and reimported as manufactured goods at a very high cost. The most important, most rewarding and most difficult phase of the process take place abroad" (Galtung, 1967: 296).

b. Critique of Donor-Driven Research

Given the ideological nature of development policies in Africa that are often driven by the neo-liberal agenda and the dictates of globalization the research agenda on gender tends to be determined by external priorities and policy orientations that reinforce the re-colonization of African social science. Donor-driven research can also undermine academic programmes if the faculty is motivated by the pursuit of funds for research especially in light of the economic difficulties of the continent and the low salaries of faculty. African researchers have to be critical of donor-driven and donor-sponsored research. Particular attention must be paid to various projects sponsored by international donor agencies and to certain types of externally designed research. Some research on health care, nutrition, agricultural production, migration and education may be designed to promote neo-liberal policies related to making African markets and labour more accessible to exploitation.

External gender research priorities can also center around concerns with fertility regulation, female circumcision, rather than to the global economic forces and liberalization policies that result in increasing malnutrition and poverty. Nor is enough attention being given to the dumping of guns, other lethal weapons, drugs, pornographic material and dirty technologies in Africa. Little interest is also shown in the illegal trafficking of young girls from Africa to Europe to be used as prostitutes and domestic servants under slavery-like conditions. The destructive impact of debt, structural adjustment policies, unemployment, export-oriented industries, sex tourism and so forth are often also overlooked.

c. Social Impact and Basic Research

Social impact research is critical. A number of studies can be conducted as intensive micro-level studies for purposes of evaluating the impact of "development projects in small communities." Although a number of international projects have an evaluation component built in, such an evaluation need not have local input and may reflect the vested interest of certain interest groups abroad. It is important that evaluative research be given a high priority by African social scientists.

Micro-level research can also be conducted as basic research that can have policy implications. Intensive research, using both qualitative and quantitative methods can be most useful and yield relevant information from which valid conclusions can be drawn. Intensive social surveys can provide useful information about food distribution, income distribution and demographic changes and can provide a good profile of the health status of a community. For example, it can lead to a clearer evaluation of the fertility rates in a given country by taking cognizance of factors such as infertility, infant mortality and mortality from the HIV/AIDS epidemic as well as fertility. Governments will then be presented with realistic projections on which to base a population policy.

d. Viewpoint and Value Orientation

The researcher is not a neutral observer. He or she brings existentialist limitations to the scholarly endeavour. The values and biases of the researcher are inevitably injected into the research. A researcher has a certain obligation to become involved in the realities and problems of the "subjects" under study. Research in Africa has to be geared towards a certain degree of involvement and intersubjectivity. The aim should be to contribute to improving the life of the people studied rather than to exploit them for professional advancement. Very often there is an indifference and a patronizing attitude to the "subjects" of research, especially when the researcher is a foreigner with vested professional interests outside of Africa. Very few researchers bring back to the community the results of their study or give anything back. The subject/object or insider/outsider dichotomy is increasingly being challenged by both Western and scholars from the South. Most scholars of the South now insist the study of culture from the inside by an insider.

The overriding problem facing Africa today is that of the destruction of African societies by forces of corporate globalization resulting in poverty, illiteracy and disease. The major mission of an scholarly endeavour in the social sciences should be the elimination of the conditions that produce massive poverty and human misery among the masses of African people. The new researcher has to be involved in improving the well being of African people. Involvement would necessitate abandoning the subject/object dichotomy of social science to one of "intersubjectivity" more akin to an indigenous model with elements of advocacy, protest and social engineering. Such approaches will also of necessity be multidisciplinary, policy-oriented as well as participatory both on the side of the researcher and of the people being studied. The aim would be to dymystify the research process itself since data gathering procedures will be linked to problem solving and can be participatory.

Quantitative and mathematical research instruments designed for use in more technologically complex societies may have limited relevance when applied to Africa. They may also be more prone to bias due to the variability of the research capacity and data base. Research instruments, data-collecting and data-analyzing procedures have to be sensitively designed and made uncomplicated to encourage participation and involvement and to have practical relevance. Research methodology from an African perspective has to be partisan i.e. dedicated to the progress and advancement of the African people. An appropriate value orientation would lead to research formulations and projects that aim to be action and policy oriented, problem solving and focused on the improvement of the African condition.

e. Time Orientation

Emphasis should be given to an analysis of social processes on a continuum that will involve the past, the present and the future. A historical perspective will be essential in understanding the role of conquest and colonization in shaping the themes and trajectory of research in Africa as well as in developing new forms of colonization such as corporate globalization. Urbanization and social change will be seen, not as inevitable processes of modernization but as a distortion of African indigenous development through economic domination. The African worldview encompasses dimensions of the past, present and future. Stated simply, the dead, the living and those yet to be born are essential for maintaining cosmological balance. This balance has been destabilized and has important gender implications leading to a loss of social status for women not only in the political and economic spheres but also in the realm of ritual and religion.

f. Geographical Orientation: Incorporating the African Diaspora

African is no longer confined to its geographical entity. The Transatlantic slave trade led to the dispersal of Africans on a massive scale. Today, Africans move as migrants, refugees and international civil servants to all parts of the world. The study of Africa must now include "Global Africa" in all its historical, socio-cultural, political and economic dimensions. In a book I edited recently, this concept was central to an analysis of Black Women of Africa and the African Diaspora within the current international economy. I advanced the notion of African Feminism as a theory and praxis for the liberation of African women from gender-based discrimination compounded by racism, the legacy of colonialism, and the injustices of the international political economy.[2]

g. Levels of Analysis

A useful orientation in terms of level of analysis is one that combines both macro- and micro-levels of analysis within a given national or international boundary. This orientation can be used to demonstrate the larger systems of interaction that exist between the rural area and the urban area. Thus, rural and urban areas can be seen as systems in a larger framework rather than as fossilized units presented in monographs. This perspective of rural/urban interaction is missing in most studies of Africa. The interconnectedness of phenomena across broad spatial domains has also been absent from most studies of African urbanization.

Orientations that show dynamic interactions rather than atomized unitary systems are essential to understanding the fluidity of the African social situation requiring linkages among the political, economic and cultural systems as well as geographical linkages between rural and urban areas and even between countries and sub-regions. This orientation will also facilitate pan-African research and the strengthening of African research networks designed to build capacity for indigenous research in which similar problems can be examined in a number of countries in Africa.

A continuum must also be maintained between the macro- and micro level and the holistic and particular. In our attempt to understand the position of African societies within the international economic system and the historical conditions that have shaped the relationship of inequality between the rich and the poor nations, a macro-level perspective of global dimensions is a useful one. Here we will need to re-examine neo-Marxist methodology in the context of Africa. Its theoretical and political significance as it affects social science research ought to be given greater attention. This will lead to an understating of how forms of imperialist domination affect a country in terms of means of production, property ownership and the relationship between class, gender and the family.

We need to study the relationship of imported ideologies, religions, educational systems and other aspects of the superstructure to the oppression of the African masses. The South has produced eminent scholars who have articulated this view. The research efforts of African scholars must continue to study the theoretical and political implication of oppositional discourses and methodologies in the context of Africa.

h. An Emphasis on Culture

Culture is a collective pattern of living that conveys the norms and values of society that is handed down from generation to generation. It is both dynamic and resilient and has positive, negative and neutral attributes. The study of African cultures have to include an inquiry into the continuities of gender discrimination and to determine where the cultural, historical, gendered and racial markers uphold, distort and undermine the "real" and the "authentic."

Because culture represents routine behavior that carry norms and values of a society, they are often not easily changed. Okeke has argued against the tendency to regard gender discrimination inherent in cultural practices as being acceptable because it is the "tradition." She shows how patriarchal continuities, even when they contain contradictions can support claims of the rightness of tradition. For an example, the contradictions between statutory and customary law and the weaknesses in statutory law can lead to the strengthening of traditional justifications that still privilege men in relation to property rights, inheritance laws, etc. This can result in "relations of power which keep in place an inequitable social structure that privileges the dominant gender" (Okeke, 2000: 6).

Essed in her study of gendered racism in Europe has shown how everyday racism is the interweaving of racism in the routine of day to day life, in a way that makes racial injustices seem normal and a part of what can be expected. She notes that the focus on everyday manifestation of systemic inequality extends outside the field of race relations as well. This contributed to granting "the everyday" generic meaning, "everyday inequalities, everyday sexism" (Essed, 2002: 210).

An examination of the role of gender in the socio-cultural construction of hierarchies and hierarchy sustaining structures has to continue as an important research agenda for African social science. For example, the gender implications of the legacies of colonialism, apartheid and racism have only been systematically studied within the last 20 years. We still do not have comprehensive studies of the role of gender as a central aspect of armed conflict, civil wars and the erosion of the African state.

Gender-based analyses are also important in our understanding of the patriarchal myth which is being sustained by forces of globalization that privilege men in cases of privatization of land, liberalization of markets, etc. and can lead to alliances among men that ordinarily would be enemies on the basis of East/West, North/South and White/Non-White divisions.

Culture has valuable and positive assets and provide effective models for gender research that can lead to the empowerment and advancement of African women. African feminism as defined in 1981 outlined the value of African women in the ideological, institutional and customary realms. Women's power bases are partly derived from cultural values that stress the potency of a female principle governing life and reproduction though motherhood and the centrality of children. Women can also control political and ritual spaces. Women's indigenous groups can provide important leveraging mechanisms for women and are instrumental in promoting sustainable development projects. So rather than dismiss African cultures as archaic, we need to conduct more studies using culture as the paradigmatic framework that has the potential of producing action-oriented research capable of transforming society and empowering women.

VII. THE CONTINUING RELEVANCE OF OPPOSITIONAL DISCOURSES: THE POLITICAL ECONOMY PARADIGM

The major problem confronting most women in Africa today is poverty. This compounds their lack of access to strategic resources, facilities, basic literacy and economic and political decision-making. In addition, they are faced with health and nutritional problems, including the HIV/AIDS epidemic and deteriorating environments that can no longer sustain them. In order to fully comprehend and address the deepening poverty in Africa, a comprehensive study is needed of the causes consequences of poverty and its chronic and protracted nature in the African context. Analysis of the conditions and processes involved in the production, reproduction of poverty and its structural nature must be conducted in its spatial and temporal context as well as from a cross-cultural perspective within Africa.

Globalization facilitates the movement of capital across national boundaries and is characterized by a deepening of markets across borders aided by communication technologies, international laws and the monitoring role of the World Trade Organization. It affects countries differently and uses traditional institutions, the informal labor market and women's labor to facilitate the process of forging a "single market" dominated by the North. While some countries are experiencing growth and market integration, others, like those in the South, especially Africa are being marginalized. The term "a market apartheid" has been applied to this process. Inequality has increased between and within countries. Even the World Bank, one of the sponsors of globalization paints a dismal picture.

"One sixth of the world's population produce 78% of the world's goods and services and get 78% of the world's income, an average of $70 per day. Three-fifths of the world's people in the six poorest countries receive 6% of the world's income; less than $2 a day. However, this poverty goes beyond income. While 7 out of 1,000 children die before age 5 in high-income countries, more than 90 out of 1,000 die in low-income countries."[3]

The Human Development Report of 1999 showed an increase in inequality between countries. Within the past decade, the number of individuals in Eastern Europe and Central Asia living on less than U.S.$1 rose to 13 million. The corresponding number of 35 million in South Asia and in sub-Saharan Africa, the number actually tripled to 39 million...[4] One can only imagine the gender implications when compounded with gender-based discrimination. Macro economic policies often makes gender disaggregated impacts difficult to assess because of the way in which they are conceptualized and the focus on official policy rather than the realities on the ground.

The World Bank figures are even higher and show that between 1987 and 2000, the number of people living on $1 or less (65 cents) a day increased by more than 80 million in sub-Saharan Africa. According to Dembele, "One of the most dramatic impacts of trade and investment liberalization in Africa has been the weakening, even the collapse of many African states. Among the factors that contributed to this collapse are the huge revenue losses, resulting from sweeping trade and investment liberalization" (Dembele, 2002: 78). African countries experience huge losses in revenues from import taxes from which they derive 90 per cent of their fiscal revenues. The losses have meant greater dependence of up to 80 per cent of their budget on external sources.

In spite of these grim realities, the policy preference for the international community controlled by the North and the IMF and World Bank, the major international financial institutions is to develop strategies for poverty reduction within the context of the market and the instruments of liberalization and privatization. The mantra is "trade not aid." Free trade is now well recognized as being anything but free, and trade liberalization is viewed as a major contributor to poverty in Africa with serious gender implications. According to Dembele, sub-Saharan Africa is the only region in the world where poverty has steadily increased during the last two decades and all development indicators reveal a continuing deterioration. Trade liberalization is a major contributor to this human crisis.

The political economy approach offers one of the best explanatory models for full understanding of the political economy of African countries that is shaping gender relations. According to Pheko, multilateral financial institutions are forcing insidious policies of liberalization and globalization, market ascendancy and the diminished roles of the state, that have been unsuccessful in industrialized countries. She urges African women to be aware of the dangers of trade liberalization and resist it. The role of gender research and gender researchers as activists in this process is crucial since privatization and the private sector are notoriously gender biased. The public sector has been the most advantageous for women's formal sector employment but Structural Adjustment Policies mandate retrenchment in the public sector and cut backs in the social sector, such as health and education, that are of extreme importance to women.

"As women, we need to continue applying a gender analysis to all trade agreements and globalization processes. The human rights analysis should also be applied while strong South/South dialogue among women should be promoted, especially regarding the impact of international trade and macroeconomic policies, in particular, their formulation and implementation. African women should also call into question, the liberalization and globalization agenda by building civil society's understanding of the issues and by bringing about mass mobilization in a global, regional and coordinated fashion" (Pheko, 2002: 105).

VIII. CONCLUSION

African feminist inquiries have articulated the strong link between Western neoliberalism and European domination that are implicated in colonial oppression and corporate globalization and bolstered by racist ideologies and institutions.

There is a need for a revisionist analysis of external concepts, canonical theories, methodologies and paradigms that have distorted gender studies in Africa. There is also a need to critically examine gendered readings of mainstream research of the West in the fields of science, history, the social sciences and the academy from an African perspective. There is also a need for an African feminism that will reflect the paradigmatic complexity of gender research in Africa.

African feminism, as I define a brand of it, operates within a global political economy in which sexism cannot be isolated from the larger political economy and economic processes responsible for the exploitation and oppression of both men and women. The result is kind of feminism that is transformative in human and social rather than in personal, individualistic and sexist terms (Steady, 1981). Given this orientation, the following are among important research questions to be asked.

- How does an academic context shaped by the injustices of the Transatlantic Slavery, colonialism and imperialism and justified by racist and sexist stereotypes and myths about Africa and Africans, affect gender research in Africa?
- How relevant is the Eurocentric search for universal women's oppression when other forms of oppression based on race, nationalism, ethnicity, class and so forth and by the global economy of whole nations and peoples threaten the very existence of most Africans?
- How do the pressures of globalization and the market economy impact on social institutions such as marriage, the family, male/female relations and positive and negative cultural practices?
- How has the donor community influenced the research agenda of Africa and distorted African realities based on preconceived assumptions and biases?
- How do we deepen our understanding of the importance of matrifocal traditions of Africa of which Diop wrote and the dynamic interplay between these traditions and patriarchal systems, especially the modernization of patriarchal domination through globalization?
- How is the link between women's roles in production and reproduction significant in understanding the continuities between the public and the private spheres and in the context of a rapidly changing political economy and a socio-cultural crisis of major proportions?
- How are gender relations in the domestic sphere supporting or impeding women's decision-making and control over their lives?
- To what extent are African womens' bodies becoming commercialized, and a potential target for trafficking and violence, in the age of globalization?
- How is the HIV/AIDS epidemic affecting notions of sexuality, fertility, gender relations, well-being and collective survival in Africa?

NOTES

1. See Diop, 1974 and Bernal, 1987 for challenges to these positions.
2. See Steady, 1981, 1987, 2000, 2001, 2002).
3. World Bank, 2000, *World Development Indicators, 2000,* New York, OUP.
4. UNDP, 1999, Human Development Report, New York, UNDP.

BIBLIOGRAPHY

Amadiume, I. 1987, *Male Daughters, Female Husbands: Gender and Sex in an African Society,* London, Zed Books.

Amadiume, I. 1997, *Reinventing Africa: Matriarchy, Religion and Culture,* London, Zed Books.

Amin, S. 1974, *Accumulation on a World Scale: A Critique of the Theory of Underdevelopment,* New York, Monthly Review Press.

Amin, S. 1997, *Capitalism in the Age of Globalization: The Management of Contemporary Society,* London, Zed Press.

Asante, M. 1990, *Kemet: Afrocentricity and Knowledge,* New Jersey, Africa World Press.

Bernal, M. 1987, *Black Athena: The Afroasiatic Roots of Classical Civilization,* New Brunswick, Rutgers University Press.

Boserup, E. 1970, *Women's Role in Economic Development,* London, George Allen and Urwin.

Dembele, M. 2002, "Trade Liberalization and Poverty in sub-Saharan Africa" in F. C. Steady, ed. *Black, Women, Globalization and Economic Justice: Studies from Africa and the African Diaspora,* Rochester, Schenkman Books.

Diop, C. 1974, *The African Origin of Civilization: Myth and Reality.* Translated from French by Mercer Cook, New York, L. Hill.

Essed, Ph. 1990. *Understanding Everyday Racism: An Interdisciplinary Theory,* Newbury Park, CA. Sage.

Essed, P. 2002, "Gendered Racism in Diasporic Locations: Opposition and the Use of Eyewitness Testimonies in Global Struggles" in F. C. Steady, ed. *Black Women, Globalization and Economic Justice: Studies from Africa and the African Diaspora,* Rochester, Schenkman Books.

Etienne, M. and Leacock, E. eds. 1980, *Women and Colonization: Anthropological Perspectives,* New York, Praeger.

Fall, Y. ed. 1999, *Africa: Gender, Globalization and Resistance,* Dakar, AAWORD.

Foucault, M. 1992, *The Archeology of Knowledge and the Discourse on Language,* New York, Pantheon.

Galt, A and Smith, L. 1976, *Models and the Study of Social Change,* London, John Wiley and Sons.

Galtung, J.1967, "After Camelot" in I. Horowitz, ed. *The Rise and Fall of Project Camelot,* Cambridge, M.I.T. Press.

Grosz-Nagate, M and Kobole, O. eds. 1997, *Gendered Encounters: Challenging Cultural Boundaries and Social Hierarchies in Africa,* New York, Routledge.

Imam, A., and Mama, A. and Sow, F. eds. 1997, *Engendering African Social Sciences,* Dakar, CODESRIA

Macquet, J. 1964, "Objectivity in Anthropology" *Current Anthropology,* vol. 5: 47–55.

Mohanty, C. "Under Western Eyes" in C. Mohanty, A. Russo, L. Torres, eds. *Third World Women and the Politics of Feminism,* Bloomington and Indianapolis, Indiana University Press.

Narayan, U. 1997, "Cross-Cultural Connections, Border-Crossings," and 'Death by Culture: Thinking About Dowry-Murders in India and Domestic-Violence Murders in the United States" in U. Narayan, 1997, *Dislocating Cultures: Identities, Tradition and Third World Feminism,* New York, Routledge.

Nnaemeka, O. ed. 1998, *Sisterhood, Feminisms and Power: From Africa to ... the Diaspora,* Trenton, Africa World Press, Inc.

Okeke, P. 2000, "Reconfiguring traditional women's rights and social status in contemporary Nigeria" in *Africa Today,* Bloomington, Winter, 2000.

Oyěwùmí, O. 1997, *The Invention of Women: Making an African Sense of Western Gender Discourse:* Minneapolis, University of Minnesota Press.

Owusu, M, ed. *Colonialism and Change,* Essays presented to Lucy Mair, The Hague, Mouton, 1975.

Pettman, J. 1996, *Worlding Women: A Feminist International Politics,* London, Routledge.

Pheko, M. 2002, "Privatization, Trade Liberalization and Women's Socio-Economic Rights: Exploring Policy Alternatives" in F. C. Steady, ed. *Black Women, Globalization and Economic Justice: Studies from Africa and the African Diaspora,* Rochester, Schenkman Books.

Rodney, W. 1981, *How Europe Underdeveloped Africa,* Washington, D.C. Howard University Press.

Sen, G. and Grown, C. 1986, *Development, Crises and Alternative Visions: Third World Women's Perspectives,* New York, Monthly Review Press.

Steady, F. C. 1977, "Research Methodology from an African Perspectives" in *Echo,* Dakar, AAWORD.

Steady, F. C. ed. 1981, *The Black Women Cross-Culturally,* Cambridge, Schenkman Publishing Company.

Steady, F. C. 1987. "African Feminism: A Global Perspective" in R. Terborg-Penn and A. Rushing eds. *Women of the African Diaspora: An Interdisciplinary Perspective,* Washington, D.C. Howard University Press.

Steady, F. C. 2001, *Women and the Amistad Connection: Sierra Leone Krio Society,* Rochester, Schenkman Books.

Steady, F. C. ed. 2002, *Black Women, Globalization and Economic Justice: Studies from Africa and the African Diaspora,* Rochester, Schenkman Books.

U.N.D.P. 1999, *Human Development Report,* New York, U.N.D.P.

World Bank, 2000, *World Development Indicators, 2000,* New York, Oxford University Press.

CHAPTER 18

THE *YUM*: AN INDIGENOUS MODEL FOR SUSTAINABLE DEVELOPMENT

Bertrade B. Ngo-Ngijol Banoum

INTRODUCTION

In the early 1990s, Bogso, a village of approximately 2500 inhabitants, located in the southern part of Cameroon, in Central Africa, was in the midst of a protracted social and economic crisis. In the face of pervasive food shortages, the Bogso peasant women, whose primary economic activity is subsistence hoe agriculture, resorted to the traditional philosophy of *Yum*, a system whereby community members do agricultural work collectively on plots of land belonging to individual members of the group. To carry forward their plan, these women, under the leadership of Teclaire Ntomp, a retired teacher, organized the Group of Common Initiative of Bogso Women Farmers (GICBAP, a French acronym), to increase the cultivation and production of cassava[1] in their village.

PROCESS AND TOOLS

The *Yum* is a form of indigenous community mobilizing and organizing rooted in the ancestral culture of solidarity that has driven endogenous development of African societies in the past. The *Yum* philosophy comes alive in the form of women's labor collectives: During the agricultural

[1] Cassava—yucca/manioc—is a tuber crop that originated in South America and is a staple in most parts of the tropic. Its massive leaf production drops to form organic matter, which recycles nutrients into the soil. Cassava thus requires little or no fertilization and produces steadily over a fairly long period. The perennial plant produces bulky roots with heavy concentration of carbohydrates, while the shoot grows into leaves that constitute a good vegetable, rich in proteins, vitamins, and minerals. When properly processed, cassava leaves and roots provide a balanced diet for millions across the globe. The location of Bogso in a forested area with sandy soil is an ideal setting for the cultivation of cassava.

season, the peasant women move from farm to farm, helping one another to tend their land and crops. Following an agreed-upon rotation schedule, the group holds "hoeing parties" to help cultivate, plant, or, later in the growing season, to weed and harvest the individual members' fields. Within the *Yum*, women are at the forefront of people's mobilisation for collective action to alleviate poverty and secure sustainable livelihoods.

Impact and Sustainability

The GICPAB initiative has had to overcome significant obstacles including social customs, structural hierarchies, leadership issues, and religious practices that impede agricultural expansion. Working previously uncultivated land with machetes and hoes alone has proved extremely difficult as has transporting harvested produce on people's heads over long-distances paths to bring it to market. Processing produce has also been labour-intensive, due to lack of adequate technology. The group also needs literacy and skills training in income management, as well as information technology, to enhance communication. Despite these difficulties the *Yum* has allowed Bogso women to pool together resources and maximise outcomes.

Sustainable cassava farming within the *Yum* cooperative has far exceeded expectations. The women have expanded their farms, increased production of cassava, diversified their crops, sought out new markets, and increased their profits. The primary goal of securing food self-sufficiency for the Bogso community, has been achieved, with a surplus production for marketing. The *Yum* has also empowered the women tremendously, consolidating the community and allowing members to expand their activities into other arenas, including the economic, socio-cultural, and educational sectors, food security, primary health care, and youth safety. The GICPAB has set up a health center and a pharmacy, a library, water pumps, public latrines and wells, a local market, a public mill, a communal kitchen, and a canteen to provide the village children with a balanced meal every school day. The Bogso women have also published a collection of 22 cassava recipes in two local languages. This cookbook has now been translated into French and English allowing wider dissemination of knowledge and generation of income. A micro-credit system has been set up to facilitate income management. Improved economic opportunities and living standards have attracted young migrants who are returning from the city to live productively in the revitalized village. This redistribution of development has gone a long way toward restoring the rural women's self-confidence, and sense of self-worth. It is an invaluable asset both for the female peasants' self-empowerment and for the well-being of their families and community.

Partnerships, Replicability and Transfers

The women farmers' *Yum* initiative in sustainable cassava cultivation has made them a mentor and role model to many sister groups. Locally, they have organized numerous peer-learning fora with other rural community-based organizations and formed networks. Nationally, they have participated in workshops and seminars focusing on poverty eradication, local governance, and sustainable development. They have won several awards of excellence for their cassava recipe book, *Fighting Hunger with Cassava: A Gift of 22 Recipes from the Rural Women of Bogso.* Regionally, the GICPAB's success in curbing hunger and poverty in their community has earned the group membership with the Coalition Africaine sur la Securite Alimentaire et Developpement (COSAO) [African Coalition for Food Security and Development], and on the Committee charged with the follow-up of the World Food Summit.

Internationally, the group has participated in several global meetings, including the Women, Development and Public Policy symposium in Haifa, the Food and Agriculture Organization 5th Anniversary in Quebec, and the Hunger and Poverty Forum in Brussels, all held in 1995. In 2000, the Bogso peasant women were selected as one of only 94 Projects Around the World to be featured within the Basic Needs pavilion of the International Fair EXPO 2000 in Hanover, Germany. For three months from June to October, Cameroon cassava was showcased in a variety of recipes and presented to the international community. During a weeklong Grassroots Women's International Academy (GWIA) organized as part of EXPO 2000, the *Yum* philosophy behind the successful cassava campaign, as well as cassava cooking methods, were shared with other rural women from around the globe. The Bogso women farmers traveled back to Cameroon with an international award crowning all of them as "Cassava Queens." All the traditional kitchen utensils manufactured and used by the GICPAB during EXPO 2000 are presently showcased at the Museum of Nutrition in Barcelona, Spain.

LESSONS LEARNED

The *Yum* practice exemplifies the benefits of doing development from the ground up and from the inside out, with indigenous natural and human resources as the driving force. At the core are the Bogso rural women with their experience, expertise, and accumulated knowledge and wisdom. As experts in everyday life, they bring unique perspectives and insights grounded in indigenous knowledge, traditional practices, local institutions, and endogenous forces. Local initiatives by local people in touch with local realities and serving their community interests are rooted in people's assets, skills, and networks, indigenous cultural practices, and traditional knowledge bases. The *Yum* has proved a productive people-centered development strategy grounded in people's solidarity and participation. Adaptive strategies and organisational structures that people have developed themselves have the potential to lead to sustainable livelihoods. The *Yum* is more proof that collective action is at the heart of poverty eradication and sustainable human development.

The GICPAB's success around the *Yum* highlights the importance of building and strengthening people's personal, social, economic, political, and environmental assets. Also important are principled alliances, coalitions, and partnerships, not only locally but also nationally and internationally, through engagement of all stakeholders including academia, the media, governments, international agencies, non-governmental organizations, the private sector, foundations, and faith-based groups. All must be involved in partnerships to address human poverty in its diverse dimensions. Poor people bring certain advantages in terms of human and natural resources—a case in point is cassava farming within the *Yum* collective framework. But alone, however well organized, they cannot force policy shifts for poverty eradication and sustainable development. People's indigenous knowledge and adaptive strategies must be the starting point for goals to be realized through responsive policies, programs and projects, relevant research and scholarship, as well as appropriate technological support. The *Yum* people-centred model is an effective way of helping communities help themselves. The *Yum* resonates with the concept of human development as articulated in the first and eighth issues of the UNDP *Human Development Report*—a process of enlarging people's choices and enhancing the quality of their lives (1990, 1997). The *Yum* participatory processes and innovative practices also fit within the implementation of the Habitat Agenda and the Agenda 21.

The Bogso rural women's achievements and their representation in discussions of global affairs herald a new era of increased grassroots women's participation in the decision-making processes affecting their lives. These areas include advocacy in poverty eradication, participatory governance, and people-centered sustainable development.

The GWIA peer exchanges prove that the Bogso solidarity-driven initiative, rooted in the people's rich historical and socio-cultural heritage and enhanced by international support, is a workable model to be replicated, transferred and expanded. The participation of GICPAB in EXPO 2000 means that the *Yum*, as a successful development strategy locally, is becoming a development model globally.

REFERENCES

"Considerations de genre et apport des associations des femmes". Pauline Biyong & Teclaire Ntomp. Symposium, Mont Carmel-Centre International de Formation "Golda Meir", Haifa, Israel. 2–8 avril, 1995.

"Production alimentaire, l'apres recolte dans les villages, precedes et difficultes pour l'ecoulement des produits des centres ruraux vers les marches urbains". Teclaire Ntomp. World Assembly on Food Security. Quebec City, Canada. 8–9 October 1995.

"La lutte pour le developpement: la lecon de Bogso". Rose Don Zoa, in *Le Mouvement Paysan en Marche*. Fevrier 1996, p. 19.

"Toward Sustainable Food Security: Focus on Farmers", in *World Sustainable Agriculture Association Newsletter*. Spring. 1996, Vol. 5, No. 2, pp. 4–5 & 10.

"Grow Food Locally, Support Women Farmers, Says NGO Coalition". Veronica Shofftall. *One Country Newsletter of the Baha'i International Community.* July–September 1996, Vol.8, Issue 2.

"The Group of Common Initiative of the Women Farmers of Bogso (GICPAB)", in *The Emerging Role of NGOs in African Sustainable Development.* Scott Chaplowe & J. Patrick Madden. UN-NADAF. WSAA. 1996, pp. 61–62. Also in *For All Generations: Making World Agriculture More Sustainable*, 1997.

"The Group of Common Initiative of the Women Farmers of Bogso (GICPAB): The Fight Against Poverty in Cameroon Through Community Work: The *Yum*". Teclaire Ntomp.

Poverty Eradication in Africa: Selected Country Experiences. UN-OSCAL, 1997, pp. 68–72.

Fighting Hunger With Cassava: A Gift of 22 Recipes from the Rural Women of Bogso. Introduced, edited & translated by Bertrade B. Ngo-Ngijol Banoum. African Action on AIDS Inc. (AAA Inc.). 1998.

Activites du GICPAB de Bogso: Activites champetres et transformation du manioc, soins de sante et securite alimentaire, activites artisanale, environnementale, culturelle et economique, Photographic Essay. 1997. 1999. 2001.

"The Bogso Women Farmers' Best Practice: From Local *Yum* Organizing to Global Networking". Submitted to the GWIA Project Selection Panel. Bertrade B. Ngo-Ngijol Banoum. 2000.

UNDP. *Human Development Report.* New York: Oxford university Press. 1990. 1997.

Section VII

Critical Conversations

Knowledge building is a call-and-response undertaking. To that extent, it is necessary that scholarship attract critical attention that is an essential step in the quest to refine concepts and build theories. Ongoing conversations among scholars are needed if the field is to develop. The first two articles in this section should be read together, because one is a direct reaction to the other. In the piece titled "Epilogue: In my Father's House" which is indeed the closing chapter of his tome on Africa's philosophy of culture, Kwame Anthony Appiah used the death of his father and the occasion of his burial to examine personal and political issues of family, belonging, inheritance, identity, gender, and culture. Appiah raises questions about the meaning of family and the rights and obligation of family members by describing a situation in which the Akan family traditions of his father, which are based on matrilineal principles, clash with the customs of his English mother, which privilege patrilineal bonds.

In "Questions of Identity and Inheritance: A Critical Review of Kwame Anthony Appiah's In My Father's House," Nkiru Nzegwu responds to Appiah. She spotlights the multiple levels and variable conceptions of family underpinning Appiah's approach to culture in the book. But one family type looms large she tells us, in Appiah's thinking, in Ghanaian contemporary realities, and indeed in feminist and non-feminist scholarly discussions of gender: the nuclear family. Nzegwu deconstructs this normative family organization: its colonial origins, its ethnocentric and gender biases, and the havoc it is wreaking in postcolonial Africa.

In "African Gender Research and Postcoloniality: Legacies and Challenges," Desiree Lewis, presents a survey of research trends in the African gender literature. She identifies five rubrics under which much of the scholarship falls to date and finds all of them wanting. They are anthropological studies of women, developmentalist approaches, state and donor-driven initiatives, post-colonialism and African feminisms. Lewis concludes by drawing our attention to what she considers a positive paradigm shift in the works of feminists who are using a poststructuralist approach.

The final chapter "African Women in the Academy and Beyond: A Review Essay," is by Godwin Rapando Murunga. It is a review of three books on gender and African women in the academy, and in society. In a very focused reading, Muranga teases out the various challenges that race, gender and class inequalities impose on African women in their bid to represent themselves, and to be included as knowledge makers in the academy.

Chapter 19

In My Father's House: Epilogue

Kwame Anthony Appiah

Abusua do funu.
The matriclan loves a corpse. (Akan Proverb)

My father died, as I say, while I was trying to finish this book. His funeral was an occasion for strengthening and reaffirming the ties that bind me to Ghana and "my father's house" and, at the same time, for straining my allegiances to my king and my father's matriclan—perhaps, even tearing them beyond repair. When I last saw him alive, my father asked me to help him draft a codicil to his will describing his wishes for his funeral. I did not realize then that in recording these requests on his deathbed and giving them legal force, he was leaving us, his children, an almost impossible mission. For in our efforts to conduct the funeral in accordance with my father's desires—expressed in that codicil—we had to challenge, first, the authority of the matriclan, the *abusua*, of which my father was erstwhile head and, in the end, the will of the king of Ashanti, my uncle.

And in the midst of it—when partisans of our side were beaten up in my father's church, when sheep were slaughtered to cast powerful spells against us, when our household was convinced that the food my aunt sent me was poisoned—it seemed that every attempt to understand what was happening took me further back into family history and the history of Asante; further away from abstractions ("tradition" and "modernity," "state" and "society," "matriclan" and "patriclan"); further into what would probably seem to a European or American an almost fairytale world of witchcraft and wicked aunts and wise old women and men.

Often, in the ensuing struggles, I found myself remembering my father's parting words, years ago, when I was a student leaving home for Cambridge—I would not see him again for six months or more. I kissed him in farewell, and, as I stood waiting by the bed for his final benediction, he peered at me over his newspaper, his glasses balanced on the tip of his nose, and pronounced: "Do not disgrace the family name." Then he returned to his reading.

I confess that I was surprised by this injunction: so much an echo of a high Victorian paterfamilias (or perhaps of the Roman originals that my father knew from his colonial education in the classics). But mostly I wondered what he meant. Did he mean my mother's family (whose tradition of university scholarship he had always urged me to emulate), a family whose name I did not bear? Did he mean his own *abusua* (not, by tradition, my family at all) from which he had named me Anthony Akroma-Ampim? Did he mean his legal name, Appiah, the name invented for him when the British colonial authorities decided (after their own customs) that we must have "family" names and that the "family" name should be the name of your father? When your father's family tradition casts you into your matriclan and your mother's claims you for your father, such doubts are, I suppose, natural enough.

Pops, by contrast, was afflicted by no such uncertainties. He was the head of his matriclan, his *abusua*, the matriclan of Akroma-Ampim, for whom, as I say, I am named. In the autobiography that was his final gift us, he wrote:

> My matrilineal ancestors were among the very early Akans of the great Fl-uone (Bush Cow) clan which originally settled at Asokore, some twenty-six miles from Kumasi, long before Ashanti was created a nation by the great warrior-King, Osei Tutu and his great Priest Okomfo Anokye. In the course of time, some of my ancestors moved to Fomena and Adanse, where other members of the clan had settled earlier. Of the long line of ancestors, Akroma-Ampim ("the hawk is never impeded in its flight") and his sister Nana Amofa later joined this migration to Fomena and established the family reputation and themselves at Mfumenam in Adanse sometime well before the beginning of the nineteenth century. . . . Being a great warrior, Akroma-Ampim had acquired a thousand personal "slaves" as his reward for his valor in various wars. These were all men captured in battle and therefore a great asset to a warrior-adventurer. My ancestor settled these men at Mfumenam, a forest-belt on the Adanse side of the Offin River. Daily, he watched the vast unoccupied forest land on the other side of the great river, until his adventurous spirit decided him to cross over with his sister and men and to occupy it all. . . . All precautions against any eventuality having been taken, he and his brave band of one thousand set out to the new lands with his famous war fetish *Anhwere* and *Tano Kofi* being carried before him. . . . Satisfied with what he had acquired, he set out the boundaries and placed his war fetish *Tano Kofi* on the western end of the boundary. . . . This settlement was named "Nyaduoni" or the place of the garden eggs.[1]

But if he was clear that this was his family, he was clear, too, that we were his family, also. In a notebook that we found after he died, he had written a message to us, his children, telling us about the history of his *abusua*, of our mother's family, and of his father, of his hopes for us. And the tenderness of his tone was all the more striking since he wrote of his own father:

> I did not have the good fortune to know him as intimately as you have known me and this for two reasons; he was reserved and what's more, it was not then the custom here for a father to get too acquainted with his children for fear of breeding contempt.

In his autobiography, he also told us how he was acknowledged head of his *abusua* after the funeral of his predecessor (the man for whom I am also named, Yao Anthony, corrupted later to Yao Antony, anglicized on my British baptismal record to Anthony—dubbed the "Merchant Prince," a businessman who, though nonliterate managed a vast empire).

> The next day's ceremonies started at about 6 AM. Leading us—the elders, my sister, and I—was a man carrying the sacrificial lamb and a bottle of schnapps. A few yards only to the broad river. I saw a huge crocodile, mount fully open, dancing in circles in middle of the river. . . . The libation, was schnapps over, the oldest among the elders and I, holding two legs each, flung the sheep into the river, to be grabbed, happily for me, by the dancing crocodile. After three dives followed by a circular dance, the crocodile vanished, holding the sheep between its mighty jaws. Firing of musketry began, amid the singing of war songs, as we made the journey back home. I had been proved to be the rightful and true successor to my recently-deceased grand-uncle, in the long line to Akroma-Ampim. Now, every word of mine was an edict—never to be challenged so long as I breathed the breath of life.[2]

My father refound his family at the funeral of his great-uncle: at his funeral I learned more about that family and discovered the ways in which it was and was not mine.

In the codicil to his will, my father instructed his church and "my beloved wife, Peggy" to carry out all the rites in association with his funeral. Not much to notice in that, you might think, but, given the centrality of the *abusua* in Asante (a centrality so clearly displayed in my father's account of his origins) it is not surprising that by Asante custom the funeral is their business. In practice, this usually means the business of one's brothers and sisters (or the children of one's mother's sisters) along with one's mother and her sisters and brothers, if they are living. Since you belong to your mother's *abusua*, the widow and children belong to a different family from their husband and father. Of course, the widow and children of a dead man are part of the furniture of an Asante funeral. But they do not control it.

Naturally, in these circumstances, the codicil did not please the *abusua*. In particular, it displeased my father's sister, my aunt Victoria, and she and her brother Jojo were determined to wrest control of the funeral away from the church, the wife, and the children. Their displeasure was compounded by the inescapable publicity of my father's deathbed repudiation of them. For the funeral, as the leave-taking of a Ghanaian statesman, a brother-in-law of the king, a leading lawyer, a member of an important *abusua* was, inevitably, a public event. Through a long career in public life. Papa (or Paa) Joe, as he was known, was a well-known figure in Ghana. His gusts of eloquence in parliament, at public rallies, when he preached at church; his cantankerous resistance to government policies he disapproved of; his mischievous anecdotes: a hundred tales in a thousand mouths would surround his coffin. The services were an occasion for the cameras of national television; for articles in the Ghanaian newspapers that told familiar stories demonstrating his reputation for incorruptibility; for tales of the corruption he had rooted out, the legendary bribes he had scorned. There were long obituaries in the national and international press; later there were editorials about the funeral. Removing the *abusua* from normal control inevitably entailed an element of public disgrace.

Speculation about my father's motives in excluding his *abusua* from his obsequies was bound to run rampant. I speculated also, since he never explained his decision directly to me. Still, I knew, along with almost everybody in Kumasi, that he had had a dispute with my aunt over properties left to them and their sister Mabel in the will of my great-great-uncle, Yao Antony. We all also knew that my aunt had refused to come and make peace with her brother even on his deathbed.

My father felt strongly about his burial rites. In his autobiography, he wrote:

> The exhibition of dead bodies to all and sundry prior to burial and subsequent unnecessary and elaborate funeral celebrations have always distressed me; there-for, I solemnly request that these abominable trappings be avoided at my passing away. I wish my family and friends to remember me as I was before my demise and to clothe themselves in white instead of the traditional black and dark browns that portray man's inevitable transition as a gloomy specter.[3]

Despite my father's codicil, neither my mother not the church sought at first to exclude the *abusua* from the funeral arrangements. Rather, we hoped to include them in a public display of solidarity around the coffin. In retrospect, it seems altogether natural that our overtures to them were rebuffed. Whatever dates we suggested, for example, the *abusua* proposed others. The issue was not convenience but control.

Within a week of daddy's death, the world around us, it seemed, took sides. On the one hand, there were the church and its leaders, the Reverend Dr. Asante-Antwi, district chairman, and the Reverend Dr. Asante, pastor of the Wesley Methodist Church; and my sisters and myself. (So far as was possible, we kept my mother out of the dispute.) Since the church was professionally preoccupied with healing breaches, and I was my mother's eldest child and only son, the leadership of "our" side—insofar as it involved confrontation—devolved upon me. (Never concise a martilineal society with a society where women are in public control.)

Leading the opposing "side" was my father's sister, Victoria, whose husband is the Asantehene, our king. She is, perhaps, the most powerful person in the kingdom. (Never assume that individual women cannot gain power under patriarchy.) By the time we began to make arrangements, Auntie Vic had begun to mobilize the considerable power of the throne (or the "stool," as we say in Asante) in an attempt to wrest control of the funeral from us.

The immediate locus of debate seems trivial. We settled on Thursday, 26 July 1990, as the day for my father's burial, which was already eighteen days after his death. That meant Wednesday night would be the wake; Friday would be a day of rest; Saturday the *ayie*, the traditional Asante funeral; and Sunday the thanksgiving service. We were keen to get the funeral over with, in part because it seemed the longer we waited the more likely it was that the church would be forced to give in and let the *abusua* take over; in part, for sundry practical considerations; in part, for the normal reason that contemplating the funeral would continue, until it was over, to be a source of strain and distress. We had explained our reasons to the *abusua* on several occasions in several forums, and they seemed to have acquiesced. Then, the week before the burial was due, a message came summoning my sisters and me to a meeting at 11:00 A.M. in the palace of the king of Asante—the Asantehene—in his capital, our hometown, Kumasi.

The summons was not altogether surprising. We had begun to hear rumors that the Asantehene was objecting to the dates we had suggested because he was planning to celebrate the anniversary of his accession to the stool on Friday, 27 July, which would place it on the very next day after the burial.

Even if, as we suspected, the event had been created as a pretext, we had to take the matter seriously, because we knew the church would. We obeyed Nana's summons.[4]

We were accompanied to the palace by our father's best friend, Uncle T.D., a journalist, who had been with my father when he died. After being kept waiting for an interval (no doubt to establish who was in charge), we were summoned along with the church committee into the huge sitting room of the palace; it is enormous, with its two sitting areas, each centered on a giant Oriental rug and surrounded by expensive, mock-antique furniture that looks as though it came from Harrods in London (probably because it did). My uncle, Otumfuo Nana Opoku Ware the Second, Asantehene, was already seated across the room.

He was surrounded by the largest collection of courtiers I had ever seen in the palace. Seated in two ranks on his right were five or six linguists, led by Baffuor Akoto, who had been senior linguist for the last king. The Sanahene, chief of the treasury, and his colleague the Banahene were also present, and there were others I recognized but whose names I did not know. Behind the Asantehene and seated to his right was the Juabenhene, whose stool is the "uncle" of the Golden Stool. Nana Juabenhene was a schoolmate of mine in primary school and went on to study engineering at the Kumasi University of Science and Technology. Though, like me, he is in his midthirties, the seniority of his stool and its relation to the Asantehene mean that he is a very important chief. There were other chiefs around, including Nana Tafohene, chief of a town on the outskirts of Kumasi, a lawyer dressed in a formal suit that he had presumably been wearing in court that morning. To the left of the king (who had himself studied law in England), and a few feet away, sat my aunt, also on a thronelike chair. As we were about to begin, Uncle George, head of my grandfather's *abusua*, a son of the last king and henchman of my aunt's, arrived through the French windows to our right and sat down on a chair beside her.

On the sofas and chairs at right angles to them and to the king, facing the serried ranks of linguists and other courtiers, were the members of the church's funeral committee and the Reverends Asante-Antwi and Asante.

We came resolved not to let the church be pressured into changing what we had agreed. Naturally, we had no intention of being pressured ourselves. But this gathering of notables was impressive and designed to intimidate. According to custom, each time my uncle, the king, spoke, his senior linguist would address us with the formal version of his remarks in his beautiful courtly Twi. And as he spoke, he others would utter various words and noises to stress the key points: "*Ampa*" (That's true), three or four of them would say; or "*Hwiem!*"—a kind of auditory punctuation, an exclamation point, at the end of a significant utterance. (If you wanted to know where the tradition of the African-American church with its cries of "Testify!" comes from, you could start by looking here.)

Baffuor Akoto had clearly been prepared by the Asantehene for what he had to say. He explained to us, as we expected, the problem about the conflict with the anniversary. Nana obviously wanted to come to as many of the ceremonies in association with his brother-in-law's deaths as he could. But he could not come in the white cloth of celebration to a burial service, and he could hardly come in the cloth of mourning to celebrate his two decades on the stool. The timing was in the hands of the church. Nana did not ask us to change anything. He had called us only to let us know of this problem.

It was striking to me how, even in this display of power, Asante kingship operates nowadays (as, perhaps, it has always operated) by a kind of euphemism. There were no orders here; there was no acknowledgment of conflict. Nana would come to as much as he could of the funeral, we were told. Obviously, if we moved it, he could come to all of it. But the decision was up to us.

The church people tried to explain the reasoning behind the choice of dates, and they were interrupted from time to time by my aunt; she was rather less euphemistic in her demands. Why were they not willing to do this little thing for Nana?

The members of the church committee responded politely but with diminishing firmness to all the questions put to them; at a certain point, it seemed that they might be beginning to waver. We faced the prospect of a funeral delayed for weeks by my aunt, while she made efforts to undo the effects of my father's codicil.

As this spectacle continued, my sisters and I grew angry. Their murmuring in my ear became increasingly urgent. Finally, when indignation had turned into the unfamiliar emotion of rage, when the blood was pounding through my head, I could not take any more. This wrangling over my father's corpse (as it struck me) by people who had ignored his suffering when he was living, apparently without any concern for those of us who had loved and cared for him, was more than I could bear. If I believed in possession. I would say that I was possessed. Despite years of training in deference to Asante kingship and its institutions, I could not restrain myself. I stood up, the violence of my movement interrupting. I think, poor old Baffuor Akoto (a longtime friend and political ally of my father's), and I walked to the edge of the rug nearest the door, with my sisters gathered around me, before I spoke.

"Everybody here knows what is going on and my sisters and I are not going to sit here and let it happen. That woman," I said pointing at my aunt, "and that man," pointing now at her cohort Uncle George, "are trying to use Nana to get their way; to force the church to do what *they* want." We were not going to be party to such an abuse of the stool; we were leaving. By now my sisters were all in tears, shouting too at them, "Why are you doing this to us?"

Pandemonium broke out. Never, they told us later, in the history of the court had anyone walked out on the king. As we hurried out to our car, crowds of agitated courtiers streamed after us, preceded by Uncle T.D. "You can't go," he said. "You can't leave like this." My childhood friend, the Juabenhene, joined him. "You must come back. You owe it to Nana." I told him that I had indeed been brought up to respect the stool and its occupant; that I was still trying to do so, but that the stool was being "spoiled" by my aunt; and that after what I had seen today, it was hard for me to hold Nana himself in respect. Nana Juabenhene was sympathetic. "But," he insisted, "you cannot leave like this. You must return."

After a few minutes that passed like hours, we had recovered enough to reenter the palace. "Don't worry," Uncle T.D. said. "What you did will have helped. Now everyone will know how strongly you feel. But you must go back now and finish this."

When we entered and everyone was settled, Nana Tafohene rose on our right. He addressed Baffuor Akoto, as chief linguist, seeking pardon from Nana for the disgraceful exhibition that had just occurred. At the height of Nana Tafohene's peroration he remarked on my trespass: "Of course, we should beat him with rods of iron until he bleeds. But then," he added after a masterful pause, "he is our child, and we would only have to tend his wounds."

Then all of the church committee and the *abusua* (even my aunt) rose and begged on my behalf for forgiveness, bending the right knee, with a hand on it, and saying the traditional formula of apology: "*Dibim.*" I joined in, clumsily, at the urging of Uncle T.D. Has I disgraced the family name after all?

Nana spoke. "We have locked what happened here in a box and thrown away the key," he said. And he meant: the matter is closed.

He couldn't have been more wrong.

As we filed out into the sunlight and into our car, trying to calm down, preparing to leave, one of the palace servants slipped over to the car where we were seated. "Wayɛ *adeɛ*," he said, smiling and grabbing my hand—"You have done something," which is the Akan way of saying "Well done." He was not expressing hostility to the king: he was telling us that he, and many others around the palace, thought it was time someone told the king's wife to stop abusing Nana's power. He was speaking out of concern for the king and respect for the stool—and, perhaps, out of love for my father.

Within a few hours, people came to the house from all over town to ask for our version of what happened, and to say to me, "Wayɛ *adeɛ*." Some in the family suggested I would now be the obvious choice for a stool—chieftaincy—at the ancestral village of Nyaduom. (The fact that I did not belong to their *abusua* was brushed aside. It was as if for them I had become truly an Asante in the act of opposing Asante tradition.) They were claiming me back, claiming back the child they had known as one of their own. Curiously, to many, defiance at court made me something of a hero.

It was clear that many people wanted us to know that they disapproved of my aunt's campaign; they came with stories of how she had influenced Nana to make bad decisions in chieftaincy disputes; they implied that his decisions could be bought by paying off his wife. These were accusations I had never heard before; before, I had been one of her favorite nephews, her favorite brother's only son. Now that we were on opposite sides, I could hear these stories. True or not, they revealed a degree of hostility to my aunt and contempt for the king of which I had been totally unaware. Someone even said: "She better get out of town fast when Nana goes," thus both breaking the taboo against mentioning the Asantehene's death and uttering threats against his wife at the same time.

But even I knew how difficult it was to lock things in a box in Asante. I got used to it a long time ago. I remember, about fifteen years ago, when I was staying in Kumasi with an English friend from college. I was teaching in those days at the University of Ghana and my father was a minister in the government, working in "the Castle," the center of government in the old Dutch slaving castle of Christiansborg in Accra. My friend James and I were alone in Kumasi for the weekend—alone, that is, except for the driver and the cook and our steward—because both my parents were away. He asked to be taken out to the discos of Kumasi. "Fine," I said, "let Boakye, our driver, take you. He'll enjoy it."

At dawn the next morning my father, then a minister in the government, called from his office in the capital. Word had reached him that our car had been seen in a "strange" part of town last night. What had we been doing? My father reminded me that our car would be recognized anywhere it went, asked that I should bear that in mind in deciding where to send the driver, and went back to his investigations of the financial dealing of another crocked multinational.

At breakfast I told James about the early morning call. Where had he been? He didn't know exactly, but the women had been very friendly. And from then on he took himself about in a taxi. The family name would not be disgraced.

The *abusua* did not limit itself to appeals to earthly powers. At the height of the tensions, my kinsman Kwaku came from the family house to tell us that a sheep had been slaughtered and buried there, in the main courtyard, and spells cast against us after the sacrifice. We met with Kwaku and worried members of our household on the landing, whispering: so as not to disturb my mother upstairs: so as not to be heard by the crowd of mourners gathered in the hall and the dining room downstairs. Kwaku had gone at once to find a malam, a Moslem medicine man, who could produce some countermedicine. A white chicken and some doves would be sacrificed. The consensus was with Kwaku: some sort of countersacrifice was obviously necessary. I arranged for it.

It was a form of remedy with which my father was highly experienced from his earliest childhood in Adum, "the hub and heart of Kumasi, even Ashanti."

> We, the true youth of Adum, spent most of our time learning to fight in anticipation of frequent raids that we made on the citizens of other areas of Kumasi who we felt were collaborators of the British usurpers in our midsts. In order to ensure victory at all times, our leaders provided us with juju, which we rubbed into our shaven leads and bodies and was meant to break or deflect bottles or other missiles thrown on us by the enemy. For this and other purposes, no chicken was really safe at night.[5]

That I myself do not believe in magic was oddly beside the point. It was my responsibility to respond to the spiritual menace, as the local head of our *abusua*, the only (and thus, I suppose, the senior) male. So what if members of "our" side were beaten up in the street by loyalists of the other "side"; at least the juju was checked by counterjuju.

Meanwhile, even more disquieting stories began to circulate: the Uncle Jojo was arranging a crowd of the notoriously tough men of Adum to "kidnap" the corpse when it arrived and take it off.

There was also talk of threats to the business interests of members of the funeral committee, to the priests, to the district chairman; on the Sunday before the burial was due to take place, we were informed that someone had entered the vestry of the Wesley Methodist Church and tried to beat up one of the priests. They wavered; their business was healing breaches, not engaging in hostilities. They urge me to have *abotarɛ*, a Twi virtue, usually translated as "patience." It was a word that came up often in the ensuing days. My sisters and I agreed that if there was one word we would like expunged from the language, this was it. In the name of *abotarɛ*, people were willing to wait and listen while the *abusua*, in general, and Uncle Jojo, in particular, took advantage over and over again of our desire to meet them halfway. It was, in part, in the name *abotarɛ* that my aunt's abuses of the stool were tolerated: in time, everyone thinks, this too will pass. To urge *abotarɛ*, so it seems to me, is to do what Moslem peasants mean when they say "if Allah wills": it is to leave in the lap of the gods what could he in the sphere of human action. But sometimes, I think, what they really meant was not "have patience" but "keep looking for compromise." We wanted to bury our father on his terms (or, at any rate, on ours): they wanted to keep the peace. We wanted what we thought was fair and just; they wanted a solution that would allow them to live together in peace. This is an old confrontation, between "abstract rights" and "social community," an opposition much beloved of those legal anthropologists who urge us to see "African values of community" expressed in our procedures of arbitration and our hostility to the colonial legal system. Yet, if I ask myself where my own concern for abstract rights came from, my own passion for fairness, I think I must answer that I got it not from my British schooling but from my father's example. And, often, so it seems to me, as in this case, those who urge compromise as an African virtue are only supporting a compromise with the status quo, a concession to those with money and power, and a little bit of concern for abstract rights might reflect not a colonized mind but an urge to take sides against the mighty, and "speak the truth to power."

I had broken with my king, with my father's *abusua*. I had crossed my father's sister, a powerful woman in her own right. This was not to be done lightly. When food from the palace was conveyed to our house, we were told it was most likely poisoned (by means of witchcraft, of course). Auntie Vic made her weight felt around town, driven around in one of her fleet of Mercedes-Benzes, cultivating a faintly plutocratic aura. The displeasure of the *abusua* was not something to be lightly incurred, either. My cousin Nana Ama, whom I had always thought of as good-hearted and put-upon, revealed the depth of feeling in the *abusua* when she warned us coldly to consider the future welfare of our mother. "Be careful," she said to my sisters and I. "You do not live here. We are here with your mother." When, my sisters challenged her to say directly if she was threatening my mother—asked her if she remembered how my mother had watched over her education—she shouted defensively that she had "said what she had said."

On the day that we retrieved my father's remains in Accra and brought him back in a military plane, the lead editorial in the *Ghanaian Times* was entitled "Paa Joe's Lesson"; explicitly, it took our side against the *abusua*. The man's wishes should be respected, it insisted. Powerful enemies we had, but it was also clear that we had popular sentiment on our side.

Flying over southern Ghana toward Kumasi, a trip I had not taken by air for nearly two decades, we could see the red laterite roads snaking through the forests to the villages and towns of Akwapim and Asante. When our city came into view I could see how much it had grown in the last years, gathering around it a girdle of new housing stretching out into what had once been farms in the forest. As we came down the runway we saw the hundreds of people gathered at the airport in red and black cloths; the priests in their robes; the hearse waiting on the tarmac for the coffin. Most of our party descended from the rear door of the aircraft, but a few of as gathered at the front by the cargo door: I leapt down the few feet to the tarmac, the black cloth I was wearing trailing behind me, and waited to lift down the coffin. We had done it. We had brought Pops home. As the wails of the mourners rose and fell, Uncle George, head of my grandfather's *abusua*, stepped forward to pour libations, (Uncle Jojo hovered nearby, plainly keen to exercise his prerogatives as self-appointed heir-presumptive to the headship of the *abusua* but aware, too, that his participation at this moment would be unwelcome. Not that he had been idle: we discovered later that he had spent the time we were in Accra trying to find a lawyer who would file an injunction to stop the burial. Because the bar was involved in the funeral arrangements—the president of the national bar, the chairman of the Asante bar, and other senior lawyers were to carry his coffin from the church—every lawyer in Kumasi knew what was going on, and, amazingly enough. Jojo couldn't find a single lawyer who would file the papers.)

Home is a house my parents built just before independence. Downstairs two doors come off the front veranda: one to the house, one to my father's legal office. As children we would go to school in the mornings past the many people who gathered from early in the morning on that veranda to see him. Many of them were very poor and they brought chickens or yams or tomatoes in lieu of money, because they knew my father never insisted on being paid. Sometimes, the people who came were not clients but constituents, who had walked miles from Lake Bosomowi to catch a "mammy-wagon" to town, to ask for his help in dealing with the government; sometimes they were not constituents but people from Nyaduom, seeking a decision about land rights or help in getting a road through, so that they could take out their crops in trucks and not in headloads.

My father's coffin traveled in under the tree that my English grandmother had planted the first time she visited that house (a tree where, as a child. I had pretended to be Tarzan, swinging from the branches, oblivious of the cultural policies of my play) and up onto this veranda, passing by the office where he had been Mr. Joe Appiah, barrister and solicitor of the Supreme Court of Ghana in his Ekuona chambers; the Honorable Member of Parliament for Atwima-Amansie, known as the Leopard. *Osebo* for his fearless opposition to the government; *Opanin* Kwabena Gyamfi, heir to Akroma-Ampim, elder and hereditary owner of Nyaduom. When, he entered into the house he was once more my mother's Joe, and our papa.

There was loud drumming and louder weeping as the body was delivered into the house on the shoulders of a half dozen young men, with cloths tied around their waists, some from my stepgrandmother's house, some simply neighbors on the street. I wrapped my cloth around my waist and joined them. In the dining room a platform had been raised, surrounded by flowers, and there we placed him, the coffin covered in his finest *kɛntɛ*, and opened the small window above his head, so that we could see his face.

A year and a half after he fell ill in Norway, nearly a year after he returned to Accra, our father, heir to Akroma-Ampim and Yao Antony, *Ɔpanin*

Kwabena Gyamfi—alias *Ɔsebɔ*, the Leopard; Papa Joe; Pops—was home for the last time.

By 10:00 A.M, of the day of the funeral, the church was full, and the Asantehene and his queen mother were seated in the royal seats, my Aunt Victoria between them. (Somebody told us later that during the service at one moment, when my aunt started weeping, the queen mother turned to her and asked, "Why are you crying? Has somebody you know died?" It was a royal rebuke to my aunt for her attempts to block the funeral.) The stalls we had set aside for VIPs were empty save for the president of the Ghana Academy of Arts and Sciences, Dr. Evans-Amfom, a family friend since his days as vice-chancellor of Kumasi's university. As the strains of the first hymn came to a close there was a good deal of noise outside, including sirens and the sounds of a cheering crowd. An official-looking person walked over from the side door to Rev. Asante and they whispered for a moment. At the end of the verse he spoke: "Would you please all rise," he said "to welcome the head of state and chairman of the PNDC, Flight-Lieutenant Jerry Rawlings and his party."

It was an electric moment, for security considerations meant that almost no one had been told he was coming. The head of state entered, dressed in a civilian suit, open at the neck, accompanied by a civilian member of the PNDC—an old friend with whom I had taught at the University of Ghana, over a decade ago—and some uniformed companions. Now I knew that people would feel we had done our father the honor he deserved of us; that at least we had honored *his* name.

Throughout the service, lawyers in their court robes stood guard at the head and foot of the coffin, taking five-minute turns to honor their colleague. If I turned to my left and scanned to the right, I could see the *abusua*, first; then the royal party; then the priests of the various denominations; then, behind the head of the chairman of the PNDC on the wall, the plaque in memory of my father's father, who had also served this church. Further to the right ware the serried ranks of the legal profession in their robes. On my immediate left was Uncle T.D.; behind me my sisters, my Nigerian in-laws and friends, my friends from America. And to my right, somber and dignified in her black cloth and black scarf, was my mother. All the identities my father cared for were embodied about us: lawyer, Asante man, Ghanaian, African, internationalist; statesman and churchman; family man, father, and head of his *abusua;* friend; husband. Only something so particular as a single life—as my father's life, encapsulated in the complex pattern of social and personal relations around his coffin—could capture the multiplicity of our lives in a postcolonial world.

"I had to play the man and restrain any tears as best I could," my father wrote about Yao Antony's funeral. "It was not the done thing for the head of a family or a leader of men to shed tears publicly."[6] I did not manage this Asante restraint as well.

Outside, the people, thousands upon thousands who had shouted, "Pops, O, Pops," the watchword of my father's friends when we arrived, turned to shouting "J.J., J.J." (Rawlings's initials) as his cortege swept away. Somehow we were hurried through the crowds (many among them dressed in the black-and-white cloth we had asked for—celebrating his life, mourning his passing; many in ordinary brown and red and cloths of mourning) toward the central police station, where our car was parked. And then we followed the hearse, led by police motocycles that cleared the way. We passed the law courts, where my father had argued so many cases, down along the main street of Kumasi, Kingsway, alongside Adum, where he was born, a curious crowd lining our way; we traveled through the Kejetia roundabouts, with the huge central sculpture—worker, soldier, and farmer, symbolizing our nation—along by the lorry park from which thousands of people travel daily out from Kumasi in every direction of the compass; we drove by our house and past the houses of a dozen of my father's colleagues and friends. We passed the Methodist Wesley College, where he had worked with the missionaries as a boy; we entered Tafo, domain of the Tafohene, and the city cemetery where my father, like his father before him, was to be buried. And as we settled in by the graveside, and the coffin was placed in the ground, Jerry Rawlings joined us. His remarks at the graveside were terse but pointed. If we truly wish to honor the memory of a great man, he said, we will not disturb his widow and children over questions of property.

In effect, his mere presence at the funeral, which he would not ordinarily have attended, was a rebuke to the Asantehene and his wife: that the words he spoke at the graveside were addressed to the heart of the dispute between my father and his sister only made this explicit. In the normal business of Ghana, the head of state and the king circle warily about each other, each aware of the symbolic and material resources at the other's disposal. To come to the Asantehene's capital to deliver this rebuke, Jerry Rawlings had to have a point to make. In the context of public knowledge, the main political effects of his presence were three: first, to claim affinity with a politician of the independence generation; second, to underline recent government decrees expanding the property rights of widows, third, to imply an awareness of the manipulations of the stool for private ends. The knowledge that he might have come for private reasons—out of personal respect, as someone told me later, for my father—did nothing to undermine these public messages.

"*Wowu na w'ayie bɛba a, wohwɛ wo yareda hɔ mu,*" our proverb says. "If you die and your funeral is coming, you foresee it from your sickbed." I do not know how much my father would have foreseen, whether he knew his funeral would provide the occasion for conflict between monarch and head of state, between Asante and Ghana. To most of my kinsmen, to be sure, his thoughts on the matter are hardly hypothetical; for them, he was a witness to the ceremonies. Some of them tell me that he would have been pleased.

My father's successor as head of the *abusua* will be named in time (the succession is still in dispute as I write), the latest in Akroma-Ampim's long line. Perhaps, if matters are properly arranged, another crocodile will seize another sheep, signaling acceptance of the choice by the powers and principalities of the spirit world. The lineage will continue.

Another proverb says: *Abusua te sɛkwaeɛ, wowɔ akyiri a ɛyɛ kusuu, wopini ho ana wohunu sɛ dua kora biara wo ne sibere*. "The matriclan is like the forest; if you are outside it is dense, if you are inside you see that each tree has its own position. "So it now seems to me. Perhaps I have not yet disgraced my families and their names. But as long as I live I know that I will not be out of these woods.

NOTES

1. Joe Appiah, *Joe Appiah: The Autobiography of an African Patriot*, 103.
2. Ibid., 202–3.
3. Ibid., 368.
4. On the way to the palace, a couple of notes on the terminology surrounding chieftaincy may be in order. The symbol of chieftaincy in Akan cultures, including Asante, is the stool. The Asantehene's stool is called the Golden Stool; his queen mother's is the Silver Stool. These are *symbolic* representations of chieftaincy and, unlike a throne in Europe, they are not sat upon in the ordinary course of things, being thought of rather as repositories of the *sunsum*, the soul, of a chief's village, town, area, or nation. Indeed, the Golden Stool has its own palace and servants. We speak in Twi (and in Ghanaian English) of the stool, the way an English person might speak of the throne, when referring to the object, the institution, and, sometimes, the incumbent chief or queen mother.

   Any person of high status, male or female, including one's grandparents, other elders, chiefs, and the king and queen, may be called "Nana."

   A chief—*Ɔhene*—is named for his place: the king of Asante is the Asantehene, the chief of the town of Tafo, the Tafohene; and the queen mother—the *Ahemma*—is called the Asantehemma or the Tafohemma. Not all chieftaincies are hereditarily restricted to a particular matriclan; some are appointive. Thus the *Kyidomhene*, the chief of the rearguard, associated with major stools, is appointed (for life) by his chief.
5. Appiah, *Joe Appiah*, 2–3.
6. Ibid., 200–201.

CHAPTER 20

QUESTIONS OF IDENTITY AND INHERITANCE: A CRITICAL REVIEW OF KWAME ANTHONY APPIAH'S *IN MY FATHER'S HOUSE*

Nkiru Nzegwu

Judeo-Christian and Anglo-Saxon forms of marriage have injected patrilineal values and companionate expectations into the Akan matrilineal family structure. As Anthony Appiah demonstrates, these infusions have generated severe strains in the matrikin social structures and, in extreme cases, resulted in the break up of families. In this essay, I investigate the ideological politics at play in this patrilinealization of Asante society.

Kwame Anthony Appiah's much-praised book *In My Father's House* is no doubt a well-crafted persuasive collection of essays in which the author draws on an impressive array of multinational writings to explore the possibilities and pitfalls of an African identity in the late twentieth century (1992, x). One of the principal aims of the project is to articulate by means of various literary strategies a transnational, transracial *new Africanist* identity that is at home in the social and economic structures of dominance of the Western cultural and intellectual traditions. Not only must this carefully crafted individual be intimately familiar with the literature and thoughts of Habermas, Adorno, W. E. B. Du Bois, the *Village Voice, T. L. S.*, and *The New York Times Book Review,* she or he must be willing to undertake the arduous task of making Africa intelligible to interested individuals in the West. When called upon, the new Africanist must provide a sweeping overview of continental events which awes, by virtue of its analytic brilliance, but which rests on old stereotypical assumptions about Africa, its social relationships, and traditions. In other words, the new Africanist must simulate the form and manner of the West and the West's imagined idea of Africa and its culture. She or he must speak more to it (the West) than to Africans about Africa and its problems; the new Africanist must project the analyses in the familiar voice the West understands, and she or he must assure it (the West) of her or his political and theoretical allegiance.

Since the desired translation of the conceptual, economic, social, and philosophical issues of Africa into Western imagination is conducted on the basis of the latter's categories of thought and its privileged philosophical explanation of reality, the new Africanist must, in most cases, forgo the meaningful issues that are of interest to Africa. She or he must necessarily ignore what is believed to be a "trifling" problem of distortions and erasures of Africa's conception of world-being that underpin family life, structures, and relationships. This, however, is a small price to pay for the golden opportunity to theorize about Africa on the world stage in a thickly veiled way that recovers African peoples and cultures as vapid forms into Western imagination.

In this review, I briefly identify the different levels and shifting conceptions of family underpinning Appiah's appropriation of an Asante identity in his discourse on culture, race, and identity. I argue that the author's appropriated identity tacitly privileges a particular conception of family to underwrite a neocolonial new Africanist career. The central problem in the book is that the preferred conception of family ignores the matrilineal implications of his father's Asante culture and the damaging consequences of that mode of family structure and organization for his assumed Asante identity. Proverbially, when a child does not really know the father, his or her effusive assertions to being the father's child diversionarily mask the fact that the child has never belonged.

To avoid the charge that the review is misdirected on the ground that it does not directly address Appiah's postulations since family issues are not the author's focus of work, it should be made abundantly clear that family issues are an integral part of the philosophy of culture that Appiah examines. Furthermore, he engages directly and sometimes by means of innuendos, allusions, and inversions in a torrid discourse on family life, family structure, and relationships and the politics that sustain them. For the moment, we may look at seven main levels and ways in which family may be construed in Appiah's work. The first is the loose form, in which the world is treated as an extended global family, an idea that is not farfetched given the multinational dimensions of Appiah's family. Second, this expansive notion of family may significantly be narrowed down to peoples of African descent once the author's focus shifts to the history and development of Pan-Africanism as it does in the first three chapters: "Invention of Africa," "Illusions of Race," and "Topologies of Nativism." Third, in the middle chapters Africa may be construed as another form of family.[1] The contours of the next four levels and types of family constructions respectively and progressively diminish in scope as one moves from the idea of the state of Ghana as a family, to that of the Asante group as a family, to the Akroma-Ampin *abusua,* and finally to Joe and Peggy Appiah's nuclear family.

Although I recognize the multiple forms in which family may be construed, my focus is on the last three variants, particularly the sociocultural interfaces and intersections of the latter two: the *abusua* and its matrilineal variant of family, and the conjugal unit with its underlying patrilineal structure of family relationship. The fundamental concern, as Ato Quayson also articulated in his e-mail review of *In My Father's House*,[2] is with the constitution of the nuclear family, its relationship to the *abusua* (the extended matrikin system of the Asante families). Of interest is the impact the latter has on child socialization and the formation of individuals' cultural identity.

I should state that the choice of focus on family as a category of analysis is dictated by three compelling factors. The first is the new Africanist's firm conviction that salient aspects of Africa's traditional values can be discarded or modified to blend with salient aspects of Euro-Americanized cultural values. The second, is the realization that Christian and court forms of marriage have injected a variegated form of companionate expectations in Akan family values that are generating great tensions and conflicts for the traditional extended notion of family and the social structures that flow from it. Last, the third factor, is that the prevalent intrafamily feuds in different parts of Africa demand serious investigation and critique. Some of them have ended up in protracted costly legal battles, as the Appiah case to a lesser extent did, and that of the late Kenyan lawyer Silvanus Melea Otiero in Kenya attests.

SETTING THE STAGE: REFERENCING FAMILIES

As earlier mentioned, the discourse in *In My Father's House* yields several possible conceptions and forms of families. Additionally, the book is also replete with articulated and unarticulated references to models and types of families. For instance, in the preface, the author explicitly comments on the expansive character of some Akan families (1992, vii). He obliquely alludes to both the polygynous nature (vii) and westernized character (viii) of some Ghanaian families. While the author's parents typify the westernized variant, for the African mind, polygyny, rather than serial monogamy, is obliquely referenced in the statement about the Asante king, Prempeh II's "first wife" (vii).[3] Later in the preface, we encounter the bi-national and bi-racial character of some Ghanaian families as Appiah chats about his trips to "mother's native country" to visit a "grandmother in the rural West Country" in England. This introduction alerts us to his unique role as a child of two worlds—Ghana and England—with a matrilineal form of family relationship in his father's Asante lineage and a patrilineal form in his mother's Anglo-Saxon lineage. The bi-national, bi-racial notion of family is quickly expanded into a multinational, multiracial one as Appiah reveals the extended global reaches of his family, consisting of a Lebanese uncle, American, French, Kenyan, and Thai cousins and, as his sisters married, Norwegian, Nigerian, and Ghanaian protrusions were added as well.

From the author's constant references and emphasis on his father, Joe Appiah, he defines a patri-focused position for his book. This strategy simultaneously recovers the father as a looming dominant figure in this global family network, and recovers a patriarchal-patrilineal model of family relationship for Akan society. The latter is consequently represented as the principal form of family relationship in present-day Asante. The prominence of his father's patrician figure and the centrality of the father-locus pole contrasts sharply with the shadowy background role Appiah chose for his Anglo-Saxon mother and the mother-locus pole. Rarely referenced, yet for African-focused thinkers, particularly matrilineal Akans who organize clan identity along the mother's line, Appiah's mother is formidably present by the sheer power of her absence. She is present in his very words and represents the image of the hidden framework he employs in judging Africa.

Further references to general and specific images of family abound in other chapters too. In the first chapter, the parents' wedding highlights the monogamous nuclear family character of the parents' conjugal unit (6, 7). Appiah goes on to explicate the differences between "race feeling" and "family feeling" and how the conflation of the two makes racism seem acceptable (17). The identification of this problem underpins Appiah's critique of Crummell's and Du Bois's conceptions of race. Also, variations of families as patrilineal and matrilineal (31) are considered as he exposes what he perceives to be Du Bois's "race-bound" philosophy. All through the rest of the book, various metaphors and models of families are invoked, deployed, and withdrawn in line with specifically assigned tasks. Finally in the epilogue, the most interesting and revealing part of the book, Appiah passionately turns to personal family affairs, events, and familial relationships. The crack in his facade provides valuable clues to Appiah's less than intimate knowledge of Asante culture, of his uneasy stance to the Akan world-sense, and of his determined aim to recast Asante culture in the name of "progress."

In the epilogue, Appiah graphically describes the controversy surrounding his father's funeral and uses the opportunity to vilify certain individuals in his father's *abusua* (181). Though extremely well written, his moral castigation of the *abusua* and his aunt as disruptive forces fails to convey the real reason for the confrontation, which is, the long-standing simmering tensions between two competing forms of family and their underlying behavioral and social expectations. It is noteworthy that Appiah's controlled description irrationalizes Asante family practices and presents the Akroma-Ampim *abusua* as the disruptive force. Epistemologically, the value of his description lies in its disclosure of Appiah's imperialist attitude toward Asante culture and his limited knowledge of Asante family dynamics. This shows precisely when Akan cultural institutions and world-sense are treated as if they lack complexity and subtlety, and as if they are transparently clear once one stands at an archimedean point and peers at them through "universal" (Euroethnic) categories.

Other direct references to family occur when Appiah obscures the *abusua* relationship to its custodial head. This allows him to suggest that lust for power and fear of public disgrace are the underlying reason for the Akroma-Ampim *abusua*'s opposition (183). Intellectual imperialism manifests itself when, in a explanatory aside, he tells us that we should never assume that individual women cannot gain power under patriarchy (184). This characterization of Asante social organization as a form of patriarchal-matriliny

(184) is simplistically premised on the assumption that the categories of men/male and women/female in Asante social practice are binarily ranked and embody the same gender connotations as in Euro-American life. It is interesting that Appiah's "informed" gender evaluation is made without prior detailed analyses of the complex social history of Asante women and gender relations in a matrilineal society. Nor for that matter, any critical reference of the variegated history of dominance of Western categories and analyses in the production of knowledge about African women. Like many feminists, Appiah naturalizes patriarchy in Africa and then takes it for granted in explaining the role and status of African women in various societies. Intellectual imperialism allows both him and some feminists to entrench the idea that women-orientedness is a Euro-American discovery and that African women should follow the path charted by Euro-American feminists.

As I halt the identification of references to family in the book, it is worthwhile to restate that I am uninterested in Appiah's more widely praised postcolonial argumentations on race and Pan-Africanism, which also ignore pertinent social and historical incidences, events, and texts that complicate the new Africanist position of the author. Since some of the problems have already been noted by others (Ofiemun, 1992; Taiwo, 1995), in the ensuing section I engage in a detailed examination of the interrelationship between patrilineality and matrilineality as I evaluate Appiah's attempt to assert an Asante identity. Of interest is his firm conviction that the differences between the two in identity formation can easily be bridged with matriliny subject to modifications, presumably because it is traditional and backward. In taking this tack, I hope to expose some of Appiah's errors of misrepresentation of matriliny and show that these derive from conceptual bias, and an imperialistic construction of knowledge of which he seems unaware.

MATRILINY: TRAITS AND CHARACTERISTICS

In the epilogue, Appiah abandons the detached "omniscient" voice of theory to engage in the real life politics that engulfed his family following the death of his father. As he presents it, the central line of dispute is drawn between his father's conjugal family and his matrikin. Under the direction of Aunt Victoria, his father's sister, the matrikin contested the rights of the conjugal family to set the date and manner of his father's funeral. Appiah presents this contestation as mean-spirited by discursively deploying problematic images of the matrikin and the Akan matrilineal ethos; these images condemn it without conceptually engaging the matrilineal character of Asante society. This avoidance strategy prevents us from seeing the negative implication of the Akan matrilineal ethos for Appiah's assumed Asante identity. With readers attention deflected by Appiah, patriliny is privileged and reproduced in Asante to ground the author's patrilinized "Asante" identity.

An informed examination of Akan social and family relationships is necessary to detect the occurrence of such glosses. For now, I will ignore Appiah's appropriation of an Asante identity and focus on his partial glosses of the often cacophonous encounter between matriliny and patriliny in twentieth century Asante. In addition, I shall determine how the constitution of these models converge in Appiah's family to shape his identity and world-sense, and how the convergence is exploited to underwrite a fictive Asante identity. In making an African sense of why Appiah side-steps the foundational questions of identity-formation at the heart of his assumed Asante personhood, I seek to problematize his customization of two opposing family structures to meet the present exigencies of a new Africanist agenda. This will uncover the "europhonic" (Appiah, 1992: 54) echo in his mode of thinking, as well as the hidden agenda to displace Asante family norms and mores for an imported one. Though radical questions of personal identity are raised in this line of interrogation, the issue at stake is not whether Appiah is the biological son of his father or whether he is a Ghanaian. Rather, it is whether or not Asante identity and all it connotes, whatever this turns out to be, can indeed be conveyed through the father in the absence of an Asante *abusua* as customarily required by the inheritance laws of a *matrilineal* society. What needs to be sorted out is whether the Anglo-Saxon-derived Marriage Ordinance of Ghana is the proper channel through which Asante identity is established in the same way it conveys Ghanaian citizenship.

The matrikin system, as Christine Oppong, an English female anthropologist writes in *Middle Class African Marriage* (1986), remains one "in which the matrilineage is the solidary important kin group for incorporating the newborn, for owning property, for supporting the dependent young and old—the unit for performance of important life-cycle rituals especially at death, and the context within which the young or old would always find a home and a source of permanent security" (1986, xx). With the dissemination of patriarchal consciousness in the nineteenth century by evangelical Christian missionaries, family problems arose for Akan individuals who embraced the patrilineal models of family organization favored by the church. Because the Akan social structure is matrilineal, the dominant tie within the system is that between mother and child and between children of the same mother (Oppong, 1986: 29). The rights of these uterine siblings override the spousal rights of wives and children since females-as-wives retain their identity as kins in their own matriclan and do not become members of a husband's matrikin. Writing in 1897, J. M. Sarbah noted in *Fanti Customary Laws* that females-as-wives are of different "families" (matrikin) from their husbands, that they can acquire and hold their own property, are not liable for their husbands debts, have their matrikin to fall back on, and can only inherit parts of their husband's estate that are willed before his death *and* ratified by the matrikin (Sarbah, 1897: 90, 105, cited in Oppong, 1986: 31). Oppong observes that Akan inheritance matters continue to be as true in 1981 as when Bosman recorded them in 1705, and that a "man and wife have no community of goods and may not inherit each other's property" (Oppong, 1986: 44).

In presenting Asante initiatives to the Judeo-Christian patrilineal ideology, Oppong refers to the 1938, 1941, and 1942 Akan Confederacy Council meetings. The Confederacy Council debated the question of inheritance rights and, to accommodate the forces of change, resolved that only witnessed gifts of *personal* property may be made to widows and children. The decision was guided by the recognition that lineage or *abusua* property, namely land and cocoa farms, are communally owned, hence may appear as a man's personal property where in fact it is not (Oppong, 1986: 42–43). Moreover, a woman's identity is seen to be properly located in her matrilineage, not in a husband's, nor as a wife. In 1948 the Asante Confederacy Council amended its own inheritance laws in response to wives' growing dependency on spouses so that a third of a man's estate could be inherited by widows and children. Despite these positive responses, the Council's decision lacked legal force as the colonial governor failed to approve the ruling preferring instead a total displacement of matriliny. Of far greater importance epistemologically is that despite the popularity of the patrilineal-patriarchal Judeo-Christian and Anglo-Saxon statutory marriages,[4] the matrilineage remains widely recognized as the salient arena of identity-formation of the Akan ethnic group: *Abusua baako mogya baako. Abusua baako nipa koro.* (One [matri]lineage, one blood. A [matri]lineage is one person.)

The sociologist G. K. Nukunya also observes in *Tradition and Change in Ghana* (1992) that "in a matrilineal system, an individual has more to do with his mother's people than his father's because the descent group to which he belongs is traced lineally through the female line" (Nukunya, 1992: 28–29).[5] Under the Asante notion of family, the matrilineal principle governs in interpersonal relations; it predominates and controls economic, social, and ideological spheres of social life (Nukunya, 1992: 33). Even though *ntoro,* which is described as the father–child axis of relationship, is recognized among the Akan, Nukunya states that it "does not serve as a serious counter to the matrilineal *abusua* and the concept of matriliny itself" (Nukunya, 1992: 31). This patri-focal ethos is so removed from what really affects the individual that it does not make a significant impact on the child's life (Nukunya, 1992: 33). This occurs mainly because in a matrilineal system a "family does not always constitute a domestic group because husband and wife after marriage may continue to live among their own kin" (Nukunya, 1992: 48). The effect is that parental functions are performed by the mother's brothers, and children are socialized to inherit from their mother's brother or brothers.

Nukunya describes the *abusua*, or lineage, as a corporate group of men, women, and children with an *abusua panin* (male head) and an *obaa panin* (female head), while the overall administration of the group is vested in the two heads (Nukunya, 1992: 30). Every Asante belongs, through the female line, to one of the society's eight clans. In line with this matrilineal principle, "inheritance and succession also pass in the female line, from a man to his brothers or to his sister's children while status and offices go first to younger brothers before going down to the sister's children" (Nukunya, 1992: 29). Consequently, the protection of a matriclan to which one owes allegiance and which forms one's identity is the ultimate responsibility of every member of the kin-group, both male and female. This investment in the matriclan continues even as marriages are contracted under the Judeo-Christian and Anglo-Saxon marriage ordinance.

In his contribution, Quayson provides critical insight into the nature of interaction between the companionate nuclear family and the wider *abusua*. His analysis puts the reason for many present-day family conflicts in Ghana in sharper perspective. As he sees it, under the companionate [conjugal] model, a wife negotiates her authority in relation to other women [the kins not the wives] in her husband's wider family, since "it is usually other women [the kins] in a man's family who pose the greatest problems to a wife." This happens because the claims of the wider *abusua* (consisting of both male and females) remain in place only as long as a man does not place his wife above his extended family. A companionate marriage model "is therefore diametrically at variance with the maintenance of the claims of the wider *abusua*" in which the matrikin regards a man's estate as theirs by right (Quayson, 1994).[6]

Quayson's emphasis highlights another model of marriage in which conjugal bonds are weaker, in which sibling relationships are much stronger, and marital relationships are not designed to weaken siblings' bonding. Under such marriage conditions, wives (and their children) necessarily seek identification in their (mothers') matrilineage or *abusua* rather than in their husbands' (fathers') *abusua*. Matrilineality is maintained and reinforced precisely because conjugality or conjugal bonding is de-emphasized. This state of affairs assigns secondary value to husbands, who are treated as reproductive mates rather than as centripetal forces in the lives of women. By valorizing only kinship ties, the matriclan system eliminates from its conceptual and societal scheme the husband-dependency syndrome created for women in the patriarchal-patrilineal model that strips them of their kin identities. This dependency is what the Anglo-Saxon statutory law of inheritance ameliorates by giving widows full rights in a spouse's estate. Indeed if anything, the distinguishing trait of the matrikin system is that it avoids this dependency by channelling women's energies and resources into the building and consolidation of their personal identity, wealth, and their *abusua*.

Fortuitously, Quayson's interjection enables us to see that modern-day intrafamily feuds occur in Akan societies precisely because a patrilineal companionate model of marriage is privileged in a matrilineal context that deemphasizes conjugality and stresses consanguinity. Though today many Asante increasingly marry under the patriarchal-patrilineal precepts of the companionate model, they still recognize, as Appiah's father's did, the centrality of the matriclan in ordering family inheritance and succession. For most contemporary Akans whose social and personal identities continue to be framed matrilineally by the histories of a mother's lineage, their patrimony is shared by the kin-group even as they affirm the Anglo-Saxon patrilineal precepts of modern marriages.

Thus, it is not uncommon to find Ghanaians today who continue to espouse matriliny, shape their identity by their mothers' *abusua*, and regulate their lives by the mores of the system. Equally true, as Oppong's research demonstrated and as Appiah's father's life proved, it is not uncommon to find some Asante who maintain their matrilineal identity and yet set up a nuclear conjugal unit in which patriliny is privileged. What is noteworthy is that those in the latter group who tend to be affluent, well-educated, and privileged inevitably create family vortices of tensions that strain conjugal and extended family relationships. They act as if Asante citizenship is assigned the same way that Ghanaian citizenship is conferred. Insulated by privilege, rarely does the question of conflict-resolution between the warring patrilineal and matrilineal models ever seriously come up for these educated, wealthy Akan. In fact, the men especially magnify the tensions and defy their monogamous marriage vows by setting up competing conjugal relationships with other women.

MATRILINY AND PATRILINY: AN ATAVISTIC STRUGGLE

From Kwasi Wierdu, the most respected African and Akan philosopher, we learn that it is to the mother that "Akans ascribe the origin of a person's *mogya* (literally blood)" (Wiredu, 1990: 244). According to him, the *mogya* "is the basis of lineage, or more extensively, clan identity" (Wiredu, 1990: 244). Because the Akan are matrilineal and the most important kinship group is the lineage, the *mogya* "is the most important constituent of a person" both socially and politically. It is the maternal marker that assigns kinship and status in the Akan network of rights and obligation. Wiredu states that "in the making of a baby, the father contributes the *ntoro* (semen) which combines... with the blood of the mother to constitute... the frame of the human being to come" (1990: 244). It is through the father's *ntoro* that a child acquires a social link to a patrilineal kinship group (Wiredu, 1990: 245). Comparatively, what the Akan conceptual scheme assigns to the father is the child's manner of being or human personality or *sunsum,* and which Wierdu contends is somewhat indefinite. On the Akan system, therefore, the father's contribution to the social being and identity of the child is of lesser importance to that of the mother (Nukunya, 1992: 31). This is why ethnic "citizenship" is set through the mother line, whereas according to the patriarchal precepts of the Anglo-Saxon-derived legal system of Ghana, it is set through the father.

That the malestrom created at the intersection of patriliny and matriliny is at the center of family disputes and feuds in Ghana today all the more problematizes and highlights the contentious nature of the title of Appiah's book. In choosing the title *In My Father's House,* as if it were unproblematic, as if patriliny is the norm in Akan culture, Appiah overwrites the explosive issue of patrilineal*ization* in Asante society. No doubt, avoiding conceptual engagement with the society allows him to present Asante identity as an inheritable trait and patriliny as the channel through which it runs. As paternity becomes the path of ethnic identity, Appiah downplays the importance of Asante matrilineal prescriptions in the assignment of identity, hence sidesteps the cultural implication of his patrilineal*ized* conception of self and personhood.

It cannot be overemphasized that by ignoring the matriliny-patriliny conflict Appiah engages in cultural mispresentation. He presses Anglo-Saxon values into Akan culture and deflects attention from the ways in which Asante identity is socially formed. This allows him to promote the idea that the Appiah nuclear family satisfies the relevant matrilineal conditions under which Asante identity is ascribed and developed. Though theoretically necessary, Appiah avoided a deconstructionist analysis of his family as a transgressive disruptive presence in Akan conceptual scheme since it is counterproductive to the new Africanist objective that has as its goal the elimination of oppositional Akan mores. It must be noted that it is the recognition of the epistemological differences between Akan and Anglo-Saxon cultures, and its implication for his identity, that underpins Appiah's ultimate objective of transforming Asante society into a "euroethnized" patrilineal society.[7] Consequently, the title of Appiah's books is at once a decoy that discursively obscures a covert colonizing moment in which theoretical manipulation is under way and a bold imperialistic statement of what he envisions Asante society to be.

It may seem that nothing is lost by the contentious nature of the title, since Appiah is focusing on the modern patrilineal*ized* condition of Ghana, the patrilineal state of his parents' family, and the future direction of a progressive Ghana. Consider that matriliny is still very much a pivotal part of Asante life and even in Appiah's own family, as his father's life demonstrates. Regardless of anthropologists' prognostication that matriliny is doomed, it has not yet been eradicated. Moreover, presenting the society as patrilineal*ized* purports to state justifiably that matriliny is an outmoded state that must necessarily be changed. The problem with the strategy is not just that it takes the Anglo-Saxon social custom of patriliny for granted and problematizes the Akan social custom of matriliny, but that it assumes the inevitability of a linear trajectory of cultural development with technologized Europe in the lead. The presuppositional level of this assumption invites our uncritical agreement that matriliny and Akan culture are lower down the evolutionary scale because they are backward and unprogressive. Quoting Appiah: "*Ideologies succeed to the extent that they are invisible, in the moment that their fretwork of assumptions passes beneath consciousness; genuine victories are won without a shot being fired*" (60).

Playing the patrilineal card to global readers through his title had enabled Appiah to succeed. Hanging his case on emotive pulleys, he simultaneously naturalizes patriliny and its father-son axis of bonding in Asante, and "others" the Akan matriclan that privileges a uterine axis of bonding. Much is gained by a discursive title that is pressed into a subversive social restructuring program to privilege a phallic axis of bonding. As a well-oiled emotive argument, his title tugs at the patrilineal*ized* hearts of *global readers* as Appiah highlights the touching image of his filial act of carrying on a father's nonracial, non-ethnocentric legacy. A lot is gained theoretically and materially when the possessive pronoun qualifier "my" in the title does double duty: first, by covering up the identity and inheritance issues at the root of the funeral controversy and, second, by reinforcing the author's legitimacy as the rightful heir of his father's patrimony. With the father's figure perpetually held high in the book, the title forces emotional commitment from unwary readers and quietly invites their condemnation of a society that sanctions the "inhumane" practice of separating a son from his father; and that structurally privileges a uterine basis of bonding over a phallic basis of bonding.

So what is wrong with emphasizing the image of the father? Should not a son rightly be in his father's house, speaking fondly of the memories he shared with him? Moreover, where else would a son's patrimony be if not in a father's estate? It is worthwhile to note that these questions show how entrenched and normal a patriliny ideology is, and how easy it is for its logic to be exploited. This clarification is important since Appiah's construction succeeds by portraying fatherhood as a natural biological act. Why is it natural that a son's patrimony necessarily lies in a biological father's house? It could lie elsewhere. Because Appiah takes patriliny as *the* only acceptable form of family relationship, he is unwilling to accept the consequences of treating fatherhood as a social act. To do so would be to accept that Joe Appiah's paternal role as *abusua panin*, at the very least, is socially equal to the paternal relation that exists between Joe Appiah and him. He would have to accept that a paternal role in the context of matri-filiation or uterine axis bonding is no less legitimate than one that occurs in a context of patrifiliation or phallic axis of bonding. He would have to accept that Joe Appiah is as much a father to members of the Akroma-Ampim *abusua* as he is to him. In other words he would have to expand his notion and conception of father and recognize the legitimacy of the rights and obligations that come with it.

Since Appiah's basis for usurping the *abusua*'s rights to inclusion is foundationally based on his filial role as a son, he is making a biological argument for fatherhood. Though Appiah may seek to deny it, he is implicitly construing fatherhood as a biological construct when he takes a father-son relationship to be superior to sibling relationships. His attack on the rights of the *abusua* succeeds because the Anglo-Saxon-derived legal system of Ghana is inherently structured to privilege filial rights and to irrationalize siblings' rights. Matters become interesting when Appiah deploys this biologized notion of fatherhood and asserts his inheritance rights. Not only does he erroneously imply that a biological child is necessarily the heir of a biological father, he implies that there is a logical entailment between reproduction and fathering. Yet how fatherhood is understood depends on the prevailing kinship system in a given society, not on some natural logical connection, which is why in Asante society the social, economic, and inheritance rights of children do not override those of the *abusua*.[8]

There is a fundamental conceptual problem when Appiah misses the preeminent ways in which parenting is social.[9] Although it may be the case that in many societies and family relationships the sociological role and the biological capacity to reproduce are fused together, nevertheless this does not imply that the two are one. It is not a necessary condition to being a father that one physically sires a child because one can parent a child that one did not sire. If biological capacity to reproduce is equivalent to fatherhood, then adoption in its Western variant would not have been invented. In some West African societies, the Igbo included, socialization and marriage provide an entry into fatherhood, a clear recognition that parenting is a social act to be exercised only by those who have formally and publicly declared their readiness to perform the role. It is for this reason that in Onitsha (Nigeria) paternity claims are not entertained on the flimsy ground that one was the biological instrument of conception.[10]

Matriliny is maligned by those who view the world through patrilineal lens and who cannot separate fatherhood from the reproductive act and recognize the ways in which uncles may be fathers.[11] When fatherhood is separated from the reproductive act, we begin to see what is socially involved in being a father. The dominant social responsibility of that role entails providing a spatiotemporal nexus of identification, an extended network of relatives and relations within which the lineage-diffused character of a self-othered identity is formed. A child belongs whether or not he or she is biologically yours. Since family relationships are socially defined roles, uncles, granduncles, and grandfathers both on the maternal and paternal sides are fathers, while patrimony is provided by the socially delineated father within the lineage. Thus the underlying insinuation that matriliny is "unnatural" because it limits the rights of sons and daughters in a biological father's house is conceptually flawed, both by the mores of Africa and the contemporary Western world.

A Euro-Nativist in Imperialist Garb

Appiah's disregard for Akan matrilineal ethos comes from deep-seated reservation of nativism, a view Appiah claims assumes that the indigenous is distinct and separate from the alien (56), and "that the 'people' have held unto an indigenous national tradition" (58). For one so against nativism in African scholarship, it is interesting that Appiah does not see himself as upholding Anglo-Saxon customs and traditions. His theoretical position is fascinating in that he perceives Asante mores from a traditional Anglo-Saxon standpoint, including its biology-focused view of fatherhood and strict biological line of inheritance. This nativist commitment to Anglo-Saxon tradition undergirds his inability to accept the matrilineal prescriptions of his father's Akan culture. Worse still, his treatment of patriliny as privileged is a colonizing act that seeks the eradication of matriliny. Anglo-Saxon imperialism is masked by representing himself as a Ghanaian man's son; and ideological recolonization is marked by obscuring the side of the equation on which salient social and cultural issues in Asante are framed and resolved: the europhonic side, or the akanphonic side. That Appiah opts for the europhonic side is displayed by his difficulty to grasp that the Akroma-Ampim matriclan's role in the funeral of its head cannot plausibly "be limited to a public display of solidarity around the coffin," as Appiah sought (184). To move beyond ideological recolonization and imperialist hand-waving, Appiah needs to rethink his conception of family as it applies to the Asante, rather than deploying the Anglo-Saxon model for the Akan.

Although one sympathizes that a family dispute erupted during the funeral and complicated matters, nevertheless one cannot but note that Appiah's description of events lacks an Akan-sense recognition of events. He presents the vast properties of Yao Antony, the former late head of Akroma-Ampim *abusua* (183) as gifts to his father without considering their fiduciary nature to the Akroma-Ampim matriclan. He underplays the property squabble between his father, the *abusua panin,* and aunt, the *obaa panin,* shortly before the father's death, hence Appiah misses the larger question of the *abusua* property implicated in Joe Appiah's wealth and which the father's codicil vindictively appropriates (183). He portrays Asante culture as insensitive to widows and children (183) and he characterizes events in such a way as to demonize the *abusua* and exonerate the nuclear family (188). He portrays himself as a swashbuckling knight forced to battle the "evil" *abusua,* checking juju with counterjuju (188), and finally breaking with his father's Akan *abusua* and his father's Akan king (189). All these converge to depict Asante *abusua* as crude and retrograde, and worthy of replacement with a "better" family model.

The new Africanists' grasp of customary affairs are facile since customs are never seen as worthy of serious intellectual engagement.[12] Hopping from text to text, the new Africanists forgo theoretical contact with material culture and destroy what they do not understand. Appiah's altercation with the Asantehene, Otumfuo Nana Opoku Ware the Second, is a case in point. It calls into question his identity claims to being an Asante and his father's son by examining his attitude toward Asante culture.[13] Summoned to the palace by the Asantehene and dissatisfied with the turn of events, Appiah abandons all respect for the Asantehene and the Stool and discourteously stalks out in rage. This action not only demonstrates his low esteem for the Asante kingship and its institutions, it reveals his disregard for the juridical wisdom of the Asante court. Insofar as his intemperate behavior prompts one to ask what he really respects about a culture he claims as his, we are reminded that claiming to be an Asante is quite a different matter from being one.

What is instructive about Appiah's disrespect is that he exonerates himself by blaming his Aunt Victoria for "unduly" influencing her husband, the Asantehene. He cannot see that his discourtesy to the Stool and his preemptive occupation of the moral high ground signal disdain and a refusal to enter the Asante world of political and cultural discourse. It may seem that his disdain derives from the "irrational" "exotic" things he takes to be African: slaughtering of sheep to cast powerful spells, poisoning of meals, a "fairytale world of witchcraft and wicked aunts and wise old women and men" (181). But it also extends to other aspects of the culture, as evidenced by his description of the courtiers and the palace decor (185). Sardonically, Appiah plays up what he see as the alien and the nontraditional quietly mocking the idea that there is an indigenous national tradition. His excoriating gaze inveighs that there is just one way of being African, which the Asantehene compromised by his education and with the decor of "Oriental rugs" and "expensive mock-antique furniture" (185). Since the twentieth century hybridity of Africans is problematic for Appiah, it must be that, like his opposition, the Afro-nativists, he holds a deeply recessed, but negative, view of Africa. His image of Africa is of a wild jungle, in which the "authentic" African is isolated, uncontaminated by the trappings of contemporary life. What Appiah misses about the intersection of Akan and Anglo-Saxon manifestations in the Asantehene's eclecticism is that the central organizing ethos remains dominantly Akan and marginally Anglo-Saxon. Whereas for Appiah, it is dominantly Anglo-Saxon and minimally Akan.

ANGLO-SAXONIZING THE MOGYA

Since *In My Father's House* proclaims his presence in his father's house, it is crucial to examine what this occupation of his father's Asante/Akroma-Ampim/personal "house" means? What does it mean for him to be in his father's *abusua*/matrikin/house "given the centrality of the *abusua* in Asante" (53) and the socially formalized paths of acquiring a lineage-centered identity in Asante?[14] How does the identity of a non-Akan woman affect a child's acquisition of an Asante identity when descent is traced matrilineally? Essentially, how does one become an Asante without all the requisite ingredients for creating that mix?

Prior to the heavy investment of modern Ghanaians in Judeo-Christian and Anglo-Saxon forms of marriage, an Asante marital unit might be nuclear and either patrifocal or matrifocal, but would typically be structured on matrilineal lines. As Appiah disclosed, the conjugal nuclear unit of his parents was patrilineal and patrifocal. Qualifications are necessary because two types of family structures converge in Appiah's father's home, which makes the issue much more complicated than he presents. It seems more likely that the patrilineal elements would be stronger in interpersonal relations when the companionate precepts of the parent's marriage prevailed. Most likely it would shift to the matrilineal pole in ancestral ceremonial and ritual matters, and when the obligations of the *abusua* call to the fore the force of his father's role as head of the *abusua*. From Appiah's descriptions of the conjugal unit, however, and his ***natural*** expectations to inherit unproblematically from his father, one could grant that the Anglo-Saxon derived patriarchal-patriliny model was the preferred form of marital interaction and child socialization conditions in the conjugal unit.

The complexity of the Appiahs' family situation, as with many others in Ghana, is that the parents' maintenance of a patriarchal-patrilineal ideology occurred in tandem with the father's recognition of the matrilineal implications of Akan ethnic identity. As Joe Appiah's notebook revealed (182), he became the head of the Akroma-Ampim *abusua* matriclan at the death of his great-uncle. Prior to that the acquired his social identity in the matrix and glorious histories of his mother's line of ancestors. Since Joe Appiah was aware that the patrilineal conception of family is at variance with the matrilineal orientation of his Akan culture, in choosing to marry an Englishwoman and as a Christian, he did two things. The first is that, as most educated Africans of the time who believed that marriage to white women signified social progress, Appiah's father set up a conflict- loaded family vortex in which to sire and raise his children as well as interact with the *abusua*. The second is that he expected his Anglo-Saxon wife to produce Asante children as if Asante consciousness is somehow stamped onto the child at birth. What he neglected in this scenario was that his Anglo-Saxon wife lacked an Asante consciousness and a requisite *abusua* within which to mold the cultural identity of children. He failed to acknowledge the implication of the *mogya* as the ascriptor of cultural identity, hence he did not consider that while the companionate patrilineal model encouraged intimacy between couples, it does so by minimizing the influence of the matrilineage on one's conjugal life and in the socialization of one's children. The existential network Joe Appiah needs to participate in order to culturalize his children is precluded by the companionate model of marital interaction with a white wife. The consequence is not only that the Anglo-Saxon woman socialized her children but also that the histories of her people prevailed in shaping the children's identity.

It is noteworthy that the emphasis on the *mogya* (the maternal compass) as the basis of Akan identity comes principally from the role of the mother in socializing children into the mores of the culture. According to Wiredu, this enrichment program begins in the innermost circle "of the grandmother, the mother, the mother's sibling, her own children, and the children of her sisters" (Wiredu, 1990: 245). After Joe Appiah sired his children, in accordance with the patriarchal-patrilineal vows he had embraced, he left it to his wife to perform her part of the patriarchal duty. Availing himself of the patriarchal advantages of his conjugal role and burdened by the pressures of political life, Appiah's father may have missed the culturally crossed connections in the cultural identity of his well-mannered children. He seemed not to realize that identity is not biologically transmissible and that Asante identity cannot be produced in a nuclear europhonic environment in which the mother lacks embeddedness in Akan culture. Asante cultural identity cannot occur where the Anglo-Saxon wife does not have the requisite existential network, oral narratives, and documented histories of the Asante and the Akroma-Ampim *abusua* to convey to *his* children. She could only convey that which is accessible to her, which are *her* father's histories, philosophies, and mannerisms.

In the light of this, Appiah may argue, but not plausibly that Asante identity, like all identities, is socially acquired and that therefore he does not need an Akan woman for a mother. Not only does this line of escape ignore the matrilineal ethos of Asante society that makes motherhood a prerequisite for identity ascription. It ignores the fact that access and membership to any of the eight Asante clans is through an Asante female. It ignores too that his

Anglo-Saxon mother does not belong and lacks the power to compel the matrikin's cultural assistance. Furthermore, without a strong Akan family network to assist in the formation of her children's cultural identities, what would be created were Anglo-Saxon identities with a dash of Asante flavoring. Literally, English children in adinkra cloth.

SUNSUM: A TENUOUS ROAD TO ASANTELAND

In an exceedingly important way, Appiah's attempt to assert an Asante identity by invoking the *sunsum* exposes his conceptual and cultural distance from the Asante philosophic scheme. Where the Ghanaian legal system conveys citizenship if one has a Ghanaian father, the Asante customary system establishes ethnic rights through the *mogya*. Only one who is not versed in the cultural nuances of the Asante ascriptive framework, or perhaps has lost his or her cultural identity like those pressed into the seminary at the age of six, would in adulthood begin the difficult journey of developing a new cultural identity. Rhetorically, why would a grown Asante man feel the need to declare his presence in his matriclan or even in a father's house? Why would an Asante assert among his own that he is Asante? To borrow Wole Soyinka's expression: a tiger does not proclaim its tigritude; and this is premised on the idea that the tiger is really a tiger. Soyinka's maxim is important if only because it allows us to probe Appiah's need to assert his identity and to establish to whom the assertions are addressed. An inspection of the character of his cultural consciousness at the formative years of life may provide some clues as to why he felt the need to proclaim his "asantitude."

Before departing for boarding school in England, Appiah, as he tells it, was raised in elite, privileged circumstances in Mbrom, a small neighborhood in Kumasi, Ghana (vii). His life behind the hibiscus hedge that framed his English mother's rose garden (vii) and where he swung on trees pretending to be Tarzan (190), was in a nuclear family structure in which patriarchal lines of relationship were dominant. Daily his father headed to the courts dressed in dark European suits, carrying the white wig of the British barrister, and with a rose from his Anglo-Saxon wife's garden in his buttonhole (vii). In true replication of the leisured colonial lifestyle of colonial wives, his mother, the daughter of Sir Stafford, a former Chancellor of the Exchequer, stayed home and was regularly visited by Muslim Hausa traders from "the North" who knew of her interest in seeing and buying the brass weights used for weighing gold (vii). Though Appiah's Mbrom home was opposite his grandparents' house, and he was aware that scores of kinfolk and dependents lived under the direction of his step-grandmother, "Auntie Jane," his family and gender consciousness were powerfully and firmly shaped by "Victorian paterfamilias" (181), the upper-class patriarchal family values of his Anglo-Saxon mother, rather than by the matrilineal *abusua* family values of his father's Akan culture.

Further examples may be called upon to elucidate the powerful presence of the mother's Victorian paterfamilias consciousness on the adult son; these examples reveal to some degree the extent of his alienation. In a terse confrontation between the nuclear family and the *abusua,* Appiah easily slid into a patriarch's role after the narrative of his mother's people to guard what he perceived as his father's personal wealth. From his patrilineal*ized* non-Asante eyes, he failed to see himself in the *abusua,* nor for that matter did he see the *abusua*'s ties to him. In his patrilineal*ized* non-Asante identity he saw his father as separate from the *abusua* and the *abusua* as removed from him. This ideology of separateness is at odds with the wider flexible understanding of family that is instilled in Akan-identified children. Appiah's conceptualization of a family as nuclear-conjugal and his belief that he can pick and choose what he wants from the Asante culture prove that he never was in his father's Asante house/*abusua,* except as a stranger/non-*abusua*. Because he has always been in his mother's Victorian paterfamilias house, Appiah now attempts to assert a false Asante identity. His presence in his father's house not only problematizes his ambiguous relationship to Asante culture, it also exposes the fact that he never was, nor lived it, before. This ambiguity clues us to the fact that Appiah is not addressing Asante and "correct-thinking" Africans. He is speaking to those who do not know that he is his mother's child.

In a certain sense, Appiah is a victim of his father's conflicting choices, for, unlike him, the son did not have the benefit of experiences in the norms of two different cultures. In recognizing the vital role of an *abusua* network in developing an Asante consciousness, the important question that must be posed is: Whose *abusua* did Joe Appiah expect his children to claim in grounding their Asante identity? Surely he must know that his *sunsum* and *kra* alone cannot ferry them to Asanteland, nor can they share his *abusua* with him. Only by initiating a radical restructuring program that patrilineal*izes* Asante and appropriates his mother's Akroma-Ampim history could a cultural locus be established for his Anglo-Saxonized children. This appropriation constitutes the making of patriarchy in contemporary Akan, and marks the gradual erasure of women's presence in the Akan, conceptual scheme. Joe Appiah achieved his objective by tilting the family balance toward patrilineal elements. At his deathbed, he converted the political prestige and economic power of the Akrom-Ampim matriclan into his personal assets. The effect is the strengthening of the patrilineal consciousness of his conjugal family at the expense of the matrilineal *abusua*. The deflation of the importance of the *mogya,* and by extension the diminuation of the role of women and the concept of matriliny, allow modern Akan men and Euro-American feminists to read patriarchy into the culture, as if it existed there all along. If patrilinization, which amounts to a distortion of Akan culture, is needed to make Appiah an Asante, then he presides in his father's house only as a transgressive force whose identity depends on the destruction of the central social structure of Asante culture. Since self-interest underlies Appiah's objective to patrilinize Akan culture, it needs to be clear that the attempt to overthrow matriliny has nothing to do with the internal inadequacies of the system or the depravity of its social values, but an emotional commitment to a nativist Ango-Saxon view of social relation.

Given this state of affairs in which Akan cultural death is the cost for Appiah's admission, biracial marriages in Africa need to be problematized, because many have unwittingly played colonizing roles in the way offspring of such unions are socialized. In a way that bi-ethnic marriages have not, biracial marriages raise to the fore the invidious issue of racial privilege. Lineage members (both men and women) have been shoddily treated and compelled to defer to these white wives. In West Africa, in the 1940s, 1950s, and 1960s, a significant number of educated African men married white women while studying abroad. On returning to Africa, the presence of some of these white wives inimically affected the relationship of the extended family to their kin. Family members were uncomfortable with the superior attitudes of white wives, and they resented the wives' curtailment of access to their kin. The general insistence by the white wife on conjugal privacy is an alienating device that forces the husband to choose between the wife and the wider family. Marriages have collapsed as a result, and those that survived did so either because the men yielded to his white wife's pressure and barred his kin from their home. Or the men resolved the problem by according the white wife her space in a clearly marked residence, and then accommodated the extended family in an alternative residence or residences that had been set up with local women whom they married.[15] Either way, destabilization occurred as the white wives brought up their children in relative isolation from the extended family, a situation that severely weakened family ties.

The major way biracial marriages function as instruments of cultural destabilization is through the molding of identities in which the narrow nuclear model of family undermines Akan family and lineage cohesiveness. While some biracial unions have been enormously successful, some have contributed to family disruption by weakening interfamily ties. An investment in nuclear family living weakens interfamily bonds by de-emphasizing family identification. Subsequently this causes the disengagement of children from the lineage. The effects of these withdrawals are felt by the extended family because of the social prominence of these children's fathers. Although the wider family loses out when illustrious sons are replaced by stranger-children, the pertinent point is that former colonial masters are incarnated in our midst as our children.

MOGYA IS SUPREME

No quick resolution is offered to the atavistic confrontation of competing family structures in Africa, in general, and in Ghana, in particular: between the extended *abusua*, and the conjugal nuclear family the matrilineal and the patrilineal, and Asante culture and English culture. The difficulty of achieving an amiable and judicious resolution in the matriliny/patriliny dispute is complicated by the fact that, under the homogenizing global pressures to conform to a social norm, the onus to adjust is placed on Africa and other cultures that are perceived to deviate from the now globalized Western norm. The issue is further complicated by the politics of middle and upper-middle-class African women. Formidable on the chorus line of people who perceive the matrilineal structure as backward are African and Asante women, who was eloquent when the focus is on their identity as wives, but switch to a different tone when the focus is on their identity as kin group. Some are not above demanding their rights to their brother's wealth but vehemently object to anyone interfering in their husband's estate. Because Appiah's portrayal in the epilogue of the matrikin system casts it as oppressive and callous to widows, and since some African women agree, it is important to explore the character of the system through Appiah's father to determine how a mother-focused system is oppressive.

As the notebook of family history Appiah's father left behind reveals (182), at the death of Yao Antony, his *great-uncle* (emphasis mine), Joe Appiah not only proudly refounded the Akroma-Ampim *abusua*, he reveled proudly in the matrix of his mother's line of ancestors as he became the custodian of the properties and wealth of that illustrious *abusua* (183). As head of the matriclan of Akroma-Ampim, he relished in its prestigious history, its closeness to the Asante Stool, and his exalted role in it. All through his life till he added the codicil at his death bed, he scrupulously maintained his Akroma-Ampim *abusua* identity, never once rejecting it.

This clarification is important for many reasons, not least of which is Appiah's attempt to play on the patrilineal and feminist sentiments of his European and North American readers to convince them of the obscurantist, outdated nature of the matrikin system.[16] What is underplayed in Appiah's narrative, and which readers ought to note, is that his father became what he was in Ghana largely on the basis of his matrikin. Apart from the fact that Joe Appiah owed very little to a father he hardly knew (182), the Asante matrikin system is one in which membership in a prestigious *abusua* confers social status. In fact, the elder Appiah had no qualms of conscience about having "coveted" his mother's brother's patrimony nor in becoming the heir of his uncle's *abusua* and its wealth instead of his children. The fact Appiah's father did not acknowledge that his good fortune entailed the dispossession of his uncle's children was not because *he* was callous, as some would now claim, or that Asante custom treats "the widow and children of a dead man as part of the furniture" (183), as his son so loudly claims today. It was because the customary protocol stipulates that a child's inheritance is with his/her mother's relatives. Likewise the inheritance of Joe Appiah's uncle's children lie in the estate of their mother's brother, just as Joe Appiah's lay in his uncle's estate. Hence Appiah's father could not rob his uncle's children of what was never theirs, as Asante customary law defined.

The charge that widows were maltreated cannot legitimately be sustained, because the matrikin system expects widows to define their identities in their matriclan home and their children's inheritance lies therein. A charge of ill-treatment arises only if an evaluator illicitly presupposes the patrilineal family as a model and applies it to a matrilineal one.[17] The oppressiveness that Appiah, and some African women too, see in the matrikin system comes either from misreading the system, or from mischievously obscuring facts to amplify personal gain. Whichever the motive, the flawed characterization of a matrikin as oppressive is premised on a biologized assumption about family relations and inheritance, and a tacit allegiance to a companionate model that stipulates that widows and children should inherit from a husband's estate. It is for this reason that the father–son bonding that Appiah manufactures and inserts into the social structure of the matrikin is problematic, because that axis of bonding was never a significant part of the matrilineal scheme, even as his father, Joe Appiah, contended (182). Unlike patriliny, matriliny affirms the mother's line and family, and offers it as the legitimate arena for nurturing a child's cultural and personal identity. It fosters sibling cohesiveness and privileges uncle-nephew bonding over father–son bonding. Thus, however much Appiah may want to dehumanize the Asante matrikin system, or restructure it to accord with his own mother's patrikin system, or recast his father (182) to accord with his cherished proper view of father–son relationship, he cannot rewrite or falsify history for self-serving ends. No amount of gesturing to a fabricated tenderness in his (father's) tone (182) can recast history and make father-son bonding a norm where it is not. The matrikin system is neither callous nor insensitive to women simply because social and family organization are differently ordered from what is the case in the patrikin system.

Indisputably, erasure plays a vital role in Appiah's construction of the matrilineal system, and the obligations and expectations that go with it. He rewrites history to justify his demonization of matriliny and to replace it with patriliny as the proper model of family in Asante. The clue to this "irrational" project may lie in this enigmatic statement of Appiah's: "When your father's family tradition casts you into your matriclan and your mother's claims you for your father . . . doubts are . . . natural enough" (182). The question that arises is: What doubts? Self-doubts are really inconceivable where the matrikin system is the dominant system and children are aware that uncle is the father-figure. So what doubts? Knowing that doubts arise only for those in contexts where a marginal model contravenes the norm, matriliny cannot be marginal or outmoded for the Akan.

It must be understood that Appiah's "natural doubts" are driven by a tacitly privileged patrilineal model. The issue at stake here is not that Appiah's doubts speak to the lack of an Asante identity, or to the factitiousness of his patrilineal*ized* identity. The issue is that cultural encounters with the father and his matrikin tradition always point to the formidable presence of the textually absent mother. They always urge us to look to the mother-locus pole for his identity. In addition, they urge Appiah to claim his inheritance from his mother's brother, who would be Sir Stafford's son, if he had any, or the estate if there is no son. An encounter with the Asante matrikin emphasizes Appiah's mother's figure and stipulates that the Stafford line provide Appiah with his inheritance, as it had admirably done for his identity; while the *abusua* patrimony of Joe Appiah, *head of Akroma-Ampim abusua,* should rightly devolve to the next in line in the *abusua*, including the children of his sister, Aunt Victoria, Appiah's protagonist. Perhaps the most infuriating aspect of all this for Appiah is that the mores of the "backward" Asante matrikin system rebuffs the cherished patrilineal father–son relationship and obligation he learned in his "advanced" English matrikin. In its place, the latter affirms the primacy of the matrikin ties which the patrilineally raised Appiah cannot accept.

FAMILY AND RACE: A QUESTION OF BEING

So why cannot Appiah go to England to claim his legacy in the way his father's culture advised him to? Why is this not the right course of action for him? Surely this is how he can best demonstrate his love and respect for his father's tradition? Why must he abide by the inheritance tenets of his father's marriage contract but refuse to abide by the inheritance tenets of his father's ritualized *abusua* contract? Why is the ritualized *abusua* contract treated as inferior to a paper marriage contract?[18] Why does he believe in the superiority of the patrilineal model and in the inferiority of the matrilineal model? Why does he hold the socialized traditional values of his Asante father in low esteem? Most especially, why does Appiah treasure and privilege the biologized anachronistic traditional notion of fatherhood he learned from his Anglo-Saxon mother? No doubt, the reason most people would give as to why he cannot claim an English inheritance is that he is his father's child. But that is to assume the legitimacy of the very issue at stake.

Biologically speaking, Appiah is as much his father's child as his mother's, so why should he be obligated to subsume his father's culture to his mother's. We cannot presuppose the validity and naturalness of the patrilineal model. Nor can we assume its superiority without proof. After all we have to remember that the Ghanaian head of state, Flight-Lieutenant Jerry Rawlings, was rejected by his Scotsman father yet claimed by the Ewe mother. In Appiah's case no rejection is implied, just the helpful gesturing to the true house where his inheritance lies even as he claims an Asante connection. He can follow the worthy footsteps of Paul Boateng, who today sits in the House of Commons in England, and is affirmed by both the matrilineal culture of his Akan father and the patrilineal culture of his English mother. If, like Boateng, Appiah really believes in the equality of his biracial background, then, his swarthiness notwithstanding, it should not be problematic for him to affirm his Anglo-Saxon identity and set himself up as Sir Stafford *in England*, hopefully with a seat in the House of Lords. Africa should not always have to bow and adjust to Europe. Africa would be better served by this new state of affairs, if race truly does not matter.

Might race and imperialism have anything to do with Appiah's decision to speak for Africa in the academic arena? Could it be that it is easier to be an "Africa expert" than a "British expert"? Ironically, in the first chapter of his book Appiah devoted considerable attention to exposing the irrationalism of race to prove that race does not exist. His argument consists in showing that there is no biological basis for race arguments, nor can biology explain cultural matters. While he systematically underplays the importance of race, it simmers in the subtext in his awe and unquestioned allegiance to European traditions, and in his constant privileging of Euro-constructed models and traditions over his father's traditions. It is important to see this as the penetration of the politics of race in his understanding of the relation between Africa and Europe, and between Asante and Britain. Race, power and imperialism repeatedly crop up in the subtext of Appiah's narratives and define the relevant framework for understanding his decision to "strengthen . . . and affirm . . . the ties that bind [him] to Ghana and '[his] father's house' " (181). It seems that the challenge of race constitutes the underlying reason that persons such as Rawlings and Appiah look to Africa for their primary identity even as they take a stick to it. As a new Africanist spokesperson, Appiah would serve Africa well by taking his race argument to his Anglo-Saxon and Germanic cousins and ensure that his Asante, Ga, and African cousins are treated fairly by his European cousins in Northern multilateral agencies. At the very least he can ensure that differential standards are not set up for East Europeans and Russians, and another for Africans.

So why does Appiah want to affirm his links to Ghana and his father's house[19] on the occasion of his father's death? The concept of *mogya* or the mother-locus pole is especially useful in probing Appiah's objective in Asante culture.

As a narrative of cultural politics, *In My Father's House* is strangely silent on the larger issues of power, neoimperialism, and neocolonialism and how these new variants manifest themselves and are operationalized in Africa. With a stranger non-Akan mother in a matrilineal system, Appiah knows that he lacks an Asante identity; his identity was never fully formed in the conventional way of having an Akan *abusua* and of learning the histories and narratives of the Asante. Nor was it reinforced in an Akan network of aunts, uncles, and cousins whose formal and informal interactions are critical to developing a full repertory of experiences and histories in the concrete context of social practice. With time out in England for his education, and having been fed a solid diet of his mother's cultural histories and philosophies since birth, Appiah developed an Anglo-Saxon rather than an Asante identity. This development relegates him to the category of non-being in an Akan matrikin system, regardless of the importance of his father and the latter's membership in an illustrious *abusua*. On the one hand, he cannot claim his father's Akroma-Ampim identity since the histories of the Akroma-Ampim *abusua* do not constitute his mother's history or lineage. On the other hand, his mother's matrikin does not belong by virtue of its foreign nature and disconnectedness from the culture.

Thus, as a son whose matriclan is English, and who already knows more of his mother's people than his father's to claim son-hood, that is, his social rights as "the Asante son of his father" is to affirm a non-Asante custom and to espouse the patrilieal ideology of his Anglo-Saxon matriclan. Indeed to "be a true son" of his father's, which involves abiding by the matrilineal codes of his father's culture, entails accepting disengagement from the father's house, traditions, and culture. Because socially embracing his father's matrilineal culture amounts to a rejection/destruction of the father, Appiah is thrust further into the house of his matrikin, knowing that his love for the father represents the cultural death of the latter. To the extent that what is affirmed is not Asante culture and that it erases the latter, Appiah's attempt to affirm and assert his links to Asante as his father's heir in accordance to the precepts of his matrikin's patrilineal system amounts to despoiling, castrating, and mutilating the Asante identity and memory of the father.

Given Appiah's penetrating insight, he must be aware of the cultural implications of wresting custodial power from the *abusua*. He must know that wresting the patrimony, the heir-ship of his father, the head of the Akroma-Ampim *abusua* is a violent rape that closes the Akroma-Ampim line in which his father Asante's identity was formed. Neoimperialism enters the picture when the closure facilitated the appropriation of the patrimony, legacies, and histories of an important *abusua* to serve as the foundation of an Anglo-Saxon matriclan in Ghana. The closure of an Akan *abusua* benefits Appiah as it clears the way for a hybrid Anglo-Saxon matriclan to be implanted into Asante culture, and to draw nourishment from it. Thus innocuous as the funeral furor may seem, it marks an important cultural event in the Asante world scheme. It marks the restaging of unfinished colonial business, in which Europe takes over from within through the legal force of a codicil. It is significant that in a manner similar to the way Appiah's father refounded his Akroma-Ampim *abusua* at the death of his great-uncle, the son chose the occasion of his father's death to establish his Anglo-Saxon matriclan. That the father's codicil facilitated the act and underwrote the closure of an Asante matrikin from which he had taken so much may seem like the greatest act of betrayal from one who swore to protect and work for the good of the *abusua*. But American, European, African, African-American, and other readers of *In My Father's House* need to gain a deeper appreciation of the subtle myriad ways in which neocolonialism and neoimperialism currently thrive in Africa to surplant its traditions with "europhonic" ones. It is through Africa's own leaders, statesmen, and children who most loudly profess to work for Africa's interest that the continent's subjugation occurs.

NOTES

This essay has been immensely enriched by a number of people who gave unstintingly of their time, ideas, and vision. Oyèrónkẹ́ Oyěwùmí (University of California, Santa Barbara) who sang the conceptual-shaking song of a truly inspired vision; Olufemi Taiwo (Loyola University) the devil's advocate, who paced us in our inspired theory dance checking for logical flaws; and Susan Babbitt (Queen's University), who encouraged and urged that this wilding begin. Others to be thanked are Sam Ebow Quainoo (Binghamton University) for generously sharing of his internet Ghanaian community, and most especially L. Ato Quayson (University of Cambridge), who graciously sent an extensively detailed e-mail file.

1. Specifically, these are "The Myth of an African World," "Ethnophilosophy and its Critics," "Altered States," "Old Gods, New Worlds," and "African Identities."

2. This is from an e-mail file sent to Sam Quainoo and received January 29, 1995. All other references to Quayson are from this source. A version of this paper titled "Alter/Natives?: Questions of Identity in the Epilogue to Anthony K. Appiah's *In My Father's House*," was presented to the Postcolonial Reading Group of Wolfson College, University of Oxford in January 9, 1995. Quayson teaches Commonwealth and International Literature in English, at Pembroke College, University of Cambridge, England.
3. Familiarity with African cultures leads one to recognize the expression "first wife" as indicating a polygynous marital relationship rather than the serial monogamy variant practiced today in the West.
4. Ghanaian statutory law was imposed in the former Gold Coast (now Ghana) during the colonial times. Though modifications have occurred to bring the law more in line with Ghanaian realities, it cannot escape its English heritage. Calling the law English-derived is a recognition of the modifications that have taken place.
5. This peculiar sentence in which "individual" is gendered and presented as masculine is one of the invidious legacies of colonialism. English language played a major role in erasing women by representing everything as male through the use of masculine pronouns.
6. Oppong deals with some of these issues (1986: 1–14).
7. Certainly documentation does exist that from the 1900s some Akan families opted for patriliny; hence Appiah cannot be represented as having begun the partinealization move. The contention of my essay is that he is working to finalize the process by means of misrepresentation.
8. Even the marriage ordinance has been modified to accommodate a tripartite system of inheritance (*abusua*, children, wives). See Oppong (1986, 45, 51 n. 46).
9. This section on avoiding the standard mistake of biologizing social and family relations has benefitted immensely from lively, passionate discussions with Oyèrónkẹ́ Oyěwùmí.
10. It is interesting to note that this process makes it possible for women to raise a child sired by a lover as the husband's child, and the child will have full rights of inheritance to the husband's estate. The proverb that makes a distinction between fatherhood and being a reproductive instrument is: One who poaches in a vagina does not father a child.
11. See Douglas (1969: 121–35) for a good sampling of anthropologists' views and negative prognoses on matriliny.
12. This comes out clearly in the chapter on "Topologies of Nativism" when Appiah presents Rattray's *Ashanti Law and Constitution* (1929) as a collection of "invented traditions that have now acquired the status of national mythology" (Appiah, 1992: 61). Rather than stating what Rattray "invented" in Asante tradition, the Ghanaian Appiah leans precariously on Terence Ranger's research on South Africa, to conclude about the situation in Ghana. Such disingenuous circuitous "proof" establishes that Appiah does not really know much about Asante culture to ascertain if Rattray invented any tradition, or to offer a coherent challenge to Rattray's construction. Appiah's problem is not that he is out to tar Rattray, but that he does not know, because he does not see Akan customs as worthy of intellectual consideration.
13. One wonders whether Appiah would behave in this petulant manner in a family court in the United States or England even if the presiding judge had ruled against him, or even if it were clear to him at the onset that he would be

discriminated against. The fact that he would have maintained the conventional standards of civility and propriety all the more underscores the low esteem in which he holds the Asantehene.

14. I would like to acknowledge the invaluable help of Ato Quayson's ideas in pointing me to my present position.
15. Typically at the death of a man severe feuds strain the family as contestations of wills ensue once the "legal wife" discovers she's been had. While this phenomena is not unique to biracial unions, it plays out differently in the latter where the white woman deludes herself about the promiscuous proclivities of African men, and lacks an expansive lineage family for a buffer.
16. Through his negative portrayal of his Aunt Victoria, the other members, and the politics of the *abusua*, Appiah conveys the "backward" oppressive nature of the matrikin system.
17. In fact, it is Joe Appiah, the minister, lawyer, and good Christian, who should be castigated for the way he repudiated for his connection to the *abusua* in his dying moments and appropriated its wealth for his conjugal family, after benefiting from the *abusua* in his lifetime.
18. The issue of the codicil is being treated in another paper, but it should be stated that a codicil cannot "speak" for the head of an *abusua* after he is dead, because by Appiah's father's own admission his word is "an edict—never to be challenged so long as (he) breathed the breath of life" (183). Only the living can decide these matters.
19. It is not clear what this means by "house," which I have read as the sum total of the father's history, legacy, lineage; in short, the *abusua*.

REFERENCES

Appiah, Kwame Anthony. 1992. *In My Father's House*. New York: Oxford University Press.

Douglas, Mary. 1969. Is matriliny doomed in Africa? In *Man in Africa*, ed. Mary Douglas and Phyllis M. Kaberry. London: Tavistock Publications.

Nukunya, G. K. 1992. *Tradition and change in Ghana*. Accra: Ghana Universities Press.

Ofiemun, Odia. 1992. Africa's many mansions. *West Africa,* 20–26 July, 1231–32.

Oppong, Christine. 1986. *Middle class African marriage*. London: George Allen and Unwin.

Rattray, R. S. 1929. *Ashanti law and constitution*. London: Oxford University Press.

Sarbah, J. M. 1897. *Fanti customary laws*. London: Clowes and Sons.

Taiwo, Olufemi. 1995. Appropriating Africa: An essay on new Africanist schools. *Issue: A Journal of Opinion* 23(1): 39–45.

Wiredu, Kwasi. 1990. An Akan perspective on human rights. In *Human rights in Africa: Cross-cultural perspectives,* ed. Abdullahi Ahmed An-Na'im and Francis M. Deng. Washington D.C.: Brookings Institution.

Chapter 21

African Gender Research and Postcoloniality: Legacies and Challenges

Desiree Lewis

Introduction

Much African gender research draws extensively on the discipline of anthropology, and the predominant emphasis in many gender initiatives on the continent remains technocratic and narrowly developmentalist. Alternatives to traditional anthropological and technicist methods and ideas have been developed by feminist scholars in a variety of fields. In historical research from the late 80s, for example, Fatima Mernissi (1988) and Bonlanle Awe (1991) explored the need for "herstory" in African historiography, with their comprehensive accounts of women's agency and subordination transcending the limitations of insular anthropology and developmentalism. Developing these themes in more recent work, Cheryl Johnson-Odim and Nina Mba in *For Women and the Nation* (1997) link the texture of historical process to a Nigerian woman's life narrative in order to approach issues of gender and development from a holistic and humanist point of view.

Certain recent studies of the state have gone especially far in extending theoretical and empirical material for understanding women and African politics. Scholars like Azza Karam, dealing with Egypt (1998), and Sylvia Tamale (1999) and Aili Tripp (2000), focusing on Uganda, examine postcolonial states in terms of gendered institutional structures, relations and cultures. In so doing, they question restrictive notions of development and enlist a much wider range of theories and subjects than those examined in traditional anthropological accounts. In the sphere of economics Aderanti Adepojou and Christine Oppong's *Gender, Work and Population in Sub-Saharan Africa* (1994) draws together a range of case studies in which women's work is explored with detailed reference to gender roles, kinship, conjugal relations and the connections between reproduction and production. Collectively showing how governments and donor agencies ignore the minutae of women's labour, and usually base development programmes on skewed notions of what this labour actually entails, this anthology offers a powerful critique of liberal "Women in Development" approaches, and also implicitly questions traditional anthropological biases.

With many contributions to recent cultural studies, African feminist scholarship has encouraged attention to the everyday, the ordinary and the seemingly insignificant. Here "culture," which is seen to encompass all socially inflected exchanges and mediations, is viewed as the site of localised struggles and transformations. Before the nineties, work on culture in relation to women and gender tended to fix or reify culture, or focused primarily on literature, visual art and music as examples of formal cultural expression; recent research has been enriched by confronting the enormous varieties of cultural communication. With this recent cultural studies work, broad attention to voice, communication and action enlarge conventional understandings of women's political agency, and transcend the "resistance" models that have often constrained understandings of women's roles as political and historical actors. The attention to popular culture and social history in particular opens up ostensibly self-evident or neutral forms of women's lives as fertile sites of self-expression, cultural creativity and political rebellion. Marking a departure from scholarship's traditional "serious" subjects, these studies usefully depart from conventional anthropological projections of culture as static and unchanging.

The range of innovative and radical feminist work on gender in Africa today is therefore considerable, with earlier models often providing the basis for recent exploration. Yet despite the steady upsurge of ideas and publications, the field of women and gender studies in Africa today continues to bear the imprint of traditional anthropology and developmentalism. This impact is often insidious and indirect. It can affect, for example, students' perceptions of gender, or biases in particular gender sources, or the orientation of gender research, or the donor specifications with which many feminist initiatives need to comply. In other words, these conservative traditions have continued to obstruct progress in African gender research and advocacy even though many feminist scholars have successfully mapped alternative paths and goals. It is a key argument of this paper that the dominance of anthropology and developmentalism need ongoing scrutiny in order for us to take progressive postcolonial agendas forward.

The paper starts with a survey of research trends that undermine the radical trajectories identified above. I focus not on the details of particular approaches, but on the epistemological and political patterns thrown up by research to date, as well as the challenges they pose for future research. In the sections that follow, I describe innovative emerging patterns.

THE IMPACT OF ANTHROPOLOGICAL STUDIES OF WOMEN

A tradition of scholarly research on African women first surfaced with studies like Denise Paulme's *Women of Tropical Africa* (1963) and Sylvia Leith-Ross'

African Women: A Study of the Ibo of Nigeria (1965). These works were powerfully shaped by the structural functionalist approaches initiated by Claude Levi Strauss. Paulme, in her introduction to the collection, describes the variety captured in the essays as follows:

> The first thing that strikes one on reading these contributions is how widely varied the modes of life are which they describe. There are agriculturalists of more or less permanent settlement, pastoralists living in straw huts and following their herds from one grazing land to another, or again a complex stratified society with masters, servants and slaves and a strict clientage where subordinates provide subsistence products for a patron who is bound to protect them from the exactions of others, this being the mode from the bottom of the pyramid to the solitary sovereign at its apex. (1963: 2)

The tone and language reflected here, as well as the subjects focused on immediately signal a particular anthropological fixation with customs, modes of life and cultural difference, an over-riding feature of which is a tendency to present African women as frozen in time and place and subjects with static rituals and customs but lacking any real history. The character of this work has been traditionally ethnographic in the sense of offering a window on non-western worlds by defining these as the complementary projections of western ones. Discrete units of analysis like the family, lineage, marriage or kinship indicate an effort to demonstrate (and inscribe) the radical difference of African from western societies. The detailed descriptions of women's social roles, their situations within marriage and their cultural roles in many ways conjures up a sense of all-pervasive "strangeness."

The codification of African women's "difference" in scholarship did not necessarily result in their being denigrated, an effect usually attributed to much western scholarship. On the contrary, scholarly imagining of African women in texts like Paulme's are often ennobling and even iconic. These portrayals continue to be a marked feature of the present, and the shrouding of African women in an enigmatic "difference" is a significant feature of recent seminal work produced by certain African scholars. Among these is Ifi Amadiume's voluminous oeuvre. In her *Reinventing Africa: Matriarchy, Religion and Culture* (1997), a work in which she outlines concerns in her oeuvre as a whole, she shows that a strong matriarchal legacy throughout Africa has allowed women to acquire unique powers and positions of authority, these distinguishing them from women in the west.

Amadiume's recourse to anthropological legacies originating in structural functionalism is registered especially clearly in her preoccupation with topics like kinship, family, lineage and ethnophilosophy. Pat McFadden acutely pinpoints the political effects of this connection when she writes: "The academic language of lineage, the family, and notions of hierarchy and status are drawn largely, in methodological and conceptual terms, from the stock of traditional ethnographical and anthropological sense making, different only in that it is applied via a claim that because it is an African female academic who is using the language, it therefore assumes a different meaning and implies different and previously unknown features and characteristics about those societies and communities" (2001: 60).

McFadden concentrates on the political effects of this "strange consonance" of "old European appropriational practices of studying Africa" and the "claims of indigenous African anthropologists" (2001: 60), dealing mainly with how problematically the latter feed off the former. What primarily concerns me here, though, is the extent to which early anthropology has functioned as a discourse for producing particular research agendas and establishing interpretive frames for ongoing study and representations of African women. In other words, the problem is that the overwhelming impact of a particular tradition within anthropology has been registered not only in anthropological work on African women and gender relations, but more pervasively—in the way that early anthropological concerns have filtered into and defined an authoritative lens in fields ranging from feminist theory and politics to gender advocacy.

The overdetermining impact of anthropology is evident in the way that certain theorists have essentialised African women in terms of binary oppositions between western and African women. A theorist like Catherine Acholonu, for example, in her *Motherism: the Afrocentric Alternative to Feminism*, uses the term "motherism" as a "multidimensional Afrocentric theory" (1995: 110) to define what she sees as being "the essence of African womanhood" (1995). Writing more recently, Gwendolyn Mikell claims that "African feminism is distinctly heterosexual and pro-natal" (1997: 15) and grants a pivotal place to the distinctively supportive roles of African as opposed to western women. For certain theorists, then, African women's ascribed roles and identities are seen to constitute the basis for their radical "alterity," with difference being imagined through the available signifiers and images offered by structural functionalist anthropology.

Another manifestation of the traditional anthropological bias in research is the leaning towards a fetishized "culture," seen to be self-contained, coherent and neatly bounded. References to culture infiltrate discussion and debate in various ways to codify and entrench the binarism of Africa and the West. Here, the fixation with an imagined African authenticity in relation to women in many ways reproduces dominant discursive constructions of Africa, constantly described in terms of everything that the west is not. This is not to deny the importance of ongoing attention to Africa's unique situation in global politics or culture, or to reject the relevance of metaphorically using terms like "the west" or "western" to decode power relations. What is disturbing, however, is the fixing of these categories as absolute entities, with meanings about Africa being formulaically measured on the basis of their being antithetical to projections about the west. In the same way that colonial discourses have imagined Africa in terms of its antithetical difference from the west, so does much recent intellectual thought and politics fixate on a binary impulse—ostensibly in an effort to contest western dominance, but often with the effect of reproducing western modes of misrepresentation and projection.

The preoccupation with cultural difference often colours the tone of debate, the kinds of agendas that define conferences or workshops, orientations in teaching and curricula design and various forms of gender advocacy. The focus of this work and politics often appears extremely radical insofar as inherited terms like "gender" or "feminism" are jettisoned in favour of a new language which seeks to register distinctively pre-colonial or postcolonial agendas.

One difficulty with the assumption that language can be overturned in favour of an entirely new lexicon and world outlook is the problematic assumption that words and their meanings can be neatly separated from a globalised cultural repertoire pervasively underwritten by centuries of western discursive dominance. The effort to salvage past modes of thought, or to invent an entirely new language, seriously underplays the extent to which current language use, terminology and theory have become irrevocably creolised. This means that what we understand, from the vantage point of the present, to be pre-colonial and what we currently imagine to be postcolonial will always be deeply implicated in western discursive practices. This dilemma seems to me best confronted not by attempting to transcend hybridisation as "contamination," but by squarely acknowledging and working with it in order to develop "new" contestatory modes and theories.

Another problem with efforts to salvage or recreate entirely new meanings by codifying a pristine "Afrocentrism" concerns ways in which organicist notions of African identity feed into conservative gender and class hierarchies. Throughout Africa, the reification of African difference has been marshalled in a variety of ways to build a sense of African unity that mystifies class and gender divides. Evidence of this abounds in the strategies and pronouncement of postcolonial political elites, in the philosophies of heads of state, and in the defensive reactions to radical women's agendas of many male politicians. Thus, the effect of Afrocentric nation-building in debates about gender on the continent is often to foreground alliances between formerly colonised black men and women to the extent of underplaying the very urgent divisions and struggles around resources, power, dignity and self-expression associated with inequalities between men and women.

This seems to me a key drawback of the extremely important intervention made several years ago by Chikwenye Ogunyemi. In a seminal work published in *Signs* "Womanism: The Dynamics of the Contemporary Black Female Novel in English," Ogunyemi launches a radical critique of the extent to which white and western women have ignored the realities and locations of African women. She goes on to coin the term "womanism" as an alternative to feminism, arguing that African women and men have been united in a common struggle against colonialism. I believe that this intervention, made in 1986, remains a crucial milestone in the efforts of radical African women to name themselves independently and to contest the appropriative ways in which many western feminists have spoken for them. But the argument about the congruence of African men and women's struggles can become tricky when a critique of colonialism and neocolonialism and white feminists' dominance is *pitted against* an analysis of gender hierarchies in Africa. There seems to be no reason why one form of oppression should be privileged above another, and why it should not be possible to critique western feminist discursive dominance while simultaneously disavowing patriarchal oppression in Africa.

When we consider the repercussions of privileging racial or national identity to the extent of ignoring structural inequalities between men and women in postcolonial African politics, it is disturbing that a celebrated African authenticity can muffle and displace crucial power relations and challenges for change in Africa. Consequently, the reification of Africa or an essentialised African identity can mystify political consequences in ways reminiscent of earlier constructions of Africa. Traditional anthropology, and in particular the legacy of structural functionalism, has therefore had a major impact not only on anthropological work on women and gender, but on the debates, discourses and frames that are sometimes generally deployed within African gender advocacy and women's and gender studies. As such, anthropology has exercised the force of a regime of truth, through which observation and description are anchored in language and interpretive methods with the force of irrefutable objectivity or scientific scholarly accuracy.

DEVELOPMENTALIST APPROACHES

Women in Development (WID) has been a feature mainly of donordriven activity and research for NGO's, handbooks, consultancies and so on. As such it has been sidelined within academic scholarship and publishing. Despite this, the impact of developmental paradigms continues to make an enormous impact on, for example, the drawing up of gender courses, university lecturers' selections of readings, the political focus of workshops or postgraduate research and thesis-writing in addition to much advocacy work and policy-making in Africa. Originating with Esther Boserup's *Women's Role in Economic Development* (1970), this paradigm defines as its aim the liberation of third world women from their entrapment in African patriarchy and under-development. The WID paradigm that was current in the seventies has been developed in the present, with gender experts couching their prescriptions in the form of knowledge specially attuned to practical agendas for African women. This has resulted in a deluge of "accessible" and "relevant" material that ostensibly sets critical guidelines for facilitating African women's "development."

The limitations of this paradigm have been extensively critiqued by Rudo Gaidzwanwa (1992), Ruth Meena (1992), Amina Mama (1996), April Gordon (1996) and many others. What still seems to warrant scrutiny is the ongoing appeal of this limited paradigm in addressing Africa's gender-related developmental problems. In other words, it does not seem sufficient simply to identify why WID approaches have been inadequate. What is important is the question of why, despite the abundant evidence of its inadequacy and the many examples of rich, innovative work on women's labour and involvement in the economy, it remains so prominent, and what this implies for the climate of progressive gender research and politics in Africa.

Liberal developmentalist approaches have been steadily critiqued, and yet the mindset and bias that makes these approaches, rather than any other, such major contributions to Africa's dilemmas are noteworthy. In a climate that prioritises an urgent pragmatism, issues of intellectual development and the need for building a critical intellectual culture that exerts an influence on state and donor-funded gender work have been consistently underplayed. One result of the emphasis on technocratic and functional development has been to limit the intellectual quality and range of gender research. From a WID perspective, gender research and advocacy can be reduced to neatly defined gender issues, while analysis and rigorous intellectual work is marginalised as secondary, not of pressing importance, the luxury of intellectual elites.

The hegemony of developmentalism has been to sever scholarship from the agendas and priorities facing African women and to delimit issues of development to narrowly economic and donor-related concerns. Stephen Arnold, in his Preface to *Culture and Development in Africa* (1990), describes this situation as "technocratic balkanisation" (1990: viii). "Technocratic balkanisation" has had a major impact on university teaching and the ethos of intellectual debate and scholarship throughout Africa, with the trend being to displace the relatively militant and independent intellectual activity of the immediate post-independence period (during the sixties and seventies) with a growing focus on Development Studies, technologies of development and intellectual agendas driven by market forces and conservative political strategies. With gender research, technocratic balkanisation has had an especially restrictive impact because "gender" has a long history of being reduced to a peripheral "hands-on" concern. The broad and wide-ranging field of gender analysis has easily been reduced to clear-cut "gender issues," fragmented topics that can be easily identified and resolved in line with transformation driven by structural adjustment and conservative post-colonial state-building.

Another effect of the functionalist emphasis driven by WID is the bias towards policy-making, rather than intellectual activism in gender advocacy. This means that short-term problem-solving and immediate action takes prior place over the careful analysis and political insight that could shape radical programmes and projects for long-term transformation. In a highly suggestive article on Ghana, Dzotsi Tsikata (1997) identifies a schism between policy activism and intellectual activism on gender in Africa, a situation that has meant that "research has not had a fundamental impact on the work of activists, organisations and on state policy formulation" (1997: 381). She goes on to claim that "while analysis has shown that state action is often both gender-blind and gender-biased, both independent and state-sponsored activists have sought to rely solely on the state to outlaw gender discrimination, with limited success" (1997: 381).

The systemic and structural nature of the problem presents difficulties that cannot easily be remedied. Tsikata's historical approach to policy is extremely valuable, since it develops more than a critique of existing state policy and considers how patterns develop, how pervasively they have affected gender research and activism and, implicitly, how they can be changed. Reviewing historical trends helps to explain the constrained dialogues between critical feminist scholarship and gender activism and the reasons for the highly visible, yet remarkably ineffectual state-inspired gender policy-making throughout Africa.

State and Donor-Driven Initiatives

The WID emphasis easily supports state-controlled developmentalist orientations that, throughout Africa, have helped to erode independent feminist initiatives in Africa. These orientations have a number of causes that vary from region to region and from country to country. Their key causes, however, are very similar throughout Africa. With the transition to independence, new ruling parties rapidly set about consolidating the diverse and militant women's organisations that had mushroomed during the struggles against colonialism. The militancy and independence of women's movements in countries like Algeria, Ghana, Zimbabwe and South Africa rapidly dissipated as women's wings were yoked to the new ruling parties. With this co-opting of many grassroots and local women's movements, political lines of difference (which might have sparked off important realignments, mobilisation and consolidation for radical women's organisation in the postcolonial period) were reduced to personality struggles and petty conflicts.

Tsikata demonstrates this situation in Ghana (1997: 393) while Gaidzanwa reflects on the co-option of the women's movement in Zimbabwe and South Africa (1992). Extending the argument to Kenya, Tripp shows how the Kenyan African National Union steadily increased its grip on women's organisations to turn the dominant *Maendeleo ya Wanawake* into a party wing eventually declared the sole representative of Kenyan women (2000: 9–10). Lazreg develops similar conclusions in her discussion of how women involved in Algeria's armed struggle were later confined by the patriarchal agendas of post-independent Algerian nation-building (1994). In an important contrastive study, Tripp shows how Ugandan organisations were able to elude state co-option. Focusing on the concept of "societal autonomy," her study is an important discussion of conditions shaping the independence of Ugandan women's movements, a position that has generated the vigorous gender struggles in the country today (2000).

A final consideration in explaining the general impact of state policy on gender concerns the fragmentation and conservativism of postcolonial policy-making. Generalising about state policy on gender in the third world, Haleh Afsar writes:

> Third Word states in general . . . do not have coherent policies abut women, nor do they usually have structural facilities for co-ordinating their decisions. Given

> the tension within bureaucracies and the almost total absence of discussion between the separate branches of the executive, it is not surprising to find the introduction of policies which have radically opposed implication for the lives of women and make at one and the same time contradictory demands of them. (1987: 3)

Many of the pioneering feminist studies of African state policy today, including Tsikata's (1997), Sylvia Tamale's (1999), and Tripp's (2000) demonstrate that it is often liberal or WID approaches that frame state policy and generate funding. Post-colonial governments, under pressure to democratise from donor agencies and an international community, have been quick to embrace ad hoc, piecemeal and uncoordinated gender initiatives. This creates situations where gender is arbitrarily woven into policy-making in the absence of any long-term vision or context for meaningful gender transformation. At times, legislation may be surprisingly radical. Yet this is often not connected to legislation in all areas, so that concerted policy-making in certain areas may be out of step with its absence in others, or particular pieces of progressive legislation may be undermined by unmonitored gender discrimination in the wider society. Tripp expands this bleak picture of state control over gender advocacy by showing how many African governments have regulated funding sources for progressive activism and planning (2000: 10–11). By monitoring NGOs, many African governments have sought to ensure that funding potentially aimed at progressive and state-independent gender initiatives is channelled through the state's agendas for development and policy-making.

The regulating of gender advocacy in relation to patriarchal anxieties about meaningful gender equity, external pressure and western prescriptions has had far-reaching consequences for women. Although the picture that emerges is of vigorous and high-profile gender activism, planning and policy-making, the reality is often evidence of government's nominal engagement with women's rights. Many African women scholars have critiqued postcolonial state initiatives in relation to the economy or health, implicitly offering guidelines for radical planning and policy-making in particular regions or throughout Africa. Yet it is usually the legacies and patterns traced above, rather than this insight and rigour that infiltrates policy-making.

The salience of the state in gender initiatives creates the impression that it offers a flourishing site or models for gender research and scholarship. It is easy to assume that the voluminous research, mechanisms and information generated by different governments creates an adequate climate for future work, especially when these are linked to donor support and international mechanisms. The fact that they have not done so poses a crucial challenge to African feminists seeking to forge connections between their work and radical activism, and to ensure that initiatives from civil society, rather than from the state, take responsibility for conceptualising and driving transformation and development in post-colonial Africa.

POSTCOLONIALITY AND AFRICAN FEMINISMS

The situation mapped above raises the importance of strategising for feminist capacity-building and research on a number of levels. Of importance here are not only efforts to enhance the quantity of the enormously important feminist work on the continent. Possibly even more urgent is the need to develop capacity-building and networking projects that address the entrenched discursive and structural legacies traced above. The legacies I have described indicate that levels of networking need to be qualitatively transformed in order to foster strong communication and fruitful crossdisciplinary exchanges. To challenge the fragmentation of knowledge and representation originating in anthropology's dominance, it is crucial to encourage communication among scholars, students and researchers who are often confined to their different niches. Secondly, reinstating and ethos of critical debate and intellectual rigour is a vital way to forge fruitful exchanges between activism and academia, to contest the current separation of activism from academia, and to undo the misconception that gender advocacy and activism can dispense with rigorous intellectual work.

Already there have been a number of exciting collaborative and networking initiatives that contest the legacies and elements reviewed above. Development organisations and research networks such as CODESRIA, the Southern African Regional Institute for Policy Studies (SARIPS) and the Association of African Women for Research and Development (AAWORD) have been hugely influential in shaping regional intellectual, cultural and political agendas. Specialist networks and organisations dedicated to particular areas for women's empowerment, like Akina Mama wa Afrika (AmwA), the African Women's Leadership Institute, Femmes Africa Solidarite (FAS), which concentrates on peace-building, ABANTU for development, dealing with organisations and development, the Council for the Economic Empowerment of Women in Africa (CEEWA), Women in Law and Development in Africa (WILDAF), AMANITARE, a recently launched organisation concentrating on reproductive rights and gender-based violence, and the Association of African Women Scholars (AAWS), which has consolidated scholarship in Africa and North America, have considerably strengthened the work of those formed in the eighties.

This tradition has allowed feminist intellectuals to "institutionalize their presence, to articulate agendas for African feminism by facilitating research and activism by African women scholars [through organising] workshops on methodology, women and rural development, reproduction, the mass media and development assistance" (Mama, 1996: 6). These networks have also offered foundations for the much-needed debate and conversation likely to address the structural legacies traced above. One of the key effects of this conversation would be to instil a strong ethos of cross-disciplinarity in African feminist scholarship. Another effect would be to strengthen traditions of intellectual rigour and so invigorate the politics, research and advocacy that have been insidiously undermined by technicist and state or donor-driven developmentalism.

Cross-disciplinarity and boundary-breaking have long been celebrated as keys to the success of feminist intellectual intervention. A definitive characteristic of second-wave feminism was the way it questioned the conventional schism between activism and academia. Moreover, disciplines blended and fused in rich and exciting ways, resulting in a pattern that made women's and gender studies in the seventies and eighties extremely difficult to place in disciplinary terms. Women's and gender studies teachers were frequently drawn from a range of disciplines, while course-work and research were often defiantly and assertively situated in-between conventional boundaries.

Although it has become increasingly clear that understanding gender dynamics and promoting gender transformation requires us to explore intersections in terms of connections among disciplines, fields, power relations and identities, enthusiasm around interaction and interdisciplinarity has not developed as far as it might in the field of African women and gender studies. There are clearly a host of reasons for this, reasons that must include the constraints on African feminist scholars to sustain interdisciplinarity in universities with very different priorities, insufficient time for exploratory research beyond conventional disciplines or limited opportunities for conference travel and scholarly collaboration. Located in disciplines where we are often constrained by heavy teaching loads or administrative duties, sometimes unaware of each other's work because of the relative paucity of African conferences in our field; unable to visit other countries and universities because of limited funding from our universities for research and conference travel; and pressured to take up important yet exhausting ideological and political battles in unsupportive institutional environments, as African feminist scholars we have far fewer opportunities to network effectively and consistently than many feminist academics in the West.

The positive impact of interdisciplinary conversation is attested to by trends in gender research that draw on a variety of fields and marshal a range of theories or genres to bring fresh insights to bear on particular subject. Laetiticia Mukurasi's *Post Abolished* (1991) springs to mind here. Exploring the iniquitous mechanisms preventing and circumscribing women's access to higher paid economic activities *Post Abolished* is a powerful autobiographical account of the author's battle against gender discrimination in Tanzania despite this country's progressive postcolonial policies. Appraising the discriminatory landscape that women workers confront, the book uses testimony and personal narrative and so enlists a genre that is often marginalised in mainstream scholarship. A study which is similar in orientation but which has the advantage of incorporating a concise introductory analysis of patriarchy and feminist research methodology is Ngaiza and Koda's *The Unsung Heroines: Women's Life Histories from Tanzania* (1991). Contributors include both established and new writers dealing comprehensively with the experiences of women ranging from migrants and peasants to urban housewives. These works are notable both for the ways in which they draw on different styles and genres and for their holistic appraisals of African women's experiences. It is clearly demonstrated that economic activity, politics and interpersonal or domestic relations are inextricably linked, even where the focus may be on a particular facet of women's social experience.

Other important developments have occurred in research with strongly literary or cultural orientations. Of importance here are ways in which a cultural or literary focus is deployed to shed light on broader questions of subjectivity and political expression. A pivotal subject here has been motherhood, with many literary critics focusing on the centrality of social and symbolic motherhood for African women to raise general concerns about ways in which women have been defined in ideologies of domesticity and to explore women's subjectivities and self-perceptions. The anthology edited by Susheila Nasta, *Motherlands* and, more recently Nnaemeka's edited collection, *The Politics of (M)othering: Womanhood, Identity, and Resistance in African Literature* (1997) are highly suggestive here. In the studies of diasporic African women's writing in these key anthologies, a range of critics bring different political perspectives to bear on their reading of women authors' concerns. At the same time, they unravel the contours and histories of the looming mother motif in African women's subjectivities.

Much cross-disciplinary research reveals an emphatic commitment to the transformation of gender relations. It is acknowledged that power relations between men and women are complex, multi-dimensional and pervasive, and that a diversity of tools and angles are needed to disentangle and contest them. Rather than simply registering women's locations and identities, or narrowly compartmentalising "women's struggles," this work intricately explores and challenges gender dynamics as the confluence of networks that shape men and women's relations *vis-à-vis* numerous past and present circumstances of power and control.

Having highlighted networking and conversation as the basis for strategic interdisciplinary work, it seems significant to raise a caution about interdisciplinarity for interdisciplinary's sake. bell hooks (1994) trenchantly observes in her discussion of the boundary-crossing in recent American cultural studies that it can easily define a new orthodoxy, with critics, researchers, students and scholars enthusiastically speaking the language of contestation and border-crossing, yet making very little effort to connect their ideas to practice. Our networking needs to be informed by the priorities and legacies that have thus far shaped the singularity of progressive feminist scholarship on the continent. While it would ideally enhance our research output and opportunities to grow, effective networking need not only lead to career consolidation and individual academic achievement. The agendas, priorities and directions that have thus far shaped progressive women and gender studies on the continent, especially the important collaboration and conversation between advocacy and women's movements and academia, would therefore be a crucial dimension of progressive exchanges and networking for activist-oriented interdisciplinary work.

CONCLUDING COMMENTS

I have singled out three major constraints in women and gender studies and gender advocacy in Africa today. At one level, these have led much African gender research to become overly preoccupied with endorsing a "difference" predicated on colonial imagining of Africa. At another level, the content of research and politics has often been constrained by technicism, state interference and the role of developmentalist discourses in shaping technologies of gender, rather than fostering critical intellectual debate. By way of conclusion, I want to highlight the paradigm shift which largely informs the radical work and focus on interdisciplinarity traced above.

Many radical third-world feminists have extensively deployed post-structuralist methods and theories, while insisting on the "postcolonial" as opposed to the "post-structuralist" or "postmodern." The use of post-structuralism in the work of certain feminists in Africa signals a major re-orientation away from earlier structuralist emphases in theory and methodology.[1] For example, Pat McFadden, in a recent article on culture and resistance, draws on Said and Gramsci to explore discourse as a site of post-nationalist African feminist struggle (2001). Amina Mama has focused on subjectivity as an entry point into cross-disciplinary explorations of women's experiences and struggles in Africa. This approach informs much of her work on politics and the state, but it is most clearly outlined in her *Beyond the Masks* (1995), a study of black diasporic women's subjectivity that yields important comparative insights into the articulation of race, imperialism and gender in Africa. Marjorie Mbilinyi's work is similarly inflected by a critical engagement with post-structuralism. Defining her origins as "European/American" and redefining herself as a "critical Third-World feminist," she writes that "Identities or positions are the product of struggle and they represent an achieved, not an ascribed trait... 'Third World Feminist' connotes a critical analysis of the imperial relations, not a geographical location or physical trait" (1992: 35). As her comments suggest, much recent work registers an emphasis on self-reflexivity and positioning for feminists. Increasingly, scholars are acknowledging that all representation and knowledge production are mediated, and that feminist research and practice, if it is not to betray its progressive thrust, is always relational and partial. Azza Karam's work on the Egyptian state (1998) is especially noteworthy in the way it directly brings Foucauldian analysis to bear on pressing questions of power in relation to postcolonial gendered practices and relations. Drawing on discourse analysis and demonstrating that power is not simply imposed from above, but infiltrates the way in which social subjects routinely police themselves, Karam offers important insights into understanding the tenacity and complexity of oppressive relations in postcolonial Africa.

The shift to post-structuralism has therefore focused on power at a range of levels, rather than on entities and constants clearly observable in real life. Efforts have been made to consider how the naturalised language and tools of scholarship are themselves implicated in multiple networks of power. The emphasis has also been placed on acknowledging how multi-layered oppression usually is. Overall, postcolonial interventions have the potential to expand work in some of the key growth areas for African women's studies and to open up for scrutiny hidden facets of power, subjectivity and society. The recourse to post-structuralism, therefore, indicates a strategic, self-conscious and extremely selective borrowing of progressive resources in order to address specifically African concerns with gender and substantive development. Far from signalling hasty efforts to "keep up" with the theoretical orthodoxy of the west, they are highly politicised and distinctively African forms of intellectual engagement.

By way of conclusion, it seems important to reflect on the role of modern information and telecommunication systems (ICTs) in relation to the impact of poststructuralism in African gender research. What is postmodern is generally considered to be uncontainable, without boundaries, fluid, what upsets the securities that we have long cherished about knowledge, information and text. The Internet is characteristically "postmodern" in the way that it opens up limitless opportunities for communication, writing and thought, in the way that it galvanises the proliferation of text freed from the mastery of authors, and in the way that—hypothetically—it makes all information the ownership of everyone. The Internet is often equated with an *apocalyptic* postmodernity, with the impact of the modern information revolution being seen as an anti-humanist movement that has, in comparison with the industrial revolution, taken the world by storm.

From this point of view, the Internet seems to occupy a place in an amorphous, dispersed and post-humanist global culture that is at worst hostile to and at best impervious to the agendas of culturally, socially and politically marginal groups. Yet to stress the generally postmodern effect of the information revolution can also mean ignoring the way that information technology is always used for particular political goals. ICTs are fundamentally a resource, requiring human agency and political intention in order to be used. In this sense, ICTs afford enormous possibility for the networking, reflection and rigour that can continue to invigorate African feminist thought. In devoting our energies to challenging conceptual and research work, therefore, we cannot risk ignoring the exciting resources and possibilities made available by a globalised "postmodern" world.

NOTE

1. Structuralism here would include not only structural functionalist anthropology, but also Marxist, Nationalist and many early feminist paradigms that assumed singular causes of oppression and that were often insensitive to the multiplicity of power relations and the encoding of power in theory and discourse.

REFERENCES

Acholonu, C. 1995. *Motherism: the Afrocentric Alternative to Feminism.* Owerri, Nigeria: Afa Publications.

Amadiume, I. 1997. *Reinventing Africa: Matriarchy, Religion and Culture.* London: Zed.

Arnold, S. 1990. *Culture and Development in Africa.* Trenton NJ: Africa World Press.

Awe, B. 1991. "Writing Women into History: The Nigerian Experience." Offen, K. *et al.* eds. *Writing Women's History: International Perspectives.* Bloomington: Indiana University Press.

Boserup, E. 1970. *Women's Role in Development.* London: Allen and Unwin.

Gaidzanwa, R. 1992. "Bourgeois Theories of Gender and Feminism and their Shortcomings with Reference to Southern African Countries" Meena, R. ed. *Gender in Southern Africa: Conceptual and Theoretical Issues.* Harare: SAPES Books.

Gordon, A. 1996. *Transforming Capitalism and Patriarchy: Gender and Development in Africa.* London: Lynne Reiner.

hooks, b. 1994. *Outlaw Culture: Resisting Representation.* New York: Routledge.

Johnson-Odim, C. and Mba, N. 1997. *For Women and the Nation: Fnimilayo Ransome-Kuti of Nigeria.* Chicago: University of Illinois Press.

Karam, A. 1998. *Women, Islamisms and the State: Contemporary Feminisms in Egypt.* London: MacMillan.

Lazreg, M. 1994. *The Eloquence of Silence: Algerian Women in Question.* NY and London: Routledge.

Mama, A. 1996. "Women's Studies and Studies of Women in Africa During the Nineties." Dakar: CODESRIA.

McFadden, Patricia. 2001. "Cultural Practice as Gendered Exclusion: Experiences from Southern Africa" in *Discussing Women's Empowerment: Theory and Practice.* SIDA Studies no. 3.

Meena, R. Introduction in Meena, R. ed. *Gender in Southern Africa: Conceptual and Theoretical Issues.* Harare: SAPES Books.

Mernissi, F. 1988a. "Women in Muslim History: Traditional Perspectives and New Strategies."

Mikell, G. 1997. *African Feminism: The Politics of Survival in Sub-Saharan Africa.* Philadelphia : University of Pennsylvania Press.

Mukurasi, L. 1991. *Post Abolished: One Woman's Struggle for Employment Rights.* London: Women's Press.

Nasta, 1991. Motherlands: Black Women's Writing from Africa, the Caribbean and South Asia. London : Women's Press.

Ngaiza and Koda. 1991. *The Unsung Heroines: Women's Life Histories from Tanzania.* Dar-es-Salaam. Research and Documentation Project.

Nnaemeka, ed. 1997. *The Politics of (M)othering: Womanhood, Identity, and Resistance in African Literature.*

Ogunyemi, C. 1984. "Womanism: The Dynamics of the Contemporary Black Female Novel in English." *Signs: Journal of Women in Culture and Society,* 11, 1.

Tamale, S. 1999. *When Hens Begin to Crow: Gender and Parliamentary Politics in Uganda.* Kampala: Fountain Publishers.

Tripp, A. 2000. *Women and Politics in Uganda.* Oxford: James Currey; Madison, Wisconsin: University of Wisconsin Press; Kampala: Fountain Publishers.

Tsikata, D. 1997. "Gender Equality and the State in Ghana." Imam, A. *et al.* *Engendering African Social Science.* Dakar: CODESRIA.

CHAPTER 22

AFRICAN WOMEN IN THE ACADEMY AND BEYOND: REVIEW ESSAY

Godwin Rapando Murunga

Publishing stands at the tail end of one academic process and at the start of another. One the one hand, it represents a culmination of a research process, a process that begins with conceptualizing a topic, setting research instruments, collecting data, analyzing it and writing up the findings into a coherent text. This is a process whose very nature is woven with the trails and travails of the academy and academic work. These involve, among other things, power and power relations within and beyond the academy. The academy reflects the culture, values and power situation of the wider society. It, in turn, reproduces these relations in its administrative and management cadres, in its curriculum and knowledge producing and imparting organs and processes. The nature of power in the wider society is also mirrored in the student admission processes, the faculty recruitment procedures, and in the academy's overall goals and the way these goals are identified, structured, processed and articulated. Power relations in the wider society, as in the academy, are structured along class, gender, religious, ideological and racial lines. These also have a bearing on the mechanisms of inclusion and exclusion, mechanisms that determine who belongs and who does not. These lines demarcate member as opposed to non-members, insiders as opposed to outsiders, and therefore have a direct bearing on access to the academy and its resources, on equity in administrative and managerial representation.

On the other hand, the post-research and writing stage connects the researcher to society through various links. These are dictated by the need for universities to disseminate their findings and knowledge to society. There are several dissemination procedures and channels. They include publications, conferences, workshops and seminars. Thus, no university is an island by itself, cut off from the rest of the society. The critiques that have been leveled against "ivory tower" mentality, especially in the developing world, are indicators of the inextricable connection between the academy and the wider society. Though the actual practical realization that the academy is part of the wider society may have come belatedly in Africa as Mamdani argues, it has become clear that society authorizes and legitimizes academic work.[1] Society provides the field of study, the resources and wherewithal for academic undertaking and influences the capacity for success or failure. Where certain university functions cannot be undertaken within, private non-state and non-university institutions step in to vouchsafe the specific needs of the academy through grants and scholarships, publications and equipment. In many other cases, like in the case of publishing, private non-university initiatives have played a significant role in boasting the channels of knowledge dissemination within society. However, these very institutions also reproduce the power relations within society and therefore participate in perpetuating rather than inhibiting the reproduction of exclusion and marginalization along gender, class, religious, racial and ideological lines in the academy.

The three books under review consider the place of women, as individuals and as a gender category, in the academy and beyond. The studies tackle specific gender aspects of the process of teaching, research and publication in the Southern and Northern academy. They illuminate the difficulties that gender, class, race, ideology and religion makers impose on women both as researchers, teachers and authors. Written from African (racial) and "feminist" (gender) and worker (class) perspectives, the studies consider and critique questions of representation, equity and access to knowledge, and the institutions and infrastructures relevant to authoring, teaching and representing women. They put the academy—as a workplace—and publishers—as dissemination channels—to task, challenging old societal assumptions about women and gender. Specifically, chapters in these volumes implicitly question the feminist claim to a universal sisterhood among women, a claim that has bundled together all women without recognizing their diversity or that merely pays lip-service attention to this diversity and its different, varied and at times, conflictual demands. The studies admonish researchers to investigate and understand "diversity not just for its own sake, but also for its strategic importance to feminist politics." The studies correctly identify both class and racial inequalities within the common fold of women and argue that there are forms of subordination and marginalization other than patriarchy and sexism that need equal attention. The chapters show that western feminism has attacked sexism and patriarchy but has not done well in understanding social struggles against western and racial hegemony. In many ways, these authors concur with Ruth Frankenberg that "white people are "raced," just as men are "gendered."[2] The studies also bring into focus, and intelligibly address, the question of experience as it relates to women's representation of themselves both in the publishing industry and in the university. With a few exceptions, they do this with admirable clarity, vigor and rigor.

Women in African Studies Scholarly Publishing is a collection of five essays initially commissioned by the Bellagio Studies in Publishing Series but rejected upon completion of the manuscript. They discuss the challenges and difficulties that women scholars face in their effort to generate and disseminate scholarly knowledge. The second study, *Women in Academia* constitutes a set of eight essays compiled under the CODESRIA program on Academic Freedom to discuss the relations between men, women and academia. The last study, *We Only Come Here to Struggle*, departs substantially from the first two studies. It is used in this review to illustrate some of the arguments contained in the previous two books. *We Only Come Here to Struggle* is a narrative of the life of one woman who has lived through the harsh realities of life as a wife and trader in Kenya. From her village in Machakos District to Nairobi, Berida ekes out a living on the meager resources she earns from her petty trade. Her story as recorded by Claire Robertson demonstrates how one western author engages an African reality. In different ways, each of these studies tackles a theme that centers on women experience within or out of the academy and forms instructive material to read.

The five essays in Veney and Zeleza were designed to examine the experience of women in African Studies scholarly publishing in the North and South. The chapters range in interest from a critique of feminist knowledge in African studies to the cultural connections between Africa, through the Black Atlantic, to its Diaspora; from the politics of women scholarly publishing in Africa and the North to an analysis of the gate keeping functions of different outlets for African scholarly productions. All the chapters concur that the tag "women" as it has been deployed by western feminism to imply universal unity and similarity of female experience is misleading. The authors insist that diversity must be accorded due attention. Basically, most of the authors in this volume would concur with Fouche that "what females in one society learn about how to think, act and live can differ enormously from what females in another society learn; in fact . . . there can be very significant differences within a given society."[3]

They, therefore, focus on the experience of women as they are differentiated by location, religion, race and class. In the process, some of the authors rightly shed light on the stereotype of universal sisterhood. The chapters argue that though western feminism has achieved remarkable strides in dealing with patriarchy and sexism, it has failed to transcend its own internal forms of exclusion along racial and class lines. There should be no doubt about the relation between race and class because "Whiteness is a location of structural advantage, of racial privilege."[4] As a result, differences along class and racial lines have been perpetuated and reinforced even when western feminists seek support for their political agenda on the basis of a unified gender category of biological females.

Nkiru Nzegwu's chapter is most vociferous in challenging the notions of universal gender category of women who are subordinate, marginalized and disempowered by men.[5] Unlike Sylvia Tamale and Joe Oloka-Onyango who emphasize "the general balance of traffic" of sexual harassment that favors men in the African academy,[6] Nzegwu pays more attention to the nuances in this traffic as a way of challenging the universalizing creed of western feminism. Quoting Oyèrónké Oyěwùmí's study on the *Invention of Women*,[7] Nzegwu argues that in both Igbo and Yoruba societies, women were not always biologically perceived.[8] She identifies the situation of "female-husbands" to demonstrate its importance in directly challenging the assumption in most western studies that define women biologically.[9] She asserts that "no Igbo female is simply a wife." The term "husband", she adds, "is not equivalent to male, it is a relational term that mainly identifies members of the family into which a female is married."[10] She further convincingly argues that the perception of women in western discourse stems from an imperialistic projection and reading of non-western societies. For Nzegwu, women were not always powerless and subordinate in all African societies. A more accurate reading of their experience would show that "provisions were made for females to negotiate their way out of unfavorable situations."[11]

Take the example of motherhood. Most western feminism perceives mothering as complicit to patriarchal subjugation and therefore antifeminist. Yet mothering means different things to different societies. Mothering is not always a domestic affair, as most western feminism would suppose. It certainly is not a confirmation of the givenness of patriarchy. In any case, the dichotomy between public and private, official and domestic spheres is false, at least going by the Igbo (African) scheme. Nzegwu argues that "a dichotomy that construes domestic and private as female sphere and the official and public as male spheres derives from the researcher's own cultural scheme, not the Igbo conceptual scheme."[12] Using specific texts to illustrate her argument, Nzegwu is emphatic that such western imperialistic reading of African societies can and ought to be rectified. More studies of women in Africa should begin by presenting the positive contributions of women, rather than the present discourse that focus on "overly negative themes of poverty, prostitution, economic and cultural disadvantages, social domination, and political and social disempowerment."[13] She cites the damning discussion of Female Genital Mutilation as an example. Nzegwu correctly notes that "even if the thesis of subordination is true, we ought to realize that histories and social structures are different, and that women are not subjugated in the same way, thus no uniform models exists, and no set of prescriptions can be universalized." In relation to Igbo society, she concludes that "there is no fixed permanent location of subordination."[14]

Nzegwu's chapter clarifies some of the issues raised by Veney and Zeleza in chapter one. In particular, Veney and Zeleza identify some gate keeping functions in African Studies that have worked in favor of white men and isolated and excluded women in scholarly publishing. The exclusion is, however, not generalized for all women, rather it also follows ideological, racial and class lines. In cases where women have been included, these have most often been white women. The reasons for inclusion change on the basis of marriage and academic networks. Thus, married women or those with access to white men are most likely to be better published than unmarried ones.[15] This trend masks the fact that given unrestricted access to research funding and publication channels, unmarried and non-western women are equally hardworking and prolific. The balance of access, they show, is in favor of white men and white women. One reason for the inequity is that networking has become a critical component for academic writing and publishing.

Access to a network depends on access to senior scholars and members of their networks. Since such networking often goes along gender, racial, ideological and class lines, and male dominance is already an established reality, those who can easily be accepted within a network are favored. These are mainly white male writers and researchers.

Further, the authors discuss gate keeping functions like the peer review procedure. For them, peer review cannot be understood outside the politics of the academy and across geographical spaces. Peer review must be seen in the context of the "publish or perish" syndrome that guides the determination of academic excellence, promotion and recognition within specific fields. Veney and Zeleza are cynical of this syndrome. They argue that "it has resulted in an inflation of publications, not in the expansion of knowledge, in which quantity matters more than quality, and mountains of papers are cannibalized from dissertations and research projects and churned out to be listed and indexed rather than read."[16] The result is an emphasis to publish without a concomitant emphasis on intellectual ethics and relevance. A critical analysis of most publications, they argue, shows the increasing distance between authorship and the very people being studied leading to what Oscar Wilde lamented as "an art for its own sake." According to Veney and Zeleza, this growing irrelevance is partly because manuscripts are "written more with the reviewer than the reader in mind."[17]

Veney and Zeleza discuss the question of access, fairness and high academic standards in relation to peer review processes.[18] For them, peer review is a process "often fraught with deceit, suspicion, and recrimination." They correctly argue that peer review is at times neither blind nor conducted by peers. Often junior scholars are paired with senior scholars. Also, the editors are the final decision-makers in determining who reviews which manuscript. Some of the editors may even know the subjective preferences of the reviewers but proceed to use them.[19] Together, all the above factors work to eliminate or reduce the level of women contribution to the understanding of themselves and their own societies. Using results from a survey they conducted, Veney and Zeleza demonstrate that women's access to publishing infrastructure is limited and the constraints have been reinforced by a tendency to devalue women's publishing and to deride gender as a valid area of research. Examples of male scholars who denigrate gender as a valid area of research are legion both in the North and the South. Fashina's chapter in the Sall's volume below documents one such instance of an established scholar at Obafemi Awolowo University advising a female colleague to proceed onto more serious themes of study since her promotion had been based solely on publication on women's issues.[20]

Veney and Zeleza correctly correlate male domination in the publishing industry with the low number of women scholarly production in African studies. By invoking the issue of originality, many publishers have ended up rejecting manuscripts submitted by women and those they ideologically disagree with. The authors add that the concept of originality is essentially empty of meaning.[21] In many cases, they argue, rejection based on originality may be motivated by gender or ideological excuse, an excuse that largely depends on the predilections and biases of the reviewer, editor and publisher. For those male publishers who do not consider gender issues to be of any value, such ideological biases inform their idea of originality. This argument is useful to Rebecca Clarke's analysis of women publishers in Africa and the North.[22]

Clarke demonstrates that women publishers are few compared to male publishers. In Africa, she shows that women are under-represented in publishing. Part of this underrepresentation is connected to a colonial legacy and the dominance of large multinational publishing firms on the continent. Part of the problem also lies in the fact that editors of books, especially literary texts, are men who fail to appreciate the contributions of women in the literary world. Clarke documents the struggles of women in the publishing sector in Africa. She writes about Serah Mwangi's Focus Publishers in Kenya, Mary Asirifi's Allgoodbooks Ltd. in Ghana, and Jane Katjavii of New Namibia Books (NNB) in Namibia.[23] Clarke extends her analysis of publishers to the North, especially the United Kingdom which offers some promising signs though the picture is not very different from Africa. This is especially depressing because publishing is better established in the North than in the South and the required technology and resources abound in the North than in the South. Even in the case of women publishing through North–South linked projects, women do not have prominent positions. Through an analysis Heinemann's African Writers Series, and the co-operation between Heinemann and NNB, Clarke argues that women representation even at the level of editorship is minimal. She concludes that "the fact that all the editors of the African Writers Series have been men, as mentioned earlier, means that women's voices and writings may not have received the prominence they deserve."[24]

Though tenable, the insinuation that women's voices can only be represented by women editors is more complicated than Clarke is willing to explain. She takes this assumption to be true; a given that does not require explanation. Given that one of the editors of this book is male, one might wonder exactly what makes a gender-conscious male editor fail to represent female voices. Let us take the analogy of minority groups in the US to make this explanation. In the US, integration of minorities or the marginalized groups has taken place without confronting the basic structure of oppression and marginalization. Tessiu Liu insists that the diversity debates in the US, with their emphasis on multiculturalism, tried to integrate the racial minorities and empower women without necessarily eliminating the structure that promote marginalization. While some achievements have been attained as a result of the emphasis on diversity of cultures, multicultural curriculum only adds color to a white background without challenging this very background. Consequently, the idea that white is the norm from which others deviate remains intact or is further perpetuated.

Quoting her own class experiences in the US, Liu writes that even though students operating under a multicultural curriculum learn to sympathize with the poor, racial minorities and women, they still consider poverty, racism and sexism other people's problems. "They condemn racism, which they believe is a problem out there between racists and the people they attack." Analogously, she adds, "many male students accept the reality of sexism, feel bad about it for women, but think that they are not touched by it."[25] This suggests that there are gender-conscious men who are however detached from actual social struggles against sexism. Clarke should have investigated the possibility of gender-conscious male editors who consider sexism a problem that is out there between sexists and women and who believe there is nothing they can do but merely sympathize. Such editors remain aloof and disconnected from the active promotion of women's writings and from the wider social struggles for empowerment. Conversely, given that race is a gendered social category, examples of feminists who think that race is a problem between racists and the so-called women of color whom racists abuse adds to this argument. The examples are not hard to come by even within US feminism, for instance. Ruth Frankenberg writes of her own shock when so-called women of color accused white feminists for being racists. Feminism, she thought, was meant to empower all women by fighting their structural oppression by men. Like many of her socialist oriented white feminist friends, Frankenberg had never realized her position of structural advantage as a white woman. She writes:

> As a white feminist, I knew that I had not previously known I was "being racist" and that I had never set out to "be racist." I also knew that these desires and intentions had had little effect on outcomes. I, as a coauthor, in however modest a way, of feminist agendas and discourse, was at best failing to challenge racism and, at worst, aiding and abetting it.[26]

For the study under review, Liu and Frankenberg's explanations are helpful in several ways. First, they bridge a gap evident in some of the essays in this study. These authors explain and challenge a dubious correlation especially evident in Clarke's chapter where male editors are equaled to male publication and female editors are equaled to female publication. Secondly, it draws attention to a failure in Clarke's chapter to effectively problematize the positions of women in their respective societies to illustrate the variations in experience, thoughts and perceptions. Clarke is content to conclude that "the state of women's scholarly publishing in African and Northern countries is firmly tied to the positions of women in their respective societies," but she does not show what positions women have.

Further, it is worth noting that many of Clarke's examples are drawn mainly from literary studies. A review of women scholarly publishing in the non-literary fields would have been helpful for the overall study so as to have a wider field of illustrations. This way, the discussion of literary and cultural production would have been reserved for Tuzyline Jita Allan's chapter which discusses feminist scholarship in Africa. Allan's chapter is valuable because it recognizes feminism for what is it, a political project. Allan talks about "feminisms" in recognition of the varieties of feminism and the contests within them that have led some scholars and activists, especially among black women in the US and South Africa, to insist on its context-specific meanings. Allan demonstrates the significance of class and race in US and South African discussions of women issues. Quoting Cheryl De La Rey, she asserts that "racism is alive and continuing in many feminist groupings in South Africa."[27] Allan examines existing historiography to illustrate the unending tensions between the internationalism of western, and predominantly white, feminism on the one hand and womanism on the other hand. The former overlooks the differences and variations within feminism and among women all in the name of advancing feminist politics. The latter is as interested in black sexual power tussles as with the world power structure that subjugates blacks.[28] Discussing the historiography on womanism, Allan shows that while feminism adopts an anti-male position, womanism is as much concerned about women as it is about men. Further, she shows that non-western feminists are also concerned about racism and power, power that has been deployed on a world scale with negative consequences of exploitation against the poor and minorities and with a double consequence for poor and minority women.

It has to be mentioned that black women in the US are products of a history of exploitation through slavery. Cheryl Johnson-Odim examines their experience by an analysis of how the literature on the Black Atlantic has grown to appreciate gendered dimensions of the Black Atlantic and the cultural connections with Africa. The Black Atlantic produced only a physical separation of the African race, but this has led to cultural breaks and innovations. The study of these innovations remains a vigorous field and Johnson-Odim tackles the cultural aspects of this historiography. Her intention is to identify and discuss changes and continuities, retention and syncretism. She insists that to be black and female "renders a certain common identity." Of all the identities relevant to her analysis like race, gender, ethnicity, religion and class, only race and sex are less mutable. Women cannot do anything to change their gender just like blacks can do nothing to change their racial pigmentation. The commonality of this identity imposes certain specific concerns that a universal feminism fails to comprehend.

However, Johnson-Odim does not ignore the differences within. Rather she uses the racial commonalities only to demonstrate that the production of knowledge on African and black experience within and out of Africa, especially in the North, has to confront problems of communication across the Atlantic. Johnson-Odim is concerned about the way questions about women are posed, what the important pivots for posing gender questions are and generally, the need to be sensitive to differing perceptions. She is concerned that much of the scholarly productions on Africa are done in North America and Western Europe, mainly by westerners of Africans resident in the North. This has allowed research and writing to proceed with little reference to Africa, African women and African voices. By reference to personal experience, she suggests several possible ways of ensuring that the African voices on the continent are heard. Johnson-Odim rightly calls for better modes of networking with African scholars resident on the continent.

There is no doubt that this is a useful and informative collection of writings on women scholarly publishing in African studies. It does not take anything for granted neither does it shy from provoking our thinking in new directions. It confronts the academic and male mainstream and invites a new look at women and Africa and their relationship to the North. It is not a surprise that a mainstream book publishing series whose stated objectives focus on "book development and publishing in the Third World" rejected the manuscript for this study. The study is a living testimony of what publishing is all about; power, ideology and subjectivity. Should we not, therefore, applaud Africa World Press for rescuing this useful and informative manuscript?

Women in Academia stands on several solid grounds. First, it belongs to a series purposely designed and launched in 1994 by CODESRIA (Council for the development of Social Science Research in Africa) to monitor academic freedom and human rights in Africa. The editor, Ebrima Sall, was until recently, also the officer in charge of the CODESRIA program on Academic Freedom. This affords the study a level of connection and consistency that is not always part of many other publications on the question of academic freedom and human rights in Africa. In introducing this study, Sall writes that this volume is the first in forthcoming thematic and sectoral studies "meant to highlight specific aspects of academic life and issues related to academic freedom, human rights and intellectual citizenship."[29] Indeed, the second solid ground for this study is the choice of theme and authorship. The theme is apt. This aptness is reinforced by the fact that most of the chapters are authored or co-authored by African women, many of them resident on the continent. As will become clear presently, many of the authors write from experience, both personal and from acquaintances, students or colleagues. This gives the study a touch that other analyses of Africa by non-African authors lack. Thus, the book implicitly reinforces the arguments contained in Cheryl Johnson-Odim's chapter above that

> African scholars (or scholars permanently based in Africa), because they are "on the ground" so to speak, are more likely to be aware of the indigenous perspective on particular issues and to generate theses and theoretical propositions that are informed by what is actually happening.[30]

Indeed, the strength of *Women in the Academia* is that it allows a look into the lives of women researchers and scholars, taking one through the harassment, double burden and the problems women face in their struggle to be recognized as scholars in their own right, not as women scholars. As Tamale and Oloku-Onyango and Saida Yahya-Othman show, female university students and intellectuals are perceived mainly "through lenses tainted by their sexuality."[31]

Thus, this study is more specific and focused than the previous one. Though the authors recognize the significant external influences to issues of gender bias and harassment in Africa, they are content to discuss internal aspects of gender and sexual harassment in the academy and how these reinforce discrimination in access to research, funding, teaching and publishing. Sall eloquently introduces the study, but Tamale and Oloku-Onyango set the pace for subsequent analyses. The remarkable contribution of this particular chapter is its eye-opening critique of existing instruments of struggle for academic freedom in Africa. Taking the example of the Kampala and Dar es Salaam Declarations on Intellectual Freedom, the authors accuse the charters for adopting a gender-neutral language.[32] These documents assume that the formal acquisition of a right is enough to solve the problem.[33] Ironically, Fashina's chapter in this very volume is written as if to confirm this assumption. But as Tamale and Oloku-Onyango caution, the assumption omits the fact that the genders in question are far from equal and the power imbricated in their socialization deserve more comprehensive political and legislative actions than the mere adoption of a gender-neutral language cares to admit.

The validity of Tamale and Oloku-Onyango's critique is reinforced by the recognition that the roots of "patriarchal oppression lie in the smallest unit of societal organization, the family, and attention on the state alone can only achieve limited reform."[34] The authors admonish against reform measures that focus on the academy alone arguing that the academy reflects the wider society. But the authors do not adequately discuss how gender discrimination in the family connects with gender discrimination in the academy. Also, because Tamale and Oloku-Onyango operate at the level of generalities, it is difficult to zero down on the culture and family being discussed in this chapter. Such knowledge is important in order to develop an understanding of the societal context within which their concept of family and their notion of academic freedom refers. There is not universally acceptable idea of academic freedom. This varies between societies, regions, cultures and over time. This makes it difficult to understand why they disagree with Florence Etta's argument "that women are themselves the chief agents of this socialization which confers inequality on their kind."[35] Thus, they correctly point to the family as the root of women marginalization but fail to demonstrate how socialization from the family affects women even at the height of their achievement. Further, the family has never been a stable unchanging unit of analysis; it is not immune to social influences from within and without. The authors do not grapple with this fact of social transformation to show how different families in different African contexts deal with female siblings. If indeed the family is the root of women marginalization, it would have helped for the chapter to identify a particular context and shed light on how influences in one culture operate to influence women and how these differ from numerous other contexts in Africa. The idea here is that there is no one overarching way in which women are socialized in the family unit and it is misleading to peg problems of academic freedom on a decontextualized family. Even if there is, this has changed over time. The authors suggest that the struggle for "academic freedom for women" ought to proceed in tandem with broader societal struggles for democracy and human freedoms. Further they suggest the promulgation of an edict on gender and academic freedom to supplement and fortify the existing Dar and Kampala documents. This is suggested even when the authors recognize that the Dar and Kampala edict lack legal binding force.[36]

In what is perhaps the best chapter of this volume, Saida Yahya-Othman examines engendering academic freedom in Tanzania. The chapter is a broad analysis of academic freedom within and beyond the university. It examines both subtle and covert practices that blatantly and consistently violate academic freedom. Yahya-Othman identifies an ironic position in Tanzania where during Julius Nyerere's era emphasis was on primary and basic education as opposed to higher education. This is the position that the World Bank adopted in the 1990s.[37] A notable negative consequence of this was the emphasis on basic education at the expense of higher education. Yahya-Othman traces the impact of this policy in Tanzania on higher education in general and on women access to education in particular. The chapter establishes the connection between basic and higher education, a connection that is often taken for granted. In Tanzania, emphasis on basic education translated into low resource input in higher education. Fever women also managed to access basic education, and due to higher attrition rates, each successive education level witnessed limited access for women. As a result, Tanzania has the lowest number of student entering university in Sub-Saharan Africa. Of those who enroll in first year of primary, only 0.3 percent finally enter university.[38] The same case is established in this volume for Senegal and Cameroon.

Tanzania has three universities and a dwindling budget for higher education. Though Yahya-Othman uses statistics, she focuses on their social import to show that the emphasis on basic education led to fierce competition for university education and access to resources. This is compounded by Structural Adjustments that place a strain on resources especially as they call for an end to state subsidy in the social sector. SAPs eroded the profitability of those sectors like agriculture where women gained earnings to educate their children almost at the same time when they promoted private education.[39] The impact on women has been negative even from the wider societal perspective. Within the university, academic violations have intensified amidst reduced state and donor expenditure on higher education. In a context that sees bright and intelligent women as an anomaly, there has intensified in the University of Dar es Salaam pathological identification and harassment of women leading, at times, to rape and death. The case of Ravina Mukassa is cited as one example.[40]

Penda Mbow's chapter on Senegal in many ways complements Yahya-Othman's though the religious aspects resonates more with Helmi Sharawy's chapter on Egypt.[41] This shows how aspects of gender inequality and academic freedom are reproduced across the continent. For instance, in terms of women representation within the structures of university teaching and management, Senegal, Tanzania and Cameroon show marked similarities. Here women are poorly represented at the professorial and assistant professorial levels. At the University of Dakar, women made up only 7.3 per cent in 1985. Of the total 449 teaching staff, only 11.1 per cent were women.[42] At the University of Dar es Salaam, only 62 women stand against 539 men, with 42 of these women being lecturers and senior lecturers. At the level of student enrollment, the figures are not better for Cameroon where the "number of women in pursuit of knowledge decreases at each successive level of education, so that only 0.5 per cent of all women reach the level of higher education."[43] Mbow has no figures for women in high academic positions in the university academic staff. But such an unequal marching affects the articulation of women concerns.

Like Fashina, Mbow critiques the gender biases that overwork women and predispose some of them to perform less than their abilities in professional undertakings. The societal gender division of labor makes women responsible for reproductive roles and domestic work and organization, plus numerous other social duties which their male counterparts do not undertake. This extra-workload is often ignored in discussion on academic freedom and social responsibilities of intellectuals. Further, those women who manage to get into academia are exposed to frustrating societal sanction and mores in the university. In Islamic societies, some women have consequently been "convinced" that involvement in women issues will further marginalize them. Using the example of female students who shun attending meetings on women issues, Mbow argues that the university has at times turned against women. The absence of women's magazines, seminars or updates on gender issues only validate this sorry state of affairs at the University of Dakar. In part, religion explains this rather lukewarm situation. Male students, she writes, tend to be hostile to or misconstrue critical lectures on religion as heretical further driving female lecturers into positions that male lecturers hardly get into. Her chapter, in some ways, provides interesting preparation on the personal experience detailed in Isabel Apawo Phiri chapter.

The structure of authoritarianism and intolerance in Malawi, as in many other countries, connects the university, civil society and the state in interesting ways. A couple of years ago, Zeleza persuasively and adeptly analyzed the nature of censorship in Kamuzi Banda's Malawi.[44] He showed that the texture of authoritarianism did not end with Banda. Tragically, Zeleza showed, authoritarianism had spread beyond the state to the wider civil society in which the culture of fear and despondency was evident even in realms where the state had little effect. Phiri's personal experience at the hands of intolerant students and inept administration is reminiscent of this culture of authoritarianism in society, a story that would be familiar to academics resident in Africa and especially on African university campuses. Phiri's story is compelling. It is about the harassment she encountered because she researched, wrote, presented and aired on the media the extent of harassment and rape directed against women at Chancellors College campus. She tells of personal harassment and injury through misguided and misplaced student activism, of administrative complicity in such harassment, of mediocre journalistic (mis)reporting that perpetuated falsehoods to the wider public and the consequences of these even at her church. What is remarkable about her narrative is the level of collegial solidarity, especially her department which not only came to her defense against the students and the administration, but, in fact, took responsibility for the research paper she had written and defended her to the hilt. As Phiri notes, many people, including men expressed sympathy and supported her within and out of the university.

Phiri's picture contrast in certain respects with Fashina's who also recounts instances of harassment and bias against women in Obafemi Awolowo University, Ile-Ife. Fashina's chapter has the most potential that is least exploited. Its strength, like other chapters in the volume, is in the use of personal experiences and observations to document cases of intolerance, harassment and derision against female academics in the university. But this is the shortest, least conceptualized and least referenced chapter dealing with women issues in the volume (note that chapter six on Mauritania does not discuss women issues). As Phiri's chapter shows, personal experience can be reconstructed from memory and other supporting evidence including oral communication, letters, memorandum, newspaper reports, staff minutes etc. In writing her chapter, Fashina relies on oral communication and observation only. These enable her to document internal cases of neglect, derision and patronage from men in relation to women issues. Fashina should have known better than to rely on UN and related declarations on rights and equality between men and women. In any case, rarely have UN declarations and resolutions been fervently pursued to their logical end when they touch on issues related to exploitation in the Third World in general and Africa in particular. Seen in the context of Tamale and Oluko-Onyango's chapter, the unproblematised appeal to the Kampala declaration on academic freedom does not make a difference either. These authors accuse the declaration of adopting a gender-neutral language that is not very helpful in confronting the basic structure of gender inequality. Fashina should have paid attention to this issue. Like Clarke's essay above, Fashina fails to explore the reasons why men, "even when they recognize that women have certain rights as human beings, still deny them such rights."[45] Tessie Liu is helpful here in reminding us that it is not just men, but men who think that sexism is a problem out there between sexists and the women they attack. This brings us to a problem of conceptualizing gender.

The problem of researching, writing and teaching gender issues as women issues is very real in this volume. Some essays in this volume treat gender and women as synonyms and proceed to discuss women issues as if they are peculiarly gender issues. Thus, some chapters are intolerant to nuance and variation on the theme of discrimination against women. The only redeeming essay is Nobert Ouendji's nuanced presentation on Cameroon. Ouendji looks at the general structure of power in Cameroon and how this has affected the university. He locates the problem in the wider contexts of global inequalities that generate poverty, want and misery even in regions that are well endowed with resources. He cites cases of generalized state harassment of academics and students and associates this to state intolerance to criticism and freedom of speech. This has unleashed student resistance to harassment. Ouendji discusses forms of abuse by university rectors against students and female students in particular. Arguing that women representation in various sectors including student leadership remain low, Ouendji insists that this is because of the overall social status of women in Cameroon.

Though Ouendji is emphatic that women are marginalized, he cautions that no generalized judgments should be made on these. For instance, Ouendji examines the state of academic crisis, collapse and near anarchy in the universities and argues that such a situation has had deleterious consequences to all, men and women. Like Ihonvbere's study of Nigeria, Ouendji accuses university administrators for corruption, malfeasance and mismanagement, but he does not spare academic and non-academic staff and students. These groups prefer to position themselves on the oppressed end of the divide though in reality some among them have been responsible for the problems afflicting universities.[46]

On the question of sexual harassment between the male academic staff and female students, Ouendji understands it within the crisis of the university in Cameroon and the consequences on academic standards. He has a two-pronged assessment. On the one hand are cases of female students who are coerced into sexual relations with male lecturers mainly because of the relations of power between the two. Lecturers are then able to impose compliance and silence with the threat of failing female students who dare report them. Students who refuse to yield to such coercion face reprisal like earning low marks or outright failing in such courses. The situation is worse for women students at the graduate level who have, as their advisors, male professors. It is surprising that none of the writers in this volume discusses the case of female graduate students. Contributors to this volume extensively discuss the male/professor-female/student aspect of sexual harassment.

Tamale and Oluko-Onyango are evidently intolerant to any other perspective that suggests female culpability. They set this tone by expelling from their discussion any other aspect of sexual relations between male lecturers and female students by simply noting that "while it is clear that there are women who harass men, the balance of the traffic is in the opposite direction."[47] Ouendji would agree with them to that extent, but the reality of STG (Sexually Transmitted Grades) compels him to admit, quoting a female student, "that the professors are not the only instigators of sexual harassment. There are also some students who are really hung up and who count on sex to get good marks."[48] Ouendji concludes that it is difficult to support "the theory of academic discrimination or exclusion of the so-called weaker sex."[49] Indeed, this is a redeeming argument because in the concern to right the wrongs of sexism, researchers have tended to overlook the wider context of poverty and ethical decay, both being problems that are gender blind. This has allowed the grading system in the universities to become a transaction between students and professors on the basis of financial and sexual favors.

Ihonvbere calls this "sexploitation." He argues that some "female students in Nigerian universities are simply objects of sex," and there exists gangs of lecturers whose job is to exchange sex for grades.[50] The motivating factors are many and complicated. They range from simple problems of laziness and ethical decay to more complicated aspects of poverty and want. The withdrawal of state subsidy on education and the introduction of student fees can also easily account for the fact that students are forced into exchanging sex for money.

A consideration of the above critique would have given a fuller picture to this text without compromising the basic fact that women are marginalized and harassed within the African academy. The aim here is not to gainsay the fact that women face specific problems that deserve urgent attention. However, that these problems vary, and reflect much more than a male versus female dichotomy is a plausible field of investigation that makes sexual harassment more, not less, intelligible. Studies have noted rising social pathologies in our societies whose sources relate to the changing economic and social situation. Unfortunately, this very important issue is minimally considered when research on the concept of gender is driven by feminism.[51] These pathologies include poverty, want, misery, and hopelessness. These have generated other vices like indiscipline, violence and harassment. Similar anger is also vented against children and juniors in families and schools. Those who are powerless or weak become easy targets leading to increased number of victims. For example, the transformation of the Dar-based student newspaper, *Punch*, from a student mouthpiece critiquing the state into a sexist instrument may in fact reflect much more than male chauvinism. In other places reports of devil worship and mysterious deaths have proliferated in our institutions of learning precisely at the time when African economies are at their lowest ebb and when external pressure to downsize is high. Notable examples of unexplained deaths abound in Nigerian universities while devil worship and mass killing of female students is reported in Kenyan schools. These all point beyond the male/female dichotomy to more serious structural problems in our societies.

In general, however, Ebrima Sall's edited collection is a refreshing contribution in the CODESRIA program on academic freedom. Perhaps, some of the questions raised in this review will be tackled in forthcoming sectoral and thematic studies. As usual, studies issued by CODESRIA have maintained a certain consistency in speaking for the African people and one looks forward to other releases. Further, CODESRIA has always allowed voices on the continent to be heard, and this volume is no exception. By refusing to go by the fads prevalent in the mainstream academia, this study, and many others from CODESRIA, stick to the local agenda and respond to internal issues with more consistency and connection. For those researchers and scholars who never have enough time to observe the African campus, this study provides a good view of the intricate politics between the African academies and the women scholars and researchers.

It should be evident so far that the two studies reviewed above set terms and raise debatable issues in relation to Africanist production and knowledge about Africa. Most of the studies are wary about knowledge on Africa produced in the west. In particular, some studies in *Women in African Studies Scholarly Publishing* point to the problems of translation, perception and communication between the North and the South. Claire Robertson's name features severally in Nkiru Nzegwu's chapter, for instance. Thus, the choice to review her co-authored study was motivated, among other reasons, by the recurrence of her works in *Women in African Studies Scholarly Publishing*. A further compelling reason for looking at her study is the issue of experience which is present in the two studies already reviewed. Indeed, Claire Robertson is not unaware of the concerns raised by Nzegwu and others. In retelling the life story of Berida Ndambuki, Robertson acknowledges some of the problems Nzegwu highlights including those of translation and perception. In reviewing *We Only Come Here to Struggle* one is naturally interested in how some of the issues raised above are tackled and resolved.

What is significant about this study is that Berida's story is not unique, neither is it exceptional. On the contrary, it is a story many ordinary African women, including my mothers and grandmothers, will tell. Like many ordinary African women, Berida belongs to "a transitional generation." According to Robertson, this is a generation that "accepted the goals and values concerning marriage of those older than themselves Â... but also presaged changes that involved those younger than themselves Â..."[52] Berida's story is worth retelling not because it is located between "tradition" and "modernity," but because she has lived through a certain axis of continuity and change diverse aspects of Kenyan history.

The study is interesting in the variety of themes it tackles simply by reconstructing Berida's life. It looks at continuities and change in the contexts of colonialism and independence, from rural to urban, from poverty to prosperity, and from marriage to "separation." Also, Robertson does not pretend to give an untainted narrative of Berida. Rather, she acknowledges her own predilections and eccentricities; things that always follow ones account of the past. For instance, Robertson is conscious of her feminist convictions, some of which were "deeply offended" by Berida's and other project members' views and perceptions.[53] Robertson gives the impression that she tried, with a high level of success, to surmount some of these challenges. But since this is a co-authored study in which Robertson as a western educated author is displaced, it is debatable who really succeeds in surmounting these problems; Berida or *Kalaya* (Berida pronounced Claire as kalaya)? Overall, Berida's life story "rescues itself from being a recounting of yet another sad patriarchal epic, just as it is not merely a saga of women subjected to puberty rites that included excision of the clitoris."[54] Perhaps, Robertson's main contribution to the historiography on gender lies in deciding to celebrate Berida's triumphs. Berida's story reads like "a triumph of sorts over male dominance." She is not "an uncontested victim, an unblemished survivor, or a triumphant empowered victor."[55]

Divided into five main chapters, the story of Berida begins in 1936 in Masii, her birthplace. From here she moved to Mwala and later Kathonzweni in 1950 upon getting married to Kiatine Ndambuki. All these was in Machakos District before she moved to Nairobi as a trader doing business mainly at Gikomba market. Berida gave birth to sixteen children in total, six of whom died as babies. She tells of the joys and sorrows of motherhood, of poverty in marriage and how she worked to surmount it, of the aspirations and unmet hopes of marriage, and of politics and the plight of petty traders in the volatile Kenyan political economy. Though Berida had a pre-arranged marriage, she successfully resisted it preferring to choose her husband. She was attracted to Ndambuki because of his smart dressing. But she captions the story of her marriage with the words "no woman can know what will happen to her in marriage." This introduces the reader to the nature of her marital problems that involve an alcoholic husband. Reading through her story one realizes just how much the western canons of historical writing mystify issues that would otherwise be presented in a simple, clear and understandable manner if told free of fads.

Three areas where Berida's story is a useful correction to previous presentations will be highlighted in the remainder of this review. First, is the story of her early life that touches on the experience of circumcision and pre-arranged marriage. Second is the experience of marriage to Ndambuki that introduces the theme of abusive marriage. Finally is her business engagement that demonstrates her ability to survive harsh marital and economic realities. As can easily be gleaned from existing literature, female circumcision, otherwise baptized as female genital mutilation (FGM) has been a thorny issue in recent feminist scholarship and western discussions. For some, FGM represents part of the age-old exploitative patriarchal structure whose main aim is to control women, their sexuality and their bodies. This theorizing has generated enormous literature and controversy part of which is done by people without credible cultural knowledge of the practice. The consequence has been sensationalism and misinformation. As a result, the privacy of African women has been violated since, in Nzegwu's word, "the vulva is acutely needed for theorizing."[56]

For Berida, the practice of excision of the clitoris "should continue."[57] To her, this practice deters immorality. "Excision does not guarantee virginity; it only assures that one does not sleep with everybody, maybe only with one friend, not moving from one man to man."[58] Some would dismiss Berida as ignorant. Others will see this as evidence of her socialization under patriarchal rule. But that misses the larger explanation which Berida offers. There were two types of initiation among the Kamba of Eastern Kenya: *nzaiko nini* (the small initiation) that involved excision and *nzaiko nene* (the big initiation) that involved a mark on the pubic area. Excision was not just about the cut which recent scholarship has reduced it to. It was broadly about education. This may explain why the excision of the clitoris was referred to as small initiation—*nzaiko nini*. What the merchants of voyeurism miss in their discussion of circumcision is the educational value of the practice. Berida explains:

> With *nzaiko nene* a lot of advice was given and information passed along to the initiates. After it the whole group would be sleeping outside on the verandah chaperoned by another woman Â.... During the *nzaiko nene* you had advisors

> who were referred to as hatchers [*awikii*], as with eggs. Our hatchers told us the bad things we should not do. They were like our mothers and were paid only, say, thirty cents for doing it. It wasn't a career but a status you inherited.[59]

Berida blames the death of this practice on whites and Christianity and that is the reason why only one of her daughters is circumcised. One can conclude from this that activism has little contribution in dealing with female circumcision if it proceeds without understanding the cultural/educational component of the practice.

Apart from having abandoned circumcision for her daughters, Berida also rejected a pre-arranged marriage to a man she did not care for. By rejecting a pre-arranged marriage, Berida ably challenged an age-old tradition of her society. Yet there is nothing novel in this because though pre-arranged marriage was practiced in Kenya, it was not such an absolutist institution. On the contrary, the very fact that Berida rejected it without social chaos is an indication that rejection was possible and many other people did reject pre-arranged marriages. Instead, she opted for one she loved. However, life in marriage has not measured up to her expectations. It has largely been a life of poverty and want coupled with a husband who gradually became an alcoholic and abusive. Rather than simply resist his many failures, Berida adjusted to, and found ways out of the problems generated by her marriage. It is at this point that Berida does not conform to western expectations. To any casual observer, especially those schooled in western feminism, the solution to an abusive marriage is separation, even divorce. On the contrary, Berida treats marriages as a lifetime relationship, a journey full of ups and downs. She recounts numerous instances of abuse including wife beating as her husband degenerated into a drunkard. Rather than divorce him, Berida saw in this an opportunity to make a claim to her life as a married woman, to resist such violence and find innovative ways of surviving poverty. Thus, an alcoholic husband, rather than being a deterrent, has in fact spurred Berida into hard work as a businesswoman. It has given her an opportunity to reconcile herself with reality and proceed in life. She remains married to Ndambuki though economically independent. What Berida shows in this is that poverty and abuse regularly reinforce each other and are at times inextricable.

Driven by an urge to avoid poverty and fed by her daring energy, Berida got into business selling cereals and related items. She did this with the blessings of Ndambuki. She lives as his wife though she spends a large part of the year in Nairobi away from her husband where she rents a house. They are still married. On the contrary, Berida has often used her earning from business to ensure that her husband is smartly dressed (something that Berida obsessively believes in) and to educate her children. Funds from her business also built a family house and she continues to feed everyone including her grandchildren. Occasionally she uses her earnings for ceremonies like her sons' wedding. Though Berida wishes she had fewer children, she continues to do all in her ability to support them. She knows that Ndambuki is a liability but still accords him status, however nominal, as a head of the household. She insists, for example, that her children cannot be referred to as the children of Berida. They are Ndambuki's children.[60]

It is important to remember that Berida told this story to Robertson who in turn recorded and transcribed it. The recorded story fulfils the relevant canons of historical writing, of periodization and "objectivity." This is done with ease because the subject of analysis, Berida, tells it from experience without bothering about theoretical frameworks or related concerns that mystify knowledge all in the name of being scientific. However, and to her credit, Robertson allows a notable and important displacement to take place in this text. Berida takes center stage in the text and yields to the west only in terms of language of communication. The authority of other authors is consigned to the footnotes where they are allowed very little interference. As a result, the narrative flows in the direction of Berida's story. Whether Berida's story fits in western expectations is not an issue for this text. Berida remains the norm for this text from which the west deviates.

But though the author largely succeeds in displacing the western mode of producing Africa, some footnote citations do not. Most footnotes are meant to provide a context of understanding Akamba history, Kamba being Berida's ethnic group. But a few end up privileging the perceptions of colonial and amateur anthropologists. For instance, footnote 5 on page 24, 16 on page 34, and 15 on page 80 all provide information that could be stated without reference to secondary citations. Indeed, some of these citations are broad generalizations that eventually compromise the specificity of the case in question. In footnote 16 on page 34, for instance, Robertson quotes in order to elaborate on Ndambuki's alcoholism. She approvingly quotes that " 'beer drinking is the favorite occupation of old men Â . . . ,' who got old before their time because of it." Such a quotation simply panders on a colonial stereotype of the Kamba written into colonial annual reports of Ukambani Province by administrators who doubled up as producers of "reliable" information on colonial "tribes." We know however that the perceived habitual drunkard of the colonial administrator was not the norm but the exception. In colonial days, time for drinking competed with labor time which is why the administrators raised complaints about the Kamba. Certainly beer drinking was regular but it was not the favorite occupation of all old men. Beer drinking had its time and rules. Therefore, a footnote to this effect perpetuates a stereotype rather than help one understand the context of beer drinking in Ukambani. Neither does it explicate Ndambuki' habit and should be treated with enough suspicion.

Overall, the story of Berida like the experiences of women highlighted in the other texts under review is worth reading. Its contribution lies in its ordinariness and the simplicity of presentation. For those who prefer to theorize gender issues in Africa, this story shows the limits of theory. Theory almost always privileges a western reading of African realities. This often ends up with a gloomy picture of misery, hopelessness, abuse, mutilation, prostitution and disease. Robertson and Berida bring to life not just the concerns, joys and sorrows of one African woman but of many others whose experiences remain untold. The dominant motif in the text is poverty and survival. Berida, like many other ordinary women of Africa, is a survivor of poverty. Abuse is less of a concern to her. Questions of female circumcision do not worry her so much. Adopting a positive attitude, she sees any challenge as part of a life to be lived and survived. Berida portrays the intricacies of this survival. In all, the three texts under review demonstrate the struggles of African women in the academy and beyond and deserve everyone's close attention.

REFERENCES

Amadiume, Ifi. Male Daughters, Female Husbands: Gender and Sex in an African Society (New Jersey: Zed Books, 1987).

Buchert, Lene and Kenneth King (eds). *Learning from Experience: Policy and Practice in Aid to Higher Education,* The Hague: Center for the Study of Education in Developing Countries, 1995.

Cherly Johnson-Odim. "From Both Sides Now: Gendering the Black Atlantic," in Veney and Zeleza (eds). *Women in African Studies Scholarly Publishing,* p. 107.

Etta, Florence. "Gender Issues in Contemporary African Education, in *Africa Development,* XIX, No. 4, 1994.

Fouche, Fidela. "Overcoming the Sisterhood Myth," in *Transformation,* Vol. 23, 1994, p. 79.

Frankenberg, Ruth. *White Women, Race Matters: The Social Construction of Whiteness,* Minneapolis: University of Minnesota Press, 1993, p. 1.

Higher Education. The Lessons of Experience, Washington D.C.: The World Bank, 1994.

Ihonvbere, Julius. "The State and Academic Freedom in Africa: How African Academics Subvert Academic Freedom," in *Journal of Third World Studies,* Vol. X, No. 2, 1993, p. 58.

Liu, Tessie. "Teaching the Differences among Women from a Historical Perspective: Rethinking Race and Gender as Social Categories," *Women's Studies International Forum,* Vol. 14, No. 4, 1991, p. 266.

Mahmood Mamdani and Mamadou Diouf (eds). *Academic Freedom in Africa,* Dakar: CODESRIA Book Series, 1994.

——. "University Crisis and University Reform: A Reflection on the African Experience," in *CODESRIA Bulletin,* No. 3, 1993, pp. 13–14.

Ndambuki, Berida and Claire C. Robertson. *We Only Come Here to Struggle: Stories from Berida's Life,* Bloomington: Indiana University Press, 2000.

Oyèrónkẹ́ Oyěwùmí. The Invention of Women: Making an African Sense of Western Gender Discourses (Minneapolis: University of Minnesota Press, 1997).

Steeves, H. Leslie. *Gender Violence and the Press: The St. Kizito Story,* Athens: Ohio University Center for International Studies Monographs in International Studies African Series No. 67, 1997.

Zeleza, Paul Tiyambe. "The Politics of Historical and Social Science Research in Africa," in *Journal of Southern African Studies,* Vol. 28, No. 1, 2002, pp. 9–24.

——. *Manufacturing African Studies and Crises,* Dakar: CODESRIA Book Series, 1997, pp. 390–404.

Contributors

Adeleke Adeeko is associate professor of English and chair of the Department of Comparative Literature at the University of Colorado, Boulder.

Emmanuel Akyeampong is professor in the Department of History at Harvard University, where he also serves as chair of African and African American studies.

Ifi Amadiume is a professor at Dartmouth College, where she holds a joint appointment in the Department of Religion and the African and African American Studies Program.

Kwame Anthony Appiah is professor of Philosophy at Princeton University.

Abena Busia is associate professor in the Department of English Literature, Rutgers University.

Babacar Fall is associate professor at The Ecole Normale Superieur (School of Education) of the University Cheikh Anta Diop, Dakar, Senegal.

Audrey Gadzekpo is a Senior Lecturer at the School of Communication Studies, University of Ghana.

Igor Kopytoff is professor of anthropology at the University of Pennsylvania.

Marnia Lazreg is professor in the Department of Sociology at Hunter College, City University of New York.

Desiree Lewis has worked as a lecturer and researcher in literary and gender studies in various South African Universities. She currently works as an independent researcher.

Godwin Rapando Murunga teaches history at Kenyatta University, Nairobi, Kenya. He is currently completing graduate studies in history at Northwestern University, Evanston.

Juliana Makuchi Nfah-Abbenyi is professor of English at the University of Southern Mississippi.

Wairimu Ngaruiya Njambi teaches women's studies at Harriet L. Wilkes Honors College, Florida Atlantic University.

Bertrade Ngo-Ngijol Banoum is associate professor of African Studies, Women's Studies, and French at Lehman College, City University of New York.

Obioma Nnaemeka is professor of French, women's studies, and African/African Diaspora studies at Indiana University, Indianapolis.

Nkiru Nzegwu is associate professor and chair of the Department of Africana Studies at Binghamton University.

Pashington Obeng is an assistant professor in the Department of Africana Studies at Wellesley College.

William E. O'Brien teaches environmental studies at Harriet L. Wilkes Honors College, Florida Atlantic University.

Achola Pala Okeyo is currently an independent scholar. She has served as head of the UNDP Africa Bureau and as senior advisor on governance to UNIFEM.

Oyèrónké Oyěwùmí is associate professor of sociology and chair of the women's studies at Stony Brook University.

Filomina Steady is professor and chair of Africana Studies at Wellesley College.

Paul Tiyambe Zeleza is a professor of African studies and history at Pennsylvania State University.

INDEX

Printed in the United States
200395BV00003B/34-60/A